Others

Others

◆

Third-Party Politics From the Nation's Founding to the Rise and Fall of the Greenback-Labor Party

Darcy G. Richardson

iUniverse, Inc.
New York Lincoln Shanghai

Others
Third-Party Politics From the Nation's Founding to the Rise and Fall of the Greenback-Labor Party

iUniverse, Inc.

For information address:
iUniverse, Inc.
2021 Pine Lake Road, Suite 100
Lincoln, NE 68512
www.iuniverse.com

ISBN: 0-595-31723-5 (pbk)
ISBN: 0-595-66397-4 (cloth)

Printed in the United States of America

In memory of my father, a highly principled and dedicated man not unlike some of the noblest souls in this book.

Contents

Preface

The first in a four-volume series, this book has changed significantly, in both length and scope, since I first began researching and writing it more than a dozen years ago. This was originally intended to be a single volume history of nationally-organized third parties in the United States, but over time grew to include parties that only existed in a single state, city or town, as well as the literally thousands of independent candidates who have challenged the two major parties at different times throughout our nation's turbulent history. This book, like the three volumes to follow, was also expanded to include far more biographical material about the men and women who labored outside the traditional two-party system to change the course of American history than originally intended.

There are many people whose support in aiding my research and writing that deserve special recognition, foremost among them being my parents, without whose generosity and encouragement these books never would have been completed. I owe a deep debt of gratitude to both of them. My only regret is that my father, who was one of those that initially inspired me to undertake this seemingly never-ending project, did not live long enough to see these books through to their completion. My mother, Shirley—one of the most voracious readers I know—was particularly helpful, painstakingly proofing and editing the final version of this lengthy manuscript. To the extent that this book withstands critical scrutiny at all, it is largely as a result of her patience and keen attention to detail.

I would also like to extend a heartfelt thanks to a number of others whose efforts over the years contributed to the completion of this book, including Michael P. Ambrose, who skillfully edited several early drafts of my manuscript, as well as my brother Bill, who also read and re-read several early versions of this volume and made many useful and valuable suggestions. The same appreciation is afforded my nephew, Kyle, a precocious and extraordinarily talented writer who gladly proofed and edited several of the earlier chapters in this volume. A special debt of gratitude also goes out to the late Timothy R. Coughlin, a former assistant Secretary of State of Missouri, whose delightful correspondence over the course of several years included many valuable insights and promising leads into some of the more obscure third-party candidates who appear in several volumes of this comprehensive history. Tim passed away in 1998 and is deeply missed.

A number of others also deserve mention, not the least being Richard Winger, the discerning and dedicated publisher of the informative San Francisco-based *Ballot Access News*, a top-notch monthly publication and the only one of its kind in the country. By far the nation's leading authority on ballot access laws, Richard—who undoubtedly wondered time and again whether these books would ever be completed—consistently provided invaluable insight and encouragement along the way. He is also the person who introduced me to Tim Coughlin and his treasure trove of hard-to-find biographical material on some of the long-forgotten third-party personalities who, at one time or another, made fleeting appearances on our national stage.

In addition, appreciation is also extended to a number of others who have from time to time provided much-needed material on this vast subject. Included in this category is history professor Mark A. Lause of the University of Cincinnati, who generously shared information and material at his disposal, including a number of *New York Tribune* articles and other hard-to-find archived material relating to the relatively little-known Simon Wing and Charles H. Matchett of the Socialist Labor Party. A gifted historian, Dr. Lause is the author of *Some Degree of Power* (University of Arkansas Press, 1991) and *The Civil War's Last Campaign: James B. Weaver, the Greenback-Labor Party & the Politics of Race & Section* (University Press of America, 2001), a copiously rich narrative and arguably the finest book ever written about the Greenback-Labor Party and the 1880 presidential election. Recognition is also due to countless others, including—to mention but a few—the extremely helpful staff at the Jacksonville Public Library, the staff of the Illinois State Historical Library in Springfield, Illinois, who were particularly accommodating in helping me find information on the relatively obscure Alson J. Streeter, the Union Labor Party's presidential nominee in 1888, and the good folks at the Utah State Historical Society in Salt Lake City, who provided assistance in tracking down some biographical information on the little-remembered Parley P. Christensen, the Farmer-Labor Party's presidential standard-bearer in 1920.

I also owe a special debt to my friends Michael L. Brown and Adeline Proctor, who had to endure countless stories about the Anti-Masonic, Know-Nothing, Greenback-Labor, Populist, Prohibition and Socialist parties—and others too numerous to mention. Their patience and continuing interest in my subject is deeply appreciated.

Darcy G. Richardson
Jacksonville, Florida
April 2004

Introduction

○ ○

"Saying we should keep the two-party system simply because it is working is like saying the Titanic voyage was a success because a few people survived on life-rafts."

—*Eugene J. McCarthy*

For nearly a century and a half, the entrenched two-party system in the United States has mystified voters and scholars alike. No one can quite explain, at least not with any degree of authority, precisely how or why a "two-party system"—as opposed to a system without political parties, or possibly a multiparty arrangement—took hold so abruptly in the young nation. After all, several of the Founding Fathers, including the gifted and worldly John Adams and James Madison, had eloquently cautioned against the development of two strong parties or factions. Even George Washington, the remarkable man whose solid character held the struggling nation together during its infancy, held a rather dim view of political parties, as did John Marshall, the broad-minded first chief justice of the United States, who complained that "nothing debases or pollutes the human mind more than a political party."[1]

Despite these warnings, two strong parties quickly developed in the fledgling Republic, beginning with the Federalists, who organized the government and were responsible for the adoption of the Constitution in 1787. Formed during Washington's presidency, the Federalist Party initially enjoyed the support of most of the nation's leading Anti-Federalists, the group that initially opposed the Constitution and insisted on the inclusion of the Bill of Rights. Thomas Jefferson's Democratic-Republican Party, a states' rights party adhering to a policy of strict construction and committed to the doctrine of a government of limited powers, emerged as the Federalist Party's chief rival during this period. Rallying the great bulk of the original Anti-Federalists and marshalling the support of yeo-

---

1.   Gerald John Fresia, *There Comes a Time: A Challenge to the Two Party System* (New York, 1986), p. 58.

man farmers and urban workers, the Jeffersonian Republicans were organized in opposition to the kind of strong federal government advocated by Secretary of the Treasury Alexander Hamilton in his sweeping proposals for funding the national debt and assuming the Revolutionary War debts incurred by the states, while establishing a national bank and providing tariff protection for American industry.

The Jeffersonian Republicans weren't exactly welcomed with open arms. As Joanne B. Freeman, an assistant professor of history at Yale University, recently pointed out, the creation of a system consisting of two strong and competing parties alarmed a number of leading politicians of the time, many of whom had labored long and hard to prevent the creation of such an arrangement, fearing that a national struggle between the Federalists, largely comprised of wealthy and elite New Englanders, and Jefferson's emerging agrarian-based Democratic-Republicans, though lacking the appurtenances of modern political parties, would inevitably destroy the fragile Union.[2]

Following more than two decades of Democratic-Republican dominance during the administrations of Jefferson, Madison and James Monroe, the once-proud Federalists faded from the scene forever in the early 1820s. As a consequence, the Democratic-Republicans were without any real opposition for a period of several years until intense rivalries between John Quincy Adams, Henry Clay and Andrew Jackson during the bitterly-contested 1824 presidential campaign, eventually led to the formation of two new parties—the Jacksonian Democrats, a precursor to the modern Democratic Party, and the National Republicans, a short-lived party founded by supporters of Henry Clay, John Quincy Adams, and later by the brilliant and illustrious Daniel Webster, an ex-Federalist who was unquestionably the greatest orator of his time. Closely resembling the Federalists of old, the National Republicans advocated a strong federal government, a national bank and protective tariffs while—not unlike either major party today—generally favoring the interests of business and industry. The National Republicans eventually gave way to the newly organized Whig Party, a party that took its name from the English antimonarchist party to symbolize its opposition to "King Andrew" Jackson. Having elected William Henry Harrison and Zachary Taylor to the nation's highest office in the 1840s, the Whig Party, in turn, slowly began to unravel and eventually disintegrated during the height of the frenzied Free Soil and Know-Nothing activity of the late 1840's and early

---

2.   Joanne B. Freeman, "The Election of 1800: A Study in the Logic of Political Change," *Yale Law Journal*, Volume 8, Issue 8 (1999).

1850's before being supplanted by the remarkable rise of the Republican Party in the middle of the latter decade.

At a time when the Whig Party was in a state of serious decline, the Republican Party was founded as an antislavery third-party in Ripon, Wisconsin, in March 1854. Attracting members of the fledgling Free Soil and dying Whig parties, the Republicans quickly emerged as the country's second major party, firmly establishing themselves as the dominant political force in the North when their presidential standard-bearer John C. Fremont carried eleven of the sixteen northern states in the 1856 presidential election. Given the regional balkanization of American politics during this period, the Republicans, having also absorbed most of the northern Know-Nothing movement into their ranks, permanently cemented their major-party status four years later when Abraham Lincoln, garnering thirty-nine percent of the popular vote, captured the presidency in a four-cornered race.

Despite the establishment of a two-party system in the United States, third parties have challenged the two major parties throughout the nation's history, beginning in the late 1820s with the founding of the Anti-Masonic Party, the country's first nationally organized third party, as well as the various local Workingmen's parties sprinkled across the American landscape. These new parties, however, weren't the first to challenge the country's political establishment. Dating as far back as the earliest days of the Hamiltonian Federalists, there were occasional candidates who ran for public office under the auspices of committees or "political associations" that weren't affiliated with either the Federalists or Jefferson's emerging Democratic-Republican organization. Although some of these voices of discontent occasionally won local office, none of them ever succeeded in winning seats in Congress or to any major statewide office.

Led nationally by New York's Thurlow Weed, Thaddeus Stevens of Pennsylvania—a master of intrigue and invective—and Weed's young protégé William H. Seward, the Anti-Masonic Party, unlike some of the earlier discordant voices that had challenged the two-party system, succeeded in electing no fewer than twenty-five members to Congress in 1832, the party's high-water mark and a year when its presidential candidate William Wirt garnered nearly eight percent of the popular vote. Having more or less achieved its goal of reducing alleged Masonic influence in American public life, the Anti-Masonic movement fizzled out as a third force in American politics shortly after that election, but not before furnishing a popular base of support for the newly-formed Whig Party, which, for all intents and purposes, was a merging of the National Republican and Anti-Masonic parties into a major party capable of competing effectively with the

Jacksonian Democrats.³ Despite its relatively short lifespan, the Anti-Masonic Party also left another huge political legacy by ushering in what eventually became the common practice of using party nominating conventions at the local, state, and national levels.

The late 1830s and early 1840s witnessed the appearance of the Liberty Party, the first political party devoted exclusively to the abolition of slavery and the promotion of equal rights for the country's downtrodden and abused African-American population. Struggling against the determined hostility of the entrenched Whigs and Democrats and spurned by most antebellum voters during its abbreviated history, the tiny Liberty Party, comprised largely of religious zealots hoping to purge the nation's Protestant churches of the sin of slavery, nevertheless succeeded in electing countless members of its party to local office, particularly in what is called the "Old Northwest." Though overlooked by most historians, the party even held a U.S. Senate seat from New Hampshire, albeit briefly, in 1847.⁴

Though failing to realize its dream of black emancipation during its relatively short existence, the Liberty Party, whose leadership ranged from such colorful figures as wealthy philanthropist, reformer and political gadfly Gerrit Smith to Ohio's insatiably ambitious Salmon P. Chase, who later served as Lincoln's Secretary of the Treasury and chief justice of the U.S. Supreme Court, nonetheless succeeded in placing the issue of slavery in the forefront of American politics. "There never was a party composed of truer or nobler spirits," said a modest Chase shortly after the party's demise in 1848.⁵ Ironically, it was Chase himself who had hurried the party's extinction when he engineered the party's defection to the fledgling Free Soil Party earlier that summer.

Unlike the more extreme Liberty Party, which sought complete emancipation, the Free Soil Party sought to prevent slavery from spreading into the territories while putting an end to the preferential treatment afforded that "peculiar institution" by breaking the Slave Power's hegemony over both major parties. Lacking the Liberty Party's radical edge, the Free Soilers, comprised of New York Barnburners and antislavery Whigs, were able to attract a wide array of pragmatic politicians to their cause, including Conscience Whigs such as John G. Palfrey, Charles Sumner and Charles Francis Adams of Massachusetts and Ohio's fiery

---

3.   William B. Hesseltine, *Third-Party Movements in the United States* (Princeton, 1962), p. 19.

4.   Richard H. Sewell, *John P. Hale and the Politics of Abolition* (Cambridge, MA, 1965), p. 82.

5.   Vernon L. Volpe, *Forlorn Hope of Freedom: The Liberty Party in the Old Northwest, 1838-1848* (Kent, Ohio, 1990), p. xv.

Joshua R. Giddings, as well as antislavery Democrats like John A. Dix, Preston King and David Dudley Field of New York. As such, the Free Soil Party enjoyed tremendous success at the ballot box, winning countless local races and electing hundreds of state legislators, more than a dozen congressmen, and three members of the U.S. Senate—an impressive triumvirate consisting of Ohio's Chase, the independent-minded John P. Hale of New Hampshire and the fiery Charles Sumner of Massachusetts. Unlike most minor parties throughout American history, the Free Soilers were able to play a decisive role in the outcome of a presidential election when former President Martin Van Buren, the party's presidential standard-bearer in 1848, siphoned enough votes from conservative Democrat Lewis Cass in Connecticut, Massachusetts, New York and Vermont to throw the election to the Whig Party's Zachary Taylor, a man many believed at the time to be sympathetic to the antislavery cause. Like its predecessor, the Free Soil Party was hardly a single-issue entity. During its short but magnificent life, the antislavery party, campaigning on the stirring slogan of "Free Soil, Free Speech, Free Labor, and Free Men," took part in a lively debate of all of the issues facing the increasingly divided nation and routinely advocated internal improvements for the country's rivers and harbors, homestead legislation, cheap postage, and later called for the repudiation of the Compromise of 1850 and the accompanying Fugitive Slave Act. Though it survived less than a decade, the Free Soil Party's principle of slavery containment, as historian Frederick J. Blue so eloquently asserted, in no small measure paved the way for the newly founded Republican Party in the mid-1850s and, ultimately, the election of Abraham Lincoln in 1860.[6]

The most potent third-party in American history also came to prominence during this period when the rapidly growing Know-Nothing Party, formally known as the "American Party," spectacularly burst upon the scene. This peculiarly named party, as George Washington University professor Tyler Anbinder—one of the most perceptive historians of our time—noted in his superb book *Nativism and Slavery*, was until only recently a peripheral subject of historical scholarship—and only then as a study of the rise of nativism as "a social phenomenon."[7] While several books have been written about various aspects of the Know-Nothing movement, including the sensationalist and error-prone

---

6.   Frederick Blue, "Free Soil Party, 1848-1850s," *The Encyclopedia of Third Parties in America*, Immanuel Ness and James Ciment, eds., 3 vols. (Armonk, New York, 2000), Vol. II, p. 267.

7.   Tyler Anbinder, *Nativism & Slavery: The Northern Know Nothings & the Politics of the 1850s* (New York, 1992), p. xii.

Brass-Knuckle Crusade, written by the prolific Carleton Beals more than four decades ago, a serious, full-length treatment of the national party is still eagerly awaited. Yet, despite this lack of serious scholarly attention, the Know-Nothing Party was inarguably the most extraordinary and intriguing third-party movement in U.S. history, particularly given its critical role and importance in the pre-Civil War political crisis.

Owing much of its electoral success to the rampant immigration of the 1830s and early 1840s, as well the escalating tension between Protestants and Catholics and the ambivalence of the Whig and Democratic parties on the issue of slavery, the Know-Nothing movement was an outgrowth of earlier nativist-oriented minor party movements, most notably the Native American and American Republican parties of the 1840s. Delivering a serious blow to the fading Whigs—a party then suffering from serious political atrophy—the anti-Catholic and anti-immigrant Know-Nothings unexpectedly captured gubernatorial races in California, Connecticut, Delaware, Kentucky, Maine, Maryland, Massachusetts, New Hampshire and Rhode Island in the mid-1850s, while winning literally hundreds of state legislative seats and as many as fifty-two seats in the U.S. House of Representatives and five U.S. Senate seats in the 34th Congress. Moreover, in 1855 the party also came close to adding the governorship of populous New York—the biggest prize of them all—to its list of impressive conquests when Daniel Ullman, a Yale-educated New York City lawyer active in the Whig Party's Silver Gray faction, came within 34,000 votes of winning in a tight and bitterly-contested four-way race. Although the party eventually broke up as a result of irreconcilable differences over the issue of slavery, ex-President Millard Fillmore, hoping to rid the Know-Nothing Party of its more despicable xenophobic aspects while transforming it into a genuine conservative movement, garnered more than 873,000 votes, or nearly twenty-two percent of the popular vote as the party's presidential standard-bearer in 1856. It was the second strongest third-party showing ever in a U.S. presidential election, eclipsed only by Teddy Roosevelt's Bull Moose candidacy in 1912.

The demise of the Know-Nothing Party in 1859, preceded by the cataclysmic collapse of the Whigs a few years earlier, led to the founding of the short-lived Constitutional Union Party by John J. Crittenden of Kentucky and other pro-Compromise border-state politicians. Deeply committed to the preservation of the Union, the Constitutional Unionists nominated former Tennessee Senator John Bell—America's original peace candidate—for president and named ex-Whig Edward Everett of Massachusetts, a former congressman, governor and diplomat, as his vice-presidential running mate in the four-cornered 1860 presidential election. Seeking peace and stability at a time when sectional strife was seriously threatening to break the Union apart, the Constitutional Unionists carried Kentucky, Tennessee and Virginia, garnering more than 590,000 votes for the Bell-Everett ticket while electing two congressmen that year. Denied its raison d'être—namely, the preservation of the Union—the Constitutional Union Party went up in smoke with the firing on Fort Sumter by Pierre Beauregard's Confederate forces the following spring.

The short-lived Labor Reform, Liberal Republican and Workingmen's parties notwithstanding, it wasn't until the Greenback movement of the mid-1870s that the country again experienced anything remotely resembling a nationally organized third-party movement. Founded in 1876, the Greenback-Labor Party—a vibrant party that existed for nearly a dozen years—enjoyed broad appeal among farmers and urban workers as a result the economic depression that followed the Panic of 1873. A successor of a number of agrarian-based statewide independent and anti-monopoly parties sprinkled across the Midwest in the early 1870s, the Greenback-Labor Party was the first third-party in American history to successfully coalesce the divergent grievances of the nation's hard-pressed and poverty-stricken farmers and the struggling industrial laborers of America's cities under a single umbrella.

During the party's heyday in the late 1870s and early 1880s, the Greenback-Laborites elected fourteen congressmen and three governors—the colorful Benjamin F. Butler of Massachusetts, former congressman Josiah Begole of Michigan and Harris M. Plaisted of Maine, all three of whom were elected on fusion tickets with the aid of the somewhat dormant Democratic organizations in those states. Additionally, Iowa insurgent James B. Weaver, a popular former Union army general and Greenback congressman who later received more than a million votes as the Populist Party's presidential standard-bearer in 1892, polled an impressive 305,000 votes, or more than three percent of the national total, in an uphill bid for the presidency on the Greenback-Labor ticket in 1880. The party's fortunes, however, took an unfortunate nosedive during the 1884 presidential campaign when the inimitable Benjamin F. Butler of Massachusetts, one of the most fascinating third-party personalities in our nation's history, garnered a disappointing 175,000 votes against his two major party rivals. During its brief but colorful appearance on the national stage, the Greenback-Labor Party, which was succeeded briefly by the farmer-dominated Union Labor Party in the late 1880s and by the Populists in the 1890s—one of the most powerful third-party movements in history—and even later by the twentieth-century Farmer-Labor Party, left an unmistakable and indelible mark on American politics. In addition to its radical demand for greenbacks—paper treasury notes that weren't specifically backed by gold, silver or any other precious metal—the party's profound legacy includes, among other things, federal regulation of interstate commerce; an eight-hour workday; occupational safety and health standards; child labor legislation; the establishment of a Bureau of Labor Statistics; women's suffrage; and equal voting rights for African-Americans—almost all of which were considered political heresy when the Greenbackers first proposed them in the 1870s and 1880s.[8]

The nation's oldest third party, the Prohibitionists, also made their debut during this period. Though regarded as something of a joke today, the Prohibition Party was once something of a significant factor in American politics. Founded by Methodist minister John Russell in 1869, the Prohibitionists have competed in every presidential election dating back to 1872, when little-known James Black of Pennsylvania garnered a miniscule 5,608 votes against President Ulysses S. Grant and *New York Tribune* editor Horace Greeley. During its long history, the dry party managed to elect thousands of local officeholders, including dozens of mayors, mostly in small towns and cities. In addition to significantly influencing the outcome of the 1884 and 1916 presidential contests, more than 270,000 voters—or one out of every forty-four—cast a ballot for the Prohibition Party's presidential ticket in 1892. The party's glorious history also includes two congressmen—Minnesota's long-forgotten Kittel Halvorson, who was elected on a Farmers' Alliance-Prohibition fusion ticket in 1890, and Charles Hiram Randall, a former newspaperman from Los Angeles who served in Congress as a Prohibitionist from 1915-1921. The party's most spectacular electoral showing, however, occurred in 1916 when Sidney J. Catts, a flamboyant Baptist minister and anti-Catholic demagogue who had been narrowly denied the Democratic nomination in a disputed and highly controversial primary election, was elected governor of Florida on the Prohibition line, easily defeating his two major-party rivals while polling more than forty-seven percent of the vote.

Much to its credit, the Prohibition Party, once an influential voice of progressivism, was the first political party in American history to endorse women's suffrage and became the first ballot-qualified party to name a woman for the vice presidency when it nominated longtime party and Woman's Christian Temperance Union activist Marie C. Brehm of California for that office in 1924. It was also among the earliest to espouse the initiative and referendum and was the first political party to call for the direct election of the U.S. Senate. Needless to say,

---

8.   J. David Gillespie, *Politics at the Periphery: Third Parties in Two-Party America* (Columbia, South Carolina, 1993), pp. 66-67.

any treatment of the Prohibition Party would be incomplete without mention of the important and sometimes crucial role played by the party in the adoption of the Eighteenth Amendment in 1919, banning the manufacture, sale, transportation, importation, or exportation of intoxicating liquors.

There was a time in American history when third party and independent candidates had much greater success at the ballot box than they enjoy today. Not only were most of the nation's newspapers and magazines far less jaded than many of the pundits in the print and electronic media today, they were also far less obsessed with the "horserace" aspect of political campaigns and rarely viewed third-party and independent candidates as potential "spoilers." Unfortunately, that's a more recent phenomenon in American politics.

On the whole, newspapers and journals in the past took their responsibility more seriously than their modern counterparts and frequently provided meaningful coverage to candidates running outside the traditional two-party system. It wasn't altogether unusual for some of the nation's largest newspapers, such as the *New York Times* or the *New York Tribune*, to provide relatively extensive coverage of a third-party's national convention, including that of the little-remembered American Party of 1888, or to publish a presidential nominee's entire letter of acceptance. Even the tiny Daniel DeLeon-led Socialist Labor Party—a party that still exists today, albeit largely as a paper organization—regularly received coverage in the mainstream press, even if vastly disproportionate to the amount of space generously provided to the country's two major parties. Occasionally, such minor-party coverage even made its way onto the front pages of the nation's newspapers. Even as late as 1940—long before the advent of the one-eyed monster—Socialist Party officials were able to persuade the nation's three major radio networks to carry a live broadcast of Norman Thomas' acceptance speech, enabling millions of Americans to hear the Socialist candidate.

Third-party and independent candidates in the nineteenth century also didn't have to deal with the increasingly burdensome ballot access barriers deliberately placed in their path by Democratic and Republican-controlled state legislatures beginning in the 1890s and continuing throughout the twentieth century, the worst of which, arguably, were enacted during the period from 1930 to 1945.[9] Before the adoption of the Australian ballot beginning in 1888, there were no government-printed ballots in the United States and political parties and voters were free to print and distribute their own ballots. For the record, it wasn't all that uncommon in those days for a third-party candidate to occasionally upset the applecart, as Minnesota's professional wrestler-turned politician Jesse Ventura miraculously managed to do in that state's hard-fought 1998 gubernatorial campaign. In fact, in the nineteenth century there were no fewer than twenty-three governors elected on third-party tickets (and many more than that if one includes the number of governors elected on fusion tickets with a minor party)—a figure that dwarfs the thirteen state chief executives elected outside the two-party system in the following century, especially considering there were fewer states in the Union during much of the nineteenth century. The contrast is even more striking when one looks at the number of seats held by third parties in state legislatures across the country during those two periods.

Including minor parties that existed solely in a single town, city, county or state, there have been well over a thousand third parties in our nation's history, many of which barely survived one or two election cycles.[10] While America's badly flawed winner-take-all electoral system has historically proven detrimental to third-party and independent candidates, during the latter part of the nineteenth century and early twentieth century the Greenbackers, Populists, Prohibitionists, Socialists and a few other minor parties, such as the Readjuster Party in Virginia, routinely captured hundreds of local offices and state legislative seats in communities and states scattered across the country. The Socialist Party, for instance, held no fewer than 1,141 elective offices in 1912—a year when the party's presidential standard-bearer Eugene V. Debs garnered over 900,000 votes—yet even that figure, as astonishing as it was, pales by comparison to the number of offices proportionately won by the Know-Nothing Party in the 1850s and the Populists at the height of their popularity in the 1890s. Even the principled yet pious Prohibition Party had its pockets of strength, as evidenced by the party's virtual sweep of rural Venango County, Pennsylvania, in 1904, when it won 205 township, borough, and county offices. That was the same year that "Fighting Parson" Silas C. Swallow, a fiery Methodist minister from Harrisburg,

---

9.   Richard Winger, "History of U.S. Ballot Access Law for New and Minor Parties," *The Encyclopedia of Third Parties*, Vol. I, pp. 72-95. Ironically, as Winger pointed out, a third-party was responsible for one of the most stringent ballot access laws in the country. In an attempt to thwart opposition from the Populists, Nevada's Silver Party—which not only controlled the state legislature but dominated politics in the Sagebrush State for the better part of a decade—changed that state's ballot access requirements for minor-party and independent candidates in 1893, vastly increasing the number of signatures on nominating petitions from three percent of the last vote cast to a staggering ten percent of the last vote cast. Despite the severity of the new law, the Populist Party somehow managed to comply with the ten percent requirement in 1894.

10.   Steven Hill, *Fixing Elections: The Failure of America's Winner Take All Politics* (New York, 2002), pp. 57, 316n.

garnered nearly 259,000 votes—or nearly two percent of the total—against President Theodore Roosevelt and his hapless Democratic challenger

Despite the notoriously hostile nature of this winner-take-all system to candidates running outside the two-party duopoly, third-party candidates were also successful in more than 350 U.S. House races during the 1800s, compared to only seventy-eight the following century. In addition, sixty-five independents—including 22 Independent-Democrats, 11 Independent-Republicans, three Independent-Whigs and an Independent-Unionist—were also elected to Congress in the period from 1809-1899, juxtaposed to the relatively meager fifteen independents and three write-in candidates who managed to scratch and claw their way to victory in the twentieth century.[11] Impressively, third parties were represented in the U.S. Senate at one time or another on at least forty occasions during the nineteenth century—a period when members of that body were chosen by their state legislatures—while only a half-dozen third-party candidates and two independents were popularly elected to that body in the last century.[12]

Throughout most of our nation's history, the idea of supporting an independent or third party candidate was not considered "wasting" one's vote or throwing one's vote away—a theme constantly drummed into voters' minds today. There was a time when third parties were viewed as viable participants in the democratic process and, as a result, tended to attract top-notch candidates for most major political offices. Among them were three former presidents who sought political comebacks on third-party tickets in an effort to reclaim the Executive Mansion—Martin Van Buren on the Free Soil ticket in 1848, Millard Fillmore on the American (Know-Nothing) Party ticket in 1856 and Teddy Roosevelt on the Progressive ticket in 1912. Fillmore himself had first been elected to public office on the Anti-Masonic ticket in 1828 when he won a seat in the New York legislature. What's more, the aloof and introspective John Quincy Adams, one of the most successful diplomats and lawmakers in American history, was returned to Congress on the Anti-Masonic ticket shortly after leaving the White House, serving as a powerful and seasoned voice of reason in the U.S. House of Representatives from 1831 until his death in 1848. One of the most uncommonly candid and principled politicians of his era, the nation's sixth president also ran for governor of Massachusetts, albeit reluctantly, on the Anti-Masonic ticket in 1833, finishing a respectable second in a four-cornered race.

---

11. Of the eighteen people elected to Congress as independent or write-in candidates in the past century, only four—William L. Carss and Ole J. Kvale of Minnesota, Frazier Reams of Ohio, and Bernie Sanders of Vermont—were not truly affiliated with one of the two major parties.

In addition, President John Tyler, borrowing the time-honored name of Thomas Jefferson's Democratic-Republican organization of an earlier generation, organized a new states-rights party in his bid for re-election in 1844. Planning to campaign against the Democrats and Whigs on a platform calling for the annexation of Texas, the 54-year-old Tyler—a man essentially without a party—aborted his third-party effort later that spring when the Democrats nominated James K. Polk at their convention in Baltimore.

While it is generally true, as J. David Gillespie suggested in his brisk and lively *Politics at the Periphery*, that the major parties, acting "like a porous sponge," eventually co-opted the ideas of many of the earlier third party movements in American history, it is equally true that many contemporary adherents of those parties would have vehemently disagreed with that assertion. When conservative Republicans charged in 1936 that Franklin D. Roosevelt had carried out most of the Socialist Party's platform through his New Deal policies, the witty and urbane Norman Thomas, the party's six-time presidential candidate—and a man who served as the nation's conscience for more than four decades—sharply disagreed. "Roosevelt did not carry out the Socialist platform." Thomas quipped, "unless he carried it out on a stretcher."[13] Years later, of course, the aging Tho-

---

12.   The six senators elected on third-party tickets in the twentieth century were Progressives Miles Poindexter, who was initially elected by the Washington state legislature in 1911, and Wisconsin's Robert M. LaFollette, Jr., son of the late "Fighting Bob" LaFollette; the Minnesota Farmer-Labor Party's Magnus Johnson, Henrik Shipstead and Ernest Lundeen; and New York's James L. Buckley, who was elected on that state's Conservative Party ticket in 1970. The two independents elected to the U.S. Senate in the twentieth century were Nebraska's "Gentle Knight" George W. Norris and Harry F. Byrd, Jr., of Virginia, a conservative Democrat who successfully sought re-election as an independent in 1970. This figure doesn't include two Republicans—Wayne Morse of Oregon, one of Capitol Hill's original doves during the war in Vietnam, and Bob Smith, a somewhat drab and unimpressive conservative from New Hampshire—who briefly switched their party affiliation to independent while serving in the Senate. This list also doesn't include Elmer A. Benson of Minnesota's Farmer-Labor Party who was appointed to fill a vacancy in the U.S. Senate in 1935, nor does it include Prohibitionist Andrew J. Houston of Texas, the 87-year-old son of the legendary Sam Houston. Appointed to fill a vacancy in April 1941, Houston, who had been the Prohibition Party's candidate for governor of the Lone Star State in 1910 and 1912, served in the U.S. Senate for two months until his death in June of that year.

13.   Gillespie, *Politics at the Periphery*, p. 4; Harry Fleischman, *Norman Thomas: A Biography* (New York, 1964), p. 171.

mas readily conceded that he took great satisfaction in having influenced one of the two major parties, telling consumer activist Ralph Nader, then a young government and economics major at Princeton University, that he was pleased that the Democrats had borrowed so many of his ideas, most notably Social Security, unemployment compensation, and regulation of the securities industry.[14]

In the first of a comprehensive four-volume series, this book examines the important and often dynamic role that third parties played in the first one hundred years of our Republic. Covering the period from the nation's founding through the collapse of the Greenback-Labor Party in the mid-1880s, this sweeping historical chronicle is also the story about some of the men and women who, usually against tremendously long odds and often at great personal sacrifice, helped to shape the course of the nation's tumultuous history through persistent third-party agitation.

---

14. *Hartford Advocate*, March 11, 2004.

1

Early Political Parties

❖

The Views of the Founders

It would not be an exaggeration to say that the Constitution was devised, in large part, to mitigate the effect of political factions. Deeply influenced by Thomas Hobbes, David Hume and Jean Jacques Rousseau—three European philosophers who regarded political parties as a threat to stable government—the founders of the new republic were acutely sensitive to the dangers presented by these entities both to the general interest, as well as to individual rights.[1] By and large, the framers of the U.S. Constitution viewed political parties as a source of weakness and division. "Nothing could be more ill-judged," wrote Alexander Hamilton in *The Federalist Papers*, "than that intolerant spirit which has at all times characterized political parties. The pestilential breath of faction," he argued, "may poison the fountains of justice" and "it will rarely happen that the advancement of the public service will be the primary object either of party victories or of party negotiations."[2]

Recognizing that "the latent causes of factions are...sown in the nature of man" and that "the spirit of party in different degrees must be expected to infect all political bodies," the proponents of the new Union saw the remedy in the form of an extended republic of continent-wide proportions, a national government of divided powers and a federal system in which the states would supplement and check the authority of the central government.[3]

---

1. Arthur M. Schlesinger, Jr., ed., *History of U.S. Political Parties* (New York, 1973), Vol. I, p. xxxiv.
2. Alexander Hamilton, James Madison and John Jay, *The Federalist Papers*, Clinton Rossiter, ed., (New York, 1961); Hamilton, Madison and Jay, *The Federalist Papers*, Isaac Kramnick, ed., (New York, 1987).
3. Ibid.

Such an arrangement, argued James Madison, a soft-spoken and scholarly Virginia lawmaker, would be particularly effective against the most dangerous kind of faction—a majority. "When a majority is included in a faction," he wrote, "the form of popular government...enables it to sacrifice to its ruling passion of interest both the public good and the rights of other citizens." A large republic, encompassing a wide variety of interests, classes and parties, would dilute the strength of any majority. The separation of powers, checks and balances, and the states would further fragment and frustrate "tyrannical" majorities.[4]

Paradoxically, then, the Founders—while deploring political factionalism and the rise of party politics—created a system that they hoped would promote *the widest possible variety* of political groups. In the best of all imaginable political worlds there would be no parties—accordingly, everyone would be an "independent." But, failing that—and such a failure was deemed inevitable—the next best situation would be a *multiplicity* of factions in as *unlimited* a number as possible, for this would be the best way of avoiding the tyranny of a self-perpetuating, self-interested and irresponsible majority.

The Framers, of course, did not prescribe the appropriate number of such factions, sects or parties. Madison favored "a great variety of parties" and a "multiplicity of interests." He was wary of a society where "the stronger faction can readily unite and oppress the weaker," which, by implication, means a society consisting of *only two* factions. Hamilton also did not seem enthralled by the prospect of two factions engaged in perpetual rivalry. "The habit of being continually marshaled on opposite sides," he wrote, "will be too apt to stifle the voice both of law and of equity." In discussing the role of parties in approving presidential nominations, Madison observed that the "choice which may at any time happen to be made under such circumstances will of course be the result either of a victory gained by one party over the other, or of a compromise between the parties. In either case, the intrinsic merit of the candidate will be too often out of sight."[5] The assumption of a two-party rivalry was a situation that he did not look forward to with much enthusiasm. John Marshall, arguably the ablest man to ever serve on the U.S. Supreme Court, also bemoaned the idea of rival parties.[6]

John Adams, anticipating the adoption of the U.S. Constitution, observed that the development of two strong political parties or factions would be the worst of all possibilities. "There is nothing I dread so much as a division of the

4.   Ibid.
5.   Ibid.
6.   Albert J. Beveridge, *Life of John Marshall* (Boston, 1916), Vol. II, p. 410.

republic into two great parties," he cautioned in 1780, "each arranged under its leader and converting issues in opposition to each other. This, in my humble apprehension, is to be dreaded as the greatest political issue."[7] In a letter to Thomas Jefferson, the principal author of the Declaration of Independence, Adams wrote that parties and factions "will not suffer improvements to be made. As soon as one man hints at an improvement," he noted, "his rival opposes it. No sooner has one party discovered or invented any amelioration of the condition of man, or the order of society than the opposite party belies it, misconstrues it, misrepresents it, ridicules it, insults it, and persecutes it..."[8] The intellectual Jefferson, likewise, held a dim view of political parties. "If I could not go to heaven but with a political party," he wrote in 1789, "I would not go there at all."[9] Even as late as 1816, the poorly educated Andrew Jackson, who had little in common with the nation's founding fathers and the scholarly Puritan that he succeeded as president twelve years later, said that it was "time to exterminate the monster called party spirit."[10]

Similarly, George Washington, who also viewed the idea of political factions and parties with more than a little disdain, kept his distance from the organizers of America's earliest political parties. In fact, the nation's first president, whose chestnut hair had already turned white, was so heartsick over the spread of factionalism that he nearly refused a second term in 1792.[11] Washington had always believed that political parties, mired in factionalism and selfishness, were inherently evil. He said in 1790 that if liberty and independence, which had cost the new nation "so much blood and treasure to establish," were to be preserved, then "we must drive far away the daemon party spirit and local reproach." Shortly before Thomas Jefferson's Democratic-Republicans overwhelmed the ruling Federalist Party, Washington expressed his displeasure toward the emerging opposition party. "Let that party set up a broomstick," he wrote sarcastically to Governor Jonathan Trumbull of Connecticut, "and call it a true son of liberty—a

7. Eugene J. McCarthy, "The Two-Party System," *The Progressive Populist* (February 15, 2004), Vol. 10, Number 3.
8. Paul Wilstach, ed., *Correspondence of John Adams and Thomas Jefferson 1812-1826* (Indianapolis, 1925).
9. Richard Norton Smith, *Patriarch: George Washington and the New American Nation* (New York, 1993), p. 47.
10. Robert A. Diamond, ed., *Congressional Quarterly's Guide to U.S. Elections* (Washington, D.C., 1975), p. 1.
11. Smith, *Patriarch*, pp. 133-134.

democrat—or give it any epithet that will suit their purposes and it will command their votes *in toto*."[12]

In spite of Adams' words of caution, Washington's avowed disapproval and the suspicions of Jefferson, Madison, Hamilton, Marshall and James Monroe, political parties quickly developed in the new nation. Although the Constitution made no provision for political parties, by 1792 two distinct parties—the Federalists and the Democratic-Republicans—were vying for control of the young nation's destiny. The parties, as one might expect, were divided by economic and ideological differences that were far greater than those that exist between the country's two major parties today. Moreover, unlike America's modern-day Democrats and Republicans, the Federalists and their rival "Republicans"—as Jefferson's party was usually referred to in those days—had leaders of extraordinary political and intellectual ability.

Led by Secretary of the Treasury Alexander Hamilton and John Adams, the Federalist Party, representing the mercantile, shipping and financial interests of New England and those of southern planters, was formed in 1789. The party grew out of the movement that drafted and worked for the ratification of the U.S. Constitution in 1787. Adhering to a broad interpretation of the Constitution, the Federalists were widely recognized as a tool of the aristocracy. Believing that the Articles of Confederation impeded the development of a strong national government, the Federalists controlled the new republic in its early days. Its constituency was drawn to the party's strong national economic policies as well as its commitment to maintaining domestic order.

The Federalists also enjoyed strong support in the press, especially from the highly influential *Gazette of the United States*, published in Philadelphia, as well as the *Washington Federalist*, the *New York Minerva* and the *Hartford Courant*, to mention but a few of the leading Federalist newspapers of the time. For a brief period they also counted ex-Tory William Cobbett's short-lived *Porcupine's Gazette*, a conservative publication that chiefly advocated reconciliation with Great Britain and perpetual war against Revolutionary France, as one of its most unflinchingly loyal advocates.[13] They also had their share of devoted pamphleteers including such gifted wordsmiths as the Yale-educated Noah Webster and Fisher Ames, the young Massachusetts congressman and Christian educator who defeated Samuel Adams, a Boston politician whose puritanical zeal and abiding hatred of the British Crown led to the American Revolution, to win a seat in

---

12. Wilfred E. Binkley, *American Political Parties: Their Natural History* (New York, 1947), p. 51.

Congress in 1788. A vicious opponent of Thomas Jefferson, Ames shared the general Federalist contempt for the masses. "The most ferocious of all animals, when his passions are roused to fury and uncontrolled, is man," he once said. "Men are often false to their country and their honor, false to duty and even to interest, but multitudes of men are never long false or deaf to their passions." Countless Federalists, including lexicographer Noah Webster who boasted in 1801 that he had spent "the largest part of eighteen years" opposing democracy, echoed this sentiment.[14]

It should be noted, however, that during their brief yet brilliant history, the Federalists went to great lengths to avoid the appearance of being an organized political party. Conventions were abhorred—anything resembling such a meeting would have reminded voters of the despised French Jacobins.[15] The Federalist organization was so concealed, in fact, that its national convention of 1808 was kept secret—totally out of public view—as was the party's oligarchic system of party management. By operating openly as a political party, the Federalists realized that they would have been granting legitimacy to the idea of political parties in America and in doing so would have unintentionally invited organized opposition.

---

13. John C. Miller, *The Federalist Era, 1789-1801* (New York, 1960), pp. 89-92, 121-122. Thomas Jefferson criticized the *Gazette of the United States* as "a paper of pure Toryism, disseminating the doctrines of monarchy, aristocracy, and the exclusion of the influence of the people" and accused its editor of using its pages to promote his archrival Alexander Hamilton for the presidency. To counteract the "poison" disseminated by the Federalist publication, Jefferson established the *National Gazette*, a Philadelphia-based newspaper edited by Philip Freneau, the Princeton-educated "Poet of the Revolution." The son of a wine merchant and close friend of James Madison, Freneau lavishly praised Jefferson in his newspaper while pillorying Hamilton as a "monarchical serpent" and devout enemy of republicanism.

14. Seth Ames, ed., *The Works of Fisher Ames* (Boston, 1854), Vol. II, pp. 79-80, 394-395; Miller, *The Federalist Era*, pp. 110-111.

15. Formed in 1789 at the outset of the French Revolution when France was one of the richest and most powerful nations in Europe, the pernicious Jacobins seized power through a parliamentary coup in 1793 and wasted little time in unleashing their notorious "Reign of Terror," resulting in the deaths of thousands, including Marie Antoinette, widow of King Louis XVI, under the guillotine. Apparently, the Federalists were unwilling or unable to distinguish between their own agrarian opponents in the United States and the Parisian proletarian *sans-culottes*, whose rebellious rioting enabled the radical Jacobins to seize power.

Nevertheless, by 1795, late in Washington's second term, the Federalist Party was virtually crystallized in the public mind. Washington, who personally eschewed political factions and parties, was generally regarded as a Federalist. In fact, the party continued to evoke his name long after his death on December 14, 1799. Moreover, Washington's vice president and successor, John Adams, a scholar, proficient writer and indefatigable advocate of a declaration of independence, was an avowed Federalist and was the first president elected under a partisan banner. Yet, despite his Federalist affiliation, Adams remained coolly aloof from party counsels during and after his term in office.

By the late 1790's—shortly before Adams succeeded Washington as the nation's second president—the Federalists, having succeeded in making the terms "Federalist" and "patriot" virtually synonymous, had reached their zenith. They controlled not only the presidency, but also both houses of Congress, as well as the Supreme Court. "Four-fifths of the talent, ability, and good sense of the country were to be found in the Federalist ranks," wrote Theodore Roosevelt nearly a century later, "for the Federalists had held their own so far, by sheer force of courage and intellectual vigor over foes in reality more numerous."[16]

It wasn't completely surprising, therefore, that President Washington sought to head off any organized opposition in his famous Farewell Address, saying that "all combinations and associations under whatever plausible character, with the real design to direct, control, counteract or awe the regular deliberation of the constituted authorities [the Federalists], are destructive of this fundamental principle and of fatal tendency."[17] Written primarily to remove his name from consideration for a third term, Washington's 32-page handwritten address, a collaborative effort with Hamilton and, to a lesser extent, John Jay, borrowed liberally from a draft prepared by the brilliant James Madison four years earlier. (Ironically, the Federalists later vilified the principal author of that text.) Every point made in Washington's valediction, observed historian John C. Miller, "had been enunciated by Washington, Hamilton, and other leading Federalists at one time or another. It contained, in short, the essence of the political philosophy of Federalism."[18]

---

16. Theodore Roosevelt, *Gouverneur Morris* (Boston, 1888), pp. 321-322.

17. *American Daily Advertiser*, September 19, 1796. Washington's Farewell Address, written on September 17, was never delivered orally, but was originally published in David C. Claypoole's Philadelphia newspaper and later appeared in several other publications, including *The Independent Chronicle* in Boston. In his widely quoted address, the nation's first president warned against the evils of political parties and entangling alliances abroad.

"There is an opinion that parties in free countries are useful checks upon the administration of the government, and serve to keep alive the spirit of liberty," Washington said in his farewell speech. "This within certain limits is probably true; and in governments of a monarchical cast patriotism may look with indulgence, if not favor, upon the spirit of party. But in those of the popular character, in governments purely elective, it is a spirit not to be encouraged...A fire not to be quenched, it demands a uniform vigilance to prevent its bursting into a flame, lest, instead of warming, it should consume."[19]

Like most Federalist leaders of that time, Hamilton—in sharp contrast to men like James Madison and Secretary of State Thomas Jefferson, both of whom had experienced the emerging democratic life of rural Virginia—knew little about the developing American frontier. Maintaining that the masses were fit only to be ruled, Hamilton, an ardent nationalist, encouraged massive immigration to provide cheap labor—including that of women and young children—for New England's commercial interests. A former aide-de-camp to George Washington who commanded a battery of artillery during the Battle of Yorktown, the West Indies-born Hamilton, whose marriage to Elizabeth Schuyler cemented his elitist social position in American life, was no great eighteenth century social reformer. As Secretary of the Treasury, for instance, he was almost single-mindedly concerned with fostering commercial and industrial development in the new nation. He had little concern for the fledgling country's poor and downtrodden population.

Yet despite such arrogance and single-mindedness, Hamilton, as Secretary of the Treasury, proved to be superbly suited for the task facing the new republic during its infancy. As Miller wrote in his absorbing and scholarly history of the Federalist era, by 1792 Hamilton had effectively reduced the burdening debt dating from the nation's struggle for independence, alleviating the financial chaos inherited from the Revolutionary War. He also stabilized the price of government securities close to their face value, while assuring that hoarded wealth had been brought out in the open. He also established the First Bank of the United States modeled after the Bank of England, as well as a federal revenue system. Moreover, the first Secretary of the Treasury created an effective system of debt management while assuring that the power of the federal government was decisively asserted over the states. Under his watch, foreign capital began flowing into the United States and the credit of the U.S. government was solidly established.[20]

18.   Miller, *The Federalist Era*, p. 196.
19.   Henry Steele Commager, ed., *Documents of American History* (New York, 1948).

The Fading Federalists

Having recently replaced the old aristocracy of the Tories in New England, many of whom fled with the British army when the patriots captured Boston, the arrogant New England Federalists expected the masses to accord them the dignity and allegiance they believed they were entitled to—a sentiment echoed by Massachusetts Federalist George Cabot, an adviser to Alexander Hamilton, who said that the people "do not think at all," they were purely creatures of emotions.[21] But the common people of Boston and elsewhere stubbornly refused to bestow them such respect. Due to their elitist political philosophy and unflinching support of commercial interests, the Federalists also had very limited appeal among the majority of voters in what was then a predominantly rural, agrarian nation. The bulk of the country's citizenry gravitated, instead, toward the more populist-oriented Democratic-Republicans led by Thomas Jefferson, the shy, retiring man from Virginia who quietly emerged as the people's champion.

The Federalists had only themselves to blame for their somewhat sudden fall from grace. Leading Federalists such as John Adams and Alexander Hamilton were now bitter enemies and the party was virtually divided into two rival groups, a schism that threatened Federalist domination in American politics. Former President George Washington died in 1799, leaving the party without a titular leader. "His death diminished greatly the chances of Federalist success," wrote Theodore Roosevelt nearly nine decades later.[22] Making matters worse, Adams retired a few years later and Hamilton was shot and killed by Aaron Burr in a duel in 1804, virtually wiping out the upper echelon of the party's leadership. In the meantime, a number of other leading Federalist figures vanished from the scene, some through retirement and others by way of death. Included in this group were such influential Federalists as Frederick Muhlenberg of Pennsylvania, the former Speaker of the House who died in 1801, and Patrick Henry, a recent convert to Federalism who passed away two years earlier. The Federalists were also shaken by the death of influential former Senator Philip J. Schuyler of New York in 1804. These losses were compounded by former chief justice John Jay's retirement in 1801 and by Samuel Sewall's decision to give up his seat in Congress to become an associate justice on the Massachusetts Supreme Court. Adding to the Federalist woes was the fact that patriot Robert Morris, once the wealthiest man in the country and a former Federalist senator from Pennsylvania, signer of the

---

20.   Miller, *The Federalist Era*, pp. 68-69.
21.   Ibid., p. 110.
22.   Roosevelt, *Gouverneur Morris*, pp. 321-322.

Declaration of Independence, and the chief financier of the American Revolution, tragically languished in a debtors' prison in Philadelphia for three years during this period.

As bothersome as these developments were, the Federalists were beset with other problems that eventually led to their demise. Anticipating a war with France, the nervous Federalists passed the controversial Alien and Sedition Acts in 1798, a law largely designed to silence their critics. Incredibly, not a single Federalist lawmaker opposed the act.[23] The new French government, of course, had good reason to be angry at the United States and had placed itself on a war footing. The French were highly incensed by the adoption of Jay's Treaty, which virtually ignored British aggression toward American shipping interests, as well as Mother England's impressments of young American sailors. The French viewed such behavior as a concession or sell-out to England at their expense—a view that was shared by most Republicans, especially Thomas Jefferson.

Like their French adversaries, the Federalists quickly prepared for war. Almost immediately, however, the Federalist war drum was drowned out by an outpouring of criticism from Jefferson and other opposition leaders, most of whom were sympathetic to the French cause. Hoping to suppress their Republican critics while simultaneously destroying the growing bloc of immigrant voters in the rival Democratic-Republican Party, the Federalists tried to link all foreigners to the issue of disloyalty by increasing the period for naturalization from five to fourteen years. Persons from unfriendly or "enemy" nations were automatically barred from becoming naturalized citizens. This draconian act also authorized the president to arbitrarily deport any alien deemed dangerous to the peace and safety of the United States. It also empowered the nation's chief executive to order the wholesale incarceration or expulsion of aliens during wartime.

In the eyes of the fatuous Federalists, most editors and writers of French and Irish descent, as well as those who had recently emigrated from England, were all "foreign liars." While visiting Pennsylvania, for example, one New England Federalist, apparently alarmed by that state's growing Irish population, wrote home of "the most God-provoking Democrats on this side of hell."[24] The influx of immigrants frightened them immensely—not unlike the anti-Catholic and anti-immigration movement that found refuge in the Know-Nothing xenophobia of the 1850s. Consequently, most naturalized foreign-born citizens were turned off

---

23.   Morton Borden, *The Federalism of James A. Bayard* (New York, 1955), p. 38.
24.   Binkley, *American Political Parties: Their Natural History*, p. 80.

by the Federalists and quickly aligned themselves with Jefferson's populist Demo-cratic-Republican organization.

Believing that they had effectively freed themselves of the immigrant threat, the haughty Federalists turned their housekeeping activities on their Republican rivals by sweeping aside the Constitution and the Bill of Rights, including the First Amendment. Under the controversial Sedition Act, Americans were prohib-ited from assembling with the "intent to oppose any measure of the government" and editors and pamphleteers were subjected to both fines and imprisonments for any "seditious" writings or utterances against the president or Congress. Given wide latitude, many Federalist judges savagely applied the new law against their opponents for what amounted to relatively harmless remarks.

Under the Alien and Sedition Acts, the Federalists successfully prosecuted an untold number of their most severe critics, including editor and congressman Matthew Lyon of Vermont, a one-time indentured servant. Thomas Cooper, a British-born philosopher and leading Jeffersonian newspaperman, was also jailed and fined for attacking the sedition law itself. In one of the most celebrated cases of all, James T. Callender, regarded by Thomas Jefferson as a true champion of liberty, was also prosecuted. Ironically, Callender—who later turned on Jeffer-son, vilifying him in a series of scathing attacks—had been persecuted in his native England for running afoul of that country's sedition laws a few years ear-lier.

Meanwhile, Thomas Jefferson, the versatile intellectual who wiled away his days as vice president under John Adams by inventing a new plow while pursuing his interests in natural science, history and the classics, grew increasingly con-vinced that the Federalists had little, if any, regard for the Bill of Rights.[25] An early critic of both the Washington and Adams administrations, the gifted Vir-ginian feared that the Federalists were being unduly influenced, if not corrupted, by aggressive nationalists like Alexander Hamilton who persuaded President Washington to adopt an unfriendly neutrality toward France during the French Revolution while reestablishing close ties with England. In 1792, shortly after Great Britain joined Prussia and Austria in engaging the new French Republic in hostilities, Jefferson, then serving as Secretary of State, urged Washington to sup-port the French but the nation's first president, heeding Hamilton's advice, ignored his counsel. Just as the American Revolution had inspired France's mid-dle-class to revolt against its tyrannical monarchy, it was Jefferson's fervent hope that the French Revolution would inspire other European nations to do the same.

When that didn't happen, the sanguine Jefferson turned his attention to other intellectual pursuits, enthusiastically burying himself in his duties as president of the American Philosophical Society—a position he retained until 1815. Jefferson's political fire, however, was re-ignited by the passage of the Alien and Sedition Acts in 1798. Obviously frustrated by his limited role in the Adams administration, Jefferson, who gained undying fame for penning the Declaration of Independence when he was thirty-three, became an outspoken critic of John Adams and the Federalists, faulting the president in general and the policies of the Federalist Party in particular. The Federalist Party, he once observed, was an "Anglican monarchical aristocratic party" whose main objective was to usher in an American version of the British government. Forced to put his political passions on hold following his narrow defeat to Adams in 1796, the "Sage of Monticello" half-expected the ruling Federalists to pass yet another act of Congress establishing lifetime terms for both the president and members of the U.S. Senate. Nothing would have surprised him at that point.

Not content to sit idly by while the Federalists attempted to illegally silence their opposition by running roughshod over the sacred Bill of Rights, Jefferson secretly drafted the Kentucky Resolutions, declaring the Alien and Sedition Acts unconstitutional and a violation of states' rights. Jefferson also contested the legality of the Alien and Sedition Acts in Virginia, where he was aided by the diminutive James Madison, an angry former congressman and father of both the Constitution and the Bill of Rights who had joined Jefferson in opposing the Washington and Adams administrations. "If no other state in the union thinks as we do," Jefferson wrote at the height of the crisis, "Virginia, the ancient, the

---

25. Though dismissed by some of his political opponents as a radical visionary because of his immense cerebral prowess, Jefferson was remarkably successful in politics, serving as governor of Virginia, minister to France, and Secretary of State under George Washington before losing narrowly to John Adams in the 1796 presidential election. Due to the peculiar double-balloting system used during the nation's first four presidential elections (1789, 1792, 1796 and 1800) under Article II, section 1 of the Constitution, each elector cast two votes without distinguishing which vote was for president and which was intended for the vice-presidential candidate, with the person receiving the highest number of votes becoming president and the person with the second highest total becoming vice president. In the 1796 election, Vice President Adams received 71 electoral votes to Jefferson's 68, while 59 electors voted for South Carolina Federalist Thomas Pinckney and thirty for New York's Aaron Burr. Forty-eight votes were cast for nine other candidates, including fifteen of Virginia's forty-two votes for the aging Samuel Adams of Boston, one of the signers of the Declaration of Independence, and two for lame-duck President George Washington. As a result, Jefferson, the Democratic-Republican presidential candidate, had the unique distinction of serving as vice president in a Federalist administration.

great, the powerful, the rich and the republican state of Virginia, still remains free and independent."[26] South Carolina was also expected to pass a similar resolution, but outrage over the recent XYZ Affair had revived Federalist strength there and the state legislature was in no mood to criticize or second-guess the nation's governing party.

Not surprisingly, Federalists throughout the country roundly criticized the Jefferson and Madison resolutions. Because the authors of the Declaration of Independence and the Constitution had reversed the Federalist pattern of constitutional theory, Henry Adams, the freewheeling romantic reactionary who authored a magnificent nine-volume history on the Jefferson and Madison presidencies, perhaps best expressed the overwhelming sentiment of the Federalists at the time when, in his uniquely supercilious way, he declared that the "Constitution of the Republican Party was the Federalist Constitution read backwards, like a medieval invocation of the devil."[27] In addition to South Carolina, six other state legislatures rejected the Kentucky and Virginia Resolutions, claiming that the Federalists had not usurped their power and that the specific statutes questioned by Jefferson and Madison were indeed constitutional. Apparently the legislators in those states thought they knew more about the subject than the cerebral Madison—the very man who had drafted the Constitution and the Bill of Rights.

Undismayed, Jefferson again sought the presidency in 1800. He was paired in the campaign with former Senator Aaron Burr of New York, a Princeton-educated soldier, politician and nebulous adventurer who had once served as New York state attorney general. Having been courted by Jefferson since 1797, Burr, who served as a staff officer under George Washington during the War of Independence, was chosen as the Virginian's running mate in large part to help turn Federalist New York City toward the Republicans, thereby tilting the balance of power in the legislature to Jefferson.[28] As in 1796, Jefferson again faced Federalist John Adams in the general election. By this time, the aging and tired Adams was an increasingly unpopular figure—even within his own party. Most Federalists

---

26. Smith, *Patriarch*, p. 338.
27. Binkley, *American Political Parties*, pp. 81-82.
28. Eugene H. Roseboom, *A History of Presidential Elections From George Washington to Richard Nixon* (New York, 1974), p. 41. In 1800, the New York legislature, like those in Connecticut, Delaware, Georgia, Massachusetts, New Hampshire, New Jersey, Pennsylvania, South Carolina, Tennessee and Vermont, chose the state's presidential electors. Only five states—Kentucky, Maryland, North Carolina (by district), Rhode Island and Virginia (at large), chose electors by popular vote.

were angered when Adams, who had prepared the nation for war in the aftermath of the controversial XYZ Affair, proposed sending a peace mission to France in 1799. They were later flabbergasted when the president, in the face of strong Federalist opposition, threatened to resign and leave the presidency in the hands of arch-rival Thomas Jefferson. Although a caucus of Federalist senators and congressmen had re-nominated Adams in May 1800, most rank-and-file Federalists never again completely trusted the short, plump New Englander. Hoping to rid themselves of the troublesome old man, Hamilton and other Federalist leaders privately tried to draft George Washington for a third term, but the former commander-in-chief, in declining health, opted to remain in retirement at Mount Vernon. Unwilling to endure four more years under Adams, the shrewd and cunning Hamilton then secretly schemed to elevate South Carolina's Charles Pinckney to the presidency.

Although not entirely happy with Adams, a majority of Federalists reluctantly rallied behind the beleaguered president, re-nominating him in May of 1800 at a caucus of Federalist lawmakers. They also named Charles Cotesworth Pinckney of South Carolina, the brother of the Federalist Party's vice presidential candidate in 1796, as his running mate, hoping that Pinckney would strengthen the ticket in the South and help offset the loss of New York—a crucial state with twelve electoral votes that had supported Adams four years earlier—which had already given the Republicans control of the New York legislature. The campaign, of course, was an excruciatingly difficult one for Adams. Not only was Hamilton, as in 1796, again scheming to elevate Pinckney to the presidency and relegating Adams to the vice presidency by manipulating the vote in the Electoral College, but several of his own cabinet members, especially Secretary of State Timothy Pickering and Secretary of War James McHenry, a physician and close ally of Hamilton, were delighting in the fact that they had obstructed some of the president's policies. McHenry resigned at the president's request, but Pickering, who denounced Adams as a doddering old man who was "influenced by the vilest passions," had to be removed from office and was replaced by 45-year-old future Supreme Court chief justice John Marshall of Virginia, a leader of the southern Federalists in Congress. Marshall had incurred the wrath of most Federalists by voting to repeal the Alien and Sedition Act and by favoring Adams's effort to make peace with France. Adams named Samuel Dexter of Massachusetts to replace McHenry. Curiously, however, Adams allowed Secretary of the Treasury Oliver Wolcott to remain in his post despite widespread knowledge that he was acting as Hamilton's spy within the administration. Meanwhile, Hamilton hardly tried to conceal his contempt for Adams. "If we must have an enemy at the head of the Government," he argued, "let it be one whom we can oppose, and for whom we are not responsible, who will not involve our party in the disgrace of his foolish and bad measures."[29]

Despite serious misgivings about Adams, the Federalists feared Jefferson's election even more and, as such, waged one of the dirtiest campaigns in U.S. history. "For a high-toned people they waved an astonishingly low-level campaign," observed one historian. "They charged that Jefferson had cheated his British creditors, obtained his property by fraud, robbed a widow of an estate worth ten thousand pounds, and behaving in a cowardly fashion as Governor of Virginia during the Revolution." Marshalling all of the forces of bigotry and intolerance to their cause, the Federalists tried in vain to prevent the election of the Virginia "Jacobin" to the presidency. The campaign was so nasty that First Lady Abigail Adams lamented that enough "abuse and scandal" had been unleashed "to ruin and corrupt the minds and morals of the best people in the world."[30] However, Jefferson, presented to the electorate as a friend of the farmer, succeeded in ending Federalist control of the White House once and for all, narrowly defeating the increasingly unpopular Adams in the Electoral College. Because of the use of the double-balloting system originally established by the Constitution in which presidential electors were required to cast two votes each for the presidency (with the second-place finisher becoming vice president), Jefferson and his running-mate Aaron Burr both tied in the Electoral College. The two men each received 73 electoral votes to 65 for Adams and 64 for Charles Pinckney with one Rhode Island Federalist casting his vote for John Jay, the nation's first chief justice of the Supreme Court. The election was then tossed into the House of Representatives, controlled by the lame-duck Federalists, where Jefferson finally emerged victorious on the thirty-sixth ballot. Burr, who was never particularly close to Jefferson, became vice president.

Jefferson's election in 1800 ended the Federalist Party's early domination of both the White House and Congress. Prior to Jefferson's ascendancy to the pinnacle of power, the Federalists had steadily maintained a relatively comfortable six-seat majority in the U.S. Senate and outnumbered their rival Democratic-

---

29. Miller, *The Federalist Era*, pp. 258-262; Paul F. Boller, Jr., *Presidential Campaigns* (New York, 1984), pp. 10-11. Hamilton, who actively campaigned against Adams in New England, was denounced by the President as the leader of a "pro-British" faction and "a bastard, and as much an alien as Gallatin"—a reference to the brilliant Swiss-born Pennsylvania Republican Albert Gallatin who later served as Jefferson's highly capable Secretary of the Treasury.

30. Boller, *Presidential Campaigns*, pp. 11-13.

Republicans by twenty-two seats in the House of Representatives. When the Seventh Congress convened on December 7, 1801, the Democratic-Republicans outnumbered the Federalists in the House by a margin of 66 to 38 and held seventeen seats in the U.S. Senate to fifteen for the rapidly declining Federalists. By 1803, two years into Jefferson's first term, the Eighth Congress was totally dominated by the Democratic-Republicans. Jefferson's party enjoyed a sixteen-seat majority in the Senate and controlled the House with 102 seats to only 39 for the fading Federalists.

Friend and foe alike conceded Jefferson's re-election as a virtual certainty as the country approached its fifth presidential contest in 1804. Realizing that he would not be named as Jefferson's running mate that year, Vice President Aaron Burr, an intensely ambitious and highly intelligent man, mounted an unsuccessful campaign for governor of New York, losing badly to Morgan Lewis, a former Revolutionary Army officer and lawyer who was among the first in that state to cast his lot with Jefferson's new Democratic-Republican Party.[31] One of the most enigmatic yet fascinating politicians in American history, the 48-year-old Burr presided over the impeachment trial of Supreme Court Justice Samuel Chase during his otherwise uneventful term as Jefferson's vice president. Following a formal caucus of Republican senators and congressmen in early February, George Clinton, the cheerful 65-year-old ex-governor of New York, was named as Burr's replacement on the Republican ticket.

Though bulldozed under by Jefferson's rising democratic movement, the Federalists—at least those who hadn't yet deserted the dying party—nevertheless went through the painstaking motion of nominating a presidential ticket in 1804. Though born into privilege, these diehard Federalists, apparently willing to put up with political penury for years to come, were not about to let their once proud party die on the vine. With little or no realistic chance of recapturing the presidency, they were determined that the Federalist banner would still ripple in the winds of American politics.

---

31. Blaming Alexander Hamilton for his overwhelming defeat in New York's gubernatorial race, Burr shot and killed his ex-Federalist rival in a duel in Weehawken, New Jersey, on July 11, 1804. After fleeing to Virginia, Burr, entertaining visions of gaining fame and power by trying to establish a separate empire in the southwest, ended up defending himself against charges of treason. In a widely watched trial presided over by Chief Justice John Marshall, the disgraced former vice president was acquitted in 1807. Following a trip to Europe where he continued to dabble in nebulous intrigues, Burr returned to the United States in 1812 and practiced law in New York City until his death in 1836.

At an informal meeting in Washington in late February of that year, these undeterred Federalists named philanthropist Charles Cotesworth Pinckney of South Carolina for president. Pinckney, who had been the party's vice presidential candidate on the ticket headed by John Adams in 1800, was one of the few remaining Federalists of national stature. The party, needless to say, was suffering from a dearth of national leaders. The venerable Rufus King of New York was selected as Pinckney's vice-presidential running mate.

A man of varied interests, the 58-year-old Pinckney was the son of a wealthy plantation owner. Educated in England, he was considered an accomplished musician and one of South Carolina's leading botanists. A gifted speaker and lawyer by training, Pinckney's plans for a career in law were sidetracked when, as a young man, he won a seat in the provincial assembly. A devoted patriot of the American cause, Pinckney served as a colonel and aide to General Washington during the Revolutionary War, but was captured by the British in Charleston in 1780. He was released as part of a prisoner exchange two years later and eventually rose to the rank of brigadier general in the Continental Army before the end of the war.

After the war, Pinckney delved even deeper into national politics, serving as a delegate to the Federal Convention of 1787 where he vigorously supported ratification of the Constitution. Pinckney was hardly an ambitious politician—he was motivated more by a strong sense of obligation, a sense of giving something back to one's country, than by any lust for power or prestige. On no less than three occasions between 1791 and 1795, he refused important appointments from President Washington, turning down offers as Commander of the Army, Secretary of War and Secretary of State. He finally relented and accepted an appointment to serve as minister to France, but the French, steaming over Jay's Treaty with Britain (which they felt was heavily biased in favor of the British), refused to receive him. Pinckney gained national prominence the following year when, as a member of a special commission appointed by President John Adams, he delivered his legendary reply to the French during the highly publicized XYZ Affair. When three French agents, representing French foreign minister Charles Maurice Talleyrand, demanded a public disavowal of anti-French statements allegedly made by Adams, along with a $12 million loan and a $250,000 bribe, Pinckney obdurately responded to the French that the United States was willing to spend "Millions for defense, but not one cent for tribute."

It was, of course, one of the most widely misquoted slogans in American history, yet Pinckney, an extraordinarily talented diplomat, became an instant hero to thousands of Americans. (In truth, Pinckney, believing that the bribe was a bit too excessive, had merely said, "No! No! Not a sixpence.").[32] President Adams published the commission's report but substituted the letters X, Y, and Z for the names of the French agents. An undeclared naval war with France followed shortly thereafter.

Despite his hero status, Pinckney's candidacy aroused little enthusiasm during the presidential campaign of 1804. In fact, the former Continental Army officer didn't bother to mount much of a campaign, busying himself with other matters instead, including leading a crusade to outlaw the barbaric custom of dueling. He had been deeply moved by the fatal duel between his close friend Alexander Hamilton and Aaron Burr. Pinckney himself had been wounded in a similar shootout in 1785.

With almost no opposition to speak of, Jefferson rolled to an easy victory, swamping his Federalist rival by an Electoral College margin of 162 votes to fourteen. Pinckney was simply no match for the tall Virginian. The Federalists' downward spiral was further evidenced by the loss of fourteen House seats and two Senate seats in the Ninth Congress. New Hampshire Senator William Plumer, then a Federalist, blamed the party's defeat on lethargy and a sense of hopelessness on the part of voters who had previously been loyal to the party.

Over the next couple of years the on-again, off-again Napoleonic Wars between France and Great Britain slowly drew the United States into the international crisis. French and British warships often interfered with American trading vessels. The British frequently stopped American ships to draft sailors from the crews, insisting that such acts of impressments involved only British subjects. But in some cases, those taken by force were actually American citizens. Massachusetts Senator John Quincy Adams, a leading Federalist who would soon break with his party, described the British behavior as an "authorized system of kidnapping upon the ocean." Although the French were hardly innocent when it came to capturing American vessels in European ports, it was England's superior navy, plundering roughly one of every eight American vessels on the high seas that eventually earned the wrath of the American people.

The final straw came in June 1807, when the American frigate, the *Chesapeake*, came under fire from Great Britain's man-of-war HMS *Leopard* after refusing to allow the British to board the ship to search for possible deserters. This unprovoked attack by the English resulted in the deaths of three American crewmen and injuries to eighteen others. Shortly thereafter, as news of the attack

---

32. Miller, *The Federalist Era*, p. 212.

spread throughout the country, the American people began clamoring for war with England.

Like his cautious predecessor John Adams during the XYZ Affair, Jefferson calmly resisted the nation's war cries and ordered an embargo instead. Hoping to preserve the peace, Jefferson enacted the ill-conceived Embargo Act of 1807, barring American vessels from entering foreign ports while prohibiting foreign ships from taking on cargo in the United States. Unfortunately, Jefferson's embargo effectively killed American exports, inflicting untold misery on merchants and manufacturers dependent on foreign trade. It had a particularly harmful economic impact in the old Federalist enclaves of New York and New England. Under the embargo, exports fell from $108 million to $22 million in its first year, while imports dropped sharply from $138 million to less than $57 million in 1808.[33]

Although it virtually crippled foreign trade, Jefferson was determined to see his "candid and liberal experiment" in "peaceful coercion" through to the end of his second term. Despite mounting political opposition from the Federalists, the erudite Jefferson desperately stuck by his general embargo. However, in the final days of his administration, the Republican-controlled Congress replaced Jefferson's flawed Embargo Act with the Non-intercourse Act, which allowed American merchants to trade with all other foreign countries except France and Great Britain. Passed in early March 1809, that legislation also provided that if either quarrelsome nation lifted its blockade against American shipping, the U.S. would lift its ban against that country. Fourteen months later, Congress also approved legislation drafted by North Carolina's Nathaniel Macon that once again opened trade with France and Britain. Macon's bill stipulated that if either foreign power revoked its restriction on neutral commerce, a policy of non-intercourse would be resumed against the other.

The escalating war between the two European nations, each seeking preeminent superpower status at the expense of the other, coupled with Jefferson's misguided remedy that struck hard at certain American industries while completely devastating the fledgling nation's maritime interests, was like a fire-bell in the night for the then-dormant Federalist Party. Although many of its more influential members had long since deserted the party, including John Quincy Adams, the Federalists seemed poised for a comeback. The 41-year-old Adams, who

---

33.   Bernard Bailyn, David Brion Davis, David Herbert Donald, John L. Thomas, Robert H. Wiebe and Gordon S. Wood, *The Great Republic: A History of the American People* (Lexington, Mass., 1981), p. 298.

rarely followed the party line anyway, had startled his Federalist colleagues by breaking completely with the party in 1807 when he supported Jefferson's embargo. Despite the defections of several other prominent party members during this period, a number of remaining Federalists were suddenly inflicted with Potomac fever as the 1808 presidential election neared. For the first time in nearly a dozen years, the Federalists were imbued with both enthusiasm and bravado.

Of course, not all Federalists believed that the time was ripe to again seize power—some thought it would be a bit wiser, especially in a period of international uncertainty, to throw their support to 68-year-old George Clinton, the lesser evil within the dominant Democratic-Republican Party. A former Anti-Federalist, Clinton had been elected governor of New York on seven separate occasions. By backing Clinton, who, in the eyes of most Federalist leaders was certainly preferable to James Madison, Jefferson's successor and a co-founder of the Democratic-Republican Party, the Federalists couldn't be blamed if the international situation suddenly turned ugly. It would be the Republicans—and not the Federalists—who would have to answer to an angry electorate if the country was dragged into an un-winnable three-cornered war. The party of George Washington and John Adams, they reasoned, would then be perfectly positioned to regain the White House and Congress in 1812.

But a majority—or perhaps it was only an undaunted vocal minority—disagreed with that strategy. In their view, the Federalist Party had been too cautious and too conservative for too long. It was time, they believed, to take their case to the American people. Exhibiting the can-do spirit of General Washington at Valley Forge, this small but courageous band of Federalist leaders, numbering no more than twenty-five or thirty, met privately in New York City in August. According to one historian, this was the first national nominating convention in American history.[34] Smelling blood, these obstinate out-of-power Federalists, while rejecting Clinton's candidacy, accepted Rufus King's recommendation that the party should nominate its own ticket and again named Charles Pinckney and New York's Rufus King for president and vice president, respectively.

By 1808, the party's best-known leaders, not the least being John Quincy Adams and John Marshall, the brilliant chief justice of the U.S. Supreme Court, had already abandoned the party, essentially giving it up for dead. Even in its former stronghold of New England, the party had suffered at the polls in recent

---

34. Samuel Eliot Morison, "The First National Nominating Convention, 1808," *American Historical Review*, Vol. 17 (1912), pp. 744-763.

years. Connecticut, where Washington's old friend Jonathan Trumbull still reigned, was one of only three states with a Federalist governor.[35] Moreover, the party clung to a mere 24 seats in the 142-seat U.S. House of Representatives and held only six of thirty-four seats in the U.S. Senate. Nevertheless, in what amounted to a three-way race against two Democratic-Republican opponents—James Madison of Virginia and New York's George Clinton—Pinckney ran better than expected, carrying the four states of New England, as well as Delaware. He also picked up two of Maryland's eleven electoral votes and three of North Carolina's fourteen, polling 47 electoral votes to Madison's 122. Clinton received six of New York's 19 electoral votes. In addition, the Federalists won gubernatorial races in every state in New England, and, though unable to increase their small bloc in the U.S. Senate, doubled their membership in the lower chamber of Congress by winning 49 seats.

In several other states the Federalists conducted competitive campaigns for the first time in more than a decade. In Pennsylvania, for example, two rival Federalist factions combined for nearly forty percent of the vote against the entrenched Jeffersonian Republicans—the largest gubernatorial vote ever amassed by Federalists in that state.[36]

The Keystone State was a most unlikely setting for a Federalist revival. Though once a Federalist stronghold, the state's leading political figures, including popular Gov. Thomas Mifflin and influential Senator William MacClay, had long viewed the Federalists with disdain. As such, Pennsylvania was the only state outside the South that Jefferson carried against the Federalist Party's John Adams in 1796. Moreover, Philadelphia's four largest newspapers had been consistently hostile to Washington's Federalist administration. Of these, Benjamin Franklin Bache's *Aurora* was the most scurrilous, accusing the "perfidious" president of padding his expenses and claiming that Adams really wanted to be King. Known as "Lightning Rod, Junior," the fiery Bache, a grandson of Benjamin Franklin, was later charged with seditious libel under the controversial Alien and Sedition Act, but died of yellow fever before his case was brought to trial.

---

35. Delaware's George Truitt, who served as that state's chief executive from 1808-11, and Vermont's Isaac Tichenor, a Princeton-educated lawyer and former chief justice of the state Supreme Court, also served as Federalist governors that year.

36. The Pennsylvania Federalists were badly divided that year. In a three-cornered race, Federalists James Ross of Pittsburgh and John Spayd polled 39,575 and 4,006 votes, respectively, against Democratic-Republican Simon Snyder's 67,975 votes. See, *The Pennsylvania Manual, 1972-73*, Vol. 101, p. 909.

There was also plenty of ill will toward the Federalists in the western part of the state. Widespread anti-Federalist sentiment had been festering in that area since the so-called Whiskey Rebellion in 1794. That year, the region's frontier settlers protested a Federalist-imposed excise tax on whiskey and were suppressed by a militia of nearly fifteen thousand troops headed by President Washington himself. Once a soldier, always a soldier, Washington's response to the rebellion was a classic case of overkill—the ragged and poorly-armed Pennsylvanians were no match for Washington's troops and were quickly dispersed. Incidentally, the militia assembled by Washington in putting down the Whiskey Rebellion was larger than any army he had commanded during the Revolutionary War and the president attempted to justify the government's excessive show of force by arguing it was time to demonstrate to the rest of the world that the United States was determined to defend its government and laws. Not surprisingly, the failed Whiskey Rebellion left a bitter aftertaste and for the next dozen years Federalist candidates were routinely swamped in Pennsylvania statewide elections.

In 1810, as the young "War Hawks," led by influential House Speaker Henry Clay of Kentucky, South Carolina's John C. Calhoun and Felix Grundy of Tennessee, whipped up widespread enthusiasm for war with Great Britain, Federalist fortunes again slipped. Having lost a dozen seats in that year's congressional elections, the antiwar Federalists were outnumbered in the House by a margin of 108 to 36 and held only a half-dozen of the thirty-six seats in the U.S. Senate. During this period, the Federalists lost some of their most renowned and brilliant members, including former Sen. William Plumer of New Hampshire, former Secretary of War Samuel Dexter of Massachusetts and Daniel Webster, who first entered Congress from New Hampshire as a Federalist in 1813 but within a few short years no longer considered himself a member of the party. The party keenly felt the loss of these talented young men. Moreover, by 1808 only two Federalists—John Marshall and Bushrod Washington, a nephew of the late president—remained on the nation's highest court. That number, however, increased when James Madison, ignoring party labels, appointed Joseph Story, a young Federalist congressman and law professor from Massachusetts, to the Supreme Court in 1811. A founder of the Harvard Law School, the 32-year-old Story, who was credited with establishing a solid foundation for the nation's admiralty laws, remained on the bench until his death in 1845.

Federalist fortunes improved, however, with the outbreak of the War of 1812. The Federalists had long opposed the idea of war with Great Britain. "Sooner would ninety-nine out of a hundred separate from the Union, than plunge into such an abyss," wrote devoted Federalist Timothy Dwight, president of Yale University, several years earlier.[37] Because of their close commercial ties to Great Britain, Federalists in New England had done everything in their power to prevent a declaration of war. Shortly after war was declared on June 18, Federalist lawmakers in Massachusetts and Connecticut defiantly refused to allow their state militias to aid the national war effort.

The party's bitter opposition to that conflict, coupled with James Madison's bungling of the American military effort, again led to a limited Federalist revival. Hoping to prevent Madison's destruction of the nation, the Federalist Party held its last formal meeting of party leaders to nominate a presidential ticket in 1812, when they endorsed electors pledged to 43-year-old DeWitt Clinton, the aristocratic and ambitious nephew of longtime New York governor George Clinton. At the time, the younger Clinton was serving simultaneously as mayor of New York City and as the state's lieutenant governor. He was joined on the ticket by the aging Jared Ingersoll of Pennsylvania, a dignified and urbane Federalist who had served in the Continental Congress and as a delegate to the Constitutional Convention of 1787.

Clinton's candidacy was sharply opposed by influential Federalist Rufus King, who believed that by backing the New Yorker the Federalists were merely substituting a Caesar for James Madison. It was a harsh comment. As in previous presidential campaigns, King again urged the Federalists to nominate their own ticket.

This time, however, a majority of the party faithful, influenced by moderate state Senator Harrison Gray Otis of Massachusetts and others, decided to support the younger Clinton. Clinton, after all, promised them that he would appoint Federalists to key government posts. For the first time since Jefferson's inauguration in 1801, Federalists would again be welcome in a presidential administration. Longing for a return to glory, the out-of-power Federalists took Clinton at his word. Yet fearing a possible backlash among Clinton's insurgent Republican followers—a group of whom had endorsed him on May 29—they didn't publicly endorse his candidacy, but quietly supported his electors. This suited Clinton perfectly, enabling him to enjoy Federalist backing without being publicly linked to the antiwar party—a party despised by many of his supporters within the Democratic-Republican ranks.

During this period, the Federalists were widely viewed with suspicion—and not without good reason. It was no secret that many Federalists favored coopera-

37. William Plumer, Jr., *The Life of William Plumer*, A. P. Peabody, ed., (Boston, 1857), pp. 282-283.

tion with Great Britain, believing that the Royal Navy was the first line of defense for the United States against France in its trade with Europe. Disenchanted Federalists in New England sold their government bonds and stubbornly discouraged enlistments in the army. A few of the more fierce Federalists, including the aging Timothy Pickering, a diplomat with a flair for the undiplomatic, and John Lowell of the so-called Essex Junto, went so far as to urge secession from the Union in order to save New England, while a few others could hardly contain their glee at news of British naval victories across the sea.[38] Lowell authored a series of stinging pamphlets that accused the Republicans of behaving like the Jacobins while making little secret of his secessionist intentions and the *Boston Gazette*, a newspaper heavily influenced by the Junto, had urged secession as early as 1808, shortly after Jefferson had enacted the embargo. "It is better to suffer the amputation of a limb than to lose the whole body. We must prepare for the operation."[39]

On the home front, there were even unsubstantiated reports that some antiwar Federalists had engaged in traitorous activities, including burning blue lights to signal U.S. ship movements to the offshore English fleet. The fact that the British exempted New England from its blockade of the country's Atlantic ports lent considerable credence to these reports. Moreover, the widely respected Commodore Stephen Decatur complained in early 1813 that blue-light signals had prevented him from setting out to sea from New London, Connecticut. Although there was no concrete evidence that the Federalists had anything to do with the treasonous blue lights, they were soon given the opprobrious label of "Bluelight Federalists" by their Democratic-Republican opponents. This disgraceful moniker stuck in the public mind until the demise of the party more than a decade later. In fact, in his diary, "Old Man Eloquent" John Quincy Adams, a one-time Federalist himself, referred to the "Bluelight Federalist" epithet as late as 1833.

---

38. In addition to Lowell and Pickering, the "Essex Junto," a term that first appeared during the period of the Articles of Confederation when John Hancock used it in a derisive reference to his adversaries in Essex County, Massachusetts, was comprised of Judge Theophilus Parsons, Jonathan Jackson, former Sen. George Cabot, Nathan Dane, Benjamin Goodhue, Fisher Ames, Theodore Sedgwick, Tristram Dalton, John Lowell, Jr., Stephen Higginson, Josiah Quincy, Caleb Strong, ex-Congressman Harrison Gray Otis, Francis Dana, and Robert Treat Paine, a signer of the Declaration of Independence and longtime Federalist who served as a prosecutor in the Boston Massacre trials of 1770. Most of its members resided in Boston.

39. John Lowell, Jr., *The New England Patriot* (San Francisco, 1940), p. 62; David Loth, *Chief Justice* (New York, 1960), p. 257.

The war, of course, was not going well for President Madison and Federalist opposition to it—at least initially—seemed to be paying huge political dividends. The Madison administration was woefully unprepared to take on their British rivals. The navy had been reduced in size and the regular army suffered cutbacks in favor of the militia. America's military strategy initially called for a three-pronged invasion of Canada, a country where two-thirds of its inhabitants were American-born. The invasions were to occur along Lake Champlain near Montreal, across the Niagara frontier and from Detroit. But by the summer and early fall of 1812, efforts to liberate British-occupied Canada were proving to be a dismal failure. General William Hull, who was later described as a latter-day "Benedict Arnold," inexplicably surrendered to the British in Detroit without so much as firing a single shot. It soon became apparent to most Americans that its war with England wouldn't be won overnight—if, indeed, it were to be won at all.

Pitted against Madison, who had been unanimously nominated for a second term by a caucus of congressional Republicans in May—a month before the nation's declaration of war against England—Clinton's appeal was not only to those who abhorred the war, especially the Federalists, but also to those who were growing increasingly unhappy with Madison's handling of the conflict. To Madison's hawkish critics, Clinton promised a more vigorous prosecution of the war and to the antiwar Federalists of New England, the young New Yorker pledged an immediate cessation of hostilities. According to at least one historian, Clinton was simultaneously a "thunderbolt of war and an angel of peace," carefully straddling both sides of the issue.

In losing to the incumbent president by a closer than expected electoral vote of 128 to 89, Clinton carried every state in New England except Vermont. Impressively, he also added New York, New Jersey and five of Maryland's eleven electoral votes to the anti-Madison column. In addition to Clinton's relatively strong showing against the somewhat colorless Madison, the Federalists picked up thirty-two seats in the U.S. House of Representatives, increasing their representation from 36 to 68 seats, while trimming the Democratic-Republican majority to only forty-four seats. The Federalists also gained three Senate seats in the 13th Congress, enlarging their meager presence in that esteemed body from six to nine.

In 1814, with the French forces deteriorating badly, the British launched a series of major assaults against the United States. In addition to an airtight blockade of the Atlantic seaboard, the British briefly occupied the nation's capitol in August, forcing President Madison and Congress to flee the burning city. The occupying British forces proceeded to scorch the Executive Mansion and several other public buildings. To make matters worse, American soldiers went weeks and months without pay, the nation's treasury was completely depleted and the British fleet had virtually captured or sunk the entire salt-water navy. As might be expected given the circumstances, American morale was at an all-time low.

Widespread discontent with the war enabled the Federalists to capture 65 House seats in the 1814 mid-term elections. The Federalists also picked up two additional seats in the U.S. Senate, bringing their total to eleven. In the meantime, the Federalists also enjoyed a resurgence of sorts at the state level, holding on to governorships in Connecticut, Maryland, Massachusetts and Rhode Island, while capturing gubernatorial races in Delaware, New Hampshire and Vermont.

The Hartford Convention

The time was again ripe for the resurgent Federalists to strike. Still dreaming of a major role in national politics, a group of New England Federalists, hoping to salvage their strong mercantile ties to Great Britain, called a regional convention to air their grievances. Meeting in Hartford, Connecticut, on December 15, 1814, twenty-six Federalists representing Connecticut, Massachusetts, New Hampshire, Rhode Island and Vermont, approved a modest agenda calling for a series of constitutional amendments. While disregarding the desire of the outnumbered Federalist extremists of the Pickering stripe who openly called for the dismemberment of the Union, the Hartford Convention, guided by Massachusetts moderate Harrison Gray Otis, hoped to lessen the growing power of the southern agrarian states by proposing to eliminate the three-fifths representation of slaves in apportioning congressional and Electoral College votes. They also demanded that the admission of new states, future embargoes (which would be limited to sixty days) and declarations of war (except in the case of an invasion) should require a two-thirds majority of Congress.

In a desperate attempt to prevent the continuation of the so-called "Virginia Dynasty"—the successive elections of Virginians Thomas Jefferson, James Madison and, later, James Monroe—the aristocratic New Englanders also approved a resolution limiting the president to a single term while preventing his successor from residing from the same state as the incumbent.

Although the convention's official report, issued in early January 1815, argued eloquently against secession, it nevertheless contained a lengthy list of indictments against the ruling Republicans, accusing that party of trying to secure perpetual control of the government at the expense of New England by excluding

Federalists from that region from influential roles in the national government. The report also charged the Republicans with unconstitutionally interfering with the nation's courts, fiscal irresponsibility, and unwarranted hostility toward Great Britain.[40]

The Hartford Convention, viewed by some as a joke yet regarded by others as a treasonous plot, concluded with the appointment of a committee of three, led by Otis, who were named to negotiate with the national government. But just as the negotiators, acting "with the confidence of emissaries on a mission that could not fail," neared the nation's capital, news of the successful Ghent peace treaty, which was concluded on Christmas eve, and Andrew Jackson's smashing victory over the redcoats in New Orleans—resulting in one of the worst British military setbacks in history—swept across the country. Realizing that it was pointless to press their case in the midst of the national jubilation over Jackson's tremendous success in New Orleans, the Federalist commissioners turned around and quietly returned home.

In hindsight, the Federalist strategy was doomed from the outset. Shortly before the Hartford Convention, the U.S. war effort had improved slightly when the British army that had occupied Washington, D.C., failed in a similar attempt to capture Baltimore. This was followed almost immediately by Thomas Macdonough's naval victory in a critical battle in Plattsburg Bay on Lake Champlain on September 11—forcing the British to withdraw and take refuge in Canada.

Other factors were also working against the Federalists. In August 1814, diplomat John Quincy Adams, a former Harvard professor and the nation's first minister to Russia, had been quietly negotiating a peace treaty with the British at Ghent. It soon became clear that England, badly shaken by the news of its devastating defeat in the Battle of Plattsburg Bay, was no longer interested in prolonging the war.

Federalist fortunes, as one might expect, fell dramatically with the advent of peace. The party could no longer rely on the support of the merchant ship owners of the Atlantic ports from Boston to Charleston. Nevertheless, some Federalists refused to wither away. In 1816, a handful of party leaders nominated New York Senator Rufus King, the politically weary and aging former ambassador to the Court of St. James, for the presidency.

Considered one of the ablest lawmakers of his time, King, a lawyer and diplomat, had faithfully labored on behalf of the Federalist cause for the better party of a quarter century, serving as his party's vice presidential standard-bearer in 1804

---

40. William Edward Buckley, *The Hartford Convention* (New Haven, 1934), pp. 20-21.

and 1808. He was an exceptional speaker who had earned the respect of most of his peers, including those in the opposing party.

Former Maryland Senator John E. Howard, 64, was named as King's vice-presidential running mate. A diehard Federalist, Howard had retired from the U.S. Senate nearly fourteen years earlier. He had previously served in the Continental Congress and as governor of Maryland, serving in the latter capacity from 1788 to 1791. A colonel in the Revolutionary Army who was honored for his gallantry at the battle of Cowpens in 1781, Howard later declined George Washington's appointment as Secretary of War.

By 1816, most Federalists, including King himself, were resigned to future Democratic-Republican control of the country. Their time had passed. "Federalists of our age must be content with the past," said King. Viewing the likelihood of a Federalist resurgence in national politics as a "fruitless struggle," King, like many other Federalists in the days immediately following the War of 1812, believed that his party should assist "the least wicked" faction of the Democratic-Republican Party.[41] This, of course, was a sharp departure from the views he held earlier when he urged the Federalists to nominate their own ticket rather than support insurgent movements led by the Clintons within the opposition party's ranks in 1808 and 1812.

Meanwhile, the entrenched Republicans, meeting in caucus, selected Secretary of State James Monroe of Virginia for president. The 58-year-old Monroe, a Revolutionary War hero and able diplomat who had served in the U.S. Senate and as governor of Virginia, was nominated by a narrow 65 to 54 margin over William H. Crawford of Georgia, a good-natured former senator who had served as Madison's Secretary of War and as Secretary of the Treasury.

The son of a moderately affluent planter, Monroe was a protégé of Thomas Jefferson. He had vigorously opposed ratification of the Constitution at the Virginia convention on the grounds that it placed too much power in a centralized government. Daniel D. Tompkins, the young and energetic governor of New York, was chosen as Monroe's vice-presidential running mate. As governor, the 42-year-old Tompkins was responsible for completely abolishing slavery in New York and had introduced a host of other liberal reforms.

Although no formal nominations were made by the Federalists that year, King, a man whose public career spanned four decades and who was one of the

---

41. Lillian B. Miller, *'If Elected...' Unsuccessful Candidates for the Presidency 1796-1968* (National Portrait Gallery, Washington, D.C., 1972), p. 69; Loth, *Chief Justice*, p. 287.

thirty-nine signers of the Constitution, received 34 electoral votes to James Monroe's 183 in the 1816 presidential election. Coming across to many voters as a somewhat "pompous and arrogant aristocrat," King was able to carry only three states—Connecticut, Delaware and Massachusetts—in his losing bid. The party's last presidential standard-bearer accepted his defeat with grace and dignity and later served his country again as minister to Great Britain during the administration of John Quincy Adams.

The once proud party of Washington, Hamilton and John Adams had all but vanished as an entity in national politics following King's devastating defeat in 1816, although a few hardy Federalists remained active at the state and local levels in a handful of states until the mid-1820s. All but the most irreconcilable Federalists had cast their lot with the Republicans during Monroe's first term. Yet the Federalist Party experienced a few noteworthy victories in its dying days, most notably in the example of former congressman Charles Goldsborough's election as governor of Maryland in 1818. A lawyer who had served in the Maryland Senate for six years and in Congress for a dozen more, Goldsborough was a member of a politically prominent family whose members had served in public office dating back to the pre-Revolutionary period all the way through the early 1950s. In Connecticut, Oliver Wolcott, Jr., a Revolutionary War veteran, served as that state's Federalist governor from 1817 to 1827 and in neighboring Massachusetts, Harrison Gray Otis served in the U.S. Senate as a Federalist from 1817-22 when fellow Federalist James Lloyd Jr., replaced him. One of the last Federalists to serve in the U.S. Senate, Lloyd, who previously served in that esteemed body from 1808 to 1813 when he was elected to fill the vacancy caused by the resignation of John Quincy Adams, was a merchant with a deep interest in foreign trade.[42]

The Federalists also continued to elect a handful of congressmen throughout the 1820s. As late as 1826, Pennsylvania sent four Federalists to Congress, including James Buchanan, a future Democratic president. First elected to Congress on the Federalist ticket in 1820—a year when the Federalists held thirty-five of the ninety-six seats in lower house of the Pennsylvania legislature and eleven of the state's thirty-one Senate seats—Buchanan didn't formally join the Democratic-Republican Party until the late 1820s. In 1827, Federalist Kensey Johns, a Princeton-educated lawyer from New Castle, narrowly defeated Republican James A. Bayard, Jr., the 28-year-old renegade son of one of the nation's staunch-

---

42. Ford, Worthington C., "The Recall of John Quincy Adams in 1808." *Massachusetts Historical Society Proceedings*, 45 (October 11-June 1912), pp. 354-375.

est Federalist families, to capture Delaware's lone seat in the U.S. House of Representatives. He was re-elected to the House as a Federalist in 1828, again defeating the young Bayard. Incredibly, as late as 1845 Anthony Colby, a long-time Whig who had already lost in two previous efforts, briefly revived the Federalist banner in an unsuccessful bid for governor of New Hampshire.

One of the last great Federalist leaders was Josiah Quincy, a former congressman and mayor of Boston from 1823-28. Clinging to the Federalist label long after the party had all but disappeared from the scene, Quincy has long been regarded as one of the best mayors in American history, playing a central role in making Boston the country's first modern city, vastly improving its public services while changing its dynamics from that of a town ruled by an elite Brahmin class to first-class city with a broad and popular electorate.[43] Born into an aristocratic family in 1772, Quincy's father was the famous patriot leader of the same name who died three years after his son's birth while returning from a diplomatic mission to Britain.

Educated at the prestigious Phillips Academy and a graduate of Harvard College, the younger Quincy practiced law with his mentor William Tudor before turning to politics. Rising rapidly in the Federalist Party, he served in the Massachusetts legislature before winning a seat in Congress in 1805. His congressional career, however, was relatively disappointing and, at times, even humiliating. In 1809, for instance, the young Federalist congressman called for Thomas Jefferson's impeachment in the waning days of his administration, only to see his motion defeated by a vote of 117-1. In the days leading up to the War of 1812, Quincy, who had a reputation as "a ranting Federal spouter," fought in vain to prevent the war, hoping that by encouraging the War Hawk faction in Congress to bang the drums of war, the administration, fearing a major conflict with England, would be sufficiently moved to offer concessions to the British. But this strategy backfired. In protest of the war, the deeply disappointed Federalist lawmaker abruptly resigned from Congress in 1813 and returned to his estate in Braintree, south of Boston.

Like most Federalists, Quincy, a wealthy WASP, didn't trust the "democratic" majority, believing that economically dependent workers would become the voting fodder of the nation's new industrialists. A Brahmin elitist, he was once accused of making statements deploring the idea of providing higher education to working-class and impoverished children. Providing moral and intellectual lead-

---

43. Robert A. McCaughey, "From Town to City: Boston in the 1820s," *Political Science Quarterly*, 80 (June 1973), pp. 202-212.

ership for the masses, Quincy firmly believed that only civic-minded members of the aristocracy could truly bring about social improvements. Ironically, however, as mayor of Boston, Quincy, representing a new generation of conservative elites, provided what can only be described as a populist brand of leadership—all the while opposing the insurgency of Jacksonian democracy.

Back home, the 41-year-old Quincy again took his seat in the Massachusetts Senate, serving until 1820. He also served in the state's lower chamber from 1821-22, the last year as Speaker of the House. Despite losing in an earlier attempt, Quincy was elected mayor of Boston in 1823, a growing city with a population of approximately 55,000. He was easily re-elected on six occasions, garnering nearly 98% of the vote in 1824 and more than 86% of the vote a year later.[44] Described by one historian as "nearly a century ahead of his time," Quincy is credited with a long list of innovative accomplishments during his six years in office. Among other things, the far-sighted mayor rebuilt the city's commercial and market sector—including enlarging the Faneuil Hall Market area—modernizing Boston's criminal justice system, providing humane treatment for the city's poor and indigent population and, like an early nineteenth-century version of New York City's Rudolph Giuliani, removed some 6,000 tons of dirt and trash from the city's streets, making the 200-year old city one of the cleanest, healthiest and safest cities in the country. He also modernized Boston's fire department and improved the city's sewage, sanitation and water supplies. It wasn't uncommon for the Federalist mayor to be seen riding horseback through the streets of his city at five in the morning making routine inspections. These early morning tours resulted in the formation of street sweeping crews, regular garbage collection and vast improvements in the city's long-neglected sewers—all of which contributed to a dramatic decrease in Boston's mortality rate.[45] "Quincy was perhaps the must successful urban reformer in early nineteenth century America," wrote one of his biographers, and "when his tenure ended, Boston was very likely the cleanest, most orderly, and best-governed city in the United States." Later generations of Bostonians referred to him as "the Great Mayor."[46]

After leaving City Hall, Quincy served as president of Harvard College for sixteen years. A brilliant administrator, the former mayor assembled a prestigious faculty, expanded the law school, built a world-famous library, and launched a

---

44.   Melvin G. Holli and Peter d' A. Jones, *Biographical Dictionary of American Mayors, 1820-1980*, p. 299.
45.   Melvin G. Holli, *The American Mayor: The Best & Worst Big-City Leaders*, p. 27-35.
46.   Robert A. McCaughey, *Josiah Quincy, 1772-1864: The Last Federalist* (Cambridge, Mass., 1974), pp. 114, 131.

fund-raising drive that led to the construction of the school's Astronomical Observatory.[47] Upon his retirement from Harvard in 1845, the former mayor pursued a literary career in which he wrote several history books, mostly about Boston, and remained involved in public life, vigorously debating the leading issues of the day. At the age of eighty-four, the last great Federalist-turned-Free Soiler ran for governor of Massachusetts as the candidate of the so-called "Bird Club"—followers of antislavery advocate Francis W. Bird of Walpole who were furious that the Republican Party had dabbled "in the dirty pool of Know-Nothingism."[48] Quincy, who garnered less than four percent of the vote in the 1856 gubernatorial contest, remained politically active for the remainder of his life, forcefully speaking out against slavery and supporting Lincoln in his struggle to preserve the Union. He died in Braintree in 1864 at the age of ninety-two. One of New England's wealthiest citizens, Quincy had accumulated a fortune of $750,000 at the time of his death. One of his seven children, abolitionist Edmund Quincy, served as vice-president of the American Anti-Slavery Society and edited the Non-Resistance Society's semi-monthly newspaper, while his namesake, Josiah Quincy, Jr., served as mayor of Boston from 1846-48.

Despite Quincy's success in Boston in the 1820s, victories were few and far between and the Federalists slowly faded from the political landscape. Much to their credit, however, the Federalist Party left an indelible mark on the new nation, demonstrating that the powers of the federal government could be used to promote the general welfare. Proving that republicanism was compatible with stability, the Federalists established procedures that were quickly emulated by their domestic opponents and eventually adopted by scores of emerging republics around the world. Unfortunately, many of those who made a parchment into a workable instrument of government went to their graves believing that their brief experiment in free government had ended in failure, convinced that the country's wisdom, virtue and talent had been discarded by demagogic politicians and an ignorant electorate. Ironically, in death, the Federalists finally achieved what they failed to accomplish in life—namely, the establishment, albeit briefly, of a one-party system.

---

47. Holli and Jones, *Biographical Dictionary of American Mayors*, p. 299.
48. John R. Mulkern, *The Know-Nothing Party in Massachusetts: The Rise and Fall of a People's Movement* (Boston, 1990), p. 152; William E. Gienapp, *The Origins of the Republican Party 1852-1856* (New York, 1987), p. 389.

The Democratic-Republicans

Despite considerable factionalism within its ranks, the Democratic-Republican Party, comprised largely of the same group that originally made up the Anti-Federalists—and before that, Patrick Henry's Patriot Party—continued to prosper long after the Federalist Party passed from the scene. The Anti-Federalists, of course, had opposed the ratification of the U.S. Constitution in 1787-88, largely on the grounds that the framers of that document had given the federal government—especially the president—too much power.

The Democratic-Republicans favored states' rights, a literal interpretation of the Constitution and popular sovereignty. Before long, the Republicans, modifying their agrarian philosophy, slowly began to resemble the party they had replaced, becoming almost as much a party of business interests as the old Federalists had been. In fact, longtime Federalist Josiah Quincy, the former mayor of Boston and Harvard University president, poignantly observed that the Republicans had "out-Federalized Federalism." The nation's banking and business communities quickly aligned themselves with the party in power.

Enjoying a healthy cash flow, the Republicans controlled both the White House and Congress for twenty-four virtually uninterrupted years, dominating national politics with no major opposition to speak of until the mid-to-late 1820s.[49]

The United States was practically a one-party nation during Monroe's "Era of Good Feeling." Although the country faced a mild economic panic in 1819, the nation's fifth president had the good fortune of governing during a period of relative calm. In fact, the Federalists, now all but a memory, failed to name even a token opponent during Monroe's bid for re-election in 1820. That suited Monroe just fine. "Surely our government may go on and prosper without the existence of parties," he asserted. Like the Founding Fathers, Monroe said that he had always considered political parties as "the curse of the country."[50] Without any organized opposition, Monroe was easily re-elected that year, capturing 231 of the 232 electoral votes cast. The sole dissenting elector was former New Hamp-

---

49. According to Binkley, the Jeffersonians owed a debt of gratitude to Alexander Hamilton and the Federalists. "It was Hamilton who had managed to integrate the then dominant elements in American society into the party that gave the new government, under the Constitution, a commanding prestige and authority in every section of the Union." See Binkley, *American Political Parties*, p. 93.
50. Boller, *Presidential Campaigns*, p. 31.

shire Governor William Plumer, an ex-Federalist and historian, who cast his lone vote for his longtime friend John Quincy Adams.[51]

The absence of serious competition from a major party opponent led to much rancor and factionalism within the dominant Democratic-Republican Party. A one-party nation was a recipe for disaster. No fewer than seventeen men, including South Carolina's John C. Calhoun, jockeyed for position in the 1824 presidential campaign. Calhoun dropped out of the race early in the year and the contest eventually dwindled down to four serious contenders—the cold and aloof John Quincy Adams, Andrew Jackson, Henry Clay and Secretary of the Treasury William H. Crawford—each seeking the presidency under the Democratic-Republican banner.

When none of the four candidates was able to obtain a majority in the Electoral College, the election was thrown into the House of Representatives, where powerful Speaker of the House Henry Clay threw his support to Secretary of State John Quincy Adams. When a grateful Adams subsequently named Clay as his Secretary of State, Jackson and Crawford partisans charged that a "corrupt bargain" had been struck.

Faced with a hostile Congress and constantly hampered by charges that he had cut a deal to win the presidency, John Quincy Adams, the eldest and most gifted son of the nation's second president, had a particularly difficult four years in the White House. Most of his program—the establishment of a national university in Washington, D.C., construction of an astronomical observatory and the building of more roads and canals—never saw the light of day. Not surprisingly, the discouraged president was soundly trounced by former Sen. Andrew Jackson of Tennessee, the rugged hero of the War of 1812, in his bid for re-election in 1828. Jackson's election marked the birth of the modern Democratic Party.

---

51. Plumer, *The Life of William Plumer*, p.283; C. O. Paullin, "The Electoral Vote for John Quincy Adams in 1820," *American Historical Review*, XXI (January 1916), pp. 318-319; Lynn W. Turner, "The Electoral Vote against Monroe in 1820—An American Legend," *Mississippi Valley Historical Review*, XLII (September 1955), p. 259. The former New Hampshire senator and governor cast his vote for Adams because he felt that the Massachusetts lawmaker and diplomat was better suited for the presidency, and not—as it was once believed—because he wanted to preserve Washington's legacy as the only man unanimously elected president of the United States.

2

Quids, Workingmen, Anti-Masons and Nullifiers

✦

America's Earliest Third Parties and Factions

While most historians insist that the Anti-Masonic Party was the country's first nationally organized third-party, a rather strong case can be made that an earlier group, known as the Quids, actually deserves that distinction. Emerging shortly after Thomas Jefferson's Democratic-Republicans seized power from the Federalists, the Quids, or "Quiddists," as they were sometimes called, were led by Virginian John Randolph, a one-time administration leader in the House of Representatives who broke ranks with Jefferson in 1805 over policy differences.

The Quids, a term derived from the Latin phrase *tertium quid*, meaning "a third something," were staunch states' rights advocates. During their brief history, the Quids opposed the acquisition of West Florida; supported Monroe against Madison in 1808; and resisted Jefferson's ill-conceived Embargo Act of 1807, which prohibited virtually all U.S. trade with the outside world.

The Quids were more than just a "Virginia, or Randolph minority," as then-Senator John Quincy Adams of Massachusetts referred to them in his diary in 1808. They were an extraordinarily independent lot—in a sense, men without a party. Of the eighty-six members of the Pennsylvania House of Representatives in 1805-06, twenty-three of them were described as Quids.[1] The Quids also held six seats in the 11th Congress from 1809-11 and Pennsylvania's William Findley, a weaver, teacher and farmer who had migrated to the United States in 1763 and immediately became a fierce advocate of independence, continued to serve in the House as a Quid until the end of the 12th Congress in 1813. Though not well-

---

1.   *Aurora*, November 19, 1806.

organized nationally, Quid leaders could be found throughout the young nation, including men like Morgan Lewis, a veteran Revolutionary War officer who had trounced Aaron Burr to win the New York governorship in 1804 in what was considered one of the most virulent campaigns in American history. Other notable Quids included Virginia agrarian philosopher John Taylor and Joseph Hopper Nicholson, a Maryland lawyer and Democrat who financed and commanded an artillery company that defended Fort McHenry during the War of 1812.

Another prominent Quid steward was Speaker of the House Nathaniel Macon of North Carolina, who, though less spectacular than Randolph, was nevertheless one of the ablest of the Quid leaders. A former private in Washington's Continental Army, the Princeton-educated Macon had opposed the ratification of the U.S. Constitution on the grounds that it gave the central government far too much power. As the Democratic-Republicans geared up for the War of 1812 the independent-minded Macon, siding with the antiwar Federalists, worked diligently to reduce the size of the navy and even called for the abolition of the army. A fiscal conservative, Macon, fearing that war with Great Britain would eventually lead to the establishment of a larger federal government, did almost everything in his power to thwart President Madison's ability to wage war—and to a large degree, he succeeded. Not only was the regular army drastically reduced in size, the Bank of the United States, the federal government's chief financial agency, was allowed to expire on the eve of the conflict with England.

An eccentric politician, Quid leader John Randolph was quite fond of quoting Latin and Greek in his speeches. In fact, after using the term *tertium quid* in one of his speeches, his followers were quickly dubbed the "Quids." An extreme extrovert by nature, Randolph was considered an authority on parliamentary procedure and was a superbly skilled debater. Few were willing to take him on. Never in particularly good health, he was best known for his sarcastic and often invective language. He rarely pulled any punches. Believing that Daniel Webster had personally insulted him, the Virginian responded by saying, "I would not attempt to vie with the honorable gentleman from Massachusetts in a field where every nigger is his peer and every billygoat his master." On another occasion, the tart-tongued Randolph reputedly described Edward Livingston, President Jackson's second Secretary of State, as "a man of splendid abilities but utterly corrupt. He shines and stinks like rotten mackerel by moonlight." It was vintage Randolph. When the Quid movement faded out around 1812, Randolph, who once fought a harmless duel with Henry Clay, remained in public life as a kind of one-man thorn in the side of whatever administration happened to be in power. In addition to serving a brief stint as U.S. minister to Russia in 1830, he served in Congress until his death three years later.

The Anti-Masonic Party

Jacksonian Democracy, marked by universal male suffrage, the popular election of public officials, shorter terms of office and political patronage, helped to usher in a number of new political parties—most notably, the Anti-Masonic Party in 1827. The Anti-Masons were, as their name implied, highly critical of the Masonic Order, as well as other secret societies of the time.

It is widely believed that the Anti-Masonic Party was formed shortly after the mysterious disappearance of William Morgan, an itinerant bricklayer and Freemason, who, along with David C. Miller, the struggling publisher of the *Batavia Republican Advocate*, apparently planned to divulge the secrets and rituals of the Masonic Order in a book that was soon to be published. Apparently, both men wanted revenge against certain Masonic lodges that had harassed them, verbally and physically, on several occasions. In one instance, local Masons tried to destroy Miller's printing presses by setting fire to his shop. Incredibly, while Morgan's book *Illustrations of Masonry* was being printed, he was arrested and jailed in the Finger Lakes village of Canandaigua on September 11, 1826, on a trumped-up charge of petty theft. Apparently, he owed an innkeeper two dollars and sixty-nine cents. The next day a Mason paid his paltry debt and he was quickly released from jail. As he left the jail, a small group of Masons allegedly kidnapped the unemployed and penniless author and hurried him via horse-drawn carriage to Fort Niagara, possibly en route to Canada. At Fort Niagara, or so the story goes, Morgan's abductors apparently tied him up and threw him into the river. His body was never found.[2]

The tale of Morgan's abduction and death was widely publicized by Thurlow Weed, the ambitious editor of the *Rochester Telegraph* and later the *Albany Evening Journal* and a dyed-in-the-wool foe of the Jackson administration, and other Anti-Masonic journalists of the time. The widespread publicity surrounding Morgan's baffling disappearance led to an investigation—one that was largely resisted by the Masons. At first, Masonic sheriffs, judges and members of the jury

---

2.   Formisano, Ronald and Kutolowski, Kathleen Smith, "Antimasonry and Masonry: the Genesis of Protest 1826-1827," *American Quarterly*, XXIX, No. 2 (1977), pp. 139-165.

prevented any indictments in the case. Almost overnight, the Masons were sharply denounced as frustrated civic and political leaders in communities all across the country resolved to oppose any Masons seeking public office.

One of the better known and most powerful of the Anti-Masonic leaders was Thurlow Weed, an imposing and forceful man who first became an influential political figure of sorts as editor of the *Rochester Telegraph*. A bitter enemy of Martin Van Buren, Weed skillfully used William Morgan's disappearance to mercilessly attack Van Buren's New York political machine, known as the "Albany Regency." Weed and his 26-year-old protégé, William H. Seward, convinced large numbers of New Yorkers that Van Buren's organization was really a front for Freemasonry and, as such, was completely opposed to any investigation of Morgan's mysterious disappearance. Weed and Seward portrayed Van Buren as being in an unholy alliance, not only with the Masons, but also with arrogant New York aristocrats—a tactic that did much to tarnish the Democratic Party's popularity in that state. Weed's blistering, non-stop assaults on Van Buren and the Democratic machinery paid huge dividends. Capitalizing on widespread resentment of Freemasonry, the Anti-Masonic Party polled roughly one-half of the popular-vote in New York's statewide elections in 1830.

A self-made man who served briefly in the New York assembly in 1825, Weed milked the "Morgan Affair" for all it was worth, skillfully using his newspapers—the *Rochester Telegraph* and later the *Antimasonic Enquirer*—to maximize public outrage over Morgan's disappearance and the sometimes blatant efforts of the ubiquitous Masons to hamper the subsequent investigations. It was a lengthy and bitter ordeal that eventually included twenty grand juries and resulted in the indictment of fifty-four Masons, ten of who were ultimately convicted and sentenced to relatively short prison terms. On at least two occasions, Weed, assuming the role of an investigative journalist, demanded that local officials exhume a badly decomposed body that had been pulled out of Lake Ontario by a group of fishermen in early October 1827—nearly thirteen months after Morgan had disappeared. The body bore almost no resemblance to Morgan. Though the corpse was later positively identified as Timothy Munroe, a Canadian fisherman who disappeared the previous spring, Weed, in a desperate effort to salvage his credibility, charged during a second coroner's inquest that the Masons had stolen and replaced the body to discredit his highly publicized investigation.[3]

---

3. In a post-bellum revival of anti-Masonry, the National Christian Association, then closely identified with the American National Party, erected a monument to the memory of William Morgan in 1880 and placed it in the cemetery near Munroe's gravesite.

In addition to the powerful and highly influential newspaper editor, the Anti-Masonic Party attracted some of the brightest men of that generation, including William H. Seward, Albert Tracy, William Maynard, Frederick W. Whittlesey, John C. Spencer, Theophilus Fenn, Myron Holley, Henry Dana Ward, Millard Fillmore and Pennsylvania's ardent antislavery advocate Thaddeus Stevens. Of these, Weed, Fillmore, Seward, Spencer, and Stevens went on to enjoy long and distinguished public careers. Described as the country's first modern political organizer, Thurlow Weed used the anti-Masonic movement to embarrass the ruling Van Buren machine in New York and later helped organize the Whig Party. A prototype of the nineteenth-century political boss, he also served as Seward's campaign manager throughout his long and dramatic political career and was later influential in Lincoln's administration. The six-foot-tall Fillmore, who began his political career by winning a seat in the New York legislature on the Anti-Masonic ticket, served as the nation's last Whig president in the early 1850s and later mounted a political comeback on the Know-Nothing ticket in 1856. Seward, who began his political career as an Anti-Masonic state senator, later served as New York's first Whig governor and as a member of the U.S. Senate from 1849-61. He was also Lincoln's chief rival for the Republican presidential nomination in 1860 and later served as Secretary of State in Lincoln's cabinet. Like many others attracted to the new party, Seward was hardly some sort of zealous Anti-Masonic crusader. Instead, he was a practical politician, as evidenced by his speech to the party's 1830 state convention in Utica. "We are impelled in this undertaking to abolish Freemasonry not by fiery excitement, or fanatical zeal, but by a deep sense of our responsibilities to perpetuate this government."[4] Thaddeus Stevens, whose botched and overzealous inquiry into the assorted evils of Masonry as a Pennsylvania legislator eventually cost him his seat, later served as chairman of the U.S. House Ways and Means Committee in a congressional career that spanned nearly two decades. A leading obstructionist in President Andrew Johnson's attempt to carry out a lenient Reconstruction policy in the South, Stevens also served as chairman of the managers named to conduct the impeachment proceedings against Lincoln's successor in 1868.

Also prominent among the Anti-Masons was Francis Granger, a lawyer and state assemblyman from New York. A leader of the anti-Masonic movement nationally, Granger had lost two difficult campaigns for governor of New York in 1830 and 1832 as the nominee of both the Anti-Masonic and National Republi-

---

4.   William Preston Vaughn, *The Anti-Masonic Party in the United States, 1826-1843* (Lexington, Kentucky, 1983), p. 36.

can parties. He eventually served in the U.S. House of Representatives as an Anti-Mason (1835-37) and later as a Whig. Though largely overlooked in American history, Granger was the Whig and Anti-Masonic parties' vice-presidential candidate in 1836, receiving 77 electoral votes against three rivals. When the four vice-presidential hopefuls that year failed to receive a majority in the Electoral College, the selection of a vice president, under the provisions of the twelfth amendment, was decided by the U.S. Senate which preferred Democrat Richard Johnson of Kentucky, Martin Van Buren's running mate, over Granger by a 33 to 16 margin.

Long after the dissolution of the Anti-Masonic Party, Granger remained active in public life, serving as Postmaster General during William Henry Harrison's administration. Because of his shoulder-length silver hair, Granger was considered the leader of the so-called "Silver Grays," the conservative pro-Union faction of the Whig Party that not only endorsed Know-Nothing candidate Millard Fillmore in the 1856 presidential election but also lent considerable support to the Constitutional Unionist movement four years later. Late in his long and distinguished career, Granger also served as a delegate to the failed peace-between-the-states conference of 1861.

New York's John C. Spencer, a former Democratic congressman and longtime state legislator from Canandaigua—twice winning a seat in the New York assembly on the Anti-Masonic ticket—was also an important figure in the fledgling party. Regarded as one of the ablest lawyers of his time, Spencer served as a special attorney general during the closely-watched William Morgan trial. He later served as Secretary of War and Secretary of the Treasury in John Tyler's administration, but resigned his position in 1844 rather than agree to the annexation of Texas. The hanging of his son Philip and two others aboard the brig *Somers* for attempted mutiny while Spencer was serving as Secretary of War shocked the country and was a bitter personal tragedy that marred his otherwise outstanding public career.[5]

Despite the party's meteoric rise, anti-masonry was hardly a new phenomenon in the United States. As early as 1737, newspapers in Philadelphia and New York had been critical of the Masonic Order, suggesting that behind its veiled secrecy was a pattern of immoral and lewd practices, not to mention an occasional murder. The initial attacks on Freemasonry allegedly occurred following a Masonic initiation of a member who was badly burned and died a few days later. A doctor

---

5.   Barnes, Joseph W., "Rochester's Congressmen, Part I, 1789-1869," *Rochester History*, Vol. XLI, No. 3, (July, 1979).

who belonged to the Masonic lodge involved in the incident and two others were subsequently tried and convicted of manslaughter. Benjamin Franklin's *Pennsylvania Gazette* insisted that the defendants in the case were not Masons at all, but Franklin's explanation only aroused more suspicion, especially since most readers were aware of the fact that Franklin, not unlike other leading figures of his time—including George Washington and Marquis de Lafayette—was a member of the controversial secret fraternity.[6]

Having attained their peak of popularity following America's war of independence, Freemasonry came under attack again in the 1790s when Congregational minister Jedediah Morse of Boston asserted that the mysterious Bavarian Illuminati had secretly gained control of the French government following that country's revolution and was seeking to do the same in the United States. As proof of a foreign plot against the United States, Morse cited a book written by an obscure Presbyterian clergyman from Scotland in which the author traced the Illuminati's activities in France and England, where they allegedly used the Masonic Order as a front, and detailed the group's clandestine plans to move on to America. A number of newspapers in New England carried stories about the Illuminati and warned of the danger of such a conspiracy. Before long a number of clergymen in New England and New York were echoing Morse's warnings, but unlike the situation some three decades later the anti-Masonic crusade of the 1790s failed to arouse much anxiety among citizens of the new republic and soon vanished as a public concern.[7]

The situation in the late 1820s, however, was quite a bit different. Morgan's book eventually hit the market, was read and widely believed and, aided by the frenzied and dramatic coverage of sympathetic newspaper editors and publishers like Thurlow Weed, the Anti-Masonic Party—the first of many nationally organized third parties—was born. Almost overnight, the Anti-Masonic movement was transformed from a grassroots protest movement with social and religious underpinnings into a national political party not to be taken lightly. By 1832, there were at least fifty-five anti-Masonic newspapers in Pennsylvania and no fewer than forty-six in New York. Hundreds of thousands of Americans were convinced that Masonry wasn't some sort of benevolent brotherhood, as its members claimed, but rather a Luciferian conspiracy to rule the United States—and the world.

---

6.   Lorman Ratner, *Antimasonry: The Crusade and the Party* (Englewood Cliffs, N.J., 1969), pp. 3-4
7.   Ibid., pp. 3-5.

In the autumn of 1827, fifteen Anti-Masons were elected to the New York Assembly. The results, remarked one observer, "astonished all—even the Anti-masons themselves—and opened the eyes of the politicians to the growing power of the new party."[8] The following year the party elected seventeen assemblymen and five state senators in New York, while demonstrating some considerable electoral strength in Pennsylvania and Ohio. That year, the Anti-Masons also elected five congressmen—Robert S. Rose, Timothy Childs, Phineas L. Tracy and Ebenezer F. Norton of New York and William Cahoon of Vermont—and played the role of spoiler in New York's hotly-contested gubernatorial election between Democrat Martin Van Buren and National Republican Smith Thompson, a 60-year-old U.S. Supreme Court justice and former Secretary of the Navy. In that race, the Anti-Masonic Party's Solomon Southwick, a somewhat eccentric politician, former Mason and editor of the *Albany National Observer*, the state's leading Anti-Masonic journal, polled the difference between his major-party rivals, garnering 33,335 votes, or twelve percent of the total, to Van Buren's 136,795 and Thompson's 106,415.[9]

From the outset, the anti-Masonic movement, which began in the hills and valleys of western New York, was such a force in the towns and villages of that region, particularly in the so-called "burned over district"—a region where religious revivals and political reform crusades were commonplace during this period—that a number of longtime incumbents who just happened to be Masons were unexpectedly tossed out of office.[10] At the same time, the anti-Masonic movement, picking up incredible steam, enabled a number of other down-and-out politicians to mount significant political comebacks, simply because they embraced the cause of anti-Masonry. These included such political relics as Martin Flint in Vermont and Solomon Southwick in New York. A veteran of the War of 1812, Flint who was reputedly the first Mason in Vermont to quit the order shortly after the Morgan affair, was perhaps more responsible than anyone in making eastern Vermont an Anti-Masonic stronghold. A former county sheriff and postmaster, Southwick emerged as a leader of the party's "purists" in New

---

8.   Jabez D. Hammond, *"The History of Political Parties in the State of New York* (Cooperstown, N.Y., 1847), Vol. II.

9.   Vaughn, *The Anti-Masonic Party in the United States*, pp. 30-31. Southwick was nominated for governor after 35-year-old state assemblyman Francis Granger, the National Republican candidate for lieutenant governor and later a prominent leader of the Whig Party's Silver Gray faction, declined the Anti-Masonic Party's gubernatorial nomination.

10.   Ratner, *Antimasonry: The Crusade and the Party*, p. 10.

York—those opposed to rapprochement with the National Republicans—and stood as the party's gubernatorial candidate in 1828.

In 1829, Joseph Ritner, the party's gubernatorial candidate in Pennsylvania, polled an astonishing 44% of the vote against George Wolf, his heavily favored Democratic opponent. After another unsuccessful try for the state's highest elective office in 1832—a year when the Anti-Masonic Party elected eight congressmen from Pennsylvania and captured thirty-two of the 100 seats in the lower house of the state legislature—Ritner, a former Speaker of the Pennsylvania House of Representatives, was eventually elected governor in a hard-fought three-way race in 1835, becoming the only third-party chief executive in the history of the Commonwealth. In addition to electing Ritner, Pennsylvania's Anti-Masonic Party also gained control of the lower house of the state legislature.

Under Ritner's watch, a new and progressive state constitution was drafted in 1837, limiting the governor's power of appointment and increasing the number of elective offices while shortening the terms of most elected and appointed officeholders. The new constitution, approved the following year, gave the citizens of the Keystone State a far greater voice in public affairs while generally safeguarding them from potential abuses of power.

The Anti-Masonic Party also enjoyed tremendous success in Vermont where William A. Palmer, a moderate former senator with a long career in state and national politics, was elected to four consecutive terms as governor on the party's ticket beginning in 1831. Palmer had run unsuccessfully for governor on the party's ticket in 1830—a year when the Anti-Masons captured 76 of the 225 seats in the Vermont assembly. A lawyer and farmer, Palmer had served in the Vermont legislature and on the state Supreme Court prior to being elected to the U.S. Senate in 1818. In the U.S. Senate, the Vermont lawyer was generally supportive of the Monroe administration but was also sympathetic to Henry Clay's American system and its protective tariff—an issue of paramount importance to the state's wool growers, of which Palmer was one.[11]

Palmer was clearly a minority governor, yet he managed to defeat his major party rivals on four occasions, polling 44% of the vote in winning the 1831 gubernatorial contest against two major party opponents. He tallied a majority of the vote in only one of his three successful bids for re-election—garnering nearly 53% of the vote in 1833 when he defeated Democrat Ezra Meech, who was then running as a fusion candidate.

---

11.   Vaughn, *The Anti-Masonic Party in the United States*, pp. 73-76.

But Palmer wasn't the only influential Anti-Masonic leader in Vermont. William Slade, who was elected to Congress on his third try in 1831, emerged as one of the party's most effective congressional leaders during this period. A graduate of Middlebury College, Slade, a vigorous antislavery pamphleteer, had served as Vermont's secretary of state from 1816 to 1823 and later held a relatively minor post in the U.S. State Department during the Monroe administration. Andrew Jackson's Secretary of State, Martin Van Buren, later removed him from that position—instilling in Slade a deep dislike and distrust of Masonry. A practical politician, Slade was a staunch supporter of Henry Clay's American system and was strongly opposed to the Jackson and Van Buren administrations. Serving in Congress from 1831-1843—the last three terms as a Whig—the Vermont lawmaker was later instrumental in leading the Anti-Masonic movement into the Whig Party upon its founding in 1834.[12]

Although there is at least a scintilla of evidence that the Federalists were the first political party to hold a national nominating convention, most historians bestow that honor on the Anti-Masons. The Anti-Masonic Party convened in Baltimore on September 26, 1831, to nominate a presidential ticket to challenge President Jackson in 1832. Unhappy with Jackson and leery of Henry Clay (who was a Mason), the Anti-Masonic leadership sounded out several presidential possibilities in the weeks and months leading up to their national convention. Overtures were made to Supreme Court Justice John McLean, a Jackson appointee who had soured on the administration, as well as 77-year-old Chief Justice John Marshall. Unlike McLean, Marshall, a longtime Federalist who did much to strengthen the nation's highest court, wasn't interested in the fledgling party's nomination. Former Treasury Secretary Richard Rush of Philadelphia, a close personal friend and confidant of James Madison, was also approached, as was the man Rush had served most recently—former President John Quincy Adams. A former Mason, the 51-year-old Rush, whose candidacy was vigorously promoted by former Pennsylvania attorney general Amos Ellmaker, had attracted the attention of the Anti-Masons when he published two lengthy letters earlier that year denouncing Masonry as a subversive force and the greatest contemporary danger to American liberties. Opposed by Seward and other party leaders, Rush, who later confounded Anti-Masonic leaders when he endorsed Andrew Jackson's re-election in the autumn campaign—an act that cost him a seat in the U.S. Senate, as well as his membership in the American Philosophical Society—formally withdrew from the race two months before the Baltimore convention.[13] Like Rush,

---

12.   Ibid., p. 77.

Adams, who was still licking the wounds from his setback to Jackson in 1828, did little to advance his own candidacy. Adams, of course, had recently returned to Congress from his home district in Massachusetts—a position he held until his death in 1848.

Even Vice President John C. Calhoun of South Carolina, the preeminent spokesman for slavery in the antebellum South, seemed to harbor faint hopes of winning the Anti-Masonic Party's presidential nomination. The 49-year-old Calhoun, who was now completely alienated from the Jackson administration, later resigned from the vice presidency and won a seat in the U.S. Senate. Journalist Duff Green, publisher of the *United States Telegram*—a newspaper once steadfastly loyal to Andrew Jackson—promoted Calhoun's short-lived candidacy for the Anti-Masonic Party's presidential nomination, but found little enthusiasm for the South Carolinian among northern Anti-Masons who were largely unsympathetic to the cause of states' rights and slavery. Daniel Webster of Massachusetts, whose strong tariff position might have been expected to attract some Clay supporters, was also occasionally mentioned as a possible presidential candidate, but his candidacy never materialized.[14]

Like Marshall and Adams, Rush, as mentioned previously, also remained above the fray. An affluent Philadelphia Democrat and former attorney general in the Madison and Monroe administrations, Rush would have been an ideal candidate for the new party. As one of the foremost proponents of Nicholas Biddle's Second Bank of the United States, Rush stood in sharp contrast to Old Hickory—a man raised as a poorly-educated orphan in the rural frontier where banks were generally despised. Perhaps the most intellectually incompetent man ever elected to the presidency, the hotheaded Jackson pinned his re-election hopes on his steadfast opposition to "Nicholas Biddle and his monster bank." Having run into serious financial trouble as a young land speculator and storekeeper in rural Tennessee, Jackson believed that credit extended by banks encouraged reckless speculation and indebtedness. In July 1832, Jackson vetoed a bill re-chartering the Second Bank of the United States and predicted that his veto would crush the Bank. A close personal friend of Biddle, the genteel Philadelphia banker, Rush believed just the opposite. He was convinced that the Second National Bank, depository of the nation's public funds, was indispensable to the nation's political and economic vitality. It not only enforced a uniform standard of currency—i.e., paper money—it also regulated state banks to prevent future financial crises

---

13. Ibid., p. 57.
14. Ibid., p. 58.

through the expansion or contraction of credit, thereby preventing state banks from lending too much or too little money. The largest corporation in the country, Biddle's bank rendered all of its services, including payment on the national debt, payment of all civil and military salaries as well as government pensions, free of charge to the federal government. Yet, Rush, whose public diffidence and appetite for irony confused and puzzled almost everyone, later supported Jackson's re-election in the fall of that year.

With Marshall, Adams and Rush out of the picture, most delegates to the historic Anti-Masonic convention in Baltimore expected to nominate Ohio's John McLean, a three-year veteran of the nation's highest court, for the presidency. Among others, the reluctant McLean had the unswerving support of Pennsylvania's Thaddeus Stevens, an ardent Jackson foe who later became a leader in the Free Soil movement while making a vocation of defending captured fugitive slaves. On the eve of the convention, McLean, apparently unwilling to sacrifice himself in what would almost certainly amount to a lost cause, abruptly sent word to the delegates that he was no longer interested in the new party's presidential nomination. McLean's statement hardly discouraged Stevens, who remained determined to draft the 47-year-old jurist. The Pennsylvanian's plans, however, were short-circuited by the shrewd and talented Thurlow Weed of New York and his young protégé, William H. Seward. After sounding out the elderly but quite lucid Chief Justice John Marshall, the powerful New York duo turned to William Wirt, the able former attorney general who lived only a few blocks from the convention hall. The sixty-year-old Wirt, who deeply despised Jackson, readily gave his thumbs up to the fledgling Anti-Masonic Party.[15]

With Weed and Seward carefully orchestrating the proceedings, the convention's 116 delegates, representing thirteen states, gave the nod to Wirt, who received 108 of the 111 votes cast on the convention's fifth ballot. (One delegate voted for statesman and diplomat Richard Rush, one of the most brilliant public speakers of his time, and two delegates abstained.) Wirt's nomination was later made unanimous.[16] The delegates then nominated 45-year-old Amos Ellmaker, a former Pennsylvania congressman, for the vice presidency. A Princeton-educated attorney, Ellmaker, who practiced law in Lancaster, Pennsylvania, served in the

---

15. Curiously, while searching for a presidential candidate Weed also met with Charles Carroll, the sole surviving signer of the Declaration of Independence. It is unclear whether Weed was actually sounding him out as a presidential possibility. After all, the frail, 94-year-old Carroll, a former Federalist Senator from Maryland, had retired from public life nearly forty years earlier. He died shortly after the 1832 presidential election.

state legislature for two years and as attorney general of the Keystone State from 1816-19 and again from 1828-29.

Though largely forgotten in the annals of American history, Wirt, who served as U.S. attorney general in the Monroe and John Quincy Adams administrations, received considerable national attention during this period as a result of his spirited defense of the Cherokee Nation against the state of Georgia. The Cherokee, also known as the Eastern Woodsmen, were among the most advanced and civilized tribes in the country. By the 1820s, they had pretty much adapted to the white man's customs—taking up farming, raising cattle and pursuing other activities of the European intruders. They even developed a written language of their own and drafted their own constitution in an effort to set up a separate state within northwest Georgia. This infuriated the recalcitrant Georgia legislature, which responded in 1828 by nullifying all Cherokee laws and placing their region under strict control of the state. Still outraged by the tribe's sophisticated attempt at self-government, the legislature passed another law two years later requiring all white men living in Cherokee territory to take a loyalty oath. This was hardly surprising. After all, this was the same reactionary legislature that offered a $5,000 reward for the capture of outspoken abolitionist William Lloyd Garrison, the pacifist publisher of *The Liberator*, in 1831.

In *Cherokee Nation v. Georgia* (1831), Chief Justice John Marshall failed to rule on the 1828 law, but in the second case (that dealing with the 1830 legislation), *Worcester v. Georgia* (1832), Marshall ruled in favor of the Indians. By then a noted Supreme Court lawyer, Wirt skillfully and passionately defended the Cherokee cause in both cases—a fact that angered President Jackson to no end. Believing that all Indian tribes had to be "removed" beyond the Mississippi, Jackson blasted Wirt, calling him a "truly wicked" man. The feeling was mutual. The former attorney general had long considered Jackson a despot and a demagogue of the worst sort. The urbane and witty former U.S. Attorney General had little time for semiliterate roughnecks like Jackson.

The son of a Maryland innkeeper who was orphaned at the age of eight, Wirt was a self-educated man and opened his own law practice by the time he was twenty. He never attended college, but was later awarded an honorary degree from Princeton University. Befriended by Jefferson, Madison, and Monroe as a

16. Vaughn, *The Anti-Masonic Party in the United States*, p. 61. McLean received 41 votes on the first ballot to Wirt's 38. Three other candidates—Granger, Webster and Rush—each received five votes or fewer. By the fourth ballot, McLean's supporters had all but given up the fight as the former attorney general amassed 94 votes to nine for the Supreme Court Justice.

young man, Wirt was prodded and encouraged by his older mentors to pursue a legal career far greater than he ever possibly imagined. Appointed Clerk of the Virginia House of Delegates by the time he was twenty-eight, Wirt, who had turned down a "sure seat" in Congress when it was offered by Thomas Jefferson earlier that year, was elected to the Virginia House of Delegates in 1808 and served until 1810. President Madison later appointed him U.S. district attorney for Virginia in 1816.[17]

A scholarly and brilliant attorney, Wirt was arguably one of the finest constitutional lawyers of his time. Having first come into the public eye while serving as counsel for muckraking journalist James T. Callender in his celebrated trial under the repressive Alien and Sedition Acts of 1798, the young Virginia lawyer later served on the prosecutorial team that tried former Vice President Aaron Burr for treason when he conspired to create a new nation in the southwest. Wirt's four-hour closing remarks in the so-called "Blennerhassett Affair"—the widely-watched trial involving Burr and his alleged co-conspirators—stands as one of the greatest courtroom summations in history.[18] He also defended the accused slayer of George Wythe, the famous lawyer and legal mentor of Kentucky's Henry Clay. As attorney general, a post he held for twelve years—longer than anyone else in American history—Wirt also presented the government's side in the landmark *McCulloch v. Maryland* case (1819), in which the Supreme Court upheld the power of the federal government to establish a bank while denying the state of Maryland the right to tax a branch of that bank.

A man of letters, Wirt was also one of the country's foremost literary figures. His book *The Letters of the British Spy*, "a controversial series of satirical essays on American society and prominent lawyers and politicians," enjoyed tremendous popularity after it first appeared in a Richmond newspaper in 1803.[19] A later book, *The Life and Character of Patrick Henry*, the first in a never-completed series of biographies of heroic American leaders, was also widely read.

In some ways, Wirt's nomination by the Anti-Masonic Party was puzzling. After all, he was a former Mason and had left the order more or less out of boredom. Unlike most party leaders, Wirt didn't believe that there was anything inherently evil in Masonry. Moreover, Wirt wasn't a politician—at least not in the traditional sense. In fact, he only held elective office on one occasion—as a delegate to the Virginia assembly for a single term. But having convinced Weed

17.   Gregory K. Glassner, *Adopted Son: The Life, Wit & Wisdom of William Wirt, 1772-1834* (Chapel Hill, N.C., 1997), p. 2.
18.   Ibid., pp. 50-54.
19.   Ibid., p. 2.

and others that he—and not Henry Clay—was the only person who could possibly unite the nation's anti-Jackson forces, Wirt, who was hoping to also capture the National Republican nomination, accepted the Anti-Masonic designation with great élan.

Wirt's enthusiasm, however, dampened considerably in December 1831, when the National Republicans, also meeting in Baltimore, rejected him and unanimously nominated the popular Henry Clay of Kentucky. Along with John C. Calhoun and William Lowndes, Clay, then serving in his third term in the U.S. Senate, was one of the chief architects of the "American System," a program for defense, transportation and high protective tariffs.

The National Republicans, forerunners of the Whig Party, developed out of a coalition of supporters of Henry Clay and John Quincy Adams in the late 1820s. Committed to the economic policies of internal improvements championed by Adams, its national leadership was furnished, in large part, by Daniel Webster and Henry Clay in the U.S. Senate. The Washington-based *National Intelligencer* served as the party's official organ.

The 156 delegates from seventeen states attending the National Republican convention never seriously considered the Anti-Masonic nominee to head their ticket—they were far more concerned with Jackson's abuse of the spoils system and his utter disregard for decisions of the Supreme Court than they were in the alleged proscriptive nature of the Masons.

Following John Quincy Adams' overwhelming setback in 1828, the anti-Jackson torch was automatically passed to long-distance runner Henry Clay, the National Republican Party's co-founder and premier propagandist. Philadelphia Rep. John Sergeant, who was then serving in his fifth term in the U.S. House of Representatives, joined Clay on the National Republican ticket. A Federalist throughout his early career, the 48-year-old Sergeant was considered one of the leading political intellectuals of his day. In terms of sagacity, the National Republicans, competing in their first presidential campaign, had nominated one of the most impressive tickets in history.

In the eyes of the National Republicans, Clay was the only man who could possibly unseat "King Andrew" Jackson in 1832. Having fallen short in 1824, this campaign was Clay's second of five tries for the presidency. The affable Kentucky lawmaker, inarguably one of the most influential political figures of his time, believed that he could win the presidency by dividing the entrenched Democratic Party over the bank issue. The old "War Hawk," as he was dubbed, had considerable political experience. He entered politics at the age of twenty-two with a ringing denunciation of the Alien and Sedition Acts and was elected to the

Kentucky legislature a few years later. He had first entered the U.S. Senate in 1806 at the age of twenty-nine—a year before he was constitutionally eligible to hold such office. He later served as Speaker of House during the War of 1812. Clay was particularly well versed in the art of compromise, as evidenced by his willingness to extend an olive branch to the British while negotiating the Ghent peace treaty in 1814. He also served as Secretary of State during John Quincy Adams' administration.

Despite his impressive record of public service, Clay wasn't without his detractors. He always had plenty of critics. Swiss-born Albert Gallatin, a western Pennsylvania farmer who served as Jefferson's Secretary of the Treasury—and possibly the most competent man to ever hold that office—once described Clay as a man devoured with ambition. Gallatin, the chief architect of the Ghent Treaty in 1814, wasn't entirely off the mark. Even one of Clay's biographers described his unquenchable thirst for the nation's highest office as a "never ending quest for a cup that would be forever dashed from his lips."

Clay was a man almost possessed by visions of grandeur. For the record, he first reached for the glittering prize—the presidency—during the 1824 presidential election, an intra-party affair featuring such heavyweights as John Quincy Adams, John C. Calhoun and William H. Crawford. Clay's ambition, of course, wasn't all that unusual. His persistent pursuit of the presidency was shared by several other outstanding figures of his era, most notably in the cases of South Carolina's John Calhoun and Daniel Webster of Massachusetts. Leading politicians in both major parties since Clay's time have followed the same trail, journeying up and down the presidential path time and again only to come up short. It's a long list including but not limited to such outstanding figures as Salmon P. Chase of Ohio, James G. Blaine of Maine, William Jennings Bryan, Robert A. Taft, Norman Thomas, Harold E. Stassen, Hubert H. Humphrey and Eugene J. McCarthy.

A Virginian by birth, Clay studied law under the tutelage of scholar George Wythe, a professor of law at William and Mary College and close personal friend and mentor to Thomas Jefferson. Among his contemporaries, Clay was considered a shrewd and brilliant criminal defense attorney. Among other things, he was the originator of the "insanity" plea. Folklore has it that none of his clients, even those charged with the most heinous crimes, were ever hanged.

As for the Anti-Masonic Party's William Wirt, who was every bit as competent a lawyer as Clay, the 1832 campaign proved to be an agonizingly burdensome ordeal. Realizing that all hope of victory was lost shortly after the National Republicans nominated Kentucky's "Great Compromiser," Wirt was convinced that he and Clay would divide the anti-Jackson vote and assure the president's re-election. As such, Wirt planned to drop out of the race. To do otherwise, he believed, would have given him the appearance of "a sickly vanity and morbid appetite for the office"—qualities he surely didn't possess.[20] Though he would have preferred to retire to the comfort of his country home to lead a literary life, New York's Thurlow Weed and other Anti-Masonic leaders persuaded him to remain in the race.

A fourth candidate, Virginia Governor John B. Floyd, a staunch defender of states' rights and slavery, also entered the 1832 presidential sweepstakes. A physician-turned-politician, Floyd, who received South Carolina's eleven electoral votes that year, was the Nullifiers' nominee for president. Of the twenty-four states in the Union at the time, South Carolina was the only state that still selected its electors through the state legislature.[21] This party was essentially the nation's first states' rights party. The Nullifiers came into existence when Congress raised duties on imported goods in 1828. Particularly hard hit by the depression of 1819, South Carolinians, led by nationalist John C. Calhoun, had long believed that the tariffs of 1816 and 1824 were an unfair tax on southern agriculture for the benefit of northern industry and, in 1828, defiantly declared the "Tariff of Abominations" null and void within the state's borders. Though never formally a political party, the recalcitrant Nullifiers sent former Governor Stephen Decatur Miller, who had done much to rile the voters of South Carolina against Congress, to the U.S. Senate in 1831. There, the 44-year-old Miller worked in unison with Vice President Calhoun, who later resigned from the nation's second highest office over states' rights differences with President Jackson.

Henry Lee of Boston, a fifty-year-old partner in the East India Trading Company, joined Floyd on the Nullifiers' ticket. A staunch free trade advocate and prolific writer, Lee had prepared the so-called "Boston Report" in 1820, a widely circulated two hundred-page pamphlet opposing higher duties on imported products. An intensely shy yet genial man, he later worked closely with former Secretary of the Treasury Albert Gallatin in championing the cause of free trade. Briefly overcoming his almost debilitating shyness, Lee, who was regarded as something of an intellectual, ran unsuccessfully for Congress in 1830, losing to National Republican Nathan Appleton.

---

20.   Miller, *'If Elected...' Unsuccessful Candidates for the Presidency 1796-1968*, p. 104.
21.   Vaughn, *The Anti-Masonic Party in the United States*, p. 68.

While Floyd, a close friend of Calhoun, was not a factor in the election's outcome, the Nullifiers managed to elect no fewer than nine congressmen during this period, including eight of nine from the South Carolina delegation, as well as one from Alabama.

The 1832 presidential election extended from October 31, when voters in Ohio and Pennsylvania went to the polls, through November 19, when Rhode Island voters finally cast their ballots. In a desperate effort to stop Jackson, the Anti-Masons joined fusion tickets with the National Republicans in New York, Ohio and Pennsylvania, but "Old Hickory" prevailed in all three states. In the end, Jackson defeated Clay in the popular vote by a margin of 701,780 to 484,205, and by an even greater margin of 219 to 49 in the Electoral College. The Anti-Masonic Party's William Wirt received 100,715 popular votes in eleven states, or eight percent nationally.[22] He also received Vermont's seven electoral votes. Nearly two-thirds of his total came from Pennsylvania, an Anti-Masonic stronghold. Wirt's overall showing, however, was a bit misleading. In New York and Ohio, for example, where the Anti-Masons fused with the National Republicans, many of the 231,462 votes cast for Henry Clay came from Anti-Masonic voters, thereby depleting Wirt's real national strength. This was offset to a certain degree, however, by the 66,706 votes cast for the fusion ticket in Pennsylvania—many of which were really cast for Clay.

For his part, the Virginia lawyer was hardly disappointed by the results of the election. "A culprit pardoned at the gallows could not be more light-hearted," he told a friend shortly after the election.[23] When the *Providence American* speculated shortly after the election that the former attorney general could be a serious contender for the presidency in 1836, Wirt quickly dismissed the idea. "I take no pleasure, but the reverse," he said, "in seeing my name the renewed subject of newspaper discussion for a purpose so remote and so contingent." He apparently had no interest in seeking the presidency again, but it turned out to be a moot point as the former attorney general, who was in fragile health, died suddenly shortly after catching a cold during the winter of 1834.[24]

More significant than Wirt's showing in the presidential election was the party's relative success in that year's congressional races. By 1833, the Anti-

---

22. The Wirt-Ellmaker ticket received popular votes in the following states: Connecticut, 3,409; Illinois, 97; Indiana, 27; Maine, 844; Massachusetts, 14,692; New Jersey, 468; Ohio, 538; Pennsylvania, 66,706; Rhode Island, 819; Vermont, 13,112; and Virginia, 3. Source: Congressional Quarterly, *Presidential Elections Since 1789*, p. 68.
23. Miller, *'If Elected…' Unsuccessful Candidates for the Presidency 1796-1968*, p. 105.
24. Glassner, *Adopted Son*, p. 134.

Masonic Party held twenty-five seats in the U.S. House of Representatives—up from 17 in the previous Congress. Running on the Anti-Masonic ticket that same year, former President John Quincy Adams—who once described Masonry as "humiliating to the human character"—was nearly elected governor of Massachusetts in a tight, four-way race won by National Republican John Davis. Though never quite demonstrating the kind of strength as exhibited in Pennsylvania, Vermont and western New York, Massachusetts had been something of a stronghold for the Anti-Masonic Party and by 1831 the party claimed 150 of the 490 seats in the lower house of the state legislature.[25]

In the meantime, Thurlow Weed, who had launched the politically puissant *Albany Evening Journal* as an Anti-Masonic organ in the early 1830s, abandoned anti-Masonry in 1834 to organize New York's Whig Party. Other party leaders soon followed suit and by 1836 the Anti-Masonic Party was but a shell of its former self. The Whigs, whose membership included such eminent figures as John Quincy Adams—who had been frequently returned to Congress on the Anti-Masonic ticket—Henry Clay and Daniel Webster, quickly evolved into a major party.

With most of its members having been absorbed by the Whigs, the Anti-Masonic Party—or what was left of it—endorsed William Henry Harrison, the Whig nominee, for president in his uphill battle against Democrat Martin Van Buren in the 1836 presidential campaign. Harrison was one of three Whig candidates in that year's presidential contest. Hugh L. White, a former Democrat from Tennessee, was the Whig standard-bearer in nine states that autumn and the extraordinarily brilliant Daniel Webster was the party's nominee in his native state of Massachusetts.

As the Anti-Masonic and National Republican parties faded into the sunset, the Whigs, taking their name from the English antimonarchists, were formed in opposition to Andrew Jackson's war on the Second Bank of the United States and his mistreatment of the Indians. A major party from the moment of its inception in 1834, the Whig Party was highly critical of Jackson for running

---

25. Davis, a conservative ex-Federalist, won the popular vote with only 40.3% of the total, receiving 25,149 votes to 18,274 for Adams, 15,493 for perennial Democratic candidate Marcus Morton and 3,459 for Samuel L. Allen of the Workingmen's Party. Adams carried Bristol, Franklin, Middlesex, Norfolk, and Plymouth counties in eastern Massachusetts while garnering over 29% of the statewide vote. Eager to avoid the same situation that led to his election to the presidency by the U.S. House of Representatives nine years earlier, the former president withdrew and endorsed the National Republican candidate when the election went to the legislature.

roughshod over the Constitution and for his proclivity to ignore Supreme Court decisions.

Believing that it was inexpedient to unite behind a single presidential candidate, the Whigs fielded three candidates—Harrison, White and Webster—in the hope of denying Jackson's successor, Martin Van Buren, an Electoral College majority in 1836. In the campaign, viewed largely as a referendum on Andrew Jackson, the Whigs endorsed internal improvements and a national bank. With an eye on the South, the Whigs also tried to link the Democrats to the issues of abolition and sectional strife. Despite running regional favorite-son candidates, the Whigs were unable to prevent Van Buren's election. The New York Democrat polled 764,176 popular votes to Harrison's 550,816, White's 146,107 and 41,201 for Webster, while amassing an Electoral College majority of 170 votes to 73 for Harrison, 26 for White and fourteen for Webster.

After 1836 there were still a few men who clung to the Anti-Masonic label, especially in the party's former stronghold of Pennsylvania where Thaddeus Stevens labored valiantly to keep the party afloat. By 1836, the party's membership in the U.S. House had dropped to a mere seven members, including Richard Biddle of Pennsylvania, a scholar who later resigned from Congress in 1840 so that he could spend more time practicing law and publishing literary works on American travel and discovery. One of the last holdovers, Joseph Ritner, Pennsylvania's popular Anti-Masonic governor, was narrowly defeated in his bid for re-election in 1838, losing to Democrat David R. Porter by a scant 5,500 votes. During this period, the party's presence in Congress dwindled rapidly. The party won just six House seats—all from Pennsylvania—in the 1838 mid-term elections. Despite the party's rapid decline, Anti-Masonic candidates continued to run for office under the party's banner into the early 1840s, occasionally winning local office.

Due to the Anti-Masonic Party's influence, it has been estimated that the number of Masons in the United States dropped from roughly 100,000 to 40,000 during the ten-year period of the party's existence. Moreover, the number of Masonic lodges in New York alone fell from 480 lodges to 82 lodges, while membership dropped from 20,000 to approximately 3,000. Freemasonry suffered similar losses in Connecticut, Massachusetts, Ohio, Pennsylvania, Rhode Island and Vermont, but by the eve of the Civil War, Masonry was again as popular as it had been prior to the Morgan affair.

The Workingmen's, Anti-Rent and Law & Order Parties

There were, to be sure, other third parties and factions in existence during this period. In the early 1820s, for example, four distinct parties held seats in the Pennsylvania legislature. In addition to the Jeffersonian Democratic-Republicans and the fading Federalists, two other parties—the Old School Party, which claimed eleven seats in state House in 1820 and the so-called "Binnites," who held three seats—were also part of the political landscape. The late 1820s saw the rise of numerous workingmen's parties in cities such as Boston, New York and Philadelphia. Similar parties were also formed in dozens of small towns sprinkled across the country. These workingmen's parties (some were called People's Party, Farmers' and Mechanics' Society, etc.) basically focused on local issues, calling for such things as free tax-supported public schools, lien laws and tax reform.

It was only fitting that the first labor party in the United States was formed in the country's birthplace of Philadelphia—where the Declaration of Independence was signed and in which the first labor strike in American history occurred—during the long humid summer of 1828. The movement quickly spread westward to Pittsburgh, Lancaster, Harrisburg, Cincinnati and elsewhere. It also spread southward to Delaware, where in 1830 a workingmen's party elected thirteen of eighteen public officials in Wilmington, and northward to New York City, Newark, Trenton, Albany, Buffalo, Syracuse, Troy, Utica and into New England. Between 1828 and 1834, independent labor parties were formed in no fewer than sixty-one cities and towns scattered throughout the North and Midwest.[26]

Anticipating the socialist movement of the late nineteenth century, these local labor parties called for profound economic and social change in America. During this shameful period of American history, most children of working-class parents were deprived of a public education and were virtually kept in ignorance while the workers themselves, who were often taxed more heavily than the country's wealthiest citizens, were frequently thrown into prison for what amounted to petty debts. It was estimated in 1834 that more than 1,250,000 children in the United States were illiterate and that a few years earlier roughly 75,000 persons were serving time in debtor prisons, more than half of them for sums of less than twenty dollars. William Cutter, a Revolutionary War veteran, was among the thousands who had been imprisoned. He owed a $12 debt. For these Americans,

---

26. Alden Whitman, *Labor Parties 1827-1834* (New York, 1943), p. 63.

the phrase "land of opportunity" had a hollow ring. It wasn't surprising, therefore, that the demand for public education and the abolition of debtor prisons
was a common theme advanced by the assorted workingmen's parties that flourished in towns and cities across the nation during this period. These early labor
parties were also concerned with the rapid decline of the traditional craft system,
which, in earlier times, had enabled trade apprentices and journeymen to climb
the economic ladder.

Another common theme found in "Workeyism"—as they were derisively
referred to in conservative circles—was the abolition of compulsory service in the
militia. While no less fearful of foreign invasion than the nation's wealthier citizens, the working poor had tired of serving in the militia at their own expense,
turning out, usually three times a year, for what amounted to an "expensive and
useless machinery of pageant and parade," while the rich avoided duty by paying
a twelve dollar annual fine. The banking monopoly was also a source of contention, as the workingmen's parties demanded the abolition of bank notes and the
payment of wages in hard currency and laws limiting the power of these financial
institutions.

Thomas Skidmore, a radical and self-educated machinist, and George Henry
Evans, the brilliant and tireless editor of the *Working Man's Advocate*, were perhaps the most influential of those who had advocated the creation of an independent labor party in the late 1820's. One of the most radical spokesmen for
American labor in the pre-Civil War years, Skidmore, a longtime advocate of a
ten-hour day, had authored *The Rights of Man to Property* in 1829, a 400-page
philosophical treatise for the working-class on how to acquire property not only
for themselves but for all future generations. The 39-year-old Skidmore, who had
been something of a child prodigy, was firmly convinced that only a revolutionary transformation of existing property laws would bring relief to the downtrodden and proposed that every man twenty-one years of age and older—and every
unmarried woman—should receive a free grant of one hundred and sixty acres of
land. While he didn't propose the immediate confiscation of large land holdings,
he nevertheless advocated a law in which the government would claim all holdings in excess of 160 acres at the owner's death—thereby eliminating the inequitable distribution of land in the country by the end of a generation. He also
hoped to abolish all inheritances, debts and monopolies. The Yankee-born itinerant teacher-turned-metal worker also hoped to outlaw all forms of discrimination
based on race, religion and sex and was one of the country's earliest advocates for
full equality, including suffrage, for African-Americans and women.

Born in England and raised in upstate New York, Evans, who had been apprenticed in the printing industry at a very young age, was a devoted admirer of Thomas Paine, the most influential political philosopher and writer of his time. Evans, who moved to New York City in 1826, later teamed up with Thomas Skidmore and launched the Working Men's Party a few years later. His *Working Man's Advocate* was arguably the most influential of the nation's early labor newspapers. While sympathetic to Skidmore's radical agrarianism, which called for the expropriation and redistribution of private property, especially land, Evans eventually steered the party toward Robert Dale Owen's more limited goals of providing a paternalistic "state guardianship" over children and fought for the establishment of public schools. Their efforts later led to the creation of the short-lived State Guardianship Party, a third-party that flourished briefly in the demise of New York's original Working Men's Party.

Another leading third-party agitator and influential organizer and speaker in the workingmen's movement was Scottish-born feminist writer and utopian socialist Fanny Wright, an antislavery, public education and birth control advocate. Moved by the egalitarian principles of the American Revolution, Wright rhetorically asked if the War of Independence had been fought merely to oppress the country's working people through a systematic pattern of neglect, poverty and starvation.

In addition to Skidmore, Evans and Wright, the workingmen's movement attracted a cavalcade of formidable but lesser-known reformers, including women such as Sarah G. Bagley, a Lowell factory worker and schoolteacher who later formed the Lowell Female Labor Reform Association. It also included long-forgotten men such as Vermont-born Orestes A. Brownson, who was later so disillusioned by Van Buren's defeat in 1840—partly the result of surrendering to the Loco-Foco movement, or so his conservative Democratic and Whig foes asserted—that he inexplicably drifted into the conservative camp, and Thomas A. Devyr, an Irish-born agrarian reformer who joined George Henry Evans' land reform movement and served as editor of the radical *National Reformer* and *Anti-Renter* newspapers. There was also Alexander Ming, Sr., who ran for the New York legislature on the Working Men's ticket in 1829 and co-edited Thomas Skidmore's *Friend of Equal Rights*. Ming's son, Alexander Ming, Jr., was also active in the workingmen's movement and stood as the Loco-Foco candidate for mayor of New York City in 1836. The younger Ming was also instrumental in organizing mass demonstrations of the unemployed throughout New York City in the wake of the Panic of 1837.

Other outstanding figures associated with the Working Men's Party in New York included Robert Dale Owen, son of the distinguished English Utopian socialist Robert Dale Owen; John Commerford, president of the Chairmakers' and Gilders' Union; and Levi D. Slamm, leader of the Journeymen Locksmiths' Union of New York and later editor of the New York *Plebian*. Like other working-class leaders during the 1820s and 1830s, Devyr and Commerford were deeply worried about the introduction of machinery in the workplace, insisting that it should be used for the masses—not for the profits of a few. Devyr described the advent of machinery as a kind of "occult power" that would render skilled trades virtually obsolete. Commerford was a bit more optimistic. The time would come, he predicted, when machinery would be used to benefit the masses and not simply to replace workers. "Machinery will not then be used, as it is now, for the benefit of the few," he told a gathering of the General Trades' Union in New York in 1835. "Governments will become the legitimate guardians of its improvements, and they will be compelled to keep machinery in operation for the comfort and convenience of the people."[27]

In Philadelphia, the Working Men's Party, founded in 1828 by William Heighton, a young and disgruntled leather worker, was comprised largely of mechanics and journeymen, most of whom were skilled craftsmen. Heighton was the editor of the *Mechanics Free Press*, believed to be the nation's first labor journal.[28] Aside from Heighton, the Philadelphia party attracted a number of other able leaders, including William English, a journeyman shoemaker who later served as president of the Philadelphia Trades' Union and as a Democratic member of the Pennsylvania Senate. The Philadelphia artisans were particularly outraged by what they perceived to be deliberately contrived low wages, fostered by unscrupulous and greedy employers who were willing to substitute child labor for what historically had been skilled adult labor. As such, they were among the first to fight for child labor legislation, almost eighty years before state legislatures began grappling with that issue. They also firmly believed in establishing a system of free public education. "The original element of despotism," proclaimed a party committee in 1829, "is a monopoly of talent, which consigns the multitude to comparative ignorance, and secures the balance of knowledge on the side of the rich and the rulers."[29]

27. Philip S. Foner, *History of the Labor Movement in the United States: From Colonial Times to the Founding of the American Federation of Labor*, Vol. I (New York, 1947), p. 169.

28. Nicholas B. Wainwright, "The Age of Nicholas Biddle 1825-1841," *Philadelphia: A 300-Year History*, Russell F. Weigley, ed., (New York, 1982), pp. 279-280.

These early labor parties were not completely unsuccessful at the ballot box. Occasionally, "Workies," as they were nicknamed, were elected to local office, often defeating major party opponents. Within a year of its founding, for example, the Working Men's Party, which routinely ran candidates for public office from 1828-31, held the balance of power in Philadelphia's city council when twenty of its fifty-four candidates, all of whom had been endorsed by either Federalists or Democrats *after* being nominated by the Working Men's Party, were swept into office. Withstanding repeated assaults from their major party opponents who attempted to disrupt their meetings through hoodlum tactics or by packing the halls with their own supporters, leaders of the Working Men's Party had mixed feelings about their initial venture into the rough and tumble of Philadelphia politics. "The result has been equal to our most sanguine expectations," commented Heighton's *Mechanics' Free Press*, but added, "yet it may not be equally as satisfactory to our friends."[30]

One of the party's best-known candidates was Stephen Simpson, who had fought in the Battle of New Orleans under Andrew Jackson. A clerk in the Second Bank of the United States and a cashier at Philadelphia's Girard Bank, he was also the author of *The Working Man's Manual*, published in Philadelphia in 1831. In 1830, the 41-year-old Simpson ran for Congress on the Federalist and Workingmen's tickets, garnering roughly a third of the vote while losing to a three-term Jacksonian Democrat. Although the party elected eight commissioners in the city's Northern Liberties community that year, the party faded out shortly after the 1831 election when it failed to elect a single candidate. The party's failure to unite into a statewide organization with the various independent labor parties sprinkled across the Keystone State undoubtedly contributed to its relatively short lifespan.

In Massachusetts, the Working Men's Party actually succeeded in electing historian George Bancroft to the state legislature on its ticket in 1830, but the Harvard-educated scholar and diplomat declined to serve. Bancroft, who entered Harvard College at the age of thirteen and graduated with honors a few years later, joined the workingmen's movement in 1832—two years after turning down a seat in the state legislature—and led an attack on the Second Bank of the United States shortly thereafter. A staunch opponent of slavery, Bancroft was a minor poet of sorts and close confidante of Abraham Lincoln. He also served as James K. Polk's Secretary of the Navy and as U.S. ambassador to Great Britain

29.   Bailyn, *et al., The Great Republic*, p. 365.
30.   Whitman, *Labor Parties 1827-1834*, p. 25.

from 1846-49—a post that provided him ample time to work on his voluminous *History of the United States from the Discovery of the Continent*, a ten-volume undertaking that took nearly forty years to complete.

In New York, labor party candidate Ebenezer Ford, president of the Carpenters' Union, stunned Tammany Hall by winning a seat in the state assembly in 1829—the first time that a labor representative had been elected to the New York legislature since the victory of a Mechanic's ticket back in 1785. Ford's victory was all the more remarkable given the fact that the Working Men's Party didn't formally enter the fray until barely a week before the election—and with only $75 in its treasury, to boot. All but one of the party's nine candidates for the assembly garnered over six thousand of the twenty-one thousand votes cast. Moreover, the third-party's success was not confined to New York City. In Salina (now Syracuse), in upstate New York, the Farmers and Mechanics' Party elected its entire slate in the spring elections of 1830 and in the cities of Troy and Albany—where the party adopted an arm and hammer superimposed over a plow as its symbol, a sort of "precursor to the hammer and sickle," as one historian noted—workingmen's parties carried all but a single ward in those two cities. Needless to say, these early successes spread terror and dismay among the state's aristocracy. Several leading journals blamed the results on universal suffrage. By giving every man the right to vote, lamented the conservative *Journal of Commerce*, "power was placed in the hands of those who had neither property, talents, nor influence in other circumstances."[31]

Unfortunately, the New York party's success was extremely short-lived. Shortly after the 1829 election, Thomas Skidmore, one of the party's founders, left to form the Poor Man's Party, which later developed into the Agrarian Party. Skidmore's party, which espoused a crude form of agrarian communism, didn't seriously damage the Working Men's Party as only a few workers followed him into the new party. The remaining elements of the workingmen's party, however, quickly broke up into separate groups, including the State Guardianship Party, which focused on the need for public education and governmental regulation, and the little-remembered North American Hotel Party, which was named after the hotel in which it was founded. The North American Hotel Party apparently opposed public education as well as almost any government interference in American life—a kind of precursor to the modern Libertarian Party. The State Guardianship Party included such radical thinkers as feminist Fanny Wright, philanthropist and utopian socialist Robert Dale Owen and printer George

---

31.   Foner, *History of the Labor Movement in the United States*, pp. 132-134.

Henry Evans, as well as other important figures in the early American labor movement.

This breakup resulted in three separate Working Men's tickets competing against each other in the campaign of 1830. The Owen-led state guardianship faction ran a full city and state ticket and endorsed other parties for Congress. A second faction opposed to Owen ran a complete city and state ticket, except for governor and lieutenant governor and Skidmore's Agrarian Party, which nominated a handful of local and state candidates, also entered the fray. Given such splintering, Tammany Hall, benefiting from thousands of workingmen who were disgusted by the factional infighting and returned to the Democratic fold, had little difficulty sweeping New York City and capturing a majority in the state assembly, as well as the governorship. Despite the movement's splintered nature, at least three candidates for Congress on the Working Men's ticket that year garnered over ten percent of the vote in New York City, including John Frazee, a former bricklayer and tombstone cutter who, without any formal training, later became one the country's leading sculptors. Combining realism and neo-classicism, Frazee's portrait bust of John Jay in the nation's capitol was the first government commission ever given to a native-born sculptor. Frazee, who then owned a marble shop in New York City, garnered 2,158 votes, or 10.5% of the total, in the city's third congressional district. Thomas Skidmore, a founder of the original Working Men's Party, was less fortunate. Running under the banner of his newly formed Agrarian Party, he polled a pitiful 116 votes for the same seat—or roughly one-half of one percent of the total.

Following that disastrous electoral experience, Skidmore tried desperately to keep the original Working Men's Party afloat and briefly published a daily newspaper called the *Friend of Equal Rights*. The party in New York completed faded out, however, shortly before his death during the great cholera epidemic of 1832.

The Working Men's Party, however, briefly clung to life in a few other places, including Massachusetts, where its 1833 gubernatorial candidate Samuel C. Allen, a Congregational minister and former Federalist congressman who had rallied the state's Working Men's Party behind Andrew Jackson's hard-money policies, garnered 3,459 votes, or 5.5% of the vote, in a four-cornered race. Allen finished last in field that included well-known National Republican John Davis, perennial Democratic aspirant Marcus Morton and former President John Quincy Adams, the Anti-Masonic Party's reluctant nominee.[32]

Beginning in Connecticut, various workingmen's parties had been formed in no fewer than twenty-one cities throughout New England during the late 1820's. For a period, the seacoast town of New London, Connecticut, with its large shipbuilding industry, was the center of the movement before it shifted to Boston with the formation of the New England Association of Farmers, Mechanics and Other Working Men in the early 1830s. The Association, which grew out of a meeting in Providence, Rhode Island, in December 1831, sought to eliminate the typical "daylight to dark" working day. The workingmen's parties in New England differed from the movements in Philadelphia and New York in at least three fundamental respects. In addition to appealing to urban laborers, the New England parties reached out to farmers, declaring that there was "an indissoluble connection between the interests of the cultivator of the soil, and the mechanics and every class of laborers" against their common enemy—"the idle, avaricious and aristocratic" classes. Secondly, the Association, asserting that farmers and mechanics were "the last hope of the American people," made little effort to organize New England's factory workers—a group comprised largely of women and children—believing that they were "already subdued to the bidding of employers." Finally, unlike its counterparts in Philadelphia and New York, the Association made a concerted attempt to branch out into the towns and villages of New England in an effort to bring all of that region's producers together.[33]

Many of those who had been active in the state's workingmen's parties, including Evans, later resurfaced with the Equal Rights Party in the early 1830s. By 1836, the Equal Rights Party had become a force of sorts in New York politics, frequently running candidates for various state and local offices. This party was a loose coalition of urban trade craftsmen and upstate "LocoFoco" Democrats. The LocoFocos were an anti-Tammany faction that earned its sobriquet when some Tammany henchmen tried to disrupt one of their gatherings by extinguishing the lights in their meeting hall. The meeting continued, however, when the resourceful participants lit candles with the newly invented matches known as "locofocos."

The Equal Rights Party was formed following a mass meeting of some 27,000 people in New York's City Hall Park protesting a court decision that found twenty-five members of the Union Society of Journeymen Tailors guilty of "conspiracy to injure trade, riot, assault [and] battery." Three months later, a convention of mechanics, farmers and laborers, elected by working people in various New York towns and cities, assembled in Utica, drew up a "Declaration of Inde-

---

32. Vaughn, *The Anti-Masonic Party in the United States*, pp. 122-123. Davis, who was subsequently elected by the National Republican-dominated Massachusetts legislature, garnered 25,149 popular votes to 18,274 for the Anti-Masonic Party's John Quincy Adams and 15,493 for Democrat Marcus Morton.
33. Whitman, *Labor Parties 1827-1834*, pp. 45-46.

pendence" from the two major parties and boldly launched the Equal Rights Party.

For a short period of time the Equal Rights Party became a third force in New York City politics, but was relatively weak as a statewide organization. The party advocated equality for all and opposed monopolies and paper money, preferring hard currency instead. While the party often ran its own candidates for public office, many of the movement's leaders didn't place a great deal of confidence in the ballot box. One such leader was Seth Luther, a self-educated carpenter from Providence, Rhode Island, who rarely minced words. "We will try the ballot box first," he told a July Fourth rally of the party faithful. "If that will not effect our righteous purpose, the next and last resort is the cartridge box." Others were also leery about the effectiveness of electoral politics. "Remember the regretted fate of the workingmen," cautioned the *Albany Microscope*. After admitting lawyers and politicians into its ranks, leaders of that party became "perverted," unwittingly "drawn into a vortex, from which they never escaped."[34]

Like many of the workingmen's parties of this period, the Equal Rights Party—though anticipating later political trends—was too weak and unstable to survive longer than a few years. The party quickly dissolved, but its remnants formed the building blocks of yet other political movements in a period of frenzied political fusion that followed.

In 1844, George Henry Evans, who had revived his then-defunct *Working-man's Advocate*, renaming it *Young America*, rallied the veterans of the earlier Workingmen's and Loco-Foco movements into the National Reform Association (NRA). Referring to the vast unsettled lands in the West as a kind of "safety valve" for farmers and workers whose opportunities were limited in the East, Evans was the first to suggest that the United States owned enough land in the West to guarantee every family a farm—an idea that was later popularized by Horace Greeley, the influential editor of the *New York Tribune* who coined the Republican slogan, "Vote yourself a farm." Specifically, the National Reform Association advocated homestead legislation and the adoption of a homestead exemption outlawing the seizure and sale of family farms for non-payment of debts. It also called for strict restrictions on the amount of land any one individual could own. The National Reform Association affiliated with the communal Fourierist movement in 1845 and launched a series of annual conventions known as the National Industrial Congresses. By the late 1840s, a number of its members had aligned themselves with the broader antislavery movement, including

---

34.   Howard Zinn, *A People's History of the United States* (New York, 1980), pp. 218-219.

active support of the fledgling Liberty and Free Soil parties. Some NRA members also joined romantic novelist George Lippard's secretive and little-known Brotherhood of the Union, which, in keeping with the mythology of other secret societies, allegedly traced its roots back to the Bavarian Illuminati. Lippard, who as a young orphan watched helplessly as creditors devoured his family's farm, eventually founded Brotherhood lodges in twenty-four states—including eight slave states—and the District of Columbia before his death in 1856. According to Joshua K. Ingalls, one of its few prominent members in the South, Lippard's southern lodges were later transformed into the Union Leagues, an anti-secessionist underground that operated secretly during the Civil War.

One of the National Reform Association's most famous members was Alvan Earl Bovay, a graduate of Norwich University and one-time speaker and propagandist in New York's flourishing anti-rent movement. An anti-Nebraska Democrat with strong ties to the Whig Party in the northeast, the bearded Bovay later chaired the famous meeting in the little white schoolhouse in Ripon, Wisconsin, on March 20, 1854, that gave birth to the Republican Party. Though historians have long argued the GOP's precise origin, this meeting of 53 citizens who were upset with the Kansas-Nebraska legislation sponsored by Democrat Stephen A. Douglas of Illinois, is generally regarded as the party's genesis. In fact, Bovay, believing that the party's name should be synonymous with equality while alluding to the name of Thomas Jefferson's earlier Democratic-Republican Party, was the one who coined the party's name at a similar meeting in Ripon a month earlier.

Expanding its horizons beyond the narrow goal of egalitarian land ownership and communitarian experiments, the radical National Reform Association also advocated the establishment of cooperative labor organizations and supported trade unionist calls for a shorter workday. Like Abraham Lincoln, the National Reformers later bitterly opposed the Mexican War and the extension of slavery in the territories, while blasting the unresponsiveness of the country's two old parties. Their main focus, however, was passage of homestead legislation, an idea first proposed by Missouri Sen. Thomas Hart Benton. Through vigorous lobbying, the NRA finally got its version of a homestead bill onto the floor of Congress in 1848 and, over the period of the next three years, waged what was then the largest petition drive in U.S. history. Although the measure finally passed in the House, it was overwhelmingly rejected in the U.S. Senate.

Like Evans himself, the tens of thousands who took part in the massive petition effort for homestead legislation in the early 1850s, gravitated toward the new Republican Party during the 1854 mid-term elections, helping that party win a plurality in the House of Representatives. Like many others in the NRA, Evans actively supported the new party, playing an important role in founding and organizing the fledgling party in New Jersey. In fact, it was on one of his many trips to neighboring New Jersey to promote the party during the winter of 1855 that he caught pneumonia and died. Overcoming hostile opposition from southern lawmakers who feared that its passage would hasten the settlement of western territories and add to the political influence of the free states, the NRA's homestead measure, which had been narrowly defeated in the Senate in 1858, was finally passed by both houses of Congress in 1859, only to be vetoed by President James Buchanan.

In no small measure, Evans and the National Reform Association, providing a "free labor" vision of the nation's future in antebellum America, contributed directly to Abraham Lincoln's victory in the four-cornered 1860 presidential election. With a sympathetic leader in the White House, the organization's goal of providing land to poor and dispossessed farmers finally became a reality on May 20, 1862, when the Homestead Act was signed into law, granting up to 160 acres of public land to any citizen willing to pay a small registration fee and who was willing to live on the land continuously for five years. It also enabled anyone willing to pay $1.25 per acre to acquire the land in only six months' time.

The Anti-Rent and Law & Order Parties

During the nineteenth century, an estimated two million acres of New York farmland was controlled by a relatively small handful of wealthy families, especially in the lush green hills of the Hudson Valley. The death of Stephen Van Rensselaer, heir to one such vast estate, in January 1839, spurred the creation of yet another third party—the New York-based Anti-Rent Party. It seems that Van Rensselaer, remembered as the congressman who cast the deciding vote that put John Quincy Adams in the Executive Mansion in 1824, didn't bother to collect any rent from his tenants. The Rensselaer family's manor had about eighty thousand tenants. Over the years, the family had amassed a fortune estimated at $41 million. When Rensselaer's heirs tried to collect his back rents shortly after his death, an anti-rent war broke out.

Shortly thereafter, anti-rent associations, led by men like Smith Boughton, a country doctor who made house calls on horseback, and Ainge Devyr, a revolutionary Irish immigrant who fled to the United States after being arrested in Ireland on sedition charges, were formed in most leasehold counties throughout the New York countryside. These associations constituted the base of the new party.

The Anti-Renters donned calico Indian costumes, not unlike those who had taken part in the Boston Tea Party as a reminder of those who originally inhabited the land. They also carried tinhorns, reminiscent of the Indians' call to arms. In no time, some ten thousand "Indians" were trained to fight for the anti-rent cause.

The anti-rent movement soon became part of a broader reform movement, not unlike anti-Masonry and temperance, and quickly developed into a formidable statewide third party movement. Through the anti-rent associations, reformers sought to promote a host of constitutional and statutory changes. The anti-rent movement appealed to discontented farmers living on worn-out and infertile farmland where landlords naturally proved to be convenient scapegoats for the poverty and uncertainty confronting them.

In the early 1840s, the anti-rent imbroglio began to draw the major parties—the Whigs and the Democrats—into the picture. A crisis developed after tenants' organizations petitioned the New York legislature for rent reform in 1840. The crisis quickly escalated after Governor William Seward's forceful suppression of anti-rent protests in the so-called "Helderberg War," precipitated when Van Rensselaer's heirs tried to collect back rents. Hoping to take credit for the investigation of the protests, both major parties blamed each other for the uprising.

Pursuing a politically shrewd course of action, the Anti-Renters devised an inside-outside political strategy. In counties where it was weakest, the minor party backed candidates nominated by one of the two major parties, usually Whigs. In counties where they had more strength, such as Albany County, they fielded their own candidates. Calling for legislative action to force landlords to make concessions to renters, in 1845 the Anti-Rent Party captured numerous local offices and elected fourteen members to the state legislature, including a state senator. A number of prominent Whigs openly supported the anti-rent movement, including journalist Horace Greeley and Ira Harris, a 43-year-old lawyer and powerful Whig state legislator. Harris was the man the third-party usually looked to for leadership.

The following year, the Anti-Rent Party backed John Young, the Whig nominee for governor, against incumbent Democratic Governor Silas Wright, a man hostile to the anti-rent movement. Wright had earned the scorn of the Anti-Rent Party by forcibly quelling tenant protests and by imprisoning several of the movement's leaders, including Dr. Boughton, one of the most respected and popular leaders in the protest movement. The Anti-Renters proved to be the difference in the hard-fought contest, enabling Young to carry the state by more than 11,000 votes.

In the 1850 gubernatorial contest, the small yet influential party was responsible for Whig Washington Hunt's razor-thin 262-vote margin over Democrat Horatio Seymour. In that election, Hunt's name appeared on ballots distributed by both the Whig and Anti-Rent parties. The Anti-Rent Party remained active in New York politics until 1851. That year, the third-party endorsed the entire Democratic ticket, leading to a walkout of those members who were sympathetic to the Whigs. That division virtually ended the Anti-Rent Party as a force of sorts in New York politics.

During its short but colorful history, the Anti-Rent Party temporarily aligned itself with George Henry Evan's National Reform Association, which actively supported the movement until purged from a leadership position by Ira Harris. Harris, who was later elected to the U.S. Senate from New York as a Republican in 1860, was a close personal friend of the Lincolns. In fact, his daughter, Clara, and her fiancée were with the Lincoln's at Ford Theatre on the night the president was assassinated.

Though the Anti-Rent Party disappeared later that year, the anti-rent movement thrived for several years thereafter. In its short history, the anti-rent movement produced some concrete results, including restrictions on the length of all new leases to not more than five to ten years and taxation of all income derived from such rents.

This same period also saw the rise of a Law & Order Party in Rhode Island. Founded by the state's aristocrats in the aftermath of the so-called Dorr Rebellion of 1842, the Law & Order Party was strongly opposed to Thomas W. Dorr's decade-long struggle to rewrite the state's antiquated constitution and liberalize Rhode Island's voting requirements.

The chief agitator in Rhode Island was none other than Seth Luther, a self-appointed radical spokesman for working people, who had lent considerable energy—and inspiration—to the Workingmen's parties of the 1820s, and, later, to New York's Equal Rights Party. A vociferous advocate of free suffrage, Luther had long argued that property-less working people should have the right to vote and frequently denounced the monopoly of political power by Rhode Island's "small potato aristocrats." Why, he wondered, shouldn't twelve thousand working people in Rhode Island have the same right to vote as the five thousand who owned land?

Working people, undoubtedly influenced by Luther, organized the Rhode Island Suffrage Association and in the spring of 1841 held a rally in Providence that was attended by thousands of supporters, many of whom carried banners and signs urging immediate electoral reform. They also organized their own "People's Party" and drafted a mock constitution that guaranteed voting rights for working people without regard to property qualifications.

In the early part of 1842, the suffrage group held an unofficial referendum in which 14,000 people, including a majority of the state's property owners, voted in favor of the new constitution. Soon thereafter, they also held a mock election in which Thomas Door, an attorney and scion to a well-to-do Providence family, ran unopposed for governor. Approximately six thousand Rhode Islanders voted for him—more than a thousand more than had actually voted for Whig Samuel Ward King, the state's official governor, later that year when he was re-elected to a third term.

On May 3, 1842, Dorr's determined supporters held an inauguration, complete with a parade of laborers marching through downtown Providence. Much to the dismay of the state's aristocracy, a newly elected "People's Legislature" was also convened. Dorr then led a daring, yet somewhat awkward attack on the state arsenal, featuring a popgun size blast from an old cannon that badly misfired. Furious at his antics, Governor Samuel Ward King ordered Dorr's immediate arrest, but the political reformer, proving too elusive for the state's law enforcement personnel, fled the state.

While in hiding, Dorr tried desperately to raise money for a private militia. He returned to Rhode Island a short time later to complete his insurrection, but was again forced to flee the state after realizing that the governor had assembled a militia of several thousand men, including several African-Americans who were angered by the fact that the "People's Constitution," over Dorr's objection, had inserted the word "white" in its voting rights clause. Meanwhile, Gov. King declared martial law and Dorr was finally captured and arrested in the fall of 1843 and was convicted of treason and sentenced to life imprisonment at hard labor. As with the Anti-Renters in New York, armed insurrection had failed.

Dorr's rebellion, however, spawned a new conservative party—the Law & Order Party, a short-lived party that quickly supplanted the Whigs as Rhode Island's predominant political force. Riding the crest of anti-Dorr sentiment, the Law & Order Party won both of Rhode Island's U.S. House seats in 1842 and elected 72-year-old James Fenner governor the following year. The aging Fenner initially held that post some thirty-six years earlier. Serving as the state's chief executive had become something of a family tradition. Fenner's father, an Anti-Federalist who opposed Rhode Island's ratification of the federal Constitution, had served as governor in the 1790s. A consummate politician, the younger Fenner, a former Democratic senator, was the first governor to serve under the state's new constitution, which had been enacted, in large part, as a result of Dorr's fierce agitation. Ironically, Fenner was personally responsible for drafting that constitution.

Facing only token opposition, Fenner was easily re-elected on the Law & Order ticket in 1844, the same year the party sent former Gov. John B. Francis to the U.S. Senate to fill a vacancy. A former Anti-Mason, Francis was serving as chancellor of Brown University at the time of his election. Fenner was defeated the following year by Charles Jackson, a Whig who favored releasing all political prisoners, including Dorr. In ailing health, Fenner decided not to seek his party's gubernatorial nomination in 1846. His death on April 17 of that year signaled the end of what was appropriately called the "Reign of Fenners."

For his part, Dorr spent twenty months in jail. But his prison stay hadn't been in vain. After a long struggle, impoverished and working-class people of Rhode Island had finally obtained the right to vote. Aristotle's axiom that if men "are equal on any count, they are equal absolutely," had been realized. The harshness of Dorr's sentence was widely condemned and in 1845 he was released from prison. His civil rights were restored in 1851 and the court judgment against him was set aside three years later.

The Law & Order Party, created as a backlash to the Dorr Rebellion, returned to power briefly in 1846 when the state's general assembly chose Byron Diman, an admirer of Kentucky's Henry Clay, as governor. By this time, the Dorr Rebellion was but a memory. Despite some lingering bitterness, Rhode Island had a new and more democratic constitution and politics in the Ocean State had returned to relative tranquility. The short-lived Law & Order Party had fulfilled its mission by maintaining law and order during one of the state's most turbulent periods.

3

The Struggle for Freedom

✦

The Liberty Party

The antislavery movement of the 1830s led to the founding of the first political party in American history devoted exclusively to the cause of abolition—the Liberty Party. By the 1830s the institution of African slavery dominated almost all aspects of southern society and played a significant role in the expansion of the South's cotton cultivation, enabling that region to increase its cotton production from roughly a thousand tons produced annually in the early 1790s to a million tons of cotton per year by 1860—the year of Lincoln's election. Despite the fact that slave importation was outlawed in 1808, the slave population in the South grew from approximately 500,000 slaves—more than half of whom resided in Virginia—to nearly four million during this same period, including an estimated 250,000 who were illegally imported prior to the Civil War. According to the 1860 census, more than 2.3 million of the nation's slaves lived in the Deep South, compared to 1.2 million in the Upper South and 432,586 in the Border States, including Delaware with a slave population of less than 2,000. The heaviest concentrations of slaves were in Mississippi and South Carolina, where nearly half the white population owned slaves and where the slave populations in those states actually exceeded the number of whites. In addition, there were more than a quarter million free blacks living in the South at this time—a figure that exceeded the number of free blacks in the North. Interestingly enough, these included a few blacks in Louisiana who owned slaves themselves. Most of the free blacks in the South, especially in the Upper South and the Border States where slavery was economically more vulnerable, were treated as second-class citizens, subject to a rash of laws that essentially reduced them to the status of slaves without masters.

Parts of the South, ranging from the low country of South Carolina and the Sea Islands and extending through the fertile Black Belt of Georgia and Mississippi to the sugar parishes of Louisiana, resembled the "slave societies" of the eighteenth and early nineteenth century colonies of the West Indies where black slaves typically made up ninety percent or more of an island's population under the control of large plantation owners and the prosperous merchants who made a comfortable living off the slave system. For all of its cruelty and inhumanity, slavery was fundamentally an economic phenomenon with the nearly four million captive slaves in the South carrying a market value of close to four billion dollars. As a result of slavery, the per capita income in the South—where the inequality of wealth between rich and poor was most pronounced and where whites of modest means had been priced out of the market—was $3,978 in 1860, compared to only $2,040 in the North. Moreover, three-fifths of the nation's most affluent citizens lived in the slaveholding South.

Yet, curiously, while the South had become a slave society dominated politically and economically by a planter oligarchy, fewer than 10,000 families out of a population of eight million belonged to the agricultural aristocracy. The vast majority of the 385,000 southern slave owners were small planters who owned fewer than twenty slaves—and half of them owned fewer than five. Moreover, fewer than 3,000 families owned more than one hundred slaves and three out of every four white southerners were not slaveholders, nor were they related to anyone who owned any slaves.[1]

In 1839, at roughly the same that the Liberty Party was founded, the *New Orleans Courier* suggested reopening the African slave trade—an idea that shocked many in the North as well as the South. After a large hue and cry, the issue subsided for more than a decade before Leonidas W. Spratt, the fiery editor of the *Charleston Standard*, again took up the issue in 1853, systematically advocating the repeal of the ban on slave traffic. Robert Barnwell Rhett's *Charleston Mercury* began championing the issue shortly thereafter.[2]

To a growing number of Americans, the notion of human bondage was incompatible with the republic's founding ideals. Though most of the nation's leading abolitionists, including William Lloyd Garrison—the most hated man in the South—agitated against slavery, they almost universally opposed the idea of political activism, a course that suited the country's two major parties just fine.

---

1. Bailyn, *et al.*, *The Great Republic*, pp. 415-416; Zinn, *A People's History of the United States*, pp. 167-168.
2. David M. Potter, *The Impending Crisis 1848-1861*, Don E. Fehrenbacher, ed., (New York, 1976), p. 396.

However, abolitionist lawyer and reformer Alvan T. Stewart, president of the New York State Anti-Slavery Society, changed all that in the late 1830s by convincing a few of his fellow abolitionists to build and support a third party that could achieve a balance of power in some of the tightly contested regions of the North, thereby pressuring the Whig and Democratic parties in those areas to deal with the "peculiar institution" of slavery. Such a strategy, it was argued, would ultimately free many Whigs and Democrats from the grip of the so-called "Slave Power," which consisted not only of southern slave owners, but also their powerful representatives in Congress as well as their obsequious business allies in the North.[3] As early as 1837, Stewart, who had been held captive in Canada briefly during the War of 1812, had argued that the Constitution, contrary to widespread belief at the time, did *not* protect slavery and was in both letter and spirit an antislavery document which, coupled with the Declaration of Independence, empowered Congress and the federal judiciary to free all of the country's slaves.[4] Like other abolitionists of the period, Stewart had grown disillusioned by the unwillingness of Whig and Democratic politicians in Congress to seriously consider antislavery petitions. "We might as well send the lamb as an ambassador to a community of wolves," he glumly remarked.[5] Though Stewart's early efforts to launch an independent antislavery party was given a cold reception by some of the country's leading abolitionists—including such men as William Goodell, Gerrit Smith and Lewis Tappan, founder of the New York Anti-Slavery Society—his idea was eventually embraced by New York's Myron Holley, a former state assemblyman and veteran of the Anti-Masonic movement, as well as a group of antislavery activists in Massachusetts, led by abolitionist editor Elizur Wright, Jr.

The Liberty Party believed that slavery was to blame for virtually all of the nation's ills, short of inclement weather. The party's leaders, including well-known Quaker poet John Greenleaf Whittier, held that the conspiratorial alli-

---

3. Richard H. Sewell, *Ballots for Freedom: Antislavery Politics in the United States 1837-1860* (New York, 1976), p. 51. Stewart first called for the creation of such an organization at an executive committee meeting of the New York Anti-Slavery Society in January 1839, maintaining that a new party was essential to waging political war on the institution of slavery. At best, he argued, the two major parties could be expected to nominate some "milk and water or a vainglorious nominal abolitionist" who would be next to worthless in the eyes of most antislavery voters.

4. Ibid., p. 50.

5. Clifford S. Griffin, *Their Brothers' Keepers: Moral Stewardship in the United States, 1800-1865* (New Brunswick, N.J., 1960), p. 156.

ance between southern slave owners and their northern minions were responsible for the country's deepening economic depression. The Libertymen, as they were called, also accused the Slave Power of undermining the civil liberties of free Americans. On this point they were most certainly correct. In the early 1830s, southern politicians had demanded guarantees that would prevent abolitionists from using the postal service to distribute their "incendiary publications." They also demanded legislation barring Congress from accepting petitions proposing the abolition of slavery in the District of Columbia.

Presidents Andrew Jackson and Martin Van Buren, ever mindful of their large Democratic constituencies in the South, urged postmasters to halt all antislavery publications at their point of origin. Moreover, many northern Democratic congressmen, ignoring the protestations of modern antislavery northern Whigs, voted with southern lawmakers of both major parties to assure the implementation of "gag rules," which automatically tabled any antislavery petitions in Congress. Despite the strenuous objections of John Quincy Adams and other antislavery congressmen, these "gag rules" were in effect from 1836 to 1844.

Ardent antislavery activists simply wouldn't stand for any of this and righteously set out to create their own political party. Led by the witty and highly principled Stewart—a man who relished in ridiculing his adversaries—and such divergent reformers as wealthy New York silk merchants Lewis and Benjamin Tappan and Gerrit Smith, America's largest landowner, the Liberty Party quickly attracted an impressive array of backers, including William Jackson, a former Massachusetts state legislator and newspaper publisher. Jackson, who was also an enthusiastic leader in the early temperance movement, felt so strong about the latter issue that he ended the daily practice of serving rum to his employees—not an altogether uncommon practice in the early 1800s—and increased his employees' wages with the money he saved. Heavily influenced by Alvan Stewart, Elizur Wright, Jr., the caustic editor of the *Massachusetts Abolitionist*, also favored the formation of independent antislavery party. Confiding in his longtime friend Beriah Green, Wright, who had initially opposed the idea of a separate abolitionist party, said that he "would like to see an antislavery candidate for the Presidency—if we can find a 'proper man.' We want a nucleus for political action—something for a practical man to look at."[6] Another prominent reformer drawn to the Liberty Party was attorney Henry B. Stanton, husband of the famous women's rights leader Elizabeth Cady Stanton.

---

6.   Wright letter to Beriah Green, October 10, 1839, Wright Papers, Library of Congress, as quoted in Sewell, *Ballots for Freedom*, p. 59.

Among the many other notable individuals who played a role in the Liberty Party was future Chief Justice of the Supreme Court Salmon P. Chase who joined the party in 1841. Chase, then practicing law in Cincinnati, was drawn to the abolitionist movement in late 1836 after a mob attacked the office of James G. Birney's *Philanthropist* newspaper. Chase defended the embattled editor during this period and the two men struck up a close personal friendship. Nathaniel Berry, a former state senator from New Hampshire, and William Goodell, a nationally recognized abolitionist, were also leaders in the fledgling antislavery party. The Reverend Owen Lovejoy of Illinois and antislavery radical Myron Holley were also among those initially drawn to the Liberty Party. Holley, who claimed to be a descendant of the man after whom "Halley's Comet" was named, was editor of the *Rochester Freeman*.

Reaching for the political heavens, the Liberty Party met in convention in Warsaw, New York on November 13, 1839, and nominated 47-year-old James G. Birney, founder and publisher of the *Philanthropist*, as its presidential candidate. Francis J. Lemoyne, a prominent Pennsylvania physician and abolitionist who was actively involved in the Underground Railroad, was chosen for vice president. Curiously, Birney had once been a slaveholder himself, a result of his wife's dowry, which included the possession of some of her family's indentured servants.

Birney thought the Liberty Party nomination was a bit premature and graciously refused to accept it. The 41-year-old Lemoyne, who later built the first crematory in the United States, also declined. However, when the Whigs and Democrats—having nominated William H. Harrison and Martin Van Buren, respectively—expressed no antislavery sentiment in their platforms, a second Liberty Party convention was held in Albany, New York, in April 1840. Delegates from six states attended the second convention. Birney was unanimously nominated for a second time and enthusiastically accepted. This time he was paired with Thomas Earle, a 44-year-old Quaker attorney from Philadelphia, Pennsylvania. A prolific writer, Earle, who had been a delegate to the Pennsylvania Constitutional Convention in 1837, was deeply involved in the American Anti-Slavery Society.

Born into wealth and culture, the Princeton-educated Birney served briefly in the Kentucky legislature before settling in Alabama where he tried his hand as a planter. As a member of the first Alabama legislature in 1819, Birney authored legislation for gradual emancipation, including a law calling for trial by jury for slaves indicted for crimes more serious than petty larceny. Remarkably, he was also responsible for the inclusion of provisions for gradual emancipation in the state's constitution. Later, he persuaded the Alabama legislature to pass a law barring the importation of slaves for sale or hire. Both measures were later repealed.

Birney failed miserably as a plantation owner. Neglect and gambling losses forced him to sell his plantation and most of its slaves in early 1823. Having already achieved considerable prominence as an attorney, Birney quickly recovered from his embarrassing financial setback. He later served as counsel to the Cherokee Nation for several years, an experience that led him, albeit slowly, into the abolitionist fold.

Though he personally found slavery repugnant, Birney's evolution from southern aristocrat to fiery abolitionist was two decades in the making. He had embraced the colonization movement in the late 1820s and later served as vice president of the Kentucky Colonization Society. The colonization movement—one of the most controversial and outlandish reform movements in American history—sought to send free blacks voluntarily back to Africa. Incredibly, a number of prominent Americans, including Henry Clay and Abraham Lincoln, at one time or another supported the idea of gradual colonization. Fortunately, the movement for repatriation had only limited success. In 1830, for example, the Society succeeded in relocating only 259 free blacks to its West African colony in Liberia. Guided as much by racial prejudice as benevolence, the movement was sharply denounced by William Lloyd Garrison and other abolitionists. Deportation, they argued, was not a substitute for social justice. After considerable soul-searching, Birney, like Lincoln, eventually saw the error of his ways, realizing that gradual emancipation and foreign asylum was hardly the solution to America's racial woes. Declaring himself an out-and-out abolitionist, Birney freed his six remaining slaves and abruptly resigned from the American Colonization Society in 1834.

The following year, Birney delivered the principal address at the American Anti-Slavery Society's annual meeting in New York. As vice president of the society, he traveled far and wide on its behalf, giving countless public speeches and addressing several state legislatures.

Dedicating himself to the nation's antislavery movement, the former state legislator moved to Cincinnati, Ohio, in early 1836 and founded the *Philanthropist*, an antislavery newspaper. With the editorial assistance of the gifted Gamaliel Bailey, a physician and one of the most powerful pens in the abolitionist movement, the *Philanthropist* quickly became the country's leading antislavery newspaper. From its pages, Birney and Bailey relentlessly attacked the Democrats and Whigs while exhorting the abolitionists to become politically involved. During his stay in Cincinnati, Birney's life was threatened and his office was looted no less than three times by unruly mobs operating with the connivance of local authorities. Long before Abraham Lincoln's famous address in which he proclaimed the doctrine that a house divided against itself cannot stand, Birney had uttered similar words. "There will be no cessation of conflict until slavery shall be exterminated or liberty destroyed. Liberty and slavery cannot live in juxtaposition." It wasn't quite Lincolnesque, but he made his point.

Although Birney forcefully argued the party's antislavery views throughout the campaign, the tiny Liberty Party really wasn't a factor in the 1840 presidential election. Like Democrat Martin Van Buren, Birney was simply no match for Whig candidate William H. Harrison, who was portrayed as a "log cabin and hard cider" friend of the poor. President Van Buren, vilified by the rugged Davy Crockett and others as an affected, wealthy aristocrat who had turned the White House into a luxurious—and effeminate—palace, also found it difficult to compete with the "victor of Tippecanoe." Using the traditional Democratic weapons of populism and grassroots organization, the Whigs captured the White House. Harrison garnered 1,275,016 votes to the incumbent Democrat's 1,129,102, receiving 234 electoral votes to Van Buren's sixty. The hapless Birney, meanwhile, mustered only 7,069 votes nationally, or less than three-tenths of one percent of the total vote.

The 1844 Campaign: A Five-Way Affair?

For a brief period, the race for the White House in 1844 was shaping up as a genuine five-way affair, featuring not only the Democratic, Whig and Liberty parties, but also two new entries—the more significant of which was a new National Democratic Party hastily created by President Tyler, "a president without a party," to bolster his lagging re-election prospects.

John Tyler, America's tenth chief executive, was the first politician to ascend from the vice presidency to the nation's highest elective office upon the death of a president. The 51-year-old Virginia planter and slave owner, an almost stereotypical southern aristocrat, had assumed power on April 6, 1841, less than 48 hours after President William Henry Harrison succumbed to pneumonia, the result of catching a bad cold while delivering his inaugural address on a damp and bitter cold day a month earlier. Like John Quincy Adams, Tyler was only the second man in American history up 'til then to switch parties before reaching the pinnacle of power. Adams, similarly, had severed his ties with the Federalists in 1807 when he supported Jefferson's controversial Embargo Act, some seventeen years before winning the White House.

Tyler's story, however, was a little different. He had angered Democrats in the Old Dominion State by his sharp criticisms of Jackson's "imperial presidency." Having supported Andrew Jackson in the presidential campaigns of 1828 and 1832, the recreant senator grew apart from the president over the issues of secession and nullification, staking out a middle position of sorts by arguing in favor of secession while opposing nullification. When Jackson sought congressional approval to use armed force to collect the federally-mandated tariff in South Carolina, Tyler strenuously objected, casting the lone Democratic vote against the so-called "force bill." Viewing Jackson as a virtual dictator, the conservative Virginian grew increasingly critical of the president and voted to censure him in 1834. Having aligned himself with Henry Clay and the Whigs, Tyler resigned from the Senate in 1836 rather than follow the wishes of the Virginia legislature instructing both of its senators to expunge the censure from the congressional record.

As a result of his opposition to Jackson, the Virginia lawyer became an instant hero to the Whigs, who promptly nominated him as Hugh L. White's vice-presidential running mate in 1836, the year that the Whigs nominated three regional presidential candidates in an unsuccessful attempt to deny Democrat Martin Van Buren an Electoral College majority. Tyler was subsequently elected to the Virginia legislature and was named Speaker of the state House of Representatives in January 1839. Considered one of the most notable states' rights leaders in the Whig Party, Tyler was again nominated for the vice presidency in 1840 and was swept into office when Harrison trounced the hapless Van Buren.

Ironically, as president, Tyler became the only chief executive in American history to have been expelled by his own party while in office. Having irked Whig nationalists—particularly the influential Henry Clay, whose bank bills he vetoed on two occasions—Tyler was cast overboard by his adopted party on September 13, 1841, barely five months after assuming the presidency. Tyler was, in effect, a president without a party. He also served without a vice president for forty-seven months—the longest period in American history in which there was a vacancy in that office.

In opposing Clay's banking legislation, Tyler had even managed to anger his own cabinet. Protesting his second veto of Clay's bank bill, his cabinet resigned *en masse* on September 11. Among those who resigned were Secretary of the Treasury Thomas Ewing, who later served as an advisor to Presidents Lincoln and Johnson, and Postmaster General Francis Granger, leader of the Silver Grays, the Whig Party's conservative wing. Southern luminaries such as John J. Crittenden of Kentucky, Tennessee's John Bell and the witty George E. Badger—all of whom later helped to form the Constitutional Union Party in the wake of the Whig Party's disintegration in the mid-1850s—also resigned their posts as Attorney General, Secretary of War and Secretary of the Navy, respectively. Tyler's entire administration had been virtually wiped out in one fell swoop. The one notable exception was that of the talented Daniel Webster, who remained in his post as Secretary of State long enough to conclude negotiations in the famous Webster-Ashburton Treaty, which settled a longstanding dispute over the Maine and New Brunswick boundary, thereby ending any threat of hostilities between Great Britain and the United States. Though he was formally read out of the Whig Party a few days later, the embattled chief executive was praised for blocking Clay's banking legislation. Tennessee Gov. James K. Polk, a Democrat, offered the highest praise, commending Tyler for "saving the country from the dominion and political incubus of the money power in the form of a National Bank."

The "Champion of the Old South," as one biographer described him, immediately appointed a new cabinet, consisting almost entirely of conservative Democrats. These appointments started the beleaguered president on a seemingly never-ending chain of cabinet selections, giving him the dubious distinction of making more cabinet changes than any other single-term president in American history. It was almost a comical version of musical chairs. At the urging of powerful South Carolina Senator John C. Calhoun, the preeminent spokesman for slavery in the antebellum South, Tyler, leaving little doubt as to where he stood on the issues of states' rights and slavery, appointed Naval Secretary Abel Upshur to the post of Secretary of State upon Daniel Webster's resignation in 1843. Upshur, a Virginian, had been openly sympathetic to slavery. Staunch proslavery men who viewed territorial expansion as a God-given right controlled an entire cabinet for the first time in American history.

Yet even after expelling him, the Whigs still weren't finished with the crusty Virginian. Demonstrating a mean spiritedness almost unparalleled in U.S. history, the Whigs tried unsuccessfully to impeach Tyler in January 1843 on the flimsy basis that he had signed a tariff measure designed to raise some much needed revenue at a time when the nation's public coffers had run dry. The vote on an impeachment inquiry, however, was overwhelmingly defeated in the House by a vote of 83 to 27.

Tyler's years in the White House were excruciatingly painful, both personally and politically. Letitia Christian, his devoted wife of 29 years and mother of the first eight of his fifteen children, passed away in 1842. Moreover, his "accidental" presidency was marred by one of the worst tragedies imaginable. On February 28,

1844, while the president and a large entourage of friends, supporters and admin-
istration officials were on a leisurely cruise down the Potomac River on the USS
Princeton, a new steam-powered warship, one of the ship's guns accidentally
exploded, killing several guests, including Secretary of State Abel B. Upshur and
Secretary of the Navy Thomas W. Gilmer. (Ironically, only a few hours earlier
Upshur had drafted a treaty for the annexation of Texas.)

The freak explosion, by far the worst tragedy to ever befall so many high-ranking U.S. officials at one time, also took the lives of David Gardiner, believed to be
one of the wealthiest men in the country, as well as John Calhoun's best friend,
newspaper editor Virgil Maxcy who was then serving as Charge d'Affaires of the
United States to Belgium. Tyler and his future wife, 23-year-old Julia Gardiner,
whose father was killed in the violent explosion, escaped with their lives because
they had gone below deck moments before to fresh their champagne. The president, in fact, carried young Julia off the burning battleship to a nearby rescue vessel. They were married four months later. Though many of the fifty-four-year-old
president's critics scoffed at the May-December relationship, his marriage to Julia
Gardiner was a long and happy one, lasting until the former president's death on
January 18, 1862. They had seven children together.

Still shaken by the deadly *Princeton* mishap, Tyler, with little fanfare, named
John Y. Mason of Virginia as Gilmer's replacement as Secretary of the Navy.
However, his choice for Upshur's replacement as Secretary of State didn't go
quite as smoothly. Hoping to place another ardent annexationist at the helm,
Tyler turned to the "Cast Iron Man" himself and nominated South Carolina's
John Calhoun for the post. In nominating the old Nullifier, Tyler faced a barrage
of criticism, especially from the nation's abolitionists. The aging John Quincy
Adams, paladin of the antislavery movement in Congress and a man always quick
to turn a memorable phrase, had earlier denounced the president and "his cabinet
of slave-drivers" who "swill like swine, and grunt about the rights of man" while
seeking to expand the "peculiar institution" of slavery across the continent. The
criticism from the antislavery forces notwithstanding, Calhoun was eminently
qualified for the post and, after considerable wrangling in the U.S. Senate, was
eventually confirmed.

Borrowing the name of Thomas Jefferson's time-honored Democratic-Republican Party, Tyler, determined to make the "re-annexation" of Texas a central
issue in the 1844 presidential campaign, created a new party that spring. Tyler's
short-lived third party, adhering to his strict constructionist views, was made up
largely of friends and supporters from both major parties. Most of those who rallied to the beleaguered president's new party were southerners unhappy that a

majority of Whigs and Democrats were adamantly opposed to the idea of adding the Lone Star Republic to the nation as a slave state.

The Democrats and Whigs had both gone on record in the early 1840s in opposition to the annexation of Texas, fearing a possible war with Mexico, as well as increased domestic tensions between the nation's antislavery forces and southern slave owners. There were several other factors that also contributed to the reluctance of the country's two major parties to admit Texas to the Union—namely the isolationist policies of Tyler's predecessors Jackson and Van Buren. Jackson, whose position wasn't entirely unlike that of South Carolina's John C. Calhoun a few years later, had urged Texans to bide their time, encouraging the Lone Star Republic to establish a claim to California in order to "paralyze" the opponents of annexation, most of whom were ardent abolitionists from the North. Old Hickory's successor, Martin Van Buren, who relied almost entirely on support from the nation's northeast corridor, proved to be too timid to directly address the question of annexation for fear that it would cost him votes—and the presidency.

Rarely one to back away from a fight, the headstrong Tyler was convinced that Texas, if not immediately annexed, would be forced to ally with Great Britain to protect itself against its menacing neighbor, Mexico. This wasn't an altogether far-fetched notion. After all, the British—with their eyes focused on the huge Mexican and Texas markets—had extended formal recognition to Texas in 1842. Though careful not to antagonize southern cotton interests of which she was so dependent, Great Britain wanted to keep Texas independent of both Mexico and the United States.

Tyler fought tooth and nail for the annexation of Texas, if for no other reason than the glory and luster it would provide his presidency—and he did so against long odds. Most Texans, after all, had already begun to look askance at the idea of annexation, preferring an independent Texas Republic instead. Even the colorful and legendary Sam Houston, once an outspoken champion of annexation, seemed cool to the idea by 1840, even in the face of a possible invasion by neighboring Mexico. By then, Houston had adopted a somewhat grandiose and imperialistic vision of an independent Texas that would eventually unite with the Oregon Territory, California and New Mexico into a transcontinental power, perhaps even absorbing some of northern Mexico's sparsely-populated region. Houston, to be sure, wasn't alone in advocating independence for Texas. Two other former presidents of the Texas Republic—Mirabeau B. Lamar, the Republic's second president and a man who liked to dabble in poetry, and David G. Burnet, an outspoken Houston adversary—were both on record as opposing annexation, as were scores of European immigrants who had recently settled in the Lone Star Republic.

Not the least bit discouraged by such opposition, the states' rights champion, who was determined to protect southern interests at any cost, pushed vigorously for an annexation treaty, only to watch helplessly as Senate Whigs, joined by eight Democrats, including Missouri's powerful Thomas Hart Benton, rejected his proposal in June 1844. Seething from the Senate's repudiation of his annexation treaty and disappointed that the Democrats appeared ready to pass him over at their national convention later that spring, Tyler was more convinced than ever that it was time to take the issue of annexation directly to the American people—and the only way to do it, he believed, was through a new political party.

This was the only occasion in American history that a sitting president sought to win re-election on a third-party ticket. (There is more than a little *prima facie* evidence to suggest that President Grover Cleveland used the vast resources of his office to aid a third-party ticket some fifty years later by lending subtle, behind-the-scenes support to the Gold Democrats in an attempt to deny William Jennings Bryan the presidency in 1896.)

In any case, the mortified Democrats looked on in disbelief as Tyler's supporters met at the Globe Hotel in Washington, D.C., on April 1. As expected, the delegates enthusiastically passed a series of resolutions praising Tyler's vetoes of Clay's bank bills and urging the re-annexation of Texas. The "Administration Party," as it was dubbed, also lambasted Democratic front-runner Martin Van Buren, who was opposed to annexation, and enthusiastically endorsed Tyler's re-election. Tyler's loyalists also made friendly overtures to former President Andrew Jackson who had recently come out in favor of annexation. Obviously, they were hoping that Old Hickory would use his influence to persuade his fellow Democrats to embrace a pro-annexation platform and nominee—or, if rebuked, to join their cause.

Resurrecting the Democratic-Republican label of the great Jeffersonian organization, Tyler's party reconvened in Baltimore's Calvert Hall in late May, at the same time that the badly divided Democrats were holding their national convention in the same city. More than 1,000 delegates, most of whom were administration employees or hangers-on, attended what amounted to a Tyler coronation. Huge banners proclaiming TYLER AND TEXAS and RE-ANNEXATION OF TEXAS—REJECTION IS POSTPONEMENT adorned the carnival-like hall. It took the festive delegates, consuming large amounts of brandy, whisky and gin, less than an hour to nominate Tyler for a second term. The party decided against naming a vice-presidential candidate, pending the outcome of the Democratic national convention at Odd Fellows Hall. Tyler's third-party maneuver impressed even his sharpest critics, including battle-scarred John Quincy Adams who confessed that the president had played his hand with considerable skill and "intrepidity."

Insisting that the issue of Texas annexation was more important than his own re-election, Tyler accepted the states' rights Democratic-Republican nomination in a statement issued on May 30. His statement was a political masterpiece, clearly leaving the door of negotiation with Polk and the Democrats ajar.

Though lost on most biographers and historians, President Tyler, the side-lined ex-Whig who was still on speaking terms with Andrew Jackson and other influential Democrats, shrewdly had a hand in shaping both the Democratic ticket and its platform that year. A lesser politician probably wouldn't have been able to pull it off. By threatening to run as a third party candidate, Tyler skillfully forced the southern wing of the Democratic Party to forsake frontrunner Van Buren and push hard for the nomination of a pro-South expansionist—namely, former Speaker of the House James K. Polk of Tennessee. Like Tyler, Polk was a slaveholder. In a genuine three-way race, the Democrats realized that their candidate would have been doomed. Tyler's third-party candidacy, siphoning votes from the Democratic standard-bearer in the southern and border states, would have virtually assured the election of the much-despised Whig candidate Henry Clay.

Having played his hand with considerable adroitness and skill, Tyler withdrew from the race in August and endorsed Polk. By holding out the threat of a third-party candidacy, Tyler succeeded in influencing the Democrats, thereby guiding the young nation on the path of its historic "Manifest Destiny," the crown jewel of which was the annexation of Texas in 1845.[7]

For a dozen years or so after leaving the White House, John Tyler, seeking vindication, believed that the Democrats would one day nominate him for the presidency, enabling him to return to power. He believed that if historians judged his administration in a positive light, then future vice presidents who succeeded to the presidency "may feel some slight encouragement to pursue an independent course" as he had. The former president remained deeply interested in

---

7.   Former New York assemblyman John L. O'Sullivan, editor of the *Democratic Review* and a man who was twice indicted for violating U.S. neutrality laws, coined the term "Manifest Destiny" to justify the country's westward expansion. O'Sullivan, who was indicted for taking part in Narcisco Lopez's failed Cuban expedition in the late 1840s, later served in a minor post during the Pierce administration.

national politics and in 1861 presided over the failed peace convention at the Willard Hotel in Washington. He was elected to the Confederate Congress in November of that year, but died suddenly in his hotel room while preparing to attend its first session in Richmond.

Joseph Smith and the Reform Party

The 1844 campaign also saw the brief participation of a Mormon-sponsored Reform Party. Holding a dim view of President Tyler and unhappy with John C. Calhoun, Henry Clay, Martin Van Buren and other prospective candidates for the presidency, the Mormons, seeking redress for the persecution they had suffered in Missouri and elsewhere, entered their own presidential ticket headed by Joseph Smith, the charismatic and controversial 38-year-old founding prophet of the Church of Jesus Christ of Latter-Day Saints. There were approximately 35,000 Latter-Day Saints in the country at the time.

Harboring few illusions that he would actually be elected, Smith's Reform Party nevertheless claimed that it was organized in almost every state in the Union. The party's national convention, held in Nauvoo, Illinois, formally nominated Smith on January 29, 1844. James Arlington Bennett, an accountant from New York City, was initially chosen to be Smith's vice-presidential running mate, but his Irish birth made him ineligible. Sidney Rigdon of Pittsburgh, a former Democrat who served on the city council and later as postmaster of Nauvoo, was then named in Bennett's place. The 50-year-old Rigdon, a one-time Baptist preacher, had run unsuccessfully for the U.S. House from Ohio in 1832, losing narrowly in a three-way race.

Hoping to establish a one-party theocracy in the United States—Smith's long-envisioned "dominion of the Kingdom"—the new party denounced the Democratic and Whig parties and called for a two-thirds reduction in the size of Congress (a position also taken by Josiah Quincy, the great Massachusetts Federalist), prison reform and the abolition of debtor prisons. Like the Liberty Party's James Birney, Smith also advocated the freeing of slaves, but, unlike Birney, favored the annexation of Texas. Smith also suggested that slaveholders should be compensated for their losses out of surplus revenues generated from the sale of public lands—a proposal, curiously enough, that was echoed by poet Ralph Waldo Emerson eleven years later.

The fourth of nine children born to poor tenant farmers in the green, rolling hills of Vermont in 1805, Smith was raised in a household of religious revivalists.

In early 1820, he claimed to have had his first mystical experience—asserting that he had a vision of God. A decade later, he published *The Book of Mormon*, a 600-page translation of sacred engraved golden plates supposedly containing the history of an ancient Christian civilization in the New World. Smith's book portrayed American Indians as depraved yet salvageable descendants of an ancient Hebrew tribe and foresaw a new American prophet who would establish Christ's Kingdom in the New World.

In 1830, shortly after the publication of his book, Smith organized the Church of Christ, which was later renamed the Church of Jesus Christ of Latter-Day Saints. He ordained countless deacons, teachers, lay priests, elders and high priests and dispatched missionaries to scout the Missouri frontier. In 1831, a few of Smith's followers established an outpost near Independence, Missouri, the eastern entry to the Santa Fe Trail. Smith immediately designated the site as New Jerusalem. As instructed in his revelations, Smith's ultimate goal was to move the saints westward to build a city of Zion. Later that same year, Smith and his followers from New York migrated to Kirtland, Ohio, near Cleveland, where Mormon missionaries had converted an entire community.

Needless to say, Smith and his followers faced religious persecution from the outset. Ministers and members of other denominations refused to accept the *Book of Mormon* as having a divine origin and Smith was personally subjected to tar and featherings and threats on his life. By 1839, the Mormons were forced out of Ohio and Missouri and sought refuge in Nauvoo, a piece of swampland along the eastern shore of the Mississippi River in western Illinois. In Missouri, proslavery "border ruffians," infuriated by rumors that the Mormons intended to bring free blacks into the state, attacked the saints unmercifully, destroying their settlements around the city of Independence. Armed encounters between the ruffians and the Mormons soon followed. Adding fuel to the fire, Gov. Lillburn W. Boggs, a former Indian trader and storekeeper, declared that the Mormons had to be driven from the state or exterminated. Shortly thereafter, nineteen Mormon men and young boys were massacred and Smith was convicted of treason and sentenced to death. Fortunately, Smith escaped shortly before his execution.

Smith and his adherents soon found refuge in Nauvoo. In 1840, the Illinois legislature incorporated Nauvoo as a kind of independent city-state, allowing the Mormons to live in virtual exclusivity. Unlike their previous experiences, the Mormons were treated favorably in Illinois. In Nauvoo, the Mormons built a model city, complete with wide streets and state-of-the-art steam sawmills, a flourmill, factories, hotels and schools, including the University of Nauvoo. In addition, they also began work on a breathtaking place of worship, supported by thirty gigantic pillars and walls of hewn stone that poet John Greenleaf Whittier described as the most splendid architectural monument in the country. In no time, Nauvoo became the envy of several neighboring communities.

But as in Missouri, the saints once again faced difficulties. Despite increasing criticism from neighboring residents who objected to the Mormon practice of polygamy, Smith was determined that he and his followers would not be chased out again. Donning a lieutenant general's uniform, Smith quickly established a private 2,000-man militia to defend his city.

Shortly after announcing his candidacy for president, the Mormon prophet allegedly founded the Council of Fifty, a secretive secular authority independent of the church hierarchy and instructed its members to build a world government to establish Christ's Kingdom on Earth. Fearing that American society would no longer tolerate the Mormons, Smith unsuccessfully negotiated with the new Republic of Texas to sponsor a Mormon colony along the disputed Mexican border. Seeking a new home for his persecuted religious movement, he also sent a secret diplomatic mission to Russia and France.

In the meantime, Smith, a frequent target of kidnappings, lawsuits and death threats, planned to air his church's grievances in the 1844 presidential campaign but was jailed in Carthage, Illinois, on a charge of inciting a riot before his campaign got into full swing. Tragically, an angry anti-Mormon mob—including members of the Illinois state militia—seeking its own brand of frontier justice, broke into the Carthage jailhouse on June 27, 1844, and murdered Smith and his brother, Hyrum. The short-lived Reform Party died with its controversial founder.

With Tyler and Smith out of the picture, the Liberty Party played a pivotal role in the extremely close presidential election that year. One hundred and forty-eight delegates from a dozen states met at the party's national convention in Buffalo in August 1843. Once again, Birney was nominated for president, receiving 108 votes on the first ballot to two for Ohio's Thomas Morris. One delegate cast his lot with longtime reformer William Jay, the 54-year-old son of the late John Jay, the brilliant statesman and New York patriot who served as the nation's first chief justice.

Having largely succeeded in popularizing the notion of an inherently wicked Slave Power conspiracy, the Liberty Party looked to Ohio, site of some of the party's most spirited activity, for a vice-presidential candidate. The state's star-studded Liberty Party, after all, was a galaxy of political talent, including the likes of Salmon P. Chase, Thomas Morris, Edward Wade (brother of Radical Republican Benjamin F. Wade), Samuel Lewis and Gamaliel Bailey, who was then editor of *The National Era,* the American Anti-Slavery Society's weekly publication. The Libertymen chose the indefatigable Morris as their vice-presidential standard-bearer on the first ballot, giving him 83 votes to Gerrit Smith's 22 and one for the New York Anti-Slavery Society's Alvan Stewart.

Born of New England ancestry, the 66-year-old Morris had the distinction of being the country's first antislavery member of the U.S. Senate when he served in that body as a Democrat from 1833-39. Undoubtedly influenced by Birney's *Philanthropist,* Morris, who had been initially silent on the issue of slavery, became an uncompromising abolitionist—so much so that his own party dumped him in 1838, replacing him with Benjamin Tappan.

Despite his overwhelming nomination at the Buffalo convention, Birney was by no means the first choice of many Liberty Party leaders. Shortly after the 1840 campaign, a number of Liberty leaders in Ohio, including Salmon P. Chase, a recent convert to the party, had been scouting about for a more appealing and better-known candidate to replace the somewhat colorless and aristocratic Birney—even if it meant going outside the party's rank-and-file to find such a candidate. Joining Chase in this effort were Thomas Morris, Gamaliel Bailey, Samuel Lewis, Leicester King and the Reverend Jonathan Blanchard. It was their hope that a more seasoned politician, running on a moderate antislavery platform, would have widespread appeal to Whig and Democratic voters alike, thereby enabling the tiny Liberty Party to build a formidable coalition in which to challenge the two major parties. As early as 1841, the names of aging former President John Quincy Adams, a hero to antislavery forces throughout the country, and William H. Seward, the ambitious Whig governor of New York, had surfaced as possible candidates to lead the Liberty Party in the 1844 presidential campaign, but enthusiasm for both men eventually waned as they refused to repudiate the Whig Party.[8]

Attention then centered on reformer William Jay of New York, the 55-year-old Yale-educated son of the nation's first chief justice of the Supreme Court. A distinguished jurist in his own right, the younger Jay served as a Westchester County judge from 1818-43. Like William Lloyd Garrison, Jay was a staunch abolitionist and outspoken critic of the African colonization movement. He also helped establish New York City's Anti-Slavery Society in 1833. An Episcopalian, he was also a founder of the American Bible Society and later served as president of the American Peace Society. A prolific writer, Jay wrote a two-volume life of his father, which was published in 1833. He also wrote extensively on slavery and

---

8.   Sewell, *Ballots for Freedom,* pp. 121-124.

other topics. His writings included *War and Peace: The Evils of the First and a Plan for Preserving the Last*, published in 1842.

In the meantime, Birney, who found it repugnant that the Liberty Party would look for a candidate outside of its own ranks, grew increasingly pessimistic about the party's chances. He lamented that the injustices of the past twelve years—the gag rules, lynch mobs, Mormon persecution, mistreatment of the Cherokee Indians, and the acquiescence of northern politicians to southern slave-holders—made it nearly impossible for the Liberty Party and its friends to prevail in such an atmosphere. "There is no reason for believing that the virtue of our own people would ever throw off slavery," he wrote to Lewis Tappan. "Slavery has corrupted the whole nation, so that it seems to me we are nearly at the point of dissolution. I must say—and I am sorry to believe it true—that our form of government will not do. My confidence in it as a political structure is greatly impaired."[9]

In the months leading up to the Liberty Party's national convention in Buffalo, Chase, Bailey, Gerrit Smith, Henry B. Stanton of New York, and others talked up Jay's candidacy, but it was all for naught as the New York jurist clung to his belief "that what little virtue there is in politicians is with the Whigs," adding that an antislavery candidate couldn't possibly expect to win even a single electoral vote. Disappointed that Adams and Seward had refused to break with the Whigs and rebuffed by Jay, Chase and Birney's other Liberty Party detractors eventually acquiesced in his nomination and actively stumped for the doomed antislavery ticket in the general election.[10]

The 1844 presidential campaign was the first of many in which dirty tricks were used against a third-party. In October, word spread that Birney had accepted the Democratic nomination for a seat in the Michigan legislature. The Whigs immediately charged that the Liberty Party had abandoned its simon-pure reputation by striking a deal with the Democrats to defeat Henry Clay. Birney tried to explain his reasons for accepting the Democratic offer but was somewhat unconvincing. In the process, he clumsily admitted his own preference for Democrat James Polk over Clay, saying that Clay, as president, would be clever and cunning enough to engineer the annexation of Texas, thereby bringing the Lone Star Republic into the Union as a slave state. Polk, he tried to explain, was far less competent than Clay and, therefore, a safer bet for the antislavery cause.

---

9.   Birney letters to Tappan, Jan. 14 and July 8, 1842, as quoted in Sewell, *Ballots for Freedom*, pp. 122-123.

10.   Sewell, *Ballots for Freedom*, p. 124.

If that wasn't bad enough, things quickly got worse for the Liberty Party standard-bearer. A day or two before the November election, a number of Whig newspapers carried a forged letter in which Birney allegedly promised not to agitate against slavery in the Michigan legislature. Known as the "Garland letter," the letter was a complete fabrication, yet Horace Greeley of the *New York Tribune* and other deceitful Whig journalists were able to convince thousands of antislavery voters that it was true. Unfortunately, there wasn't enough time remaining in the campaign for Birney to refute the false charge and the fledgling Liberty Party consequently lost an indeterminable number of votes in the campaign's closing hours.

Despite the dirty tricks leveled against him, Birney's candidacy was nevertheless the deciding factor in the razor-thin contest between Democrat James K. Polk and Whig Henry Clay. Aided in no small measure by Tyler's withdrawal from the race in August, Polk garnered 1,337,243 votes to Clay's 1,299,068. Receiving votes in the six states of New England, New York, New Jersey, Pennsylvania, Ohio, Illinois, Indiana and Michigan, Birney polled 65,608 votes, or slightly more than two percent of all votes cast. The Liberty Party candidate polled an impressive 15,812 votes in New York, mostly in the western part of the state, a Whig stronghold. By siphoning off a relatively large number of antislavery votes, the Liberty Party had, in effect, enabled Polk to squeak out a 5,000-vote margin in populous New York, thus denying Clay the office he so strongly coveted. Had Clay captured New York's 36 electoral votes, he would have become the nation's eleventh president. Instead, he lost to Polk in the Electoral College by a margin of 170 to 105. Birney also polled enough votes in Michigan, which had entered the Union seven years earlier, to deny Clay that state's five electoral votes.

The leaders of the abolitionist party felt little, if any, remorse in helping to deny Clay the presidency. After all, it was Clay, they reasoned, who acquiesced to southern interests in drafting the Missouri Compromise of 1820, which, except for Missouri, excluded slavery from the Louisiana Purchase lands north of latitude 36°30′, thereby allowing Missouri to enter the Union as a slave state. The issue of slavery wasn't something that could be negotiated or compromised. In the eyes of the Liberty men, it had to be abolished everywhere.

The Liberty Party made significant strides in the 1846-47 mid-term elections. Owen Lovejoy, brother of the martyred Elijah Lovejoy, garnered over sixteen percent of the vote in a three-cornered race for Congress from Illinois. At the time, the 35-year-old Congregational minister, who had been widely acclaimed at the party's national convention in Buffalo a few years earlier, was one of those who initially defended the party's objective of remaining a single-issue party committed to ending slavery, rather than developing into a broader reform party, as advocated by Salmon P. Chase and others. "We must cling to the one idea," he fiercely asserted at the time. "If we could not succeed with that, we might as well give up all hopes of success, and call on the Whigs to perform our funeral services," he said. "If the Liberty Party must adopt a narrow party policy or be ruined, let it gather about it the drapery of death and descend into its grave without the hope of resurrection."[11]

The antislavery party also waged strong campaigns in at least eleven other U.S. House districts in New England. The party's strongest showing took place in Maine's sixth district where Jeremiah Curtis tallied eighteen percent of the vote against Democrat James S. Wiley, a Dover lawyer, and Whig Sanford Kingsbury. Another impressive race occurred in the state's third congressional district where Seth May, who later served as an associate justice of the Maine Supreme Court, received a sixth of the vote in a three-way race won by Whig Hiram Belcher, a former state legislator. Theologian Jared Perkins also waged a spirited campaign on the Liberty Party ticket, finishing a respectable third in New Hampshire's third congressional district. Perkins, who served briefly in the state legislature, was later elected to Congress in 1851 on a Whig-Free Soil fusion ticket. The party also had reason to celebrate when Amos Tuck, its candidate for Congress in New Hampshire's first district, won a runoff election as an independent, defeating his Democratic rival by more than 1,400 votes. A Dartmouth-educated lawyer, the 37-year-old Tuck, a close friend and ally of New Hampshire Senator John P. Hale, was re-elected to Congress on the Free Soil ticket in 1849 and 1851 before losing his seat in 1853.[12]

The Liberty Party also made a splash of sorts in several gubernatorial campaigns during this period, including polling double-digit percentages in Maine, New Hampshire and Vermont. Liberty Party organizer Nathaniel S. Berry, a tannery operator, polled nearly nineteen percent of the vote in New Hampshire's hotly contested 1846 gubernatorial race between Democrat Jared W. Williams and the Whig Party's Anthony Colby and waged another strong campaign the following year. Berry, who ran unsuccessfully for governor of the Granite State at least a half-dozen times on the Liberty and Free Soil tickets, was later elected as a Republican, serving as governor of New Hampshire from 1861-1863. Vermont's

---

11.   *The Liberty Tree*, 1846, Illinois State Historical Library.
12.   Tuck was one of two independents elected to the 30th Congress. The other was George Petrie of New York.

Lawrence Brainerd, who also ran as an antislavery third-party candidate for governor on five occasions, polled over fourteen percent of the total against his Whig and Democratic rivals in that state's gubernatorial contests in 1846 and 1847. A businessman from St. Albans, Brainerd later served briefly in the U.S. Senate as a Free Soiler from October 1854 to March 1855.[13] In Massachusetts, perennial candidate Samuel E. Sewall, a one-time Garrison abolitionist, regularly polled between 6,300 and 10,000 votes while running for governor of that state between 1842 and 1847.[14]

There was also considerable cause for optimism in Ohio, where Samuel Lewis, a former Superintendent of Public Instruction, waged an extraordinary campaign for governor. A native of Massachusetts, the fiery Lewis was one of the most eloquent antislavery spokesmen in the country. Campaigning on a platform crafted primarily by Salmon P. Chase, Lewis promised to abolish the state's longstanding Black Laws, which restricted African-American access to state and local courts, schools and other public facilities. To almost everyone's surprise, Whig candidate William Bebb took an almost identical position, but placated his party's conservative wing by asserting that he opposed equal political and educational rights for blacks, suggesting that a special tax should be levied on their land to keep former slaves from migrating to Ohio. The Democratic candidate, on the other hand, was strongly opposed to repealing the infamous Black Laws. Conducting a whirlwind speaking tour of Ohio, Lewis polled an impressive 10,799 votes, or more than four percent of the total, in a race decided by 2,300 votes. The Liberty Party's vote probably would have been much greater if the winning Whig candidate hadn't come out in favor of repeal, albeit insincerely.[15]

Like so many other minor parties throughout American history, the Liberty Party had no shortage of perennial candidates, those true believers who were willing time and again to carry the party's banner against extremely long odds. One of them was Francis J. Lemoyne, the party's original vice presidential nominee in 1840. Lemoyne ran for governor of Pennsylvania on the Abolitionist ticket three times between 1841 and 1847, but never polled as much as one percent of the

13. Brainerd was elected by the Vermont legislature to fill the vacancy caused by the death of Whig Senator William Upham. See *Dictionary of American Biography* and the *Biographical Directory of the United States Congress*.

14. One of the party's gubernatorial candidates during this period was James G. Birney, the party's presidential standard-bearer in 1840 and 1844. The two-time presidential candidate garnered nearly eight percent of the vote as the Liberty Party's candidate for governor of Michigan in 1845.

15. Smith, *The Liberty and Free Soil Parties in the Northwest*, pp. 91-93.

vote. Samuel E. Sewall of Massachusetts and Samuel Fessenden of Maine, a lawyer who ran repeatedly for Congress and governor on the party's ticket, were also
frequent Liberty Party candidates. Another perennial Liberty Party candidate was
Francis Gillette of Connecticut, a Yale-educated former state representative who
played an important role in the Liberty Party's fight for black voting rights.
Gillette's persistence paid off several years later, in 1854, when he was elected to
the U.S. Senate by a coalition of the state's Whig, Free Soil and temperance
forces. Gillette, a founder of the Republican Party in Connecticut, was a silent
partner in the influential *Evening Press,* the GOP's official organ in that state.
Shortly after his election, he arrived in Washington just in time to vote against
the Kansas-Nebraska Act. Long after leaving the U.S. Senate, the longtime third-
party adventurer ran for governor of Connecticut on the Prohibition ticket in the
early 1870s.

Although frequently overlooked in history, the antislavery party's greatest
political achievement occurred in 1846, when Joseph Cilley of New Hampshire,
a full-fledged member of the Liberty Party and a perennial candidate for Congress on its ticket, was elected to the U.S. Senate by the state legislature. A 55-
year-old farmer and former aide-de-camp to the governor, Cilley was elected in
June of that year to fill the remaining nine months of Democrat Levi Woodbury's term. A former Secretary of the Treasury, Woodbury left the Senate the
preceding autumn to take a seat on the U.S. Supreme Court and, as it turned out,
also to unsuccessfully seek the Democratic presidential nomination. Cilley, who
ran for Congress on the Liberty ticket in 1843 and 1845—garnering a respectable
4,827 votes in the latter contest—was elected only three days after a coalition of
Whigs, Liberty men and independent Democrats in the New Hampshire legislature, with barely a vote to spare, elected former antislavery congressman John P.
Hale to fill the long-term vacancy caused by Woodbury's resignation. The long-
forgotten Liberty Party senator served in the U.S. Senate until early March 1847
when Hale finally took his seat.[16]

Following the 1844 presidential election, the Liberty Party essentially split
into three factions. One group, headed by Ohio's Salmon P. Chase, looked to
build a coalition with antislavery Democrats and Whigs. A second group opposed
the idea of coalition and hoped to remain a single-issue party committed to the
eradication of slavery. A third group, led by Birney, wanted to broaden the
party's appeal by adopting a more comprehensive platform. But compromise
with the Whigs or Democrats was the last thing Birney wanted. Longing for a

---

16.   Sewell, *John P. Hale and the Politics of Abolition,* pp. 80-83.

third presidential nomination again in 1848, the Kentucky-born abolitionist believed that the Liberty Party had to be prepared to deal with all of the issues facing the country—not just slavery. Tragically, however, leadership of his faction fell to wealthy landowner and self-styled philanthropist Gerrit Smith and William Goodell when the party's two-time presidential standard-bearer was partially paralyzed in the summer of 1845, the result of falling from a horse. Though he later regained most of his physical strength, the accident impaired his speech and essentially ended his public career.

Renaming itself the Liberty League, the Goodell faction—comprised of the Liberty Party's most unwavering and idealistic element—held a national convention in Macedon Lock, New York, in June 1847. Acting independently of the regular Liberty Party organization, the Liberty Leaguers adopted a comprehensive platform denouncing slavery as an "illegal, unconstitutional and anti-republican" institution and called for the abolition of monopolies, including the postal service. Crafted by Goodell and the ingenious Lysander Spooner, the party's platform, known as the "Nineteen Articles," also called for the elimination of wars, tariffs, liquor, land monopolies and secret societies. It also sharply criticized the U.S. war with Mexico.

The Liberty League also proceeded to nominate a national ticket. Although no fewer than four names were bandied about for president, including American Anti-Slavery Society founder and Congregational minister Beriah Green, a 52-year-old former professor of sacred literature at Western Reserve College, and abolitionist Frederick Douglass, this was unmistakably a pro-Smith gathering. The 51-year-old "Sage of Peterboro," as expected, was easily nominated for the highest office in the land and was joined on the ticket by the "learned blacksmith" and well-known pacifist Elihu Burritt of Worcester, Massachusetts. The 37-year-old Burritt, who was lecturing in England at the time of his nomination, later declined and was replaced on the ticket by the rather obscure Charles C. Foote, a 36-year-old minister from Michigan. A graduate of Oberlin College, Foote, who worked as an agent in the Freedman's Aid Society following the Civil War, was later active in the American National and Prohibition parties, running for governor of Michigan on the former ticket in 1882.

Many of those who were sympathetic to the aims of the original Liberty Party were steadfastly opposed to the events that had taken place in Macedon Lock. The *Cincinnati Herald*, for instance, called Goodell's universal reform party a "betrayal" of the Liberty Party and on July 14 the Wisconsin Liberty Association denounced the new party as completely unnecessary.[17] Only two abolitionist newspapers—the *Albany Patriot* and the New York-based *Cortland True American*—came out in favor of the new movement.[18]

Meanwhile, the original Liberty Party held its national convention in Buffalo on October 20, 1847. For several months, leading antislavery newspapers from Maine to Illinois had been beating the drum for a Liberty Party ticket headed by New Hampshire Senator-elect John P. Hale, with either Samuel Lewis, an ex-Whig and chairman of the Buffalo convention, or Salmon P. Chase of Ohio as a possible vice-presidential running mate. Although Chase and others, eyeing a possible broader coalition with antislavery Democrats and Whigs—possibly under the guise of a non-partisan anti-slavery league—desperately wanted to postpone the nomination of a presidential ticket until the following spring after the major parties held their national conventions, the delegates, anxious to put a candidate in the field, proceeded to nominate a somewhat reluctant Hale for the presidency.[19]

Read out of the Democratic Party two years earlier for having the audacity to oppose his party's call for the annexation of Texas, Hale easily defeated the Liberty League's Gerrit Smith by a margin of 103 to 44 on the convention's only ballot. Leicester King of Ohio, a former Whig judge and president of the Ohio Anti-Slavery Society, was named as Hale's vice-presidential running mate.[20] The 58-year-old King, who labored tirelessly but in vain as a state senator to repeal Ohio's notorious Black Laws, was narrowly nominated over Owen Lovejoy, a noted abolitionist minister from Illinois. Lovejoy, whose martyred brother Elijah was murdered by proslavery thugs in 1837, is perhaps best remembered as the man who later urged Abraham Lincoln to become the spokesman for a new party—the Republican Party. Lovejoy believed that Lincoln was the only person

---

17. Smith, *The Liberty and Free Soil Parties in the Northwest*, p. 102.

18. Rayback, *Free Soil: The Election of 1848* (Lexington, Kentucky, 1970), p. 110.

19. Frederick J. Blue, *The Free Soilers: Third Party Politics, 1848-1854* (Urbana, Illinois, 1973), p. 12; Rayback, *Free Soil: The Election of 1848*, p. 111. By a vote of 144 to 72, the delegates, led by Smith's Liberty Leaguers and members of the Liberty Party's old guard, rejected Chase's resolution to postpone the nominations until May 1848. This figure, taken from the Boston *Emancipator* of October 27, 1847, and the *Cincinnati Herald* of November 3, 1847, differs from the 137-28 margin reported by Theodore Clarke Smith in *The Liberty and Free Soil Parties in the Northwest*, p. 119.

20. Owen Lovejoy of Illinois, who initially hoped to maintain the Liberty Party as a single-issue party, led on the convention's first ballot, garnering 76 votes to King's 72. Hoping to avoid an all-out battle between the Liberty Party's old guard and Chase's Ohio coalitionists, the Congregational minister then graciously conceded to his rival, a seasoned leader of Ohio's Liberty Party.

who could mold the country's "ragtag bobtail" antislavery forces into an effective political movement. King, a longtime promoter of the Pennsylvania and Ohio Canal, later withdrew from the race.

Because Hale wasn't technically a member of the Liberty Party, his nomination caused a great deal of discontent among some of the party's extremists, especially among Gerrit Smith's Macedonian supporters in the East, as well as among party members in Wisconsin, where that state's Liberty Association viewed the former New Hampshire lawmaker with suspicion. As late as the spring of 1848, the Wisconsin Liberty Party seriously toyed with the idea of throwing its support to Goodell's fledgling Liberty League. "We are slow to believe it necessary to leave the circle of noble men who have been the life of the cause," declared one antislavery newspaper in that state. "We will put his name at the head of our columns, but do not wish to be considered pledged." Even James G. Birney, the Liberty Party's presidential standard-bearer in 1840 and 1844, had a difficult time accepting Hale's nomination and protested by resigning from the American and Foreign Anti-Slavery Society when that organization nodded its approval of the New Hampshire lawmaker's candidacy. Similar rumblings were heard from New York's Lewis Tappan and other members of the Liberty Party's old guard.[21] By the summer of 1848, this was a moot issue as far as Hale was concerned. Having lost the Free Soil nomination, the nation's only independent senator eventually withdrew from the race and endorsed former President Martin Van Buren, the Free Soil Party nominee.

Repudiating the Free Soil "heresy" of Van Buren, the Liberty Party faithful—or what remained of them—later reconvened in Buffalo, renamed themselves the National Liberty Party, and ratified the ticket nominated by the Liberty League in Macedon Lock the previous June.[22] They also denounced the Free Soil Party, arguing that any party that acknowledged the constitutionality of slavery in the states and called only for containment rather than outright abolition wasn't worthy of their support. Smith picked up a third nomination when the Industrial Congress endorsed the Liberty League aspirant at its annual meeting in Philadelphia on June 13, 1848.[23] The Industrial Congress was a spin-off of George Henry Evans' National Reform Association. Evans long argued that the nation

---

21. Rayback, *Free Soil: The Election of 1848*, pp. 112, 250.

22. As expected, Smith was easily nominated on the first ballot, garnering 99 of the 104 votes cast. Then serving a Congregational Church in Whitesboro, New York, longtime reformer Beriah Green was preferred by two delegates and Frederick Douglass, Charles C. Foote, and little-known Amos A. Sampson each received a single vote.

owned enough land in the West to guarantee every family a farm—a slogan that was later popularized by editor Horace Greeley in the 1850s.

Born in Utica, New York, Gerrit Smith used a sizeable inheritance to fund a variety of social causes, including prison reform and women's suffrage. A cousin of dynamic women's rights activist Elizabeth Cady Stanton, he had long advocated equal rights for women. It was no surprise, therefore, that a number of leading feminists such as Antoinette Brown Blackwell—an Oberlin College seminary graduate and the first woman ordained as a minister in the United States—and antislavery advocate Jane Swisshelm of Pittsburgh, a schoolteacher-turned-antislavery newspaper publisher who later served on the Underground Railroad and, as a correspondent for Horace Greeley's *New York Tribune*, became the first woman to ever sit in the Senate press gallery, were attracted to the bearded Smith and the Liberty Party almost from its founding. As a leader in the American Peace Society, Smith also helped to finance the Irish and Greek independence movements. No stranger to third-party politics, Smith was more than willing to finance a new political party for virtually every cause he espoused, contributing generously to the Liberty, Liberty League, Anti-Dramshop and Prohibition parties.

Perhaps best remembered for his later works in the antislavery movement, Smith was part of the infamous "Secret Six," a group that surreptitiously financed John Brown's bloody scheme to invade the South. Following Brown's violent raid at Harpers Ferry in 1859, Smith, who vehemently denied any complicity in the attack, went temporarily insane but quickly recovered. A man of a thousand causes—ranging from vegetarianism to temperance—he once attempted to set up a black colony in the Adirondacks. That experiment failed, however, when the inhabitants found the Adirondack wilderness too harsh. The generous and bearded philanthropist was also active in the Underground Railroad and personally financed the Free Soilers' campaign to settle Kansas as a free state, thereby keeping it out of the slave column. Later in his life, Smith teamed up with Dr. Edward Cornelius Delavan of Albany, New York, a retired businessman who made his fortune in real estate, hardware and wine, to form the post-Civil War Anti-Dramshop Party. Delavan accused local brewers of using water from a polluted slaughterhouse and glue-works pond to make their beer.

---

23. *New York Tribune*, July 1, 1848. Delegates to the Industrial Congress convention nominated William S. Waite of Illinois for vice president, but Waite later withdrew from the race.

Unlike William Lloyd Garrison and other abolitionists, Smith firmly believed in political action and played an active role in politics for fifty years, frequently as a candidate himself. Running under the "Ultra-Abolitionist" label, Smith, who liked to wear his politics on his sleeve, was elected to Congress in 1853. An impatient man, he quickly grew disillusioned with the House of Representatives and resigned before the end of his term. In addition to his election to Congress and his frequent bids for the presidency, Smith ran for governor of New York on an antislavery People's Party ticket in 1858, campaigning on a platform that included, among other things, temperance, land reform and opposition to slavery.

During the Civil War, Smith lectured and wrote frequently in support of the Union, which eventually led him into the Republican fold. He contributed generously to John Fremont's campaign in 1856 and actively campaigned for Lincoln in 1864 and for the hard-drinking and gritty Ulysses S. Grant four years later.

Joining Horace Greeley and New York attorney Charles O'Conor, Smith was one of the signers of Jefferson Davis' bail bond in 1867 and, like Greeley and O'Conor, advocated a moderate reconstruction policy toward the South following the war. Always a third-party man at heart, Smith was also one of the founders of the national Prohibition Party in 1869.

Despite its lack of support at the ballot box, the Liberty Party played an important role in American politics during the 1840s. Not only was it the *first* political party to attack slavery head on, it was also the first in a long series of reform-minded third parties to play the role of the nation's conscience at a time when the major parties preferred to bury their heads in the sand. Time and again, whether the issue was slavery, land reform, women's suffrage, child labor, social reform or war and peace, third parties have often taken the lead only to see their issues co-opted by one of the major parties. The Liberty Party introduced the issue of abolition in American politics, wrote George Washington Julian nearly four decades after the tiny antislavery party vanished from the scene, "and no man who cherishes the memory of the Free Soil Party, and of the larger one to which it gave birth, will withhold the need of his praise from the heroic little band of sappers and miners who blazed the way for the armies which were to follow, and whose voices, though faintly heard in the whirlwind of 1840, were made significantly audible in 1844." Though largely misunderstood and frequently misrepresented, the Liberty Party clearly understood its task and courageously spoke for America's better self. "Their political creed was substantially identical with that of the Free Soilers of 1848 and the Republicans of 1856 and 1860," he wrote. "They were anything but political fanatics, and history will record that their sole offense was the espousal of the truth in advance of the multitude, which slowly and finally followed in their footsteps."[24]

---

24.   George W. Julian, *Political Recollections, 1840 to 1872* (Chicago, 1884), p. 43.

4

Barnburners and Conscience Whigs

✦

Martin Van Buren and the Free Soil Party in 1848

The acquisition of vast new territories as a result of the Mexican War of 1846-47 placed the issue of slavery at the very forefront of American politics, where it would remain until the Civil War. The South had maintained its "peculiar institution," in large part, as a result of the Missouri Compromise of 1820 when it achieved parity with the North in the Union, and, therefore, in Congress. A "free" state's admission into the Union, under the provisions of the compromise, had to be balanced by the addition of a "slave" state. The slave states also benefited enormously from the presence of a number of pro-southerners in the White House throughout the 1840s and 1850s.

This was one of the principal reasons most proslavery lawmakers had enthusiastically supported the Mexican War—a contrived conflict incited by President Polk that ultimately claimed the lives of 13,000 U.S. soldiers and a far greater number of Mexicans while extending America's boundaries to the Pacific. Even Ulysses S. Grant, a veteran of that conflict, called it the "most unjust war in history."[1] It is also why so many other northerners, including the sinewy Abraham Lincoln, a 38-year-old Whig congressman from Illinois, had staunchly opposed that war.[2] Lincoln, who was not yet in Congress when the war began, had demanded to know the precise spot where American blood was allegedly shed on U.S. soil, earning him the pejorative nickname of "Spotty." Sharply opposed to

---

1.   Patrick Buchanan, "Jimmy Polk's War," *The National Interest*, Issue 56 (Summer 1999).

the extension of slavery into the new territories, many antislavery politicians and abolitionists in the North viewed the war—with more than a little justification—as a naked land grab, a conspiratorial effort cooked up by proslavery southerners to provide additional raw material for new slave states. A handful of antislavery congressmen, including Ohio's bold and courageous Joshua R. Giddings who denounced the conflict as "an aggressive, unholy, and unjust war," voted against all measures for the war, including funding for U.S. troops and supplies. "In the murder of Mexicans upon their own soil, or in robbing them of their country, I can take no part either now or hereafter," Giddings proclaimed. "The guilt of these crimes must rest on others—I will not participate in them."[3] The apoplectic proslavery elements, on the other hand, feared that the banning of slavery in the territories would eventually lead to an overwhelming majority of free states and the ultimate abolition of slavery.

In 1846, a 32-year-old antislavery Democratic congressman from Pennsylvania named David Wilmot attached an amendment to an appropriations bill prohibiting slavery in the new territories acquired during the Mexican War. Drafted by Ohio lawmaker Jacob Brinkerhoff, the Wilmot Proviso was considered a direct challenge to "Mr. Polk's War" and all of its ramifications. Although many northern senators ignored the wishes of their own state legislatures (by whom they were chosen), fourteen state legislatures endorsed Wilmot's proposal and the House of Representatives approved the measure on several occasions.

The "free soil" issue haunted the Whigs and Democrats alike from 1847 to 1850, creating irreparable sectional rifts within both major parties. Many southern Whigs sharply opposed the idea of excluding slavery from the territories as an affront to the rights of the southern states and John C. Calhoun's supporters even went so far as to unite all southerners in an obdurate defense of sectional rights by opposing any candidate who refused to repudiate the Wilmot Proviso.

Meanwhile, Free Soil Democrats led by "Prince" John Van Buren, the flamboyant and politically ambitious son of the former president, had gathered in Herkimer, New York, in late October 1847 to discuss their options in the 1848 presidential election. Churchill C. Cambreleng, a somewhat unscrupulous supporter and friend of former President Martin Van Buren who had wielded tremendous power as chairman of the House Ways and Means, Commerce, and

2.   Despite the strenuous opposition of John Quincy Adams and a small group of Whigs, the war resolution easily sailed through both chambers of Congress, winning approval in the House by an overwhelming 174–14 margin and by a lopsided vote of forty to two in the U.S. Senate.

3.   Zinn, *A People's History of the United States*, pp. 151-152.

Foreign Affairs committees during the Jackson and Van Buren administrations, presided over the gathering. Pennsylvania congressman David Wilmot opened the meeting by attacking slavery extension and stressing the merits of his Proviso while the younger Van Buren gave what amounted to the keynote address, attacking the Democratic Party's "Hunker" faction and charging that the party's statewide ticket that fall had been nominated by fraudulent methods. The "Prince"—a nickname he earned by dancing with the future Queen Victoria while his father served as minister to England in the early 1830s—was clearly breaking with the party of his father. While stopping short of formally severing their ties with the Democratic Party, the Herkimer gathering, proclaiming their devotion to "Free Trade, Free Labor, Free Soil, Free Speech and Free Men," adopted a resolution opposing any Democratic presidential nominee in 1848 who was on record as favoring the extension of slavery.[4]

Former President Van Buren, meanwhile, was somewhat taken aback by his son's actions, but the younger Van Buren assured his father that he knew what he was doing. "I can therefore, hurt no one but myself—and on my own account I will never submit to imposition and rascality a moment."[5]

It probably wasn't too much of a stretch to suggest, as one of Van Buren's biographers asserted, that the 1847 Herkimer convention "was an important preliminary to the formation of the Republican Party."[6] With the eyes of the nation riveted upon them, the Herkimer conclave put the country's two major parties on notice—the issue of slavery could no longer be swept under the rug. Indeed, Salmon P. Chase of Ohio, one of the men who helped organize the Republican Party in the mid-1850s, was convinced that the Herkimer convention signaled a significant political development in the antislavery movement. "It was a great blow for liberty and right, that struck at Herkimer," he wrote the leaders of the New York movement. "The conventions of both parties in your state had repudiated the only measure, which during the last quarter of a century, has been brought forth, of an anti-slavery character."[7] Chase had been laboring long and hard during this period to build a mass antislavery party comprised of Free Soil Democrats, New York Barnburners, Conscience Whigs and Liberty Party mem-

4.   Blue, *The Free Soilers*, pp. 31-32.
5.   Ibid., p. 32; John Van Buren to Martin Van Buren, November 13, 1847, in Van Buren Papers (Library of Congress).
6.   Edward M. Shepard, *Martin Van Buren* (Boston and New York, 1899), pp. 418-419.
7.   Dodson, S. H., "Diary and Correspondence of Salmon P. Chase," *Annual Report of the American Historical Association*, 1902, Vol. II, p. 142.

bers. When the Free Soilers' brief history came to a close in the mid-1850s, wrote Free Soil Party historian Frederick J. Blue, it was clear that they had played a critical role in the decline of the Whigs and the emergence of the Republican Party. "It would be their principle of containment, which had been too advanced for voters in 1848 and 1852," Blue noted, "that would be the focus of the Republican appeal in 1856 and place Abraham Lincoln in the White House in 1861."[8]

In the meantime, the "Conscience Whigs," a group centered in Massachusetts and led by Charles Sumner, Charles Francis Adams, and Henry Wilson, were also discussing their future plans. During this period, the Conscience Whigs of Massachusetts and most antislavery Whigs in New Hampshire and Ohio had pinned their hopes first on Sen. Thomas Corwin of Ohio and later on Judge John McLean, believing that one of them would take up their cause and seek the Whig Party's presidential nomination.[9] Working closely with Daniel Webster, the conservative Corwin tried to forestall the Wilmot Proviso in 1847 by arguing vehemently against the war with Mexico, believing that it would lead to civil war at home.[10] Though believed by many Whigs to be the strongest northern candidate, Corwin, whose candidacy failed to gain momentum outside of Ohio, disappointed the antislavery Whigs by taking his name out of consideration rather early in the process.[11]

As Corwin's potential candidacy fizzled, Conscience Whig John G. Palfrey, the brilliant Massachusetts scholar turned politician, made a desperate plea to McLean, a nineteen-year veteran of the nation's highest court and the last and best hope of the antislavery Whigs, to endorse the idea of non-extension. In a desperate attempt to stop the boom for Mexican War hero Zachary Taylor, the Conscience Whigs fervently hoped that their party would turn to McLean in a deadlocked convention. But McLean, though clearly eyeing the Whig Party's nomination, refused to endorse the Wilmot Proviso, believing that it was safer to "straddle the fence" and thereby minimize the risk of alienating any large group of delegates, particularly the large bloc of moderate Whigs.[12]

As Zachary Taylor's candidacy continued to gain momentum, Charles Francis Adams, Charles Sumner, Henry Wilson and other Conscience Whigs met in Boston in late May and tentatively agreed that if the Whigs nominated the Mexi-

---

8.   Frederick J. Blue, "Free Soil Party, 1848-1850s, *The Encyclopedia of Third Parties in America*, Vol. II, p. 267.

9.   Sewell, *John P. Hale and the Politics of Abolition*, p. 95.

10.   Foner, *Free Soil, Free Labor, Free Men*, p. 188.

11.   Rayback, *Free Soil*, p. 164.

12.   Blue, *The Free Soilers*, p. 50.

can War general or any other candidate who wasn't opposed to slavery extension, they would bolt from the party and nominate their own ticket committed to the Wilmot Proviso.[13]

As feared, the Whig Party's national convention in Philadelphia that summer was an utterly disappointing experience for the country's antislavery Whigs. The much hoped for deadlock never materialized as frontrunner Zachary Taylor, who was sold to the American public as a gallant knight in the tradition of a Napoleon, rolled to a relatively easy victory on the convention's fourth ballot, trouncing Henry Clay, Winfield Scott and the ailing and battle-scarred Daniel Webster. In the pandemonium that ensued, Massachusetts Whig Charles Allen frantically denounced the proceedings, warning his fellow delegates that "the Whig Party is here and this day dissolved" and Henry Wilson, another Conscience Whig, told the delegates that he wouldn't be bound by the convention's proceedings, adding that he would return to Massachusetts and do all he could to defeat the Whig ticket. Few paid any attention to the New England duo. An antislavery delegate from Ohio then tried to introduce a resolution favoring the Wilmot Proviso, but was immediately ruled out of order. When Whig leaders moved to nominate wealthy Boston industrialist Abbott Lawrence for the vice presidency, the Conscience Whigs went ballistic, bitterly denouncing the party for trying to have "cotton at both ends of the ticket." After all, Lawrence, who was expected to contribute at least a hundred thousand dollars to the Whig campaign, had made his enormous fortune largely through his commercial ties with the slaveholding South. As it turned out, Lawrence's candidacy stalled after the first ballot and the party ultimately turned to New York state comptroller Millard Fillmore, a handsome, six-foot former congressman, on the next ballot. Fillmore's candidacy was seen as a sop to Henry Clay's disappointed supporters—and certainly wasn't designed to placate the disgruntled antislavery Whigs.[14]

Without a moment's rest, Henry Wilson met with fifteen disaffected delegates before leaving Philadelphia and proposed holding a national convention open to everyone opposed to the extension of slavery and the Taylor and Cass candidacies. Appointing a committee to plan for a convention to be held in Buffalo in early August, it was agreed to include the fledgling Liberty Party, led by Ohio's Salmon P. Chase and others, in their plans. The Liberty Party, as previously mentioned, had already nominated New Hampshire's independent-minded Senator John P. Hale for president at its convention in Buffalo the previous autumn.

---

13. Ibid., p. 51.
14. Ibid., pp. 51-53.

Meanwhile, the Barnburners, who had formally split with the Democrats at the party's national convention in Baltimore in the spring of 1848, were also making plans for the autumn campaign. Their complete break from the party, of course, had only been a matter of time and when the Democrats dodged the issue of slavery in the territories and nominated the weak and colorless Sen. Lewis Cass of Michigan on the fourth ballot, the Barnburners dramatically stormed out of the convention. An unimaginative and conservative former diplomat, Cass had undoubtedly played a pivotal role in the "vile intrigue" which cost Van Buren the party's presidential nomination in 1844. As the angry Barnburners left Baltimore's Universalist Church, the Democrats added insult to injury by selecting William O. Butler of Kentucky, a veteran of the War of 1812 and a strident opponent of the Wilmot Proviso, for the vice presidency.[15]

Blending Locofoco ideals with antislavery sentiment, the Barnburners—a nickname, incidentally, that grew out of a story about a Dutch farmer who allegedly burned down his own barn to drive the rats out—were loosely organized back in 1843. Angered by President Polk's decision to divert all of New York's patronage, including the plum prize—the collectorship of the Port of New York—to Secretary of War William L. Marcy, leader of the state's proslavery "Hard-shell" Democrats or "Hunkers," the Van Buren or "Barnburner" Democrats had been subjected to one slight after another at the hands of the party's conservative faction, culminating in the rejection of resolutions endorsing the Wilmot Proviso and the nomination of a man who not only had favored the annexation of Texas but was also opposed to the Wilmot Proviso.

The Barnburners, to be sure, were a formidable group, capable of creating more than a little havoc for their former party. Among others, they were led by the talented Benjamin F. Butler, a former attorney general who doubled as Secretary of War in the closing days of Andrew Jackson's administration (not to be confused with the indomitable Benjamin F. Butler of Massachusetts); Preston King, publisher of the *St. Lawrence Republican* and an outspoken foe of federal centralization who incongruously favored states' rights but opposed the spread of slavery; and New York Senator John A. Dix, a lawyer who later served briefly as President James Buchanan's Secretary of the Treasury and as minister to France during Andrew Johnson's administration. As Secretary of the Treasury for a few months in the closing days of Buchanan's administration in early 1861, Dix wired an order to a subordinate in New Orleans, stating that "if anyone attempts to haul down the American flag, shoot him on the spot."[16] He then resigned to

---

15. Ibid., p. 49.

become a Union Army general for the next four years. David Dudley Field, who had introduced the Wilmot Proviso plank at the Democratic state convention in 1847—only to watch it go down in flames—was also among those who helped organize the Free Soil Party and later insisted that the party should nominate former President Martin Van Buren for the presidency.[17]

The Barnburners also included such movers and shakers as William Cullen Bryant, the poet and longtime editor of the *New York Evening Post*, and, of course, "Prince John" Van Buren, the gifted and ambitious son of the former president. The Barnburners also enjoyed some support outside of their New York bailiwick. Among others, Chicago Mayor James H. Woodworth, an ex-New Yorker and one-time flour merchant, heartily endorsed the Barnburners' cause that year. The 43-year-old Woodworth, an ardent opponent of slavery who later served as Chicago's first Republican congressman, had been elected mayor of the Windy City as an independent Democrat earlier that spring.

While many Barnburners, such as King, Bryant and Field, were motivated by strong antislavery convictions, many others—including the Van Burens, John A. Dix, Benjamin F. Butler and Azariah Flagg, a former New York state comptroller—entered the Free Soil movement reluctantly, motivated as much by revenge as by any deeply held opposition to slavery.[18] Butler and Flagg, of course, were upset that President Polk, ignoring Van Buren's recommendation, had passed them over for coveted appointments as Secretary of State and Treasury Secretary, respectively. Rubbing salt in their wounds, the 49-year-old Polk—the country's youngest president up to that time—named two of Van Buren's bitter enemies instead, choosing Mississippi's Robert J. Walker for the treasury post and the lackluster James Buchanan of Pennsylvania as Secretary of State. Realizing that he had antagonized Van Buren's powerful allies, Polk later tried to mollify the New Yorkers by offering Butler the position of Secretary of War, but Van Buren's former law partner, believing it to be an inferior post, flatly turned it down. Polk then completely angered the Barnburners by foolishly appointing William L. Marcy, leader of the rival "Hunker" faction, to the post—leaving Van Buren's men in New York furious at Polk for having completely capitulated to their enemies.[19]

16.   Dan Morris and Inez Morris, *Who was who in American Politics* (New York, 1974), p. 194.
17.   Eric Foner, *Free Soil, Free Labor, Free Men: The Ideology of the Republican Party before the Civil War* (London, 1970), p. 153; Frederick J. Blue, *The Free Soilers*, p. 60.
18.   Ibid., p. 153.
19.   Blue, *The Free Soilers*, pp. 24-25.

This was especially difficult for the Van Buren forces to comprehend. After all, it was one of their own—the popular Silas Wright—who had given up a safe seat in the U.S. Senate to wage a difficult campaign for governor against the Whig Party's Millard Fillmore in 1844, thereby strengthening the national ticket in New York and enabling Polk to squeak out a narrow 5,000-vote victory in the nation's most populous state. Without the state's thirty-six electoral votes, Henry Clay—and not James K. Polk—would have been sworn in as the country's eleventh president.[20]

The Barnburners, as it turned out, were dealt a severe blow in August 1847 when Wright—a man who had turned down the Democratic Party's vice-presidential nomination three years earlier—died suddenly of a stroke after tending to chores on his farm in the blistering August heat. A popular vote getter, the 52-year-old Wright was a member of the politically potent Albany Regency and, were it not for his untimely death, almost certainly would have been the Free Soil Party's presidential standard-bearer in 1848.

Deprived of Wright, the grieving Barnburners held a parley in Albany and later met with delegates from five other northern states in Utica, New York, on June 22, 1848. Sparked by the splendid oratory of Preston King, Benjamin F. Butler and John Van Buren, the delegates adopted a platform endorsing the Wilmot Proviso and called for a national convention of the nation's antislavery forces. After taking a serious look at Missouri's Thomas Hart Benton—a man who opposed the annexation of Texas in 1844 and did much to slow the extension of slavery in Missouri and Maryland—the New York Barnburners then proceeded to nominate former President Martin Van Buren by acclamation for his old job and named former Massachusetts governor Marcus Morton as his vice-presidential running mate. The 64-year-old Morton, a lawyer who had been the Democratic candidate for governor of Massachusetts on an almost regular basis from 1828-1843—winning twice during that period—had serious reservations about breaking with the Democratic establishment. When he declined the nomination, the Barnburners quickly turned to Sen. Henry Dodge of Wisconsin, a wealthy lead mine operator and staunch supporter of the Wilmot Proviso.[21] Senator John A. Dix, who had also been seriously discussed as a possible presidential candidate, was nominated for governor of New York against his wishes and Seth M. Gates, a former Whig congressman and prominent abolitionist, was named

20. Ibid., pp. 23-24.
21. On an informal ballot before nominating Van Buren by acclamation, the delegates cast 69 votes for Van Buren and fourteen for Addison Gardiner, a former New York lieutenant governor. Two Barnburners cast their ballots for John A. Dix.

for lieutenant governor. Like Van Buren, Dix, who had been praised earlier as "a most worthy successor of the late lamented Silas Wright," was initially opposed to the idea of fielding a separate ticket in 1848. Although Dodge later took his name out of consideration, Van Buren and Dix reluctantly agreed to run under the Free Soil banner.[22]

Although the movement began strictly as a Democratic bolt confined to the state of New York, other antislavery groups, including the Conscience Whigs of Massachusetts, were keeping a close eye on developments. As such, the eventual merging of the Barnburners and the Conscience Whigs into a formidable third-party movement during the 1848 presidential campaign was no mere happenstance. At the instigation of Ohio's Salmon P. Chase, leaders of the Barnburner faction in New York, Conscience Whigs and prominent members of Chase's antislavery party had been exchanging letters for nearly two years, discussing the possibility of building a mass coalition party consisting of the fledgling Liberty Party and the steadily increasing antislavery wings of the country's two major parties. Deeply disappointed by Birney's relatively poor showing in the 1844 election, Chase, agreeing with Gamaliel Bailey that "no new and small party can live simply by holding its own," had slowly come to the conclusion that the Liberty Party could never aspire to be more than a single-issue party, a protest vehicle of sorts. But that was all about to change.[23]

As the Conscience Whigs, Barnburners and Liberty Party faithful looked forward to the grand convention of the nation's antislavery forces in Buffalo, there was plenty of speculation about possible candidates to lead the new party's ticket in the fall campaign against Cass and Taylor. While the Barnburners looked favorably at their wily old chief, Martin Van Buren, a number of antislavery Whigs talked up the candidacies of Judge John McLean of Ohio and diplomat Charles Francis Adams of Massachusetts, son of the late John Quincy Adams, Van Buren's old nemesis, while still others considered Ohio's Joshua Giddings, a Whig congressman with impeccable antislavery credentials. The 41-year-old Adams, a former Whig member of the Massachusetts legislature, initially had serious doubts about Van Buren's candidacy and had been working feverishly since early June to prevent the Barnburners from dictating the party's nominee. "We do not seek to make them Whigs," he groaned. "They ought not insist upon making us Democrats, so far as obnoxious nominations are concerned."[24]

22. Blue, *The Free Soilers*, pp. 46n, 56.
23. Foner, *Free Soil, Free Labor, Free Men*, p. 124; Gamaliel Bailey quoted in Sewell, *John P. Hale and the Politics of Abolition*, pp. 88–89.
24. Blue, *The Free Soilers*, p. 67.

Though the feelings expressed by Adams toward Van Buren were typical of most Conscience Whigs, some of the antislavery Whigs in Massachusetts hoped to entice Daniel Webster, a statesman of great stature and brilliance, into the race. Noting that Webster, who was on record as supporting the principle of the Wilmot Proviso, had been unusually silent regarding Taylor's nomination, a few Conscience Whigs believed—or hoped—that he was so disillusioned by the recent Whig convention in Philadelphia that the great orator might be willing to break with his party and join the Free Soil movement. That turned out to be wishful thinking. In the end, Webster, who really never showed much sympathy for the third-party movement, reluctantly acquiesced and publicly endorsed General Taylor in September—some three months after his nomination. His decision not to march under the Free Soil banner no doubt came as a huge relief to some of the Conscience Whigs, particularly Palfrey and Adams, who in the past had been highly critical of the Whig statesman's tendency to vacillate on important issues.[25]

In the meantime, letters continued to fly back and forth between Charles Sumner, Giddings, Chase and others regarding the possibility of nominating Judge John McLean on an antislavery third-party ticket.[26] McLean, incidentally, was Chase's father-in-law. But the overly cautious McLean kept everyone guessing, wavering back and forth throughout most of the summer, indicating at first that he wouldn't be a candidate for the Free Soil Party's nomination, only to do a complete turnaround several days later by saying that he "might not refuse the nomination" if there was a groundswell for his candidacy. Despite his mixed messages about a possible presidential bid, the longtime Supreme Court jurist made it clear throughout this period that he wasn't the least bit interested in running for the vice presidency on a ticket headed by Van Buren—an idea later advanced by Sumner and other Massachusetts Conscience Whigs once it became clear that the Barnburners had enough strength to put their own man over the top in Buffalo. In the end, however, the 63-year-old McLean lacked the courage to break with the two-party system.[27]

Complicating matters even further was the candidacy of John P. Hale, the independent senator from New Hampshire who had been nominated by the Lib-

---

25.   Ibid., pp. 68-69; Frank Otto Gattell, *John Gorham Palfrey and the New England Conscience* (Cambridge, Mass., 1963), p. 166.

26.   Smith, *The Liberty and Free Soil Parties in the Northwest*, p. 141.

27.   Blue, *The Free Soilers*, pp. 64-65. In trying to convince McLean to accept the party's vice-presidential nomination, Sumner assured the Justice that, regardless of the outcome in 1848, the party would surely turn to him to lead the Free Soil ticket in 1852.

erty Party nearly ten months earlier. One of the most principled yet good-natured men to ever seek the nation's highest office, Hale's candidacy, though denounced by some of the Liberty Party's more extreme elements such as that represented by Gerrit Smith, had been welcomed in most antislavery circles.[28] Even abolitionist William Lloyd Garrison's *Liberator*, while opposed in principle to direct political action, congratulated the Liberty men on finally nominating "a reputable candidate." Salmon P. Chase, among others, had repeatedly urged Hale to decline the Liberty Party's nomination, arguing to do otherwise would virtually eliminate him from consideration later by a broader antislavery movement. Chase clearly had Hale's best interests at heart. After all, the Ohioan had engineered Hale's nomination at the Liberty Party convention in Buffalo the previous October.

Despite Chase's warnings, Hale plunged ahead with his candidacy. Though waiting more than two months, he finally accepted the Liberty nomination in a New Year's Day letter to Sam Lewis, president of the Liberty Party's national convention. In his letter of acceptance, however, the New Hampshire lawmaker was careful to point out that if a broader-based antislavery coalition were to be formed—and such a coalition was likely—he would be happy to step aside and count himself "among the humblest privates who will rally under such a banner." Cheered on by John Whittier Greenleaf, the poet-laureate of the antislavery movement, Hale selflessly carried his party's tiny and tattered banner as the 1848 campaign approached, dutifully carrying out his responsibilities as a candidate—albeit, as his biographer noted, "with the gloomy fatalism of a man bailing water in a sinking boat."[29] Van Buren's nomination by the Barnburners in June and the strong likelihood that the former president's candidacy would be ratified in Buffalo created a somewhat ticklish political situation for Hale and his Liberty Party managers.

Under a huge tent, the Free Soil Democrats, the Conscience Whigs, New York's Barnburners and the lion's share of the Liberty Party's leadership convened in the sweltering heat of Buffalo on August 9, 1848. Everyone was there, including Gerrit Smith's stridently antislavery Liberty Leaguers, disappointed Clay Whigs led by Joseph L. White of Indiana, a sprinkling of land reformers

---

28. According to Gerrit Smith, the Liberty League opposed Hale's candidacy not because they doubted his sincerity or commitment to the antislavery cause, but because it was "too much to admit a stranger into the very sanctuary" of the Liberty Party—especially one who had never belonged to the party. See Smith's letter to the New Hampshire Liberty Party leaders, published in the *New Hampshire Patriot*, April 20, 1848, as quoted in Sewell, *John P. Hale and the Politics of Abolition*, p. 258.

29. Sewell, *John P. Hale and the Politics of Abolition*, pp. 94–96.

from New York and a handful of labor representatives. Led by Joshua Leavitt and Lewis Tappan, there was also a large contingent of Liberty Party enthusiasts who were intent on nominating Hale. The latter group had strong reservations about Van Buren, agreeing with Leavitt that the former president, regrettably, was still a northern man with southern principles.[30]

Resembling a camp meeting, the Free Soil convention was attended by a throng of 15,000 sweating, yet enthusiastic onlookers who listened patiently to speech after speech condemning slavery. Among those in attendance were several African-American leaders, including outspoken abolitionist Frederick Douglass, the runaway slave turned orator. Orator Samuel Ringgold Ward, Presbyterian minister Henry H. Garnet, Charles Lenox Remond and Henry Bibb, an ex-slave and former Liberty Party member, were also on hand. A gifted speaker, Remond was the Anti-Slavery Society's first African-American lecturer and later recruited black soldiers for the Union army in Massachusetts during the Civil War, while Bibb, the son of a white Kentucky state senator, later worked with Josiah Henson, another former slave, in forming the Refugees' Home Colony in Canada for escaped slaves in 1851.

While thousands milled about in the sweltering Buffalo heat under a huge tent brought in from Oberlin, Ohio, the convention's real work was conducted by 465 determined delegates at a nearby Universalist church who patched together a political miracle of sorts, essentially unifying four diverse factions—old Liberty Party members, New York Barnburners, assorted Free Soil Democrats and Conscience Whigs—that, while generally agreeing on the issue of slavery extension, essentially held disparate positions on most economic issues, such as banking and tariff legislation.

The Barnburners and the bolting Whigs from Massachusetts were far and away the most politically shrewd of those attending the Buffalo convention, which is not to imply that Chase and the Liberty Party faithful were rank amateurs. They were far from it. It was the Liberty Party, after all, that had issued the clarion call against slavery—and it was no political novice who inserted a plank in the party's platform condemning the southern practice of employing slaves in public works rather than paying free laborers.

United behind Van Buren, the Barnburners were able to get an upper hand at the Buffalo convention. It was generally understood that they would accept nothing less than Van Buren's nomination and, failing in that, would more than likely desert the new party, essentially leaving it stillborn. "We have nominated him

---

30. Ibid., p. 95.

against his consent and wishes," explained David Dudley Field, "but having placed him in the position, we cannot, under any circumstances, abandon him."[31] The ex-Whigs, on the other hand, were somewhat divided. Some antislavery Whigs sought to place the name of Supreme Court Justice John McLean in nomination, but the self-educated jurist turned thumbs down to the idea. Others leaned toward the imperturbable John P. Hale of New Hampshire or diplomat Charles Francis Adams, while about two-dozen or so preferred Whig Congressman Joshua Giddings of Ohio's Western Reserve.

Giddings, who was the father-in-law of antislavery congressman George W. Julian of Indiana, was a remarkable and complicated man and was among the first to propose using force to end slavery. An unrelenting enemy of that "peculiar institution," the schoolteacher-turned-lawyer, served in the Ohio legislature as a Whig before winning a seat in Congress in 1838. A longtime friend and partner of Benjamin F. Wade, the Radical Republican who came within one vote of becoming president during Andrew Johnson's impeachment trial in the spring of 1868, the two men shared an office in Ashtabula County in Ohio's Western Reserve for several years. Interestingly, Giddings' home in Jefferson, Ohio, was used as a station in the Underground Railroad prior to—and after—his election to Congress. Using his own carriage, Giddings frequently drove abolitionist speakers around his congressional district, introducing them at various speaking engagements.

Serving as a moral catalyst in Congress for more than twenty years, the physically powerful Giddings first gained national attention in 1841 when 135 slaves on the *Creole*, a ship sailing from Virginia to New Orleans, Louisiana, was commandeered, killing one of the men on board. Led by Madison Washington, a slave, the ship sailed to the British West Indies—which had abolished slavery eight years earlier—where the British refused to return them to the United States, declaring most of them free. In the diplomatic melee that ensued, Giddings argued that once the ship was outside U.S. territorial waters, the slaves were entitled to their liberty and any attempt to bring them back would be unconstitutional. Giddings resigned from Congress after a majority of the House of Representatives, spurred by Secretary of State Daniel Webster's incessant bullying, voted to censure him for his remarks. Described as "a political pariah for much of his career, and a maverick for all of it," the stubborn Ohio lawmaker was promptly re-elected in 1842, garnering more than 57% of the vote against Democratic and Liberty Party opposition.[32] In Congress, he courageously voted

---

31. Blue, *The Free Soilers*, p. 60.

against the Mexican War and opposed the annexation of Texas, fearing that both measures were part of a plot to spread slavery. While in Congress, he developed a close friendship with Abraham Lincoln, a Whig congressman from Illinois. Lincoln carefully studied the Ohio lawmaker's speeches and frequently gleaned from them ideas that he later implemented as president.

The Free Soilers proceeded to nominate former President Van Buren over New Hampshire Sen. John P. Hale, the reluctant nominee of the badly splintered Liberty Party. Though by this point in the proceedings Van Buren's nomination was pretty much a foregone conclusion, the former president barely polled a majority, receiving 244 votes to Hale's 183 on the convention's first and only ballot. Five-term Ohio Rep. Joshua Giddings garnered 23 votes and thirteen delegates preferred Charles Francis Adams, while four votes were cast for others. Except for Chase, Leavitt, Henry B. Stanton of New York and a few others, most Liberty men stuck loyally with Hale to the bitter end.[33] The Liberty Party's Joshua Leavitt, the fiery editor of the antislavery *Emancipator*, moved to make Van Buren's nomination unanimous and Samuel Lewis of Ohio, who had worked vigorously for Hale, seconded the motion. If it wasn't for the behind-the-scenes bargaining between Chase and the Barnburner leadership, as historian Theodore Clarke Smith maintained, Hale might have had a fighting chance.[34]

Van Buren's nomination marked the first of three occasions in which a former president of the United States attempted to reclaim the White House on a third-party ticket. (Millard Fillmore, the Know-Nothing nominee in 1856, and Teddy Roosevelt, running on the Bull Moose ticket in 1912, also tried to recapture the Executive Mansion on third-party tickets.)

The delegates, representing eighteen states—including three slave states—then tapped permanent convention chairman Charles Francis Adams, son of John Quincy Adams and a favorite of the Conscience Whigs, as Van Buren's running mate. Adams, who had studied law under Daniel Webster, was honored to receive the nomination, saying "it places me somewhat near the level of my fathers."[35] Sadly, the elder Adams, a quintessential public citizen, had collapsed at his desk in the House of Representatives in February of that year and died two days later. In mourning for his father, Adams had worn a black band around his white hat throughout the convention.

32.   James Brewer Stewart, *Joshua R. Giddings and the Tactics of Radical Politics* (Cleveland, 1970), p. x.
33.   Sewell, *John P. Hale and the Politics of Abolition*, pp. 102-103.
34.   Smith, *The Liberty and Free Soil Parties in the Northwest*, p. 142.
35.   Blue, *The Free Soilers*, p. 79.

In exchange for Van Buren's nomination, the Barnburners virtually gave Salmon P. Chase and other Liberty Party leaders a free hand in drafting the party's platform, a document, according to Gamaliel Bailey's *National Era*, that went about as far as a political party could possibly go in opposing slavery by constitutional means and therefore pleased most of the radical abolitionists.[36] Proclaiming "Free Soil, Free Speech, Free Labor and Free Men," the Free Soil Party's platform urged voters to forget "all past political differences in a common resolve to maintain the rights of Free Labor against the aggressions of the Slave Power, and to secure Free Soil for a Free People." Among other things, it denied Congress the power to establish slavery in new territories; favored cheap postage; and advocated river and harbor improvements. Compelled by "honor and patriotism," the party also favored a tariff to assure "the earliest practical payment of the national debt." Throwing a bone to labor and western farmers, the Free Soilers, in keeping with an idea long advocated by Andrew Jackson and powerful Missouri Senator Thomas Hart Benton, also called for a Homestead Act—an idea that would not only enable anyone to become a self-sufficient farmer, but would also stymie southern control of the trans-Mississippi West.

When New York's Benjamin F. Butler read the proposed platform to the overheated and profusely sweating throng gathered under the convention's huge tent, the delegates and spectators roared their approval after every sentence, breaking out in thunderous applause and spontaneous shouting while wildly waving their hats and handkerchiefs. "In my whole life," recalled the usually imperturbable Charles Francis Adams, "I never witnessed such a scene."[37]

Unlike the radical platforms of the Liberty Party in 1840 and 1844, the Free Soil Party, while opposing slavery, virtually ignored the rights of free blacks. Most of the northern Democrats who helped organize the new party opposed the notion of black suffrage and, on occasion, actually exploited the racial prejudices of white northerners. As a consequence, many blacks that had supported the more radical Liberty Party throughout most of the 1840's were frankly offended by the Free Soil Party's attention to women's rights and communitarian experiments while overlooking the promise of racial equality. Although Frederick Douglass was permitted to briefly address the convention, most black delegates did not feel welcome in Buffalo. One African-American delegate later complained that Douglass was only grudgingly recognized at the convention because, in truth, the delegates really "didn't want a 'nigger' to talk to them." The majority

36.   Foner, *Free Soil, Free Labor, Free Men*, p. 125; *National Era*, July 8, 1852.
37.   Sewell, *Ballots for Freedom*, p. 157.

of Free Soilers paternalistically believed that African-Americans were inferior human beings who needed the direction and guidance of whites—a point eloquently made by Samuel Ringgold Ward. Distressed by the fact that the Free Soil platform failed to include an equal rights plank, Ward, a minister and editor who had been dubbed "the black Daniel Webster" because of his eloquence, later threw his support to Gerrit Smith's fledgling National Liberty Party during the 1848 campaign, arguing that the Barnburners were "as ready to rob black men of their rights now as ever they were." Agreeing with Frederick Douglas, who bounced back and forth between the Liberty and Free Soil parties that year, Ward argued that the Free Soil Party didn't truly represent the country's anti-slavery movement.[38]

Like the quickly emerging Know-Nothing Party of the same period, the Free Soil Party attracted an interesting array of political figures to its cause. One of the party's founders, Charles Sumner of Massachusetts, a fiery speaker and devoted abolitionist, was once beaten so severely by South Carolina Congressman Preston Brooks in a scuffle over slavery that he was unable to attend any sessions of the Senate for nearly three years. The beating took place shortly after Sumner delivered his legendary two-day "The Crime Against Kansas" speech before an overflow crowd in the Senate. "Murderous robbers from Missouri," he asserted, "hirelings picked from the drunken spew and vomit of an uneasy civilization" had raped "a virgin territory, compelling it to the hateful embrace of slavery." Sumner, who rarely minced words, was referring to the invasion of Kansas by Missouri "border ruffians" intent on swelling the proslavery vote in that territory.

Other notable leaders of the new party included John A. Andrew, a future governor of Massachusetts and prominent fundraiser for John Brown's legal defense. A lifelong opponent of slavery, Andrew was the first governor in the nation to send his militia to war in answer to President Lincoln's call for troops after the attack at Fort Sumter in the early spring of 1861. Andrew also organized one of the war's first all-black regiments. "I stand or fall," he proudly stated, "as a man and a magistrate, with the rise and fall in history of the Fifty-fourth Massachusetts Regiment."

The Free Soil Party also attracted able men such as Judge Philemon Bliss, an ex-slaveholder from Ohio, and editor Francis P. Blair, Sr., a member of Andrew Jackson's kitchen cabinet and one of the nation's most influential voices during the antebellum years. Leonard Bacon, pastor of New Haven's First Church for forty-one years, was also a key party member. A theologian and not a politician,

---

38.   Blue, *The Free Soilers*, p. 117-119.

Bacon was firmly committed to the antislavery cause, frequently using his pulpit to sermonize about the need to drive slavery from the land. In 1848, he co-founded and edited the *Independent*, a Free Soil newspaper.

Van Buren was by no means the first choice of many of those assembled at the Free Soil convention, especially among the Liberty men and Conscience Whigs who remembered the former president as a proslavery Jackson Democrat. Congregational minister Joshua Leavitt of Massachusetts, in particular, was disturbed by the former president's publicly stated opposition to abolishing slavery in the District of Columbia, a key point in the abolitionist program. As the longtime editor of the *Emancipator* and later of *The Chronicle* in Boston—the country's first antislavery daily newspaper—the 53-year-old Leavitt, who also served as chairman of the Liberty Party's national committee from 1844-47, was one of the most respected voices in the abolitionist movement. Van Buren's position, he lamented, "requires us not only to go into the canvass on the one narrow issue of non-extension, but to tie up our hands from every aggressive movement, however legal or constitutional, which tends to weaken the slave interest within its present bounds."[39] Van Buren, he charged, had been chosen by the Barnburners more "to avenge his old quarrel with the Hunkers" than for any deeply held sympathy for the antislavery cause."[40]

A number of other Liberty men and Conscience Whigs in attendance—those with elephant-like memories—also had serious reservations about the ex-president's commitment to the antislavery movement. Though he had consistently opposed the extension of slavery into the newly acquired territories and spoke out against the immediate annexation of Texas in 1844, they recalled all too well that it was Van Buren, as Andrew Jackson's vice president, who cast the deciding vote in the U.S. Senate suppressing "incendiary" abolitionist literature in the slave states, and it was the same Van Buren, as the nation's eighth president, who had opposed the abolition of slavery in the District of Columbia without the consent of the slaveholding states. They recalled, too, his support of the controversial gag rules, effectively tabling antislavery petitions in Congress. Nor could they forget the time that the "Little Magician" tried to force black mutineers back into slavery through an executive order during the widely watched trial of the coastal trader *La Amistad*—at one point ordering a vessel to wait in the New Haven harbor to carry the Africans, if convicted, back to Cuba and almost certain death.

---

39.   Foner, *Free Soil, Free Labor, Free Men*, p. 124.
40.   Blue, *The Free Soilers*, p. 80.

"Van Buren is too old a sinner to hope for his conversion," remarked one skeptical Liberty Party member.[41]

Despite the misgivings of some antislavery activists, former Whig Charles Sumner of Massachusetts helped to save the day for the little Magician. "It is not the Van Buren of 1838 that we are to vote," he told the delegates, "but the Van Buren of *today*." The Van Buren of 1848, after all, opposed slavery in the territories and had recently endorsed its abolition in the District of Columbia. Moreover, his Barnburner supporters had denounced slavery as "a great moral, social, and political evil—a relic of barbarism which must necessarily be swept away in the progress of Christian civilization."[42] Even the once skeptical Leavitt, a Hale supporter and founder of the old Liberty Party who labored alongside the late John Quincy Adams against the congressional gag rule on antislavery petitions—a measure Van Buren had supported as president—later moved that the former president's nomination be made unanimous. "The Liberty Party is not dead," he told teary-eyed delegates, but had merely taken on a new dimension.[43]

In nominating the former Democratic president, the Free Soilers demonstrated unusual political acumen. A man with a grudge against a party that he had served so loyally and capably was the ideal standard-bearer for an insurgent party looking to wreck havoc on the two old parties. Though he had waffled a bit on the slavery issue during his four years in office, he had now come out strongly against it, railing against the evils of slavery at almost every opportunity. The "Magician," as he was dubbed early in his career as a result of his amazing ability to produce behind-the-scenes results, came out swinging in the 1848 campaign. At times, he appeared almost eager to destroy his former party. The Democrats, after all, had rejected him four years earlier for the lackluster Polk. A man of undeniable charm, Van Buren proved to be a major factor in the election of 1848.

The self-made son of a tavern keeper, Van Buren was Andrew Jackson's hand-picked political heir and the first president born as an American citizen rather than as a British subject. His ancestors, curiously enough, had found their way to the new land from the Netherlands as indentured servants. Fluent in the Dutch language, Van Buren was admitted to the bar in 1803 when he was twenty years old and began practicing law in Kinderhook, New York, shortly thereafter.

---

41.   Ibid., p. 61; Sewell, *John P. Hale and the Politics of Abolition*, p.97.
42.   James M. McPherson, *Battle Cry of Freedom: The Civil War Era* (New York, 1988), p. 62.
43.   Blue, *The Free Soilers*, p. 78.

When he was twenty-nine, Van Buren was elected to the New York state Senate as a Democrat, quickly rising to become leader of the powerful Albany Regency political machine. The Regency so completely dominated politics in New York through the spoils system that the Federalists could offer only token opposition. Van Buren became state attorney general in 1816 and five years later was elected to the U.S. Senate, joining his old friend Rufus King, a Federalist, as the state's junior senator.

Van Buren's meteoric rise to national power was nothing short of spectacular. In the short span of twelve years, he served in the U.S. Senate, as governor of New York, Secretary of State, U.S. minister to Great Britain, vice president and president of the United States. In the latter role, Van Buren made it clear that he intended to continue most of his predecessor's policies, serving as a kind of caretaker for the Jackson administration. He even retained most of Jackson's cabinet. Van Buren's first major crisis was the Panic of 1837, when the nation's leading banks suspended payments of gold and silver for paper money. The new chief executive responded to the crisis by calling a special session of Congress in September of that year, at which time he called for the establishment of an independent treasury system to ensure federal control over the nation's tax revenues.

As firmly committed to the idea of limited government as Thomas Jefferson, Van Buren warned Congress against aiding downtrodden citizens and hard-pressed communities that suffered embarrassing losses and setbacks during the economic downturn. "All communities are apt to look to government for too much help," he cautioned. "The framers of our excellent Constitution and the people who approved it with calm and sagacious deliberation acted at the time on a sounder principle," he said. The seemingly cold-hearted president was merely following the wise advice of the nation's Founding Fathers.

A short, plump, balding man with shocking white sideburns and a ready smile, Van Buren lacked Jackson's personal popularity and charisma. His dapper appearance, in fact, made him an easy target of scoffers, including that of frontiersman Davy Crockett, who claimed that Van Buren used cologne and "laced himself in corsets"—very damaging stuff in the rugged frontier age. Whig detractors also depicted him as an effeminate man who drank wine from a silver-cooler and ate his meals on gold plates. He was also criticized for spending public money to install a hot-water tank in the White House to warm his bath water.

Despite the scathing and all-too-personal criticism hurled in his direction, Van Buren proved to be one of the most fiscally responsible chief executives in American history. It wasn't the government's role, he contended, to make men rich or to subsidize them through direct grants. Congress, albeit slowly, eventually adopted Van Buren's economic measures, but his proposal for an independent treasury system didn't go into effect until July 1840, less than four months before he again faced the voters. By then, it was too late to salvage his presidency. Though the country experienced a mild economic upswing during the winter of 1839-40, the economy slid back into depression-like conditions toward the end of his term. The economic slump persisted until 1845.

Plagued throughout his administration by a sluggish economy, which included bank suspensions, record bankruptcies, falling stock prices, soaring food costs and rising unemployment, Van Buren skillfully guided the country in a prudent yet remarkably progressive fashion. Among other things, he was responsible for introducing vast improvements in the nation's working conditions. Influenced in part by a demonstration of laborers outside the White House, the president boldly instituted a 10-hour workday for federal employees, winning him accolades from labor organizers across the country.

In other areas, however, Van Buren proved to be a bit too timid. Straddling the controversial slavery issue throughout his years in the White House—hoping to placate both the North and the South—he ultimately angered partisans on both sides of the increasingly divisive issue. The antislavery forces adamantly opposed his support for a war against the Seminole Indians in Florida, believing it would lead to Florida's eventual entry into the Union as a slave state. On the other hand, proslavery advocates criticized the New York Democrat for failing to annex Texas as a slave state. In foreign affairs, Van Buren's administration was hampered by sporadic armed clashes with the British along the Canadian border, but much to his credit, Van Buren avoided a full-scale confrontation with England.

The Democrats nominated Van Buren unanimously when they convened in Baltimore in May 1840. The party's delegates, however, were unhappy with Van Buren's controversial Vice President Richard Johnson of Kentucky and refused to nominate him for a second term. Johnson's critics had accused him of indulging in "experiments in race amalgamation." The reputed killer of the great Shawnee chief Tecumseh, Johnson had apparently fathered two daughters with a slave inherited from his father and in blatant disregard for the social mores of the South, he also had the audacity to have his daughters educated and presented in polite society. The Democrats, preferring to leave the vice-presidential decision to the Electoral College, refused to name a vice-presidential running mate for Van Buren.

Blamed for the nation's lagging economy, Van Buren carried only seven states in the fall election, losing to Whig William Henry Harrison. In his final State of the Union address on his 58th birthday, Van Buren, in an unusually lengthy speech, listed his accomplishments in office. He was proudest of the fact that his administration had preserved the fiscal integrity of the federal government, leaving the country with a $1.5 million surplus. He also defended his decision not to spend federal money on public works to relieve the depression of 1837 on the grounds that it would have been unconstitutional to do so.

The "Red Fox of Kinderhook" again sought the Democratic presidential nomination in 1844, only to watch helplessly as what appeared to be a certain first ballot victory slipped away when the delegates at the Baltimore convention unexpectedly turned to Tennessee's James K. Polk. Though Van Buren led with 146 of the 266 votes cast on the first ballot—just eleven votes shy of the two-thirds majority needed for nomination—the former president's support slowly eroded. Polk, the first real "dark-horse" to ever capture a major party's presidential nomination, was unanimously chosen on the ninth ballot. Van Buren's principled opposition to the annexation of Texas as a slave state had doomed his candidacy.

The son and grandson of presidents, Charles Francis Adams, Van Buren's vice-presidential running mate on the Free Soil ticket, began his political career as a Democrat but switched to the Whig Party over the slavery issue, serving in the Massachusetts legislature from 1840-45. After spending his boyhood in Europe, he graduated from Harvard in 1825 and began practicing law in Boston where, among other things, he tended to his father's business affairs and founded the *Boston Whig*. A prolific writer and editor, Adams also found time to write articles on American history for the *North American Review*. The 41-year-old lawyer later represented his father's old congressional district as a Republican and was appointed by Lincoln as ambassador to the Court of St. James in 1861, playing a crucial role in keeping Britain somewhat neutral during the Civil War and in settling the *Alabama* claims after the war.

Back on the campaign trail in 1848, Van Buren faced Whig Zachary Taylor, a Mexican War hero and former slave owner, and Lewis Cass, a somewhat sluggish and stout northern Democrat with undeniable southern sympathies. The Democrat-turned-Free Soil ex-president made a concerted effort to attract antislavery Whigs to the Free Soil banner, but with the exception of the Conscience Whigs in Massachusetts and the Herculean efforts of Giddings and Chase in Ohio, the Free Soil Party didn't have too much success in siphoning northern Whig votes from Taylor.

Similarly, the Van Buren-Adams ticket proved only moderately successful in attracting votes from antislavery Democrats who were displeased with the nomination of Senator Cass, a man who once advocated "squatter sovereignty"—that is, the right of settlers in the territories to decide the question of slavery for themselves. Cass's abysmal record, coupled with the Democratic Party's failure to address the issue of slavery extension in its platform, made Van Buren's candidacy quite attractive to large numbers of antislavery Democrats, including such noteworthy partisans as the powerful Blair family of Missouri. Holding political court at his estate outside of Washington, the elder Blair, a longtime Jacksonian Democrat and former editor of the influential *Washington Globe*, enthusiastically joined the Free Soil cause, as did his son, Francis P. Blair, Jr., who organized the antislavery party in Missouri and actively campaigned for Van Buren. Massachusetts Gov. Marcus Morton also endorsed Van Buren, but not the normally phlegmatic Charles Francis Adams, whom he described as "the greatest iceberg in the Northern Hemisphere."[44] Missouri's Benton, in the meantime, remained aloof, fearing a possible backlash among his state's large proslavery population. Democrats David Wilmot of Pennsylvania and former congressman Jacob Brinkerhoff of Ohio also lent support to the new party. In the forefront of the antislavery cause, the 38-year-old Brinkerhoff, who later served on the Ohio Supreme Court, was believed by many to have been the person who actually penned the Wilmot Proviso.

For a while, it appeared likely that Van Buren would also face an independent proslavery southern nominee. Sparked by former Alabama congressman William L. Yancey's walkout at the Democratic national convention in Baltimore, the movement for a southern third-party ticket quickly picked up steam in South Carolina when the fire-eating Yancey—a man who once argued that the African slave trade should be resumed—stopped in Charleston on his way home from the convention and delivered a stinging diatribe against Democratic nominee Lewis Cass.[45] In his sharply-worded address, the colorful ex-lawmaker accused Cass of being sympathetic to the Wilmot Proviso and urged the South to unite behind a third-party ticket committed to the so-called "Alabama Platform"—a litmus test of sorts that vowed to withhold public support from any national candidate who wasn't "openly and unequivocally" opposed to the exclusion of slavery in the territories.

---

44. Martin B. Duberman, *Charles Francis Adams, 1807-1886* (Boston, 1960), p. 152.
45. Potter, *The Impending Crisis*, pp. 80-81. Yancey bolted from the Democratic convention when the delegates soundly rejected his plank incorporating the "Alabama Platform." His attempt to lead a walkout of the southern delegates, however, was a complete failure as Yancey left the hall with only one follower—"a Quixote with his Sancho Panza."

Yancey, who married a wealthy widowed plantation owner about a decade ear-lier, had resigned his seat in the U.S. House of Representatives in 1846 partly due to policy differences with his northern colleagues. He drafted the Alabama Plat-form for the state legislature the following year, shortly before the Wilmot Pro-viso was formally introduced in Congress. A succinct statement, his platform argued that the territorial legislatures lacked the authority to ban slavery and stated that slave owners had the right to take their property into the territories under congressional protection. Yancey's platform, which was eventually adopted by several southern states, also urged the Democratic Party to only nominate pro-slavery candidates for national office. Within a matter of weeks, the names of 73-year-old Littleton W. Tazewell, a former governor and senator from Virginia, Jef-ferson Davis of Mississippi, and South Carolina's perennial favorite-son prospect John C. Calhoun—who seemed almost eager to head the movement—were being mentioned as possible presidential candidates on a southern-based inde-pendent ticket. The movement, however, received a cool reception outside of South Carolina and the idea was eventually abandoned.[46]

There was always an element of suspicion surrounding Van Buren's candi-dacy. Many Democrats and some antislavery Whigs believed that the former president possessed a bull-sized taste for revenge and was doing everything in his power to deny his former party the presidency, a scenario given more than a little credence by the offhand comments of Chase's lieutenant, Edward S. Hamlin, publisher of the *Cleveland True Democrat* (now the *Cleveland Plain-Dealer*). A former Liberty Party enthusiast and one-time Whig congressman, Hamlin glee-fully remarked on the eve of the Free Soil convention in Buffalo that the party's real aim was to throw the election into the House of Representatives where "we might trust Van Buren to do the rest by cheating."[47]

Despite the best efforts of Whig and Democratic leaders to soft-peddle the sla-very issue during the 1848 campaign, most Americans were beginning to form strong feelings on the subject. Lewis Cass, in fact, won the Democratic nomina-tion in the spring of that year precisely because he was ambiguous on the slavery question. His rather vague proposal for "popular sovereignty" didn't specify pre-cisely *when* voters might choose in favor or against slavery—during the territorial stage or when adopting a state constitution. Though he was opposed by South Carolina's powerful John C. Calhoun, who feared the Michigan lawmaker's pro-posal would violate the property rights of slaveholding settlers, and by antislavery Democrats who were strongly opposed to the advance of slavery into the territo-ries, Cass was able to capture the Democratic nomination at the party's national convention in Baltimore by persuading enough southern delegates that his proposal wouldn't harm their interests. Having served as territorial governor of Michigan for eighteen years, Cass held a variety of civil and military positions, including a stint as Andrew Jackson's Secretary of War and Minister to France. A New Englander by birth, Cass was nominated on the fourth ballot, defeating James Buchanan of Pennsylvania and New Hampshire's puritanical Levi Woodbury, a member of the Supreme Court.

Likewise, Zachary Taylor, a man without any discernible political opinions, was also vague on the issue. "Old Rough and Ready," it turns out, didn't belong to either political party and had never even bothered to vote before capturing the Whig Party's presidential nomination that year. The Whigs as a whole were so vague on the issue of slavery that year that they didn't even trouble themselves with drafting a platform. A career army officer, the 63-year-old Taylor—the last president born before the Constitution was adopted—had risen to fame during the Mexican War when his small band of about 5,000 men gallantly withstood

---

46. Rayback, *Free Soil: The Election of 1848*, pp. 267-274. Curiously, the South Carolinians, meeting in Charleston on July 20, endorsed the Whig Party's Zachary Taylor for president and named William O. Butler, the Democratic nominee for vice president, as his running mate. Taylor's bungling of the Charleston endorsement, in which he gladly accepted it and said he would have also accepted the national Democratic nomination in Baltimore if it had been tendered, nearly proved disastrous for the national Whig campaign. A number of northern Whigs, especially disappointed Clay supporters who were unaware that the Charleston gathering had been a predominately Democratic undertaking, mistakenly viewed it as an attempt by southern Whigs to dump vice presidential candidate Millard Fillmore from the ticket. Angry Whigs in Poughkeepsie and several other New York towns and cities responded by abandoning Taylor and proposing to nominate a new Whig ticket headed by Henry Clay with Fillmore as his vice-presidential running mate. Preparations were even made for a huge Clay-Fillmore rally at New York's Vauxhall Gardens. Despite the pleadings of Abbott Lawrence and other prominent Whigs, Clay had bitterly refused to endorse Taylor's candidacy. Clay, whose deeply disappointing loss to James K. Polk in 1844 was compounded when he lost his party's presidential nomination to Taylor a few months earlier, was initially in no mood to stump for a political novice like the "Hero of Buena Vista." However, when he realized the seriousness of the situation in New York—where there was even speculation that powerful Whig leader Thurlow Weed was ready to bolt for Clay—the three-time presidential candidate had second thoughts. The Kentuckian, after all, was a loyal party man, a kind of Whig's Whig. "I am utterly opposed to the use of my name as a candidate for the Presidency," he wrote in the *New York Express* on September 8, adding that he had given "no countenance, or encouragement" to such a movement. It collapsed shortly thereafter.

an assault by 20,000 of Santa Ana's troops at Buena Vista in February 1847. Despite his lack of political experience—Daniel Webster called him "an illiterate frontier colonel"—Taylor, perhaps the least qualified man to ever occupy the White House, was chosen on the fourth ballot at the Whig convention, defeating such luminaries as Henry Clay, Winfield Scott and Daniel Webster.[48] Taylor, who had initially considered running as an independent, led on the first ballot at the party's convention at the Museum Building in Philadelphia, garnering 111 votes to Clay's 97, Winfield Scott's 43, twenty-two for Webster and a scattering of six votes for Delaware's longtime Sen. John M. Clayton and John McLean of Ohio. Reaching for the brass ring for the final time, the colorful Clay, who was obviously frustrated and adamantly refused to stump for the Whig nominee in the autumn campaign, lamented that he wished he could "kill a Mexican." Other prominent Whigs, including Webster, who despite his advancing years still had his eye on the glittering prize, reluctantly campaigned for Taylor.

Curiously, one of Taylor's most enthusiastic supporters was little-known Abraham Lincoln of Illinois, the only Whig sent to Congress from that state during the disastrous mid-term elections of 1846. For some time, the 33-year-old congressman belonged to the "Taylor-for-President" club in the U.S. House, a comparatively youthful group known as the "Young Indians" and headed by Georgia's legendary Alexander H. Stephens. The club's members included William B. Preston, Thomas S. Flournoy, and John S. Pendleton of Virginia; Robert A. Toombs of Georgia; and Connecticut's Truman Smith, who later directed Taylor's successful campaign as chairman of the Whig Party's national committee.[49]

Like New York's William H. Seward, Lincoln attacked Van Buren and the Free Soilers, arguing that their position on slavery in the territories was virtually the same as that of Zachary Taylor and the Whigs. He also charged that by siphoning votes from antislavery Whigs, the Free Soil Party was indirectly aiding Democrat Lewis Cass, who would be less likely to promote freedom in the territories than Taylor. Having extracted a pledge from Taylor not to interfere with the legislative process and to use his veto power only sparingly, Lincoln believed that Taylor's position on potentially divisive issues such as slavery should be the same. Therefore, if Congress passed the Wilmot Proviso prohibiting the extension of slavery into the territories acquired from Texas—a highly unlikely pros-

47. *Ohio State Journal*, August 7, 1848.
48. Webster quoted in Roseboom, *A History of Presidential Elections*, p. 139.
49. Rayback, *Free Soil: The Election of 1848*, pp. 37-38.

pect given the southern domination of the U.S. Senate—Taylor would *not* veto it. Predicting "a most overwhelming, glorious, triumph" for the Whigs that year, the willowy Illinois legislator toiled away at the Whig Party's national headquarters during most of the campaign, corresponding with Whig leaders in the crucial battleground states of Illinois, New York and Pennsylvania.

At the request of the Whig National Committee, Lincoln later stumped throughout New England, championing Taylor's candidacy and trying to prevent Whig defections to the Free Soil Party by reminding audiences in Boston, Cambridge, Lowell, New Bedford, and Worcester, that a vote for Van Buren was really a vote for Cass and slavery extension—the very thing the abolitionists and Conscience Whigs were so adamantly opposed to. Seward echoed the same thing, warning that if all of the nation's antislavery forces rallied to the Free Soil banner, the two major parties—and, indeed, the Union—would then be controlled almost entirely by southerners.[50]

The campaign of 1848 was one of the nastiest in American history. The Democrats lambasted Taylor, describing him as an undignified semi-illiterate, a slave master and too cheap to buy decent clothing. They also compared him to Caesar, Cromwell, and Napoleon and warned that he would put the country on a war footing. The Democrats were merciless in their attacks, so much so that Taylor himself lamented that he had been subjected to the "vilest slanders of the most unprincipled demagogues this or any other nation was ever cursed with, who have pursued me like bloodhounds." The Whigs were equally savage in their treatment of Cass, occasionally referring to him as a windbag and a "pot-bellied, mutton-headed cucumber." They also accused him of once sponsoring legislation in the Northwest to affect the sale of white vagabonds into slavery.[51]

While avoiding the slavery issue like a plague, the two major parties willingly brought the issue of nativism into the campaign, with each party accusing the other of hostility to foreigners. On this issue, the Whigs were at a distinct disadvantage. Their only real knock against Cass was that he had once voted against a federal appropriation for relief in famine-stricken Ireland—a measure introduced in Congress by Kentucky's John J. Crittenden. The Democrats, on the other

---

50. Stephen B. Oates, *With Malice Toward None: The Life of Abraham Lincoln* (New York, 1978), pp. 89-91; David Herbert Donald, *Lincoln* (New York, 1995), pp. 80, 127-128. This wasn't the first time that Lincoln had attacked Van Buren in a presidential campaign. While stumping for William Henry Harrison in 1840, the fiercely partisan Lincoln occasionally resorted to demagoguery, chastising the aristocratic Van Buren for having supported voting rights for free blacks in New York.

51. Boller, *Presidential Campaigns*, pp. 85-86.

hand, had plenty of ammunition, reminding the voters that Zachary Taylor had been nominated by the "church burning" Native Americans at a convention in Philadelphia in September 1847—long before receiving the Whig Party's nomination. They were also quick to point out that virtually every nativist newspaper in the country, including Lewis C. Levin's inflammatory *Philadelphia Sun*, had enthusiastically endorsed his candidacy.[52]

While both major parties virtually ignored the issue of land reform, the Free Soilers made a concerted effort to win over the support of the National Reformers—a group headed by George Henry Evans that threw its support to the Liberty League's Gerrit Smith earlier in the campaign—by demanding the "appropriation of the public domain in limited quantities to actual settlers, and to actual settlers only," as opposed to land grants to monopolies and speculators. In an effort to "elevate and dignify labor," the Barnburners dovetailed the land reform issue with an appeal to workingmen, reminding them that Van Buren was the author of the ten-hour workday for employees on federal public works projects and driving home the old argument that permitting slave labor in the territories would degrade free labor while virtually excluding workingmen looking for new opportunities from seeking gainful employment in those areas. By the campaign's end, the issue appeared to have some traction as a number of land reform journals abandoned Smith's hopeless Liberty League candidacy and endorsed Van Buren and the Free Soil Party.[53]

The refined Van Buren appeared almost saint-like compared to his two major-party rivals, who spent most of the campaign trading insults. Having endured cries of "Van, Van's a used up man" in his bid for re-election in 1840 and having suffered the indignity of being passed over by the Democrats four years later, the former president harbored only faint illusions of victory in 1848. A shrewd politician nevertheless, the 65-year-old ex-president was able to split the Democratic vote in the nation's most populous state of New York, thereby enabling Whig candidate Zachary Taylor, carrying eight of the nation's fifteen slave states, to sneak into the White House with barely 47% of the popular vote.

The results of the November 7 balloting gave Taylor 1,360,099 votes to 1,220,540 votes for Cass and 291,263 votes for Van Buren. A shift of only 3,227 votes in Georgia, Maryland and Delaware would have given the election to Cass rather than Taylor. Philanthropist Gerrit Smith, running under the Liberty League, Industrial Congress and hastily formed National Liberty Party banners,

---

52. Rayback, *Free Soil: The Election of 1848*, pp. 266-267.
53. Ibid., pp. 264-266.

garnered a paltry 2,733 votes, the vast majority of which were cast in New York. There were also a few hundred scattered votes, many of them for the sulking Henry Clay of Kentucky.

For Van Buren, who received roughly five times as many votes as had been cast for the Liberty Party's James G. Birney in 1844, the outcome revealed neither victory nor defeat. Impressively, the former president finished ahead of the Democratic candidate in Massachusetts, New York and Connecticut and polled the difference between Taylor and Cass in eleven of the seventeen states where the Free Soilers had distributed ballots. One of his strongest showings occurred in Massachusetts where the deep divisions between "Cotton" and "Conscience" Whigs had virtually rendered that party asunder. However, despite capturing nearly twenty-nine percent of the vote there, Van Buren wasn't able to prevent Whig candidate Zachary Taylor from carrying the state by nearly 23,000 votes. Outside of the northeast, Van Buren ran strongest in those communities that had been settled by antislavery New Englanders. Though failing to win any electoral votes, the former president carried ten counties in Illinois, eight in New York and six each in Ohio—where he swept the entire Western Reserve—and Wisconsin, where he garnered a staggering 26.6% of the vote.

In New York, where the ex-president carried eight counties and finished second in twenty-two of the state's fifty-nine counties, Van Buren ran strongest in the central party of the state, encompassing Delaware County in the southeast, St. Lawrence and Monroe counties in the northwest and Allegany County in the southwest. Heavily populated by transplanted New Englanders, this region had been particularly strong for the Anti-Masons more than a decade earlier and was undoubtedly influenced by Charles Grandison Finney's religious revivalism. In that region, the Free Soil nominee received over forty percent of the vote in seven counties and an absolute majority in two counties. In St. Lawrence County, home of the late Silas Wright and antislavery congressman and publisher Preston King, Van Buren garnered a bulging 59 percent of the vote against his Whig and Democratic rivals.[54]

The not-too-shabby 15,702 votes cast for Van Buren in Illinois—about one-eighth of the state's total—included winning a plurality in Chicago where he enjoyed the support of popular independent Democratic mayor James H. Woodworth, an ex-New Yorker who had embraced the Barnburner cause and later led the movement against the Compromise of 1850.[55] While the Free Soil standard-bearer failed to carry a single state and garnered a somewhat disappointing four-

---

54. Ibid., p. 283.

teen percent of the popular vote in the North, the antislavery party virtually supplanted the Democrats as the second party in Massachusetts, New York and Vermont.

On Ohio's Western Reserve, where the Free Soil ticket swept Ashtabula, Cuyahoga, Geauga, Lake, Lorain and Trumbull counties, it was believed that the party's vote might have been even greater were it not for an undercurrent of anti-Van Buren sentiment among antislavery ex-Whig voters in that area. Turnout in that region dropped from nearly 52,000 in 1844 to 43,000 in 1848. Edward S. Hamlin's *Cleveland True Democrat*, a paper that initially favored Justice John McLean, even went so far as to suggest that if the Free Soil Party had nominated McLean or perhaps New Hampshire's John P. Hale—or any other candidate, for that matter—the party probably would have garnered 10,000 additional votes on the Reserve alone.[56]

For his part, the aging ex-president, who never truly expected to win, was hardly discouraged by the results. "Everything was accomplished by the Free Soil movement that the most sanguine friend could hope for and much more than there was good reason to expect," he wrote shortly after the election.[57] If success can be measured in terms of keeping Democrat Lewis Cass out of the White House, Van Buren's campaign surpassed all expectations. In that regard, Daniel Webster's jibe that the movement should have been called the "Free Spoil" Party wasn't completely off the mark.[58] Meanwhile, the jubilant Whigs virtually ignored Van Buren and the Free Soilers while celebrating Taylor's victory, but the Democrats were quick to point an accusing finger at the former president, charging that he had played the role of a spoiler and, single-mindedly motivated by revenge, was personally responsible for placing a political neophyte like Taylor in the White House.

Though polling just over ten percent of the popular vote in the presidential election, the Free Soil Party won thirteen seats in the U.S. House in the 1848-49 congressional elections, giving them the balance of power in that body. In addition, Salmon P. Chase of Ohio joined New Hampshire's John P. Hale as a Free Soil member of the U.S. Senate in March 1849. Though some of the party's lead-

55. Rayback, *Free Soil: The Election of 1848*, pp. 283-287. The former president received 2,120 votes in Chicago to Taylor's 1,708 and 1,622 for Democrat Lewis Cass. In addition to Cleveland, which Van Buren carried by a narrow margin, Chicago was one of only two major urban areas carried by the ex-president.

56. Smith, *The Liberty and Free Soil Parties in the Northwest*, p. 155.

57. Blue, *The Free Soilers*, p. 144.

58. Mitchell, *Horatio Seymour of New York*, p. 110.

ing lights, including Owen Lovejoy of Illinois and Charles Sumner of Massachusetts, went down to defeat in congressional races that year, Free Soil candidates finished second—ahead of one of their major party opponents—in at least twenty-two House races across the country. Impressively, the Free Soil Party also held the balance of power in no fewer than eleven state legislatures during this period.

Among the victorious congressional candidates were ex-Whig Charles Allen, a former Massachusetts state legislator, and 42-year-old heavyset newspaper publisher Preston King of upstate New York—a man once characterized by historian and writer Henry Adams as "the most amiable, fat old fanatic that ever existed."[59] Ironically, King, who served two previous terms in the House as a Democrat, was a states' rights advocate yet firmly opposed the spread of slavery and compromise with the South. A former Common Pleas Court judge, the 51-year-old Allen had served several terms in the Massachusetts state House and Senate. He was also a grandnephew of Samuel Adams, the selflessly devoted revolutionary whose abiding hatred of the British crown triggered America's war of independence.

Other Free Soilers elected to Congress in 1848-49 included Walter Booth of Connecticut, George Washington Julian of Indiana, William Sprague of Michigan, Amos Tuck and James Wilson of New Hampshire, Lewis D. Campbell, Joshua R. Giddings and Joseph M. Root of Ohio, David Wilmot, though still nominally a Democrat, and lawyer John W. Howe of Pennsylvania, and Wisconsin merchant Charles Durkee, a former member of the Liberty Party and founder of the city of Kenosha. Running in a staunchly free soil district in southeastern Wisconsin, the 42-year-old Durkee, a former member of the territorial legislature, combined support for the Wilmot Proviso with a platform calling for internal improvements to unseat a popular Democratic incumbent in a close three-way race. Running with Democratic support in his predominately Whig district, Indiana's George W. Julian, the Free Soil Party's vice-presidential standard-bearer in 1852, was denounced by the Whigs as an "apostle of disunion" whose victory would lead to disaster. Despite a barrage of negative campaigning, Julian eked out a narrow victory, defeating Whig Samuel W. Parker by a scant 154 votes. The Free Soil congressman, however, lost a rematch with Parker two years later.

The Free Soil Party also made a noticeable splash in several gubernatorial campaigns that year, drenching Democrats' hopes in New York and causing the

---

59.   Henry Adams letter to Charles Francis Adams, Jr., January 17, 1861, as quoted in Gienapp, *The Origins of the Republican Party*, p. 78.

Whigs all kinds of fits in several other states. In New York, John A. Dix, whose term in the U.S. Senate was coming to a close, threw a genuine scare into his major party rivals in that state's hard-fought gubernatorial campaign, garnering more than twenty-seven percent of the vote in a three-way race. A 50-year-old lawyer and railroad executive, Dix polled a staggering 123,360 votes to Whig Hamilton Fish's 218,280 votes and 114,457 for acid-tongued Democrat Reuben Walworth, a longtime jurist who had once been nominated for the U.S. Supreme Court, but wasn't confirmed by the U.S. Senate. Incredibly, Walworth was so unpopular that several New York courts, including that of state chancellor, had been abolished simply to remove him from the bench. In addition to Dix's strong showing, the Barnburners also captured fourteen seats in the state assembly, to only six for the Hunkers.[60]

In Maine, the Free Soil Party's Samuel C. Fessenden, a Portland attorney and veteran of the old Liberty Party who later served in Congress as a Republican during the first two years of Lincoln's presidency, waged his third consecutive campaign for governor, losing to Democrat John W. Dana in a three-cornered race. The son of an antislavery activist and brother of Thomas A. and William Pitt Fessenden—the latter who served in the U.S. Senate from 1854-65 and as Lincoln's Secretary of the Treasury—Samuel Fessenden's 1848 campaign was hampered by a lack of newspaper support and by the unwillingness of the state's leading political figures, such as Democrat Hannibal Hamlin, to break with their parties and endorse the third-party ticket. Ironically, among those who refused to support his candidacy was Fessenden's older brother, William Pitt, a prominent Whig who had staunchly supported the Wilmot Proviso but, like many other Conscience Whigs, was highly suspicious of Van Buren's true motives during the 1848 campaign. The older Fessenden had nothing but contempt for scheming politicians such as the powerful Thurlow Weed of New York, whose selfish aims, he believed, had thrust a novice like Taylor on the unsuspecting Whigs, but his suspicion of Van Buren's real motives apparently outweighed his contempt for Weed and other Whig kingmakers. "The principle of the free soil movement had my sympathy and respect," the older Fessenden confessed, but added that Van Buren's candidacy wouldn't have any practical result other than electing General Cass.[61] Despite personal appearances by Charles Sumner of Massachusetts, John

---

60. Herbert D. A. Donovan, *The Barnburners: A Study of the Internal Movements in the Political History of New York State and of the Resulting Changes in Political Affiliation, 1830-1852* (Philadelphia, 1974), p. 109. Taking full advantage of the split in the Democratic ranks, the Whigs captured 108 seats in the New York Assembly and elected 31 of the state's 34 congressmen.

P. Hale of New Hampshire and New York's John Van Buren, the 33-year-old Congregational minister-turned-lawyer barely garnered fifteen percent of the vote.[62]

Another spirited gubernatorial campaign was waged in Vermont where Oscar L. Shafter, a 36-year-old Wesleyan graduate who had studied law at Harvard, finished a strong second in a three-way race won by the Whig candidate. Shafter's father, a county judge, was also a third-party veteran, having twice waged campaigns for governor of Vermont on the Liberty Party ticket and once—years later—on the fledgling Temperance ticket. An ex-Liberty Party member himself and grandson of a Revolutionary War veteran, the younger Shafter's candidacy was aided by an unexpected endorsement from William Slade, a former Whig governor who enthusiastically threw his support to Van Buren and the Free Soilers in the 1848 campaign. Though ridiculed by a Democratic newspaper, which amusingly described the party as "the free-soil, free-speech, free-labor, free-any-thing-else-you-can-catch-a-stray-vote-party," Shafter garnered a whopping 15,018 votes in the September election to the successful Whig candidate's 22,132 and 13,477 for Democrat Paul Dillingham.[63] Shafter, who moved west in 1854, later served as an associate justice on the California Supreme Court before resigning due to failing health in 1867.

In Massachusetts, Stephen C. Phillips, a Harvard-educated former Whig congressman and one-time mayor of Salem, waged a spirited race for governor against the Whig Party's George N. Briggs—a former congressman who later advocated congressional prohibition of slavery in the territories and the abolition of slavery in the District of Columbia—and Democrat Caleb Cushing, a diplomat and former pro-southern congressman who was sympathetic to slavery. John Mills, a former Democrat, was named for lieutenant governor on the Free Soil ticket. The 47-year-old Phillips, who later perished on the steamer *Montreal* when it tragically burst into flames and sunk to a watery grave in the St. Lawrence River in Canada during the summer of 1857, waged three hard-fought campaigns for governor of Massachusetts on the Free Soil ticket between 1848 and 1850. In his maiden effort against Briggs and Cushing, Phillips was unable to break the grip of the powerful Whig machine in Boston, but nevertheless finished a respectable second in the race, garnering 36,011 votes, or twenty-nine percent, to 61,640 for the Whig Party's Briggs and 25,323 for Democrat Cushing.

---

61.   Blue, *The Free Soilers*, p. 117.
62.   Ibid., p. 139.
63.   Ibid., pp. 139-140.

In neighboring Connecticut the following year, the aging John M. Niles polled the difference between his Whig and Democratic rivals in a losing bid for governor, despite garnering only 3,520 votes. Gideon Welles, a young Van Buren Democrat who later served as Lincoln's Secretary of the Navy, organized the Free Soil campaign in that state. A one-time Jacksonian Democrat, Niles had twice served in the U.S. Senate and as postmaster general in the Van Buren administration. He had also waged unsuccessful campaigns for governor as a Democrat, losing to a Whig incumbent in 1839 and 1840. Joining Welles, Missouri's Francis P. Blair and Benjamin F. Butler of New York, Niles, a lawyer and founder of the *Hartford Times*, was one of the few close friends and advisors to the late Andrew Jackson—the first candidate to win the presidency under the auspices of the modern Democratic Party. He later embraced the Republican Party upon its founding in the mid-1850s.[64]

Ironically, the Free Soil Party's most significant impact was felt in Ohio—a state where party leaders wisely decided not to enter their own slate. In that state's razor-thin gubernatorial contest, the Whig Party's Seabury Ford, a longtime member of the Ohio legislature and staunch opponent of slavery, appealed directly for Free Soil support in his nip-and-tuck battle against Democrat John B. Weller, a former congressman who was widely believed to be a southern sympathizer. In fact, Weller not only voted for the antislavery gag rules while in Congress, he was also the congressman who moved to censure antislavery lawmaker Joshua Giddings in 1842.[65] Sadly embarrassed by the nomination of slave owner Zachary Taylor at the Whig Party's national convention in Philadelphia earlier that year, the 47-year-old Ford, at Salmon P. Chase's urging, adamantly refused to endorse his party's presidential candidate during the autumn campaign and, under growing pressure from Free Soil leaders, vigorously urged repeal of the state's notorious Black Laws—an issue near and dear to antislavery activists in Ohio.[66]

In the closest gubernatorial election in the state's history—and the only one ever decided by the Ohio legislature—Ford garnered 148,766 votes to Weller's 148,452 with a scattering for a little-known Native American candidate. Since neither candidate polled a majority, the disputed contest was then thrown into the general assembly, which was evenly divided between the Whigs and the Democrats with a handful of Free Soilers, mostly from the Western Reserve—once an

---

64. Foner, *Free Soil, Free Labor, Free Men*, p. 150.
65. Smith, *The Liberty and Free Soil Parties in the Northwest*, pp. 152-153.
66. Blue, *The Free Soilers*, pp. 138-139.

impregnable Whig stronghold—holding the balance of power. As expected, the Free Soil lawmakers threw their support to the Whig candidate and Ford was sworn in as Ohio's twentieth governor shortly thereafter. During his inaugural address, Ford, who deeply disliked public speaking, made a prophetic and impassioned speech on the preservation of the Union, warning his audience of the fatal consequences that were likely to follow a breakup of the nation on sectional grounds.

Shortly after the 1848 election, Van Buren and most of the New York Barnburners abandoned the Free Soil Party, essentially decimating the party in that state, and returned to the Democratic fold where they worked tirelessly against the new Whig administration. Ex-Liberty Party member Henry B. Stanton was one of those who followed the Barnburners back to their former party, saying that the third-party had served its purpose. "In my sober judgment the day for 'third parties' on the slavery question is gone," he said.[67] A large chunk of the Conscience Whigs, likewise, returned to the Whig flock and forged a somewhat precarious working alliance with the so-called "Cotton Whigs," a group of pro-southern Whigs headed by Daniel Webster and influential New England textile manufacturers such as Abbott Lawrence and Nathan Appleton, both of whom hoped to continue their profitable trade arrangements with the cotton-producing South.

Following the election, a hale and hearty Van Buren retired for a second time to the serenity of his thirty-room mansion in Lindenwald, a two hundred-acre estate about two miles from the center of the small village of Kinderhook in New York's Hudson Valley. Living comfortably on the income derived from about $200,000 in real estate and investments, the former president began work on his political memoirs while traveling extensively through Europe in the early 1850s. He wrote about 850 pages, but never completed the manuscript, partly because he had been sidetracked into writing a long essay called *An Inquiry into the Origin and Course of Political Parties in the United States*, which was published posthumously in 1867. His memoirs were eventually published in 1920—some fifty-eight years after his death. During his European travels, the former president had audiences with Queen Victoria and Pope Pius IX.

When he returned from Europe in 1855, Van Buren was seventy-two years of age and, though still in relatively robust health, rarely ventured away from Lin-

---

67.   Ibid., p. 180. The return of Van Buren and the Barnburners to the Democratic ranks was sharply denounced by Gamaliel Bailey's *National Era*, which charged that a "more shameless profligate abandonment of principle is not on record."

denwald, despite frequent urgings to attend political dinners or run for political office. Though retaining a keen interest in politics, the ex-president even turned down a suggestion that he should preside over the Democratic national convention in 1856. Remaining loyal to the Democratic Party, Van Buren nevertheless served as an elector for Pierce in 1852 and supported Buchanan in 1856. Almost alone among the ex-Free Soilers—most of whom had long since rallied to the Republican banner—Van Buren, deeply worried that the Republicans would exacerbate the slavery issue, strongly endorsed Stephen A. Douglas against Lincoln in 1860. Moreover, the former president wholeheartedly supported Lincoln and the Union cause during the Civil War—a conflict he did not live long enough to see resolved. He died in the early morning hours of July 24, 1862, about four months shy of his eightieth birthday.[68]

While the departure of Van Buren's Barnburners and many of the Conscience Whigs certainly wasn't a fatal blow to the fledgling Free Soil Party, their exodus was clearly felt in the 1850-51 mid-term elections. Despite fielding more candidates than in 1848, the antislavery party won only eight congressional seats, down from thirteen in the previous Congress. No fewer than three of its members, including New York's Preston King, defected to the major parties. Moreover, several of the party's incumbents, including Indiana's George W. Julian and Ohio's Joseph Root, went down to defeat. Julian lost narrowly to his Whig opponent in a hard-fought race in Indiana's so-called "Burnt District" while Root, garnering only eight percent of the vote in Ohio's twenty-first congressional district, was literally drubbed by his Whig and Democratic rivals. Party founder and Harvard lecturer Charles Sumner, unquestionably the party's most fervid speaker, was also a landslide loser that year, polling only fifteen percent of the vote in a special election for a U.S. House seat from Massachusetts. Sumner, however, was elected to the U.S. Senate by the Massachusetts legislature the following year, joining Free Soilers John P. Hale of New Hampshire and Ohio's Salmon P. Chase in that esteemed body.

Only four incumbent Free Soilers—Charles Allen of Massachusetts, Amos Tuck of New Hampshire, Charles Durkee of Wisconsin and Ohio's Joshua Giddings—were re-elected on the party's ticket in the 1850-51 mid-term congressional elections. The party also played an important role in the election of no fewer than five Whig Free Soilers, including Orin Fowler of Massachusetts, New

---

68. Joseph G. Rayback, *Martin Van Buren* (New York, 1982), pp. 31-32; William A. DeGregorio, *The Complete Book of U.S. Presidents* (Fort Lee, N.J., 2001), pp. 132-133.

Hampshire's Jared Perkins, Samuel Brenton of Indiana and Michigan's Ebenezer J. Penniman and James L. Conger. The party also played a key role in Galusha Grow's victory on a Democratic-Free Soil fusion ticket in Pennsylvania. The Free Soilers also sent three antislavery veterans back to Washington on its own ticket. The most famous of the three was incumbent Whig Congressman Horace B. Mann of Massachusetts. Mann was initially elected to Congress in 1848 when he won the seat held for seventeen years by the late John Quincy Adams. As founder and secretary of the state board of education, Mann had completely revamped the Massachusetts public school system, making it a model for the rest of the nation. Running on the Free Soil ticket, Mann swamped his Whig and Democratic rivals to win a second term in Congress. Two other members of Congress re-elected on the Free Soil ticket in 1850 were James D. Doty of Wisconsin, a one-time land speculator, and Pennsylvania's John W. Howe, a Whig congressman. Like Mann, Doty was a longtime Democrat who had grown disillusioned with his party over the slavery issue. In seeking re-election on the Free Soil ticket, the 51-year-old incumbent lawmaker and one-time Mississippi River explorer piled up more than 67% of the vote against his hapless Democratic rival. In addition, Thomas Bartlett, Jr., a 44-year-old lawyer and former state legislator from Vermont, was also elected to Congress that year on the Free Soil ticket, garnering 55% of the vote against his Whig and Democratic opponents to capture one of the state's four U.S. House seats. Bartlett lost his seat two years later after his district was gerrymandered as a result of congressional reapportionment when Vermont lost one of its four U.S. House seats.

Though the Free Soil Party held only eight seats in the 32nd Congress, the antislavery party came within an eyelash of winning in the 4th congressional district of Massachusetts, where former Whig congressman John G. Palfrey, a 54-year-old Unitarian minister and former state legislator who broke with the Whigs over the Wilmot Proviso, lost a heart-breaking race to an incumbent Whig by only 87 votes in a contest that included three runoff elections. A graduate of Harvard, Palfrey had come to grips with the issue of slavery in 1843 when his father, who owned a sugar plantation in Louisiana, passed away and left him twenty slaves. He freed the slaves and brought them to Boston at his own expense. A former editor of the *North American Review*, the scholarly Palfrey later angered those in his own party when he harshly condemned the Cotton Whigs while outlining the South's offenses in a series of scathing articles under the heading "Papers on the Slave Power."[69]

---

69.   Foner, *Free Soil, Free Labor, Free Men*, p. 92; Blue, *The Free Soilers*, p. 37.

In addition to Palfrey, the Free Soilers also waged competitive races in at least a half-dozen other House contests in Maine, Massachusetts and Vermont. In the second district of Massachusetts, for example, perennial Free Soil candidate Samuel E. Sewall, a 51-year-old lawyer, veteran Garrisonian abolitionist and ex-Liberty Party member, polled over twenty-two percent of the vote against his Whig and Democratic rivals, and in Vermont, a Free Soil congressional candidate garnered over twenty-eight percent of the vote in a three-cornered race won by a Whig.

5

Free Democrats, Southern Rights and Native Americans

❖

Third-Party Movements in the Early 1850s

The Liberty and Free Soil parties, however, weren't alone in their single-minded preoccupation with the slavery issue. A small pro-slavery states rights party centered in Alabama and Georgia, known as the Southern Rights Party and operating independently of both the national Whigs and the Democrats, was quite concerned with the issue, too, but obviously for very different reasons. Infuriated and embittered by the growing prospect of a peace treaty with Mexico that might include the Wilmot Proviso, southern politicians, led by former Georgia governor Charles J. McDonald and Henry L. Benning, a fiery Georgia Democrat who favored his state's withdrawal from the Union and the creation of a Southern Republic, met in Nashville, Tennessee, in June 1850 to discuss an appropriate political strategy for the South. Fearing that slavery might be banned in the vast new territory in what is today the entire southwestern part of the United States, there was much talk of secession at the convention, but the delegates adjourned without agreeing on a specific course of action.

While the southern delegates were gathered in Nashville, Henry Clay, Daniel Webster, Georgia congressman Alexander Stephens and other national leaders worked feverishly to iron-out a compromise, which was eventually adopted by Congress. The Compromise of 1850, adopted in five separate measures, was designed to placate southern moderates as well as northerners opposed to the extension of slavery into the territories, permitted California to enter the Union as a free state, prohibited slavery in the District of Columbia and satisfied Texas in her disputed boundary claims. The Compromise also included the adoption of a new fugitive slave law and, to the delight of proslavery southerners, dropped the much-dreaded Wilmot Proviso.

While Clay, Webster and others worried about how the Compromise would be received in the South, most southern politicians looked to Georgia, the "Empire State" of that region, for guidance. Georgia was expected to decide the question at a convention scheduled for the fall in Milledgeville. Needless to say, a spirited campaign for delegates to the Milledgeville convention ensued.

The secessionists waged an all-out effort to win delegates, importing such notable speakers as Robert Barnwell Rhett, the colorful former South Carolina congressman who carried his heartfelt dream of a separate and free South to his grave more than a quarter-century later. Rhett, the invective publisher of the *Charleston Mercury*, succeeded the legendary John C. Calhoun in the U.S. Senate following Calhoun's death in 1850 and later helped organize the Confederacy. (Rhett, of course, later grew deeply embittered when he failed to win the presidency of the Confederacy and was then passed over by Jefferson Davis for a cabinet post in the newly formed southern government that he had worked so diligently to create.) They also heard from Alabama's William Yancey, a cotton grower and well-known secessionist. The 36-year-old Yancey was once elected to the U.S. House but resigned before the end of his term because he felt Congress had too little power. Sparing few adjectives, Rhett and Yancey vigorously denounced the Compromise of 1850.

Along with renowned Whig congressmen Alexander Stephens and Robert Toombs, Howell Cobb, the Democratic Speaker of the U.S. House of Representatives, rallied the state's anti-secessionist forces and was able to hold sway over the Milledgeville gathering in December. Stephens' presence in the anti-secessionist movement no doubt made the difference. After all, the man who would later become vice president of the Confederacy was respected, if not revered, by Georgians on both sides of the issue.

Lamenting the fact that the South had suffered great provocation, the Milledgeville delegates adopted the famous "Georgia Platform," which recommended acceptance of Henry Clay's Compromise of 1850 as the only way to preserve the Union. But the Georgia delegates, in no uncertain terms, made it clear to the North that they had reached their limit and would recede no further. As expected, the other southern states, ignoring the desperate pleas of Rhett, Yancey and other outright secessionists, followed Georgia's lead and opted to stay in the Union, at least temporarily.

The Compromise of 1850 sharply divided politics in the Deep South, seriously undermining the Second American Party System in that region. Two new parties—the Union and Southern Rights parties—sprang up from this division in Georgia, Alabama, and Mississippi, temporarily replacing the Democratic and Whig parties in those states. Nowhere was this break more pronounced than in Georgia. In that state, radical states' rights advocates, deeply dissatisfied with the outcome of the Milledgeville convention, organized the short-lived Southern Rights Party and nominated Charles J. McDonald, a leader at the Nashville convention, for governor in 1851. The Southern Rights Party was also active in neighboring Alabama and Mississippi.

The 58-year-old McDonald, a former Democrat, had served as governor of the Peach State from 1839-43. Frustrated not only by the lingering economic effects of the Panic of 1837, but also by a Whig-dominated legislature, McDonald, as governor, pushed for the establishment of a State Supreme Court, biennial sessions of the legislature and improved education. Not afraid to take unpopular positions, he called for increased taxes during his second term to reduce the state's mounting debts—an idea that was widely rejected by the Whig legislature. McDonald retaliated by threatening to withhold the legislators' salaries until all of the state's general expenses were paid, but his threat ultimately proved empty.

Meanwhile, the state's moderate forces, led by Cobb, Toombs, and Stephens, formed the Constitutional Union Party, a forerunner of sorts to the party of 1860 that shared its name. The moderates nominated Cobb for governor. A 36-year-old member of the wealthy plantation class that dominated politics in the antebellum South, Cobb, who had a relatively safe seat in Congress from a predominately non-slaveholding district in Georgia's hill country, had little trouble defeating his Southern Rights rival in the 1851 gubernatorial campaign, garnering 57,414 votes to McDonald's 38,824. In addition to Cobb's overwhelming success at the polls, the Unionists also elected ten congressmen, including six from Georgia, three from Mississippi and one from Alabama. Suddenly, the southern Unionists replaced the antislavery Free Soilers as the leading third-party bloc in the U.S. House of Representatives. Georgia's Alexander Stephens and Robert Toombs were among the successful Union Party congressional candidates that year, with Stephen's winning a seat in the House and Toombs taking a seat in the U.S. Senate. In Alabama, where the Unionists had trounced their prosecession Southern Rights opponents led by the fiery William Lowndes Yancey in the state's 1851 legislative elections, playwright and newspaper publisher William R. Smith eked out a narrow 59-vote victory over a Southern Rights Democrat, becoming one of eight other Unionists to win a seat in Congress. In Mississippi, the Union Party's Henry S. Foote, a pro-Compromise Democratic senator, narrowly defeated Southern Rights Party candidate Jefferson Davis, an outspoken critic of the Compromise of 1850, to win that state's hard-fought gubernatorial race.[1]

The Southern Rights Party also enjoyed some modest success at the ballot box that year, winning two U.S. House seats in Georgia and one in Mississippi, the latter being Albert Gallatin Brown, a former governor and congressman who had been in the forefront of most congressional debates during this period. The 38-year-old Brown, a wealthy lawyer and planter, had been frequently mentioned as a possible candidate for the presidency.

With the signing of the Compromise of 1850, a number of Whigs and Democrats in the North and South alike hoped to use the measure as a springboard for a new national party committed to the Compromise as a final solution to the troublesome question of slavery. Though Free Soil advocates sharply opposed the Compromise of 1850 and the accompanying Fugitive Slave Law, many of them, including Ohio's Joshua R. Giddings, welcomed a breakup of the country's two major parties, believing that neither party had dealt honestly with the issue of slavery and predicting that the Whigs and Democrats would "soon be swallowed up by the Unionists."[2]

Taking note of the relatively nonpartisan nature of Zachary Taylor's successful campaign in 1848, Daniel Webster of Massachusetts, who still thirsted for the presidency, was one of the first prominent figures in either major party to call for the creation of a Union Party made up of pro-Compromise Whigs and Democrats. Dating back to the 1820s, Webster, a one-time Federalist, had long deplored the rise of mass political parties. Impressed by recent nonpartisan mass meetings in the North in support of the Compromise—including a huge Castle Garden meeting organized by New York Democrats on the eve of that state's 1850 elections—Webster believed it was time to abandon the old parties. "If any considerable body of the Whigs of the North shall act in the spirit of the recent convention in New York," he said in the fall of that year, "a new arrangement of parties in unavoidable. There must be a Union Party, and an opposing party under some name, I know not what—very likely the party of Liberty." Webster then set out to win the nomination of the party that hadn't yet been formed—and never would be.[3] But the former Massachusetts lawmaker wasn't alone. The highly regarded Henry Clay of Kentucky, arguably the most promi-

1.   Michael F. Holt, *The Political Crisis of the 1850s* (New York, 1978), p. 92.
2.   Michael F. Holt, *The Rise and Fall of the American Whig Party: Jacksonian Politics and the Onset of the Civil War* (New York, 1999), p. 617.
3.   Holt, *The Political Crisis of the 1850s*, p. 91.

nent Whig in the country, also spoke out in favor of a new Union Party. Speaking at a barbeque in Lexington, Kentucky, in October of that year, Clay endorsed the idea of a new party and in a speech a month later before a special joint session of the Kentucky legislature, predicted that opposition to the Compromise and the Fugitive Slave Law "will lead to the formation of two new parties, one for the union and the other against the union."[4]

Despite the sincere efforts of some of the southern pro-Compromise men in Georgia, Alabama, and Mississippi—almost all of whom pushed for the formation of a new national Union Party—the effort soon fizzled out and Webster, having failed to engineer a spontaneous presidential endorsement under the movement's banner in Massachusetts, geared up for another forlorn quest for the Whig Party's nomination.[5]

John P. Hale and the Free Democrats

At its last national convention, a rousing affair held in Pittsburgh in August 1852, the Free Soilers, formally adopting the name "Free Democratic Party," nominated Senator John P. Hale of New Hampshire for president. Facing only token opposition, the quick-witted Hale received 193 votes on the first ballot to a scattering of fifteen votes for radical abolitionist Gerrit Smith, Ohio's Salmon P. Chase and a handful of others. Smith, who declined the National Liberty Party's presidential nomination earlier in the year, hoped to influence the Free Soil platform, but his minority plank was apparently too radical for a majority of the Free Soilers. His minority plank, which called for political rights for everyone regardless of race or sex, was overwhelmingly rejected in a favor of resolutions written by Ohio's Joshua Giddings.

The party's vice presidential nomination unexpectedly went to Indiana's George Washington Julian, a former Free Soil congressman whose Quaker upbringing propelled him into the antislavery movement. In a race that initially included Kentucky's abolitionist sensation Cassius M. Clay, Julian stunned almost everyone—including himself—by polling 104 votes on the first ballot to 83 for front-runner Samuel Lewis and a scattering of 23 votes for others. Lewis, a Free Soil leader in Ohio and one of the party's most popular vote getters, was

---

4.   Clay's speech to the Kentucky legislature, November 15, 1850, Henry Clay MSS (Library of Congress), quoted in Holt, *The Rise and Fall of the American Whig Party*, p. 607.

5.   Holt, *The Political Crisis of the 1850s*, pp. 91-94.

reportedly hampered by the behind-the-scenes machinations of Salmon P. Chase and Judge Rufus P. Spalding, who quietly abandoned their home state favorite in favor of Julian, who just happened to be Chase's son-in-law. A staunch supporter of homestead legislation while in Congress, Julian was also aided by the presence of a hardy contingent of land reformers at the Pittsburgh convention who initially hoped to nominate George Henry Evans, but later threw their support to the former Indiana congressman when it became clear that Evans wouldn't be selected as Hale's running mate. Julian's nomination came as such a surprise that even his uncle, Henry Hoover, a devoted supporter of the Free Soil Party who would have been delighted by Julian's nomination, failed to mention his nephew's name earlier in the year when he expressed his preference for a Hale-Clay ticket.[6] In any event, the 35-year-old Julian, a splendidly literate and persuasive writer who rarely failed to get his point across, was a superb choice for the gritty and fearless antislavery party.

As in 1848, the party again adopted a forward-looking platform, which attacked slavery, condemned the Compromise and Fugitive Slave Law, advocated a homestead policy, cheap postage and river and harbor improvements. In foreign affairs, the Free Soilers called for peaceful arbitration of international disputes and championed independence for Haiti, suggesting that it should be given "most favored nations" status. Taking a swipe at the emerging Know-Nothing Party, the Free Soil platform stated that, "emigrants and exiles from the Old World should find a cordial welcome to homes of comfort and fields of enterprise" in the New World and asserted that any attempt to abridge their right of attaining citizenship and property "ought to be resisted with inflexible determination."

A man of unusual wit and eloquence, John Parker Hale, the eldest of twelve children, was born in Rochester, New Hampshire, in 1806. He was educated at the prestigious Phillips Exeter Academy before enrolling at Bowdoin College in Brunswick, Maine, where he studied law. After graduating, Hale established a law practice in Dover, New Hampshire. A compelling and gifted speaker, the young lawyer developed a reputation for his uncanny ability to sway juries. In 1832, Hale was elected to the state legislature and two years later President Jackson, impressed by the young legislator's persuasive skills, appointed him to the post of U.S. Attorney for the district of New Hampshire. From early in his career, Hale had always championed the rights of blacks and defended fugitive slaves in court

---

6. Patrick W. Riddleberger, *George Washington Julian: Radical Republican, A Study in Nineteenth-Century Politics and Reform* (Indianapolis, 1966), pp. 85-86.

on numerous occasions, earning him a testimonial from African-Americans in Boston. In the late 1850s, while serving in the U.S. Senate, he joined James Harlan of Iowa, New Hampshire's Daniel Clark and Charles Durkee of Wisconsin in attempting to have a provision for the education of African-American children included in the District of Columbia school bill. And a few years later, while a number of prominent Republicans were seriously debating the idea of adding a colonization plank to the Republican Party's 1860 platform, Hale denounced it as "one of the most absurd ideas" ever proposed.

Hale's political career was anything but ordinary, particularly for a politician of the 1850s. He was elected to Congress as a Democrat in 1843, but running for re-election as an independent was defeated two years later, finishing ninth in a crowded field for one of the state's four at-large seats. A man of strong convictions, he was literally drummed out of the Democratic Party that year because of his strong abolitionist views, prompting a "Hale storm," which prevented his replacement from winning election to Congress. New Hampshire legislators had ousted Hale shortly after the independent-minded lawmaker wrote a letter to his constituents denouncing the annexation of Texas. Supporters throughout the state—and, indeed, from across the country—immediately rallied to his defense. Among them was poet John Greenleaf Whittier, who heartily praised Hale's uncommon courage and commitment. A short time later, Hale returned to the state legislature where, without any partisan support whatsoever, he was elected to the U.S. Senate as an independent in 1847—becoming only the second full-fledged antislavery member of that body.

As the only independent in the Senate, Hale was initially ignored and frequently denounced by his fellow lawmakers. Much to his credit, however, he was able to keep most of his detractors at bay with his quick wit, sarcasm and good-natured personality. "He kept down the ire of his enemies by compelling them to laugh at the moral grotesqueness of the attitude in which he placed them," recalled George W. Julian, Hale's vice-presidential running mate in the 1852 campaign.[7] During his first two years in office, Hale virtually stood alone against the powerful proslavery interests in the Senate and basked in his role as agitator. "I glory in the name of agitator," he told his colleagues. "I wish the country could be agitated vastly more than it is." Though perhaps best known for his ardent antislavery views, the fiercely independent-minded reformer took the greatest sat-

---

7.   Julian, George W., "A Presidential Candidate of 1852," *The Century Magazine*, October 1896.

isfaction in his efforts to secure legislation prohibiting flogging in the navy and for his tireless work in improving conditions for the nation's naval seamen.

Having survived a charge of influence peddling as chairman of the Senate's Naval Affairs Committee, the colorful Hale was not without controversy. Much later in his career, he was removed from his post as Andrew Johnson's minister to Spain for allegedly dallying with the Queen. Upon his return to New Hampshire in 1870, shortly after the scandal broke, the popular former lawmaker was given a hero's welcome.

George W. Julian, Hale's co-star in the 1852 campaign, was not only a fervent abolitionist but also a sharp critic of the growing nativist movement, which he described as the "crowning and indelible shame of our politics." Long after the Free Soil Party vanished from American life, Julian continued in public service. In addition to being one of the founders of the Republican Party in Indiana, he was elected to five more terms in Congress and, much later in his life, served as President Grover Cleveland's surveyor general of New Mexico from 1885-89.

The Compromise of 1850 and the Fugitive Slave Law haunted the country's two major parties in the months leading up the 1852 presidential election. Anti-slavery Whigs in the North, convinced that the Compromise was a sell-out to the "Slave Power," and reactionary southern states' rights Democrats, believing that the Compromise largely benefited the North, tried as they might to influence the Whig and Democratic parties. Opposition to the Compromise within the two major parties was so great at times that there was even some talk among its supporters of forming a third party—a so-called "Union Party"—to rally support for the widely-disparaged compromise legislation.

While Hale launched his national campaign, Gerrit Smith's miniscule National Liberty Party, hoping to pressure Hale and the Free Soil Democrats into adopting a stronger antislavery position, nominated 59-year-old William Goodell for president. The party's platform, penned by Smith, called for an end to racial discrimination in the North and prophetically predicted that the Free Democrats would suffer the same fate as the Free Soilers of 1848 if they didn't call for immediate abolition, rather than the mere containment of slavery.

Believing that slavery was unconstitutional and could no longer be protected by Congress, Goodell helped to organize the American Anti-Slavery Society in 1833 and began publication of the *Emancipator*, the Society's official organ, a short time later. One of the original founders of the Liberty Party in 1840, Goodell authored at least five books on the subject of slavery. In 1843, he established a church in Honeoye, New York, where he preached a steady diet of temperance and abolitionist views to his parishioners. Convinced that the Liberty Party platform was too narrow, the self-styled minister left the party in 1847 and founded the Liberty League in Macedon Locke, New York, later that same year. His new party, which nominated Gerrit Smith for president the following year, advocated prohibition and called for an immediate end to slavery, tariffs, land monopolies and secret societies. In the meantime, Goodell's 1852 candidacy petered out almost before it got started, but not before winning public endorsements from Frederick Douglass and several other prominent African-American leaders.

Having passed over such notables as Lewis Cass, the party's aging 1848 nominee, Pennsylvania's James Buchanan, former Secretary of War William L. Marcy of New York and brash newcomer Stephen A. Douglas of Illinois, the Democrats chose little-known Franklin Pierce of New Hampshire on the forty-ninth ballot at their June convention in Baltimore. Pierce's nomination was owed, in large part, to the tireless efforts of former congressman Edmund Burke, a 39-year-old New Hampshire newspaper editor, who had painstakingly cultivated the support of party leaders in the South. Senator William R. King of Alabama, a 66-year-old plantation owner and former minister to France, was nominated for the vice presidency. As in 1848, the Democrats again approved a "safe" platform, promising to "abide by, and adhere to" the Compromise of 1850 and the Fugitive Slave Law.

Virtually unknown to most voters, Pierce, a fluent if not gifted speaker, served in both houses of Congress with little distinction. In some respects, this was an asset. Having retired from Congress in 1842—long before the issue of slavery came to dominate the nation's political discourse—the 47-year-old former lawmaker had few political enemies and almost no political baggage. Pierce clearly didn't achieve the hero status of his Whig opponent, General Winfield Scott, but he had compiled a fairly impressive war record during the Mexican War. Unfortunately, Pierce allegedly had a drinking problem earlier in his life and the Whigs made the most of it during the campaign, describing the New Hampshire Democrat as "a hero of many a well-fought bottle."[8]

Passing over Daniel Webster, arguably the country's most respected lawyer and statesman, while simultaneously rejecting President Millard Fillmore's bid for the nomination, the tired Whig delegates nominated General Scott on the fifty-third ballot at their national convention, which was held at Baltimore's Maryland Institute Hall eleven days after the Democrats adjourned from the same building. William A. Graham of North Carolina, the Secretary of the Navy,

---

8.   Stefan Lorant, *The Glorious Burden: The American Presidency* (New York, 1968), p. 210.

was chosen as Scott's vice-presidential running mate. The Whigs adopted a platform that upheld states' rights and acquiesced in the Compromise while condemning further agitation on the slavery issue.

In nominating the 66-year-old war hero, the Whigs hoped to repeat their earlier electoral successes of General William Henry Harrison in 1840 and General Zachary Taylor in 1848. Harrison and Taylor were the only Whigs to ever win the presidency. Taylor, of course, died in office in 1850 and was succeeded by Vice President Millard Fillmore. Naturally, Whig politicians were quick to jump on the Scott bandwagon, hailing the Mexican War hero as a kind of reincarnated Andrew Jackson and latter-day savior of the American frontier. Holding only two-dozen of the 62 seats in the U.S. Senate and winning only 88 seats in the 1850-51 mid-term congressional elections, the Whigs were a party in serious decline. They needed a winner—and they needed one badly.

A bear of a man, Scott, who stood six-feet-six and weighed 250 pounds, was a career soldier and actively served every president from Jefferson to Lincoln. A Virginian by birth, he first received public acclaim for his courage at Chippewa and Lundy's Lane in the War of 1812. He also fought in the Black Hawk War in 1832 and led the Creek and Seminole campaigns in Florida in 1836. In peacetime, Scott also proved to be something of a diplomat, safely transporting some 16,000 displaced Cherokee Indians across the Mississippi in the late 1830s, helping to ease border tensions with Canada, and bringing about concessions that ultimately averted war with Great Britain during the Maine boundary imbroglio. Scott, who was seriously considered for the Whig presidential nomination in 1840 and 1848, was named General-in-Chief of the Army in 1841—a post he held for the next twenty years. In that role, he modernized the country's military administration and improved the army's officer training program. His most brilliant hour, however, came during the Mexican War, which erupted shortly after the annexation of Texas in 1845. Hampered by political backstabbing in Washington and an ill-equipped army, Scott devised an ingenious military strategy in which he led his troops through the rugged mountainous terrain from Vera Cruz to Mexico City, routing the Mexican army in the process. As was the case with Zachary Taylor four years earlier, the Mexican War served as a launching pad for Scott's presidential candidacy—one that proved virtually unstoppable.

In many respects, "Old Fuss and Feathers"—a nickname he earned due to his meticulous manner and penchant for gaudy uniforms—was an ideal candidate for the down-and-out Whigs. Like Pierce, he didn't have a political record that had to be explained away. By the same token, he was no political novice. His years in Washington made him keenly aware of the rough and tumble of Ameri-

can politics. Whig leaders were confident that Scott, a southerner with unquestionable loyalty to the Union, would be discreet enough on crucial issues,
especially slavery, to prevent the Whig Party from splitting in two. Though the
general had personally lobbied for passage of the Compromise in Congress, his
advisers cautioned him to steer clear of the issue for fear of alienating antislavery
Whigs in the North. Moreover, they believed that a majority of voters would
simply vote for him based on his war record in much the same way they had supported Zachary Taylor four years earlier.

But the Whig strategists were wrong. Scott's silence on the Compromise actually caused a greater schism within his own party than if he had spoken out forthrightly on the issue. As a consequence, Whigs on both sides of the issue were
looking for an alternative in the election—the antislavery Whigs in the North
finding their home in Hale's insurgent Free Democratic candidacy.

There were also rumblings from disenchanted southern Whigs, many of
whom were deeply disappointed by Scott's failure to state his position on the
Compromise and the Fugitive Slave Law. William H. Seward's strong support of
Scott only served to intensify the suspicions of many Whig leaders in the South.
Deeply disturbed by Scott's nomination, nine southern Whig lawmakers, led by
Georgia's Robert Toombs and Alexander Stephens, spearheaded a drive to run
70-year-old Daniel Webster, a one-time states' rights advocate, on an independent ticket in the fall. These southern Whigs had nowhere else to turn. Similarly,
a group of Webster's supporters in his native Massachusetts also intended to support electors committed to their favorite son.

For all intents and purposes, the Webster movement was launched at a
national convention of the tiny Native American Party in Trenton, New Jersey,
in early July. Delegates from nine states—Georgia, Illinois, Maryland, Massachusetts, New Jersey, New York, Ohio, Pennsylvania and Virginia—attended the
convention. Following a lengthy debate on whether or not to field a ticket in the
1852 presidential election, a number of nativist delegates bolted from the Trenton convention. The remaining delegates then proceeded to nominate Webster
on the twelfth ballot, giving the ailing Massachusetts statesman 27 votes to Kim-
ber Cleaver's four. The little-known Cleaver had been the party's gubernatorial
candidate in Pennsylvania in 1851. Webster's nomination was later made unanimous.

This was the second attempt by the fledgling anti-foreign and anti-Catholic
party to field a presidential ticket. Meeting in Philadelphia in September 1847,
the small nativist party nominated Mexican War hero Zachary Taylor—the eventual Whig nominee—and Mayor Henry A. Dearborn of Roxbury, Massachusetts,

for president and vice president, respectively. A lawyer and prolific writer, the 64-year-old Dearborn had served in the Massachusetts state Senate and in the U.S. House as an independent.[9]

After nominating Webster, the anti-immigration party then selected George C. Washington, a grandnephew of America's first president, as Webster's vice-presidential running mate. While Webster neither accepted nor declined the party's nomination, Washington, learning of his nomination from newspaper accounts, declined the honor. The Native Americans then replaced Washington with Dr. Reynell Coates, a Quaker from Camden, New Jersey. Coates had initially opposed the idea of fielding a presidential ticket that year.

The little-known Coates lived a varied life. His pursuits included medicine, science, politics and poetry, to mention but a few of his many interests. One of his most curious enterprises was the founding of the Patriotic Order, Sons of America, a highly secretive nativist society started in Philadelphia in 1847. His organization, limited to white, native-born anti-Catholics, was quite powerful during the Know-Nothing period of the 1850s but languished during the Civil War. Long outliving its founder, the Order was still spewing white supremacy at the turn of the century, claiming to be fighting for "those cherished ideas that have made us a distinctly separate and prosperous race"—ideas that they insisted were facing "utter annihilation" in 1900. As late as 1960, Coates' organization still existed and maintained a small headquarters in Chicago.

The draft-Webster movement fizzled out when the great orator died on October 24, only nine days before the election. Learning of Webster's death, the Native Americans quickly substituted Jacob Broom of Philadelphia as their presidential standard-bearer while Webster's Whig supporters in Georgia, Massachusetts and elsewhere still had an opportunity to vote for presidential electors pledged to their fallen leader.

---

9. Curiously, New York's Barnburner faction also considered Zachary Taylor as a presidential possibility during this period, partly because the Mexican War hero had indicated a willingness to seek the presidency as an independent and partly because he had expressed tacit approval of some of the Barnburners' ideas. Among others, former President Martin Van Buren, who later emerged as the Free Soil Party's candidate for president in 1848, mentioned the possibility of a Taylor candidacy if the Barnburners were to bolt from the Democratic Party. As such, the Barnburners apparently concocted an elaborate strategy to deny Taylor the Whig Party's nomination, thereby freeing him to run as a third-party candidate. See *New York Herald*, June 13, 1848; Blue, *The Free Soilers*, pp. 46n, 53n.

The adamantly proslavery Southern Rights Party also made a cameo appearance in the presidential campaign of 1852. Earlier that year, the party tried to draft George Michael Troup, Georgia's militant ex-governor, for the White House with former Mississippi Gov. John A. Quitman, one of the South's most vocal secessionists during the crisis of 1850, as his running mate. Both men, however, refused the party's nominations.

The 71-year-old Troup, who waged a protracted battle with the federal government over removal of the Creek Indians, had retired from active politics nearly two decades earlier while the fire-breathing Quitman, a brigadier-general in the Mexican War, was too busy mending political fences in Mississippi following his acquittal on charges of violating the nation's neutrality laws, to undertake a national campaign.

Of the two, Quitman, a staunch states' rights advocate, was probably the most controversial. A one-time Lutheran seminary student and adjunct professor of English, Quitman moved to Natchez, Mississippi, while in his early twenties and began a law practice. Though born and raised in New York, Quitman was southern to the core, embracing the values and culture of his adopted state. Winning a seat in the Mississippi House of Representatives when he was twenty-eight, the transplanted New Yorker quickly climbed the political ladder, serving as president of the State Senate in 1835 and as acting governor following the resignation of Hiram G. Runnels later that fall. During the Mexican War, he served with General Zachary Taylor in northern Mexico and with General Winfield Scott in his assault on Mexico City in 1847, later serving as the civil and military governor of Mexico City during the U.S. occupation—the only American to ever serve in that capacity. Returning to Mississippi following the war, Quitman was a serious contender for the Democratic vice-presidential nomination in 1848 and was elected governor of the Magnolia State in 1849, garnering fifty-nine percent of the vote against his Whig rival.

One of the region's most outspoken slavery advocates, Quitman, who had threatened secession during the Compromise crisis of 1850, believed that the nation's slaveholders had been swindled out of a part of Texas by a boundary dispute that favored the territory of New Mexico. He was also frustrated by what he perceived as southern interests being hemmed in by the western territories and the northern states. Seeking the extension of slavery outside the U.S. borders, Quitman helped finance revolutionary leader Narciso Lopez's efforts to recruit mercenaries for a Cuban uprising. The expansion of slavery, of course, was a high southern priority. "The desire that Cuba should be acquired as a Southern conquest, is almost unanimous among Southern men," remarked one observer at the time.[10]

Before approaching Quitman, Lopez, a handsome and charismatic Cuban exile, had asked Mississippi Sen. Jefferson Davis and Robert E. Lee, a veteran of the Mexican War, to lead his soldiers of fortune against the Cuban aristocracy, but both men declined. Quitman, on the other hand, was intrigued by the idea and, though unable to abandon his responsibilities as governor and personally lead Lopez's troops, raised a considerable amount of money for the 600-man mercenary army. Although the uprising never materialized—Lopez and his army were forced to flee to Key West, barely outracing a Spanish warship after capturing the town of Cardenas in northwest Cuba and burning the governor's mansion—Quitman, Lopez and several other prominent southerners were later indicted for violating U.S. neutrality laws.[11] Facing arrest, the Mississippi governor threatened to use his state's militia to thwart federal marshals, but eventually resigned from office and surrendered. The charges against Quitman and the other conspirators were later dropped when three hung juries failed to convict one of the defendants, a Mississippi planter.

Aside from the controversial Compromise of 1850, which both major candidates avoided talking about, the hopelessly dull presidential campaign of 1852 was virtually issueless and the campaign quickly degenerated into a name-calling free-for-all, with both parties trading scurrilous personal accusations on an almost daily basis. Democrat Franklin Pierce was unfairly labeled a coward for his role in the Mexican War and, although he hadn't had a drink in years, was frequently criticized as a drunkard. On the other hand, Winfield Scott, the swashbuckling Whig candidate who appeared in full military regalia during a campaign swing of the North, was ridiculed as a "pompous ass."

With the admission of California to the Union two years earlier, thirty-one states took part in the 1852 presidential election. On Election Day, Pierce, carrying every state except for Kentucky, Massachusetts, Tennessee and Vermont, swamped his Whig rival by a margin of 1,607,510 to 1,386,942, tallying 254 electoral votes to Scott's forty-two. Free Soil candidate John P. Hale, who polled 155,210 votes nationally, finished ahead of one of his major party opponents in no fewer than 153 counties and carried eight counties in Iowa, Ohio, Vermont and Wisconsin. Decimated by the return of the Barnburners to the Democratic

---

10. McPherson, *Battle Cry of Freedom*, p. 107.
11. Cuban officials executed Lopez and fifty others following a subsequent attempt to free Cuba from Spanish rule in 1851.

fold in New York, Hale's showing represented a forty-seven percent decline from Van Buren's total on the Free Soil ticket four years earlier. Moreover, the party captured only 6.6 percent of the vote in the free states. "The moral tone of the Free States never was more thoroughly broken," lamented Charles Francis Adams shortly before the election.[12]

Meanwhile, little-known Jacob Broom, the Native American Party's last-minute substitute for the late Daniel Webster, polled a dismal 2,566 votes in three states and the reluctant Southern Rights ticket of Troup and Quitman, carrying Barbour and Lowndes counties in Alabama, tallied 2,331 votes, or less than one-tenth of one percent of the national total. Apparently preferring a dead orator to two living mutes, nearly 7,000 voters in Georgia and Massachusetts cast their ballots for the late Daniel Webster.

The Free Soil Party, which fielded a total of seventy-nine candidates in the 1852-53 congressional elections, captured only four seats in the U.S. House of Representatives, including the race in New York's twenty-second district where wealthy philanthropist and abolitionist Gerrit Smith, garnering in excess of forty percent of the vote, defeated his Democratic and Whig opponents.[13] While Free Soil candidates waged competitive races in almost every congressional district in Massachusetts, only one of the party's eleven candidates for the U.S. House was successful. Even Charles Francis Adams went down to defeat, losing a closely-contested runoff election to Whig J. Wiley Emands by 438 votes in a four-cornered race. The Free Soil Party's Gershorn B. Weston also came up short, narrowly losing a similar runoff election to Whig Samuel L. Crocker, a wealthy copper manufacturer, by a scant 154 votes in the state's second congressional district. Educator Horace Mann garnered 38,763 votes while placing a close third in the state's gubernatorial contest. Elsewhere, the party also waged somewhat competitive gubernatorial campaigns in New Hampshire and Vermont where former state treasurer John Atwood and ex-Liberty Party activist Lawrence Brainerd garnered 15.7% and 19.6%, respectively. In Michigan, lawyer and newspaper publisher Isaac P. Christiancy, a former state senator who later served as chief justice of the Michigan Supreme Court and as a Republican member of the U.S. Senate, garnered seven percent of the vote against his Democratic and Whig rivals.

The stridently anti-Catholic and anti-immigration American Party, which fielded ten candidates for the U.S. House in New Jersey, New York and Pennsyl-

---

12.   Potter, *The Impending Crisis*, p. 228.
13.   The other Free Soilers elected to Congress in 1852-53 included Alexander DeWitt of Massachusetts and Joshua R. Giddings and Edward Wade of Ohio.

vania, failed to win a single seat. The party's strongest showing occurred in Philadelphia's first congressional district where former congressman and lawyer Lewis C. Levin, the fiery publisher of the native American *Sun*, received more than 26% of the vote against his Democratic and Whig rivals in a failed attempt to regain his former seat. The party also made a strong showing in Philadelphia's fourth congressional district when Oliver P. Cornman, a former Native American Party member of the Pennsylvania Senate, garnered 2,063 votes, or more than sixteen percent of the total, while losing to a Democrat in a four-cornered race. Two independents—William H. Bissell of Illinois and Caleb Lyon of New York—also won seats in the 33rd Congress. A Democrat-turned-Republican, Bissell later served as governor of Illinois and the 29-year-old Lyon, a world traveler, poet, author and artist who was once described as a "polished misfit," later served as the Lincoln-appointed territorial governor of Idaho—a post from which he successfully negotiated a treaty with the Shoshone Indians.

6

Parties in Disarray

◆

The Nativist Movement Gains Ground

Given a name perhaps more aptly suited for both major political parties in America today, the Know-Nothing Party was founded in 1847. By far the most successful third party in American history, the party's origins can be traced back to local third-party movements of the 1830s and early 1840s.

Curiously, one of the first nativists to run for public office on a third-party ticket was Samuel F.B. Morse, better known as the author of the Morse code and the inventor of the telegraph. Born and raised in Charlestown, Massachusetts, Morse was the son of prominent minister Jedidiah Morse. His father, like many other Protestant revivalists of his day, frequently denounced Catholicism and "Popery" from his pulpit and occasionally launched into sermons against the Bavarian Illuminati, the mysterious secret order that he and others claimed had taken control of the French Revolution and was now seeking to gain control of America. Upon graduating from Yale, the younger Morse studied painting in England before returning to the United States in 1815. As an artist specializing in history painting for which there was a very limited market, he was barely able to eke out a living. He was particularly disappointed when his depiction of "The Old House of Representatives" failed to bring him the kind of prominence enjoyed by Charles Wilson Peale, Gilbert Stuart, Col. John Trumbull and other famous artists of the period. Dejected, Morse became an artist-for-hire, turning to painting portraits to support himself.

In 1829, the 38-year-old Morse traveled to Europe, hoping that success abroad might boost his reputation in the United States. Morse's visit to Europe, however, pointed the struggling artist in an entirely new direction. While visiting Rome, Morse was callously shoved to the pavement by a soldier when he failed to kneel down in front of a Catholic procession, thereby instilling in him a newly intensified anti-Catholicism. The bayonet-wielding soldier struck Morse's hat from his head when he was knocked to the ground and his trampled hat thereafter became something of a symbol to those in the American nativist movement. Under the pen name of "Brutus," the wily inventor, who once admired the beauty of Catholic ceremony, wrote a series of scathing newspaper articles in which he claimed that the monarchies of Europe had enlisted the aid of the Catholic Church in a scheme to subvert American democracy by flooding the American West with hordes of Catholic immigrants. With a substantial power base in the West, coupled with uncontrolled rampant Catholic immigration along the eastern seaboard, the Papacy, Morse argued, would eventually put the United States under the sway of Roman Catholic despotism.[1]

Anti-Catholicism certainly wasn't a new phenomenon in the New World. Nor was it a recent development in New York. Fear and mistrust of Catholics had long festered on these shores. In fact, Jacob Leisler, New York's German-born colonial governor, founded a vigilante group in 1688—comprised of farmers, workers and assorted opponents of the aristocrats—to guard against a rumored Catholic conspiracy in the wake of the removal of James II, a Catholic, as England's ruling monarch. He also ordered the arrest of "reputed Papists" and began an extensive campaign of routing alleged Romanists from the colony.[2]

Morse quickly became a leading spokesman for nativism and ran for mayor of New York City in 1836 as the candidate of the Native American Democratic Association, capturing a few thousand votes, or roughly six percent of the total. Founded in March 1835 by James Watson Webb, the nativist editor of the *New York Courier and Inquirer*, the organization was so successful that it soon had its own newspaper called the *Spirit of '76*. In addition to opposing the Catholic Church and the immigration of paupers and criminals to the United States, the Native American Democratic Association's platform also opposed the idea of foreign-born citizens holding public office. A schism in the fall of 1835, precipitated by the departure of a group that wanted to direct all of the organization's activities against Catholics, severely weakened the organization, but not before chapters were founded in Brooklyn, Cincinnati, Paterson, New Jersey, and New Orleans—the latter a hotbed of nativist activity.[3] During a second campaign for mayor the following year, Morse's candidacy was viciously sabotaged when newspapers on the morning of the election published a fraudulent letter stating that

---

1. Ray Allen Billington, *The Protestant Crusade 1800-1860: A Study of the Origins of American Nativism* (New York, 1938), pp. 122-123.
2. Ibid., p. 8.
3. Ibid., pp. 131-132.

inventor had withdrawn from the race and, as a result, he garnered only 77 votes in that contest while a nativist Whig ticket headed by Aaron Clark was swept into office. A highly successful banker and lottery owner, Clark—the only Whig to ever serve as mayor of New York City—tried unsuccessfully to discourage foreign immigration into the city during his two one-year terms in office. [4]

No less instrumental than Morse in fanning the fires of anti-Catholic bigotry was the fire-and-brimstone preacher Lyman Beecher, father of the famous author Harriet Beecher Stowe. From his pulpit at the Hanover Street Congregational Church in Boston, Beecher routinely railed against "the whoredom of Babylon," the "foul beast of Roman Catholicism" and the Papacy.

Shortly after his second failed attempt to capture the New York mayoralty, Morse organized the vehemently anti-Catholic American Protestant Union to preserve civil and religious liberties. Beecher became president of the organization and Morse served as one of the group's vice presidents. The Reverend Horace Bushnell of Hartford, Connecticut, soon joined them in this endeavor. Undoubtedly the most vociferous agitator in the organization, Bushnell regularly ranted against slavery, infidelity and Roman Catholicism. In his book *Barbarism Is the First Danger*, the Hartford minister predicted that the influx of Catholic immigrants would lead to national decline, resulting in savagery and Romanism.

Holding considerable sway over the Whigs and Democrats in New York City through his own Protestant Union Party, which controlled the school board, Morse's group succeeded in convincing both major parties in that city to keep foreign-born and Catholic candidates off their respective tickets. Under school superintendent William L. Stone, a former newspaperman, the Protestant Union Party-controlled school board mandated the use of the Protestant Bible in the city's public schools, prompting Bishop John Hughes to form his own third party at a mass meeting at New York's Carroll Hall.

Conceding that there was no alternative for Catholics but to build their own schools, the Bishop proceeded to organize a third party committed to the interests of the city's growing Catholic constituency. Hughes also urged his parishioners to send their children to Catholic schools. "It is a sacrifice we must make," he said. With the creation of the Carroll Hall Party, as it was named, came charges that Hughes and other Catholics really intended to rule the country. Denying any desire to affect New York's political life beyond protecting the

---

4.   Scisco, Louis Dow, "Political Nativism in New York State," *Columbia University Studies in History, Economics and Public Law* (New York, 1901), Vol. XIII, pp. 30-31.

rights of Catholics, the Hughes-led Carroll Hall Party entered New York's municipal campaign—the first and only time in American history that an all-Catholic party competed in an election. The Catholic ticket polled roughly 2,000 votes, finishing well ahead of the Native American ticket and enabling the Whigs to eke out a slim 300-vote victory.

A chorus of liked-minded anti-Catholic nativists across the country soon joined Morse, Beecher and Bushnell. Included in the choir were such respectable newspapers as the *Cincinnati Gazette* and the *Detroit Journal*, to mention but a few. Nativism also began to take hold in the South. In Louisiana, for example, a new party committed to the protection of "American" principles and the exclusion of foreigners from public office had been operating independently of the two major parties since 1841. Due to its lax immigration laws, the Cajun State was almost literally overrun by foreign arrivals. For years, the Europeans had been dumping the unwanted occupants of their almshouses, insane asylums, hospitals and prisons on America's doorstep, a disproportionate number of whom ended up in New Orleans. While many immigrants eventually made their way up the Mississippi Valley, it was Louisiana that felt the initial burden of these unwanted guests.

The American Republicans

In the North, the American Republican or Native American Party, a precursor to the national Know-Nothing Party, was founded in New York City in June 1843. The new party was used primarily as a protest vehicle against immigrant voters and, not surprisingly, both major parties tried to curry favor with its members, especially in closely contested elections. Within four months of its founding, the new party established the *American Citizen*, a staunchly nativistic newspaper, and in the autumn elections astounded most political observers by garnering more than eight thousand votes.[5] Whig Henry Clay and Democrat James Polk both angled for the party's backing during the 1844 presidential campaign. Because most foreign-born voters aligned themselves with the Democrats, Clay and other Whig candidates were able to make a stronger appeal for nativist support than their Democratic opponents.

The American Republican Party, which carried municipal elections in Boston, Philadelphia and New York City—including the election of the mayor of New York and six members of Congress in 1844—endorsed the Whig ticket of Henry

---

5.   Billington, *The Protestant Crusade 1800-1860*, pp. 200-201.

Clay and former Sen. Theodore Frelinghuysen in that year's hotly-contested presidential campaign. Hailing from neighboring New Jersey, the Princeton-educated Frelinghuysen, a former mayor of Newark, had been active in various anti-Catholic evangelical and Bible societies.

The party's endorsement of Clay in exchange for Whig support of American Republican legislative and congressional candidates prompted an immediate response from the Democrats, who accused the Whigs of being in league with "church burning" bigots. Agreeing with that sentiment, Democrats in Congress reacted by speeding up the naturalization process for Irish and German immigrants.

Under the direction of campaign manager and shrewd political strategist John Lloyd, the American Republicans swept New York City, electing four congressmen, a state senator, and fifteen assemblymen. Despite the strenuous objections of Whig leader William H. Seward, the vast majority of Whig voters in the city supported the American Republican ticket. Even Horace Greeley, who later emerged as one of the country's most outspoken critics of Know-Nothingism, supported the American Republican candidates in his district. Ironically, so did Bishop John Hughes, who cast his first vote as an American citizen that year.[6] The four American Republicans elected to the U.S. House from New York—William W. Campbell, Henry I. Seaman, Thomas M. Woodruff and William S. Miller, a fanatical nationalist and one-time follower of French philosophers Voltaire and Rousseau whose works and ideas deeply influenced that nation's revolution—were joined in Congress by publisher Lewis C. Levin and lawyer and former state legislator John H. Campbell of Philadelphia. The party nearly picked up a seventh seat in the U.S. House when Jacob Shearer lost a heartbreaking three-cornered race to incumbent Democrat Charles J. Ingersoll in Philadelphia's fourth congressional district. The son of Jared Ingersoll, a member of the Constitutional Convention of 1787, the younger Ingersoll, a man of considerable erudition who found time to write a four-volume history of the War of 1812, defeated his American Republican rival by the slimmest of margins, garnering 4,235 votes to Shearer's 4,060 and Whig Thomas W. Duffield's 1,581.

While Henry Clay failed to carry New York, the staunchly anti-immigration American Republicans gained a voice in both Albany and Washington, D.C. Party leaders were ecstatic and began to think in terms of widening their power and influence. "At the only two points where our principles are understood,"

---

6.   Carleton Beals, *Brass-Knuckle Crusade: The Great Know-Nothing Conspiracy 1820-1860* (New York, 1960), pp. 96-97.

boasted the *Native American* newspaper, an official party organ in Philadelphia, "we have triumphed by overwhelming majorities. Let us regenerate perfectly the city and country, and then each become a missionary for the next four years to redeem this country from foreign influence."[7]

Buoyed by their early success, the American Republicans launched the *National American* in September 1844. This national publication was followed shortly thereafter by the publication of the *Native Eagle and American Advocate*, a stridently nativist newspaper committed to protecting the interests of American labor against competition from immigrant workers. Several national magazines were also founded during this period, including the New York-based *Metropolitan Magazine and Republican Review* and the *American Republican Magazine*, both founded as party organs and featuring articles attacking Catholicism and foreign immigration. In addition to news of party activity around the country, the first issue of the *American Republican Magazine*, published in October 1844, contained a number of patriotic stories as well as articles entitled, "The Insolence of Foreigners" and "The Constitution."[8]

In July 1845, the American Republicans held a national convention in Philadelphia at which time they officially changed the party's name to the Native American Party. Representing every state and territory in the Union, the delegates to the convention drafted a legislative program denouncing foreigners and Catholics and calling for a 21-year waiting period for citizenship—legislation that the Know-Nothings failed to enact even at the height of their influence in the mid-1850s.

The nativist movement continued to gain popularity in the forties and early fifties as a result of the nation's growing intolerance toward immigration, especially from Ireland, where hundreds of thousands of people facing starvation as a result of that country's devastating potato famine sought refuge in the United States. Moreover, a large number of Germans, hoping to escape the general economic misery that was sweeping Europe, also found their way to America's shores. With more than a little justification, many Americans naturally feared the prospect of losing their jobs to these new immigrants. With the influx of cheap workers, the fledgling labor movement lost much of its momentum and wages in general were rising at a much slower pace than in previous years.

Unfortunately, the Irish "paddies" and their German counterparts were blamed for a number of the country's ills, including an increase in the nation's

---

7.   *Native American*, November 4, 1844; Billington, *The Protestant Crusade*, p. 202.
8.   Billington, *The Protestant Crusade*, pp. 210-211, 219n.

crime rate. The new immigrants, by virtue of their lifestyles, were also running afoul of traditional WASP practices, such as temperance and the strict observance of the Sabbath. Street fights, attacks on German social clubs, and random acts of vandalism against Catholic church property were not uncommon in the 1830s and 1840s.

Anti-Catholic parties, using various labels, sprouted up in several cities during this period. With the aid of the Whigs, who fielded a straw candidate, the nativists captured the New York City mayoralty in the spring of 1844 with the election of James Harper, head of a New York publishing house. Harper, who ran on a platform promising bipartisan patronage (Whig and American Republican), municipal reform and lower taxes—all standard campaign fare—defeated his Democratic and Whig rivals, garnering 24,509 votes to the Democrat's 20,538 and the hapless Whig candidate's 5,297.[9] A militantly anti-foreign, anti-Catholic crusader, Harper was aided as much by the fact that New Yorkers had finally tired of the graft and corruption that had mushroomed during the previous Democratic administrations than he was by the party's vitriolic appeals to nativism—of which there were many. "If I had the power," shouted one fiery nativist orator, "I would erect a gallows at every landing place in the city of New York and suspend every cursed Irishman as soon as he steps on our shores."[10]

Although his administration had taken giant strides in cleaning up corruption, Harper, running without Whig backing, was soundly defeated in his bid for a second term in 1845. Though snowed under by the Democrats, Harper nevertheless finished some 10,000 votes ahead of his out-manned Whig opponent. Without Whig support, however, the American Republicans were only able to elect a single ward constable from Brooklyn in that year's devastating municipal elections.

The Know-Nothings

Anti-foreign sentiment was clearly on the rise in the 1840s and early 1850s. During this tumultuous period, nearly three million immigrants arrived in America, including a large number of Irish Catholics. This massive immigration spawned a number of xenophobic secret societies, most notably Charles B. Allen's Supreme Order of the Star-Spangled Banner, whose main purpose was to prevent foreign-

9. *New York American Republican*, April 26, 1844, as cited in Billington, *The Protestant Crusade*, p. 214.
10. Beals, *Brass-Knuckle Crusade*, p. 94.

born persons from holding public office. Other like-minded groups included the United Sons of America and the Sons of the Sires. These groups worked together to form the American (Know-Nothing) Party for the expressed purpose of safeguarding America from the "insidious wiles of foreigners."

Meanwhile, anti-Catholic violence spread like wildfire across the American landscape. Some of the worst violence occurred in Philadelphia, the "City of Brotherly Love." Spurred by the Protestant clergy and laity, the popular press and Native American politicians, Philadelphia experienced the worst mob violence in its history. In one incident between nativists and newly-arrived southern Irish immigrants during the spring of 1844, thirty Irish homes were destroyed, three Catholic churches, including St. Michael's and the Church of Saint Augustine, were burned to the ground and an estimated fifty persons were injured, several of them seriously. Two months later, fifteen persons were killed and another fifty wounded in a clash between the two groups. While thousands of respectable citizens across the country deplored the carnage and looked askance at a party that seemed to be sanctioning mob rule, nativist editors desperately tried to put a positive spin on the horrible events that had unfolded in Philadelphia. Claiming that he cared little for the riots and abhorred the bloodshed, the editor of New York's *American Republican* wrote that it was "idle to suppose that Americans can be shot down on their own soil, under their own flag, while in the quiet exercise of their constitutional privileges, without a fearful retribution being exacted."[11]

Other cities experienced similar outbreaks of violence. In Baltimore, for example, ruthless gangs such as the Plug Uglies and the Blood Tubs helped to keep immigrants from the voting precincts on Election Day, thereby assuring Know-Nothing dominance at the polls, earning the city a reputation as a mob-town. "Wherever there is a Know-Nothing success, bloodshed, disorder and a disregard for everything have signaled its triumph," charged the appalled Democrats in that city.[12] Riots between nativist thugs and recent immigrants took at least four lives in New Orleans, ten in St. Louis, seventeen in Baltimore and no fewer than twenty-two in Louisville during the mid-1850s.

Like members of other secret societies, including the early Masons, the Know-Nothings used forms of communication and identification known only to the initiated, including special handshakes and passwords. Like the Masons, they

---

11. Elizabeth M. Geffen, "Industrial Development and Social Crisis 1841-1854," *Philadelphia: A 300-Year History*, pp. 357-358; Billington, *The Protestant Crusade*, pp. 220-237; New York *American Republican*, May 8, 1844.

12. Jean H. Baker, *Ambivalent Americans: The Know-Nothing Party in Maryland* (Baltimore, 1977), p. 124.

even had their own ceremonial rites. Among other things, members of the party were required to take an elaborate oath and were instructed not to discuss their activities with non-members. If asked about the American Party, a member would simply say, "I don't know"—hence, the party's nickname of "Know-Nothing," a term originally coined by journalist Horace Greeley.

The anti-Catholicism that fueled the Know-Nothing movement reached a crescendo by the early 1850s. Almost all of the Irish immigrants and nearly one-half of the Germans who recently entered the country were Catholic. Many Protestant Americans, incredulous as it may seem, were convinced that some sort of elaborate Vatican plot was underway. Rumors that Catholic churches contained hidden arsenals—and that Roman Catholics were awaiting word from the Papacy to begin their conquest of America—spread throughout the country.

While many Americans of the "old stock" were genuinely concerned about the unprecedented numbers of new immigrants flooding the nation's shores, a few of the more politically astute natives, particularly those in small towns and rural areas, worried about the effect of massive immigration on American politics. They realized that unscrupulous urban political bosses wouldn't be the least bit averse to receiving political support from the new arrivals crowding into the slums of America's big cities. Their concerns were not completely without merit. Urban ward heelers readily exchanged easy naturalization for votes. As a consequence, this period saw the rapid rise of big city machines.

One of the earliest and most enthusiastic advocates of Know-Nothingism was William W. Campbell of New York, who campaigned on the slogan that "Americans should rule America." As a congressman (1845-47), Campbell tried unsuccessfully to have naturalized Irish-American citizens barred from polling places during the height of the Irish migration to the United States. Other prominent Know-Nothing leaders included Lewis Levin, the editor and publisher of the *American Sun*, a penny daily newspaper in Philadelphia. Riding the crest of the Philadelphia anti-Irish riots of 1844, Levin, a South Carolinian by birth, was elected to the first of three terms in Congress on the American Party ticket. In Congress, Levin labored tirelessly for the nativist cause, pleading for immigration restrictions and tougher naturalization laws. Nativism seems to have shaped his view on virtually every issue. In his mind's eye, foreign intrigue lurked behind every problem facing the country.

Typical of many of those attracted to the Know-Nothing movement, Levin was a demagogue of the worst sort and was personally responsible for much of the anti-foreign fanaticism that swept Philadelphia in 1844. Yet he defended the nativists to the hilt, remaking in the House of Representatives that Native Americans carried no weapons and "stood armed only with moral power."[13] In his world, it was merely moral strength that burned St. Michael's Catholic Church and rectory to the ground that violent spring, with the parish priest barely escaping with his life. And it was apparently moral force that set St. Augustine ablaze, as well as a nearby firehouse. Moreover, it was evidently this same virtuous power that destroyed thirty homes and sent cannon balls hurling against another Catholic church, killing several militiamen and Irish immigrants.

Like Boston and New York, Philadelphia was a stronghold of sorts for the early Native American Party. In addition to sending Levin to Congress three times between 1844 and 1848, the party also elected Henry Lelar sheriff in 1846. Two years earlier, eight Native Americans were elected to the Pennsylvania House and one to the Senate from Philadelphia County. In 1848, five Native Americans were elected to the state House, holding the balance of power when the legislature organized in 1849.[14]

Though Levin was the only American Party incumbent re-elected to Congress in 1846, the party was able to make inroads elsewhere. Among the successful Know-Nothing candidates that year was Peter G. Camden, a 45-year-old lawyer who was elected mayor of St. Louis. Under Camden's leadership, St. Louis established a regular police department to replace the night watchmen and a few daytime patrols that previously policed the city. The city also issued $25,000 in bonds to repair the eastern shore of the Mississippi River, a project vital to the city's continued prosperity.

The tiny nativist party made its first attempt at running a national ticket as early as 1848, but it wasn't until 1856—with the nomination of former President Millard Fillmore—that the party was finally able to mount a serious bid for the White House. As it turned out, the party's limited efforts to capture the presidency in 1848 and 1852 were little more than hard-to-find footnotes in American history. A national convention of one hundred delegates from six eastern states and Ohio met in Philadelphia in September 1847 and proposed Zachary Taylor, who was later nominated by the Whigs, for president. At the time, "Old Rough and Ready" was seriously considering an independent bid for the nation's highest office. Like others, Taylor was convinced that a large immigrant vote for the Democrats would destroy any prospect of a Whig victory in 1848. The dele-

---

13. *Congressional Globe*, 29th Congress, 1st Session, Appendix, p. 49.
14. In addition, little-known Eman C. Reigart, the Native American Party candidate for governor of Pennsylvania, polled over 26% of the vote in populous Philadelphia County, while garnering 11,247 votes against Democrat Francis R. Shunk and Whig James Irvin in the state's 1847 gubernatorial contest.

gates also endorsed Mayor Henry A. Dearborn of Roxbury, Massachusetts, for vice president. Dearborn, whose father had served as Jefferson's Secretary of War, was a former congressman and state adjutant general who had been dismissed from the latter post in 1843 for lending arms to Rhode Island to help quell the Dorr Rebellion.

Among other things, the Native American Party passed a series of resolutions stating that the Bible and an American education should be "the only passport to the American ballot box" and that no one should be eligible to vote "unless born on our soil." The convention was disrupted when several delegates tried to push through another resolution stating that only native-born Americans should be eligible for citizenship.

The fledgling anti-immigration party took another stab at presidential politics four years later when it nominated a reluctant Daniel Webster for president. The choice of the aging Webster—the highest paid attorney of his time—to head the fledgling third party ticket wasn't altogether surprising. Though he personally shied away from attacks on foreigners and Catholics, Webster's patriotic blustering and his sponsorship of the controversial Fugitive Slave Law and other compromises earned him the respect of most nativists, as well as the undying affection of many southern Whigs. The ailing Webster, undisputedly the finest orator in a period marked by many eloquent speakers, was certainly available. The sagacious lawmaker, after all, was never exactly reticent about his desire to occupy the Executive Mansion. For a man like Webster who had accomplished so much in forty years of public service, the presidency was the most important prize—only from that exalted position could his "glorious dreams" of immortality finally be realized. Reaching for the brass ring in 1852 as the crowning achievement of his long and brilliant career, Webster, a one-time frontrunner for the Whig Party's presidential nomination that year, watched in horrified disbelief as the Whigs passed him over and nominated General Winfield Scott, a political neophyte, for the presidency at their national convention at Baltimore's Maryland Institute Hall in mid-June.

Born of humble beginnings in the granite hills of New Hampshire, the Dartmouth-educated Webster was first elected to Congress as a New Hampshire Federalist in 1812, serving two terms in which he quickly developed a reputation as an ardent states' rights advocate—a position he later relinquished. Like many other New England Federalists, Webster, reflecting the will of his region's commercial and shipping interests, had opposed the general embargo of 1807, as well as the War of 1812. He moved to Boston toward the end of his second term and again served in the House from 1823-27 and in the U.S. Senate from 1827-41 and again from 1845-50. Abandoning his earlier states' rights position, the Massachusetts lawmaker became a leading proponent of a strong federal government, championing federal action to stimulate the economy through protective tariffs and advocating a national bank. While in the U.S. Senate, Webster took part in an unlikely "triumvirate" with two other legendary lawmakers—Henry Clay, his on-again, off-again adversary, and John C. Calhoun of South Carolina, a one-time militant nationalist and diehard states' rights advocate. By 1832, all three men had proven themselves as spellbinding speakers, often dazzling their colleagues with their Olympian-like oratory. The Webster-Clay-Calhoun trio was arguably the most formidable coalition of senators in American history.

Webster also contributed considerably to the development of American constitutional law. Under Chief Justice John Marshall, the Supreme Court adopted a number of Webster's legal arguments in important cases, including *Dartmouth College v. Woodward* and *McCulloch v. Maryland*. These cases strengthened the federal government against state governments and the judiciary against the legislative and executive branches of government.

Appointed Secretary of State by President William H. Harrison in 1841, Webster skillfully negotiated the famous Webster-Ashburton Treaty, which settled a longstanding border dispute with Canada along the Maine and New Brunswick boundary, thereby ending the threat of a third war between Great Britain and the United States. The treaty also provided for a joint effort between the two countries in suppressing the Atlantic slave trade, a provision that was sharply denounced by South Carolina's John C. Calhoun and most Democrats. In the face of growing criticism from the Tyler administration, Webster resigned in 1843 and was promptly replaced by Virginian Abel P. Upshur, a Tyler and Calhoun ally who was openly sympathetic to southern slaveholders.

Considered one of the ablest men to ever hold the office, Webster served a second stint as Secretary of State under President Millard Fillmore, the nation's last Whig president. Webster won accolades in 1850 from Whigs and Democrats alike for his famous reply to Chevalier Hulsemann, the Austrian charge d'affaires, who formally protested U.S. involvement in his country's affairs and its recognition of the revolution that was taking place there. "The power of this republic, at the present moment," Webster said, "is spread over a region, one of the richest and most fertile on the globe, in comparison with which the possessions of the House of Hapsburg are but a patch on the earth's surface." Such tough talk again appeared to make Webster a front-runner for the Whig Party's presidential nomination in 1852.

Like many politicians before and after him, the Massachusetts lawmaker had long been criticized for trying to be all things to all people. Moreover, many voters in the South had never completely forgiven him for his drastic treatment of South Carolina during its fight for nullification. The high tariffs that he championed while in the Senate, many believed, favored New England's commercial interests at the expense of the rest of the country, particularly the South. There were also those, such as Free Soil Congressman Charles Allen of Massachusetts, who believed that Webster was a pawn of the bankers and brokers—and, indeed, was almost constantly on their payroll. Allen once accused Webster of pocketing $50,000 for working out a deal in which the federal government would borrow money at an unfavorable interest rate. Like Henry Clay, Webster was also criticized for his heavy drinking, a trait that alienated the growing temperance crowd. It was widely known that, given his lavish lifestyle—he liked to entertain and be entertained by Boston's aristocracy—Webster was almost constantly in debt.

At the Whig Party's 1852 national convention in Baltimore, Webster, who had failed in previous bids for the presidency in 1832, 1836 and 1848, received only 29 votes on the first ballot. President Fillmore led the field with 133 votes and Winfield Scott, whose campaign was skillfully directed by New York's William H. Seward, was a close second with 131 votes. The ailing Webster hung in the race through forty-nine ballots. Fillmore's supporters, sensing that their man wasn't going to win the nomination, coyly indicated that they would throw their sizeable bloc of delegates to the former Massachusetts lawmaker if he could raise his total to forty-one—an arbitrary number that Webster was unable to reach. Fillmore's managers never explained why the aging Whig hopeful had to reach that magic number before they would throw their support to him. Meanwhile, Seward held Scott's delegates firmly in place and put his man over the top on the convention's fifty-third ballot.

The heartbroken Webster, whose health was failing rapidly, realized that his lofty, lifelong ambition would never be fulfilled. When nominated by the tiny Native American Party in Trenton the following month, the elder statesman, who had been brooding about his humiliation at the Whig national convention in Baltimore for several weeks, refused to accept the honor—but, curiously, he also refused to formally turn it down. Potomac fever, it seems, is nearly impossible to cure. To the 70-year-old Webster, turning down a presidential nomination was akin to refusing a lucrative legal retainer—he simply couldn't say no. Webster's ambivalence, however, proved to be a moot point. The great orator passed away on October 24, less than two weeks before voters went to the polls that year.

Following his death, the Native American Party's national committee hurriedly named little-known Jacob Broom of Philadelphia as Webster's replacement.

The 44-year-old Broom was born in Baltimore, Maryland, and received a classical education as a young man and later studied law. In 1840, he was appointed deputy auditor of Pennsylvania and became clerk of the Philadelphia Orphan's Court eight years later. Broom, who was later elected to Congress on a coalition American-Whig ticket, was a weak substitute for the popular Webster and netted only 2,566 popular votes in the 1852 presidential election.

7

The Brass-Knuckle Crusade

❖

The Emergence of the Know-Nothing Party

It wasn't until the spring of 1854 that the Know-Nothing Party really began to flex its muscle when entire slates of little-known candidates were swept into office across the country, many of them by write-in votes. Dozens of local elected officials, Democrats and Whigs alike, were tossed out of office that year, many of them by men they had never even heard of. Incredibly, several bewildered office-holders thought they were running unopposed only to be shocked by massive Know-Nothing write-in votes on Election Day.

Nowhere was the party's showing more devastating to the fabled two-party system than in Massachusetts. The American Party swamped both major parties in that state, capturing an astonishing 63% of the vote while sweeping virtually every office in the commonwealth. Polling over 65% of the congressional vote, the new party won all eleven seats in the U.S. House. Among the successful Know-Nothing congressional candidates from the Bay State that year were Alexander De Witt, who garnered a staggering 77% of the vote against his startled and outmatched Democratic and Whig opponents, ex-Free Soiler Anson Burlingame and the venerable Nathaniel P. Banks. Remarkably, Banks, who later became the only third-party Speaker of the House in U.S. history, was elected to ten non-consecutive terms in Congress as a candidate of *five* different parties spanning a period of 38 years. Merchant Henry J. Gardner, the party's gubernatorial candidate, was also elected in the American Party landslide, piling up a massive 40,000-vote majority over his Whig and Democratic opponents.[1] "I no

---

1. The 36-year-old Gardner, a former president of the Boston Common Council, demolished his major party opposition, garnering 81,503 votes to the incumbent Whig governor's 27,279 and his Democratic rival's 13,742 votes.

more suspected the impending result," wrote a startled Whig journalist, "than I looked for an earthquake which would level the State House and reduce Faneuil Hall to a heap of ruins." Other stunned observers looked at the seismic destruction, shaking their heads in disbelief.[2]

Though precise figures are difficult to ascertain, the Know-Nothing Party claimed at least fifty-one seats in the 34th Congress. Among the successful congressional candidates were Jacob Broom of Pennsylvania and Aaron Cragin, a 33-year-old New Hampshire lawyer who later had the distinction of serving as one of the party's last members in the U.S. Senate. Running on the Native American ticket, Broom, who opposed the Nebraska Act during his campaign but said that he wouldn't vote for its repeal unless his southern colleagues agreed to it, garnered 53% of the vote against his lone Democratic rival. Also elected in the unexpected Know-Nothing uprising was George Eustis, a 26-year-old Louisiana lawyer who later served as secretary of the Confederacy's legation in Paris during the Civil War. Other notable Know-Nothing congressmen who served in the 34th Congress included Indiana's Lucien Barbour, who was elected on a fusion ticket consisting of the Free Soil, Know-Nothing and Temperance parties, Sidney Dean of Connecticut and Thomas R. Whitney, one of the original members of the Order of the American Union and a prime manipulator of the so-called "good government" City Reform League, a front group established to bolster James Harper's mayoral candidacy in 1844. Barbour, who had been appointed district attorney for Indiana by President Polk, was an ardent antislavery advocate. A former Democrat who later served in Congress as a Republican, Barbour was frequently engaged as an arbitrator between the state of Indiana and private corporations.

In 1855, the legendary Sam Houston, an ardent nationalist who harbored strong presidential ambitions, became the first American Party member to serve in the U.S. Senate. A longtime Democrat, Houston believed that his former party had gotten itself into a "prodigious pickle" over the slavery issue and was convinced that the Know-Nothing Party was the only political party truly committed to maintaining "the perpetuity of our free institutions." Within two years, there were five Know-Nothing members in the U.S. Senate.[3]

In the meantime, the Know-Nothings won gubernatorial contests in Connecticut, Delaware, Kentucky, New Hampshire and Maine, nearly captured the New

---

2.   McPherson, *Battle Cry of Freedom*, p. 139.

3.   In addition to Houston, John Bell of Tennessee, John B. Thompson and John J. Crittenden of Kentucky and Maryland's Anthony Kennedy also served as Know-Nothing members of the U.S. Senate from 1857-59.

York governorship in a close and confusing four-way tilt and played a pivotal, if not decisive, role in Pennsylvania's 1854 gubernatorial campaign.

In Connecticut, where the Know-Nothing Party captured all four U.S. House seats in 1855 and controlled both houses of the state legislature—holding 18 of 21 state Senate seats and 161 of 226 seats in the lower house—the third party elected William T. Minor, an ex-Whig, as the state's chief executive. Running on a strongly nativistic platform, the 40-year-old Minor garnered over forty-three percent of the popular vote while defeating perennial Democratic candidate Samuel Ingham, a former congressman who ran on a platform denouncing the state's new prohibitory law while trying to sidestep the issue of slavery, and Henry Dutton, the incumbent Whig governor who had joined the nativist society in a calculated—and transparent—attempt to win re-election. Minor, who was easily elected by the Know-Nothing controlled legislature, tallied 28,080 popular votes to Ingham's 27,291 and a paltry 9,162 for the incumbent Whig governor. Incredibly, Dutton, running on the Whig and Free Soil tickets, carried only one township in the entire state. The results were devastating for the state's two major parties. "Our election has resulted in a rout and break up of the old parties," conceded Gideon Welles, a fussy anti-Nebraska Democrat who later served as Secretary of the Navy in the Lincoln administration. The unexpected Know-Nothing avalanche also effectively destroyed the state's fledgling Free Soil and Temperance parties, whose leaders lamented that the cause of liberty and prohibition were being "swallowed up by the 'one idea' that Roman Catholicism is the great bugbear and the only question that interests the freemen of this country."[4]

Promising to restore America to "its pristine purity," Minor warned against the "pernicious influence of foreign immigration" in his inaugural address, claiming that immigrants made up a majority of the inmates in the nation's prisons and asylums. "Our taxes are largely increased," he said, "for the support of our foreign population." As governor, Minor espoused a litany of anti-Catholic and anti-immigrant ideas, including a longer residency requirement for naturalization. In one of his first acts as governor, he targeted the state's Catholic institutions, requiring all Catholic Church property to be vested in the hands of congregations rather than the church hierarchy, while exempting non-Catholic denominations from such a law. It was a flagrantly unconstitutional act. During his first term, the Know Nothing-dominated legislature proposed a state constitutional amendment for a voter's literacy test that, ironically, denied countless non-aliens the right to vote and passed a law denying the right of state courts to

---

4.   Holt, *The Rise and Fall of the American Whig Party*, p. 921.

naturalize aliens. In an otherwise popular move, the Know-Nothing governor further angered the state's swelling immigrant population by disbanding six predominately Irish militia companies. Minor, who was re-elected in 1856, renewed his attacks on foreigners, but accomplished little in terms of promoting the nativist agenda during his second term.

The head of the Know-Nothing order in Connecticut was Nehemiah D. Sperry, a 27-year-old stonemason and Whig alderman from New Haven who served as secretary of state during Minor's administration. From its founding in 1853 when the first Supreme Order of the Star-Spangled Banner was established in the state, its aim was to resist "the murderous policy of the church of Rome, and all other foreign influences against the institutions of our country," and to elect "none but native-born Protestants."[5] But the Know-Nothing Party in Connecticut was more than an anti-Catholic, anti-immigration movement. Under Sperry's leadership, the Connecticut Know-Nothing order adroitly blended nativist concerns with growing antislavery sentiment, enabling Minor to narrowly win a second term in 1856. It was under Sperry's guidance that the Connecticut delegation had walked out of the American Party's national council meeting in Philadelphia in June 1855, in protest of Section Twelve, the party's proslavery plank. Defending the walkout, Gov. Minor said that the Know-Nothing Party "would have been blown to atoms in every Northern state" if Section Twelve had been accepted.[6] Yet Sperry, an immensely talented political operative, initially opposed fusion with Fremont and the Republicans in 1856 and continued to support an independent Know-Nothing Party in Connecticut as late as 1858—long after most other antislavery party members in New England had found refuge in the emerging Republican Party. Interestingly, he served as state chairman of the Republican Party in Connecticut during Lincoln's campaign in 1860 and was rewarded by an appointment as postmaster of New Haven, a position he held off and on until the end of the nineteenth century. He also served in Congress from 1895 until his death in 1911 at the age of eighty-four.

---

5.   *Hartford Times*, February 26, 1856, as quoted in Beals, *Brass-Knuckle Crusade*, pp. 231-232.
6.   Gienapp, *The Origins of the Republican Party*, p. 275.

The Temperance Parties

In 1854, a full year before the Know-Nothings swept Connecticut, the tiny Temperance Party—a third-party generally overlooked by historians in the flurry of Know-Nothing and Free Soil activity of this period—had seriously threatened the two major parties in the Constitution State when it fielded a nearly full slate of legislative candidates on a ticket headed by gubernatorial candidate Charles R. Chapman, a well-known Hartford lawyer. Democratic Gov. Thomas Seymour's veto of a local-option temperance law, coupled with the Whig Party's nomination of Henry Dutton, a notorious wet, and the Free Soil Party's abandonment of Francis Gillette, the party's pro-Maine Law gubernatorial candidate in 1853, prompted the prohibitionists to field their own ticket that year. Regarded as something of a gifted storyteller, the 55-year-old Chapman, a former Whig congressman and one-time editor of the *New England Review*, represented Hartford in the state legislature on several occasions. Remarkably, his 1854 candidacy drew 10,672 votes, or more than eighteen percent of the total—easily outpolling his Democratic, Whig and Free Soil rivals in the April voting. Moreover, the Temperance Party elected seven men to the lower house of the Connecticut legislature, compared to 110 seats for the Whigs, 89 for the Democrats, and seventeen for the Free Soilers—an increase of six over the previous legislature. Shortly thereafter, the amiable Chapman was seriously considered for the U.S. Senate seat of retiring Whig lawmaker Truman Smith, but the Whig-dominated legislature ultimately chose the Free Soil Party's Francis Gillette to fill the remaining ten months of Smith's term while selecting Lafayette Foster, the Whig Party's unsuccessful gubernatorial candidate in 1850 and 1851, to the new six-year term beginning in March 1855.[7]

As William E. Gienapp asserted in his splendidly written and exceptionally well-researched book on the origins of the Republican Party, the temperance movement—or, more precisely, the Temperance Party—has long been neglected in American political history, especially as it relates to the disruption of the second party system in the 1850s.[8] Even renowned partisans such as David Leigh

---

7.   Ibid., pp. 85-86; Holt, *The Rise and Fall of the American Whig Party*, pp. 832-833, 1145n. Dutton garnered 19,465 votes to Democrat Samuel Ingham's 28,538 and the Free Soil candidate's 2,560. Whig Henry Dutton, whose anti-Nebraska candidacy was hampered by the nagging liquor question and by the refusal of Connecticut's Democrats to endorse the Kansas-Nebraska Act, was subsequently elected governor by the Whig-controlled state legislature.

8.   Gienapp, *The Origins of the Republican Party*, p. 466n.

Colvin (*Prohibition in the United States,* 1926) and Roger Storms(*Partisan Prophets,* 1972) skipped somewhat lightly over this antebellum party in their otherwise magnificent works on the national Prohibition Party.

The temperance movement and the fledgling Temperance parties that sprouted up in the antebellum era attracted a wide array of reformers, including no small number of self-righteous moralists, responding to what they perceived to be a genuine social problem. During the early nineteenth century, per capita consumption of hard liquor was rampant—far exceeding the highest twentieth-century levels—and contributed immensely to lost productivity, child abuse, crime, public disorder, poverty and other social ills.

Relying almost exclusively on moral persuasion, the Temperance movement had become a significant, if overlooked, force in American politics during this period. As the sale and use of alcoholic beverages increasingly became a potent political issue, demands for stronger enforcement of existing laws and the passage of new ones restricting the sale and consumption of liquor and beer were enacted in eight states by 1856. In many states, temperance and abolitionism worked in tandem with the nativist movement, frequently joining forces in attempts to break away from the old parties. As such, the nation's temperance forces, in no small measure, played an integral part in the Know-Nothing and Free Soil movements, as well as in the founding of the Republican Party.[9] "While Whigs and Democrats split over antislaveryism and over other matters," observed Clifford S. Griffin in his resplendent book *Their Brothers' Keepers,* "former partisans of both groups became Know-Nothings. These politicos also became prohibitionists, and out of such ingredients came the potpourri of Republicanism."[10]

Various temperance parties, as such, played critical roles in several hotly contested campaigns during this period, occasionally providing the margin of victory for major-party candidates running on fusion tickets, such as that of New York's Myron Holly Clark in 1854, as well as in Lucien Barbour's narrow election to Congress from Indiana against a Nebraska Democrat that same year. Temperance parties, including Neal Dow's Maine Law Party—arguably the most successful of the temperance parties—and Gerrit Smith's Anti-Dramshop Party, founded in 1842, were active in several states during this period, including Connecticut, Georgia, Indiana, Maryland, New York, New Jersey, Ohio and Pennsylvania. Occasionally winning local office or state legislative seats, these early

---

9.   Joseph R. Gusfield, *Symbolic Crusade: Status Politics and the American Temperance Movement* (Urbana, 1963), pp. 51-57.

10.   Griffin, *Their Brothers' Keepers,* p. 218.

prohibition parties frequently competed in congressional and gubernatorial campaigns, especially when the major parties nominated candidates who were inexorably hostile to the anti-liquor cause. In addition to taking part in numerous fusion campaigns with Democrats, Whigs, and Know-Nothings during this period, the Temperance Party fielded its own congressional candidates on at least five occasions in the early 1850s and came remarkably close to electing John W. Hazelton to Congress from New Jersey's first congressional district in 1854. A 39-year-old farmer from rural Gloucester County, Hazelton later served in Congress as a Republican in the early 1870s. The party also made a strong showing in New York's first congressional district that year when wealthy merchant Gabriel P. Disosway—a temperance, antislavery and American Colonization Society supporter—garnered over fourteen percent of the vote in a five-cornered race narrowly won by "Soft" Democrat William W. Valk. As early as 1853, local temperance parties had contested state legislative and local races in several states including Michigan, Pennsylvania, and Maryland—where a temperance ticket swept normally Democratic Baltimore. "So many Democrats are voting for the prohibitory ticket and so many combinations are against it that I am afraid of the results," complained a Philadelphia Democrat.[11]

Although the temperance movement as a whole was weakest in the South, one of the more fascinating races featuring a Temperance Party candidate during this period took place in Georgia's 1855 gubernatorial campaign where Basil H. Overby, a prominent Atlanta lawyer and occasional Methodist preacher, challenged entrenched Democratic incumbent Hershel Vespasian Johnson and the Know-Nothing Party's Garnett Andrews, a 57-year-old lawyer and state legislator, for that state's highest elective office.

Georgia seemed a most unlikely setting for a political party committed to prohibition in the antebellum South. Oddly enough, one of the first acts by James Oglethorpe and the English trustees of the colony of Georgia shortly after its founding in 1733 as a refuge for debtors and criminals and as a buffer of sorts between Carolina and Spanish Florida, was to ban the importation of rum and brandy. While the trustees of the utopian colony allowed the early inhabitants to drink English beers, they made it illegal to consume rum within the confines of the province. "He keeps a strict discipline," remarked a visitor from South Carolina in 1734, "I neither saw one of his people drunk nor heard one swear all the time I have been here."[12] Rum smuggling from South Carolina and the failure of

---

11. Holt, *The Political Crisis of the 1850s*, p. 131.
12. Robert Wright, *A Memoir, General James Edward Oglethrope* (London, 1867), p. 64

local juries to convict rumrunners, coupled with a general relaxation of the colony's strict prohibitory laws, virtually doomed Oglethorpe's earlier efforts to enforce temperance. "From the records of the futile attempts to make this prohibition effective one could write tales of adventure and romance, comparable to the modern short stories which have cast a glamour over violations of the Volstead Act," wrote historian John Allen Krout in 1925. With greater ease and less fear of detection than was later experienced by twentieth century bootleggers, observed Krout, eighteenth century rumrunners "landed their valuable cargoes in secluded Georgia coves or packed their heavy loads along the wilderness trails from a neighboring province."[13] Despite occasional clamoring from the Washingtonians, the short-lived Flournoy movement and other temperance organizations, more than a century had passed since the death of the colonial rum law before prohibition advocates, led by the Georgia Temperance Society—a group that once eschewed politics but had grown increasingly frustrated by the unwillingness of the state's Whig and Democratic parties to take up the issue—decided to take direct political action to suppress the state's free-flowing liquor traffic.[14]

An ardent Whig prior to winning the Temperance Party's gubernatorial nomination, the 41-year-old Overby was born and raised in rural South Carolina before relocating to Georgia as a young man. After a brief stint as a schoolteacher, Overby was admitted to the Georgia bar at the age of twenty-one and established a law practice in rural Jefferson, Georgia, where he developed a reputation as one of the best lawyers in the area. Attracted by the phenomenal growth of a new railroad center in DeKalb County, which turned that thickly covered wilderness where Cherokee Indians once roamed freely into one of the largest and most thriving cities in the South, Overby moved to Atlanta in 1853 and formed a partnership with Logan E. Bleckley, an intellectually inquisitive and self-educated lawyer destined to become chief justice of the Georgia Supreme Court. John Brown Gordon, a 22-year-old University of Georgia dropout who later served as governor of Georgia and as a member of the U.S. Senate on two different occasions, joined the law firm shortly thereafter. Gordon, who had fought brilliantly during the Civil War and led the last charge at Appomattox—forever endearing him to the voters back home—has long been regarded as one of Georgia's most

---

13. John Allen Krout, *The Origins of Prohibition* (New York, 1925), p. 90.
14. Led by the flamboyant Josiah Flournoy, a Methodist planter from Eatonton, the Flournoy movement tried unsuccessfully to organize a statewide campaign to elect a legislature sympathetic to the temperance cause in the late 1830s. Leaders of both parties taunted Flournoy in the bitter campaign that ensued. His meetings were frequently disrupted and his property was destroyed.

influential political figures and, along with powerful party leaders Alfred H. Colquitt and Joseph E. Brown, constituted a third of the so-called new triumvirate of Georgia's postwar Democratic establishment that believed that the state's future lay more in the development of industry than in agriculture.

Though less known in the annals of Georgia history than Bleckley or Gordon, Overby, a man of deep religious convictions, was nevertheless considered, in the words of one historian, as "one of the brainiest men and one of the best lawyers" in the state. A jovial and witty man, Overby was highly regarded by his contemporaries "To get at justice without injustice and cruelty was the way he served," said a fellow lawyer. Overby was also something of an eloquent public speaker, achieving "his crowning glory as a public speaker" when delivering talks on his favorite topic of prohibition.[15]

Waging his first campaign for public office, Overby was nominated for governor at the State Temperance Convention in Atlanta during the winter of 1855, defeating William H. Crawford, the son of the late Secretary of the Treasury and defeated 1824 presidential candidate of the same name. A lawyer with a deep interest in politics, religion and literature, the younger Crawford received twenty-two votes on the convention's only ballot to fifty-eight for Overby.[16] Almost immediately, Overby's candidacy drew sharp criticism, especially from old Whig newspapers such as the *Southern Recorder*, which argued that Overby's campaign was designed to divide Governor Johnson's opposition and assure his reelection.

Not intent on waiting for the Democratic and Know-Nothing parties to make their nominations, Overby began a whirlwind tour of the state in April, addressing large crowds in Savannah and elsewhere. In a speech in Macon on May 18, he defended the Temperance Party's decision to field a separate ticket in 1855, maintaining that Democrats and Whigs in the legislature had ignored the issue of prohibition. He also argued that the "injurious, demoralizing and depreciating effect of the liquor traffic" upon Georgia's slave population constituted more of a danger to that peculiar institution than all of the abolitionist agitation in the North.[17]

Although Gov. Johnson was generally recognized as one of the strongest temperance proponents in the state, the Democrats virtually ignored the issue of pro-

15.   Allen P. Tankersley, "Basil Hallam Overby: Champion of Prohibition in Ante Bellum Georgia," *The Georgia Historical Society Quarterly*, Vol. XXXI, No. 1 (March 1947).

16.   Ibid.

17.   Henry A. Scomp, *King Alcohol in the Realm of King Cotton* (Blakely, Ga., 1888), pp. 509-510.

hibition in their platform that year, focusing instead on the need to resist any congressional action on slavery in the District of Columbia and in the territories that would injure "the rights and honor of the slave-holding states." Concentrating most of its firepower on foreigners who posed a "dangerous" threat to the country while harshly condemning the "union of Church and State," the Know-Nothing Party, meeting in Macon on June 27, also failed to address the liquor question in its platform.[18]

The campaign proved to be a difficult one for Overby as the Democrats and Know-Nothings began spreading rumors that he was withdrawing from the race, a rumor that was quickly quelled by a Temperance Party spokesman. "Nothing short of Divine Power, or an imperious demand by the party which nominated him, of which there is not the remotest possibility, will he withdraw." Shortly thereafter, a second Temperance Convention in Marietta on July 11 ratified Overby's nomination and passed a resolution urging "the support of all persons who desired the overthrow of the grogshop dynasty in Georgia."[19] Hampered by a lack of newspaper support, Overby had to rely on the *Temperance Banner* for favorable coverage, but it was too small to make much of a difference. Plans for the publication of a larger newspaper in Marietta, tentatively called the *Georgia Prohibitionist*, apparently fell through, but Overby's candidacy received a boost late in the campaign when businessman and former Atlanta mayor Jonathan Norcross, an avid supporter, purchased the *Atlanta Republican*, a paper initially hostile to Overby and the Temperance Party.[20]

The campaign also grew ugly, with the two major candidates exchanging barbs. Johnson, who later served as Stephen A. Douglas's vice-presidential running mate on the ill-fated Northern Democratic ticket in 1860, blasted the Know-Nothing Party in no uncertain terms. "I showed its hostility to the great ideas of our American institutions—how it sought to fetter freedom of speech, the press and the right of religious toleration," he later recalled. "In a word, that it was the most dangerous and the most wicked political organization that had ever existed in our country."[21] Though the incumbent Democrat virtually ignored his candidacy, Overby wasn't spared the same kind of fate at the hands of the Know-Nothings and their supporters in the press. The Macon-based *Georgia Journal*

18. *Southern Recorder*, June 12, 1855, July 3, 1855.
19. Tankersley, "Basil Hallam Overby;" Scomp, *King Alcohol in the Realm of King Cotton*, pp. 510-511; *Southern Recorder*, July 7, 1855.
20. Ibid., p. 21.
21. Percy Scott Flippin, *Herschel V. Johnson of Georgia, State Rights Unionist* (Richmond, 1931), p. 69.

and Messenger, a staunchly pro-American Party newspaper, accused the Atlanta lawyer of harming the temperance movement in Georgia by leading it "to an overwhelming and crushing defeat"—one from which it was unlikely to ever recover.[22]

Overby never had a chance. When all the votes were tallied, Johnson was easily re-elected to a second term, garnering 54,136 votes to 43,358 for the Know-Nothing Party's Andrews and 6,333 for the long shot Temperance standard-bearer. In 1857, the Georgia Temperance Party called a convention in Atlanta for the purpose of again nominating a gubernatorial candidate, but the turnout was so small that the party gave up. As for Overby, he joined the Know-Nothings and wholeheartedly supported Millard Fillmore in the 1856 presidential campaign. The following year, he lost narrowly in a bid for the state legislature on the Know-Nothing ticket.[23]

In the meantime, the American Party, aided by massive defections from both major parties, cruised to victory in several other states during this period. One of the those victories occurred in Delaware where Peter F. Causey, a former Whig who lost in two previous bids for governor, was finally elected governor of that tiny state on the Know-Nothing ticket in 1854, narrowly defeating his Democratic rival by 697 votes. Causey served as governor from 1855 to 1859. Likewise, New Hampshire voters also waved the Know-Nothing flag by electing Ralph Metcalf, a former teacher and farmer, to the first of two consecutive gubernatorial terms in 1855, and the Know-Nothing's Anson P. Morrill was swept into the governor's chair in Maine. The American Party also gained control of the legislature in Rhode Island and acted as an equal partner in Gov. William W. Hoppin's Whig administration from 1855-57. The party's success in that state was largely due to the *Providence Journal,* which had fanned prejudice toward recent Irish Catholic immigrants, enabling the Know-Nothings to sweep city, town, and state elections. In Kentucky, where the Know-Nothings gained control of the state legislature and won six congressional seats, the party was able to put Charles Slaughter Morehead, a prosperous lawyer, planter and slave owner, in the governor's mansion.

The 57-year-old Metcalf, a graduate of Dartmouth, was a former state legislator and local official in Sullivan County. He defeated three rivals in narrowly winning the New Hampshire governorship in 1855 and was re-elected a year later by the legislature after finishing 88 votes ahead of his Democratic opponent

---

22.   Scomp, *King Alcohol in the Realm of King Cotton,* p. 512.
23.   Tankersley, "Basil Hallam Overby."

in a multi-candidate field. As governor, Metcalf campaigned tirelessly against the public sale of liquor and against Roman Catholicism and immigration.

Anson P. Morrill's stunning victory in Maine in 1854—a tribute to the flinty character and steadfast independence of voters in that state—was the result of a serious split within the state's Democratic Party over the temperance issue, as much as anything else. The political situation in Maine, as elsewhere in New England, was very fluid during this period, due more to the divisive nature of the state's strict prohibitory liquor law than the creeping presence of Know-Nothing-ism or the political fallout from the controversial Kansas-Nebraska legislation. A tough measure designed to prohibit the sale and manufacture of alcoholic beverages anywhere in the state, the "Maine Law" was passed by the legislature and signed into law by Gov. John Hubbard, a Democrat, in June 1851. The law's enactment was the result of two decades of tireless campaigning on the part of Portland Mayor Neal Dow and ex-Liberty Party leader James Appleton, author of a lurid and influential 1837 report on the effects of alcohol. Originally, Dow and Appleton, both of whom were also fervent antislavery advocates, persuaded the state legislature to enact a prohibitory law in 1846, but that legislation was riddled with so many loopholes, including lax enforcement and weak penalties, that it proved entirely ineffective. The new tougher law was quite a different story. It had badly divided the two major parties in the state legislature, with the Democrats supporting its passage by a 56-35 majority and the Whigs favoring it by a 34-15 margin. Only the Free Soil Party remained united on the issue, with all nine members in the legislature supporting the measure.[24] Almost immediately, the Maine Law created a serious rift in both major parties and seriously blurred the lines between the various parties, making it almost impossible at times to distinguish between the competing parties.

The first signs of this split had taken place during the 1852 gubernatorial election when Democrats opposed to the Maine Law bolted and formed the Liberal Party, popularly known as the Anti-Maine Law Party, and ran Anson G. Chandler for governor. Chandler, whose candidacy was financed largely by liquor interests in Boston and New York, garnered an impressive 21,589 votes, or 23%, to incumbent Democrat John Hubbard's 41,616 and Whig William G. Crosby's 29,129. The prohibitory law not only split the Democratic Party, but also created havoc within Whig ranks. "A good many temperance Whigs voted for Hubbard and a good many rum Whigs voted for Chandler," remarked political humorist Major Jack Downing.[25] Despite his large plurality, Hubbard, a prominent sur-

24. Gienapp, *The Origins of the Republican Party*, pp. 47-48.

geon and former state senator who later helped negotiate the Reciprocity Treaty with Great Britain during the Buchanan administration, was denied re-election as governor when a number of "wet" Democrats in the legislature threw their support to the Whig Party's William G. Crosby.

In 1854, the dominant wing of the state Democratic Party nominated a gubernatorial candidate who was opposed to the state's prohibitory law while a separate faction endorsed a candidate who favored the "Maine Law." Meanwhile, the Free Soil Party, hoping to take advantage of the Democratic split, nominated Morrill, a one-time Democrat who had bolted from his party over the issue of slavery, in the hopes of rallying those opposed to the Kansas-Nebraska Act behind its antislavery banner. When the Democrats, hoping to avoid the same fate they experienced a year earlier, nominated a candidate opposed to the Maine Law for governor in 1853, Morrill entered the race and waged a spirited campaign on a "Wildcat" ticket—a hodge-podge of Democrats who favored the Maine Law, Free Soilers and temperance Whigs—and garnered over 13% of the vote in a four-way race won by the Whig candidate. Moreover, Morrill Democrats captured 19 seats in the legislature that year, the Free Soilers—whose gubernatorial candidate Ezekiel Holmes, an editor, explorer and discoverer of America's first gem mine, garnered nearly 11% of the vote, or nearly a six-fold increase over his1852 showing—claimed eight seats, and each of them held the balance of power between the Whigs and the regular Democrats, who won 64 and 60 seats, respectively.

During the 1854 gubernatorial campaign, the Know-Nothings, with an estimated 15,000 to 20,000 lodge members in the state, enthusiastically endorsed Morrill's third-party candidacy, as did Neal Dow's fledgling Maine Law Party. The Democrats nominated Albion K. Parris, a temperance man who had defeated Neal Dow for mayor of Portland. Meanwhile, the Whigs, hoping to take advantage of the serious split within Democratic ranks, fielded their own candidate in the person of Isaac Reed and adopted a platform devoted almost exclusively to the issue of slavery—by far, the most pronounced antislavery platform of the four parties competing in Maine's crowded electoral contest that year.[26] But

---

25. Ibid., p. 49.
26. Ibid., pp. 131-132. The Whig Party's statement of principles sharply condemned the Kansas-Nebraska Act, opposed the admission of new slave states and the expansion of slavery into the territories, and called for a modification of the Fugitive Slave Act to secure the rights of the accused. As Gienapp pointed out, Maine's Whig Party, while steadfastly refusing fusion, was in such a weakened state prior to 1854 that not even the Nebraska issue could possibly revive it.

Reed's efforts were undercut when several Whig leaders, including the popular Israel Washburn and, to a lesser extent, William Pitt Fessenden, urged the state's Whig leadership to unite behind Morrill's fusionist ticket.

Complicating matters even further was the candidacy of longtime state legislator Shepard Cary, one of the most vociferous opponents of the Maine Law. Having failed to win the Democratic gubernatorial nomination in two earlier tries, Cary, a wealthy lumberman who had served briefly in Congress in the early 1840s, decided to enter the race on the Liberal Party ticket, proudly campaigning as the so-called "Rum" candidate. In a confusing four-way race, Morrill, a former state legislator and county sheriff, finished with a 16,000-vote plurality against his Democratic rival, but fell just short of winning a majority with 49.5% of the vote. Whig Isaac Reed and the Liberal Party's Cary combined for nearly twenty percent of the total. Morrill was then elected by the Maine legislature. By then, a clear majority in the legislature favored the state's prohibitory law, including the entire state senate. Even Speaker of the House Sidney Perham, who headed the state's Sons of Temperance, was a devoted advocate of prohibition.

While it is impossible to say precisely whether Morrill owed his election to Know-Nothing membership in the legislature, as editor James G. Blaine keenly observed, or to those who favored the Maine Law, or perhaps to the growing number of legislators who were sympathetic to the free soil movement—or possibly a combination of all of them—one thing was sure: Morrill's third-party candidacy had turned the state's two-party system on its head and provided the nucleus for the state's emerging Republican Party.

Long active in Kentucky politics, Charles S. Morehead, the state's Know-Nothing governor and a devoted friend and supporter of the late Henry Clay, had served in the state legislature and in Congress. He was also a former state attorney general. The 53-year-old Morehead, who owned plantations in Kentucky, Louisiana and Mississippi, was a former Whig who strongly advocated neutrality between the North and South at the outbreak of the Civil War. As governor, he also vastly expanded and improved the state penitentiary and began funding an annual state fair to encourage agricultural development and production. After leaving office, Morehead, who had participated in the ill-fated Peace Convention earlier that year, was imprisoned for four months in 1861 because of his anti-administration sympathies, particularly his denunciation of Lincoln's policy of cutting off all trade with the South. Following his release from prison, the beleaguered ex-governor traveled to England where he resided until the end of the war.

The American Party also came within a whisker of winning the Missouri governorship in 1857. In that state, the Know-Nothing movement found itself in a political situation quite different than that experienced in other border states. In that slaveholding state the Know-Nothings had to compete with two Democratic parties—the regular Democrats and another faction led by powerful ex-Senator Thomas Hart Benton, the westward expansionist who had briefly opposed the annexation of Texas in 1844 because he believed that it would lead to war with Mexico and whose brilliant thirty-year Senate career came to a screeching halt as a result of his undaunted support of antislavery constitutions in California, New Mexico, and Oregon. In addition, the Missouri Know-Nothing Party also had to contend with old Whig leaders in the state who were determined to maintain their party at least through the end of 1855, a year in which the Know-Nothings swept the municipal elections in St. Louis. The following year, the American Party nominated Judge Robert C. Ewing for governor, pitting the Unionist against Democrat Trusten Polk, a proslavery apologist, and 74-year-old Benton, who was running as a "Benton Democrat." Running poorest in the state's rabidly proslavery sections, Ewing polled 35% of the vote statewide, finishing about 6,400 votes behind the victorious Polk while the aging Benton polled 27,615 votes, or nearly a quarter of the total. The Know-Nothing candidate for lieutenant governor lost a contested race by only 386 votes.[27]

In 1857, the Know-Nothings threw their support to former Whig legislator and Columbia lawyer James S. Rollins in a special election to fill a vacancy in the governor's office created when Gov. Polk was elected to the U.S. Senate. The 45-year-old Rollins, a veteran of the Black Hawk War and one of only two Constitutional Unionists elected to Congress in 1860, had failed in a previous bid for the state's highest office in 1848, losing to Democrat Austin A. King. As a state legislator, Rollins, one of the largest slave owners in his county, emerged as a leader of the free soil forces in the Missouri legislature and had boldly opposed the extension of slavery in the territories. Pitted against Robert S. Stewart, an ardently proslavery anti-Benton Democrat, in the 1857 gubernatorial contest, Rollins, a former publisher of the *Columbia Whig*, campaigned under the "American" and "Emancipationist" labels. Though a slave owner himself, the former state lawmaker and ex-newspaperman came out in favor of protecting slavery in the state, but tempered his remarks by saying that the time might come when it would be in Missouri's best interest to abandon that peculiar institution. In one of the clos-

---

27.   Floyd Calvin Shoemaker, *Missouri's Hall of Fame: Lives of Eminent Missourians* (Columbia, Missouri, 1918), pp. 637-640.

est races in the state's history, Stewart edged out his American Party rival by a margin of 47,975 to 47,619, a difference of only 356 votes. Most Missouri historians concede that Rollins, who rolled up a 1,700-vote majority in St. Louis County, was probably the true winner, but was a victim of massive vote fraud on the part of the state's anti-Benton Democrats.[28]

Critical Know-Nothing support also enabled Whig gubernatorial candidate James Pollock to carry Pennsylvania in the autumn of 1854. Pollock, who later served as director of the Philadelphia Mint, is probably best remembered in American history for coining the motto, "In God We Trust" on U.S. coins. Pollock, who defeated ex-Free Soiler William Larimer of Pittsburgh to win the Whig Party's gubernatorial nomination, was aided immensely by the state's Know-Nothing forces, which opted against fielding a separate ticket in the general election. Pollock, it seems, won the Know-Nothing nomination in an unofficial statewide primary of sorts in which Know-Nothing lodges throughout the state chose candidates nominated by the regular parties—the Democrats, Whigs, and Native Americans—and forwarded those results to the State Council, which tallied the results and declared Pollock the overwhelming victor at the party's state convention in Philadelphia on October 3. According to the Know-Nothing Council, Pollock defeated the Native American Party's Benjamin Rush Bradford by more than 32,000 votes out of approximately 80,000 votes cast by lodge members.[29]

Pollock, a lawyer and three-term ex-congressman, also received a significant boost when antislavery Democrat David Wilmot decided not to enter the race as an independent anti-Nebraska candidate. Wilmot, whose candidacy had been encouraged by Gamaliel Bailey of the *National Era*, later endorsed Pollock, but only after convincing the fusion candidate to issue a strongly-worded antislavery statement in which he unqualifiedly favored the abolition of slavery in all existing and future territories. Running on a fusion ticket comprised of Whigs, Know-Nothings and the state's anti-Nebraska forces, Pollock, a former Whig congressman from Northumberland County, overwhelmed incumbent Democrat William Bigler, a former railroad executive, by a margin of 203,822 to 166,991. Bigler had become a special target of the state's Know-Nothing forces for having

---

28. W. Darrell Overdyke, *The Know-Nothing Party in the South* (Gloucester, MA, 1968), pp. 270-271.
29. Anbinder, *Nativism & Slavery*, pp. 58-59. Journalist and occasional politician Alexander McClure disputed the results in his memoirs, asserting that the state's Know-Nothing Council had fabricated the results after gaining patronage concessions from Whig leaders.

appointed James Campbell, a Catholic leader from Philadelphia, as state attorney general—a post from which he was later plucked to serve as postmaster general in the Pierce administration. Nativists throughout the state were outraged, including more than a few Democrats who, agreeing with a Catholic critic, believed that Campbell was an "imbecile and ignoramus" whose sole qualification was his Catholicism.

While most Free Soilers supported Pollock in the gubernatorial race, a small faction backed the Native American Party's Benjamin Rush Bradford. The little-known Bradford, however, was never a factor in the contest, tallying a dismal 2,194 votes, or less than one percent of the total turnout. Bradford, incidentally, had replaced the relatively obscure David Potts Jr., the original Free Soil candidate who was widely regarded as a stalking horse for David Wilmot. Incredibly, an estimated 120,000 Know-Nothing votes—motivated more by anti-Catholic sentiment than any other genuine nativist concerns—were cast for Pollock in that election and his 55% majority was the best showing by any Whig, including presidential candidates William H. Harrison and Zachary Taylor, in the state's history. Moreover, he was the only Whig to win a statewide race in Pennsylvania that year.[30]

Actual Know-Nothing strength in the Keystone State was best illustrated in the three-way statewide battle for a seat on the state Supreme Court—the only statewide race where the Know-Nothing Party supported its own candidate rather than endorse one of the major party candidates. In that race, the Native American Party's Thomas H. Baird ran against Democratic incumbent Jeremiah S. Black and his Whig challenger. Black won with 167,010 votes, virtually the same number of votes cast for Bigler in the gubernatorial contest, while third-party candidate Baird tallied 120,576 votes, or 32.9%. The hapless Whig candidate finished a distant third in that race, garnering only 78,571 votes.[31]

Bidding for Power in New York

Capitalizing on irreconcilable rifts within the Democratic and Whig parties, the Know-Nothing Party nearly captured one of the biggest prizes of all in the fall of 1854—the New York governorship. All hyperbole aside, the four-cornered 1854

30. Gienapp, *The Origins of the Republican Party*, pp. 94, 140-147; Michael F. Holt, *Forging a Majority: The Formation of the Republican Party in Pittsburgh, 1848-1860* (New Haven, 1969), p. 151.

31. Holt, *The Rise and Fall of the American Whig Party*, p. 885.

New York gubernatorial race was one of the most fascinating political campaigns in U.S. history. In that race, the Know-Nothing Party's Daniel Ullman polled over a quarter of the vote in a hard-fought race narrowly won by Whig Myron Clark. Despite Ullman's defeat, the American Party in New York had plenty to cheer about when it elected four congressmen in its own right, including trenchant Order of United Americans mover and shaker Thomas R. Whitney. The party also took part in the successful fusion campaigns of nine other candidates for the U.S. House of Representatives. Moreover, forty-five Know-Nothing candidates, all of whom were members of the powerful Order of United Americans or the Supreme Order of the Star-Spangled Banner, captured seats in the state legislature. One of the party's biggest setbacks, however, occurred earlier in the year when James W. Barker, a stodgy dry-goods salesman and controversial behind-the-scenes party manipulator, was defeated in his bid to become mayor of New York City.

The four-cornered New York governor's race was a wild and wooly affair. Facing national extinction, the Whigs were virtually split in half that year, with the conservative "Silver Grays," led by former President Millard Fillmore on the one side, and the so-called "Wooly Heads," directed by William H. Seward, on the other. Ex-President Fillmore, of course, was still stinging from his devastating setback to General Winfield Scott at the 1852 Whig convention in Baltimore—a loss he largely blamed on Seward, who had enthusiastically supported his chief rival.

Seward was also deeply disliked by those attracted to the Know-Nothing movement. After all, he firmly believed that participatory democracy should include everyone—people of all races and creeds. A man well ahead of his time, Seward wasn't afraid to speak his mind and his views frequently drew sharp criticism. An outspoken foe of slavery, he was once criticized by the illustrious Daniel Webster, who had a rather charitable view of the South, as a "subtle and unscrupulous" man committed only "to the idea of making himself president." Webster knew all about that, for he longed for that elusive office more than any of his contemporaries, including Seward. But the New York Whig leader never shrank in the face of such criticism. Almost alone among Whig politicians—many of whom could be described as reactionaries—Seward, marching to the beat of a different drummer, also welcomed immigration and deplored the fact that so many children, especially in New York City with its large Irish Catholic population, were deprived of an education due to sectarian and racial prejudices. As governor of New York from 1838-42, he insisted that Catholics should be allowed to teach in the New York public school system—a somewhat radical notion in those days.

Seward's casual style, unruly hair and twinkling eyes made him popular among New York voters. Elected to the U.S. Senate by the Whig-dominated New York legislature in 1849, he quickly emerged as one of the most prominent Whig leaders in the country, opposing Henry Clay's compromise proposals in 1850 and promoting Winfield Scott's ill-fated bid for the presidency two years later. Like Lincoln, he held aloof from the emerging Republican Party while denouncing the Know-Nothings. Possibly eyeing the party's presidential nomination in 1856, Seward fervently tried to maintain the Whig Party as a national entity in 1854 and beyond and realized that capturing the New York governorship would go a long way in revitalizing the Whigs as a national entity.

Yet for all his brilliance, Seward's leadership of the Whig Party in New York was in serious jeopardy as the state's 1854 gubernatorial campaign got underway. For starters, he had been badly burned by the inept Winfield Scott during the 1852 presidential campaign. Tiptoeing around the issue of slavery, the Mexican War hero somehow managed to alienate voters on both sides of that crucial issue, driving countless northern Whigs into the Free Soil Party while forcing thousands of Whigs in the South to stay home on election day.

Facing a challenge from the conservative wing of his own party, and a more ominous third-party threat from the bigotry-riddled Know-Nothing crusade against Catholics and immigrants, Seward, refusing to be outmaneuvered, acted swiftly, throwing his support to state Senator Myron Holley Clark on the eve of the Whig Party's state convention. Clark, a 47-year-old hardware merchant-turned-politician, was a delicious Seward touch, appealing to almost every constituency imaginable. A former sheriff from Canandaigua, he was also something of a hero among the state's growing temperance electorate for sponsoring a prohibitory law that was eventually vetoed by Gov. Horatio Seymour. Like Seward, Clark, who was enthusiastically endorsed by the state's growing Anti-Nebraska forces, was also an outspoken opponent of slavery and as a deputy U.S. marshal once vowed never to enforce the Fugitive Slave Act. Moreover, the Ontario County lawmaker also claimed to be a third-degree member of the Supreme Order of the Star-Spangled Banner (SSSB), the secretive patriotic organization founded by Charles B. Allen in 1849, thereby making him acceptable to large numbers of voters who otherwise might have voted for the Know-Nothing ticket.[32]

Seward's forces controlled a solid two-to-one majority over the Silver Grays and a noisy bloc of Know-Nothing delegates when the Whigs convened at their state convention in Syracuse on September 20. Casting aside better-qualified Whig candidates such as state treasurer and ex-Buffalo mayor Elbridge G. Spaulding and former lieutenant governor George W. Patterson—both of whom initially enjoyed Thurlow Weed's powerful blessing—the Whigs enthusiastically nominated Clark for governor on the convention's third ballot. The Whig delegates then unexpectedly dug even further into the Know-Nothing Party's natural constituency by naming Henry J. Raymond of the *New York Times*, a paper generally sympathetic to the nativist movement, for lieutenant governor. A former state legislator and one-time managing editor of *Harper's Monthly*, the 34-year-old Raymond, like Seward, had been instrumental in Winfield Scott's drive for the Whig Party's presidential nomination in 1852. Unlike his gubernatorial running mate, Raymond was also an outspoken foe of the Maine Law. Under Seward's shrewd leadership, the delegates adopted an antislavery platform that carefully avoided any derogatory references to the Know-Nothing movement.

A large numbers of Whigs were unhappy with Clark's nomination, especially the conservative Silver Gray faction, a group loyal to former President Fillmore who had attended the convention with an eye on writing Seward's political obituary. Most of the conservative Whigs viewed the party's nominee not only as being rabidly antislavery, but also something of an intellectual lightweight, a man totally unfit for the state's highest elective office. "Mr. Clark is a respectable citizen without a single qualification" for the office, fumed Francis Granger, the aging Silver Gray leader, predicting later that thousands of moderate and conservative Whigs would oppose the ticket or boycott the election altogether. Contrary to reports in the *Buffalo Commercial Advertiser* and other leading Silver Gray newspapers erroneously suggesting that Clark's nomination was a repudiation of Thurlow Weed's leadership, Granger believed—and accurately so—that Clark was really Weed's handpicked candidate and warned former President Fillmore and other Silver Gray leaders that if the ticket wasn't disavowed, then he and other National Whig leaders in Canandaigua would consider it "as a formal disbanding of the Silver Grays."[33] But Granger wasn't the only Whig complaining about the Clark-Raymond ticket. The Silver Grays aside, a number of hard-

---

32. Anbinder, *Nativism & Slavery*, pp. 77-78. Following the Whig convention in Syracuse, a number of Know-Nothing leaders strenuously denied that Clark belonged to the Order, arguing that he had joined a counterfeit lodge in Canandaigua established by powerful Whig leader Thurlow Weed in order to gain Know-Nothing support in his bid for the Whig Party's nomination. This story, which was later corroborated by Canandaigua's original Know-Nothing council, led many Know-Nothings to conclude that Clark was not a bona-fide member of the Order.

33. Holt, *The Rise and Fall of the American Whig Party*, pp. 901-902.

drinking Whigs, viewing the party's gubernatorial standard-bearer as something of a fanatic on the prohibition issue, were also turned off by Clark's candidacy.

At a second convention held in Auburn in late September, Seward, Weed and other Whig leaders successfully fended off an attempt to fashion a genuine fusion ticket by substituting a Barnburner in place of Raymond for lieutenant governor and secured an endorsement of the entire Whig ticket. That convention, which was attended by the remnants of the Free Soil Party, assorted abolitionists, Seward Whigs, state temperance advocates and delegates to the Saratoga convention the previous month, adopted a number of resolutions wholly unacceptable to the majority of Silver Grays. Unlike the platform adopted in Syracuse, the delegates to the Auburn convention, in addition to calling for an exclusively northern national convention to nominate a presidential ticket in 1856, sharply repudiated the national platforms of both major parties of 1852 and vigorously denounced the Compromise of 1850 and the Fugitive Slave Act. In the convention's closing hours, the remaining Free Soil and anti-Nebraska delegates, with no opposition to speak of, essentially launched the state's Republican Party by agreeing to name a state committee.

The Auburn convention, as it turned out, was the final straw for those Silver Grays who desperately clung to the belief that the old Whig Party could yet be salvaged. While some conservatives may have been initially inclined to support the party's ticket following the Syracuse convention on September 20, it was now almost impossible to find any Silver Grays who were willing to support the Clark-Raymond ticket. Following the developments at Auburn, a number of Silver Grays toyed with the idea of throwing their support to one of the two Democratic factions as a way of defeating the Whig ticket while others considered sitting out the election. In the end, however, most Silver Grays supported the Know-Nothing ticket while still managing to maintain their own political identity.

Meanwhile, the Know-Nothing Party, under the firm grip of the colorful James W. Barker, convened in New York City on October 4. As leader of the secretive Supreme Order of the Star-Spangled Banner, the political arm of the powerful Order of United Americans, Barker was able to pack the convention with his own people, virtually assuring the nomination of Daniel Ullman, a 44-year-old Yale-educated New York City lawyer and prominent member of the Silver Grays who first gained public attention as an unsuccessful Whig candidate for state attorney general three years earlier. A number of Whigs and "Hard Shell" Democrats also attended the convention, hoping that the Know-Nothing Party would endorse their respective tickets. But Barker, who was hell-bent on flexing his new party's muscle, decided to field his own ticket, believing that the burgeoning American Party would prevail in a four-way race. Following a walkout of nearly half the delegates—mostly Clark supporters—Ullman, who had been a contender for the Whig nomination at the Syracuse convention a few weeks earlier, unexpectedly captured a plurality on the first ballot, garnering 256 votes to nativist Whig Joseph W. Savage's 114 and 45 for Order of the United Americans founder Thomas Whitney, while nearly a hundred delegates cast votes for several other candidates.[34] Although his handpicked candidate hadn't received a majority, Barker, fiercely banging his gavel on the podium, declared Ullman the winner.

As startled as anyone by the abruptness of his nomination, Ullman, a longtime Fillmore follower who nearly won the Whig Party's 1852 gubernatorial nomination, jumped to his feet and immediately accepted the party's nomination. Militia officer Gustavas A. Scroggs, a Hard-Shell Democrat from Erie, was named for lieutenant governor. In an effort to reach out to yet another political faction, the Know-Nothing delegates named Joseph B. Williams, a respected Ithaca businessman, for canal commissioner. A Seward Whig, Williams, who had never been a member of the Know-Nothing Order nor a spokesman for the nativist cause, later declined the nomination. The Know-Nothing convention failed to adopt a platform, but issued a lengthy statement on patriotism in which it accused the Roman Catholic hierarchy of "trying to divide the American people, create party strife, and destroy their cherished institutions."[35]

The choice of Ullman to head the party's ticket was most curious, especially given the fact that Barker and other Know-Nothing leaders had opposed his nomination at the Whig convention in Syracuse only two weeks earlier. At that convention, the Know-Nothing president had worked vigorously on behalf of Joseph W. Savage, a longtime nativist and former secretary of the Native American Democratic Association, while other Know-Nothing leaders had rallied behind former American Republican congressman William W. Campbell, a lawyer and historian with impeccable nativist credentials. Then serving as a Superior Court judge, the 48-year-old Campbell was one of the founding members of the politically potent Order of United Americans. Although Savage and Campbell possessed stronger nativist credentials, Barker turned to Ullman, a somewhat lackluster lawyer and perennial Whig candidate of sorts, to lead the Know-Nothing Party in the crucial 1854 election in an attempt to gain the support of the Sil-

---

34. Anbinder, *Nativism & Slavery*, p. 79n.
35. Beals, *Brass-Knuckle Crusade*, pp. 242-243.

ver Grays, whose deep pockets were expected to provide the necessary funding for the printing and distribution of Know-Nothing ballots, literature and campaign posters.[36]

While the Whig Party's Silver Gray faction failed to publicly endorse Ullman's candidacy, the conservative Whigs did provide some badly needed behind-the-scenes support, enabling the Silver Grays to maintain their political independence while avoiding a backlash among the Know-Nothing Party's rank-and-file membership, many of whom regarded the Silver Grays as "pompous blue-bloods"—or worse. Maintaining that he planned to take "no part in politics this fall," former President Millard Fillmore, who also refused to publicly endorse Ullman's candidacy, nevertheless hoped his friend and longtime supporter would be successful and began privately urging his old friends in the Whig Party to join Know-Nothing lodges.[37] By this time, most Silver Grays, or "National Whigs," as they preferred to be called, accepted the Know-Nothing Party as natural allies, a point made clear by Alexander Mann, the influential editor of the *Rochester Daily American*. "If a judicious course is pursued, we may sweep the Union in '56," he wrote Ullman. "We may carry 25 states at least. But shall we fight as *'National Whigs'* or as the *'American Party?'*" That seemed to be the only question.[38]

Ullman's prospects of victory, like those of his Whig rival, were enhanced considerably by the continuing rift in the state's Democratic organization, pitting the so-called Hunker or "Hard Shell" faction led by conservative, pro-slavery ex-Senator Daniel S. Dickinson, against the "Soft Shell" Democrats, nominally led by Gov. Horatio Seymour and Secretary of State William L. Marcy. The deepening division in the party, which, in truth, had as much to do with the personalities of the faction's leaders as anything else, had cost the Democrats dearly in the 1853 statewide elections and, washing away the last vestiges of the once proud party of Thomas Jefferson and Andrew Jackson, threatened to do so again in 1854.

Supportive of internal improvements and the liberal chartering of state banks, the "Hard Shell" Democrats were generally sympathetic to the slaveholding states and were adamantly opposed to the return of former President Martin Van Buren and the Barnburners to the Democratic ranks following the bitterly con-

---

36. Anbinder, *Nativism & Slavery*, pp. 77-79. "Of all the New York factions," wrote the author, "only the Silver Grays lacked a candidate, so Barker probably threw his weight behind Ullman in the hope that Silver Gray support would make victory possible for the Know Nothing candidate."

37. Holt, *The Rise and Fall of the American Whig Party*, p. 905.

38. Foner, *Free Soil, Free Labor, Free Men*, p. 197.

tested 1848 presidential election. Running on the Free Soil ticket that year, Van Buren ran a respectable second in heavily populated New York behind Whig Zachary Taylor, while Democratic standard-bearer Lewis Cass finished a distant third. Still smarting from that campaign, the Hunkers long believed that Van Buren's third-party candidacy was specifically designed to punish the party's establishment for passing him over in favor of James K. Polk four years earlier—a belief later borne out by the somewhat circumspect public conduct of "Prince" John Van Buren, the former president's dapper and spectacularly sarcastic son whose vehement opposition to slavery seemed to have vanished shortly after avenging his father in the 1848 campaign. The younger Van Buren not only supported the Compromise of 1850—legislation bitterly opposed by the nation's abolitionists—but also apparently had few pangs of conscience when he openly backed the pro-southern Pierce and Buchanan administrations.[39]

In the meantime, much of the conservatives' anger was directed at Seymour, who personally agreed to allow the Barnburners back into the fold at the Democratic Party's raucous state convention in Rome during the hot and humid summer of 1849. In doing so, argued one disgruntled editor, Seymour let the Barnburners get the better of the bargain at Rome, foolishly allowing the radicals to eventually capture the state Democratic machinery.[40]

Supported financially by some of the state's leading merchants—those dependent on trade with the South—the "Hard Shell" Democrats convened on July 12, long before any other party met, and nominated former state attorney general Greene C. Bronson of Utica for governor. The irascible Bronson, who was viewed as Dickinson's puppet, had also served briefly in the lucrative post of Collector of the Port of New York, but was deeply offended when Secretary of the Treasury James Guthrie, in a series of far-reaching financial reforms, did away with the collectorship's profitable fee-based salary. President Pierce removed him from the post shortly thereafter. A martyr of sorts, Bronson and other Hunkers sought to punish the Pierce administration by fielding a separate Democratic

---

39. Stewart, *Horatio Seymour of New York*, pp. 111-113; Henry Wilson, *History of the Rise and Fall of the Slave Power in America*, Vol. II, p. 142. Vice President Henry Wilson, a one-time Free Soiler, later maintained that the younger Van Buren would have been one of the most prominent leaders in the Republican Party if only he had remained true to his antislavery principles. Reuben E. Fenton, the Republican governor of New York from 1865-68, seemed to concur, believing that Van Buren—and not John C. Fremont—would have been the Republican nominee for president in 1856 if he had stayed the course.

40. Ibid., pp. 110-113.

ticket in New York's 1853 statewide elections, virtually dividing the party in half and enabling the Whigs to carry the state. A former chief justice of the New York Court of Appeals and, ironically, under whose tutelage Seymour had studied law back in the 1830s, Bronson's candidacy was aided immensely by the personal efforts of the white-haired Dickinson, who stormed up and down the state during the autumn campaign, railing against the Pierce administration and denouncing Seymour while colorfully characterizing the dominant issue of the campaign as "Bronson and good liquor, Seymour and bad liquor and Clark and no liquor at all."[41]

Though silent on the issue of nativism, Dickinson and the "Hard Shell" Democrats, having endorsed the Nebraska bill, were hopeful that the Silver Grays and the Know-Nothings—sure to be rejected by Seward and the Whigs—would turn to their ticket in November, but such support never materialized. Bronson's personal opposition to prohibition and his support of the Kansas-Nebraska Act—positions essentially taken by the "Soft Shell" incumbent—seriously dampened his prospects of winning in a four-way race.

In addition to Bronson's candidacy, the "Hard Shell" faction fielded dozens of state legislative and congressional candidates against "Soft" Democrats, including candidates in at least twenty-seven of the state's thirty-three U.S. House districts, thereby dividing the Democratic vote and enabling Whigs to win in twenty-four of those contests.[42]

Meanwhile, the "Soft Shell" faction, enjoying the support of a majority of the state's growing Irish and Catholic populations, convened in Syracuse in mid-September and re-nominated a somewhat reluctant Horatio Seymour to a second term. Disapproving of nativism and temperance, the "Soft Shell" Democrats, hoping to maintain the support of New York's wealthy manufacturers, carefully straddled the slavery issue, vaguely supporting the Pierce administration's veiled pro-slavery position. Seymour, who had vetoed Clark's controversial prohibitory legislation a few months earlier, had confided in William L. Marcy that he really wasn't really interested in a second term, telling the former Secretary of War that he would prefer to serve as governor of the Nebraska Territory if it was offered to

---

41. Gienapp, *The Origins of the Republican Party*, p. 156.
42. While finishing ahead of their "Soft Shell" opponents in nine of the state's thirty-three congressional races, the "Hard Shell" Democrats claimed only one of New York's U.S. House seats in 1854, that of incumbent John Wheeler in New York City's sixth congressional district. The "Soft Shell" Democrats and the American Party each captured four seats. Moreover, the Know-Nothing Party endorsed nearly half of the successful Whig congressional candidates that year.

him, or possibly spend the next couple of years in Europe—a deeply held desire that he was never able to fulfill.[43]

With his party badly divided, the 1854 campaign proved a difficult one for the embattled Democratic incumbent. Disgusted by President Pierce's mishandling of political affairs in New York and attacked almost daily by Whig candidate Myron Clark on the hot-button issues of slavery and temperance, while the Know-Nothing Party's Daniel Ullman pounded away at foreigners and Roman Catholicism and the crotchety old Greene C. Bronson, nursing grudges, jeered at the Pierce administration in an effort to siphon Democratic votes away from him, Seymour, a remarkably serene man who later refused to order a recount in an election clearly marred by fraud, would have privately preferred to retire quietly from political life. It was only after a great deal of prodding and soul-searching that he eventually agreed to seek a second term—and nearly won.[44]

Were it not for Thurlow Weed's persuasive efforts, the 1854 New York gubernatorial contest might also have included a Republican ticket, thereby dooming Myron H. Clark and the Whigs in what almost certainly would have been a confusing and crowded five-way free-for-all. Such a ticket might also have paved the way for a Know-Nothing victory. It seems that the state's burgeoning anti-Nebraska forces—those responsible for founding the state's Republican Party that tumultuous summer—also called a statewide convention in Saratoga Springs on August 16, leading to speculation that Horace Greeley of the *New York Tribune*, one of the new party's leading proponents, would be nominated for governor. It was no secret that the colorful journalist fervently hoped to launch a new party on an anti-Nebraska and temperance platform that autumn.

Curiously, a number of "Hard Shell" and "Soft Shell" Democrats also encouraged such a movement, possibly in a Machiavellian effort to further speed up the Whig Party's disintegration. In fact, it was a "Hard Shell" Democrat who introduced a resolution to form a Republican Party at the enthusiastic Saratoga convention. A few Silver Grays, hoping to lure antislavery Seward men away from the Whig Party so that they could gain control of the organization, also lent public support to the idea of a Republican fusion ticket. Appealing to his antipathy toward the menacing nativist movement and suggesting that a Republican fusion ticket would split the antislavery vote, virtually dooming Clark's candidacy and all but guaranteeing a Know-Nothing victory, Weed finally convinced Greeley,

---

43.   Stewart, *Horatio Seymour of New York*, p. 163.
44.   Ibid., p. 168.

who chaired the resolutions committee at the Saratoga convention, to abandon the idea of putting yet another ticket in the field.[45]

As was the case with its two major party rivals that year, the Know-Nothing Party also experienced a considerable amount of fission during the 1854 gubernatorial campaign. As in the case of the Democrats, the split proved fatal to the American Party's hopes of capturing the governor's mansion that year. No sooner had Ullman entered the race than a separate group of nativists, hoping to establish an order independent of "Czar Barker," met in Utica and accused the Know-Nothing nominee of being a German Jew. This organization, consisting of roughly thirty SSSB councils and headed by Alfred Cobb, also claimed that Ullman had been born in Calcutta, India—a humorous, but totally incorrect assertion originally made by one of Ullman's classmates at Yale. For the record, Ullman was born in Wilmington, Delaware. Nonetheless, a number of observers found it hilarious that the anti-immigrant Know-Nothing Party was being accused of nominating a foreign-born candidate for high public office.

If that wasn't bad enough, the Know-Nothing ticket also faced vehement opposition from Supreme Order of the Star-Spangled Banner founder Charles B. Allen, whose original organization had been hijacked by the cunning Barker. Following Barker's buccaneering, Allen, scheming in other dark circles, wasted little time in putting together a new nativist organization, called the "Firsters." With 157 chapters in New York and thirty in neighboring New Jersey, Allen's group worked diligently on behalf of Whig candidate Myron Clark in an effort to defeat Ullman and the regular Know-Nothing ticket.[46]

Despite the twin opposition from Know-Nothing defectors and Allen's rival organization, initial returns from small towns and cities in upstate New York indicated an overwhelming Know-Nothing victory in the 1854 gubernatorial election. At first, Ullman appeared headed for a landslide victory over incumbent Democrat Horatio Seymour and the Whig Party's Myron Clark. It wasn't until a day or two after the polls had closed, when the strongly pro-temperance rural vote began to trickle in, that Clark finally pulled ahead. In the final tally, the Whig candidate, running on a fusion ticket that included the state's temperance and anti-Nebraska forces, narrowly upset Seymour, garnering 156,804 votes to the Democrat's 156,495—a difference of only 309 votes. Running strongest in the state's southeast counties, the Know-Nothing's Ullman carried seventeen counties, polling 122,282 votes, or 26.1% of the statewide total. Slicing into Sey-

---

45.   Holt, *The Rise and Fall of the American Whig Party*, pp. 895-896.
46.   Beals, *Brass-Knuckle Crusade*, p. 243.

mour's total, Hard-Shell Democrat Bronson Greene received 33,850 votes, or slightly more than seven percent of the total. Though finishing ahead of Seymour in Broome and Warren counties, the governor's one-time legal mentor failed to carry a single county.

Given the party's declining influence in national politics, Clark's stunning victory kept the Whig Party alive nationally—at least momentarily. While Whigs were naturally buoyed by Clark's success, no fewer than *three* minor parties, including the state's fledgling Temperance Party, legitimately claimed to have provided the difference in his razor-thin victory.[47] No insignificant player in New York politics, the Temperance Party—an antecedent of the national Prohibition Party founded some fifteen years later—waged spirited campaigns in at least two New York congressional districts that year. The party's strongest showing, however, occurred across the river in New Jersey's first congressional district where its candidate, John W. Hazelton, polled an impressive 27% of the vote in a close three-way race against Whig and pro-Nebraska Democratic opposition. (Interestingly, the Maryland Temperance Party, with strong backing from the Know-Nothing's United Sons of America, won ten legislative seats in Baltimore a year earlier—thereby holding the balance of power in the Maryland legislature.)

Despite Ullman's setback at the polls, leaders of the Know-Nothing movement in New York had plenty to cheer about when forty-five Know-Nothings, belonging to the Order of United Americans or the Supreme Order of the Star-Spangled Banner, were elected to the state legislature. The party also captured four seats in Congress. The victorious House candidates included OUA founder Thomas R. Whitney, William W. Valk, Bayard Clarke and Francis S. Edwards, a 37-year-old lawyer who was later implicated in an influence-peddling scandal. A surgeon from Flushing, Long Island, Valk, a native of South Carolina, won his seat with nearly 31% of the vote, defeating his "Hard Shell," Whig, "Soft Shell" and Temperance Party rivals, while Whitney, Edwards, and Clarke, a 39-year-old former attaché to General Lewis Cass during his stint as minister to France in the late 1830s, were elected with formal Whig backing.

The results in New York notwithstanding, the Know-Nothing Party proved that it was still a party to be reckoned with when it picked up yet another gubernatorial victory in 1855. That year, J. Neely Johnson, an ex-Whig, was elected governor of California on the Know-Nothing ticket, becoming the first of two

47. These included not only the Free Soil and Temperance parties, but also the anti-Nebraska (Republican) forces led by the *New York Tribune's* Horace Greeley, the latter of which attempted to launch a fusion ticket earlier that summer—a ticket, incidentally, that almost certainly would have proven fatal to Clark's candidacy.

third-party governors in that state's history. (The other, of course, was Progressive Hiram Johnson). In the 1855 gubernatorial campaign, Johnson, who once drove a mule train, upset two-term incumbent Democrat John Bigler by 4,900 votes. Having been lured to California in search of gold in 1849, Bigler, a former Speaker of the Assembly and the first California governor to win re-election, was the older brother of Pennsylvania Gov. William Bigler, a Democrat who was also defeated by Whig and Know-Nothing opposition a year earlier. Completely absorbing the state's moribund Whig Party and aided by intra-party squabbling among the Democrats, the Americans also took control of the California legislature, winning 56 seats in the assembly to 23 for the Democrats. Thomas M. Coombs, an independent from Alameda County, held the other seat. The Know-Nothing success marked the first time in the state's brief history that a party other than the Democrats controlled the state legislature.

That same year, the Know-Nothing Party, aided immensely by a secret order called Freedom's Phalanx, swept Sacramento's municipal election, winning all but one aldermanic seat while electing James L. English mayor of that city. English later served as state treasurer when the Know-Nothing Party's Dr. Henry Bates was impeached in 1857 for stealing $124,000 in a scandal first uncovered by James McClatchy's six-day old *Sacramento Bee*.[48]

Running under the Citizens' Reform label in a crowded and confusing race that at one time or another included a "Know Something" slate and no fewer than four separate Democratic tickets, the Know-Nothing Party also swept San Francisco's municipal election, putting Stephen Palfrey Webb in the mayor's office. Remarkably, Webb polled 43% of the vote while easily defeating ex-New Yorker Cornelius K. Garrison, the embattled incumbent mayor who polled only eleven percent of the vote, in a race that also included an independent "Cuidado" ticket headed by Lucien Hermann, a Roman Catholic who sharply denounced "the bigotry and intolerance" of Webb's Know-Nothing supporters. The 50-year-old Webb had previously served in the Massachusetts legislature and as mayor of Salem before relocating to San Francisco in 1853. A Harvard-educated lawyer, Webb's tenure as mayor of San Francisco, coming in the aftermath of the California Gold Rush in 1849, was marked by a wave of lawlessness—there were a thousand murders in San Francisco between 1849 and 1856, few of them ever solved—and a flurry of Vigilante activity in which citizens often took the law into their own hands, frequently serving as judge, jury and executioner. Shortly after taking office, Webb became the bearer of bad news, informing city residents that

---

48. Beals, *Brass-Knuckle Crusade*, p. 220.

he had inherited an $840,000 deficit—most of which had been stolen by alderman Henry Meiggs, who absconded to Chile shortly after the election. The Know-Nothing mayor also revealed that the city had accumulated a whopping debt of some two million dollars. Following his stint as mayor, Webb returned to Massachusetts and was again elected mayor of Salem, serving in that capacity from 1860-62. [49]

During this period, the Know-Nothing Party also demonstrated its political might in hundreds of other towns and cities across the country. In Philadelphia, for example, businessman and ex-Whig journalist Robert T. Conrad, promising to recruit a police force of 900 native-born men, was elected mayor on the American Party ticket in 1854. Voters in the City of Brotherly Love had made their presence felt at the ballot box long before that year's municipal election. In 1844, for example, Philadelphia voters had sent eight men to the state House and one to the state Senate on a nativist third-party ticket. Four years later, they also elected five Native Americans to the state House, thereby giving the party the balance of power when the state legislature reorganized in 1849.

In many ways, Conrad was typical of those who gravitated toward the Know-Nothing Party during this period. He was not some sort of zealous xenophobe, but rather a practical politician who viewed the Know-Nothing Party as a realistic replacement for the moribund Whigs. A man of letters, Conrad showed far greater interest in journalism, poetry and as a playwright—contributing several dramas to the American theater—than he did to the narrow nativist cause. To the extent that he expressed any anti-Catholic or anti-immigrant prejudices, it was usually in a dignified and respectable manner.

Voters in Pittsburgh, some 288 miles to the west, also elected a Know-Nothing mayor, choosing William Bingham, a 48-year-old freight forwarder, in a confusing five-way race. Bingham, who had no idea that he might actually win, was as surprised as anyone by the election returns. In Chicago, moreover, voters elected the Know-Nothing Party's Levi Day Boone, a grandnephew of the legendary Daniel Boone, as mayor of that city. As mayor, Boone, who defeated incumbent Mayor Isaac Milliken by a scant 346 votes, increased the city's liquor license fee from $50 to $300 and mandated that licenses be renewed every three months instead of once a year in an attempt to drive small, immigrant saloonkeepers out of business. Like Philadelphia's Conrad, he also replaced foreign-

---

49. Ibid., pp. 216-218; Anbinder, *Nativism & Slavery*, p. 56; Peyton Hunt, "The Rise and Fall of the 'Know Nothings' in California, *California Historical Society Quarterly*, No. 9 (1930), pp. 24-33; *San Francisco Almanac* (Chronicle Books, San Francisco, 1975), p. 80.

born policemen with native-born officers and used his police force to crack down on those bar owners who ignored the city's Sunday closing law. In Rochester, New York, Charles J. Hayden, an ex-Whig and owner of a large furniture factory, was elected mayor on the Know-Nothing ticket in 1855. In his inaugural address, Hayden launched into a bitter attack on immigrants and Roman Catholicism, stirring so much resentment that little was accomplished during his administration. But that wasn't all. In St. Louis, where the American Party's Peter G. Camden served as mayor in the mid-1840s, voters elected two Know-Nothing mayors during this period—Luther Martin Kennett (1850-53) and Washington King (1855-56)—and in Louisville, a city with a large immigrant population, the American Party's John Barbee ran unopposed in that city's 1855 mayoralty race, largely because the incumbent mayor mistakenly claimed that his term of office didn't expire until the following year.

One of the party's most impressive victories occurred in Boston, where physician Jerome van Crowninshield Smith, a 54-year-old anatomy and physiology professor, was also swept into office on the Know-Nothing ticket. A longtime editor of the *Boston Medical and Surgical Journal* whose famous textbook on anatomy went through eleven editions, Smith had been elected port physician of Boston nearly three decades earlier. Receiving at the time what was the largest vote ever cast in a Boston mayoral contest, Smith, who had failed in a previous bid for mayor, ran on a populist, working-class platform during his remarkable 1854 campaign, promising to cut taxes, reduce the city's water rate and put the unemployed to work on public works programs designed to beautify the city and improve the city's roadways. As mayor, he also advocated selling city lots at cut-rate prices to enable citizens of lesser means to acquire or build their own homes—a radical measure that was ultimately squashed by Boston's predominately conservative city council. Although he was a member of the Know-Nothing Party, Smith was by no means typical of those attracted to the new party. Personally harboring little animosity for Catholics, he had once sculpted a bust of John Bernard Fitzpatrick, Boston's longtime Catholic bishop, and during the Civil War he helped recruit a regiment of Irish immigrants to fight for the Union cause. Smith, however, wasn't without controversy. The Free Soilers labeled him "the Black Huntsman of Shawmut" for calling out the militia to return the celebrated Anthony Burns, an escaped slave, back to his owner in the South. Despite strong opposition from Boston's antislavery forces, Smith was nevertheless easily re-elected to a second term, defeating his opponent by nearly 2,000 votes. Know-Nothing candidates running on various "Citizens" tickets also swept municipal elections in other Whig strongholds in Massachusetts, including Cambridge and

Roxbury and, over the next several months, scored victories in Chelsea, Lynn, Marblehead, Stoneham, Waltham and elsewhere. [50]

In Baltimore, little-known businessman Samuel Hinks, a wealthy, self-made grain and flour merchant, was swept into office on the Know-Nothing ticket in October 1854, beginning what historian Jean Baker described in her scholarly book *Ambivalent Americans* as "Maryland's brief, torrid, and sometimes violent political affair with the American party."[51] Hoping to create confusion among the city's electorate, Know-Nothing leaders printed ballots containing the same blue stripes as used by the Democrats. Hinks' election was all the more incredible given the fact that virtually nobody knew he was running until two weeks before the election when the *Baltimore Clipper*, the city's leading and oldest nativist newspaper, publicized his candidacy. Moreover, Hinks, a former Democrat, did not actively campaign and it wasn't until the day of his inauguration that he finally gave his first public address. In addition to electing Hinks, the Know-Nothings scored significant victories in several other Baltimore races, displacing the entrenched Democrats in both branches of the city council.

While most Democrats were stunned by the party's overnight success, many observers believed that it was a political fluke, an inexplicable occurrence that wasn't likely to be repeated. One newspaper editor commented that the Know-Nothings were like a "mushroom party" that seemed "to have sprung into existence like fungi after a summer's rain." Thomas F. Bowie, a Whig-turned-Democratic congressman, predicted that the American Party would, "like a big fish out of water, flop and flounder for a while, soon to die of premature exhaustion."[52] Bowie and other Democrats, however, quickly discovered that the party's early success was no fluke when the American Party, running exceptionally strong on the Eastern Shore and in western and southern Maryland, carried the state in a landslide the following year, electing a state comptroller, a lottery commissioner, four of the state's six congressmen, 54 of 74 seats in the House of Delegates and winning eight of the eleven state Senate seats up for grabs that year. While holding a commanding majority in the House of Delegates, the Know-Nothings also held a plurality in the Maryland Senate with the Whigs holding nine seats along with one Democrat and one Union Party member. In its stronghold of Baltimore, the party captured all ten seats in the assembly as well as the city's lone

50.   Mulkern, *The Know-Nothing Party in Massachusetts*, pp. 68, 80, 108-109; *Pittsfield Sun*, August 24, 1879; Holli and Jones, *Biographical Dictionary of American Mayors, 1820-1980*, pp. 333-334.

51.   Baker, *Ambivalent Americans*, p. 1.

52.   Ibid., p. 2.

state Senate seat. The Know-Nothings even ran reasonably well in the tobacco counties of Calvert and Anne Arundel. Remarkably, only six of the sixty-two men elected to the Maryland legislature on the Know-Nothing ticket in 1855 had previously served in the legislature. In short, the elections of 1854 and 1855 represented a basic political realignment in Maryland—one that would continue until the late 1860s.[53]

"For the rest of the decade," observed scholar Jean Baker, "the Know-Nothings were not, as in other states, a temporary third-party organization soon to dissolve as voters moved in the North to the Republicans, or in the South to the Democrats; rather, they were part of the basic two-party system typical of American politics."[54] In fact, Maryland was the only state carried by former President Millard Fillmore in his ill-fated political comeback on the Know-Nothing ticket in 1856. Even after Fillmore's loss, the Know-Nothing Party continued to flex its muscle in Maryland. In 1857, when the party was clearly on the decline elsewhere, Thomas H. Hicks, a former Dorchester County sheriff, was elected governor on the party's ticket, garnering nearly 55% of the vote against his Democratic rival. By then, the Maryland American Party controlled not only the state House and Senate, half of the state's congressional delegation—including U.S. Senator Anthony Kennedy who was chosen by the Know-Nothing legislature in March 1857—but also numerous municipal and county governments throughout the state. Even as late as 1860 when 41,760 Know-Nothing voters in Maryland voted for the Constitutional Union Party's John Bell—nearly enabling the former Tennessee lawmaker to carry the state—while electing twenty-eight Know-Nothings to the state House of Delegates and four to the state senate, many political observers believed that the Know-Nothing Party would again emerge as a power in statewide politics. Comparing the party to Noah's Ark, the *Baltimore Clipper* predicted a year earlier that the party would survive regardless of what happened in the 1860 presidential election. "When the waters of sectionalism subside, the American Party will step from the ark."[55]

Like their counterparts in Massachusetts, the first Know-Nothing legislature in Maryland, preferring to ventilate rather than legislate, passed few nativist bills—opening themselves to charges of political opportunism by critics clamoring for longer naturalization requirements and investigations into the state's Catholic convents—and instead were bogged down by routine local and state

---

53. Ibid., pp. 81-82.
54. Ibid., p. 2.
55. *Baltimore Clipper*, February 19, 1859, quoted in Baker, *Ambivalent Americans*, p. 151.

issues, such as administration of the state government, the election of a U.S. Senator, the awarding of patronage and the naming of a state printer. While generally sympathetic to the temperance movement, blaming the scourge of alcohol on whiskey-drinking Irish and beer-guzzling Germans, the Know-Nothing legislators also neglected that issue, ignoring their own James Lester, a former member of the Temperance Party who had been elected to the assembly on the Know-Nothing ticket. Much to his chagrin, Lester's tireless efforts to prevent taverns from doing business without the consent of the heads of households within a mile radius of such an establishment, was never passed.[56]

Because their history in the legislature was so short—by 1860 they no longer controlled the House of Delegates or the Senate—the Know-Nothing legislative legacy in Maryland was limited to a few nativist laws that included prohibiting foreign agents from selling insurance in the state and removing certain Catholic properties from tax-exempt status. Their legacy also included reforming the state's patronage system, establishing a public education system under the direction of a state superintendent, and enacting several judicial and tax reform measures, the latter two of which were generally applauded by Democratic newspapers. Their biggest disappointment, however, was in their failure in 1858 to convince Maryland voters to approve a constitutional convention at which time they hoped to enact a series of far-reaching reforms, including several nativist measures as well as one to correct the state's badly apportioned legislature. In the end, the Know-Nothing legacy in the Maryland legislature, while avoiding some of the embarrassing episodes that plagued their counterparts in Massachusetts, wasn't particularly nativist or reform-oriented.

In New Orleans, long a hotbed of nativist activity, voters elected three Know-Nothing mayors between 1856-62, beginning with wealthy businessman Charles M. Waterman, whose stormy administration was marred by violence, bloodshed and controversy. Among other things, he sold licenses to prostitutes for $300 and kept all of the records in his personal possession. Waterman, who virtually deserted his post in 1858, was later impeached and was succeeded in office by the Know-Nothing's Gerald Stith, a newspaper foreman who served until 1860 when he was succeeded by stevedore John T. Monroe, the city's last Know-Nothing mayor and a man who served in that capacity long after the party disappeared from the national scene. Waterman, the city's first Know-Nothing mayor, was as controversial in death as he had been in life. He simply vanished one day without

---

56.   Baker, *Ambivalent Americans*, pp. 88-91.

a trace. A suicide note was apparently left behind and a hat bearing his initials was later found on board a ferryboat, but his body was never recovered.

Owing significantly to the cultural and political battles between the Creoles and the Anglo-Saxons who settled in the region following the Louisiana Purchase in 1803, the Know-Nothing Party was the dominant force in New Orleans politics from the mid-1850s until the invasion of federal troops in April 1862.[57] The party initially ventured forth in New Orleans, a rogue's gallery of corruption throughout most of its history, under the guise of the Independent Reform Party in the city's March 1854 municipal election. Some Democrats in the city concluded that the Independent Reformers were really ex-Whigs trying to resuscitate their former party, but many Creoles, a bit more perceptive than the Democrats, correctly identified the new party as the Know-Nothings in disguise—a charge that the new party chose not to deny. "Body snatchers should not be afraid of ghosts," they responded, adding that a party that frequently brought entire graveyards back from the dead to vote for a straight Democratic ticket shouldn't be afraid of rumors regarding the Know-Nothing Party.[58] The Independent Reformers made some headway in the March election, but failed to dislodge the entrenched Democrats, who maintained control of the city by appealing to the city's large Creole, Irish and German populations and, in part, by stuffing the ballot boxes and manipulating the returns. In one Democratic precinct, for example, the total votes cast exceeded the number of registered voters in the district by some 750 votes. In another instance, Democratic officials, fearing that they had lost the election in that district, seized control of the ballot boxes and proceeded to count the ballots. That autumn, the Know-Nothings returned the favor by routing the Democrats in the state elections while electing a state senator and two state representatives in New Orleans by wide margins.[59] The following year, the American Party was swept into power, winning thirty-four of thirty-five offices. Louisiana's bayou of nativism remained a Know-Nothing stronghold longer than in most other parts of the nation.

The party was somewhat less successful in other parts of the South, in large part because most areas in that region didn't experience the kinds of massive immigration felt in New Orleans or, for that matter, in Louisville and St.

57.   Leon Cyprian Soule, *The Know Nothing Party in New Orleans: A Reappraisal* (Baton Rouge, 1961), pp. 3-26. The differences between the Creoles and the Anglo-Americans were as distinct as night and day. While visiting Louisiana, renowned Scott geologist Sir Charles Lyell observed that both groups cared little for the other.

58.   *Daily Crescent*, March 19, 1854.

59.   Soule, *The Know Nothing Party in New Orleans*, pp. 47-60.

Louis—the chief cities on the inland waterway into the heart of the agricultural South and West. Consequently, in 1850 those cities contained the largest foreign-born populations in the entire South. St. Louis, in fact, had a larger immigrant than native-born population and New Orleans was almost evenly divided during this period. In 1849, the southern states spent over one and a half million dollars on paupers, the vast majority of that on immigrants who swelled the nation's indigent population, flooding the public hospitals and charitable organizations.[60]

Nevertheless, the Know-Nothing Party was still a force to be reckoned with in other parts of the South. One of the most picturesque Know-Nothing leaders in the Upper South was William G. Brownlow of Tennessee, an itinerant Methodist minister and fiery editor of the *Knoxville True Whig*, a paper he had launched in 1849 which eventually grew into the largest weekly in the South.[61] Best known for his caustic and trenchant editorials, the "Fighting Parson" despised the Catholic Church, suggesting at one point that Catholicism and its "corrupt clergy," if left unchecked, would "overturn the civil and religious liberties of the United States."[62] Catholics were gaining power in the United States, he sneered, because "the worst class of American politicians, designing demagogues, selfish office-seekers, and bad men, calling themselves Democrats and 'Old-Line Whigs'" were wooing them to win elections.[63] A lifelong Whig, the vitriolic 49-year-old preacher-turned-editor joined the American Party shortly after its' founding and labored tirelessly to promote the party in Tennessee and elsewhere in the South. An early Know-Nothing enthusiast, the fiery editor, like other crestfallen Whig converts, predicted that the American Party would "swallow up all other parties" while holding itself aloof "from the trading, huckstering spirit of party, which has divided and distracted the Whig Party."[64]

Brownlow campaigned vigorously for former Whig congressman Meredith P. Gentry in his uphill campaign against folksy Democratic incumbent Andrew Johnson—the orphan-tailor and a man Brownlow personally abhorred—in Tennessee's razor-thin 1855 gubernatorial campaign. During that bitter campaign, the "Hell Hound," as his enemies derisively referred to him, lashed out against a rival Nashville editor who was supporting Johnson, calling him a "dirty lying and

---

60. Overdyke, *The Know-Nothing Party in the South*, pp. 10-11.
61. E. Merton Coulter, *William G. Brownlow, Fighting Parson of the Southern Highlands* (Chapel Hill, 1937), p. 50.
62. Overdyke, *The Know-Nothing Party in the South*, p. 231.
63. Holt, *The Rise and Fall of the American Whig Party*, p. 847.
64. Ibid., p. 926.

unscrupulous Abolitionist" who edited "a dirty scurrilous sheet." Like a fish that only thrived in dirty water, Brownlow argued, "the *Nashville Union and American* would not exist a week out of the atmosphere of slander and vituperation," adding that the Nashville newspaper was a fitting mouthpiece for those who rallied "under the dark piratical flag of Andrew Johnson and his progressive Democracy."[65] The colorful Knoxville editor continued to rail against the Catholic Church and against Johnson throughout the hard-fought campaign, but it wasn't enough to prevent the future vice president and president from garnering a 2,000-vote majority.[66]

A longtime partisan of John Bell, Brownlow enthusiastically supported Tennessee's senior senator for the Know-Nothing Party's presidential nomination in 1856—placing Bell's name atop his *Knoxville True Whig* editorial column—and campaigned vigorously for the Constitutional Union standard-bearer during the four-cornered 1860 presidential campaign. Though favoring slavery, the fiery editor later opposed secession with such vehemence that he was arrested and jailed by the Confederacy. Following his release, he traveled to the North where he gave a series of hard-hitting speeches attacking the Confederacy and becoming a hero of sorts above the Mason-Dixon line. Returning to Knoxville while hostilities were still raging, Brownlow revived his paper and was elected governor in 1865. Despite ill health, he was later elected to the U.S. Senate as a Republican, serving from 1869-75.

By the mid-1850s, various Know-Nothing organizations, including the Supreme Order of the Star-Spangled Banner, claimed to have five million members nationally and were reportedly gaining 5,000 new adherents a week. While their figures were undoubtedly inflated, there is little question that the movement was growing by leaps and bounds. Disenchanted Whigs in the North, as well as proslavery southern Whigs who couldn't stomach the idea of joining their longtime nemesis—the Democrats—joined the Know-Nothing Party in droves. Even President Ulysses S. Grant admitted in his memoirs that he had joined the party briefly, if only out of curiosity. The party's numbers, of course, were also increased by hundreds of thousands of voters from both major parties who feared the specter of a Papal domination of America.

Like every successful political movement, the Know-Nothing Party had hundreds of people who claimed to have given birth to the party, but none were as

65.   Overdyke, *The Know-Nothing Party in the South*, p. 179.
66.   Despite Johnson's victory, the Know-Nothings, in coalition with the state's Whig Party, gained control of the Tennessee legislature. They also elected five of the state's ten congressmen.

colorful—and less credible—than widely read dime-store novelist Ned Buntline. Best known for his more than 400 novels, Buntline was the person who first discovered William Cody, dubbed him "Buffalo Bill" and went on to write a series of dime novels based on his life's story. Incredibly, he also launched Cody's theatrical career in a play written in less than four hours. A stocky, red-bearded man with a gift for storytelling, the amazing Buntline (a pseudonym for Edward Zone Carroll Judson) lived an extraordinarily adventurous life and, indeed, was the founder of a quasi Know-Nothing group called the Guard of Liberty, which operated mainly in New England. Modeling itself after a military unit, the Guard of Liberty was apparently organized to counterbalance the growing number of Irish militia units that sprang into existence during this period. A thoroughly fascinating character, Buntline ran away to sea as a young boy, serving as a midshipman in the Navy when he was barely fifteen years of age. Following a few incredible adventures in the Seminole Wars and later in the fur trade in the northwest, Buntline was tried for murder in Nashville when he was twenty-three and barely escaped with his life when an unruly mob tried to lynch him.

Buntline, who had as many enemies as friends, was also a somewhat unscrupulous character and was frequently in trouble with the law and almost always financially strapped. He was accused of blackmail on several occasions. Unabashedly pro-American and bitterly anti-British—a stance that often put him in sharp conflict with his wife and in-laws—Buntline was implicated in the 1849 riot at Astor Place Opera House in New York City in which twenty-three people were killed and dozens more injured. The Astor Place riot, one of the bloodiest riots in U.S. history, took place during the Oregon boundary dispute when a wave of strong anti-British sentiment was sweeping the country. It involved a bitter rivalry between two popular Shakespearean actors—Britain's snobbish William Charles Macready and American tragedian Edwin Forrest, a brawny and melodramatic stage idol whose dashing and athletic style had captivated thousands. He was also a personal friend of Ned Buntline. The rivalry between Macready and Forrest dated back to the early 1840s when Forrest dogged the English actor during a tour of North America. A few years later, Macready's audiences boycotted the American actor when he toured Europe. While in Edinburgh, the confrontational Forrest stood up in his private box and hissed out loud during the British actor's performance of *Hamlet*. When Macready, a former lawyer, returned to the United States for a second tour in 1848-49, Buntline denounced the British actor in his paper, *Ned Buntline's Own*, and prodded them to action. A rowdy crowd had jeered and hissed at Macready during an appearance on May 7, prompting the British actor to denounce them as paid hecklers. "So fair and

foul a day I have not seen," he said. "Be off with you!" During a repeat performance of *Macbeth* on May 10, thousands of New Yorkers—many of them at
Buntline's urging—swarmed in and around New York's Astor Place Opera
House. Buntline, dressed in a blue frock coat with gilt buttons and a stovepipe
hat, was one of those in attendance. Following a disturbance during the first act
in which several people in the audience were forcibly removed by police officers,
all hell broke loose, with fists and cobblestones flying and policemen, who had
rushed in to the quell the disturbance, firing indiscriminately into the crowd, killing and wounding dozens. When it was all over, twenty-three people were dead.
Buntline, who was arrested and charged with conspiracy to riot, was later found
guilty and sentenced to one year at hard labor on notorious Blackwell's Island.[67]

There's little question that Buntline, a self-styled political reformer who was
known to get drunk after delivering temperance lectures, strongly embraced the
Know-Nothing movement. He even modeled his own Guard of Liberty after the
popular nativist party. But he certainly wasn't its founder. "Buntline had no more
to do with its origins than the man in the moon," insisted one Massachusetts
Know-Nothing.[68]

Nathaniel P. Banks: Third-Party Speaker of the House

With the Democrats sharply divided over the Kansas-Nebraska Act and the
Whigs virtually on life-support, the Know-Nothing Party was positioned, at least
for a short duration, to replace one of the country's two major parties. By carefully avoiding the controversial slavery issue, Know-Nothing leaders believed they
could avoid the same pitfalls that had ripped the country's two major parties
asunder. Succeeding in that, Know-Nothing leaders were confident that they
would win the presidency in 1856. They were hardly alone in this belief. The
New York Herald, for instance, virtually conceded that the new party would carry
ten states with 140 electoral votes and possibly enough to reach the magic thresh-
old of 149 needed to elect the next president.

As with the Free Soilers in the 31st Congress, a third party again held the balance of power in the U.S. House of Representatives. The newly-formed Republi-

---

67.   In fairness to Buntline, several other newspapers, including James Gordon Bennett's
       New York Herald, Horace Greeley's *New York Tribune* and William Cullen Bryant's
       New York Evening Post, also helped to inflame the city's passions during this period.
68.   Anbinder, *Nativism & Slavery*, p. 22n.

can Party, whose candidates ran under a variety of labels in the 1854-55 mid-term congressional elections—including that of the Anti-Nebraska, People's and decimated Whig parties—controlled 101 seats in the new Congress; the Democrats, who lost 76 seats in the mid-term elections, held a mere 81 seats; while fifty-one out-and-out Know-Nothings held the balance. At least one source places the number of Know-Nothings in the 34th Congress as high as seventy. Even more astonishing is the fact that nearly two-thirds of the Republicans elected to the House in 1854-55 enjoyed at least some degree of Know-Nothing support and many of them had at least a nominal connection to the nativist movement. In Pennsylvania, for instance, seventeen of the state's twenty-five congressmen, including twelve of the fifteen Whigs elected that year, were or would become members of the Know-Nothing Order.

The American Party was clearly a party to be reckoned with and nowhere was its presence more sharply felt than in the protracted and bitterly contested election of Nathaniel P. Banks, "the Bobbin Boy of Massachusetts," as Speaker of the U.S. House of Representatives. That election, which took nine weeks and 133 ballots, demonstrated just how much influence a third party, holding the balance of power, can really wield on Congress. As such, the Know-Nothings impact on the 34th Congress was unparalleled in American history.

No stranger to third-party politics, Banks, who was considered "the very bone and sinew of Free Soilism," was first elected to Congress on a Democratic-Free Soil coalition ticket in 1852. Remarkably, three of the four original candidates for Speaker of the House that year had been elected on the American Party ticket and the other, a nominal Whig, enjoyed considerable Know-Nothing support.

The party's new-found clout was most vividly illustrated by the fact that the Democrats, having been shellacked in the mid-term congressional elections, didn't bother to put up their own candidate and instead threw their support to the Know-Nothing's Humphrey Marshall of Kentucky, a former minister to China, while the Republicans nominated the antislavery Banks. The Massachusetts congressman, who wore his convictions on his sleeve, firmly believed that the repeal of the Missouri Compromise was an act of dishonor and vowed to do everything in his power to assure that the institution of slavery would not benefit from its repeal. Moreover, the Know-Nothing caucus in the House, led by Alabama's William R. Smith and Thomas R. Whitney of New York, put up yet another candidate for Speaker—Henry W. Fuller, a Pennsylvania Whig with strong nativist leanings. Complicating matters even further, most northern Know-Nothing congressmen decided to back four-term Ohio Rep. Lewis D. Campbell, an ardent antislavery advocate. The 44-year-old Campbell, a farmer and former Union army officer who had been active in the Free Soil Party, was easily re-elected to Congress in 1854 on an Anti-Nebraska fusion ticket, trouncing Democrat Clement L. Vallandigham.

A unified Know-Nothing Party probably could have put Pennsylvania's Fuller over the top in the early balloting, but it became increasingly clear that the American congressmen, lining up behind four different candidates, were as badly split over the slavery issue as the Democrats and Whigs. While the Democrats and the Know-Nothings traded horses several times through the exhaustive balloting, the Republicans continued to stick with Banks. After all, he wasn't a quitter. One of the most persistent political figures of his time, Banks was first elected to the Massachusetts legislature in 1849 on his *eighth* try.

In ballot after ballot, Fuller and Banks both fell short of the 118 votes needed to win. Throughout the nine-week ordeal, Know-Nothing leaders William Smith, Thomas R. Whitney, Leander Cox of Kentucky and Jacob Broom, one of the party's most electrifying speakers, made prolonged and virulent attacks on Catholics and immigrants. Mississippi's long-winded Stephen Adams, a Know-Nothing who had been elected as a Union Democrat to replace Jefferson Davis in 1852, delivered similar diatribes in the U.S. Senate.

Determined to thwart Banks' chances, the Democrats and southern Know-Nothings (dubbed the "South Americans"), traded horses several times after Humphrey Marshall dropped out of the race on the twenty-eighth ballot, supporting William A. Richardson of Illinois, who held Stephen A. Douglas' old seat in Congress. They later switched to South Carolina's James L. Orr before finally throwing their support to three-term Democrat William Aiken, a wealthy plantation owner and former governor of South Carolina. During the Civil War, Aiken, who at one time had been steadfastly opposed to secession, was arrested by Union authorities for making heavy donations of cash and supplies to the Confederacy.

Hoping to end the nine-week struggle and believing that they could muster enough support to elect Aiken, twelve Democrats joined with the Republicans in adopting a plurality resolution on February 2, 1856. The Speaker no longer needed a majority. Much to their chagrin, however, Banks was narrowly elected on the 133rd ballot (the fourth vote taken under the new plurality resolution adopted earlier that day), receiving 103 votes to Aiken's 100. Pennsylvania's Fuller, who dropped out of the race *three* times during the prolonged battle, received a half-dozen votes, Lewis D. Campbell of Ohio received four and one congressman voted for Daniel Wells, Jr., a Wisconsin Democrat. In the final analysis, nearly half of the Know-Nothing congressmen sided with the Democrats while the rest supported Banks. However, a handful of Know-Nothings, including Broom and Whitney, stuck with Fuller until the bitter end.

The election of the antislavery Banks—the only third-party Speaker of the House in U.S. history—sent shockwaves throughout the South. His election was considered the most serious setback to slavery since the passage of the Henry Clay-inspired Missouri Compromise of 1820.

Lacking a formal education, Nathaniel Prentiss Banks, the eldest of seven children, was forced to go to work in his father's cotton mill at an early age to help the family make ends meet. Refusing to allow his humble origins hold him back, the self-educated Banks obtained some command of Latin and Spanish and seized every opportunity to engage in public speaking, lecturing on temperance and taking part in a local debating society as a young man. He also studied to become an actor and made an appearance in Boston as Claude Melnotte in *The Lady of Lyons* before turning to other pursuits. He was admitted to the Massachusetts bar in 1839, worked as an inspector in the Boston customs house, and later served as publisher and editor of a small weekly newspaper.

Turning to politics—his first love—the ambitious Banks lost seven bids for a seat in the lower house of the Massachusetts legislature before finally winning a seat in 1849 as a Democrat. He became Speaker of the state House two years later and was elected president of the state constitutional convention of 1853—a convention described by one historian as "the ablest body that ever met in Massachusetts." Banks was first elected to Congress as a Democrat in 1852, narrowly defeating Whig Luther V. Bell, a physician-turned-politician who as superintendent of the McLean Hospital for the Insane wrote a paper describing a form of insanity that became known as "Bell's Disease." In the House, the freshman congressman demonstrated considerable independence and courage by voting against the Kansas-Nebraska legislation. Having alienated so many of his Democratic supporters by his staunch antislavery advocacy, Banks ran for re-election on the Know-Nothing ticket in 1854, amassing over 73% of the vote against his major-party rivals.

Banks viewed the Speaker's job as an executive parliamentary post rather than a partisan political position. Serving during a period of bitter partisanship, Banks rose above the fray and demonstrated considerable tact and impartiality. Regarded as one of the most capable Speaker's in history, his decisions were always prompt and impartial and not one of them was ever overruled. Though he gave the antislavery forces bare majorities on a number of committees, he named several of his most ardent opponents as committee chairmen. He served as Speaker until 1857.

Despite winning the coveted Speaker's post and holding a clear balance of power in the 34th Congress, the Know-Nothing lawmakers were unable to push through even a modest portion of their party's agenda, including its longstanding demand for a twenty-one-year period for naturalization. As was the case in 1850 when Philadelphia's Lewis C. Levin, then the only Native American member of Congress, tried unsuccessfully to introduce the measure in the House of Representatives, the issue aroused scarcely any interest from most Whig and Democratic lawmakers. Despite an impassioned plea by Mississippi Democrat Stephen Adams in the Senate and the tireless efforts of New York's Thomas R. Whitney in the House, the Know-Nothing proposal died without a vote ever being taken. The failure of the Know-Nothing lawmakers to force a vote on one of their most important measures cost the party dearly and no doubt hastened its decline.[69]

Quickly outgrowing his association with America's Know-Nothing Party, Banks was re-elected to Congress as a Republican in 1856. The following year, he became the first Republican governor in the history of Massachusetts when, after vigorously barnstorming the state, he defeated three-term Know-Nothing Gov. Henry J. Gardner by more than 23,000 votes in a three-cornered race with Democrat Erasmus D. Beach.

Though the Know-Nothing Party initially attracted many outstanding antislavery leaders such as House Speaker Nathaniel Banks, Representative Lucien Barbour of Indiana, an Amherst College-educated lawyer who once defended a fugitive slave, and Senator Henry Wilson of Massachusetts, to name but a few, the party was not without its antislavery critics. The *New York Tribune's* Horace Greeley, not surprisingly, was the most vociferous, attacking the party as a "swindle" and tool of the powerful slave interests. On another occasion, the colorful newspaper editor denounced the party "as devoid of the elements of persistence as an anti-Cholera or anti-Potato rot party."[70]

Know-Nothing critics, to be sure, abounded. George W. Julian, the Free Soil Party's vice presidential standard-bearer in 1852, also believed that Know-Nothingism was part of a sinister plot masterminded by the slave oligarchy. Its birth, coinciding with the repeal of the Missouri Compromise, "was not an accident," he said. "It was a well-timed scheme to divide the people of the free states" with trivial side issues, a diversion that enabled the South to remain united in its great cause—the preservation of slavery. By fueling "Protestant jealousy" and hatred against the Pope in a crusade against Catholics and immigrants, Julian main-

69.   Billington, *The Protestant Crusade*, pp. 410-411.
70.   Horace Greeley, *Whig Almanac for 1854*, p. 10.

tained that slaveholders believed they could continue their peculiar institution into perpetuity. "On this ground, as an antislavery man, I opposed it with all my might from the beginning to the end of its life," Julian later recalled. "It was not only irresistible in numbers, but it fought in the dark."[71]

A few groups, such as Joseph Medill's little-remembered "Know-Somethings," which hoped to drive men out of the Know-Nothing movement and into the Republican Party, relished in attacking the American Party's methods and secretive nature. Launched in January 1855, Medill's covert organization was designed to provide a vehicle in which the nativists and antislavery elements could cooperate. "It is the best that can be done to keep Know-Nothingism from doing mischief until the fever for secret societies is past," said Medill.[72] And there were men like Thomas D. English, a Philadelphia-born physician and lawyer who delighted in crusading against nativism. A poet and playwright and friendly adversary of Edgar Allen Poe, English, who later served two terms in Congress as a Democrat in the early 1890s, routinely castigated the Know-Nothings. Of this strange new and seemingly xenophobic party, Abraham Lincoln, refusing to give up the Whig ship even as its deck was being flooded by the rising tide of the Know-Nothing tidal wave, had this to say in a letter to his longtime friend Joshua F. Speed:

> Of their principles, I think little better than I do of the slavery extensionists...Our progress in degeneracy appears to me to be pretty rapid. As a nation we began by declaring 'all men are created equal.' We now practically read it 'all men are created equal, except Negroes. When the Know-Nothings get control, it will read 'all men are created equal, except Negroes, foreigners, and Catholics.' When it comes to this I should prefer emigrating to some country where they make no pretense of loving liberty—to Russia, for instance, where despotism can be taken pure, and without the base alloy of hypocrisy.[73]

Yet even as late as the 1860 presidential campaign, Lincoln's opponents tried to make political hay out of the situation by spreading rumors that Lincoln had once belonged to a Know-Nothing lodge in Quincy, Illinois, thereby hoping to force the Republican presidential standard-bearer to deny the charge—possibly costing him the support of thousands of former Know-Nothings. "Our adversaries think they can gain a point if they could force me to openly deny the charge

---

71. Julian, *Political Recollections*, pp. 141-142.
72. Gienapp, *The Origins of the Republican Party*, p. 180.
73. McPherson, *Battle Cry of Freedom*, p. 141. Lincoln nevertheless conceded that many of his friends in central Illinois were Know-Nothings and that their support was needed to combat the state's pro-Nebraska Democrats.

which some degree of offense would be given to the Americans," he wrote privately.[74]

The party also had its fair share of proslavery critics. Couching his criticism in the euphemism of "secret societies," Thomas W. Ligon, the Democratic governor of Maryland, was highly critical of the order, saying it was his duty to point out the "baneful consequences" of Know-Nothingism which had done more "to sever the ties which should bind together our whole people" than anything that occurred since the founding of the Republic.[75] William T. Barry, a young Democratic congressman from Mississippi, was also a severe critic of the party. In a heated debate with Nathaniel Banks and other Know-Nothing lawmakers on the House floor, the Yale-educated lawmaker from rural Greenwood, Mississippi, argued that the Pope exercised no temporal power and as such Catholicism was of no threat to the United States.[76] Perhaps the most eloquent of the southerners who criticized the Know-Nothing movement was Gov. Henry A. Wise of Virginia. A staunch defender of slavery, the maverick Virginia politician had been the guiding force behind the controversial Gag Law, which prevented antislavery petitions from reaching the floor of Congress, much to the consternation of John Quincy Adams and other antislavery lawmakers. He was also the governor who helped quell John Brown's bloody raid.

Having survived a bitter campaign against fierce Know-Nothing opposition in Virginia's 1855 gubernatorial contest, thereby severely damaging the new party's prestige in the South, Wise sharply attacked the party's "dark lantern" tactics. As early as September 1852, Wise, then a member of the U.S. Senate, questioned the party's conspiratorial secrecy. Just what is the Know-Nothing Party, he asked. "Nobody knows. To do what? Nobody knows. How organized? Nobody knows. Governed by whom? Nobody knows. How bound? By what limitations and restraints? By what rules? By what oaths? Nobody, nobody knows." If the party stands for something good, he asked, then "why not speak it, write it, act it out openly and aloud? Or is it evil," he asked, which loves "darkness rather than light?"[77]

In Tennessee, Governor Andrew Johnson, running for re-election against stiff Know-Nothing opposition in 1855, also sharply denounced the secretive party. Despite receiving a number of death threats, the intrepid future president lashed

---

74. Ollinger Crenshaw, *The Slave States in the Presidential Election of 1860* (Gloucester, Massachusetts, 1969), p. 20.
75. Baker, *Ambivalent Americans*, p. 89.
76. *Congressional Globe*, 33rd Congress, 2nd Session, Appendix, pp. 53-60.
77. Beals, *Brass-Knuckle Crusade*, pp. 143-144.

out against the nativists. Speaking in an open debate packed with hostile Know-Nothings in Murfreesboro, Johnson assailed the party's secret rites and shallowness and denounced the party's strident anti-Catholicism as religious persecution. "Show me a Know-Nothing," he said, "and I will show you a loathsome reptile, upon whose neck the foot of every honest man ought to be placed." Like the hyena, he said, the Know-Nothings "come from their lairs after midnight to prey upon human carcasses."[78]

Greeley, Lincoln, Johnson and other critics of the new party weren't completely off the mark. Nor was Wise, for that matter. There was more than a grain of truth in their harsh assessments of the party. In reality, however, the Know-Nothing Party was not some sort of conspiratorial proslavery or antislavery plot, as some of its critics charged. It was exactly what it appeared to be—a genuine nativist movement. For the record, many of the politicians who flocked to the party's banner—such as Nathaniel Banks and Philadelphia Mayor Robert Conrad—were by no means Catholic haters or rabid xenophobes, but political pragmatists who recognized that the country's fastest growing political party was becoming a bona-fide force in American politics. Not unlike its major-party rivals, the Know-Nothing Party had a certain allure that attracted well-intentioned politicians of all persuasions.

Henry Wilson of Massachusetts, a founder of the Free Soil Party in the late 1840s, is a prime example of the type of well-intentioned men who were attracted to the party. The "Natick Cobbler," as he was dubbed, was certainly not some sort of dyed-in-the-wool nativist by any stretch of the imagination. As publisher of the *Boston Republican*, Wilson, who later served as vice president during Grant's second term, launched his political career as a Whig and helped organize the Free Soil Party in 1848 when the Whigs refused to support the antislavery Wilmot Proviso. The shoemaker-turned-lawyer harbored little, if any, ill will toward Catholics or those who had been born outside the United States. Indentured by his impoverished parents to a farmer as a young boy, the Massachusetts politician, hoping to hitch the Know-Nothing wagon to the Republican horse, vowed to transform the Know-Nothing Party into a genuine antislavery party—or, failing that, to destroy it. Elected to the U.S. Senate in 1855 by the Massachusetts Know-Nothing legislature, Wilson ignored most of the party's nativist concerns while devoting almost all of his energy to the antislavery cause.

Likewise, Sam Houston of Texas, who had converted to Catholicism in 1833 and was elected governor in 1859 on a coalition ticket backed by the Know-

---

78. Ibid., p. 166.

Nothings and the state's pro-Union independent Democrats, could hardly be considered some sort of despot, as Lincoln once implied. Ohio's Salmon P. Chase, while insisting that slavery was the most important issue of the day, was another prominent political figure willing to work with the Know-Nothings. Unlike Lincoln, Chase, a veteran of the old Liberty Party, was willing to concede that there were at least some grounds for concern against Papal influences and organized foreignism. Significant Know-Nothing support made the difference in Ohio's hard-fought 1855 gubernatorial election, enabling the ambitious Chase to eke out a victory with 49% of the vote to 43% for the Democratic incumbent and eight percent for a separate Know-Nothing ticket headed by septuagenarian Oren Trimble, a conservative former Whig governor whose candidacy was denounced by the president of the Ohio Know-Nothing Party as a cunningly devised Democratic trick "to catch gullible Know Nothings" and, if successful, would be interpreted in the South as "an endorsement...of the Kansas-Nebraska swindle."[79] It's worth noting, too, that Chase, who was willing to make at least a symbolic gesture to the concerns of Ohio's growing Know-Nothing constituency while carefully stressing his antislavery position as the "paramount" issue, was elected governor of Ohio that year, while Lincoln, an unabashed critic of the Know-Nothing movement who was still clinging tenuously to the dying Whig Party, lost the first of two U.S. Senate campaigns in Illinois that year.

In many respects, the Know-Nothing Party was far less provocative and inflammatory than suggested by some historians. This was particularly true in Massachusetts where the party captured the governorship, all of the state's congressional seats and—incredibly—373 of the legislature's 376 seats (the Democrats, Free Soilers and Whigs each claimed one seat). Despite being swept into office on the Know-Nothing ticket, the Bay State legislature was almost entirely abolitionist and remarkably progressive.

Aside from establishing a somewhat silly and embarrassing "Nunnery Investigating Committee," enacting a literacy qualification for voting and passing a measure disbanding several Irish militia units (which had provided much of the manpower in returning fugitive slaves to bondage), the Massachusetts legislators deliberately ignored most of the Know-Nothing agenda, including Governor Henry J. Gardner's proposal excluding pauper aliens, and passed a new personal liberty law and legislation prohibiting racial segregation in the public schools—the first law of its kind in the country. The Know-Nothing legislature also approved a series of forward-looking measures that, ironically enough,

---

79.   Anbinder, *Nativism & Slavery*, pp. 178-179.

earned them a reputation as one of the most liberal legislative bodies in the state's history. These included laws abolishing imprisonment for debt, the creation of a state insurance commission and funding for the compulsory vaccination of school children. It also elected Henry Wilson to the U.S. Senate in 1855. Wilson, who did a great deal for the antislavery cause, later served as Ulysses S. Grant's vice president during his second term.

The Know-Nothing dominated legislature, however, wasn't without its embarrassing episodes. Know-Nothing lawmakers created a hue and cry when they increased their own salaries and further angered some of the Bay State's electorate when they conducted a highly publicized investigation into the state's Catholic institutions. Headed by lawmaker Joseph Hiss, the special investigating committee conducted a probe of the state's theological seminaries, academies, convents and Catholic boarding schools, beginning with a visit to Holy Cross College in Worcester. The lawmakers, most of whom were inebriated, wanted to appear impartial at the investigation's outset and gave the college a clean bill of health.

A subsequent visit to the Roxbury Girls' School was quite a different story. Storming boisterously through the school's hallways, poking their heads into closets looking for "dead babies," the Know-Nothing legislators scared the living daylights out of most of the school's female students. After creating such an upheaval, the lawmakers then proceeded to a banquet where copious amounts of champagne was consumed—and charged to unsuspecting taxpayers. In yet another embarrassing incident, committee members submitted expenses that not only included unreasonably high dinner and liquor costs, but also billed the taxpayers for the services of one Mrs. Parker—a reputed local prostitute—following a visit to a convent in Lowell. Hilariously, one committee member actually submitted a voucher seeking reimbursement for $71.80 that he claimed had been stolen from his pocket when nuns supposedly got him drunk.

The whole sordid yet delightfully humorous affair, which was covered extensively in the pages of the Boston *Daily Advertiser*, quickly blossomed into a major scandal. Concerned with possible voter backlash, the Know-Nothing lawmakers expelled Hiss from the legislature by a vote of 137 to 15. Not surprisingly, 224 Know-Nothing legislators—an overwhelming majority—avoided casting a vote in the Hiss case by sneaking out of the chamber shortly before the vote was taken. Despite the Epicurean indulgences of the Hiss committee, the record of the Massachusetts Know-Nothing legislature was, on the whole, a rather progressive one.

Despite the Nunnery Investigating Committee scandal and the defection of Henry Wilson's free soil faction to the Republicans, the Massachusetts Know-

Nothing Party swept all of the statewide contests in 1855—albeit by a smaller margin than the previous year—while retaining control over both houses of the legislature. Polling a plurality, Henry J. Gardner, the Know-Nothing incumbent, was elected to a second term as governor, defeating Republican Julius Rockwell, an antislavery ex-Whig, and Democrat Erasmus D. Beach in a four-cornered race. Gardner received 51,497 votes to Rockwell's 36,715 and 34,728 for Beach. The Whig Party's Samuel H. Walley, a former congressman and longtime ally of the late Daniel Webster, brought up the rear with 13,296 votes, or roughly ten percent of the total.

The situation in Maryland, a state with a violent and sanguinary nativist history, was a little different. The story of the Know-Nothing Party in Maryland, perhaps the most crucial border state during the Civil War, is a remarkable one, not only because it outlived the party elsewhere—including the party's birthplace of New Orleans which elected a Know-Nothing mayor as late as 1860—but because of the unique circumstances that enabled the party to survive beyond the bloody war-between-the-states. The party's long survival in Maryland is all the more remarkable given the fact that nearly half of the state's population supported the North during the Civil War while the other half openly sympathized with the South. Interestingly, the Maryland Know-Nothing Party still clung to a seat in the U.S. Senate as late as 1868—more than ten years after the demise of the national party.

The roots of the Maryland American Party can be traced back to the violence of the notorious "Blood Tub" gang in the party's Baltimore stronghold. Similar nativist groups, adopting such names as the Plug Uglies, the Thunderbolts, the Black Snakes, the Rough Skins and others existed in numerous other towns and cities dotting the American landscape. Their sole purpose was to intimidate and, if necessary, physically abuse Irish Catholics and foreign-born voters. Among the myriad of nefarious and reprehensible acts employed by the Baltimore Blood Tubs, members routinely dunked German and Irish voters in tubs of bloody water and then chased them away from the city's polling places, often kicking them all the way down the street. This act of intimidation not only scared off hundreds of German and Irish voters, but also repelled a number of other citizens from attempting to vote.

Nativist violence reached a crescendo during the 1856 municipal election in Baltimore, leaving seventeen dead and 67 wounded in the wake of Know-Nothing Thomas Swann's successful mayoral campaign. The threat of similar violence in the 1857 municipal election prompted Governor Thomas Ligon, a Democrat, to proclaim martial law and place state militiamen throughout the city on Election Day in order to keep the peace. The intrepid governor also assembled a volunteer army and borrowed 2,000 rifles from Gov. Henry A. Wise of neighboring Virginia, an unrelenting critic of the Know-Nothing movement.

Meanwhile, Thomas Swann, the controversial Know-Nothing mayor, responded in-kind by trying to recruit a special police force to fight shoulder-to-shoulder with Know-Nothing thugs against Ligon's militia. Fortunately, widespread violence was avoided in that election. There were, however, a few isolated instances of violence, fraud and intimidation during Swann's re-election effort in 1858. Swann, the scion of a wealthy Virginia family and former president of the Baltimore & Ohio Railroad, swamped independent Augustus Shutt by a margin of 24,008 votes to 4,859 in that race, but was widely lambasted in the press for failing to curb Election Day intimidation. In some cases, when unsuspecting voters refused to take a red-striped Know-Nothing ballot, they were jabbed in the legs and backs by Know-Nothing poll workers who carried concealed awls or other sharp objects in their shoes. The sporadic Know-nothing violence during the 1858 mayoralty election included an attack on the German-owned *Deutsche Correspondent* newspaper. It wasn't Baltimore's finest moment.

Upon leaving office, Governor Ligon, whose career was cut short by violent Know-Nothingism, angrily denounced the lawlessness in Baltimore, saying that it had bordered on anarchy. The Know-Nothing Party, he asserted, stood as an archenemy of law and order and good government. Bitterly assailing the party as a "conspiracy," Ligon demanded a full-scale investigation of the party and other secret societies. A subsequent legislative investigating committee later issued a whitewash of its probe into the party, denouncing the Democratic governor and demanding proof that any secret societies actually existed.

Despite the violence and intimidation that marred his mayoral campaigns, Swann, who brought the Baltimore and Ohio Railroad from the brink of financial collapse in the early 1850s, actually compiled a rather impressive record as Baltimore's chief executive. Among other things, he modernized the city's fire companies, introduced a street railway system and beautified the city's park system. A staunch secessionist during the Civil War, Swann outlived the Know-Nothing Party and was subsequently elected governor of Maryland on the Union Party ticket in 1864 and was elected to the U.S. Senate by the Democratic legislature three years later.

Already a major factor in the city of Baltimore, the American Party made its mark in statewide politics with the election of little-known Thomas H. Hicks in the 1857 gubernatorial election. Hicks, who denounced Gov. Ligon's attempt to enforce free and open elections in Baltimore by the use of rifles and bayonets, piled up an impressive four-to-one majority in that city, enabling him to defeat his Democratic rival by more than 8,000 votes. All of the party's other statewide candidates were also swept into office that year, including a predominantly Know-Nothing legislature. The party also captured three of the state's six congressional seats.

A somewhat obscure 62-year-old former sheriff of Dorchester County and the first of two Know-Nothing governors of Maryland, Hicks is perhaps best remembered for his role in preventing his state from joining the Confederacy during the Civil War. Like Sam Houston of Texas, Hicks faced strong secessionist sentiment, but unlike Houston—who eventually failed to prevent secession in the Lone Star State—the little-remembered Know-Nothing governor of Maryland courageously resisted the extralegal steps taken by his state's secessionist forces.[80] At the beginning of the war—and at great personal risk—Hicks, a professed Unionist, deliberately delayed calling a special session of the state legislature as a way of blocking Maryland's secession. It was a highly unpopular decision and numerous threats were made on his life. A riot, fueled by the arrival of federal troops in Baltimore on April 19, 1861, took the matter out of his hands, but not before his delaying tactic left the state's secessionists powerless to act.

---

80. Potter, *The Impending Crisis*, p. 510.

8

A Fleeting Three-Party System

✦

Know-Nothings and Republicans Replace the Moribund Whigs

Nationally, the year 1855 proved to be critical in the history of the rapidly grow-ing Know-Nothing Party. At a national council meeting in Philadelphia chaired by "Czar" James W. Barker, party leaders wrangled over the slavery question, cul-minating in a walkout of antislavery delegates led by Senator Henry Wilson of Massachusetts, a staunch free-soil advocate who was committed to shaping the Know-Nothing Party into a genuine antislavery party or destroying it altogether. During the hot and humid June gathering, southern delegates, led by Virginia's Alexander R. Boteler, viciously denounced Wilson and other antislavery delegates from Massachusetts.

The divisive meeting also featured a verbal assault on Charles Gayarre, a well-known historian, playwright and former judge who headed the Louisiana delega-tion. In his address to the convention, Gayarre, a prominent Catholic, told the delegates that Louisiana Catholics were "free from those gross superstitions which you attribute to the church of Rome" and argued that Catholics in the Cajun State were "enlightened" and "would not permit the most distant ecclesiastical interference with politics."[1] Several Know-Nothing leaders agreed with the former judge, including Virginia's John Minor Botts, an ambitious and articulate ex-Whig who for some time had advocated allowing Catholics to join the party. Despite his impassioned defense of Catholics, Gayarre, who had served in the U.S. Senate as a Jacksonian Democrat back in the 1830s, was later disqualified from the meeting when a resolution allowing Catholics to participate in the party

---

1.   Soule, *The Know Nothing Party in New Orleans,* p. 66.

was overwhelmingly rejected. The deeply disappointed Gayarre eventually left the party.

Prior to the defection by the party's antislavery delegates, the Know-Nothing Party was arguably better positioned than the fledgling Republicans, founded a year earlier, to replace the moribund Whigs as the country's second major party. Had it not been for the issue of slavery, it is possible—indeed, probable—that the two major parties in America today would be called the Democrats and Americans. The antislavery Republicans, one could argue, probably would have gone the way of the earlier Liberty and Free Soil parties and vanished forever. Or, possibly, the Grand Old Party might have survived as a persistent third party much like the age-old Prohibitionists or the modern-day Libertarians. After all, Republicans, as the witty and perceptive Eugene J. McCarthy once noted, never really die. "They're somewhat like the lowest forms of plant and animal life," McCarthy quipped. "Even at their highest point of vitality there is not much life in them; on the other hand, they don't die."[2]

At a second meeting in Philadelphia in February 1856, only days before the party's presidential nominating convention, the American Party's national council adopted a platform calling for a 21-year residency requirement for naturalization, the limitation of elective office to native-born Americans and tough measures designed to prevent paupers and criminals from legally entering the United States. The Know-Nothings also endorsed popular sovereignty, an idea championed by Democratic Sen. Stephen A. Douglas of Illinois as a solution to the slavery crisis. The Illinois lawmaker's proposal, of course, had virtually split the Democrats and Whigs in two while hastening the founding of the Republican Party, allowing the territories themselves to decide whether they would join the Union as slave or free states.

Caught in a moral spider web over slavery, the fastest growing third party in American history experienced a near-suicidal split at its national convention in Philadelphia, leading to yet another defection by antislavery delegates. By a 141 to 59 vote, the party's delegates rejected a resolution urging the nomination of candidates who favored restoring the Missouri Compromise of 1820. This overwhelming setback caused most antislavery delegates, including almost all of the New England delegations, to storm out of the Know-Nothing convention. The bolters quickly formed the rival North American Party and scheduled their own convention for June.

---

2.   Lewis Chester, Godfrey Hodgson and Bruce Page, *An American Melodrama: The Presidential Campaign of 1968* (New York, 1969), p. 183.

Meanwhile, the remaining Know-Nothing delegates had to choose among several prominent candidates seeking the party's presidential nomination that year. Chief among the presidential hopefuls were former President Millard Fillmore and the enigmatic and rugged Sam Houston of Texas. Other leading aspirants included George Law of New York, the flirtingly ambitious 71-year-old Supreme Court Justice John McLean and former Kentucky lawmaker Garrett Davis, a bitter anti-Catholic lawyer and close friend of the late Henry Clay. The ambitious, if not impulsive, Robert Stockton of New Jersey had also thrown his hat in the ring.

Millard Fillmore, who had joined a Know-Nothing lodge in 1855, was clearly regarded as the party's front-runner. The former chief executive had won the hearts and minds of many nativists when, echoing other disgruntled Whigs, he flayed against the growing influence of foreign-born voters, claiming that they were "fast demoralizing the whole country; corrupting the ballot box—that great palladium of our liberty—into an unmeaning mockery where the rights of native born citizens are voted away by those who blindly follow their mercenary and selfish leaders."[3]

Meanwhile, the legendary Sam Houston, an erratic expansionist and surreptitious schemer, had stoked the fire of his presidential ambitions when he commissioned Charles Edward Lester to write an official "campaign biography," which was originally published in 1850. A self-serving book, Lester's biography was a transparent attempt to acquaint the American public with Houston's heroism, wit and unselfish nature. But it turned out to be an almost embarrassing self-aggrandizement of the ambitious Texan's life. Read by thousands, Lester's book drew the wrath of several of those who were intimately familiar with Houston's life story. One of the book's sharpest critics was Thomas Jefferson Green, who had been in charge of recruiting for the Texas army during the war for independence from Mexico. Green was one of several critics who gnashed his teeth at "Sham Houston's" book.

Adopted by Cherokee Indians when he was sixteen, Houston's life was marred by a string of failures and despair, including a lifelong struggle with alcoholism. It was also graced with tremendous political and military success, including two terms in Congress and one term as governor of Tennessee in the 1820s; commander in chief of the Texas Army during its war for independence with Mexico in 1836, culminating with his victory over Santa Ana at San Jacinto; first president of the Texas Republic; and, after statehood, one of the state's first two mem-

---

3.   Billington, *The Protestant Crusade*, p. 326.

bers of the U.S. Senate. He later served as an anti-secessionist governor of Texas from 1859-61, before being deposed for failing to take the oath of allegiance to the Confederate States.

A volatile and controversial figure, Houston had puzzled many of his support-ers in 1852 when he failed to actively seek the Democratic presidential nomina-tion when it almost certainly could have been his for the asking. Considered a frontrunner by many Democratic insiders, Houston inexplicably stayed on the sidelines that year, a conspicuous absentee in a year when the Democrats were desperately scouting about for a genuine war hero to run against the Whig Party's Winfield Scott. Representative Andrew Johnson of Tennessee, who was later picked as Lincoln's vice-presidential running mate in 1864, was one of those who tried unsuccessfully to prod the Texan into the race, saying that he was "the only man in our ranks that can defeat General Scott." But Houston whittled away his first real chance at the presidency, while dark-horse candidate Frank Pierce of New Hampshire, an obscure colonel in charge of volunteers at the outset of the Mexican War, won the Democratic nomination on the 49th ballot and went on to clobber his better-known Whig rival in the general election.

There is little question that Sam Houston, who had blown an earlier shot at the presidency, wanted the Know-Nothing nomination in 1856—and wanted it badly. He realized that this was probably his last chance at history and he wasn't about to skimp on it.[4] As such, the illustrious Texas senator quickly aligned him-self with the Know-Nothing Party, publicly announcing his adherence to the new party on July 24, 1855. His change of party was such big news in Texas that the *Texas State Times* and the Austin *Confederate* printed special editions of their papers. Houston's transition to the Know-Nothing cause was a smooth one. After all, he had been exposed to nativism in the 1840s while recuperating from wounds suffered at San Jacinto in the home of New Orleans nativist leader Will-iam Christy, the fiery founder of Louisiana's Native American Party in the mid-1830s.

Shortly after switching parties, Houston set out on a speaking tour through the remainder of that year and the early part of 1856, repeatedly hammering away at the other three parties—the Democrats, Whigs and Republicans. The Democrats, he told an American Party barbeque in Austin, had gotten itself into a "prodigious pickle" over the slavery issue at the expense of other crucial issues, such as immigration. The one-time Democrat later said that his former party

---

4.   Actually, Houston ran again four years later when he unsuccessfully sought the Con-stitutional Union Party's presidential nomination.

"has more wings than the beast of Revelations." The Whigs, he said on another occasion, live on "only in the memory of its great name" and the antislavery Republicans were far too radical, sectional and single-minded to lead the country.

After stumping for several months, Houston seemed to have built a powerful base of support, not the least of which included that of ambitious Know-Nothing Governor Henry J. Gardner of Massachusetts. Gardner, an antislavery moderate, had spent most of 1855 preparing to seek the American Party's vice-presidential nomination on a ticket headed by the quirky yet somewhat visionary Houston. Gardner was convinced that a ticket headed by a southern ex-Democrat and a northern ex-Whig would be next to impossible to defeat in a three-cornered race. He might have been right. The legendary Texan also enjoyed the active support of Andrew J. Donelson, a nephew of the late Andrew Jackson and one of the biggest names in the party. Moreover, the New York *Sun* also championed Houston's candidacy, urging him to run as an "independent"—which Houston seriously considered.

Assuming that he would eventually emerge as the Know-Nothing nominee, the 63-year-old Houston suggested that the party should drop its platform altogether and simply campaign on the slogan, "Union and the Constitution"—a slogan later adopted by the Constitutional Union Party. He also made it clear that under no circumstances would he support Millard Fillmore for the presidency, criticizing the former president for flying about furtively like a blind "bat," whose leathery wings flapped as "bird or beast, as victory may incline."[5] Such language, as one can imagine, hardly helped him win friends in the Know-Nothing Party. Houston also predicted—accurately, as it turned out—that the American Party would carry only one state (a border state) if Fillmore headed its ticket.

Yet despite the dogged determination displayed by Houston in late 1855 and early 1856, the legendary Texan did little to win the Know-Nothing nomination as the party's convention neared. One of the most perplexing political figures in American history, he even seemed to have sabotaged his own candidacy by going out of his way to inform the party's leadership that he didn't plan to attend the party's national convention in Philadelphia. True, his leading rival, Millard Fillmore, didn't plan to attend the Know-Nothing gathering either, but at least the former president had a legitimate excuse for his absence—he was conducting a whirlwind tour of Europe, which, ironically enough, included an audience with the Pope.

---

5.   Beals, *Brass-Knuckle Crusade*, p. 266.

Other names considered by the American Party included Senator John Bell of Tennessee, a moderate ex-Whig who had opposed the Mexican War in 1846 and in the late 1850s undauntedly refused to follow the instructions of his state legislature to have slavery forced upon Kansas. Trial balloons were also floated on behalf of Jacob Broom, the party's last-minute presidential standard-bearer in 1852, and Commodore Robert F. Stockton of New Jersey. Though respected by the party's leadership, Broom was relatively unknown to most of the party's rank-and-file membership. And while the delegates owed him a debt of gratitude for his brief but earnest spadework four years earlier as well as for his untiring devotion to the cause of nativism, it was highly unlikely that the party would turn to the relatively obscure Philadelphian again in a year when it had a chance of actually winning the presidency. The sixty-year-old Stockton had participated in the capture of California's Mexican capital in 1845 and had organized a civil and military government there, briefly assuming the title of governor and commander-in-chief. Longtime Kentucky Senator John J. Crittenden, who did not actively pursue the Know-Nothing nomination but intimated that he wouldn't shrink from or decline the honor if it was offered, was also mentioned as a possibility. Added to the laundry list of prospective candidates was North Carolina's Kenneth Rayner, a flamboyant and rabidly anti-foreign and anti-Catholic lawmaker.

Probably the most colorful candidate in the field, the 48-year-old Rayner was the son of a rural Baptist minister. A staunch states' rights Whig, Rayner idolized South Carolina's John C. Calhoun and had worked closely with the legendary lawmaker until his death in 1850. Rayner, who had been briefly considered as Zachary Taylor's vice-presidential running mate in 1848, lived a comfortable life, largely the result of income derived from his large plantations in Arkansas and Mississippi. His rather stormy congressional career featured a number of quarrels, including coming to blows on one occasion with a colleague from his own state. An enthusiastic member of the Know-Nothing Party's Grand Council, Rayner tried to stifle talk of possible secession in the South by drafting language in the party's constitution obligating party members to protect, maintain and defend the Union under any and all circumstances.

A florid speaker, Rayner rarely pulled punches. Everyone always knew where he stood. When the Maryland Know-Nothing Party tried to soft-pedal the issue of Catholicism in an attempt to ameliorate the state's many conservative, wealthy Tidewater families, Rayner came out swinging, leaving little doubt as to the party's real position on the Catholic question. Addressing a large rally in Baltimore's Monument Square in 1855, the fiery North Carolina lawmaker delivered a gloves-off diatribe against foreigners and Catholics. "The foreign population, which, like the serpent, through your kindness taken from the most abject poverty and warmed into life, repays your hospitality by stinging your vitals, by attempting to destroy your freedom," he declared. Arguing that the Know-Nothing Party was "fighting for the Bible and the right of religious liberty," Rayner passionately claimed that no one could be "a true American and a true member of the Catholic Church, for his allegiance to the priesthood is stronger than that which he bears to his country."[6]

A somewhat perplexing southern figure, Rayner proudly fought for his beliefs. He believed in the Union as deeply as any Conscience Whig in the North, even after the outbreak of the Civil War. However, apparently feeling double-crossed by Lincoln, he later found himself wholeheartedly in favor of secession. Yet, he didn't care much for Jefferson Davis and stood in sharp opposition to his Confederate administration. Moreover, he secretly backed a peace movement led by North Carolina's William W. Holden in 1863 and later openly supported Andrew Johnson's Reconstruction policies.[7] He also anonymously authored the *Life and Times of Andrew Johnson*, a wholly sympathetic look at the rags-to-riches southern president in the immediate post-Civil War era.

While Houston's candidacy fizzled out, the venal George Law of New York, who had been actively plotting his own candidacy for more than a year, soon emerged as Fillmore's most serious challenger. Always suspicious of Fillmore's commitment to nationalism, Law, one of the party's most generous donors dating back to the early 1850s, was intent on derailing the former president's comeback bid. The two men had been bitter enemies for years.

To foster his candidacy, the 49-year-old Law began purchasing newspapers throughout the country, including dailies in such places as Albany, New Orleans,

---

6.   Beals, *Brass-Knuckle Crusade*, pp. 182-183.
7.   As editor of the Raleigh-based *North Carolina Standard*, Holden had resisted secession until the last conceivable moment. Convinced that the South couldn't possibly win the war, the former Democrat, emphasizing the theme of a rich man's war and the poor man's fight, believed that conscription, "military despotism" and economic ruin were a far greater threat to southerners than the idea of reuniting with the North. Beginning in the summer of 1863, the 45-year-old newspaper editor, who later served as the state's first Republican governor during Reconstruction before being impeached and removed from office in a corruption scandal, organized more than a hundred antiwar meetings in the South while urging negotiations with the North for an "honorable peace"—even to the point of suggesting that North Carolina should open separate negotiations with the Lincoln administration.

Pittsburgh and elsewhere. Law was the "respectable visage" of Know-Nothing-ism's dark and seamy side, known by many for his bribes of alderman and legisla-tors in pursuit of larger profits for his streetcar line, railroads, shipping companies, and banking conglomerate. A genuine "robber baron," as one writer described him, he was mega-millionaire Cornelius Vanderbilt's most unrelenting competitor in battling for lucrative steamship subsidies and for control of the nation's railroads and waterways. The son of an immigrant dairy farmer from Protestant Ireland, the self-made New York millionaire settled in upstate New York not far from the Vermont border. He was a first-rate engineer and had risen from the lowly position of common laborer—shoveling cow manure and chip-ping stones—to become one of the country's leading industrialists. Moreover, he was the largest landowner in Colombia in South America and a promoter of the Panama Railroad, where he vied with Vanderbilt for control of the lucrative Pan-ama-California shipping trade. Law also headed the Dry Dock Bank and owned the Staten Island Ferry, several streetcar lines and railroads, as well as sixteen ves-sels on the high seas.

A man who could nearly always be found lurking behind the advancing Amer-ican flag, Law frequently dabbled in international affairs—usually out of self-interest. In 1851, for instance, he was an arms merchant for Hungarian revolu-tionary Louis Kossuth and later profited handsomely from schemes to grab land in Cuba, Mexico and Nicaragua.

A former Democrat, Law had endeared himself to the nativist movement in New York City by bringing alleged murderer Lew Baker to justice following a dramatic chase on the high seas. Denouncing the "cold-blooded murder" of a fine American, Law put his private clipper yacht *Grapeshot* at the disposal of the police when Baker, a low-level Tammany henchman, fled the country after gun-ning down Bill "the Butcher" Poole—one of the toughest and most ruthless of the Know-Nothing thugs in the city.[8]

Earlier, a minor international incident involving a purser on one of Law's ships fueled a controversy that propelled Law, "a fearless, red-blooded American," into the national limelight and sparked a long and bitter feud with President Fill-more. When Law's employee was accused of peddling unfavorable news about Cuba, the governor-general of that country, threatening seizure, ordered the *Northern Light*, one of Law's many vessels, to stay out of Cuban waters. The undaunted steamship magnate demanded immediate protection from the U.S.

---

8.   Beals, *Brass-Knuckle Crusade*, pp. 19-20; David H. Bennett, *The Party of Fear: From Nativist Movements to the New Right in American History* (Chapel Hill, 1988), p. 125.

government, but the Fillmore wisely refused to honor Law's request unless the shipping tycoon agreed to keep the purser off of ships entering Cuban waters. Law's newspapers across the country harshly criticized the president, questioning not only his resolve but also his patriotism.

Blowing the issue all out of proportion and hoping to embarrass Fillmore by creating an international confrontation, Law defiantly sent the *Northern Light* on its usual run with the ticket officer at his regular post. Fortunately, the Cuban government looked the other way and a potentially explosive incident was avoided. It was anticlimactic, but Law's anger toward Fillmore lingered, its apparition manifesting itself in the 1856 battle for the Know-Nothing presidential nomination.

While Law harbored strong antislavery sentiments, he rarely aired them publicly so as not to alienate the party's southern element. Although he was only one generation removed from County Down, Ireland, Law quickly emerged as a serious contender for the Know-Nothing Party's presidential nomination, receiving the endorsement of the Pennsylvania legislature in 1855. He also enjoyed the wholehearted backing of powerful party chairman James Barker. Barker, who had worked closely with Fillmore in the past, felt that the former president was too closely aligned with proslavery interests to have much impact in the North—especially in heavily populated New York, a state with 35 electoral votes. Known as the "King of Know-Nothingism," Barker worked feverishly to line up support for Law in the New York delegation. The New York businessman-turned-politician also enjoyed the support of Philadelphia's Lewis C. Levin and New York's Bayard Clarke, one of four Know-Nothing congressmen elected from that state in 1854. More importantly, James Gordon Bennett's New York *Herald*, the city's most widely read newspaper and one of the most influential publications in the country, also championed Law's candidacy at every opportunity. Bennett, who had dubbed Law as "Live Oak George," came up with the idea of creating "Live Oak" clubs to support Law's candidacy. Despite his Irish heritage, Law had impeccable nativist credentials and, if nominated, he might have been able to mollify the party's proslavery and antislavery factions—if, indeed, that was humanly possible.

With so many northern delegates bolting from the convention, the South had the run of the 1856 Know-Nothing convention at Philadelphia's historic National Hall. Nevertheless, moderate and conservative Whigs and Democrats watched with intense interest as the American Party prepared to make its first serious bid for national power. The convention, which was chaired by Ephraim

Marsh of New Jersey, was one of the most tumultuous in history and received front-page coverage throughout the country.

As expected, Fillmore received a plurality on an informal first ballot, garnering 71 votes to 27 for George Law; the reluctant Garrett Davis received 13 votes; Stockton, 8; McLean, 7; Houston, 6; Bell, 5; and seven votes were scattered among a handful of others, including William F. Johnston, the former governor of Pennsylvania. On the formal second ballot taken later that day, Fillmore received a clear majority, polling 121 votes to Law's 34. Garrett Davis tallied 25 votes; the coquettish Justice McLean, 19; Houston and Rayner, 8 apiece; and Commodore Stockton was the choice of five delegates. Once it became apparent that Fillmore had a majority, the delegates began switching their votes in droves, giving the ex-President 179 votes. The cheering delegates then made his nomination unanimous.

Andrew Jackson Donelson, who had switched from Houston to Fillmore after the first ballot, was then nominated for the nation's second highest office, defeating, among others, a field that initially included North Carolina's Kenneth Rayner, General Richard K. Call of Florida, Gov. Henry J. Gardner of Massachusetts and Percy Walker and William R. Smith, both of Alabama.

A life-long Democrat, the 56-year-old Donelson, who had grown disillusioned by the growing sectionalism within his party, enthusiastically accepted the third-party's nomination. In his acceptance speech, Donelson, who owned more than one hundred slaves, told the delegates that he felt at home in the new party. If Old Hickory was still alive, he told the cheering delegates, there was little doubt that he would be found in the ranks of the American Party. The late Daniel Webster and Henry Clay would have also joined the new party, he insisted.

Raised by Andrew Jackson from the time he was a young boy, Donelson was a graduate of West Point where he completed four years of study in only three years time and ranked second in his graduating class. A lawyer, the young Donelson served as an aide-de-camp to Jackson during the Seminole War and later served as his personal secretary during the presidential campaigns of 1824, 1828 and 1832. He was also a valued member of Jackson's co-called "Kitchen Cabinet." Much sought after by later presidents, Donelson, who owned a cotton plantation in Mississippi, was asked by President Tyler to negotiate with the new Texas Republic and President Polk later kept him on in the same capacity. Polk subsequently appointed him to the post of minister to Prussia, a position he held from 1846 to 1849. He later served as editor of the *Washington Union*, a somewhat influential Democratic newspaper.

Firmly believing that "the man who can look upon a crisis without being willing to offer himself upon the altar of his country is not fit for public trust," Fillmore enthusiastically wired his acceptance from Paris. Hoping to mollify the party's Catholic critics and turn the Know-Nothing Party into a genuine conservative party, Fillmore had recently visited with Pope Pius IX. Upon his return to New York, America's thirteenth president was greeted by a huge, carefully orchestrated demonstration, complete with a fifty-gun salute. His followers also presented him with a key to the city and urged him to return to the White House to remove the "vermin" that had gathered there. In a major campaign address, Fillmore appealed to patriotism and the Union, criticizing the sectional interests of the Democrats and Republicans—a party that wasn't even organized in most of the border and southern states—and reminding his audience of how he held the Union together during an earlier sectional crisis.[9]

While Fillmore's supporters celebrated their hero's return, George Law, the ex-president's longtime nemesis, was plotting yet another scheme to derail the former president's political comeback.

The North Americans

Although his own presidential prospects dimmed considerably at the Philadelphia convention in February, the revenge-minded George Law kept the barely burning ambers of his candidacy alive by staking out an openly antislavery position in the weeks and months following the Know-Nothing convention. Hoping to spike Fillmore's chances in the general election, Law, continuing to spend lavishly, set out to capture the nomination of the bolting northern Know-Nothing faction. In the days and weeks immediately following the regular Know-Nothing convention, the wealthy industrialist emerged as a serious contender for the North American Party's presidential nomination. He was aided in this effort by his ever-loyal Live Oak Clubs and by a few sympathetic Know-Nothing journalists who kept his name in the news.

However, most North Americans, including the ambitious George Law—at least initially—were completely unaware that an inner clique of North American leaders were secretly working to lead the unsuspecting splinter group lock, stock and barrel into the Republican fold. Prominent among those aiding and abetting the Republicans in this clandestine effort were former Pennsylvania governor William F. Johnston, who longed for the North American and Republican vice-

---

9.   Miller, *'If Elected...Unsuccessful Candidates for the Presidency 1796-1968*, p. 170.

presidential nominations, former Know-Nothing mayor Robert T. Conrad of Philadelphia and Lieutenant Governor Thomas H. Ford of Ohio, the latter desperately wanting a lucrative federal appointment. Hoping to forge an alliance between northern antislavery forces within the American Party and the spanking new Republican Party, it was their intention to nominate House Speaker Nathaniel P. Banks—a tried and true antislavery advocate—as a stalking horse for Republican John C. Fremont.[10]

The North American Party's convention, which opened at the Apollo in New York City on June 12, was every bit as divisive as the regular Know-Nothing convention back in February. Police had to be called to protect the North American delegates from an angry mob of regular Know-Nothings who had gathered outside the hall during the second day of the convention. But the real trouble was taking place inside the hall where party manipulators carefully plotted to lead the anti-Fillmore element straight into the Republican fold by nominating Banks. Incredibly, Law, who delivered a stirring keynote address at the convention, turned out to be a willing accomplice in this effort when he and almost the entire New York delegation supported Banks in the early balloting. By this time, Law, who had been wooed by New York Republicans dating back to the regular Know-Nothing convention in February, had virtually abandoned his presidential candidacy and was now eyeing the Republican gubernatorial nomination in New York. Eventually wise to the Republican scheme, some of Law's supporters switched to the antislavery McLean on later ballots. McLean's candidacy, it's safe to say, wasn't part of any Machiavellian Republican plot. The aging justice had too much integrity and was too independent for such intra-party mischief. On the other hands, Banks, who wanted slavery ended even at the cost of disunion, could be used—and was. If there was any doubt, his immediate withdrawal from the race upon Fremont's nomination a few days later is all the proof anyone needed.

McLean was an intriguing candidate, seemingly full of contradictions. His passionate dissenting opinion in the famous *Dred Scott* case had angered proslavery politicians in both major parties, especially in the South, yet his decision in another case involving the kidnapping of an alleged runaway slave outraged the nation's abolitionists. In that case, the aging jurist ruled that a "higher law" didn't permit anyone to harbor fugitive slaves. Described as one of "the most high-toned federalists on the bench," McLean was viewed by many as a politician. But there is little in his record to suggest that he ever allowed partisan political con-

---

10. Gienapp, *The Origins of the Republican Party*, pp. 330-331.

siderations to influence his decisions. It would be unfair to suggest, as many of his contemporaries did, that McLean longed for the presidency. He wanted it, to be sure, but only on his terms—and that's the only kind of president worth having.

Cognizant of the Republican machinations, the New Jersey delegation quickly bolted from the convention, taking with them a scattering of delegates from other states. Their abrupt adjournment from the North American convention drew cheers and applause from the regular Know-Nothing demonstrators who had gathered outside the Apollo. For a few days, the idea that three separate Know-Nothings tickets would be competing for votes in the autumn campaign loomed as a real possibility.

Undeterred by the latest split, the remaining North American delegates proceeded to nominate a presidential ticket. As expected, Nathaniel Banks led on the first ballot, receiving 43 votes to Republican John C. Fremont's 34 and 19 for Justice McLean. Commodore Stockton, Pennsylvania's William F. Johnston and Salmon P. Chase of Ohio divided the remaining thirty votes. (The convention might have nominated Fremont right then and there were it not for the fact that his handlers felt that his nomination by the North Americans might damage his chances at the June 17 Republican convention in Philadelphia.) Although he was nearly overtaken by McLean on the sixth ballot—receiving 45 votes to 40 for the self-educated lawyer—Banks continued to lead through the first nine ballots and was finally nominated on the tenth, receiving 53 votes to McLean's 24 and 18 for Fremont.

The party's vice-presidential nomination went to former Pennsylvania Gov. William F. Johnston, a 47-year-old ex-Whig with strong antislavery tendencies. Johnston's nomination was in large measure a peace offering to the large Pennsylvania delegation that had held firmly for aging Justice McLean throughout the presidential balloting. As governor, Johnston often found himself at odds with the Whig administration in Washington and was a sharp critic of the 1850 Fugitive Slave Law, refusing to allow state officials to assist federal authorities in the capture of runaway slaves who had found refuge in the Keystone State.

Having nominated Banks and Johnston, the North Americans called a recess to see what the Republicans, meeting in Philadelphia, would do at their convention. Only the most naïve North Americans—and there were a few—believed that the Republicans, fearing a split in the antislavery vote, would actually endorse their presidential candidate. They hoped, however, that the Republicans, as a token of cooperation, would endorse Johnston, their vice-presidential standard-bearer. When the Republicans nominated Fremont, Banks immediately withdrew from the race and threw his support to the "Pathfinder." The North

American rump convention then reconvened and also endorsed Fremont, but his nomination was by no means unanimous. Unhappy that their candidate had withdrawn in favor of Fremont, a few delegates, apparently bothered by the fact that Fremont's father was a Catholic, voted to support Fillmore, the regular Know-Nothing nominee. Disgruntled by the Republican Party's repudiation of their vice-presidential candidate, the North Americans stood firm with Johnston and refused to endorse William Dayton, Fremont's vice-presidential running mate on the Republican ticket. After all, Republican leaders, including Fremont himself, had promised to replace Dayton with the former Pennsylvania governor.

Johnston's supporters, a determined group of seasoned ex-Whigs and Free Soilers, were convinced that their man's presence on a Republican-North American fusion ticket was the only way to deny Democrat James Buchanan Pennsylvania's twenty-seven electoral votes—and possibly the presidency. Despite the fact that Republican leaders in Pennsylvania wanted no part of a Johnston candidacy, North American chairman Francis H. Ruggles, a former New York state senator but a man with little previous national political experience, tried in vain to coax the conservative Dayton out of the race in favor of Johnston, at one point even suggesting that Dayton and Johnston should both withdraw in favor of a third, mutually agreeable vice-presidential standard-bearer. The two parties continued to negotiate over the choice of a vice presidential candidate throughout most of the summer before Johnston finally withdrew from the race, apparently with an understanding from Fremont that his friends would not be overlooked in the event of a Republican victory in the fall.

In the meantime, the seceding New Jersey North American delegates gathered at New York's Palace Hall. They were joined by sparse delegations from New York, Massachusetts, Illinois, Iowa, Delaware Indiana and Tennessee. Calling themselves "the true American Convention," this small group adopted the name "Conservative North American Party" and approved a somewhat nebulous platform condemning Charles Sumner, the cultured Massachusetts martyr, while denouncing the repeal of the Missouri Compromise. These renegades proceeded to nominate Robert Stockton for the presidency and chose North Carolina's flamboyant Kenneth Rayner as his vice-presidential running mate.

Hoping to persuade the bolters to return to the regular Know-Nothing fold and support Fillmore, Rayner declined the Conservative North American Party's nomination and late in the autumn campaign urged fusion between the regular Know-Nothings and the Republicans to defeat Buchanan. Unlike his North Carolina running mate, Stockton, who had served briefly in the U.S. Senate from New Jersey as a Democrat in the early 1850s, was somewhat coy. Then serving as president of the Delaware & Raritan Canal Company, Stockton accepted the party's nomination in a letter published in the *Mercury*, a New Jersey newspaper, on June 23.[11] It was no secret that Stockton held a grudge against Fremont dating back to the days of Fremont's Bear Flag battalion in southern California—and was now about to exact his revenge.

From the outset, Stockton, a grandson of one of the signers of the Declaration of Independence, was under tremendous pressure to withdraw from the race. The *New York Times*, among others, urged the former naval commander to withdraw from the contest and endorse Fremont. The former Secretary of the Navy eventually followed their counsel, but shocked nearly everyone by throwing his support to the Know-Nothing Party's Millard Fillmore rather than Fremont.

With Stockton out of the race, the 1856 presidential campaign became a genuine three-way race between Democrat James Buchanan, Republican John Fremont and ex-President Fillmore, the American Party candidate.

A fourth candidate, Gerrit Smith, had been nominated by a radical antislavery convention in Syracuse, New York, prompting William Lloyd Garrison to ask if "anything more ludicrous than this could be found inside or outside of the Utica Insane Asylum? It is really sad to see so good a man as Gerrit Smith befooled in this manner." Viewing his latest candidacy as strictly an opportunity to agitate against slavery, the New York philanthropist and perennial candidate didn't actively campaign for the presidency that year. In fact, the bearded abolitionist personally contributed $500 to Republican John C. Fremont's presidential campaign.[12]

The son of a poor frontier farmer, Fillmore was one of nine children and was forced to go to work as an apprentice to a cloth maker when he was barely fourteen years of age. Five years later, he fell in love with Abigail Powers, a school teacher who inspired him to give up his apprenticeship, purchase a dictionary and pursue a teaching career of his own. Fillmore later studied law and was admitted to the New York bar when he was twenty-three.

Like his archrival William H. Seward, the former president was first elected to the New York legislature as a member of the Anti-Masonic Party, serving in the lower House from 1829-1831. As a young lawmaker, Fillmore sponsored legislation to end the antiquated and long-abhorred practice of imprisoning debtors. He later served four terms in the U.S. House, generally following the leadership of Henry Clay. During his third term, he became chairman of the powerful

---

11. *Mercury*, June 23, 1856.
12. Sewell, *Ballots for Freedom*, p. 287.

House Ways and Means Committee where he secured passage of important tariff legislation in 1842.

Fillmore gave up his seat in Congress in 1843 to run for governor of New York, losing to popular Democrat Silas Wright by slightly more than 10,000 votes. Three years later, the good-looking, six-foot tall attorney was elected state comptroller, a relatively obscure post from which he was plucked by Henry Clay and the Whigs to be Zachary Taylor's vice-presidential running mate in 1848.

As vice president, Fillmore calmly presided over the U.S. Senate, a body rife with angry emotions over the divisive slavery issue. Fate then intervened and Fillmore became America's thirteenth president upon Taylor's untimely and tragic death on July 9, 1850. Few of Fillmore's contemporaries honestly believed that he was presidential timber. In their estimation, he had already risen far above his modest abilities.

The new president, like most conservative and moderate Whigs of that period, felt that compromise on the slavery question was the only way to preserve the Union. As chief executive of the increasingly divided nation, the one-time Anti-Mason signed the Clay-inspired Compromise of 1850, as well as the controversial Fugitive Slave Act—deeds that earned him the severe and everlasting condemnation of the nation's abolitionists. The Fugitive Slave Law, formally a part of the Compromise of 1850, empowered federal authorities to issue warrants, gather posses and force citizens, under penalty of fine or imprisonment, to help in the capture of runaway slaves seeking refuge in the North. Under the draconian law, the accused escapees were denied both a jury trial as well as the right to testify in their own behalf. They were often sent back to the South merely on the flimsy basis of a supposed owner's affidavit. The law also stipulated that federal authorities deciding the fate of the fugitives were to be paid ten dollars for every runaway slave that they returned to southern claimants, but only five dollars for every accused slave set free. Many observers at the time believed that had he lived, President Taylor might have vetoed both the Compromise and the Fugitive Slave Law. Daniel Webster was one of them. In fact, the brilliant Massachusetts lawyer was convinced that Taylor's unexpected death actually prevented the outbreak of a war between the states in 1850.

The Death of the Whigs

While postponing the inevitability of a civil war, Millard Fillmore's accidental presidency severely injured the Whig Party with two strokes of the pen, wounding it in such a way that it would never recover. First, he christened the Compromise of 1850 as "a final settlement" of all sectional strife and followed that by signing the controversial Fugitive Slave Act—a concession to the slaveholding states in return for the admission of the territories acquired in the Mexican War into the Union as free states. While few Whigs in the North rejoiced over the vicious Fugitive Slave Act, many agreed with Rufus Choate of Massachusetts who argued that the return of fugitive slaves was a small sacrifice in the larger question of keeping the Union together.

Viewed as a pompous man and a puppet of southern slave interests by many Whigs in the North, Fillmore was denied his party's presidential nomination in 1852, thereby infuriating a large number of southern Whigs. Hoping to repeat the electoral success they enjoyed by nominating Mexican War hero Zachary Taylor in 1848, the Whigs unceremoniously cast the incumbent aside and nominated the blustering General Winfield Scott for the presidency. Scott's nomination had been engineered in part by New York's Thurlow Weed and William H. Seward, two of Fillmore's bitterest enemies. Old "Fuss & Feathers," of course, proved that being a war hero didn't necessarily translate into votes and, waging one of the most inept campaigns in American history, was soundly defeated that year by Democrat Franklin Pierce, an affable former senator from New Hampshire.

It's quite probable that nothing could have saved the badly divided Whig Party in the early 1850s. The Whigs, increasingly regarded as a party of imperious aristocrats, had won only 71 House seats in the 1852-53 congressional elections and held only 22 of the 62 seats in the U.S. Senate. Moreover, by 1853 the Whigs claimed only four governorships, barely holding onto the state houses in Massachusetts, Tennessee, Vermont and Wisconsin. While there is little question that Fillmore had seriously injured the party by signing the Compromise of 1850 and the Fugitive Slave Law, it was the passage of the Kansas-Nebraska Act in 1854 that finally finished off the party as a viable national entity. The Kansas-Nebraska legislation badly divided the Whig Party, with all forty-five northern members of the party opposing the bill and most southern Whigs in Congress joining their Democratic colleagues from the South as well as about half of the northern Democrats in supporting Douglas' legislation. For all intents and purposes, the Kansas-Nebraska Act resulted in the ultimate disruption and disintegration of the Whig Party.

Northern Whigs, after all, were convinced that the Compromise of 1850 had answered the slavery question once and for all. In 1852, the Whigs, while desperately trying to portray themselves as the "lesser evil," had come out in favor of states' rights and for limitations on the power of the federal government. The party's platform that year also called for obedience to the controversial fugitive-slave law. Within a few years, the Whigs, who captured only 55 seats in the U.S. House of Representatives during the 1854-55 mid-term congressional elections, had been virtually relegated to third or fourth-party status by the nascent Know-Nothing and Anti-Nebraska (Republican) movements. Having proven itself virtually worthless as an antislavery force, the Whig Party had long since assumed a secondary role to the Democrats as an effective and useful instrument to the slave interests and were now on the verge of extinction. As Whig pandering to the slaveholders became more and more obvious, the party grew increasingly irrelevant. By 1854, the Whigs were hardly distinguishable from the Democrats, at least in the minds of those opposed to slavery. "They are in fact of one heart and one mind," said abolitionist Frederick Douglass in a speech early that year.

Despite the frantic efforts of some northern Whigs, including New York's William H. Seward, to revive the party on an anti-Nebraska platform, most northern voters during this period were motivated, as historian Michael F. Holt observed, more by "prohibitionist zeal and anti-Catholic, anti-immigrant, and antiparty rancor as by any anti-Nebraska sentiment."[13] Moreover, a large number of northern voters who were motivated by the antislavery cause gravitated to candidates of the embryonic Republican or Free Soil parties.

Nationally, as Holt painstakingly pointed out, the Whig Party had hoped to portray the Nebraska Act as a Democratic violation of sectional peace that threatened to rip the country in two, but they were frustrated in this effort by the tiny bloc of Free Soilers in Congress who managed to define the issue as a bold attempt to spread slavery against the expressed wishes of the North, rather than an ill-advised Democratic scheme to divide the country. As a consequence, northern and southern Whigs were unable to come together in a show of unity against their Democratic opposition in the 1854-55 mid-term elections as many northern Whigs railed against the Nebraska Act while most southern Whigs were goaded into supporting it. Moreover, a number of Whigs in both regions tried to straddle the issue—a cowardly position sharply denounced by Free Soilers, Republicans and Anti-Nebraska men alike. The Whigs, recalled former Free Soil congressman and vice-presidential candidate George W. Julian, "talked far more eloquently about the duty of keeping covenants, and the wickedness of reviving slavery agitation, than the evils of slavery, and the cold-blooded conspiracy to spread it over an empire of free soil." The northern Whigs, it should be noted, hastened their own fate that year by resisting fusion with anti-Nebraska forces

---

13.   Holt, *The Rise and Fall of the American Whig Party*, p. 957.

and others, except when made on their own terms. This was especially true in the party's strongholds of Massachusetts, New York and Pennsylvania.

Declaring that the Whig Party was deader than a doornail, a Democratic editor from Illinois predicted in early 1855 that the Whigs, in a few short years, "will be as few and far between as the old Federalists, the National Republicans, the National Bank, or the Tariff party men."[14] While most Whigs understood this to be true, a few diehards, including New York's Washington Hunt, desperately tried to keep the party afloat. While conceding that the Whigs probably couldn't win the White House in 1856, the former New York governor nevertheless called for a national convention "to demonstrate that we are still alive as a national party." Believing that the Know-Nothing and Republican parties wouldn't survive beyond the 1856 presidential election, Hunt was of the opinion that most Whigs would return to the fold after the election and "do battle again for national Whig principles."[15] In the end, Hunt, who was joined in this effort by editor Robert A. West of New York's Whiggish *Journal of Commerce* and the aristocratic James A. Hamilton, son of the famous Federalist, had badly miscalculated the Republican Party's momentum and staying power.

Following their shellacking in the 1854-55 mid-term congressional elections, many northern Whigs, especially the conservative Silver-Greys, affiliated with the Know-Nothing Party, while others attempted to mold the Republican Party in the Whig image. At first, a number of Whigs, including New York's William H. Seward and Abraham Lincoln of Illinois, resisted joining the new antislavery party. Seward, who was considered by many to be the Whig Party's likely presidential nominee in 1856, had difficulty abandoning his old party. Lincoln, too, believed that the Whig Party could still be reconstructed and resented those who tried to "un-Whig" him. "I am a Whig," he said at the time, "but others say there are no Whigs, and that I am an abolitionist." But that wasn't true, he said, because he was doing no more than merely opposing "the *extension* of slavery," which had long been the position of most northern Whigs.[16] When he challenged Stephen A. Douglas for the U.S. Senate in 1855, Lincoln did so as a Whig. During the campaign the lanky former congressman made it clear that he opposed the Kansas-Nebraska Act as a Whig, not as a Republican, and certainly not as an abolitionist. Initially believing that the Republicans were too extreme to attract a wide following, Lincoln didn't join the new party until early 1856.

---

14. Ibid., p. 959.
15. Ibid., p. 960.
16. David Herbert Donald, *Lincoln*, p. 189.

During the 1856 presidential campaign, the northern Whigs were badly divided. The Silver-Grays and old southern Whigs, for the most part, rallied behind Fillmore's candidacy on the Know-Nothing ticket while a number of northern moderate Whigs supported Supreme Court Justice John McLean, a fixture in presidential politics who was then seeking the Republican nomination, on the unlikely theory that the Ohio jurist's nomination would lead to Fillmore's withdrawal and an alliance between southern Know-Nothings and northern Republicans. McLean's candidacy, wrote Murat Halstead, was "an attempt made by the antediluvian Whigs...to reorganize the defunct Whig Party under a thin disguise of Republicanism" while demanding restoration of the Missouri Compromise. It was a moot point. McLean, whose campaign was badly bungled, was defeated by John C. Fremont on the first ballot at the Republican national convention in Philadelphia.

Although the Whig Party claimed twenty-five of fifty-two seats in the U.S. Senate shortly after its founding in 1834, it never controlled either house of Congress during its twenty-year history. Despite its minority status, the Whigs managed to capture the presidency with William H. Harrison and Zachary Taylor in 1840 and 1848, respectively, and came close to winning a majority in the U.S. House of Representatives during the 31st Congress (1849-51), when it held 109 seats compared to 112 seats for the Democrats.

Following the party's demise, a number of ex-Whigs drifted briefly into the Know-Nothing Party. Alienated by that party's nefarious attraction to nativism and angered by the Buchanan administration's attempt to force the Lecompton constitution on Kansas, a number of prominent former Whigs in the South formed a short-lived Opposition Party in the late 1850s. This short-lived movement attracted a galaxy of moderate ex-Whig leaders, including John Bell of Tennessee, John J. Crittenden of Kentucky, New York's Washington Hunt, Tom Corwin of Ohio, William A. Graham and George Badger of North Carolina, former congressmen Henry W. Hoffman of Maryland and William C. Rives of Virginia, among others.

Attracting unconditional Unionists, former Know-Nothings, and disaffected Democrats worried about the growing proslavery obstinacy of their former party, the Opposition Party emerged as the only viable opponent to the Democrats in several southern states in the 1859 congressional and state elections, winning nineteen congressional seats in the 36th Congress—including seven out of Tennessee's ten seats and four of North Carolina's eight seats. The successful Opposition candidates included several men of considerable ability, including Georgia's Joshua Hill, Zebulon Vance of North Carolina, Francis M. Bristow of Kentucky and Tennessee's Emerson Etheridge—the latter winning his seat by a mere seven votes. By far, the most colorful of the Opposition leaders elected to Congress that year was Andrew Jackson Hamilton of Texas, an ex-Democrat and outspoken critic of slavery and southern secessionists. The long-bearded Jackson, a native of Alabama, won his seat by narrowly defeating a Democrat in the state's second congressional district in West Texas. A vocal Unionist, "Colossal Jack" Hamilton later fled to Mexico shortly after the outbreak of the Civil War to avoid alleged plots against his life. He was later appointed military governor of Texas in absentia by President Lincoln and Andrew Johnson, Lincoln's successor, later appointed him governor of the state during the stormy and tumultuous period of Reconstruction in 1865.[17] Ex-Whig John J. Crittenden of Kentucky, Henry Clay's successor, represented the Opposition Party in the U.S. Senate and the party also claimed one governorship—that of the legendary Sam Houston of Texas—while coming close to capturing gubernatorial races in Kentucky, Tennessee, and Virginia.[18]

The Opposition Party's strong showing in the Border States and in parts of the lower South in the 1859 elections deeply concerned the Democrats. According to Nathan Sargent, Democrat Stephen A. Douglas, a frontrunner for his party's presidential nomination, confided in friends that if the Opposition leaders coalesced around Missouri's Edward Bates in 1860 they would defeat any other parties in the field. Given the fact that three-quarters of the American people were opposed to the kinds of strident proslavery and antislavery ideas espoused by southern Democrats and northern Republicans, the Opposition Party appeared to be ideally positioned to play a decisive role in the 1860 presidential election.[19]

17. John Hoyt Williams, *Sam Houston: A Biography of the Father of Texas* (New York, 1993) p. 351.
18. In Kentucky, moderate Democrat Beriah Magoffin narrowly defeated the Opposition Party's Joshua F. Bell by a margin of 76,631 to 67,504, while in Tennessee radical proslavery Democrat Isham Harris defeated Opposition leader John Netherland by a count of 76,226 to 68,218. In Virginia, the Opposition Party's William L. Goggin polled over 48% of the vote while losing to moderate Democrat John Letcher by a closer-than-expected margin of 77,112 votes to 71,543.
19. Allan Nevins, *The Emergence of Lincoln: Prologue to Civil War 1859-1861* (New York, 1950), Vol. II, pp. 67-68.

The Birth of the Republican Party

The Republican Party was founded as a single-issue party in Ripon, Wisconsin, on March 20, 1854, shortly after Stephen A. Douglas introduced legislation for the organization of the Nebraska territory, incorporating the principle of "popular sovereignty"—that is, the right of people in the territories to decide whether they would enter the Union as a free or slave state. Coming only four years after the Compromise of 1850, Douglas' Kansas-Nebraska bill declared the Missouri Compromise of 1820, which had set limits on slavery expansion, null and void. The Kansas-Nebraska Act, its critics argued, virtually opened the floodgates for slaveholders to expand their peculiar institution into the territories.

The notion of "popular sovereignty" and the struggle against the Kansas-Nebraska legislation was the final straw for the country's antislavery forces—out-and-out abolitionists, Whigs, Democrats and Free Soilers alike—and led to the founding of a mass party that quickly replaced the dying Whig Party. While this place in history could easily have belonged to the Free Soil Party if it hadn't wilted in the heat of the Know-Nothing inferno of 1854-55, the Republicans, fearing the prospect of an expanded slaveholding region spanning from the Gulf of Mexico to Canada, quickly surpassed their Know-Nothing rivals and the good-as-dead Whigs to become the nation's second largest party. The Republican ascendancy was unprecedented. Within a few short months of their founding, the Republicans had become the second largest political party in the United States.

Inflamed by the passage of the Kansas-Nebraska Act, thousands of anti-Nebraska men, Conscience Whigs, independent Democrats, Free Soilers and others—including many in the temperance movement who mistakenly believed that the Republicans would take up their cause as soon as slavery was abolished—joined the new antislavery party. At a mass meeting of these disparate groups in Jackson, Michigan, on July 6, 1854, the Republicans dedicated themselves to oppose slavery in the new territories by every constitutional means available.

Antislavery sentiment was so strong in the North during this period that the Republicans were bound to succeed. Unlike their Democratic and Know-Nothing rivals, the Republicans refused to waffle on the most serious sectional controversy in American history. "Bleeding Kansas" became their battle cry. In fact, Stephen Douglas, author of the controversial Kansas-Nebraska Act, once joked that he could travel from Boston to Chicago at night by the light of his own burning effigies.

Myron Holley Clark's narrow but successful campaign for governor of New York in 1854 on a Whig-fusionist ticket, comprised largely of anti-Nebraska, temperance and Free Soil forces, ushered in the new Republican Party in the nation's most populous state. Among the party's early successes were the election to the U.S. Senate of such outstanding antislavery advocates as William H. Seward of New York, Henry Wilson of Massachusetts, John P. Hale of New Hampshire—the Free Soil Party's presidential standard-bearer in 1852—former Postmaster General Jacob Collamer of Vermont and Lyman Trumbull of Illinois, a man whose third-party experience ranged the gambit from the Free Soil Party of the 1840s to 1890s Populist. Almost overnight, the Republicans were a force to be reckoned with.

Though founded less than eight months earlier, the Republicans, campaigning under a variety of labels—including the American, Anti-Administration, Anti-Nebraska, Free Soil Democrat, People's, Union and Whig labels, as well as various combinations thereof—captured more than a hundred seats in the U.S. House of Representatives during the 1854-55 mid-term congressional elections, thereby positioning themselves to vie seriously for the presidency two years later. Most political observers, even the most seasoned veterans, didn't know exactly how to interpret the party's sudden success—or precisely how many seats the party actually controlled in Congress. Due to the strength of the Know-Nothings, who captured anywhere from forty-three to seventy seats in the mid-term elections, an exact figure is all but impossible to determine. The *Tribune Almanac 1856* (formerly the *Whig Almanac*) puts the Republican total at 118, but mistakenly lists New York's Francis E. Spinner, a staunch opponent of the Kansas-Nebraska Act, as a Democrat, while Michael J. Dubin, in his magisterial volume on U.S. congressional elections, breaks down party representation in the 34th Congress at the time each member was elected as follows: Democrats 81; Whigs 55; Americans 52; Anti-Nebraska 22; Republicans 13; People's Party nine, along with one Free Soil Democrat and an Independent Whig. By the time the new House convened in December 1855, the Whig label had all but disappeared and many members who had been elected on the Whig ticket aligned themselves with either the Americans or the Republicans. Needless to say, it was a terribly confusing period as party labels and loyalties were blurred almost beyond recognition.[20]

---

20. *Tribune Almanac 1856,* as quoted in Gienapp, *The Origins of the Republican Party,* pp.240-241; Michael J. Dubin, *United States Congressional Elections, 1788-1997* (Jefferson, North Carolina, 1998) p. 174.

The Republican Party, as historian Wilfred E. Binkley pointed out, was "a unique phenomenon" in that "it originated spontaneously without the aid of an outstanding leader, such as Washington was of the Federalists, Jefferson of the first Republicans, Jackson of the Democrats, or Clay of the Whigs."[21] Ohio's Salmon P. Chase, a veteran of the Liberty and Free Soil parties, was, arguably, the most prominent of its founding members. Yet, from the outset the party also attracted other big names, including the powerful Thurlow Weed of New York and journalist Horace Greeley of the *New York Tribune*. Supreme Court Justice John McLean also joined the party, as did William H. Seward, who officially cast his lot with the Republicans in 1855. The party's list of founding fathers read like a "Who's Who" of nineteenth century liberal politicians and included such able men as abolitionist Owen Lovejoy of Illinois, Indiana's George Washington Julian and Pennsylvania's David Wilmot, a former antislavery Democrat.

Despite the party's auspicious beginning, a number of leading Republicans were pessimistic about the party's chances in 1856, especially given the strength of the Know-Nothing Party in the 1855 elections. Gamaliel Bailey, the longtime editor of the *National Era*, a close ally of Ohio's Salmon P. Chase and a man who had labored tirelessly to keep the Free Soil Party afloat after the party's historic 1848 campaign, was decidedly bleak about Republican prospects in the 1856 presidential election, believing that the Know-Nothings would divide the vote in the North, thereby enabling the Democrats to again capture the presidency. "There is just now little prospect for a respectable fight next year," he lamented. Theodore Parker, another antislavery advocate, concurred, suggesting that with rival Republican and Know-Nothing tickets in the field, "the latter will get the most votes."[22]

Aided by the endorsement of an anti-Nebraska convention in Pittsburgh the following February, as well as by the proslavery mob's ransacking of Lawrence, Kansas, and the brutal physical assault on Massachusetts Senator Charles Sumner by South Carolina Congressman Preston Brooks in the spring of that year—a beating that George Washington Julian later described as having done "more to stir the blood of the people of the northern states than any of the wholesale outrages thus far perpetrated"—the Republicans were determined to play a major role in the 1856 presidential sweepstakes.[23]

21.   Binkley, *American Political Parties*, p. 206.
22.   Gienapp, *Origins of the Republican Party*, p. 239.
23.   Julian, *Political Recollections*, p. 153.

Convening in Philadelphia on June 17, 1856, the Republicans nominated explorer John C. Fremont for the nation's highest office. In the 43-year-old "Pathfinder," the illegitimate son of a French refugee father, the Republicans had a romantic yet highly controversial candidate, best known for his explorations of the Far West and for his widely-publicized elopement with Missouri Senator Thomas Hart Benton's dazzling 16-year-old daughter, Jessie. The party's vice-presidential nomination went to former Whig Senator William L. Dayton of New Jersey who defeated little-known former Whig congressman Abraham Lincoln of Illinois, a recent and somewhat reluctant convert to the new party. Borrowing liberally from the Free Soilers, the Republicans also adopted the slogan, "Free Soil, Free Speech, Free Men, Fremont." While sharply condemning the Pierce administration, the Republicans approved a Whig-like platform that opposed "those twin relics of barbarism, polygamy and slavery" in the territories and demanded the admission of Kansas as a free state.

Curiously, the Democrats were the first to approach Fremont about a possible presidential candidacy that year. After all, he was a former Democratic senator from California and given his hero status and decidedly aloof position on slavery, they believed he would have been an attractive candidate to countless Democrats in the South. Among those who urged him to seek their party's nomination was ex-Gov. John Floyd of Virginia, the Nullifiers' presidential standard-bearer in 1832. But Fremont leaned toward the Republicans and enjoyed considerable support of influential men like publisher John Bigelow, Francis P. Blair, Sr., of Missouri and Nathaniel Banks and Henry Wilson of Massachusetts.

In nominating the impetuous Fremont, the Republican delegates passed over such luminaries as New York's William H. Seward, Salmon P. Chase of Ohio and Supreme Court Justice John McLean, a slavery foe with close ties to the Know-Nothing Party and a man Lincoln believed to be ideally suited for the presidency. All three men arguably possessed more experience and better qualifications than Fremont, but each of them had serious drawbacks. Seward was highly unpopular among nativist voters; Chase was considered too close to the radical abolitionists; and McLean, a septuagenarian, was probably regarded as too old to wage an effective campaign. Nevertheless, the aging McLean, whose ties to the burgeoning Know-Nothing movement was largely viewed as an asset, especially in doubtful but critically important states such as Illinois, Indiana and Pennsylvania—a state crucial to the party's fortunes that year—provided Fremont with his most formidable opposition at the Philadelphia convention before his candidacy was virtually sabotaged by his inept campaign manager, Judge Rufus R. Spalding of Ohio, who inexplicably withdrew McLean's name from consideration shortly before the balloting began. The deliberative Supreme Court justice was everything Fremont wasn't; he had the ability to see around corners and was able to distinguish political subtleties.

A moderate with few political enemies, McLean was viewed as the one candidate who could rally the old Whigs and the northern business community—two groups skittish about free soil extremism—to the Republican banner. This was a view apparently shared by Abraham Lincoln, a former Whig congressman from Illinois. In a letter to Lyman Trumbull shortly before the Republicans convened in Philadelphia, Lincoln predicted that a number of conservative and moderate Whigs would bolt to Democrat James Buchanan unless the 71-year-old jurist was nominated. "I think they would stand Blair or Fremont for Vice-President—but not more," he wrote.[24] Apparently agreeing, McLean's managers were convinced that a McLean-Fremont ticket would be unbeatable. An angry McLean never forgave Spalding for bungling what might have been his last shot at glory. The jurist's candidacy, however, was nearly salvaged by Pennsylvania's quick thinking Thaddeus Stevens. A longtime champion of the poor and downtrodden and a strident leader of the free soil forces in Congress, Stevens and others objected so strongly to Spalding's action that the Ohio judge quickly rescinded McLean's withdrawal. But it was too late. The damage had already been done. On the convention's first informal ballot, Fremont received 359 votes to McLean's 196.

The party's vice presidential nod went to William L. Dayton, a somewhat lackluster former Whig senator from New Jersey. Fremont, it turned out, was less than thrilled by Dayton's nomination and regarded his selection as one of the chief causes for his defeat that year. Fremont personally preferred Pennsylvania's Simon Cameron, a 57-year-old newspaper publisher, business entrepreneur and former member of the U.S. Senate, as his vice-presidential running mate. Having grown impatient with the Democrats over the slavery issue, Cameron, who had quietly ingratiated himself with the Know-Nothings, later built one of the most powerful statewide Republican organizations in the country. New York's Thurlow Weed and others believed that Cameron, a former Buchanan henchman—a man who knew where all the Democratic bodies were buried—could seriously threaten Buchanan's candidacy in Pennsylvania and possibly throw that state's 27 electoral votes into the Republican column. But Cameron's candidacy never materialized and Dayton defeated little-known Abraham Lincoln of Illinois, the former Whig congressman, on the first ballot, garnering 259 votes to Lincoln's

24.   Paul M. Angle and Earl Schenck Miers, eds., *The Living Lincoln* (New York, 1992), p. 193.

110. Nathaniel Banks of Massachusetts received 46 votes; Free Soiler David Wilmot of Pennsylvania, a recent convert from the Democratic ranks, 43; Charles Sumner, 36; and 58 votes were scattered among ten other candidates, including two for stubborn North American Party vice-presidential nominee William F. Johnston. The melodious voiced Wilmot, a former schoolteacher, Democratic congressman and one-time leader of the Free Soil Party who did as much to end slavery as anyone of his era, had been rejected as a possible compromise candidate for the vice presidency at the North American convention a few days earlier.

Pitted against two tired old men—Fillmore and Buchanan—Fremont was viewed as a fresh young leader with no political past to speak of. But he did have a past—and a somewhat controversial one at that. Born in Savannah, Georgia, in 1813, the precocious Fremont served briefly in the navy before serving as an assistant engineer and second lieutenant in the U.S. Army Topographical Corps, where he explored the plateau between the Mississippi and Missouri rivers. Later he helped pave the way for the Oregon Trail and traveled the Great Basin between the Rockies and the Sierra Madre. His frequent excursions, including an exploration of the Arkansas, Rio Grande and Colorado rivers, earned him the sobriquet of "the Pathfinder."

Arriving in California during the Mexican War, Fremont, who possessed an almost "kinetic temperament," played a prominent role in the conquest of California. Though somewhat hesitant at first, he inspired the American settlers in Sacramento Valley to begin the Bear Flag revolt and actively cooperated with Commodore Stockton's forces in the capture of Los Angeles in August 1846. While Fremont was in northern California recruiting a larger force, the Mexicans wrested control of Los Angeles from the Americans. Fremont returned in time to assist Stockton and General Stephen W. Kearny—who only weeks earlier had spectacularly captured Sante Fe for the United States—in the final conquest of Los Angeles. Almost immediately thereafter, Fremont became embroiled in a bitter and longstanding quarrel between Stockton and Kearny over their respective authorities. Fremont sided with Stockton in the dispute and was later appointed civil governor of California, serving in that capacity for two months before Washington established Kearny's authority. Kearny proceeded to humiliate Fremont, at one point taking him to Fort Leavenworth as a virtual prisoner. There, he was found guilty of mutiny and insubordination and was court-martialed for executing—without trial—several prominent Mexican prisoners. President Polk, under tremendous pressure from Fremont's powerful father-in-law Missouri Sen. Thomas Hart Benton, later remitted the Pathfinder's sentence. With public sentiment on his side, Fremont indignantly resigned from the service.

Returning to civilian life, Fremont, who shared his father-in-law's vision of acquiring the entire Far West, embarked on a disastrous exploration of the upper waters of the Rio Grande. Midway through his journey, Fremont, whose expedition had been generously financed by Benton and a few wealthy St. Louis businessmen who were interested in laying the foundation for a Pacific railroad, began to run low on supplies. Refusing to heed the warnings of Washo Indians who insisted that the region was virtually impassable in winter, Fremont foolishly ventured forth, losing eleven men to the harsh elements, including several who died of starvation. Rescued by frontiersman Kit Carson, Fremont proceeded to California where he made a small fortune in gold on seventy square miles of land in the Sierra foothills. A man who put principles above profit, Fremont refused to use slave labor in his gold mines.

Aided by a few wealthy friends, Fremont quickly acquired large realty holdings in San Francisco and enjoyed a relatively comfortable life in Monterey. Turning to politics, Fremont was elected to the U.S. Senate as a Free Soil Democrat in December 1850, but served only six months before losing his seat to John B. Weller, a former Democratic congressman from Ohio, in a protracted legislative battle for the seat. Incredibly, only eight legislators voted for Fremont on the first ballot. Maintaining his California residence until the Civil War, the restless adventurer nevertheless spent a considerable amount of time outside the state, pursuing his lifelong ambition of opening the vast territory of the Far West. Perhaps more than anything else, the Pathfinder hoped to equal the great feats of earlier explorers Lewis and Clark and Zebulon Pike. His far-reaching travels during this period included a family hiatus in London and Paris in 1852-53 and a small expedition to central Utah in search of reasonably safe passages for a southern railway to the Pacific in 1853-54.

In many respects, Fremont was an ideal candidate for the new Republican Party. A man of considerable fame and fortune, he didn't come across as some sort of wild-eyed radical abolitionist. While strongly opposed to the extension of slavery into the territories, he favored gradual emancipation and once proposed that the federal government should compensate former slaveholders—an idea abhorrent to men like Gerrit Smith, Wendell Phillips and other leading abolitionists.

Meanwhile, the Democrats—still the dominant political force in the country—met in Cincinnati on June 2. Marred by factional strife, the Democratic convention featured a three-way battle for the party's presidential nomination, pitting President Pierce, the embattled incumbent who enjoyed considerable support in the South and a somewhat weakened base in New England, against Illinois Senator Stephen A. Douglas, the party's most assertive policy maker, and Pennsylvania's bland and colorless James Buchanan, a widely-respected former senator and Secretary of State who served as Pierce's minister to the Court of St. James.

There was also some speculation that the Democrats would again turn to 73-year-old Lewis Cass, who had been the party's presidential standard-bearer eight years earlier. Raised in a heavily Federalist environment in Exeter, New Hampshire, Cass possessed an almost unparalleled record of public service, serving with distinction as a brigadier-general in the War of 1812, as military and civil governor of the Michigan Territory (1813-31), minister to France, and as Secretary of War in the Jackson and Van Buren administrations. He also served twice in the U.S. Senate. His narrow loss to Zachary Taylor in 1848 was largely attributed to the New York Barnburners, who worked vigorously for third-party candidate Martin Van Buren. Regarded as one of the country's leading defenders of the Missouri Compromise, Cass once gave a two-day speech in its defense from the Senate floor, arguing in favor of the right of the people to regulate their own affairs—a precursor of sorts to the Kansas-Nebraska Act of 1854. The aging Cass, one of the nation's most honest public servants, had been a strong contender for the Democratic presidential nomination in 1852 when he enjoyed the support of countless pro-Compromise delegates. As a reluctant and long-shot candidate for the Democratic nomination in 1856, the Michigan lawmaker received some favorable press in the South for his sharp denunciation of Charles Sumner's dramatic and insulting "Crime against Kansas" speech in May, calling it "the most un-American and unpatriotic" speech he had ever heard. Sumner's antislavery speech, riddled with sexual metaphors, cruelly targeted South Carolina Senator Andrew Pickens Butler, a stroke victim, as a shameful imbecile and a disgrace to the nation. In the end, however, Cass wasn't a factor at the Democratic convention in Cincinnati, garnering only five votes on the first ballot. Stephen A. Douglas, the "Little Giant," and author of the Kansas-Nebraska Act had stolen most of his thunder.

Aided by circumstances—including the brutal caning of Charles Sumner on the Senate floor and John Brown's murderous raid on the homes of proslavery settlers along the Osawatomie River in Kansas—Pennsylvania's James Buchanan jumped to an early lead in Cincinnati and was unanimously nominated on the convention's 17th ballot. The party's vice-presidential nod went to Kentucky's John C. Breckinridge, a former two-term congressman and close friend of Stephen A. Douglas. Breckinridge, who had turned thirty-five only a few months earlier, was a lawyer who had served briefly in the Kentucky legislature before winning a seat in the U.S. House of Representatives in 1850. The party's plat-form endorsed Lewis Cass' doctrine of popular sovereignty, embraced the contro-versial Kansas-Nebraska Act and pledged to thwart all attempts to rekindle the slavery issue. The Democrats also condemned the Know-Nothing movement, asserting that it was contrary to the American ideals of tolerance and enlightened freedom.

In large measure, the conservative Buchanan, safely tucked away in England, was nominated precisely because he had managed to avoid the Kansas contro-versy. Incredibly, Buchanan, who longed for the presidency for more than a decade, had no pre-convention strategy and merely happened to be at the right place at the right time. Lady luck was obviously looking his way. A former legisla-tor, cabinet member and longtime diplomat, Buchanan was a descendant of a long line of Federalists and one-time member of that extinct party. As Secretary of State, he settled the Oregon dispute, feuded with Whig Winfield Scott and tried unsuccessfully to purchase Cuba from Spain. He and his cohorts in diplo-matic circles helped draft the controversial Ostend Manifesto, a secret memoran-dum justifying the forceful seizure of Cuba if Spain wouldn't agree to sell the island to the United States. Though he once favored a constitutional amendment legalizing slavery and had supported the Fugitive Slave Act, Buchanan somehow managed to avoid close identification with most of the great issues of his time, including the Missouri Compromise, the Compromise of 1850 and the Kansas-Nebraska Act.

While Buchanan proudly carried the Democratic torch in the 1856 campaign, lame-duck President Franklin Pierce, rejected by his own party, quietly packed his bags for the long trip back to New Hampshire, lamenting that there was nothing left to do but "get drunk."

For his part, the Know-Nothing Party's Millard Fillmore waged a genuine national campaign, fighting Buchanan tooth and nail in the border-states and in the Deep South—which clung to the Democratic Party and its unimaginative standard-bearer in almost breathtaking fashion—and locking horns with the sophomoric Fremont in the North, whose campaign in that region was being waged with all the enthusiasm and emotional frenzy of a religious crusade. In that section of the country, Fillmore was at a distinct disadvantage. Though most pundits at the time gave him only a slight chance for success in Maryland, Ken-tucky and Louisiana—where the party's stronghold in New Orleans might pro-vide the difference in a close race with Buchanan—Fillmore assailed the Democrats as beholden to southern commercial interests, while painting the Republicans as a party dominated by radical abolitionists. However, the former president's recent utterances against slavery came back to haunt him, virtually dooming his candidacy in the South—a region that Know-Nothing leaders thought he would carry. To the extent that he appealed at all to the party's virulent anti-Catholic constituency—in the North and the South—Fillmore did so with grace and dignity. "In my opinion," he said in several campaign statements that summer, "Church and State should be separate, not only in form, but fact—religion and politics should not be mingled."[25] More than anything else, the former Whig president hoped to transform the Know-Nothing Party into a truly national conservative party—cleansing the party's of its anti-Catholic, anti-immigration stain—yet an endorsement from some old-time conservative Whigs, meeting in Baltimore in mid-September, did little to enhance his prospects. These old Silver Grays, who preferred to be called "National Whigs," endorsed the American Party's ticket but not its platform. The only thing that really mattered to these once-proud Whigs was the preservation of their beloved Union. Fillmore's message hadn't completely fallen on deaf ears.

Unfortunately, things didn't look much brighter for the Know-Nothing standard-bearer in the North. The Democrats were quick to remind northern businessmen of the lucrative southern markets and investments that were at stake in the election and the Republicans, exploiting Fremont's youth, assailed Fillmore as being too old and out of touch. Given almost no chance of success in his native state of New York or in Connecticut and Massachusetts, where the American Party had piled up such an impressive victory two years earlier, the former President was forced to appeal to the same general constituency as Buchanan and the Democrats. The antislavery forces, after all, were firmly committed to the Fremont-Dayton ticket.

Playing their trump card, some American Party activists of the Levin-stripe charged that Fremont, an Episcopalian, was really a Roman Catholic. During the campaign they published numerous pamphlets asserting that Fremont's father was a Catholic and that the candidate's adopted daughter had attended a Catholic school. At one point in the campaign, the Know-Nothing Party even produced witnesses to vouch for the statements.

Dismissing anti-Catholicism and anti-immigration as relevant issues, Fillmore was joined on the stump by his former rival Sam Houston, who actively campaigned for the Know-Nothing ticket. Though he personally knew and liked

---

25. God & Country: Religious Views of the Founding Fathers, Presidents, and Vice Presidents, http://www.geocities.com/peterroberts. geo/Relig-Politics/MFillmore.html.

Democrat Buchanan, the legendary Texan feared that Buchanan's candidacy was doomed and that Republican John Fremont, whom he considered an inflammatory abolitionist, would win by default. Though Houston's public support for Fillmore, while symbolically important, made little difference in Texas as voters in the Lone Star State gave Fillmore only slightly more than a third of the state's popular vote. Nevertheless, Houston's active support helped to set the stage for his own successful gubernatorial campaign three years later on a coalition ticket that included the Know-Nothings. With the exception of his longtime nemesis George Law and a few others, most American Party leaders, including noisy nativist Lewis C. Levin of Philadelphia, also stumped vigorously for the Fillmore-Donelson ticket. The fiery Levin, a pathologically xenophobic and anti-Catholic demagogue who went insane shortly after the election, urged voters to wash their hands of what he called "Black Republicanism," describing the antislavery party as an instrument of the Pope.

For his part, George Law, who was rejected by both the Know-Nothing and North American parties—and subsequently expelled by the Supreme Order of the Star-Spangled Banner—devoted his time and energy to further expanding his vast commercial and financial holdings. He found time, however, to write a public letter strongly endorsing Fremont's candidacy, as did several other prominent Know-Nothings, including former national president James W. Barker and Ephraim Marsh, the man who had presided over the national convention in Philadelphia that had nominated Fillmore in February. Unlike Law, Marsh actively stumped for Fremont during the autumn campaign.[26]

From the beginning, Fillmore's strategists believed that their candidate would, at the very least, carry the eight states that voted for the Know-Nothing ticket in 1855—California, Delaware, Kentucky, Louisiana, Maryland, Massachusetts, New York and North Carolina—with the possibility of picking up Missouri, Pennsylvania and Tennessee, thereby giving the former president 139 electoral votes, just nine short of a majority. But as the campaign dragged on, it became clear that Fillmore's only hope was to throw the election into the House of Representatives where a majority of lawmakers in both major parties belonged, at one time or another, to one of the various Know-Nothing lodges.

Meanwhile, in a desperate attempt to derail Buchanan's candidacy, the Republicans initiated fusion negotiations with Know-Nothing leaders in a number of critical northern states, including heavily populated Pennsylvania. For the most part, these last-minute efforts at fusion failed miserably. This was due, in

---

26.   Gienapp, *The Origins of the Republican Party 1852-1856*, p. 367.

large part, to the belief, echoed by Pennsylvania's Henry D. Moore and other Know-Nothing chieftains, that fusion was really a Republican ploy to destroy the growing nativist party. Moreover, Moore argued that the Know-Nothings should concede Pennsylvania "rather than lose our identity as a national conservative party"—a view apparently shared by presidential standard-bearer Millard Fillmore. In New Jersey, the American Party's Charles D. Deshler blocked such an arrangement, believing that any sign of cooperation with the Republicans would cost the Know-Nothing Party dearly in the South, where it still hoped to carry a couple of states. Fusion also failed in Indiana when Republican leaders initially balked at the idea of a fusion ticket composed of eight Fremont and five Fillmore electors. A last-ditch attempt at fusion in that state was also scuttled when conservative Know-Nothing leader Richard W. Thompson, who later served as Secretary of the Navy during the Hayes administration, refused to endorse it. A similar fusion strategy was also rejected in Illinois.

Recognizing that their candidate could not possibly win the election without Pennsylvania's twenty-seven electoral votes, Fremont's desperate managers made an all-out effort to fashion a fusion ticket in that all-important state. Overcoming the vehement opposition of Lewis C. Levin and other Know-Nothing leaders in Philadelphia, a fusion campaign of sorts did take place in the Keystone State, once a fever swamp of anti-Catholicism and nativism. In fashioning a fusion ticket, Republican strategists had to convince Know-Nothing leaders that Fremont could win and that Fillmore didn't have a "shadow of a chance," as Pennsylvania's seedy Simon Cameron described it. In the end, the Republicans were able to persuade a majority of Know-Nothings to join a Republican-American "Union" fusion ticket during the October elections and nearly carried the state, narrowly losing to the Democrats by 3,000 votes out of more than 432,000 votes cast. However, a large number of Know-Nothings, especially ardent anti-Catholic nativists and those opposed to Fremont and the radical abolitionists, either voted for the Democrats or boycotted the October state elections altogether.

Having come so close to dislodging the Democrats in the October elections, another fusion scheme was hurriedly put forward only days before the presidential election on November 4. Under this complicated arrangement, a joint "Union" electoral ticket featuring *both* Fillmore and Fremont was printed for mass distribution throughout the state. If the fusionist "Union" ticket carried the state, then the state's twenty-seven electoral votes would have been divided in proportion equal to the number of votes cast for each ticket, but if Pennsylvania's electoral votes could provide the margin of victory for either candidate in the Electoral College, then, as it was mutually agreed, twenty-six of the state's twenty-seven votes would be cast for that candidate (with the twenty-seventh vote split and thus lost.) All hopes of a fusion victory in Pennsylvania, however, were dashed when John P. Sanderson, the Know-Nothing Party's intractable state chairman, announced that the original slate of American Party electors would also remain in the field, thereby diluting the strength of the "Union" fusionist ticket. Fremont's men were furious and put all kinds of pressure on the anti-fusionists to withdraw their ticket, but to no avail. North Carolina's Kenneth Rayner stumped in Pennsylvania, speaking in favor of "Union and Fillmore." In Philadelphia, where tens of thousands turned out to hear him speak, the fiery North Carolinian urged Whigs and Republicans to join with the Know-Nothings in all-out effort to stop Buchanan.

At this point, only Fillmore's direct intervention could have forced the anti-fusionist Americans to withdraw from the race, but the former president, believing—incorrectly, as it turned out—that he already controlled enough electoral votes to throw the election into the House of Representatives, merely advised them to "do as our friends there think best," which was, as historian Tyler Anbinder noted, "tantamount to an endorsement of their position."[27] Fillmore's refusal to intervene on the side of the fusionists is all the more baffling given his behind-the-scenes maneuvering in Indiana where, as late as October 29, he sent an emissary into the Hoosier State to convince Know-Nothing leaders in that state to get behind Fremont to help him carry the state in a last-ditch effort to throw the election into the House of Representatives. Fillmore's proposal, which had the blessing of national president E. B. Bartlett of Kentucky and other Know-Nothing leaders, was dismissed only because it was made so late in the campaign.

Earlier, the Fillmore campaign was delivered a serious blow when Henry J. Gardner, the ambitious and powerful Know-Nothing governor of Massachusetts, decided to oppose the ex-president's candidacy in late June, only days before the American Party in that state was scheduled to ratify Fillmore's nomination at its state convention in Springfield. Gardner, a former archconservative Whig who was seeking a third term as governor that year, had spent much of the previous year promoting himself for the party's vice-presidential nomination on a ticket headed by Sam Houston of Texas, but his campaign collapsed when Houston's presidential candidacy failed to catch fire. Gardner's unexpected move stunned Fillmore and the national Know-Nothing leadership, especially since the *Boston Bee*, the party's official organ in Massachusetts, had enthusiastically trumpeted

---

27.   Anbinder, *Nativism & Slavery*, p. 242.

Fillmore's candidacy from the time of his nomination in February. As if on cue, the *Bee* wasted little time removing the names of Fillmore and Donelson from the top of its editorial page and replacing them with Fremont and Johnston.

Much to the chagrin of Fillmore's loyalists in the state, Gardner, who was looking for Republican support in his bid for re-election, then led the Massachusetts Americans straight into the Republican camp, enabling John C. Fremont to edge out the former president by a margin of 280 to 187 at the boisterous Springfield convention. The governor's unprecedented actions forced Fillmore's followers, led by Order of United Americans sachem Albert Brewster Ely, a former mayor of Springfield, to break ranks with the Gardner Americans and field their own statewide slate that, in addition to wholeheartedly endorsing the Fillmore-Donelson ticket, included a challenger to the sitting Know-Nothing governor.[28]

Know-Nothing leaders were also disappointed by the way things turned out in Fillmore's home state of New York. From the outset, they strongly believed that the former president had at least a fighting chance of capturing the state's thirty-five electoral votes. Moreover, they were convinced that the Empire State would be the party's strongest northern state. After all, the American Party had carried the state by 12,000 votes in 1855, while electing seven state senators and forty-four assemblymen. Adding to their confidence was the fact that more than half of New York's congressional delegation had at least a nominal connection to the Know-Nothing movement.

Until then, James Madison in 1812 was the only presidential candidate in American history to win the presidency while failing to carry the populous Empire State. It wasn't surprising, therefore, that all three parties made a concerted effort there. Buchanan, it seems, had benefited immensely from the actions of party leaders at the Democratic national convention in Cincinnati, who urged the party's two warring factions—the "Soft Shells" and "Hard Shells"—to put aside their differences and unite behind a single ticket. Fremont, too, was aided tremendously in that state by massive defections from the Know-Nothing ranks

---

28. Mulkern, *The Know-Nothing Party in Massachusetts*, pp. 146-153. Having been rebuffed again at the party's next state convention at Faneuil Hall on July 24 and for a third time at the state council's quarterly session two weeks later, the Fillmore Americans, meeting at Boston's Music Hall shortly thereafter, unanimously nominated textile magnate Amos A. Lawrence, a staunch Fillmore supporter and a favorite of the Brahmins, for governor. When Lawrence declined, the party turned to 70-year-old former congressman William Appleton, but he too refused the nomination, at which point the nomination went to George W. Gordon, a little-known Whig cotton dealer who had served briefly as postmaster in the Fillmore administration.

following the ransacking of Lawrence, Kansas, and the brutal caning of Charles Sumner at the hands of South Carolina states' rights lawmaker Preston Brooks, prompting Fillmore to observe that if Fremont was elected, he would owe his election to the troubles in Kansas and the martyrdom of Sumner. "The Republicans ought to pension Brooks for life," he quipped.[29]

It wasn't long before the Know-Nothings realized that they had vastly overestimated Fillmore's strength in New York. Decimated by the departure of the North Americans in upstate New York, particularly in the state's western counties—once a Know-Nothing stronghold—and by the disastrous gubernatorial candidacy of conservative newspaper publisher Erastus Brooks, Fillmore's candidacy was clearly in trouble as Election Day approached. Brooks, whose candidacy once held so much promise for the Know-Nothings, probably ended up hurting rather than helping the Fillmore-Donelson ticket.

Elected to the state Senate on the American Party ticket a few years earlier, the 41-year-old Brooks, a graduate of Cornell University's law school, was the long-time publisher and editor of the *New York Express*, one of the most conservative organs in the Know-Nothing Order. A former Whig, he had gained a great deal of favorable attention in early 1855 during a well-publicized imbroglio with Archbishop John Hughes over the issue of whether church property should be controlled by lay trustees or by the clergy. During that heated dispute, the Know-Nothing lawmaker, urging passage of legislation designed to curb a dangerous concentration of wealth by church leaders, asserted that Hughes controlled nearly five million dollars in real estate and later backed it up by producing documentation showing that the Archbishop held forty-five property deeds valued at $5,000,000—all of which, Brooks claimed, was to be turned over to the Pope on demand.[30]

Brooks, who chaired the party's state convention in Auburn later that autumn, was regarded as one of the most popular figures in the New York movement—his name had even been bandied about as a possible presidential candidate on the

29.   Anbinder, *Nativism & Slavery*, pp. 235-236.
30.   Ibid., pp. 139-140; Billington, *The Protestant Crusade*, pp. 298-299, 316-317. The legislation authored by Brooks and Know-Nothing Senators Thomas R. Whitney and James O. Putnam, provided that church property held by a deceased clerical officer was to be escheated to the state and that the escheat was only to be granted to the congregation after it had incorporated itself as provided under New York's laws of incorporation enacted in 1784. This legislation, which was eventually repealed in 1863, was deemed injurious only to the Catholic Church, since most Protestant denominations usually employed a method of lay control of such holdings.

Know-Nothing ticket—and most party leaders felt he would sweep to victory in the three-cornered gubernatorial race against Republican John A. Dix, a one-time Free Soiler, and Democratic congressman Amasa J. Parker, a relatively nondescript former state Supreme Court justice whose most lasting claim to fame was the fact that he once resided in a boardinghouse with future presidents Millard Fillmore and James Buchanan. But Brooks' popularity soon began to fade as his lively *New York Express* launched into a series of vitriolic attacks on John C. Fremont, accusing the Republican standard-bearer of being a Roman Catholic and transforming the question of Fremont's religious background into a major campaign issue. A number of leading New York publications, including at least one newspaper that had previously championed his cause, quickly turned on the conservative editor, accusing him of sabotaging the anti-slavery movement with malicious and fabricated stories.[31]

All hope of an outright victory for Fillmore in New York—and nationally—came to a screeching halt in August when the returns from the state elections in Arkansas, Iowa, Kentucky, Missouri and North Carolina began to trickle in, showing a decisive defeat for the Know-Nothing tickets in those states and convincing many voters in the North that Fillmore could not possibly win in November. The Know-Nothings captured only three of the eleven congressional races in the August elections, including a special election in Missouri. Worse yet, the party was unable to take advantage of a severe split in the Democratic ranks in Missouri, where Thomas Hart Benton, fearing that the issue of slavery would destroy the Union, ran as a "Benton Democrat," siphoning off nearly a quarter of the vote. In that race, the regular Democratic candidate finished more than 6,300 votes ahead of the Know-Nothing nominee while the aging Benton—the first man to ever serve thirty consecutive years in the U.S. Senate—ran a respectable third. The size of the Know-Nothing defeat that summer left many voters pondering whether a vote for Fillmore would be a "wasted" vote, leading to a mass exodus in the South where countless American Party voters—those who had clamored for Fillmore's nomination at the party's convention in Philadelphia—switched to Buchanan in the last hour in an effort to save the Union. Such defections, although to a lesser extent, also took place in the North. Among them was Ephraim Marsh, the former New Jersey legislator who had presided over the convention that nominated Fillmore back in February.

As the campaign drew to a close, some thirty Know-Nothing congressmen, including several from the South, issued an emotional appeal to the nation's vot-

---

31. Ibid., pp. 224, 236.

ers, arguing that the two major parties were dividing the country on sectional grounds that would lead to civil ruin. Neither party, they concluded, was prepared to prevent the country's fate from resting in the hands of the "mighty masses fresh from the monarchies of Europe." Another joint appeal "to save the Union" was issued on October 29 and signed by leading Know-Nothing officials in Kentucky, Massachusetts, New York and Pennsylvania.

Meanwhile, Democrat James Buchanan, who hardly possessed a magnetic personality, appealed to conservative voters and ex-Whigs in the North and South, insisting that Fillmore couldn't possibly win and reminding northern businessmen of lucrative southern markets and investments that were at stake. He also sharply denounced Fremont, claiming that the Pathfinder's election would lead to disunion and possibly civil war. By and large, the Democratic campaign, relying heavily on the printed word, was a negative one. Democratic newspaper editors manufactured unsavory stories about Fremont's birth and unfairly described the Republican nominee as a drunkard, a rapacious exploiter of Mexicans in California and as an unprincipled man who thought nothing of using his public position for private gain. As a result, Buchanan, who once said that there was "no middle course" on the slavery issue and condemned it as "a great political and a great moral evil," carefully finessed the issue by sticking to the middle of the road where, as the amiable and gifted Eugene J. McCarthy once observed, the worst accidents usually occur.

The Republicans, for their part, highlighted Fremont's youth and vigor while assailing his two major rivals as being over the hill. Unlike their Democratic and Know-Nothing opposition, the Republicans contested the election solely on sectional grounds, ignoring the South altogether. Like most other candidates of that period, Fremont didn't actively campaign. His acceptance speech, in which he recommended that Kansas should be admitted to the Union as a free state, was his one and only public appearance during the intensely bitter campaign. Heeding the advice of his mentors, the Pathfinder spent the duration of the campaign at his home on Ninth Street in New York City.

In Fremont's absence the Republicans flooded the North with their best and brightest speakers. William Cullen Bryant of the *New York Evening Post*, Salmon P. Chase, Schuyler Colfax, Horace Greeley, John P. Hale, Abraham Lincoln, Wendell Phillips and Missouri's Carl Schurz, among others, gave speeches on Fremont's behalf. Poet John Greenleaf Whittier and others churned out campaign lyrics and Fremont's supporters formed clubs of "Wide Awakes" in the East and "Bear Clubs" in California and held numerous rallies and torchlight marches complete with colorful floats and transparencies. Laying claim to youth, morality and religion, the Republicans campaigned with unmatched fervor, portraying Buchanan and the Democrats as a bunch of corrupt and tired old fogies.

Among the Republican stump speakers pressed into service that year were ardent antislavery advocates such as Thaddeus Stevens of Pennsylvania and *New York Times* founder Henry L. Raymond. Neither man pulled any punches. A leader of the antislavery forces in Congress, Stevens charged that Buchanan was "dead of lockjaw. Nothing remains but a platform and a bloated mass of political putridity," he said. Raymond also went for the jugular. "Remembering that he was a slaveholder," the New York publisher told an audience in Boston that if he had the chance he would have "spit on George Washington." Though jeered, Raymond, who spent much of that autumn telling lurid stories about slavery, made his point. A number of former Know-Nothing politicians, including such luminaries as Nathaniel Banks, Anson Burlingame and Henry Wilson of Massachusetts, also spoke frequently for the Republican ticket. Former New York City district attorney Chauncey Shaffer, another prominent North American, also campaigned for Fremont, believing that a Republican victory was the only way of ending the wicked and aggressive slave trade.

Despite conducting a spirited campaign, Fillmore, winning only the eight electoral votes of Maryland, ran a distant third to Buchanan and Fremont. Carrying nineteen of the nation's thirty-one states—including the entire South—Buchanan rolled to an easy victory, garnering 1,838,169 votes to Fremont's 1,341,264 and Fillmore's 874,534. Abolitionist and perennial candidate Gerrit Smith, running on the tiny Land Reform ticket, received a miniscule 484 votes. The race was much closer than the popular vote indicated. If Pennsylvania, for example, where a last-ditch fusion effort with the Know-Nothings nearly paid off, and Illinois, where a scant 9,253 votes separated Buchanan and Fremont, had voted for the Republican nominee, the election would have been thrown into the House of Representatives—a scenario that the Know-Nothing Party's Fillmore had fervently hoped for.

Capturing 21.5% of the popular vote nationally, the Know-Nothing Party's Fillmore placed a respectable second to Buchanan in no fewer than fourteen states. Running strongest in Baltimore, where he received 63% of the vote, the former president garnered nearly 55% of the vote in Maryland—a slight increase over the party's impressive showing in 1855—compared to 45% for Buchanan and a pathetic 285 votes for Republican John Fremont out of 86,860 votes cast. Moreover, a switch of only a few thousand votes in Kentucky, Louisiana, and Tennessee, would have given those states to the former president and would have thrown the election into the U.S. House of Representatives where, conceivably,

Fillmore might have emerged victorious. Though he personally harbored strong antislavery convictions—he wanted to abolish the institution "without destroying the last hope of free government in the world"—the former president polled an astonishing 44% of the popular vote in the slaveholding states, but garnered a somewhat disappointing thirteen percent of the vote in the North. Only one other third-party presidential candidate in American history—Teddy Roosevelt in 1912—garnered a larger share of the popular vote than the Know-Nothing's Fillmore. Even billionaire Ross Perot, whose lavish $67 million independent bid for the White House in 1992, was unable to match Fillmore's national percentage. (Perot, of course, polled 19% of the vote in his three-cornered race with Democrat Bill Clinton and Republican incumbent George H. W. Bush.) Moreover, casting one's vote for president back in the mid-1800s was a far more complicated procedure than it is today. In the nineteenth century, voters were faced with choosing between lists of electors pledged to individual candidates and they didn't have the luxury of voting directly for a presidential candidate. In fusion situations, such as that in Pennsylvania, the situation was even more confusing.

The American Party, which now claimed five seats in the U.S. Senate, won only fourteen House seats in the 1856-57 congressional elections—down from fifty-one in the previous Congress.[32] The party also came ever so close to winning another seat when William Appleton of Massachusetts, running on an American-Democratic fusion ticket, lost to Republican lawmaker Anson Burlingame, a one-time Know-Nothing, by a mere 69 votes in that state's fifth congressional district. Only nine Know-Nothing incumbents—Humphrey Marshall and Warner L. Underwood of Kentucky, James B. Ricaud, J. Morrison Harris and Henry Winter Davis of Maryland, George Eustis of Louisiana, Robert P. Trippe of Georgia and Tennessee's Charles Ready and Felix K. Zollicoffer, a one-time Indian fighter and former Whig—retained their seats in Congress. Despite their heavy losses in the congressional races, the Know-Nothings managed to elect several new faces to the House, including Joshua Hill, a lawyer from Georgia, and Horace Maynard, a one-time mathematics professor from Tennessee. Other newly elected Know-Nothing congressmen included lawyers Thomas L. Anderson and Samuel H.

---

32. The fourteen Know-Nothing lawmakers were later joined in the 35th Congress by North Carolina's fiercely independent Zebulon Vance who, running on the American Party ticket, won a special election in August 1858 to fill a vacancy caused by the resignation of a Democratic congressman. The 28-year-old Vance, who was later elected governor of North Carolina as a Conservative, resigned his House seat in 1861 following Lincoln's build up of troops and later served as an officer in the Confederate Army.

Woodson of Missouri, the latter of whom was re-elected on the American Party's ticket in 1858—one of only seven congressmen, including two fusionists, who were sent to Washington on the party's ticket during that period.[33] Another party member who survived the 1856 Fillmore drubbing was John A. Gilmer, a 51-year-old ex-Unionist Whig from North Carolina. Gilmer, who initially opposed secession, eventually sided with the South during the Civil War, but only after turning down a cabinet post in the Lincoln administration.

The Know-Nothing Party also fared rather poorly in that year's gubernatorial contests, losing all but three of the contests in which the party had fielded a candidate. The only successes occurred in Connecticut and New Hampshire, where William T. Minor and Ralph Metcalf narrowly won re-election. The party also enjoyed a modicum of success in Rhode Island when William W. Hoppin, the Whig-turned-Know Nothing incumbent, was re-elected on an American-Republican fusion ticket, defeating his Democratic rival with more than 58% of the vote. The 49-year-old Hoppin had joined a Know-Nothing lodge in late 1854, just as the Whig Party was collapsing. The party's biggest disappointment, however, occurred in New York when outspoken nativist publisher Erastus Brooks, though winning a plurality in several downstate counties, ran a distant third in that state's hard-fought gubernatorial contest, hopelessly garnering 22% of the vote.

Another disastrous campaign took place in Massachusetts. In that state, businessman George W. Gordon, the little-known "Fillmore American" candidate, barely tallied 10,000 votes while finishing a distant third in a crowded and star-studded field that included two other candidates running outside the traditional two-party system—octogenarian Josiah Quincy, the former mayor of Boston who ran on Francis W. Bird's hastily-fashioned "Honest Man's Ticket," and physician Luther V. Bell, a longtime Whig and a favorite of the Brahmins, whose background as the chief administrator of an insane asylum naturally made him the unwitting target of political punsters. The Know-Nothing's Gordon, a fiscal conservative who campaigned on a platform promising action against foreign paupers and criminals while barring naturalized citizens and Roman Catholics from holding public office, was never a factor in the race.[34]

---

33.   In addition to Woodson, the seven House candidates elected on the Know-Nothing ticket during the 1858-59 mid-term congressional elections included Edwin H. Webster, J. Morrison Harris and Henry Winter Davis of Maryland, and John E. Bouligny of Louisiana. Two successful fusion candidates—George Briggs of New York and Christopher Robinson of Rhode Island—eventually took their seats with the Republicans when the new House organized on December 5, 1859.

Fillmore's overwhelming defeat signaled the end of the Know-Nothing Party. The American National Council held its last meeting in Louisville in June 1857 and adjourned *sine die*. The party, barely sputtering along, held only five congressional seats during the 36th Congress in 1858-59. Among its successful candidates during the party's decline was John E. Bouligny, the only Louisianan to keep his seat in Congress after that state seceded from the Union in 1861, and Green Adams, a former Kentucky circuit court judge.

Meanwhile, Millard Fillmore, who occasionally sallied forth to make his views known, virtually retired from national politics after his overwhelming defeat in 1856. Nevertheless, he remained active in civic affairs in his home city, serving for a while as chancellor of Buffalo University and as president of the Buffalo Historical Society from 1862-67. His name was mentioned occasionally as a possible presidential candidate on the Constitutional Union Party ticket in 1860, but the former president did little to advance such a candidacy. In the winter of 1861 Fillmore hosted Abraham Lincoln while the president-elect was en route to Washington for his inauguration. He later opposed secession and called for the defense of the Union at the outset of the war-between-the-states. Although he had wholeheartedly supported the Union cause during the Civil War, the former president publicly backed Democrat George B. McClellan against Lincoln in the 1864 presidential campaign. Following Lincoln's assassination in April 1865, the exterior of Fillmore's home in Buffalo was vandalized by a grief stricken and unruly mob that angrily remembered his support of the Fugitive Slave Act and other prewar attempts to mollify the slaveholding South. Following Lincoln's tragic death, Fillmore vigorously endorsed President Andrew Johnson's relatively mild Reconstruction plan for the South. Enjoying excellent health until only a couple of weeks before his death, the former Whig president died on March 8, 1874, after suffering two life-threatening strokes a few weeks earlier.[35]

Though the Know-Nothing Party clung to life in places like Kentucky and in its strongholds of Maryland and New Orleans—where it elected John T. Monroe mayor in 1860—the party all but vanished in the South by 1858. In the North, the party continued to put up a brave front for a few years but with increasingly disastrous results. In Pennsylvania, Isaac Hazelhurst, a staunch anti-fusionist and the Know-Nothing Party's gubernatorial candidate in 1857, was snowed under against Democrat William F. Packer and antislavery advocate David Wilmot,

---

34. Mulkern, *The Know-Nothing Party in Massachusetts*, p. 150; Gienapp, *The Origins of the Republican Party*, p. 389.
35. David C. Whitney, *The American Presidents* (New York, 1978), pp. 117-118; DeGregorio, *The Complete Books of U.S. Presidents*, pp. 193-194.

who was running on a "People's" fusion ticket consisting of Republicans, Know-Nothing and ex-Free Soilers. Running strongest in Philadelphia, where he polled nearly 28% of the vote, and in a few of its surrounding counties, Hazelhurst polled less than eight percent of the statewide vote, garnering only 28,168 votes to Packer's 188,846 and 146,139 for Wilmot. The Know-Nothings did only slightly better in New York when Lorenzo Burrows, a former Whig congressman and ex-Know-Nothing state comptroller, polled 61,137 votes, or just over twelve percent of the total, in that state's 1858 gubernatorial contest while losing a three-cornered race to Republican Edwin D. Morgan. Last rites were performed the following year when the party's statewide ticket garnered a hopelessly meager 23,800 votes.

9

Rising from the Ashes

❖

John Bell and the Constitutional Unionists of 1860

Rising from the ashes of the dying Whig and Know-Nothing parties, the short-lived Constitutional Union Party was founded in December 1859 by Kentucky's John J. Crittenden and other conservative, pro-compromise lawmakers in the border slaves states who desperately wanted to preserve the Union. Adopting the slogan, "the Constitution of the Country, the Union of the states, and the enforcement of the laws," the Constitutional Union Party made its one and only splash in American history when it entered the hotly-contested four-way race for the White House in 1860.

In a last-ditch effort to save the Union, the Constitutional Unionists, whose genesis could also be found, albeit to a lesser degree, in the deep Democratic divisions over the Lecompton constitution, convened in Baltimore on May 9, 1860, only a few days after the antislavery Republicans nominated Abraham Lincoln for president at their historic national convention in Chicago. Washington Hunt, the former Whig governor of New York who was personally appalled by the rapidly growing Republican movement, served as the convention's permanent chairman. In his keynote address, the former New York governor urged the party to avoid the divisive issue of slavery in the adoption of its platform. "I trust we shall not be very much embarrassed in the construction of a platform," he assured the delegates. "We ought not to endeavor strongly to establish uniformity of opinion on a question which we all know and understand—a question that every man will at least think and feel according to his own judgment."[1]

Like Hunt, most of the delegates in attendance were die-hard former Whigs, aging men of the faith of Henry Clay and Daniel Webster. In fact, few delegates at the Baltimore convention were under the age of sixty and a disproportionate number of them hobbled around on canes. This "Old Gentlemen's Party," as it was dubbed, was treated rather savagely in the press. Noting that some of the delegates seemed intent "to galvanize petrified whiggery" while some of the delegates hoped "to whitewash embalmed Americanism," or possibly join hands with the Republicans in Chicago while still others hoped "to harness up a squatter sovereignty team," one observer quipped that the party's nominee would most likely be "an old rusty Whig fossil or an American mummy."[2] James Gordon Bennett's *New York Herald*, never at a loss for words, described the Constitutional Union convention as a "Great Gathering of Fossil Know-Nothings and Southern Americans" and the *New Orleans Daily Delta* wryly commented at the close of the convention that, "the ancient optimists and fossils quietly wended their way home by slow stages, in the full consciousness of having saved the republic."[3] Such descriptions, of course, were something of an exaggeration. Many of those who flocked to the Constitutional Union Party's banner in 1860 were younger men, including 27-year-old John Marshall Harlan, a future Supreme Court justice who served as an elector for the Bell-Everett ticket in Kentucky.

In the months leading up to its national convention, there was more than a little speculation that former President Millard Fillmore, the defeated Know-Nothing candidate in 1856, might head the Constitutional Union ticket, but his candidacy never materialized. There was also considerable speculation that Edward Bates of Missouri, a border-state moderate with antislavery leanings, would seek the party's nomination, but his assertion that Congress had jurisdiction over slavery in the territories clearly put him in the Republican camp. Winfield Scott, the 74-year-old retired general whose inept presidential campaign in 1852 hastened the Whig Party's demise, also expressed an interest in obtaining the Constitutional Union Party's nomination.[4] Meanwhile, a number of other prominent politicians were actively seeking the party's nomination, but among them only two—Sam Houston of Texas and John Bell of Tennessee—were realistically viewed as viable candidates.

---

1.   Dwight Lowell Dumond, *The Secession Movement, 1860-1861* (New York, 1973), pp. 92-93. A wealthy lawyer and farmer, the 49-year old Hunt had been offered the Democratic vice-presidential nomination that year, but declined.

2.   Parks, *John Bell of Tennessee*, p. 353.

3.   *New York Herald*, May 9, 1860; Melvin L. Hayes, *Mr. Lincoln Runs for President* (New York, 1963), p. 96.

4.   Potter, *The Impending Crisis*, p. 417.

The 67-year-old Houston, who had been swept into the governor's office in 1859 on the so-called "Opposition" ticket—a loosely organized party comprised of ex-Whigs, Know-Nothings, disaffected Democrats and assorted Unionists—had considerable support in the lower South, especially among those who wanted to prevent sectional strife. On April 27, 1860, a small group of the governor's friends met in Tyler, Texas, and elected four delegates to attend the Constitutional Union Party's convention in Baltimore. The four delegates pledged to Houston included lawyer Benjamin H. Epperson, one of the wealthiest men in Texas, former Know-Nothing congressman Lemuel D. Evans of East Texas, railroad magnate Abram M. Gentry, and Anthony B. Norton, editor of the Austin-based *Southern Intelligencer*.[5]

In a March 25 statement announcing his candidacy, Houston, who had opposed the Kansas-Nebraska bill, said that the country's growing sectional crisis had virtually destroyed the two major parties and assailed those who had been laboring for a quarter of century "to promote disunion" under the guise of democracy. The hero of San Jacinto then proceeded to enumerate the qualifications of an ideal presidential candidate, explaining that such a person must be a "bold, national man," who supported an American protectorate over Mexico—something that he alone among the presidential candidates that year had advocated.[6]

As with the Know-Nothing Party in 1856, Houston again let it be known that he was available, but in his typically baffling manner did little to secure the party's presidential nomination. He didn't even bother to attend the party's national convention in Baltimore. "Had Houston campaigned, had he been in Baltimore to speak, had he exerted any real effort," wrote one of Houston's biographers, "he could have had the nomination." Given the "fractured state of American politics" that year, wrote John Hoyt Williams, it was even conceivable that he could have been elected in a four-way race against Lincoln, Douglas and Breckinridge.[7]

While the *New York Sun*, the *Augusta Chronicle and Sentinel*, the *Arkansas Gazette* and dozens of other large and medium-sized newspapers across the country welcomed his candidacy, Houston—unlike his chief rival John Bell—had more than his fair share of detractors. The *Columbus Times* of Georgia, in a particularly harsh and mean-spirited condemnation, regretted that "a well-directed

5.   James Alex Baggett, "The Constitutional Union Party in Texas," *Southwestern Historical Quarterly*, No. 82 (January 1979).
6.   Crenshaw, *The Slave States in the Presidential Campaign of 1860*, pp. 289-290.
7.   Williams, *Sam Houston*, p. 328.

Mexican bullet did not ensure his fame by removing him while so much glory was his," and the *State Gazette* in Austin, Texas, denounced the state's favorite-son as an ostentatious showman who was "testy in temper, crafty in policy and shallow"—certainly not a man who was fit for the presidency.[8] Other criticism abounded. The *Constitutional Union* described the hero of San Jacinto as "a rather good old soul," but also one of "the most shallow of the shallow politicians" and a man who merited little consideration. "We take old Sam Houston to be a low, spiteful, cunning, hypocritical man," wrote longtime adversary Sam D. Carothers. Even his old friend "Rip" Ford, the legendary Texas Ranger, expressed serious doubts about Houston's qualifications for the nation's highest office.[9]

Interestingly, no fewer than ten candidates received votes on the convention's first ballot. One of them was Kentucky's John J. Crittenden, a moderate on secession and slavery and a man who worked feverishly to preserve the Union at all cost. While refusing to actively seek the party's nomination, the longtime Kentucky lawmaker let it be known that he wouldn't refuse the honor if it were offered. Like Tennessee's John Bell, the courageous Crittenden had vigorously opposed the Buchanan administration's attempt to force the pro-slavery Lecompton constitution on Kansas in 1858.

Other candidates seeking the Constitutional Union Party's presidential nomination included the ambitious John Minor Botts of Virginia; Edward Everett of Massachusetts; William L. Goggin of Virginia; William A. Graham of North Carolina; 75-year-old Supreme Court Justice John McLean of Ohio; Virginia's William Cabell Rives; and William L. Sharkey of Mississippi. It was an interesting and dynamic field, to say the least. Even Missouri's Edward Bates, who was then actively seeking the Republican presidential nomination, held out a faint hope that the Constitutional Union Party would turn to him on the possibility that he would also be nominated by the Republicans the following week, thereby effecting a powerful coalition in the northern and border states. It was a strategy shared by the aging McLean—a man who had been seeking the presidency since 1832, if not earlier.

Virginia's Botts was perhaps the most intriguing of those seeking the Constitutional Union Party's presidential nomination. Like Crittenden, Botts, a 58-year-old Richmond lawyer, initially hoped to engineer a seemingly unlikely fusion of old Whig and Know-Nothing elements with the Republicans in the 1860 presidential campaign. A forward-looking and articulate ex-Whig leader,

8.   Crenshaw, *The Slave States in the Presidential Campaign of 1860*, p. 291.
9.   Williams, *Sam Houston*, p. 327.

Botts was a former member of the Virginia House of Delegates and had served three terms in the U.S. House of Representatives, his last term ending in 1849. In Congress, he was a staunch supporter of Henry Clay's "American System" of protectionism and, unlike the vast majority of his colleagues in the South, had strongly opposed the extension of slavery in the territories. As a young lawmaker he had also supported John Quincy Adams in his fight against the antislavery gag rule and later denounced the annexation of Texas—highly unusual positions for a southern congressman.

William L. Goggin of Virginia, an occasional adversary of John Minor Botts, was also in the hunt. A former congressman, Goggin was a leader in Virginia's Opposition (Whig) Party and had been its unsuccessful candidate for governor in 1859, losing narrowly to Democrat John Letcher, a lawyer, newspaper editor and former congressman who was later a prime mover in the ill-fated peace-between-the-states convention in Washington in 1861. William L. Sharkey, another presidential aspirant, had served as president of the Southern States Convention in 1850. A 63-year-old lawyer from Jackson, Mississippi, Sharkey was a former state legislator who had turned down an offer to serve as President Fillmore's Secretary of War in 1851. Rounding out the field was William Cabell Rives of Virginia, a Democrat-turned-Whig former congressman and minister to France who served in the U.S. Senate from 1832-34 and again from 1836-45. Rives later attended the peace convention in Washington in 1861, but eventually sided with the Confederacy when hostilities broke out.

When the Constitutional Union Party's national convention opened on the ninth of May, the nomination was still very much in doubt. While Tennessee, Arkansas, Pennsylvania, Ohio, and Delaware were expected to go for Tennessee's John Bell, most observers felt that Sam Houston would eventually emerge as the party's nominee.[10] Bell, who led Houston by a narrow 68 ½ to 57 margin on the first ballot, was subsequently nominated on the second ballot, garnering 138 votes to Houston's 69 and 18 and one-half for North Carolina's William A. Graham, a former senator and governor who had served as Winfield Scott's vice-presidential running mate on the Whig ticket in 1852.[11] Six other candidates received a scattering of 27 ½ votes on the second ballot. Tennessee's "Eagle Orator" Gustavus A. Henry, a grandson of patriot Patrick Henry, gave an impassioned and eloquent speech thanking the delegates for honoring his state by

10.   Parks, *John Bell of Tennessee*, p. 355.
11.   The reluctant John Crittenden, who made it clear that he didn't want the party's nomination, received 28 votes on the first ballot; Everett, 25; Graham, 24; McLean, 19; Rives, 13; Botts, 9 ½; Sharkey, 7; and three delegates voted for Goggin.

nominating Bell.[12] The delegates then unanimously selected a somewhat reluctant Edward Everett of Massachusetts for vice president. The party's brief platform, one of the shortest in American history, ignored the issue of slavery altogether and called for the preservation of the Union and the enforcement of its laws—prompting the Republicans to facetiously refer to them as the "Do-Nothings."[13]

Described as a man with "Roman-like integrity and honor," the 63-year-old Bell had been frequently mentioned as a possible Republican presidential candidate that year. A former two-term senator, he had once served as President William Henry Harrison's Secretary of War but resigned shortly after Harrison's tragic death in 1841 because he could not in good conscience support the rigid states' rights agenda of John Tyler, Harrison's successor. As a senator, the stern-faced Bell took moderate positions on most issues but joined Lincoln and other Whigs in openly opposing Democrat James K. Polk on the war with Mexico. A graduate of a teachers college, Bell reluctantly supported the provisions of the Compromise of 1850 that he felt would help preserve the Union, but a few years later sharply opposed the Kansas-Nebraska legislation, which allowed the two new territories of Kansas and Nebraska to determine whether or not they would enter the Union as slave or free states. Though once a large slave owner himself, Bell was the only southern senator to vote against the Kansas-Nebraska Act of 1854.

Born in Mill Creek, Tennessee, in the winter of 1796, Bell graduated from Cumberland College in Nashville in 1814 and began a law practice shortly thereafter. He was elected to the state senate at the remarkably young age of twenty-one and resumed his law practice after serving one term. A Jacksonian Democrat, Bell, who had seven children through two marriages, was elected to Congress in 1827 and served seven consecutive terms, during which period he affiliated with the nascent Whig Party. During his long service in the House, Bell, who entered Congress when John Quincy Adams was president, personally opposed President Jackson's popular veto of the charter renewal for the Bank of the United States, but felt politically compelled to support the president. The populist president, of course, considered the bank, under the control of Nicholas Biddle, an elitist institution that monopolized the banking industry at the expense of the country's working people. Bell later opposed Jackson's efforts to remove $11 million in fed-

---

12.   Joseph Howard Parks, *John Bell of Tennessee*, pp. 354-355. Henry's speech was printed in its entirety in the *Republican Baner and Nashiville Whig*, May 16, 1860.

13.   Oates, *With Malice Toward None*, p. 199.

eral funds on deposit at the national bank and distributing the money to various "pet" banks. In Congress, Bell waged several losing campaigns for Speaker of the House before finally winning the coveted post in 1834 when he defeated fellow Tennesseean James K. Polk, the Democratic chairman of the House Ways and Means Committee and chief spokesman for Jackson's anti-banking policies. The two men, developing an intense rivalry that would last for years, squared off again in December of the following year when Polk returned the favor by defeating Bell for the same position.

Bell, who helped defeat Polk in his home state of Tennessee during the razor-thin 1844 presidential election, was returned to the state senate in 1847 and was promptly elected to the U.S. Senate by the Whig majority in the legislature, where he served for a dozen years before retiring in 1859. Lamenting that the "glorious old Whig Party" was dead, Bell announced in October 1855 that while he could never join its secret fraternity, he intended to support the Know-Nothing Party because it was a conservative organization dedicated to preserving the Union and wholeheartedly supported former President Millard Fillmore during the three-cornered 1856 presidential election.

Everett, 66, was a politician of a different stripe. Born in Dorchester, Massachusetts, he graduated from Harvard College with highest honors when he was only seventeen and earned a divinity degree three years later. He preached for a short while at the famous Brattle Street Unitarian Church in Boston before accepting a teaching position at Harvard. While on the Harvard faculty, he studied at the prestigious Gottingen University in Germany, where he received his doctorate in 1817. He traveled and studied throughout Europe for the next two years before returning to Harvard in 1819. During this period, he also became editor of the *North American Review*, the country's leading literary journal.

The one-time professor of literature at Harvard was considered something of a brilliant public speaker, yet in 1863 when he shared the platform with Lincoln in Gettysburg where the president delivered his epoch address, the former teacher droned on for nearly two hours, boring those assembled beyond belief. The long-winded diplomat didn't come close to saying in two hours what Lincoln was able to convey in only two minutes. As a politician, Everett's career was marred by a tendency to vacillate on important issues. In a public career that spanned nearly four decades, Everett, who was closely aligned with John Quincy Adams, served in Congress as a National Republican from 1825-35. During his five terms in the U.S. House, the Massachusetts lawmaker, a father of six, consistently promoted industrialization, protectionism, a national bank, and vigorously opposed the forcible removal of Cherokee Indians and other tribes from lands in the nation's southern and western regions. Cognizant of the close economic ties between Massachusetts's textile industry and southern cotton plantations, Everett was extremely reticent about openly criticizing slavery. He also served as governor of Massachusetts as a Whig from 1836 to 1840 when he narrowly lost a bid for a fifth term to perennial Democratic candidate Marcus Morton. As governor, he supported funding for public education and established the country's first teachers' college.

A founding member of the Whig Party in his home state, Everett also served in the U.S. Senate for fifteen months, resigning amid a firestorm of protest from antislavery advocates in Massachusetts shortly after failing to cast a vote on the important Kansas-Nebraska Act, apparently due to illness. He also served as ambassador to England in the Harrison administration and as Fillmore's Secretary of State for four months following Daniel Webster's death in the fall of 1852. As Secretary of State, the former Massachusetts lawmaker negotiated a commercial treaty with Japan and issued a sharply worded denunciation of a British-French proposal to guarantee Spain's permanent control of Cuba. He also served as president of Harvard from 1846 to 1849. In his latter role, African-American men were permitted to take the school's entrance examination for the first time ever, though, curiously, none of the prospective students scored well enough to gain admittance into the prestigious Ivy League school.

Having taken his name out of consideration for the party's presidential nomination when he realized the growing strength of the Bell and Houston candidacies, Everett was not entirely pleased with his vice-presidential nomination. "It looks like favoring an officer with the command of a sloop-of-war," he facetiously wrote his daughter, "after he had magnanimously waived his claim to the flag of the Mediterranean Squadron, in favor of a junior officer."[14]

While most northern Know-Nothings supported either Lincoln or Douglas in the 1860 presidential contest, a number of Fillmore's former supporters in that region rallied to the Constitutional Union Party's banner. Among those who helped to found the new party were such notable Know-Nothing leaders as Erastus Brooks of New York, Philadelphia's Jacob Broom, and the aging Nathan Sargent, a former Whig-turned-American who, like Brooks, had actively spread rumors of Fremont's Catholicism during the 1856 presidential campaign. A longtime Washington correspondent for the *United States Gazette* who was perhaps best known for his graphic memoirs of the long era from Monroe to Fillmore, Sargent was instrumental in organizing the new party, believing that

---

14.   Paul R. Frothingham, *Edward Everett, Orator and Statesman* (Boston, 1925), p. 410.

through the Constitutional Unionists the old Whig Party could yet be revived. Washington Hunt, the former Whig governor of New York who served as permanent chairman of the Constitutional Party's national convention in Baltimore, was another Fillmore supporter who worked diligently for the Bell-Everett ticket.

Some of the prominent personalities in the South who gathered under the party's banner during its brief existence included Benjamin H. Hill, a moderate from Georgia who wore several political hats—Democrat, Whig and Know-Nothing—in an effort to find middle ground on the issue of secession. The new party also attracted the support of Joshua Hill, a Know-Nothing congressman from Georgia, who later struggled in vain to promote peace during the Civil War. Secretary of the Treasury Howell Cobb, who had been elected governor of Georgia in 1851 under the Constitutional Union banner, was also a member, as was former Secretary of the Navy George E. Badger, a noted humorist and former senator from North Carolina.

Virginia congressman Alexander R. Boteler, who later served on Stonewall Jackson's staff during the Civil War, served as director of the Constitutional Union Party's executive committee and directed much of the 1860 campaign's day-to-day activities. A graduate of Princeton, the 45-year-old Boteler had moved from the Whigs through the Know-Nothings and into the Opposition Party when he was finally elected to Congress in 1859. A gifted speaker, he later gave what was once described as one of the two most eloquent speeches ever given in Congress. Boteler played a critical role at the Constitutional Union convention in Baltimore, leading delegates from New York and New Jersey as well as the entire Alabama, Florida, and Georgia delegations into the Bell camp when some of the delegates in Bell's home state were wavering.[15] In addition to enjoying the unflinching support of the Washington-based *National Intelligencer*, long a voice of conservatism, the Constitutional Unionists also established the *Union Guard*, a weekly newspaper with a decidedly protectionist and Unionist tone. Under the editorial direction of Bell's friend James C. Welling, the *Union Guard*, frequently assailing an alleged secessionist clique, sharply denounced Breckinridge and the Southern Democrats, while repeatedly referring to Lincoln as a dyed-in-the-wool "Sumnerite."[16]

For the most part, the Constitutional Unionists were treated with ridicule and scorn during the hard-fought campaign of 1860. The Republicans, brooking no compromise on the issue of slavery, described the party's platform as "worthy to

15.   Nevins, *The Emergence of Lincoln*, Vol. II, p. 66; Park, *John Bell of Tennessee*, p. 354.
16.   Crenshaw, *The Slave States in the Presidential Election of 1860*, p. 31.

be printed on gilt-edged paper" and "preserved in a box of musk" and the adamantly pro-slavery Southern Democrats, who were running their own ticket, sharply denounced the resurrected Whigs for "insulting the intelligence of the American people" by attempting to avoid the issue of slavery.[17] Everyone was a critic. A southern congressman suggested facetiously that the Constitutional Unionists should have nominated Rufus Choate, the Massachusetts statesman, for the presidency. When reminded that Choate had died a year earlier, the lawmaker said that he was aware of that fact, adding, "but he hasn't been dead a very long time."[18]

Of course, not everyone belittled the fledgling Constitutional Unionist Party. The *Daily Chicago Herald* praised the ticket, stating that it was a respectable party with noble purposes and worthy candidates, adding that the only thing it lacked was a constituency.[19] The moderate *Staunton Spectator* of Virginia, a voice of reason in that region, also praised the Bell and Everett ticket, as did countless other newspapers, including the *Harrison Flag* in Marshall, Texas, and the *Fort Worth Chief*, to mention but a few.

Curiously, Sam Houston, whose diehard supporters refused to give up, remained in the race as an independent long after the Constitutional Union convention adjourned, prompting one newspaper to quip that his platform was even shorter than that of the Constitutional Unionists, consisting merely of his "old Indian blanket."[20] In the days and weeks following the Constitutional Union Party's national convention, the enigmatic Hero of San Jacinto continued to conduct an independent campaign for the White House. In fact, two weeks after the Baltimore convention, he enthusiastically accepted a nomination that had been offered to him earlier that spring during a gala celebration at the San Jacinto battlefield on the twenty-fourth anniversary of his famous victory over Santa Ana, saying that he would run as the "people's" candidate. With astonishing swiftness, his acceptance was followed by mass rallies in New York City, including a huge affair at Union Square. Other rallies were held in Texas and elsewhere. On May 30—some three weeks after being rejected by the Constitutional Union Party convention in Baltimore—James Gordon Bennett's *New York Herald* endorsed Houston's fledgling "people's candidacy," arguing that his independent candidacy might provide the solution to the "ugly problem" confronting the nation. Bennett's newspaper, incidentally, had been all over the board that year, first sup-

---

17. McPherson, *Battle Cry of Freedom*, pp. 221-222.
18. Melvin L. Hayes, *Mr. Lincoln Runs for President*, pp. 96-97.
19. Hayes, *Mr. Lincoln Runs for President*, p. 97.
20. Ibid., p. 97.

porting John Breckinridge then switching to the legendary Texan before finally shifting to the Constitutional Union Party's John Bell in August following Houston's formal withdrawal from the race. Moreover, the *New York Sun* had been beating the drums for the old warrior for months and the *New York Express* suggested Houston's name as a possible coalition candidate supported by all of the elements opposed to the Republicans. Believing that he might actually win in a five-way race, Houston declared his independence from the country's four leading political parties. "The Constitution and the Union embrace the only principle by which I will be governed if elected," he confidently asserted.

As late as July 31, Houston apparently still believed he had a chance. "My only hope is that all men who sincerely desire the preservation of the government will unite together in the present contest against sectionalism," he said. While reiterating his continued opposition to abolitionism, sectionalism and the reopening of the African slave trade, Houston said that the major issue in the campaign was whether union or disunion would prevail after the election.[21]

By early August, however, Houston realized this his independent campaign was doomed, as one newspaper after another, including many Texas journals that were previously in his corner, abandoned his candidacy and fell in line behind one of the four other candidates. He was also deeply disappointed when the Democrats swamped his candidates in the Texas elections on August 6.[22] In the Lone Star State, where the race was shaping up as a showdown between southerners Bell and Breckinridge, a number of newspapers, including the *Belton Independent,* the *McKinney Messenger* and Anthony B. Norton's *Southern Intelligencer*, had already thrown their support to the Constitutional Union ticket. By then, it was painfully clear that Houston probably couldn't even carry his home state. Shortly thereafter, the *Houston Telegraph* urged the Texas governor to withdraw from the race and do a political somersault by endorsing John C. Breckinridge, the Southern Democrat—a suggestion that Houston, who was adamantly opposed to secession, never seriously considered.[23] Making matters worse, the *New York Times*, which was solidly behind Lincoln, published a vicious article on August 15 charging Houston with cowardice during the battle of San Jacinto and suggesting that the legendary Texan was neither a hero nor a particularly skillful political or military leader.[24]

---

21. Crenshaw, *The Slave States in the Presidential Election of 1860*, p. 292.
22. Williams, *Sam Houston*, p. 330.
23. *Houston Weekly Telegraph*, August 7, 1860, in Crenshaw, *The Slaves States in the Presidential Election of 1860*, p. 292.
24. *New York Times*, August 15, 1860.

Admitting that his cause was hopeless, Houston formally withdrew from the contest two days later, but without endorsing any other candidate. In late September, he endorsed the Union fusion campaign in Texas, a ticket consisting of two Bell and two Douglas electors. On September 22, he delivered a stinging Unionist address in which he lambasted the state's "transplants from the South Carolina nursery of disunion" and warned his fellow Texans that once out of the Union and unprotected by the Constitution, aristocracy would again rear its ugly head and that the common people would suffer an untold fate. He later gave a few rather lackadaisical stump speeches for the Constitutional Union Party's John Bell, while, in a complete about-face, privately confiding in a friend that he personally preferred Breckinridge to any other candidate in the race.[25]

The 1860 presidential campaign also included the candidacy of Gerrit Smith, the aging abolitionist who was nominated for the presidency by the tiny Union Party, a remnant of the old Liberty Party. Smith, who once said that he could "never vote for any person who recognizes a law for slavery," had contributed five hundred dollars to the Fremont campaign in 1856. This little-remembered abolitionist party called for the preservation of the Union and was adamantly opposed to secession. Nobody, including Smith himself, took the 63-year-old philanthropist's candidacy very seriously that year.

The Democrats Split

The Democrats, for their part, were badly divided in 1860. Meeting in Charleston, South Carolina, in April of that year, the Democrats were unable to select a presidential nominee, due, in large part, to southern opposition led by Alabama's fiery William L. Yancey, an uncompromising secessionist and white supremacist. Though Democratic front-runner Stephen A. Douglas of Illinois had captured a majority of the party's delegates during the convention's balloting, he was unable to gain the necessary two-thirds support needed to win the party's nomination. (It wasn't until 1936 that the Democratic Party amended its rules requiring a simple majority for nomination.)

The Charleston convention ended after several days of rancorous infighting when several southern delegations stormed out of the proceedings. Despite repeated attempts to bring the two warring sides back together, a gulf the size of the Grand Canyon developed between the northerners and their brethren from the South.

---

25. Williams, *Sam Houston*, p. 333.

Seven weeks later, the Northern Democrats, reconvening in Baltimore on June 18, nominated the 47-year-old Douglas for president. Yancey and other southern bolters from the original convention demanded to be included in the proceedings only to walkout again. Former Gov. Herschel V. Johnson of Georgia, a states' rights Democrat, was later named for vice president by the Democratic National Committee, but only after Alabama's Benjamin Fitzpatrick declined the convention's nomination.

As a leading advocate of "popular sovereignty" and the man who drafted the controversial Kansas-Nebraska Act of 1854, Douglas entered the campaign with plenty of baggage. Born in Brandon, Vermont, in 1813, Douglas went to work as an apprentice cabinetmaker when he was a teenager. Politically inspired by Andrew Jackson's presidential campaign in 1828, Douglas became a lifelong Democrat. He moved west as young man, studied law and finally settled in Jacksonville, Illinois, in the autumn of 1833. Elected state's attorney at the age of twenty-one, he quickly became a leader in the Illinois Democratic Party. In 1836, he won a seat in the state legislature, but moved to Springfield the following year. Four years later, he became secretary of state, but served only a year before being appointed to the Illinois Supreme Court—becoming the youngest justice ever appointed to the state's highest court.

In 1838, the ambitious Illinois lawyer ran for Congress from the state's third congressional district, losing to Whig John T. Stuart by a scant thirty-five votes out of more than 36,000 votes cast. Though just shy of constitutional eligibility—he was only 29—Douglas ran unsuccessfully for the U.S. Senate in 1842 before winning a seat in the U.S. House two years later. He served two terms in the House before winning the first of three consecutive terms in the U.S. Senate in 1846.

Nicknamed "the Little Giant," Douglas, who stood only five-feet, four-inches tall, quickly emerged as a leader of the northern Democrats in the Senate, playing a pivotal role during one of the nation's most divisive periods. An avid Unionist, Douglas was an unapologetic expansionist, supporting the country's "Manifest Destiny," including the annexation of Texas and the entire Oregon Territory. As chairman of the House and later the Senate Committee on Territories, he sponsored bills to establish six other territories—Minnesota, Utah, New Mexico, Washington, Kansas and Nebraska. He was also a vigorous supporter of the war against Mexico—a conflict opposed by his Illinois rival, Abraham Lincoln. He also advocated homestead legislation and promoted the federal subsidization of a transcontinental railroad from the Mississippi Valley to the Pacific Coast.

Staking out a middle position on the question of allowing slavery in the new western territories, Douglas proposed the idea of "popular sovereignty," allowing voters in the territories to decide for themselves whether or not slavery should be allowed. He was also instrumental in the passage of the Compromise of 1850, legislation that enabled the Utah and New Mexico territories to be organized on the basis of popular sovereignty, while permitting California to enter the Union as a free state—a position supported by a majority of its residents.

Douglas's Kansas-Nebraska Act of 1854 repealed the Missouri Compromise ban on slavery in that area, setting off a political maelstrom that led to the collapse of the Whig Party and a dangerously widening rift between northern and southern Democrats. His legislation also led to intense guerilla warfare in Kansas where proslavery elements from neighboring Missouri clashed violently with antislavery forces, a deadly debacle that presaged even bloodier battles to come. In 1857, the U.S. Supreme Court ruled in the *Dred Scott* case that slavery was constitutionally protected from interference by federal or territorial governments, thereby effectively undercutting the Illinois lawmaker's remedy of popular sovereignty. Later that winter, Douglas, a powerful speaker, alienated himself from most of his party's southern wing and their northern allies when he sharply condemned President Buchanan and the controversial Lecompton Constitution in Kansas, which had been drafted by the proslavery faction in the Kansas legislature.

Running for a third term in the U.S. Senate in 1858, Douglas was challenged by Abraham Lincoln, a relatively unknown 49-year-old ex-Whig congressman and lawyer from Springfield who ran unsuccessfully for the U.S. Senate three years earlier. Douglas showed nothing but respect for his challenger. "He is the strong man of his party—full of wit, facts, dates—and the best stump speaker, with his droll ways and dry jokes, in the West," he said. In a series of seven hard-hitting debates that drew considerable national attention, Lincoln became a household name as a result of his famous "House Divided" acceptance speech while Douglas, who was forced to explain in his so-called Freeport Doctrine how the *Dred Scott* decision could be circumvented to allow for popular sovereignty, was re-elected by the Democratic-controlled state legislature. Although Douglas was ostensibly the winner, the Lincoln-Douglas debates catapulted the former one-term Whig congressman into serious contention for the Republican Party's presidential nomination in 1860.

Throughout the 1850s, Douglas had been a serious contender for the Democratic presidential nomination, losing hard-fought campaigns to Franklin Pierce and James Buchanan in 1852 and 1856, respectively. Then a brash newcomer to presidential politics, Douglas stitched together a motley crew consisting of land and railroad speculators, government lobbyists and a "Young America" group favoring expansion and an aggressive, interventionist foreign policy, in a bid for his party's presidential nomination in Baltimore in 1852—and he nearly pulled it off, running neck-and-neck with his party's frontrunners through countless ballots before the delegates turned to Franklin Pierce of New Hampshire, the darkest of all dark-horse candidates, on the forty-ninth ballot.

Few men have ever campaigned harder for their party's presidential nomination than Douglas in 1856. He took to the field long before the Charleston convention, canvassing with energy and determination, frequently seen in the Senate lobby, in hotels and on the nation's sidewalks shaking hands and urging potential delegates to support his candidacy. "Probably no other candidate for a presidential nomination ever played his hand so openly and boldly," observed one of Horace Greeley's correspondents.[26]

It was Douglas's great misfortune that he finally won his party's top honor in 1860—a year when his party was so badly divided. With the bolt of the party's southern wing, quipped the *Daily Chicago Herald*, the Northern Democrats resembled "the wolf who was silly enough to get his tail cut off in a steel trap and then endeavored to persuade others that it was fashionable."[27]

From the moment of his nomination in Baltimore, the legitimacy of Douglas' nomination was seriously questioned by his party's seceding southern faction, which maintained that Breckinridge was the party's rightful nominee, especially since the vice president had the tacit support of the Buchanan administration. While it was customary for presidential candidates not to actively campaign for the office, Douglas broke with tradition and waged a valiant effort, which included conducting a speaking tour in areas where he was the most unpopular—namely, in New England and the South. In the latter region, the Illinois lawmaker, dodging raw eggs and over-ripened fruit, urged southerners, in rather powerful rhetoric, not to leave the Union if Lincoln was elected. "I would hang every man higher than Haman who would attempt to resist by force the execution of any provision of the Constitution which our fathers made and bequeathed to us," he told audiences in Raleigh, North Carolina. Continuing to stake out a moderate position on slavery—a position he maintained throughout his public career—Douglas said that he was "for burying Southern disunion and Northern abolitionism in the same grave."[28]

26.   Nevins, *The Emergence of Lincoln*, Vol. II, pp. 201-202.
27.   Hayes, *Mr. Lincoln Runs for President*, p. 92.

Meanwhile, the Southern Democrats convened at the Maryland Institute Hall in Baltimore on June 23, while the regular reassembled Democratic convention was still in session. Their convention, chaired by the surprisingly youthful-looking Caleb Cushing of Massachusetts—a sixty-year-old man of enormous intellectual prowess who opposed slavery yet believed that the North had no constitutional right to interfere in southern affairs—nominated Vice President John C. Breckinridge of Kentucky for the nation's highest office. The battle for the southern party's presidential nomination boiled down to two main contenders—Breckinridge and former New York Sen. Daniel S. Dickinson, the 59-year-old white-haired leader of New York's so-called "Hard Shell" faction.

A lawyer possessing the deadly combination of an analytical mind and biting wit, "Scripture Dick," as he was dubbed, had served in the New York legislature and as lieutenant governor before winning a seat in the U.S. Senate in 1844. As a member of that "esteemed" body, he once calmly disarmed a colleague who had drawn a pistol against another senator during a rancorous debate over the issue of slavery. During his single term in the U.S. Senate, Dickinson supported the annexation of Texas and the Oregon Territory and served as chairman of the finance committee. During the war with Mexico, he ignored the instructions of the New York legislature and voted against the Wilmot Proviso barring the expansion of slavery into the territories acquired from Mexico—earning him the everlasting wrath of the nation's Free Soilers. One of the first to introduce the idea of popular sovereignty, the New York lawmaker also introduced several resolutions that would have allowed the territorial governments to determine their own domestic policy. Following the Mexican War, he served on a special committee that helped to draft the Compromise of 1850. After leaving the Senate in 1851, Dickinson declined President Pierce's offer to serve as collector of the port of New York—a rather lucrative and powerful post—and returned to his law practice instead.

Breckinridge, as expected, defeated Dickinson by a vote of 81 to 24 on the first ballot at the Southern Democratic convention in Baltimore. At age thirty-five, Breckinridge was the youngest man ever elected to the vice presidency. Oregon Senator Joseph Lane, a Mexican War hero, was chosen as Breckinridge's vice-presidential running mate. A rump convention in Richmond, comprised largely of South Carolinians, later ratified these nominations. The Southern Democrats approved a platform calling for federal protection of slavery in the territories and demanded strict enforcement of the Fugitive Slave Law. Hoping to

---

28. Miller, *'If Elected...' Unsuccessful Candidates for the Presidency, 1796-1968*, p. 183.

expand the institution of slavery, they also boldly called for the acquisition of Cuba.

President Buchanan, to utterly no one's surprise, endorsed his vice president in the autumn campaign. So, too, did former Presidents John Tyler and Franklin Pierce.[29] Breckinridge also picked up an endorsement from Lewis Cass, the Democratic presidential standard-bearer in 1848. Remarkably, Breckinridge was also endorsed by eight of the ten Democratic senators and four-fifths of the Democratic House members from the North. By contrast, Martin Van Buren was the only former Democratic president to endorse Stephen A. Douglas and only a handful of southerners, including Pierre Soulé of Louisiana, veteran Mississippi unionist Henry S. Foote, who was then living in Tennessee, and John Forsyth of the *Mobile Register*, supported the Northern Democratic nominee.[30]

John C. Breckinridge was born into a politically active family. His father, who died when the younger Breckinridge was only two years of age, had been a state representative with great promise before his life was cut short at the age of thirty-four and his grandfather, John Breckinridge, had served in the U.S. Senate and as attorney general during Thomas Jefferson's administration. After earning a degree in 1841 from Transylvania University in Lexington, Kentucky, the younger Breckinridge opened a law practice, hanging out his shingle in Burlington, Iowa, but returned to his native state two years later where he continued to practice law.

Having served as a major in the Mexican War, Breckinridge was elected to the Kentucky legislature as a states' rights Democrat in the late 1840s before dramatically winning Henry Clay's old seat in the U.S. House in 1851 against a strong Whig opponent. Breckinridge was returned to Congress in 1853, defeating Whig Robert P. Letcher by 526 votes. In Congress, Breckinridge didn't sponsor any major legislation but played a key role in adding an amendment repealing the Missouri Compromise ban on slavery to Stephen A. Douglas's controversial Kansas-Nebraska Act in 1854. He also helped win its final approval. That same year, the young Kentucky lawmaker turned down President Franklin Pierce's offer of an ambassadorship to Spain. Breckinridge didn't seek re-election in 1855 and his seat in Congress went to the Know-Nothing Party's Alexander K. Marshall. In 1856, the 35-year-old ex-congressman was named as James Buchanan's vice-presidential running mate at the Democratic national convention in Cincinnati and subsequently became the youngest vice president in American history. Although

29.   Boller, *Presidential Campaigns*, p. 100.
30.   Nevins, *The Emergence of Lincoln*, Vol. II, p. 282.

he was firmly committed to the southern cause, as vice president, Breckinridge, who was excluded from most of the important policy-making decisions in the Buchanan White House, nevertheless presided over the U.S. Senate with a great deal of impartiality

The Immortal Lincoln

Unlike the party's 1856 national convention, which was marked by the presence of hundreds of somber-minded abolitionists, the festive Republican convention of 1860 had a distinct carnival-like atmosphere. But it was anything but a gala celebration. "What seems a brilliant festival," wrote one journalist, "is but the rally for battle; it is an army with banners." Buoyed by their strong showing in the 1858-59 mid-term congressional elections, the Republicans, meeting in Chicago on May 16, were indeed poised for battle—and confident that this time they would emerge triumphant.

Like the Constitutional Unionists and the Democrats that year, there was no shortage of candidates for the party's presidential nomination. Far better organized than in 1856, the crowded Republican field included frontrunner William H. Seward of New York, Ohio Gov. Salmon P. Chase and the aging Edward Bates of Missouri, a man with moderate antislavery leanings who had presided over the Whig Party's last presidential nominating convention in 1856 and had briefly flirted with the idea of seeking the Constitutional Union Party's nomination earlier that year. Wealthy Pennsylvania Republican leader Simon Cameron, who was willing to sell-out to the highest bidder, the ubiquitous Nathaniel P. Banks of Massachusetts, and the somewhat drab and elderly Supreme Court Justice John McLean, still entertaining visions of grandeur, were also in the hunt.[31] Dubbed the "Winnebago Chief"—a derisive nickname he acquired years earlier for allegedly cheating an Indian tribe in a supply contract—the 61-year-old Cam-

---

31.   Despite his advanced age, the 75-year-old McLean still had a number of strong supporters around the country. In endorsing him early in the campaign, an Indianapolis newspaper argued that while he was old, he was also "vigorous, and his temperate, regular life is a better assurance that he will fill his term than the dissipated vigor of younger men..."—a point subtly challenged by Lincoln. "If Judge McLean was fifteen, or even ten years younger," wrote Lincoln in early April, he would be a stronger candidate in Illinois than Seward, Chase or Bates, "but his great age, and the recollections of the deaths of Harrison and Taylor have, so far, prevented his being much spoken of here." See *Illinois State Journal*, April 23, 1860; Angle and Miers, *The Living Lincoln*, p. 323.

eron was the sleaziest aspirant in an otherwise impressive field. Abraham Lincoln was also in the race. Coming off back-to-back losses for the U.S. Senate interspersed by an unsuccessful bid for the party's vice-presidential nomination four years earlier, Lincoln, a former one-term Whig congressman, was regarded as a long shot—at best.

Although some Lincoln biographers, including historian David Herbert Donald, argue—and accurately so—that Lincoln, enjoying the unanimous support of the large Illinois delegation, "was not a dark horse" by the time the delegates convened in Chicago's Wigwam that spring, there is plenty of evidence to suggest that his nomination seemed highly unlikely only a few months earlier. Even his candidacy, coming on the heels of a losing campaign for the U.S. Senate in Illinois, came as something of a surprise to many of the nation's leading political pundits, including writer David W. Bartlett, who, in his exhaustive 360-page biographical sketch of possible candidates for the presidency in 1860, completely omitted Lincoln's name. Bartlett's book, which was published by A. B. Burdick in the fall of 1859, included in-depth biographies of no fewer than twenty-one active or potential candidates for the presidency, including such minor figures as New York's Daniel S. Dickinson and former House Speaker James L. Orr of South Carolina.[32] Similarly, Lincoln's name was also excluded from a list of forty-five prospective presidential candidates that appeared in the *Philadelphia Press*, then Pennsylvania's leading daily newspaper, during the autumn of 1859.[33] Even when his name was mentioned as a possible candidate for the Republican presidential nomination, Lincoln's chances were often dismissed. "As for Lincoln," wrote a Boston observer, "I am afraid he will kick the beam again as he is in the habit of doing."[34]

Unlike the Democrats, the Republican convention had no unit rule or two-thirds rule to quarrel over. A simple majority was all that was needed for nomination. As the opening gavel sounded, nearly everyone agreed that William H. Seward would be nominated. Even Horace Greeley of the *New York Tribune*, who was hardly beating the drum for his fellow New Yorker, conceded as much, saying on the eve of the convention that since the opposition to Seward couldn't agree on a candidate, his nomination was virtually assured. Murat Halstead of the

---

32. Nevins, *The Emergence of Lincoln*, Vol. II, p. 277. Bartlett, a Washington correspondent for the *New York Evening Post* and the *New York Independent*, quickly atoned for his oversight by writing the *Life and Public Services of the Hon. Abraham Lincoln*, a 354-page book published in 1860.

33. *Philadelphia Press*, November 28, 1859.

34. Donald, *Lincoln*, p. 236.

Cincinnati Commercial and Henry Raymond of the *New York Times* concurred, agreeing that the former New York governor was the party's presumptive nominee.[35] Seward's friends and neighbors were so confident of victory that they placed a cannon on his front lawn in Auburn, New York, to blast the news of his expected triumph.[36] His supporters reportedly also spent eight hundred dollars on a huge, beautifully colored banner bearing his likeness that was to be unfurled at the convention upon his nomination.[37] As expected, the adroit New York senator and former governor jumped out to a comfortable lead on the convention's first ballot, polling 173 ½ votes to Lincoln's surprisingly strong showing of 102. Cameron, Chase and Bates combined for 147 ½ votes while a dozen delegates voted for the 75-year-old McLean. There was also a scattering of votes for several favorite-son candidates, including the starchy and tactless Jacob Collamer of Vermont, William L. Dayton of New Jersey, the party's vice-presidential candidate in 1856, and antislavery firebrand Benjamin F. Wade of Ohio—a man with an incurable aversion to blacks who was nonetheless as devoted to equal rights as anyone in the party.

Like a bolt out of the blue, Lincoln then unexpectedly cut deeply into Seward's lead, trailing his New York rival by a slight margin of 184 ½ to 181 on the second ballot. Refusing to give up the fight, perennial hopeful Salmon P. Chase garnered 42 ½ votes on the second ballot, while 35 delegates stuck with Bates of Missouri. A handful of votes were cast for others, including two for Kentucky's Cassius M. Clay. Then, lightning struck. Abraham Lincoln, the "rail splitter" from Illinois, easily wrapped up the nomination long before the third ballot was officially announced. It was a stampede as never seen before—or since.

"To believers in the hand of Providence in American history," wrote Eugene H. Roseboom, the insightful chronicler of presidential campaigns, "the Chicago nomination must afford an amazing example of its mysterious ways. Midnight conferences of liquor-stimulated politicians, deals for jobs, local leaders pulling wires to save their state tickets, petty malice and personal jealousies—a strange compound, and the man of destiny emerges."[38] In the final analysis, however, it was the behind-the-scenes maneuvering and deals worked out by Lincoln's clever and often unscrupulous convention managers David Davis and Norman B. Judd, a former Democrat who broke with his party over the Kansas-Nebraska Act, that eventually paved the way for Lincoln's unexpected nomination. One of those

---

35. Fite, *The Presidential Campaign of 1860*, pp. 270-271.
36. Nevins, *The Emergence of Lincoln*, Vol. II, p. 239.
37. Hayes, *Mr. Lincoln Runs for President*, p. 75.
38. Roseboom, *A History of Presidential Elections*, p. 180.

deals was cut with Pennsylvania's Simon Cameron, the slippery Republican boss who threw his state's large delegation to Lincoln in exchange for a cabinet post. Lincoln's stunning and unforeseen victory over frontrunner William H. Seward, observed Murat Halstead, "was the triumph of a presumption of availability over preeminence in intellect and unrivaled fame—a success of the ruder qualities of manhood and the more homely attributes of popularity, over the arts of a consummate politician, and the splendor of accomplished statesmanship."[39]

No fewer than nine candidates, including celebrated Kentucky abolitionist Cassius M. Clay, received votes for the vice presidency on the first ballot. Senator Hannibal Hamlin of Maine, a former Democrat who switched parties shortly after passage of the Kansas-Nebraska Act, was then chosen as Lincoln's running mate on the second ballot, easily defeating Clay by a margin of 367 to 86.

Retreating from the radicalism of 1856, the Republicans adopted a relatively conservative platform restricting slavery in the territories and calling for the admission of Kansas as a free state. Less than a third of the party's platform dealt with slavery—a sharp contrast to the document approved four years earlier. In addition to criticizing the corruption of the Buchanan administration, the Republicans also blasted John Brown, denouncing the "lawless invasion by armed force of the soil of any state or territory, no matter under what pretext, as among the gravest of crimes." The platform also promised a protective tariff, designed specifically to placate the large Pennsylvania delegation, as well as a homestead law and internal improvements of the nation's rivers and harbors. The Republicans also supported the construction of the transcontinental railroad, a position also championed by the Douglas Democrats.[40]

A disarmingly unpretentious and plainspoken man, Abraham Lincoln, who was named after his paternal grandfather, was born in a crude log cabin in rural Hardin County, Kentucky, during the winter of 1809. Like so many other frontier farmers in the early nineteenth century who spent their lives in an endless struggle against poverty and other hardships encountered in the wilderness, Lincoln's parents, worried about the validity of their land claim in Kentucky, moved their family across the Ohio River to Indiana seven years later where young Abe helped clear the land for the family farm. Lincoln, whose formal education was limited to only a few months in a one-room schoolhouse, was an avid reader and read virtually every book he could lay his hands on—an attribute that his father,

39.   Baringer, *Lincoln's Rise to Power*, p. 309.
40.   Emerson David Fite, *The Presidential Campaign of 1860* (Port Washington, N.Y.), pp. 124-125.

Thomas Lincoln, mistook for laziness. Their relationship was never a good one and evidence of just how strained it really was became evident years later when the younger Lincoln refused to visit his ailing father when he was near death. He also refused to attend his funeral. Lincoln moved with his family to central Illinois in 1830 and the 21-year-old struck out on his own the following year, settling in New Salem and working in a variety of jobs, including store clerk, postmaster, surveyor, mill hand and partner in a general store. During the Black Hawk War of 1832, he was named captain of the volunteer militia, but his company didn't see any military action.

Apparently bitten by the political bug during this period, Lincoln, who had sharpened his speaking skills in the local debating society, waged an unsuccessful campaign for the state legislature in 1832. After waging a rigorous campaign throughout the district, he was elected by a wide margin two years later. He was re-elected three times. Politically, Lincoln was a devoted Whig and a disciple of Henry Clay and his "American System" of government involvement in the nation's economic and social affairs. He served in the Illinois legislature from 1834-1842, serving as a Whig floor leader and was instrumental in moving the state capital from Vandalia to Springfield in 1837. Though hardly an abolitionist, he also gained some attention as a legislator by criticizing a resolution condemning antislavery societies. Lincoln, who studied law while in the legislature, started practicing law in 1836 when he became a law partner of John Stuart, a fellow Whig lawmaker.

Deciding not to seek re-election in 1842, Lincoln then formed a law partnership with Judge Stephen T. Logan and developed a prosperous practice that was eventually dissolved in 1844, at which time he established a new partnership with William H. Herndon—a partnership, incidentally, that was never formally dissolved, even after Lincoln took the oath of office as the nation's sixteenth president. Though not widely read in law nor deeply grounded in precedent, Lincoln quickly developed a reputation as one of the finest lawyers in Illinois. In 1842, he also married Mary Todd, the educated and cultured daughter of a prominent Kentucky banker.

Lincoln's political fire was never really extinguished and, after patiently waiting his turn, was elected to Congress as a Whig in 1846, defeating Democrat Peter Cartwright, a circuit-riding Methodist evangelist, by a margin of 6,340 to 4,829 in a three-cornered race in which little-known Elihu Walcott of the antislavery Liberty Party garnered 249 votes, or roughly two percent of the vote. Not quite forty years old when he entered Congress, Lincoln was regarded by his colleagues as a genial and cheerful man, but really didn't stand out as an exceptional lawmaker. While he generally voted against measures introducing slavery in the territories, he failed to support a bill abolishing slavery in the District of Columbia and instead introduced alternative legislation calling for the white voters themselves to decide the issue—a proposal not unlike the one introduced by Stephen A. Douglas in 1854. Lincoln's proposal, quipped New York's Horace Greeley, was akin to "submitting to the inmates of the penitentiary a proposition to double the lengths of their respective terms of imprisonment."[41]

However, Lincoln, who had campaigned vigorously for Henry Clay in the 1844 presidential campaign, emerged in the U.S. House as a vocal opponent of the expansionist war with Mexico, demanding proof of the exact spot on American soil in which the Mexicans had allegedly attacked U.S. soldiers, earning him the nickname of "Spotty." He also supported the Wilmot Proviso, which, if adopted, would have banned slavery from any territory acquired during the Mexican War. Due to the Whig Party's peculiar one-term rotation system in his district, Lincoln was prevented from seeking a second term in 1848. This was probably fortunate for the one-term Whig lawmaker, especially given the unpopularity of his opposition to the war. In fact, Stephen T. Logan, Lincoln's former law partner who sought to replace him in the 31st Congress, was narrowly defeated in a bid for Lincoln's seat, losing to his Democratic rival by 106 votes.

Not one of Lincoln's colleagues, recalled Greeley, could possibly have imagined that the quiet and deferential Whig congressman would later be elevated to the presidency. "He seemed a quiet, good-natured man, who did not aspire to leadership and seldom claimed the floor," Greeley said.[42]

Upon leaving Congress, Lincoln returned to his law practice, quickly becoming one of the leading lawyers in Illinois, commanding an annual income of $5,000—a tidy sum in those days. Lincoln's interest in politics was sparked again in 1854 when Democratic Senator Stephen A. Douglas of Illinois introduced the Kansas-Nebraska Act, repealing the Missouri Compromise ban on slavery in the territories gained in the Louisiana Purchase and placing the issue of slavery center stage in American politics. From that moment until his election to the presidency six years later, Lincoln, who had rarely commented publicly on the issue of slavery, gave approximately 175 antislavery speeches, not the least of which was his epoch "House Divided" speech in 1858.

---

41. Don C. Seitz, *Horace Greeley: Founder of the New York Tribune* (Indianapolis, 1926), p. 219.
42. Ibid., pp. 219-220.

Returning to the Illinois legislature as an anti-Nebraska Whig in the fall of 1854, Lincoln, eyeing an opportunity to displace his old antagonist James Shields, resigned his seat in the legislature before being officially sworn in to run for the U.S. Senate. Convinced that preventing the expansion of slavery in the territories and isolating it within southern boundaries would eventually lead to its demise, Lincoln mounted a strong bid for the seat and led on the first six ballots in the state legislature, garnering 45 votes on the first ballot to 41 for Shields and five for anti-Nebraska Democrat Lyman Trumbull, a former state Supreme Court justice. Though he led through six ballots, Lincoln's support gradually dwindled and he received only fifteen votes on the ninth ballot. In an effort to stave off an eleventh-hour bid by supporters of affluent Democratic Gov. Joel A. Matteson—a man allegedly not adverse to using his wealth and patronage to bribe lawmakers—Lincoln, acting decisively, withdrew on the tenth ballot and threw his support to Trumbull, who prevailed. According to his friends, Lincoln was deeply disappointed by the outcome and vowed that he would never seek public office again. Given his strength in the early balloting, Lincoln found it particularly galling that his supporters in the legislature were forced to yield to Trumbull—a dark-horse candidate who had received only five votes on the first ballot. "A less good humored man than I," he grumbled privately, "perhaps would not have consented to it." Possessing a nobility of character rarely seen in American politics, Lincoln, who was all smiles, gave no public indication of the depth of his disappointment and heartily congratulated the winner at a reception in Trumbull's honor shortly after the election.[43]

Though disappointed, Lincoln remained politically active and formally joined the new Republican Party in the spring of 1856—long after most other antislavery Whigs had already joined the party. That summer, he was a favorite-son candidate for the vice-presidential nomination at the party's national convention in Philadelphia, but lost overwhelmingly to William Dayton, a nondescript former Whig senator from New Jersey, on the first ballot.

It was no surprise that the Illinois Republicans again turned to Lincoln as the logical challenger to Stephen A. Douglas in 1858. By this time, Lincoln was as clearly the leader of the party in that state as William H. Seward was in New York or the powerful Simon Cameron in Pennsylvania—and his prospects of joining them in the U.S. Senate appeared pretty good. After all, Douglas, who was finan-

---

43. Donald, *Lincoln*, pp. 183-185. Matteson received 47 votes on the ninth ballot—three shy of a majority—while Trumbull, the anti-Nebraska candidate, garnered 35 votes.

cially strapped and in declining health, seemed particularly vulnerable following his break with President James Buchanan over the administration's endorsement of the proslavery Lecompton Constitution in which the voters of Kansas were given only a choice between limited and unlimited slavery, resulting in the abstention of the state's antislavery majority—those who wanted Kansas to enter the Union as a "free state." Although less than one in every twelve eligible voters in Kansas went to the polls to elect delegates to the constitutional convention in Lecompton, Buchanan—keenly aware that 119 of his 174 electoral votes in 1856 came from slaveholding states—exerted the powers of the presidency to pressure Congress into admitting Kansas as a slave state. Believing that the Kansas vote represented a total subversion of popular sovereignty, Douglas, who privately believed that slavery was a cancer that should be eradicated, was infuriated and harshly criticized Buchanan for trying to force the constitution on the people of Kansas in opposition to their wishes.

Lincoln's nomination for the U.S. Senate in 1858 was highly unusual in that it occurred even before the state legislative elections were held that year. His early selection was designed by Illinois Republican leaders, in large part, to stymie the efforts of the ambitious and enormously popular "Long John" Wentworth of Chicago, the first Republican mayor of a major American city and Lincoln's lone challenger for the party's nomination.[44] Realizing that it would be difficult to unseat Douglas, the sagacious Lincoln, using a Biblical metaphor perhaps unconsciously borrowed from Edmund Quincy, the brilliant abolitionist son of former Boston mayor Josiah Quincy, set the tone for his senatorial campaign—as well as his presidential bid two years later—with his famous "House Divided" acceptance speech before 1,000 hot and perspiring delegates and onlookers at the Republican state convention in Springfield on the evening of June 16, 1858: "A house divided against itself cannot stand," Lincoln stated. "I believe this government cannot endure permanently, half *slave* and half *free*. I do not expect the Union to be *dissolved*—I *do* not expect the house to fall—but I do expect it will cease to be divided. It will become *all* one thing, or *all* the other."[45]

Coming some five months before William H. Seward, the red-haired, blue-eyed Whig leader from New York delivered his incendiary "irrepressible conflict" speech, Lincoln's widely acclaimed and statesmanlike speech—perhaps the most radical statement delivered by a prominent Republican up to that point—cata-

---

44. Allan Nevins, *The Emergence of Lincoln: Douglas, Buchanan, and Party Chaos 1857-1859*, Vol. I, pp. 357-359.
45. Donald, *Lincoln*, p. 206.

pulted him into the national limelight.[46] It also prompted an immediate response from Douglas when he returned to Chicago from Washington after finally succeeding in defeating the Lecompton Constitution. In addition to taking credit for the defeat of the Lecompton Constitution—calling it a victory for the idea of popular sovereignty—Douglas, who personally abhorred slavery, referred to Lincoln, who was sitting behind him on the balcony, as "a kind, amiable, and intelligent gentleman, a good citizen and an honorable opponent," before launching into an attack on his Republican opponent, insisting that his rival was advocating, in no uncertain terms, a war between the states. Appealing to the racial anxiety of the nation's voters, the Democratic lawmaker also denounced Republican criticism of the Dred Scott decision, stating that its critics were ignoring the fact that the Republic was founded on a "white basis" and that by advocating equal rights for African-Americans, the Republicans failed to comprehend that "any mixing or amalgamation with inferior races"—something Lincoln had never suggested—could only lead to "degeneration, demoralization, and degradation."[47]

Lincoln, it should be understood, was hardly some sort of flaming abolitionist in the tradition of Gerrit Smith and Wendell Phillips or some of the other leading antislavery figures of the time. In fact, he was far from it. "I am not, nor ever

---

46. Seward delivered his controversial "irrepressible conflict" speech while stumping for New York Republican gubernatorial candidate Edwin D. Morgan in Rochester on September 25, 1858. In his speech, Seward derided the fact that the country had two different systems of labor—one free and the other slave—and said that these two conflicting forces were heading for a collision. "It is an irrepressible conflict between opposing and enduring forces," he said, "and it means that the United States must and will, sooner or later, become either entirely a slaveholding nation, or entirely a free-labor nation." Under the Democrats, he asserted, the government had been surrendered to the nation's slaveholding interests and predicted that eventually northerners would strike back "and overthrow, by one decisive blow, the betrayers of the Constitution and freedom forever." Needless to say, Seward's speech, which was far more radical than Lincoln's, alarmed and angered thousands of southerners and northerners alike, including James Gordon Bennett's *New York Herald*, which denounced the speech as a dangerous and bloody manifesto. See Nevins, *The Emergence of Lincoln*, Vol. I, pp. 409-412.

47. Donald, *Lincoln*, pp. 202, 209-210. Lincoln bluntly rejected Douglas' twisted logic, challenging his rival's conclusion that, "because I do not want a black woman for a *slave* I must necessarily want her for a *wife*." The authors of the Declaration of Independence, argued Lincoln, never intended "to say all were equal in color, size, intellect, moral developments, or social capacity," but they "did consider all men created equal—equal in 'certain inalienable rights, among which are life, liberty, and the pursuit of happiness.'"

have been, in favor of bringing about in any way the social and political equality of the white and black races," he said, when questioned if he favored perfect equality between the races. "There is a physical difference between the white and black races which I believe will forever forbid the two races living together on terms of social and political equality," he said. As long as the two races remained together this distinction would have to be made, he concluded, adding that he, as much as any other man, was "in favor of having the superior position assigned to the white race."[48]

This is not to suggest, however, that Lincoln was some sort of out-and-out racist, as *Ebony* magazine editor Lerone Bennett, Jr., provocatively asserted in his recent book *Forced into Glory: Abraham Lincoln's White Dream*. Yet there's little doubt that the nation's leading abolitionists, including William Lloyd Garrison, viewed him with deep suspicion. Oberlin College president Charles Grandison Finney, the famous Protestant evangelical theologian, shared Garrison's serious reservations, deploring the fact that Lincoln seemed to have a low opinion of African-Americans. Wendell Phillips, the Boston patrician and arguably radical abolitionism's most gifted expositor, was also suspicious of Lincoln from the beginning, once referring to him as "that slave hound from Illinois." His opinion hadn't changed much by 1860. "Who is this huckster in politics?" he asked, shortly before launching into an attack on the Republican nominee's tepid support for gradual abolition in the District of Columbia. "The ice is so thin that Mr. Lincoln, standing six feet and four inches, cannot afford to carry any principles with him onto it!"

Black abolitionists, at least early on, were also highly suspicious of Lincoln. "If we sent our children to school, Abraham Lincoln would kick them out, in the name of Republicanism and antislavery!" exclaimed H. Ford Douglass, an African-American preacher from Chicago who campaigned extensively for the antislavery cause. Even Frederick Douglass, inarguably the most important black American leader of the nineteenth century who later grew to admire the nation's sixteenth president, had once denounced Lincoln as "an itinerant Colonization lecturer, showing all his inconsistencies, his pride of race and blood, his contempt for Negroes, and his canting hypocrisy."[49]

From the outset, Lincoln's efforts during the 1858 campaign were unwittingly undermined, at least to a certain degree, by the pronunciations of Horace Greeley

---

48.   Angle and Miers, *The Living Lincoln*, p. 265.
49.   Allen C. Guelzo, "Lincoln and the Abolitionists," *The Wilson Quarterly*, Vol. 24, Issue 4 (Autumn 2000).

of the *New York Tribune*—a paper with about five thousand subscribers in Illinois—former House Speaker Nathaniel P. Banks, Massachusetts Sen. Henry Wilson and other leading Republicans who suggested that Douglas, having courageously broken with the administration over the Lecompton Constitution, deserved their support in his bid for another term. Some deluded Republicans, including Greeley, believed that Douglas, a dyed-in-the-wool Democrat, might even eventually join their party—a notion the Illinois lawmaker never seriously entertained. Lincoln was understandably furious, questioning the motives of Greeley and others in their constant praise of Douglas. "Have they concluded that the Republican cause, generally, can be best promoted by sacrificing us here in Illinois?" he asked facetiously. "If so we would like to know it soon; it will save us a great deal of labor to surrender at once."[50]

Douglas' candidacy, likewise, was hampered by the efforts of Democrats unflinchingly loyal to the Buchanan administration. Derisively dubbed the "Danites" after an alleged secret order of Mormons, these Democrats worked feverishly to undermine the Illinois lawmaker's re-election effort. Led nationally by Georgia's Howell Cobb, Senator John Slidell of Louisiana, Secretary of the Interior Jacob Thompson, a former Mississippi congressman, and Jeremiah S. Black, the eccentric and absentminded attorney general, many Buchanan Democrats in Illinois openly supported Lincoln's candidacy while others launched a separate National Democratic ticket in order to divide the Democratic vote. Acting partly out of vindictiveness, Buchanan, who once referred to Douglas as "that perfidious man," began removing Illinois postmasters and other federal officials loyal to Douglas and replacing them with inveterate enemies of the senator. Eventually, all but a handful of Douglas' appointees were removed from their federal posts.[51]

Lincoln, who had no secretarial staff, full-time assistants or designated campaign manager during his 1858 Senate race, initially employed a strategy of following Douglas throughout the state, usually rising at the end of Douglas' speeches to offer a rebuttal. It was, observed the *New York Herald*, a somewhat odd spectacle, that of an incumbent senator personally stumping the state "and another who wishes to be Senator following in his wake." It was also a strategy questioned by Lincoln's own supporters, especially Norman B. Judd, a former railroad official and attorney who served as Lincoln's unofficial campaign man-

---

50.   Lincoln letter to Hon. Lyman Trumbull, Dec. 28, 1857, quoted in Angle, *The Living Lincoln*, p. 207.

51.   Donald, *Lincoln*, pp. 212-213; Nevins, *The Emergence of Lincoln*, Vol. I, p. 371.

ager in northern Illinois. A former Democrat who angrily abandoned that party in the wake of the Kansas-Nebraska Act, Judd seriously doubted the wisdom of chasing Douglas around on the campaign trail, pointing out that such a strategy enabled the Democratic incumbent to constantly put Lincoln on the defensive. Lincoln, who usually followed his own counsel, eventually abandoned the strategy.[52]

Agreeing to a series of seven joint debates in various towns and cities throughout the state, Lincoln, who was initially slow to react to the *Dred Scott* ruling in 1857—in part due to his enormous respect for the law and the judicial process—spent the remainder of the campaign addressing the moral issue of slavery, focusing, in particular, on the controversial Supreme Court decision in which the nation's highest court ruled that the Constitution prohibited Congress and the territorial governments from banning slavery in the territories. Like his fellow Republicans, Lincoln feared that the Supreme Court would eventually extend the Dred Scott precedent to prohibit individual states from outlawing slavery altogether—prompting his Democratic rival, skillfully playing the race card, to accuse his challenger of pitting section against section with the kind of language that would eventually drive the South toward secession. Lincoln's "House Divided" thesis, inferred Douglas, almost certainly meant war between the North and South.

Lincoln wasted little time in firing back. Towering over his rival during the widely-watched debates, the tall, thin, and bony Lincoln accused Douglas, as the author of the Kansas-Nebraska Act, of re-opening the slavery issue and thereby threatening disunion, while Douglas, who had a knack for going for the jugular, falsely portrayed his Republican rival as an out-and-out abolitionist. The real issue, Lincoln told the audience during their final debate in Alton, was what he defined as a conflict "on the part of one class that looks upon the institution of slavery *as a wrong*, and of another class that *does not* look upon it as a wrong," concluding that the issue would "continue in this country when these poor tongues of Judge Douglas and myself shall be silent. It is the eternal struggle between these two principles—right and wrong—throughout the world," he said. "They are the two principles that have stood face to face from the beginning of time; and will ever continue to struggle. The one is the common right of humanity and the other the divine right of kings."[53]

---

52. Ibid., p. 210.
53. Ibid., 224.

In what was expected to be an extremely close contest, Lincoln's candidacy suffered a fatal blow on November 2, 1858, when the Republicans, though winning the statewide popular vote and electing their candidates for state treasurer and superintendent of education, failed to gain control of the state legislature—the body that would ultimately elect the next U.S. Senator.[54] Several major factors contributed to Lincoln's defeat, not the least of which was John J. Crittenden's unexpected endorsement of Douglas, an act that undoubtedly influenced thousands of former Whigs and Know-Nothings in central and southern Illinois. An unfair apportionment of the legislative seats that failed to take into account the large population increase in the state's northern counties—a region friendly to Lincoln and the Republicans—and a large Know-Nothing vote for the Douglas ticket in central Illinois also enabled the Democrats to retain control of the legislature, thereby sealing Lincoln's fate. In the aftermath of the election, a number of Republicans accused the Illinois Central Railroad of bringing in illegal voters to help the Democrats in key counties, and William Herndon, Lincoln's law partner, charged that "thousands of roving—robbing—bloated pockmarked" Irish Catholics had been brought into the state from Philadelphia, St. Louis and other major cities to help defeat Lincoln. A few Republicans blamed the lukewarm support of Greeley and other eastern Republicans for Lincoln's defeat. Douglas, as expected, defeated his Republican rival two months later during the formal joint balloting in the legislature, garnering 54 votes to Lincoln's 46.[55]

As in 1855, Lincoln was again bitterly disappointed by the outcome, but was glad that he had made the race. "It gave me a hearing on the great and durable question of the age, which I could have had in no other way," he wrote an old friend, "and though I now sink out of view, and shall be forgotten, I believe I have made some marks which will tell for the cause of civil liberty long after I am gone."[56]

---

54. Ibid., p. 227. The Republican candidate for state treasurer garnered 125,430 votes to the Douglas Democratic candidate's 121,609. John Dougherty, the pro-Buchanan National Democratic candidate who hoped to siphon enough votes to throw the election—and the legislature—to the Republicans, ran a distant third, receiving a pitiful 5,071 votes, or two percent of the total.

55. Ibid., p. 228; *Illinois State Journal*, Nov. 10, 1858. Pointing out that the average Republican district in Illinois had a population of 19,655, while Democratic districts, on average, had 15,675 inhabitants, the *Journal* argued that under a fair apportionment of the state's legislative districts, the Republicans would have had a majority of seven in the House of Representatives and three in the state Senate.

Though a somewhat melancholy Lincoln was sure that his political career was over, a few voices, most notably those of the *Chicago Press and Tribune* and John Wentworth's *Chicago Democrat*—both of which were feuding for supremacy in that city—began suggesting Lincoln for the presidency.[57] Although a story of dubious credibility in the *Sandusky* (Ohio) *Commercial Register* calling on Republicans to nominate Lincoln received the most attention, it was probably the relatively obscure *Illinois Gazette*, in the small town of Lacon in the north central part of the state, that first seriously proposed his name as a candidate for president. Before long, several other newspapers, including the *New York Herald*, the *Rockford Republican*, and the *Reading Journal* in Pennsylvania were running favorable stories about a possible Lincoln candidacy in 1860. A group of Cincinnati Republicans, reported the *New York Herald*, was floating a trial balloon for a ticket headed by Lincoln with John P. Kennedy of Maryland as his vice-presidential running mate on a platform embracing protectionism, improvement of western rivers and harbors, and opposition to the extension of slavery in the territories.[58]

Though far from disinterested in the Republican Party's role in the coming election, Lincoln, who was busy tending to his law practice, didn't take these suggestions very seriously. "I must, in candor, say I do not think myself fit for the Presidency," he wrote the admiring editor of the *Rock Island Register*.[59] He also casually told the shrewd and able Jesse W. Fell, a Bloomington politician and successful land speculator, that it was pointless to talk about seeking the Republican presidential nomination in 1860, especially when their were more deserving and better-known candidates such as Seward, Chase and others. "Everybody knows them," he told his longtime acquaintance. "Nobody, scarcely, outside of Illinois, knows me. Besides, is it not, as a matter of justice, due to such men, who have carried this movement forward to its present status, in spite of fearful opposition, personal abuse, and hard names? I really think so."[60]

While amused by what appeared to be the stirrings of a presidential boom, Lincoln continued to scoff at such talk and devoted himself almost exclusively to his law practice in the opening months of 1859 and refrained from openly dis-

---

56. Ibid., pp. 228-229.
57. Nevins, *The Emergence of Lincoln*, Vol. I, p. 398; *Chicago Tribune*, November 19, 1858.
58. Donald, *Lincoln*, p. 235; Nevins, *The Emergence of Lincoln*, Vol. I, p.398; William E. Baringer, *Lincoln's Rise to Power*, pp. 51-62.
59. Ibid., pp. 235-236.
60. Baringer, *Lincoln's Rise to Power*, pp. 66-67.

cussing the possibility of mounting a presidential candidacy throughout the remainder of the year. It wasn't until August of 1859 that Lincoln, who had only given three political speeches outside of Illinois during the preceding five years, decided to increase his visibility, cautiously agreeing to a speaking tour of Iowa, Wisconsin, and Ohio where he gave speeches in Columbus, Dayton, Hamilton, and Cincinnati. His triumphant tour made quite a splash in the press and before long the Illinois dark horse was again being touted as a possible contender for the Republican presidential nomination.

Lincoln's first major break took place in late February when he addressed a large gathering at New York City's Cooper Union—a speech he thought was originally scheduled for Henry Ward Beecher's church in Brooklyn. In his profound speech, Lincoln compared the principles of the Republican Party to those held by George Washington and deftly defended his party against the charge that John Brown's bloody raid on Harper's Ferry was a byproduct of Republican antislavery agitation. "Slave insurrections are no more common now than they were before the Republican Party was organized," he told his audience of 1,500. There was growing sentiment in the country against slavery, he said, adding that such sentiment couldn't be suppressed "by breaking up the political organization which rallies around it." In his speech, riddled with a healthy dose of anecdotes, the lanky former Illinois lawmaker urged his fellow Republicans to refrain from deliberately provoking the South, but also urged his party to avoid "groping for some middle ground" between right and wrong. "Neither let us be slandered from our duty by false accusations against us, nor frightened from it by menaces of destruction to the government, nor of dungeons to ourselves, he concluded. "Let us have faith that right makes might, and in that faith let us to the end dare to do our duty as we understand it."

His speech was a smashing success, as evidenced by the glowing reaction of the *New York Tribune's* Noah Brooks, who called Lincoln "the greatest man since St. Paul." Never before, wrote Brooks, had anyone made such a tremendous first impression in an appeal to a hardened and jaded New York audience. "The tones, the gestures, the kindling eye, and the mirth-provoking look, defy the reporter's skill," he confessed. The willowy ex-Whig politician followed that speech with a highly successful tour of New England, where large and enthusiastic crowds greeted him at every stop. Lincoln's cautious and low-key campaign for the Republican nomination was off to an auspicious start.[61]

---

61. Ibid., pp. 156-159

Reaction to Lincoln's nomination was varied. The proslavery *Floridian and Journal* in Tallahassee, Florida, said that Lincoln "appears to be a man after Joshua R. Giddings' own heart—vile and brutal abolitionist as he is." The *Daily Chicago Herald*, a Democratic newspaper, said that the Republican nominee represented "the deadliest and most determined sectionalism" in the country and urged voters to "tear off the flimsy disguise, and strike the devilish aggressor to the earth"—a sentiment echoed by countless newspapers in the slaveholding states. The *Rochester Union and Advertiser*, in a swipe at Lincoln's comparative obscurity, said that choosing the little-known Illinois backwoodsman was akin to buying "a pig in a poke," while the conservative *Washington Constitution* asserted that the Republican convention had been a "disgraceful burlesque." The *New London Daily Star* in Connecticut offered a backhanded compliment to Hamlin, Lincoln's vice-presidential co-star, saying that the Republicans had nominated a "kangaroo ticket. The strength is all in the hind legs." The embittered *St. Paul Pioneer*, a paper sympathetic to Seward, criticized the Republicans "for cowardly rejecting the great apostle of Republicanism," for a man whose meager political record included losing two campaigns for the U.S. Senate.[62]

Taking a completely different view, the *Newark Daily Advertiser* praised Lincoln's nomination, saying that a "nobler specimen" was "nowhere to be found" and the *Weekly Illinois State Journal* described Lincoln as a guileless, incorruptible patriot and fearless champion of liberty, while the Washington correspondent for Horace Greeley's *New York Tribune* insisted that Lincoln had left Congress more than a decade earlier with a reputation as an able, genial man of unquestioned integrity.[63] Hailing a return to the "age of purity," the *Chicago Press & Tribune*, in an effort to jump-start Lincoln's autumn campaign, praised his nomination, maintaining that it was an indication that voters, "wearied and outraged by the malfeasance" of a succession of presidents who had been beholden to the interests of the nation's slaveholders, longed for "a return to the sterling honesty and Democratic simplicity which marked the Administrations of Jefferson, Madison, Adams, and Jackson."[64]

While the other three parties competing in the 1860 election named geographically balanced tickets that year, Lincoln and his vice-presidential running mate made little pretense at being national candidates. The Republicans, as it turned out, were the only truly "out-and-out sectional party" in the race. Unlike

62.   Hayes, *Mr. Lincoln Runs for President*, pp. 74-80.
63.   Ibid., pp. 73-74.
64.   *Illinois State Register*, May 24, 1860; Baringer, *Lincoln's Rise to Power*, p. 307.

Democrat Stephen A. Douglas, who courageously withstood verbal taunts and occasionally had to dodge rotten eggs from hostile southern audiences, the Republicans, realizing that the vast majority of voters in the South wouldn't have given Lincoln the time of day, didn't even bother to have ballots printed and distributed in ten southern states. In an interview with a reporter from the *New York Herald*, Lincoln, who did not actively press the flesh during the autumn campaign, half-heartedly intimated that he would have welcomed an opportunity to speak in the South, but refrained from doing so out of concern for his personal safety—a sad and pathetic confession for a major presidential candidate to make and one that spoke volumes about the truly sectional and divisive nature of the Republican organization during this period.[65]

The Republican Party's seeming disregard for the South wasn't lost on John Bell and other leading Constitutional Unionists. The Republicans think it's their duty to destroy the white man, declared Senator John J. Crittenden of Kentucky, one of the party's founders and a man firmly opposed to secession. Echoing other leading southerners, he prophetically cautioned that the South would secede if Lincoln won the election. The Republicans, on the other hand, thought such rhetoric amounted to little more than an idle threat. After all, they had heard this kind of campaign hyperbole once before. Four years earlier, the Democrats made similar threats to frighten northerners into voting for Buchanan against Fremont. Though it may have been a "cardinal error," as one historian put it, to ignore such threats, Lincoln himself didn't take this seemingly run-of-the-mill campaign rhetoric very seriously. "The people of the South have too much good sense and good temper, to attempt the ruin of the government," he said. "At least, so I hope and believe."[66]

Meanwhile, Southern Democrat John Breckinridge, campaigning with what Allan Nevins described as "gentlemanly decorum," found it next to impossible to provide much grace and dignity to a party hell-bent on disunion and destroying Douglas' candidacy. As such, it was difficult for the self-reliant and highly principled vice president—a man who, ironically, was personally opposed to secession—to separate himself from such volatile fire-eaters as Alabama's William L. Yancey, South Carolina's Robert Barnwell Rhett, and other southerners who used the Southern Democratic organization to make secession virtually unavoidable. Despite the fact that many of his supporters in the South were breathing secession and advocating an uncompromising policy when it came to slavery,

---

65. Fite, *The Presidential Campaign of 1860*, pp. 211-212.
66. Crenshaw, *The Slave States in the Presidential Election of 1860*, p. 20.

Breckinridge eloquently defended his own name against charges of disunion. "The man does not live," he said, "who has power to couple my name success-fully with the slightest taint of disloyalty to the Constitution or the Union..."[67]

Though considered dull and uneventful—the *New York World* called it the calmest presidential election since Monroe ran unopposed in 1820—the election of 1860 was nevertheless one of the most pivotal presidential campaigns in American history.[68] More than ever before, voters in the border and southern states abandoned the two major parties in droves and found refuge in the Constitutional Union and splinter Southern Democratic parties.

New York's William Seward, the party's most gifted oracle, ably carried the Republican message throughout the fall campaign, delivering a seemingly endless series of speeches in New York, Pennsylvania, Ohio, Indiana, Michigan, Illinois, Kansas, Missouri, and Wisconsin. His speeches, wrote historian James Ford Rhodes, were "the most remarkable stump-speeches ever delivered in this country."[69] Every speech given by the New York lawmaker was fresh and filled with a certain literary quality and originality lacking in the tired stump speeches of his rivals in the other parties. Returning time and again to the theme of the "irrepressible conflict"—a topic that he had briefly abandoned while in pursuit of the Republican nomination—Seward, while rarely mentioning Lincoln by name, focused his attacks on the evils of slavery, the need to curtail the expansion of slavery in the territories, and the utter absurdity of secession. Believing himself vastly superior to Lincoln and more deserving of the party's presidential nomination, the conceited and domineering New Yorker snubbed his party's nominee on several occasions, including once during a brief stop in Lincoln's hometown of Springfield, Illinois, when he refused to disembark from his railroad car to meet with his party's presidential standard-bearer. Apparently taking the insult in stride, the ever-humble Lincoln nudged his way through the crowd gathered at the railway depot and climbed aboard the train to shake hands with his one-time rival, at which point Seward grudgingly got up from his seat and gave a short speech before departing.[70]

Although the Constitutional Unionists were, for the most part, hardheaded political realists who really didn't expect to win a plurality of the popular vote, a number of party leaders nevertheless held out some hope of putting their candi-

67. Nevins, *The Emergence of Lincoln*, Vol. II, p. 282; Miller, *'If Elected...' Unsuccessful Candidates for the Presidency*, p. 186.
68. Fite, *The Presidential Campaign of 1860*, pp. 230-231.
69. Roseboom, *A History of Presidential Elections*, pp. 181-182.
70. Ibid., pp. 212-213.

date in the White House—and if not Bell, possibly his running mate, Edward Everett. Hoping to run strong enough in the border-states and in the lower North to deny Lincoln a majority in the Electoral College, the Constitutional Unionists believed they could throw the election into the House of Representatives, where each state was entitled to one vote. Given the fact that neither major party controlled a majority of the congressional delegations—the Republicans controlled 15 of 33 states, two short of a majority—the Constitutional Unionists hoped to position Bell as a compromise candidate among the three anti-Lincoln candidates.[71] If the House failed to name a president by March 4, 1861, the vice president elected by the Democratic-controlled Senate would then become acting president. Although Breckinridge's running mate, Joseph Lane, would seem to have the inside track in such a scenario due to his fierce loyalty to the Buchanan administration, there was also a possibility, albeit remote, that the U.S. Senate might turn to the Constitutional Union Party's Edward Everett. In a tight four-way race, the possibilities were endless, or so it seemed.

However, Bell, who agreed to take part in fusion efforts with Douglas and Breckinridge to stop Lincoln in New York, New Jersey and Rhode Island, held out little hope that he could actually win in the U.S. House of Representatives. His only chance, he believed, was to win in the Electoral College and to do that he felt it was critical that he sweep most of the South and all of the border-states while defeating Lincoln in one of the large electoral states of Pennsylvania, New York or Ohio—a tall order, to put it mildly.

Meanwhile, Bell consented to take part in a fusion campaign with Douglas in populous New York, a state with thirty-five electoral votes and where Lincoln was believed to have an almost insurmountable lead. Realizing that it was all for naught if they couldn't deny Lincoln a plurality in New York, Pennsylvania, New Jersey, Illinois, or Indiana, Washington Hunt and other Constitutional Unionists in the Empire State began considering a coalition with Douglas' supporters in an effort to form a joint electoral ticket as early as June, barely a month into the campaign. Working closely with Democrat Horatio Seymour—his good friend and a man he had twice run against for governor—Hunt was convinced that such an arrangement was the only means of defeating Lincoln in heavily-populated

---

71. The Democrats controlled fourteen states in the House, including eleven slave states, and the Opposition Party had a majority in Tennessee and was evenly split with the Democrats in Kentucky and North Carolina, while Maryland, still a hotbed of Know-Nothing activity, was evenly divided between the Democrats and the American Party. In Illinois, an Anti-Lecompton Douglas Democrat held the balance of power in that state's nine-man delegation.

New York and thereby throwing the election into the House of Representatives where he believed the Constitutional Union Party's nominee stood at least a fighting chance. Bell apparently gave his tacit approval to the idea and the two parties, meeting in Syracuse on August 14, put together a fusion ticket consisting of ten Constitutional Unionists and twenty-five Douglas supporters.[72]

The so-called "Syracuse juggle" was sneeringly denounced as a "Dry Goods Electoral Ticket," a desperate and odd amalgamation whose only purpose was to deprive Lincoln of the state's thirty-five electoral votes. Horace Greeley called it a "confusion" ticket designed to capture the votes of former Know-Nothing voters, as well as the support of Irish and German voters—a strange and seemingly incongruous combination. Pulling no punches, Greeley's *Tribune* later alleged that the New York fusionists were trying to raise a million dollars—a staggering sum in 1860—to defeat the Republican nominee and there is some evidence that Lincoln himself seemed to have been disturbed by news of this somewhat unexpected and bizarre development.

Despite such criticism, at least one major New York newspaper—James Gordon Bennett's *New York Herald*—strongly endorsed the fusion ticket. Believing that the Lincoln's defeat would save New York commerce and industry by preserving the region's extensive trade with the South, Bennett argued that the Constitutional Union-Democratic fusion ticket was an honorable attempt to build "a new and powerful Union Party—just as the palaces of the Eternal City were built out of the materials of the Coliseum and other temples of pagan Rome." Though disappointed that only ten Bell men were placed on the ticket, Hunt was reassured by a number of Douglas' associates that their electors would support Bell in the Electoral College if their votes were needed to put him over the top. In return, the former Whig governor assured the Douglas Democrats that, if elected, Bell would "not fail to appreciate their patriotism." At a huge ratification meeting in New York City on October 8, the fusion ticket, which had been initially resisted by the state's "Hard Shell" Democrats, was amended to include seven Breckinridge electors, changing its composition to eighteen Douglas electors, ten for Bell, and seven for the Southern Democratic nominee.[73]

---

72.   Parks, *John Bell of Tennessee*, pp. 370-371; Fite, *The Presidential Campaign of 1860*, pp. 223-224; Stewart Mitchell, *Horatio Seymour of New York* (New York, 1938), pp. 217-218; *New York Herald*, August 15, 17, 1860.

73.   Fite, *The Presidential Campaign of 1860*, p. 224; Mitchell, *Horatio Seymour of New York*, pp. 217-218; *New York Herald*, August 29, Sept. 19, 1860; Parks, *John Bell of Tennessee*, p. 371.

Late in the campaign, Jefferson Davis, foreseeing the inevitability of Lincoln's election and the disastrous consequences that might follow, apparently tried in vain to unite all of the opposing forces behind a coalition candidacy headed by ex-Gov. Horatio Seymour of New York. In his 1881 memoir, *The Rise and Fall of the Confederate Government*, Davis, a staunch Breckinridge supporter, explained that he had received assurances from Bell, whose main goal was preservation of the Union, and Breckinridge, who was "young enough to wait," that they would withdraw from the race if Douglas, the northern Democratic candidate, could be persuaded to do likewise.[74] Although Davis' account of the events have never been fully substantiated, the scheme apparently fell apart when Douglas refused to drop out of the race on the grounds that his supporters would probably vote for Lincoln—and not a compromise candidate—if he withdrew from the race. But such plotting aside, there were a number of other leading figures in both the North and the South who feared what would happen if Lincoln won. Among them was New York's Samuel J. Tilden, who, in a lengthy letter on the subject, shrewdly and prophetically warned of the dangers in electing a sectional president who hadn't received a single electoral vote from the South. Tilden, a Democrat, urged his fellow countrymen to defeat Lincoln by any means possible. Former President John Tyler, who later followed Virginia out of the Union, was also deeply distressed by the possibility of Lincoln's election, but blamed its inevitability on Douglas as well as the eight southern delegations that had walked out of the original Democratic convention in Charleston. "Let things result as they may," said the gloomy Virginian, "I fear that the great Republic has seen its best days."[75]

Spurning tradition, Douglas, who campaigned vigorously from Maine to New Orleans, was doomed to playing the role of a Cassandra. He spoke forthrightly to the American people in the North as well as the South, warning northern voters that the election of a purely sectional candidate such as Lincoln would result in disunion and cautioning southern voters that secession, as urged by many of Breckinridge's supporters, would result in deadly punishment and untold misery for the region. The election of a presidential candidate in conformity with the Constitution—even one as feared and disliked as Lincoln—he told one southern audience, "*would not justify any attempt at dissolving this glorious confederacy.*" There was nothing finer in Douglas' long public career, wrote Roseboom, "than

---

74. Jefferson Davis, *The Rise and Fall of the Confederate Government*, Vol. I, p. 52.
75. *New York Evening Post*, October 30, 1860; Mitchell, *Horatio Seymour of New York*, pp. 220-221.

his sturdy speeches in Virginia and North Carolina, where he declared that no grievance could justify secession, and that he would support the President in enforcing the laws." Unfortunately, his warnings, as the late David M. Potter observed, fell on deaf ears. Voters in the North thought he was trying to frighten them away from voting for Lincoln, while voters in the upper and lower South were convinced that the Illinois lawmaker was merely employing a clever strategic device to frighten them away from voting for Breckinridge.[76]

Smashing Republican victories in the Pennsylvania and Indiana gubernatorial races in early October convinced Douglas that his campaign was doomed. Moreover, he realized that the Union was in great peril. "Mr. Lincoln is the next President," he said wistfully. "We must try to save the Union." After fulfilling speaking engagements in Wisconsin, Illinois, and St. Louis, Missouri, Douglas, at great personal risk, headed into hostile territory, giving speeches in Tennessee and Georgia before ending his campaign in Mobile, Alabama. Despite being savagely denounced by southern secessionists and repeatedly threatened by ruffians—there were even plots to derail the trains on which he traveled—the Illinois lawmaker courageously persevered. "Never had he made a more heroic effort," wrote historian Allan Nevins, who was certainly no Douglas admirer.[77]

Nearly 4.7 million voters went to the polls on November 6, 1860—an increase of more 600,000 over the number who had turned out four years earlier during the three-way race between Buchanan, Fremont and Fillmore. On Election Day, former President Millard Fillmore, repudiating sectionalism, cast his vote for New York's Union fusion ticket consisting of Douglas, Bell and Breckinridge electors. In Worcester, Massachusetts, 100-year-old Ebenezer Mower, who claimed to have voted for George Washington in 1789, dutifully went to the polls, as did another centenarian, Ralph Farnham, who reportedly walked six miles to cast his vote in Maine. Farnham was believed to be the sole survivor of Bunker Hill during the Revolutionary War.[78]

During the relatively quiet campaign, the Constitutional Union Party's John Bell waged a surprisingly strong effort in the slave states and ran particularly well in the eight border-states. Incredibly, his efforts below the Mason-Dixon line nearly paid off. Breckinridge, his chief rival in the region, received 44.4% of the vote in the slaveholding states, barely edging out the Constitutional Union stan-

76. Allen Johnson, *Stephen A. Douglas: A Study in American Politics* (New York, 1908), pp. 432-433; Roseboom, *A History of Presidential Elections*, p. 182; Potter, *The Impending Crisis*, p. 516.
77. Nevins, *The Emergence of Lincoln: Prologue to Civil War 1859-1861*, Vol. II, p. 295.
78. Hayes, *Mr. Lincoln Runs for President*, p. 209.

dard-bearer by 54,079 votes (570,053 to 515,974). Bell's 41% of the vote in that region was only four percent less than the Know-Nothing Party's Millard Fillmore received in what was essentially a two-way race in the South in 1856. Moreover, the Bell-Everett ticket carried Kentucky, Tennessee and Virginia and came within an eyelash of winning in Maryland, Missouri and North Carolina. A change of only 362 votes from Breckinridge to Bell in Maryland would have given him that state and a switch of 215 votes from Douglas would have given him Missouri. In all, Bell won 39 of the 303 electoral votes at stake. Despite the presence of a well-known northern running mate, Bell polled a disappointing 72,905 votes, or less than five percent, in the free states. Only in Edward Everett's home state of Massachusetts, where he garnered thirteen percent of the vote, did he poll anything resembling a respectable showing in the North. The Constitutional Unionists, to be sure, were particularly disappointed by his showing in Pennsylvania, where he garnered only 12,776 votes out of a total of 476,442.

One can only wonder what effect there might have been on the drive for secession if a pro-Union moderate such as Bell, rather than an ardent proslavery advocate like Breckinridge, had actually won the popular vote in the South. As it was, Bell and Douglas, the two Unionist candidates, combined for 49 percent of the vote in the seven states of the original Confederacy, compared to 51 percent for Breckinridge.[79]

Carrying eight southern states along with the border-states of Delaware and Maryland, the Southern Democrats' Breckinridge garnered 72 electoral votes. Like Bell, the vice president was much less of a sectional candidate than Lincoln. In fact, Breckinridge himself, while carefully refusing to say whether Lincoln's election would be grounds for secession, argued in his Ashland speech that the Southern Democrats were not a party of disunion and supported the "Union and Constitution" as interpreted by the Supreme Court. A number of northern newspapers endorsed the Breckinridge-Lane ticket and a newspaper in Barnstable, Massachusetts, added their names to its masthead within a half-hour of their nominations. In addition to enjoying the support of an estimated four-fifths of the Democratic congressmen from the North, Breckinridge was also supported by eight of the ten northern Democratic senators, including William M. Gwin of California, William Bigler of Pennsylvania, and Indiana's Jesse D. Bright, a slave owner who was later expelled from the U.S. Senate for writing a letter "To His Excellency, Jefferson Davis, President of the Confederate States" during the Civil

---

79.   Thomas B. Alexander, "Persistent Whiggery in the Confederate South, 1860-1877," *Journal of Southern History*, Vol. XXVII (1961), p. 307.

War. Breckinridge also had the backing of such party luminaries as New York's Daniel S. Dickinson and former attorney general Caleb Cushing of Massachusetts, a surprisingly youthful-looking sixty-year-old delegate-at-large who originally supported Jefferson Davis' candidacy at the Charleston convention. Three former Democratic presidential candidates—Cass, Pierce and Buchanan—were also in Breckinridge's corner.[80]

Aided by the endorsement of the Buchanan-led Democratic state committee in Pennsylvania, the Southern Democratic ticket polled an astonishing 37.5% of the vote and carried a dozen counties in the Keystone State—a state where a straight-out Northern Democratic ticket supporting Douglas polled less than four percent of the statewide vote. Despite strong backing in the state, Breckinridge finished nearly 90,000 votes behind Lincoln in Pennsylvania. The vice president also finished a close third to Lincoln and Douglas in California and came within a whisker of winning in Oregon—Lane's home state—losing to Lincoln in the latter state by a mere 254 votes. Unlike Lincoln, who failed to receive a single vote in ten southern states, Breckinridge received votes in every northern state, excluding New Jersey, New York and Rhode Island where the Southern Democrats joined in fusion efforts with the Bell and Douglas campaigns in a desperate, last-minute attempt to deny Lincoln the presidency. Incredibly, Buchanan's vice president polled more than 29,000 votes in the antislavery stronghold of New England, including more than nineteen percent of the vote in Connecticut, where he placed third, only 1,059 votes behind his Northern Democratic rival. He also garnered more than six percent of the vote in Maine.

Capturing Missouri's nine electoral votes plus three of New Jersey's seven (the other four went to Lincoln), beleaguered Northern Democrat Stephen A. Douglas, who waged one of the most courageous yet futile campaigns in American history, won a relatively meager twelve votes in the Electoral College. The Douglas campaign was undoubtedly hampered by Breckinridge's ability to attract large numbers of northern Democrats—something Douglas was unable to reciprocate among southern Democrats. The Illinois lawmaker nevertheless polled fifteen percent of the vote in Alabama and Louisiana, nearly eleven percent in Georgia, and almost ten percent in Virginia—a remarkable fact given the candidacies of southerners Breckinridge and Bell.

The victorious Lincoln, winning in fourteen northern states plus California and Oregon while splitting the electoral vote in New Jersey, received 180 electoral votes—twenty-eight more than required. Lincoln's stunning election was all

---

80. Nevins, *The Emergence of Lincoln*, Vol. II, p. 282.

the more remarkable given the fact that the Republican Party was considered a third-party only six years earlier when it exploded on the scene against the entrenched Democrats and the wilting Whigs in the 1854 congressional elections. Striking his own name from the top of the ballot before casting a straight Republican ticket at his local precinct in Springfield, Lincoln garnered 1,865,908 popular votes to 1,380,202 for Democrat Stephen Douglas. Southern Democrat John C. Breckinridge polled a not-too-shabby 848,019 votes and Constitutional Unionist John Bell, running strongest in old Whig and Know-Nothing quarters in the Border States, garnered 590,901 votes, or a relatively respectable 12.6 percent of the popular vote nationally. Perennial antislavery gadfly Gerrit Smith, running this time as a Union Party candidate—a label Abraham Lincoln later adopted in his bid for re-election during the Civil War in 1864—polled a scant 171 votes in Illinois and Ohio. Lincoln, who didn't receive any votes in ten southern states, did only slightly better in the slaveholding Border States, polling only 2,294 votes in Maryland, 1,364 in Kentucky, and 1,887 in Virginia. His strongest showings in states where slavery was still legal occurred in Delaware where he garnered more than 23% of the vote, and in Missouri—a state Douglas narrowly carried over Bell—where one out of every ten voters cast a Republican ballot. In George Washington's hometown of Alexandria, Virginia, Lincoln received fewer than twenty votes out of more than 1,500 votes cast.[81]

Lincoln's overwhelming victory, as the late David M. Potter astutely pointed out, marked the "sectionalization" of American politics. Lincoln had carried seventeen free states and no slave states, while Breckinridge carried eleven slave states and no free states. The country's two truly bisectional parties that year—the Constitutional Unionists and the Douglas Democrats—managed to win only four Border States and three of New Jersey's seven electoral votes between them. "The election marked the crystallization of two fully sectionalized parties," wrote Potter. "But it was the party of the northern section that won, and by winning the presidency, it became the government for ten states in which it had not even run a ticket."[82]

What is even more remarkable about Lincoln's victory in 1860 is the fact that nearly sixty-one percent of the electorate voted for one of the three other candidates—a fact that has led some observers to mistakenly conclude that the Republican standard-bearer was elected because his opposition was so badly divided. But that was hardly the case. Even if his opposition had united behind a single

---

81.   For Lincoln's vote in Alexandria, see Hayes, *Mr. Lincoln Runs for President*, p. 213.
82.   Potter, *The Impending Crisis*, pp. 446-447.

candidate—an idea advocated by Jefferson Davis and others late in the campaign—Lincoln still would have been elected with barely thirty-nine percent of the popular vote, perhaps even less. It was almost as if fate had intervened. Lincoln's clear majorities in the populous northern states were such that he would have won against any single opponent. In fact, he could have even failed to carry California, Oregon and New Jersey—the three states that he won without a clear majority—and still have been elected. Incredibly, he would have won even without the eleven electoral votes of his home state of Illinois, a state he barely carried against Douglas with 50.7% of the popular vote. He also could have afforded to lose in neighboring Iowa, with its four electoral votes.

Given the heavily-populated states in which he won absolute majorities, it is theoretically possible (if one cares to do the math) that Lincoln, polling bare majorities in thirteen states, could have achieved an electoral majority as a sectional candidate that year with less than thirty percent of the popular vote, or slightly more than 1.3 million votes out of more than 4.6 million votes nationally, *against any single opponent*. This little-known phenomenon is one of the most startling facts in the annals of American presidential elections. Given the circumstances, it was almost as though he was destined to win, regardless of what kind of opposition he faced, or how united and strong that opposition might have been. The truth is that Lincoln could have won with even fewer popular votes against a single rival like Horatio Seymour—or some other compromise candidate—than Stephen A. Douglas, finishing dead last in the Electoral College, actually received in the four-way race with Lincoln, Bell and Breckinridge. What sort of constitutional crisis that scenario might have created is an interesting one to ponder, but almost certainly there would have been a great deal of clamoring, especially in the South, to abolish the Electoral College.

Nobody was more thrilled by Lincoln's election than the aging Joshua Leavitt, a thirty-year veteran of the antislavery crusade and a founder of the old Liberty Party. "Thank God!" Leavitt exclaimed. "Lincoln is chosen! It is a joy to have lived to this day." It wouldn't be long now before slavery was a thing of the past. Unfortunately, many of Leavitt's old friends and colleagues in the antislavery third-party movement, including party founders Alvan T. Stewart and Myron Holley, Ohio's Samuel Lewis, publisher Gamaliel Bailey and two-time presidential candidate James G. Birney, didn't live long enough to see the election of a bona-fide antislavery president.[83] Charles Francis Adams, the Free Soil Party's

---

83.   Leavitt letter to Salmon P. Chase, Nov. 7, 1860, quoted in Sewell, *Ballots for Freedom*, p. 3.

candidate for vice president in 1848, shared Leavitt's enthusiasm. "There is now scarcely a shadow of a doubt that the great revolution has actually taken place," he wrote in his diary the day after Lincoln's victory, "and that the country has once and for all thrown off the domination of the Slaveholders."[84] Poet Henry Wadsworth Longfellow was also delighted by the results. "This is a great victory," he exulted. "It is the redemption of the country. Freedom is triumphant."[85]

Viewing it as an ominous development, many white southerners were deeply alarmed by Lincoln's victory. "The differences between North and South have been growing more marked for years, and the mutual repulsion more radical, until not a single sympathy is left between the dominant influences in each section," commented the *Daily Constitutionalist* of Augusta, Georgia, shortly after the election.[86] Accustomed to the ranting and grim prophecies of Robert Barnwell Rhett, William L. Yancey and other fire-breathing southerners, many voters below the Mason-Dixon line were convinced that the new president—a deeply-despised man who had been hung in effigy in public squares throughout the South—would free the more than four million slaves in the region and give them all the federal jobs while urging—as absurd as it sounds—the newly-freed African-Americans to copulate with and marry their white daughters and sisters.[87]

Such rhetoric was rampant in the South during the campaign. "These [Northern] people hate us, annoy us, and would have us assassinated by our slaves if they dared," thundered one southern leader.[88] "A party founded on the single sentiment...of hatred of African slavery, is now the controlling party," lamented the *Richmond Examiner*. No one could possibly be deluded "that the Black Republican party is a moderate" party, declared the *New Orleans Delta*. "It is, in fact, essentially a revolutionary party."[89] Lincoln's election, reported the *Baltimore Sun*—a newspaper that couldn't bring itself to congratulate the new president—"has created a profound sensation all through the South. 'Minute men' are forming in several of the slave States." The paper went on to report that a "volunteer rifle corps" of one hundred young men was being equipped in Charleston and that they would be at the governor's beck and call in the event of an emer-

84. Charles Francis Adams Diary, Nov. 7, 1860, quoted in Foner, *Free Soil, Free Labor, Free Men*, p. 223.
85. Hayes, *Mr. Lincoln Runs for President*, p. 221.
86. Potter, *The Impending Crisis*, p. 215.
87. Oates, *With Malice Toward None*, pp. 203-204.
88. Bailyn, *et al.*, *The Great Republic*, p. 466.
89. *New Orleans Delta*, Nov. 3, 1860, and *Richmond Semi-Weekly Examiner*, Nov. 9, 1860, quoted in McPherson, *Battle Cry of Freedom*, pp. 232-233.

gency. If there was any doubt as to the veracity of the *Sun's* report, such disbelief was soon laid to rest. "The tea has been thrown overboard—the revolution of 1860 has been initiated!" exclaimed the *Charleston Mercury*, a paper that had once described Lincoln as a "horrid looking wretch" and of "the dirtiest complexion." The rabidly proslavery Rhetts, the fiery father and son team that edited the Charleston newspaper, had long been itching for an all-out fight over sectional rights and slavery.[90]

Yet it is folly, as Mary Scrugham observed in her long-forgotten book *The Peaceable Americans of 1860-1861*, to suggest or imply that a majority of southerners were "aggressively proslavery and bent on maintaining slavery," even at the cost of disrupting the Union. Given the large number of votes received by nonsectional candidates Stephen A. Douglas and the Constitutional Union Party's John Bell, who together outpolled Breckinridge in the slaveholding states of the Deep South as well as the Border States, Scrugham argued that it was clear that most of those in the South hoped to maintain the Union—with or without slavery.[91]

A cursory analysis of the returns from the slaveholding states, moreover, reveals some interesting patterns, some of which seem to give credence to Scrugham's contention. Breckinridge, who was widely regarded in the North as well as in the South as the "secessionist" candidate despite personal utterances to the contrary, won outright majorities in only six southern states—Alabama, Arkansas, Florida, Mississippi, North Carolina, and Texas. Nearly 56% of the voters in the slaveholding states voted against Breckinridge, including 26,395 voters in Delaware, Kentucky, Maryland, Missouri, and Virginia who supported Lincoln. Moreover, in eighteen southern cities with populations greater than 10,000, Breckinridge won clear majorities in only two and in large cities like Memphis, Mobile, and New Orleans, he garnered less than thirty percent of the vote against unionist candidates Douglas and Bell. He ran no stronger in Norfolk and Richmond.

Even more interesting, however, is the fact that the Southern Democratic nominee seemed to have run strongest in southern counties with relatively small slave populations, garnering approximately 64 percent of the vote in those counties in the states that made up the original Confederacy. Paradoxically, he garnered only 52 percent—barely a majority—in counties with the largest

90. Hayes, *Mr. Lincoln Runs for President*, pp. 219-220; Fite, *The Presidential Campaign of 1860*, p. 210.

91. Mary Scrugham, *The Peaceable Americans of 1860-1861* (New York, 1921), reprinted by Octagon Books, 1976, p. 52.

proportion of slaves, suggesting that even in areas where slavery was most heavily concentrated there was significant sentiment for keeping the Union intact. According to sociologist Seymour Martin Lipset, Breckinridge carried almost two-thirds of the counties with relatively small slave populations while nearly half of the counties with large numbers of slaves voted for Bell and Douglas, both of whom were trying desperately to find common ground in the country's growing sectional cleavage.[92]

In addition to winning the presidency with only a large third of the popular vote, the Republicans also widened their comfortable majority in the U.S. House of Representatives, winning 106 seats to only seventy for the combined opposition parties. Among the successful congressional candidates that year were two Constitutional Unionists and several independents. Included in the more than two-dozen men who served in the 37th Congress from outside the traditional two-party system were three Union Party congressmen—Rhode Island's George H. Browne, who worked vigorously to prevent the impending war-between-the-states, and William P. Sheffield, a Harvard-educated lawyer and longtime state legislator who later served in the U.S. Senate as a Republican, and ex-Whig George P. Fisher, a former state attorney general from Delaware—as well as a number of States' Rights Democrats, including Milledge L. Bonham and William W. Boyce of South Carolina, the latter of whom, fearing that Black Republican "fanaticism" would become the law of the land, argued vehemently for secession, even if it meant South Carolina should secede on its own.

Among the many former third-party adventurers elected to Congress on the Republican ticket that autumn were George W. Julian, the Free Soil Party's vice-presidential candidate in 1852; Samuel C. Fessenden of Maine, a veteran of the Liberty and Free Soil parties who, like his brothers William and Thomas, carried on his father's antislavery legacy; and Anson P. Morrill, the former Know-Nothing governor of Maine. A number of other minor-party veterans were also re-elected to Congress on the Republican ticket that year, including Pennsylvania's Galusha A. Grow, a former Free Soil-Democrat who was re-elected to a sixth term in David Wilmot's old district; ex-Liberty Party member Owen Lovejoy of Illinois, a friend of Lincoln's who once denounced slavery as "the sum of all villainy"; and Charles Francis Adams, Van Buren's vice-presidential running mate on the Free Soil ticket in 1848. Pennsylvania's ardent slavery foe Thaddeus

---

92. Potter, *The Impending Crisis*, pp. 442-445; Seymour Martin Lipset, "The Emergence of the One-Party South—the Election of 1860," in *Political Man: The Social Bases of Politics* (New York, 1960), pp. 345-354.

Stevens, a one-time member of the Anti-Masonic Party and a leader of the free soil forces in Congress, was also re-elected to Congress on the Republican ticket in 1860, running virtually unopposed. Like Lincoln, Stevens, who eschewed the Free Soil Party in 1848, didn't formally break from the Whigs until 1855.

Some of the newly elected Republicans that year included the mellifluously-named Socrates N. Sherman, a surgeon from Ogdensburg, New York, and Robert B. Van Valkenburgh, a 39-year-old lawyer and former New York assemblyman who later organized seventeen regiments for the Union army during the Civil War. During his long and illustrious career, the long-forgotten Van Valkenburgh also served as ambassador to Japan during Andrew Johnson's administration and as a justice on the Florida Supreme Court from the mid-1870s through the late 1880s.

One of the most interesting congressional races that year featured John Commerford, a chair and cabinetmaker and tireless leader in the antebellum labor movement. Commerford had previously sought a seat in Congress on the Land Reform ticket in 1846. A former president of the General Trades' Union of New York and veteran of the Workingmen's and Loco-Foco movements, Commerford was the Republican candidate for the U.S. House in New York's fourth congressional district, losing a three-way race to James E. Kerrigan, a 31-year-old Mexican War veteran who later became a staunch Irish Nationalist. Running as an "Independent Democrat," Kerrigan, who was one of several independents elected to the House of Representatives that year, defeated his major-party opponents, garnering 5,145 votes to the Democrat's 3,989 and 3,324 for Commerford. Serving only one term in Congress, Kerrigan, who was a colonel in the Union army during the Civil War, later led a company of Irish Nationalists across the Canadian border during a planned Fenian invasion of that country spearheaded by Civil War veteran John O'Neill in 1866. In another attempt to strike a blow against England, the former congressman later commanded *Erin's Hope*, a doomed gunrunning vessel that ran ashore while trying to deliver arms and ammunition to the Irish coast in 1867.

The 1860 election also brought to a close the brief but colorful congressional career of antislavery advocate Eli Thayer, an inventor, educator and conservative two-term Republican lawmaker from Massachusetts. A graduate of Brown University, Thayer, a good natured man who condoned rather than condemned the shortcomings of others, taught at Worcester Academy and served as its principal before founding the Oread Institute in 1848, a woman's college located in Worcester. A prolific inventor, he conceived of the first hydraulic elevator and invented a sectional safety steam boiler, as well as a sediment extractor. A longtime slavery foe, Thayer was elected to the Massachusetts legislature as a member of the Free Soil Party in the early 1850s. Hoping to populate Kansas with a large antislavery citizenry, Thayer, with an eye on ending slavery and another on turning a profit, was instrumental in founding the Massachusetts Emigrant Aid Company in the spring of 1854, shortly before the passage of the Kansas-Nebraska Act. Working closely with abolitionist Unitarian clergyman and author Edward Everett Hale and Alexander H. Bullock, a former Whig legislator and longtime editor of the *National Aegis*, Thayer's investment company was established to provide economic assistance to those who were willing to relocate to Kansas. The Massachusetts Emigrant Aid Company, originally chartered with $5,000,000 in capital, was later consolidated with the Emigrant Aid Company of New York and Connecticut and assumed a new name—the New England Emigrant Aid Company.

Charles Robinson, a physician who took part in the California gold rush—later helping to establish that vast territory as a free state—served as an advisor to the company. Robinson later served as governor of Kansas in the period immediately following its admission into the Union in 1861. Samuel C. Pomeroy, who later became one of the state's first two members of the U.S. Senate, also served as one of the company's agents. The first group of thirty settlers departed for Kansas even before the company was formally organized, arriving in Lawrence on August 1, 1854. Five other parties soon followed, bringing the number of settlers to about 450 by year's end. The ransacking of Lawrence by proslavery "border-ruffians" in May 1856 only served to stimulate the Kansas aid movement. In all, some 1,250 settlers eventually relocated to Kansas under the auspices of the New England Emigrant Aid Company—far short of its goal of 20,000, but enough to make a crucial difference in establishing Kansas as a free state. Though his venture proved far from a financial success, Thayer's far-sighted plan was widely hailed by the nation's antislavery forces. Charles Sumner of Massachusetts later said that he would "rather have the credit due Eli Thayer for his work in Kansas than be the hero of the battle of New Orleans." That was pretty high praise.

Thayer, who later formed the "Kansas League" to promote continued emigration into the territory, was elected to Congress from the ninth congressional of Massachusetts in 1856, defeating two-term Know-Nothing lawmaker Alexander De Witt, a textile manufacturer and one-time Free Soiler, in a bitterly-contested three-cornered race. In Congress, Thayer chaired the Committee on Public Lands from which he endorsed the idea of popular sovereignty in the territories. He was easily re-elected in 1858, piling up over seventy percent of the vote against his hapless Democratic rival. Thayer, however, angered some Republicans by criticizing what he called the "political Cassandras" within his own party, those "who are continually saying that slavery has always had its own way, and always will have it; that slavery under the Dred Scott decision, will yet be established in Massachusetts and New Hampshire." Those "Cassandras," of course, included such Republican luminaries as Abraham Lincoln and New York's William Seward, both of whom had stated publicly as late as 1858 that if not eradicated, slavery could eventually spread into the free states—a notion Jefferson Davis described as "absurd."

Denied re-nomination by his own party in 1860, Thayer ran for re-election as an independent. Supported by Democrats and Constitutional Unionists within his district, he was narrowly defeated by Republican Goldsmith F. Bailey, a lawyer and state representative from Worcester. After leaving Congress, the one-time Free Soiler was appointed by President Lincoln as a special agent of the Treasury Department. He later served as a land agent for the Hannibal and St. Joseph Railroad. In 1872, Thayer mounted a comeback for his old seat in the House, but lost badly. After writing *A History of the Kansas Crusade*, published by Harper & Brothers in 1889, Thayer spent the remaining years of his life working on numerous and far-flung his inventions.

Republican Anson Burlingame of Massachusetts, diplomat extraordinaire and a veteran of the Free Soil and Know-Nothing parties, also lost his seat in Congress in 1860 when the Constitutional Union Party's William Appleton, a former Whig congressman, defeated him by 258 votes in one of the closest House races in the country. An 1846 graduate of Harvard Law School, Burlingame was one of the most intriguing public officials of his time. A widely respected man, his admirers included no less than writer Mark Twain, who never forgot Burlingame's encouragement and magnanimity in "throwing away an invitation to dine with princes and foreign dignitaries" to help him break a story about fifteen starving men who had been lost at sea for forty-three days. The three-column story, which received front-page coverage in the *Sacramento Union*, marked a turning point in the young writer's career.

Joining the Free Soil Party shortly after graduating from law school, Burlingame, who had married the daughter of a prominent Cambridge family a year earlier, actively campaigned for the Van Buren-Adams ticket in 1848. Exuding an abundance of personal magnetism and a gifted speaking style, the 31-year-old lawyer was elected to the Massachusetts state senate in 1852 and won a seat in the U.S. House of Representatives during the Know-Nothing sweep of Massachusetts two years later, trouncing the same man who unseated him six years later.

Like "Bobbin Boy" Nathaniel Banks, "Natick Cobbler" Henry Wilson and other antislavery politicians in the Bay State, as John R. Mulkern stated in *The Know-Nothing Party in Massachusetts: The Rise and Fall of a People's Movement,* Burlingame gravitated to the mysterious new party not simply to join the crowd—like almost every other Free Soil politician in Massachusetts—but to lead it.

Burlingame's transition from the ranks of the Free Soil Party to the Know-Nothings was much smoother than some of his Free Soil colleagues, such as the pernicious Wilson, who vowed to convert the Know-Nothing Party into a true antislavery party or to destroy it. Burlingame, after all, was perfectly capable of appealing to the party's virulent anti-Catholicism, as evidenced by his nominating speech on behalf of gubernatorial candidate Nathaniel Banks in 1857—a speech that was described as "more American" than anti-slavery. He once suggested that the origin of African slavery could be traced back to a papal decree promulgated by Pope Martin V in the fifteenth century, arguing that there can be "no real hostility to Roman Catholicism which does not embrace slavery, its natural co-worker in opposition to freedom and republican institutions." On another occasion, Burlingame quoted the Bishop of St. Louis as saying that a Catholic hierarchy would soon dominate the United States, at which point religious liberty would cease to exist.

Affiliating with the Republicans during this period, Burlingame was re-elected to Congress in 1856 and 1858. Running on the American Party ticket, he was barely re-elected in 1856, defeating Appleton by 69 votes and had only somewhat less difficulty running as a Republican two years later when he defeated Democrat John F. Heard by a margin of 6,214 to 5,823. While in Congress, Burlingame sharply chastised South Carolina Congressman Preston Brooks for his brutal caning of Massachusetts Senator Charles Sumner following his famous "The Crime Against Kansas" speech in 1856, prompting the young States' Rights Democrat to challenge him to a duel. Burlingame wasted little time in accepting the challenge, choosing rifles as the weapons to be used and the Navy Yard on the Canadian side of Niagara Falls as the site. Fearing for his safety in passing through "the enemy's country," the South Carolina lawmaker backed down, enabling Burlingame to be hailed as a hero in the North.

After narrowly losing his bid for a fourth term in 1860, President Lincoln named Burlingame as ambassador to Austria, but the Austrian government, then headed by Emperor Francis Joseph I—a man who ruled that country for 68 years—objected because of the former congressman's public support for Hungarian and Sardinian independence. Burlingame was then appointed U.S. minister to China, where he quickly earned the trust and respect of the Emperor and his

Chinese government for his efforts in maintaining that country's territorial integrity. Having urged China to send a diplomatic mission to meet with the Western powers, Burlingame must have been surprised when the Ta-Tsing Empire asked him to head such a delegation. After careful consideration, Burlingame agreed and resigned as U.S. ambassador to China.

Burlingame's Chinese mission first visited the United States in March 1868 and a treaty, known thereafter as the Burlingame Treaty, was signed by both nations four months later. Among other things, the two countries agreed to respect the territorial sovereignty of the other, to preserve the privileges and immunity of those living in the host country, to guarantee religious liberties and, most significantly, to recognize and honor the principle of free immigration. Burlingame and his Chinese delegation also visited representatives in several European nations, including Great Britain, France, Denmark, Holland, Sweden and Prussia, negotiating treaties with all of them except France. Burlingame had just started negotiations with the Russian government in early 1870 when he was stricken with pneumonia and died a few days later.

The treaty's immigration provision, of course, later provoked great controversy and resentment in the United States, especially on the west coast. Within a decade, anti-Chinese sentiment, exacerbated by Denis Kearney's vociferous attacks on the "coolies," gave birth to the xenophobic Workingmen's Party of California. By 1880, both major parties adopted strong anti-Chinese immigration planks in their national platforms.

The 1860 presidential election was the Constitutional Union Party's one and only appearance in national politics. Shortly after the 1860 election, the thin gray ghosts of the Whig and Know-Nothing parties moaned inaudibly and then vanished from the scene forever. As a minor consolation, the Constitutional Unionists managed to chalk up victories in two congressional races that year, electing Missouri's James S. Rollins, an ex-Whig state legislator and veteran of the Black Hawk War, to the first of two terms in Congress and returning former Whig congressman William Appleton of Massachusetts to the House of Representatives after a two-year absence. Appleton, who ran on a Constitutional Union, Democratic, and Breckinridge Democratic fusion ticket, defeated Republican Anson Burlingame by a scant 258 votes to regain his seat. A cousin of Nathan Appleton, the powerful New England textile manufacturer, philanthropist and high-tariff politician, the 74-year-old Constitutional Unionist resigned from Congress after only five months in office due to failing health. The Constitutional Union Party, which fielded a total of twenty-nine candidates for the U.S. House that year—including a handful of fusion candidates—also came close to winning three other seats in Missouri and nearly re-elected Whig congressman Eli Thayer from his Worcester district in Massachusetts. Like Horace Greeley of New York, Thayer was a delegate to the Republican national convention from Oregon earlier that year. Former Whig congressman Henry M. Fuller of Pennsylvania was one of the many Constitutional Unionists who went down to defeat with the Bell-Everett ticket in 1860. A Princeton-educated lawyer who had been the choice of the Know-Nothing congressional caucus for Speaker of the House against Nathaniel P. Banks some five years earlier, the former Whig lawmaker barely polled 13% of the vote in a three-cornered race won by Republican Edward J. Morris.

Lost in the luster of the Lincoln landslide that year, the Constitutional Union Party was a valiant attempt by conservative statesmen from the South and border-states to resist the growing sectionalism that was dividing the nation and to prevent an outbreak of hostilities between the North and the South. "Your position is a proud and enviable one," wrote New York's Washington Hunt in a letter to John Bell three weeks after the election. "It enables you to render important aid in the work of reconciliation. History will do full justice to you and to the gallant band of union men who rallied under your banner."[93] Unfortunately, Hunt, who served as permanent chairman of the Constitutional Union Party's national convention that year, was sadly mistaken. History has never done justice to Bell or his heroic effort in the 1860 presidential campaign. In fact, only one full-length biography has ever been written about him—and that was in 1950, nearly a century after his death. Though largely overlooked in the annals of U.S. history, the low-keyed and phlegmatic former Tennessee senator was, for lack of a better phrase, America's original peace candidate. He was also one of the most principled men of his era. "Mr. Bell was the only national candidate," wrote Oliver P. Temple, a close friend and confidant of the candidate. "His election would have prevented secession. If the North had been as anxious in 1860 to save the Union as it became in 1861," it almost certainly would have supported Bell.[94] It's an interesting point to ponder and may very well be true.

During the impending "winter crisis" that immediately followed the 1860 presidential campaign, Bell, who never believed that Lincoln was an extremist, broke his silence and issued a tepidly written letter denouncing the legitimacy of secession on the eve of Mississippi's decision to join South Carolina in holding a

---

93. Hunt letter to John Bell, November 21, 1860, as quoted in Parks, *John Bell of Tennessee*, p. 389.
94. Oliver P. Temple, *East Tennessee and the Civil War* (Cincinnati, 1899), p. 294, quoted in Parks, *John Bell of Tennessee*, p. 388.

secessionist convention. While believing that Lincoln's election was certainly "a bold experiment upon the temper and forbearance of the South, and upon the strength of their loyalty to the Union," the former Tennessee lawmaker proceeded to analyze Lincoln's election, claiming that about a third of Lincoln's supporters voted for him because of a "strong and inveterate" dislike of the Democrats and another third supported the Republican ticket as a way of expressing their displeasure with the repeal of the Missouri Compromise and the Buchanan administration's heavy-handed "attempt to force the Lecompton constitution upon the people of Kansas." The balance of Lincoln's supporters—a clear minority—was the most worrisome, Bell contended, because they were either indifferent to the future of the Union or "actually desirous of a separation" between the country's free states and the slaveholding states of the South.[95]

Recognizing the potentially disastrous consequences resulting from the election of a purely sectional president, the former Tennessee lawmaker insisted in his letter that southern grievances could still be satisfactorily resolved by constitutional means without disrupting the Union. Even indignity and insult should be pardoned, he maintained, in the interest of "peace and harmony." After all, he said, the South wasn't completely blameless in the growing hostility between the two sections. In his concluding paragraphs, Bell criticized Mississippi for endangering the peace and security of the other states in the South "without previous consultation" and without exploring every possible means of redress. Under no laws or by any code of moral conduct, he insisted, would Mississippi or any other state be justified, under existing circumstances, in seceding from the Union. Insisting that he wasn't saying that under no circumstances would he ever agree to separation, Bell urged Mississippi's lawmakers and those in other southern states to "exhaust every constitutional means for the redress of our grievances" before considering the dissolution of the Union. "I am not willing that one state should be withdrawn from the Union—that one star should be stricken from that bright cluster which now emblazons the national flag," he concluded.[96]

In late January 1861, the former Constitutional Union Party standard-bearer addressed a large Nashville audience and again spoke out against the secessionist movement. Bell, whose name had been suggested to Lincoln by Henry J. Raymond of the *New York Times* as a possible cabinet appointee, was widely denounced by the state's secessionist forces. Henry S. Foote, a colorful trans-

---

95.   Parks, *John Bell of Tennessee*, pp. 390-391.
96.   *Republican Banner and Nashville Whig*, December 8, 1860; Parks, *John Bell of Tennessee*, pp. 391-392.

planted former Democratic senator from Mississippi and then one of Tennessee's leading secessionists, accused Bell of being an "an intimate friend and co-conspirator" of William H. Seward, Lincoln's newly-appointed Secretary of State. Foote, who later served in the first and second Confederate Congresses and, ironically, briefly spent some time in a Confederate jail, predicted that within a few weeks Bell would be named to a cabinet post. That, of course, never happened.[97]

Heeding Bell's advice, the voters of Tennessee narrowly rejected a popular referendum on secession on February 9, 1861, defeating the measure by a margin of 68,282 to 59,449. The election took place after voters in South Carolina, Georgia, Mississippi and the other Gulf states, stimulated in part by Republican intransigence in Congress—steadfastly opposing all plans of compromise offered by Crittenden, Douglas, Ohio's George E. Pugh and other committed unionists—had already approved secession ordinances in their respective states. Each of those states voted for Breckinridge during the recent presidential election.[98]

In the meantime, Bell traveled to Washington to attend Lincoln's inauguration and to meet personally with the president-elect. Though little has been recorded of Bell's meeting with Lincoln, the former Tennessee lawmaker urged Lincoln to proceed with the greatest caution and told the president that he shouldn't be deceived by the February 9 vote against secession in Tennessee, telling Lincoln that it was a vote of confidence in the new president in the belief that he would adopt a just and conciliatory policy toward the South. He also urged Lincoln and his cabinet to evacuate the federal forts in the South to avert a possible showdown and to allow for a badly needed cooling-off period. If the seceding states rejected conciliation, then "the wisest course would be to let them go in peace," Bell told the president. Though Lincoln and his cabinet members refused to make any specific commitments, Bell, who was somewhat impressed with Lincoln's conservative tone during their face-to-face meeting, left the nation's capitol confident that the new president would adopt a policy of conciliation.[99]

Tennessee finally seceded from the Union almost two months after General Pierre Beauregard's Confederate troops opened fire on Fort Sumter in the early morning hours of April 12, 1861. A deeply distraught Bell, who personally felt

---

97. Parks, *John Bell of Tennessee*, p. 394; *New York Times*, November 12, 1860.
98. Charles A. Miller, *The Official and Political Manual of the State of Tennessee* (Nashville, 1890), pp. 167, 170; Parks, *John Bell of Tennessee*, pp. 394-395; Dumond, *The Secession Movement*, pp. 167-168. Curiously, the total number of Tennessee voters casting ballots on the question of secession was 17,602 less than had voted in the 1860 presidential election.
99. Ibid., pp. 395-396.

betrayed by Lincoln, reluctantly endorsed secession after his state's Democratic governor—a staunch Breckinridge supporter during the 1860 campaign—declared that Tennessee "will not furnish a single man for the purpose of coercion, but fifty thousand if necessary for the defense of our rights and those of our Southern brothers." Speaking in Nashville on April 23, a deeply pained Bell announced his support for a united South in "the unnecessary, aggressive, cruel, unjust wanton war which is being forced upon us" by Lincoln's mobilization of a Union militia.[100]

However, the man who had supported the Compromise of 1850, voted against the Kansas-Nebraska Act, opposed the admission of Kansas under the proslavery Lecompton Constitution, and had tried unsuccessfully to unite ex-Whigs and moderate Republicans in a last-ditch effort to save the Union in 1860, initially urged his home state to resist the clamor of the seceding states as well as the military demands of the Union. In a statement issued along with ten other Tennessee conservatives only six days after the firing on Fort Sumter, Bell warned that to side with either section would render the state ineffective as a possible peacemaker between the bellicose cotton states of the South, led by Jefferson Davis of Mississippi, Georgia's Robert Toombs, and the fiery white supremacist William L. Yancey of Alabama—men Bell could hardly tolerate—and the equally obstinate federal government headed by Lincoln. Tennessee's role in the crisis, they maintained, should be that of a defender of the "union and peace of the country against all assailants, whether from the North or South." Within a few days, however, Bell was beginning to sound like a rebel, urging the state to organize a well-equipped militia in the event Tennessee is dragged into the war and suggesting that there were thousands of citizens in the state opposed to secession who wouldn't hesitate to take up arms in defense of the South.

While keeping a close eye on developments in neighboring Kentucky, Bell was careful to avoid suggesting that Tennessee should join the rebellion by adopting an ordinance of secession. Recognizing that further resistance was probably futile, he still held out some hope that the two states, acting as a bloc, might somehow play a critical role in preserving the Union—a suggestion echoed a week earlier by the *Republican Banner and Nashville Whig*, which eloquently urged Tennessee and Kentucky to stand together "until the last beacon light of hope twinkles out in the distance, as we are drifted into an unknown and tempestuous sea."[101]

---

100. McPherson, *Battle Cry of Freedom*, pp. 274-277. Lincoln issued a proclamation on April 15 calling for a militia of 75,000 men to put down what he described as an insurrection "too powerful to be suppressed by the ordinary course of judicial proceedings."

By June, however, shortly after the voters of Tennessee overwhelmingly ratified a secession ordinance, any such hope that the state could hope to mediate a peace in the great conflict had long since faded. For his part, Bell was severely—and unfairly—raked over the coals for supporting the secessionists, albeit grudgingly and with great remorse. He had held out as long as he possibly could. Yet the criticism was venomous. "A more sudden, and utter, and inglorious defection was never suffered by a sacred and imperiled cause," lamented George D. Prentice of the *Louisville Journal*, an avid supporter of the Bell-Everett ticket in 1860. John Minor Botts, who had campaigned arduously for the Constitutional Union ticket, accused Bell of having embraced the party's platform as long as there was a chance he could be elected, but once the election was over "he knocked the platform from under his feet" and assisted those who were attempting to destroy the Union. Horace Greeley of the *New York Tribune*, however, lodged the cruelest comment of all a few years later when he charged the former third-party presidential candidate with "complicity in the crime of dividing and destroying" the country, adding that of all the men who were beguiled into supporting the secession movement, "no name whereon will rest a deeper, darker stigma than that of John Bell."[102] Those were pretty strong words from a man who in 1860 had floated Bell's name as a possible presidential candidate on a Republican-Opposition fusion ticket.

Most of the criticism hurled at Bell ignored the fact that there was little that he or any other southern unionist could do after the firing on Fort Sumter. Public resistance at that point was futile. The Constitutional Union Party now but a distant memory, Bell lived a quiet, somewhat isolated existence for the duration of the bloody conflict. He died on September 11, 1869, at the age of seventy-three.

In the aftermath of the 1860 election, Kentucky's aging and sagacious John J. Crittenden also tried unsuccessfully to avert the Civil War by proposing a series of six constitutional amendments and four resolutions. Known as the "Crittenden Compromise," these amendments and resolutions enjoyed considerable popular support and were even endorsed by Lincoln's incoming Secretary of State William Seward. Crittenden's proposals prohibited the abolition of slavery on federal land in slaveholding states, restored the Missouri Compromise line and compensated owners of runaway slaves. Additionally, one of the Kentucky lawmaker's amendments guaranteed that future constitutional amendments could

101. Ibid., pp. 397-400; *Republican Banner and Nashville Whig*, April 16, 1861.
102. Parks, *John Bell of Tennessee*, pp. 400-401.

not change the other five amendments, nor could future laws change the Constitution's three-fifths and fugitive slave clauses. A majority of the Republicans in Congress, however, believed that Crittenden's proposals made too many concessions to the South and refused to enact it. The Constitutional Union Party founder, a moderate on secession and slavery who had labored long and hard to avert the Civil War, was also deeply torn during the war with two of his five sons fighting on opposite sides of the conflict. The aging Kentucky lawmaker died in July 1863, less than two years before Robert E. Lee, telling his weary and hungry men to lay down their arms, surrendered on the steps of the Appomattox Courthouse.

This does not necessarily mean that Lincoln's party killed the last best hope to save the Union, or that the Republicans could necessarily be defined as the war party. By this time, it was probably already too late to prevent secession. Leaders in the Deep South feared that a compromise wouldn't be enough to secure peace unless the Republicans unequivocally repudiated their anti-slavery principles—a highly unlikely prospect. Secession was certainly in the air. "No human power can save the Union," huffed Jefferson Davis, "all the cotton states will go." And so it was.

In his March 4 inaugural address, Lincoln, who arrived in Washington dressed incognito in the dead of night to avoid a possible assassination attempt, had promised that there would be no use of force against the seceding states, unless provoked. He also assured the American people that he had no intention of interfering with the institution of slavery in the states where it already existed. "In *your* hands, my dissatisfied fellow-countrymen, and not in *mine,* is the momentous issue of civil war. The government will not assail *you.* You can have no conflict without being yourselves the aggressors." His voice tempered with sadness, America's sixteenth President told the American people that they had no heavenly right to destroy the United States, reminding them of the oath of office that he had just taken—an oath to preserve, protect and defend the government of the United States. "We are not enemies, but friends. We must not be enemies," he concluded. "Though passion may have strained, it must not break our bonds of affection. The mystic chords of memory, stretching from every battlefield, and patriot grave, to every living heart and hearthstone, all over this broad land, will yet swell the chorus of the Union, when again touched, as surely they will be, by the better angels of our nature."[103]

---

103. Oates, *With Malice Toward None*, p. 237.

Like Bell, John C. Breckinridge, the Southern Democratic standard-bearer in 1860, also worked to prevent secession and civil war in his new role as a member of the U.S. Senate from Kentucky, when he replaced the retiring John J. Crittenden in March 1861. However, after the firing on Fort Sumter on April 12, 1861, the former vice president urged Kentucky to secede from the Union. He was expelled from the U.S. Senate on December 4 of that year, but that was rather meaningless given the fact that he had already been commissioned as a brigadier-general in the Confederate army a month earlier. Having seen action in the battles of Shiloh, Chickamauga and New Market, where his rag-tag rebel force of 5,000—including 247 young cadets, some as young as fifteen, from the Virginia Military Institute—drove back a larger and better equipped Union army, Breckinridge was promoted to the rank of major general in the spring of 1862 and was later put in charge of a territorial command in western Virginia. He later succeeded the embattled James Alexander Seddon as the sixth and last Confederate Secretary of War in February 1865, barely two months before Lee's surrender on April 9. At the war's conclusion, Breckinridge fled via Florida and Cuba to England and finally to Canada where he remained until Christmas Day 1868 when he was granted amnesty and returned to his home in Lexington, Kentucky. Breckinridge, who urged reconciliation between the North and South and denounced the Ku Klux Klan, never returned to public life. He served as a railroad executive until his death in 1874 at the relatively young age of fifty-four.

Democrat Stephen A. Douglas also desperately sought a compromise that would save the Union following Lincoln's election. Among other things, he courageously campaigned against secession in hostile Mississippi, delivering a stirring speech in Vicksburg in which he called for the preservation of the Union. As expected, the Illinois lawmaker pledged his wholehearted support to the new president once hostilities heated up. Tragically, the "Little Giant" died a few months later while traveling to Illinois to enlist his state's support in the Union cause.

10

The Civil War Years

◆

The National Union Party, Copperheads and the Cleveland 400

As the 1864 presidential campaign approached, the prospect of a Union victory on the battlefield appeared slim. General Ulysses S. Grant, Lincoln's renowned commander of the Union army, had been stalled by Robert E. Lee's troops in Virginia and William T. Sherman, who was then in charge of the Union's western armies, had been halted en route to Atlanta, the heart of the Confederacy.

The heavy losses incurred by Grant's troops sent shock waves throughout the North. Some people, horrified by the mounting casualties, suggested postponing or canceling the 1864 elections altogether. Lincoln, of course, refused to seriously entertain such advice, saying that if the rebellious South forced the nation to postpone its national election, our southern rivals can claim to have already "conquered and ruined us."[1]

Discontent with the Lincoln administration was widespread. In Congress, dominated by the radicals, Lincoln had been dealt a setback when Indiana's Schuyler Colfax, an ally of John C. Fremont, defeated his candidate for Speaker of the House. Things weren't much rosier in the U.S. Senate where, among others, Charles Sumner, the icy and pontifical Massachusetts lawmaker, was growing increasingly critical of Lincoln's handling of the war, as were Lyman Trumbull of Illinois and John P. Hale, the nagging New Englander and one-time Free Soil candidate for president. Even staunch Lincoln allies like Zachariah Chandler of Michigan were urging a fuller prosecution of the war. As if things weren't bad enough, Lincoln was dealt an even more serious blow when Benjamin F. Wade's radical-dominated Committee on the Conduct of the War issued a stinging

---

1.   Boller, *Presidential Campaigns*, p. 115.

report on April 3—only two months before the Republicans were scheduled to convene in Baltimore—calling for a more vigorous prosecution of the conflict.[2]

As the war dragged on, with casualties mounting on both sides and no victory in sight, Lincoln, barraged by a firestorm of public criticism, watched helplessly as the list of his potential challengers in 1864 continued to grow. For a while, his nomination appeared to be in serious doubt as many leading Republicans apparently agreed with Massachusetts Gov. John A. Andrew when he said that Lincoln "was essentially lacking in the quality of leadership."[3] Horace Greeley of the *New York Tribune* was among them, claiming that Lincoln's re-nomination would lead to a Democratic victory and ultimately the nation's ruin.[4]

Leading the pack of prospective rivals was none other than Lincoln's own Secretary of the Treasury, Salmon P. Chase. The ambitious 56-year-old former senator and Ohio governor, whose vigorous opposition to slavery was so strong that he was known as the "attorney for runaway Negroes," was gearing up to challenge the hemorrhaging president for the Union Party's nomination.

By this stage in the campaign, the Republicans had dropped their name altogether and had become part of a new Union Party, a wartime coalition of regular Republicans and pro-war Democrats. Lincoln's Union Party attracted an unusually large number of Democrats to its banner, including many of those who had supported the late Stephen A. Douglas in 1860. Lincoln felt strongly that the urgency of the war necessitated the creation of a new party distinguished in both purpose and personnel from the pre-war Republican Party. The Union Party, as such, was a genuine major party coalition with prominent Democrats and Republicans taking part. As a result, political patronage flowed freely from the Lincoln White House to members of both camps.

The movement to nominate Ohio's Salmon P. Chase for president on the Union Party ticket began to take shape during the winter of 1863-64. Chase, of course, believed that he was much better qualified for the presidency than Lincoln—and wasn't the least bit reluctant to say so. "Chase is a good man, but his theology is unsound," quipped Ohio's Benjamin Wade. "He thinks there is a fourth person in the Trinity."[5] A rather humorless and somewhat self-righteous man, Chase enjoyed the backing of powerful Philadelphia financier Jay Cooke, whose firm, Jay Cooke & Company, profited handsomely during the Civil War

2.   Allan Nevins, *Fremont: Pathmaker of the West* (Lincoln, Nebraska, 1992), p. 564.
3.   Bailyn, *et al., The Great Republic*, p. 516.
4.   Boller, *Presidential Campaigns*, p. 116.
5.   John C. Waugh, *Reelecting Lincoln: The Battle for the 1864 Presidency* (Cambridge, MA, 1997), p. 38.

by selling government war bonds for the U.S. Treasury headed by Chase. Generally regarded as an incorruptible man, the Treasury Secretary also had the unwavering support of prominent Senators Samuel C. Pomeroy and John Sherman of Kansas and Ohio, respectively. Pomeroy was angry with Lincoln for apparently favoring his rival fellow senator, James H. Lane, in the distribution of political patronage in Kansas. Chase's inner circle later expanded to include Representative James A. Garfield of Ohio. Though backed by such luminaries as Cooke, Pomeroy and Sherman, the Secretary's biggest booster was undoubtedly his own daughter, Kate Chase Sprague, whose greatest obsession was to reign as hostess of the White House for her widowed father. An attractive Washington socialite, Kate was both shrewd and calculating and had reputedly married Senator William Sprague, a wealthy Rhode Island manufacturer, to further enhance her father's chances of attaining the pinnacle of power that he so strongly coveted.

Chase's supporters made their move in February of 1864 when they issued a harshly worded yet anonymous pamphlet titled, "The Next Presidential Election," which contended that the people had "lost all confidence" in Lincoln's ability "to suppress the rebellion and restore the Union." It also criticized the president's vacillation and indecision, "the feebleness of his will" and his "want of intellectual grasp." Without mentioning Chase by name, the pamphlet asserted that the next Republican presidential candidate must be "an advanced thinker; a statesman profoundly versed in political and economic science, one who fully comprehends the spirit of the age."

Kansas Sen. Samuel C. Pomeroy, one of the most crooked men in public life, caused a major stir later that month when he apparently authored a private letter that quickly found its way into several Washington newspapers, including the conservative *National Intelligencer.* The letter stated that Lincoln's re-election was "practically impossible" and heaped praise on Chase, stating that he was "a statesman of rare ability" and had consistently demonstrated "more of the qualities needed in a President" than any other candidate, including the incumbent. Disavowing any connection to what became known as the "Pomeroy Circular," a mortified Chase apologized to Lincoln and offered to resign as Secretary of the Treasury. After allowing Chase to dangle in the wind for more than a week, Lincoln, a rather forgiving man, refused to accept his resignation. Others were less forgiving. "It is a matter of surprise that a man having the instincts of a gentleman should remain in the Cabinet after the disclosure of such an intrigue against the one to whom he owes his portfolio," blurted Francis P. Blair, Jr., who simultaneously launched a vicious attack on corruption in the treasury department, clearly laying the blame for wrongdoing at Chase's feet.[6] As it turned out, the circular backfired as most state Republican leaders rallied to Lincoln's defense, piercing Chase's hot air balloon in the process. Making matters worse, the Republican national committee, many of whom were Lincoln appointees, met in Washington on February 22 and overwhelming endorsed Lincoln's re-election. Deeply disappointed, Chase officially withdrew from the canvass on March 5.[7]

Aside from Chase's rapidly deflating candidacy, a number of other leading Republicans wanted to nominate Ulysses S. Grant in Lincoln's place, but the general was adamant in his refusal to run. Grant preferred to focus all of his attention on the assignment at hand—namely, capturing the Confederacy's "store house" in Georgia and routing Robert E. Lee's pesky troops in Virginia. Meanwhile, a number of others looked for salvation in the person of Benjamin F. Butler of Massachusetts, the former military governor of New Orleans and one of the most popular generals in the Union army.

On the Democratic side, a battle was brewing between party regulars who supported the war but were unhappy with its progress and the so-called "Peace Democrats," or Copperheads, led by the eloquent Clement L. Vallandigham, an exiled former antiwar congressman from Ohio. The son of a Presbyterian minister and lifelong admirer of British philosopher and statesman Edmund Burke, the 40-year-old lawyer had been one of Lincoln's most unrelenting opponents during the war. The renegade Ohioan was arrested a year earlier and, tried by a hastily created military commission, was found guilty of making disloyal statements. A former schoolteacher, Vallandigham, who claimed that he had been imprisoned in a "military Bastille for no other offense than my political opinions," was a states' rights Democrat who frequently denounced slavery as "a moral, social, and political evil," but wished to preserve the Union by conciliation rather than bloodshed. Like most antiwar Democrats, Vallandigham had been particularly critical of Lincoln's usurpation of power in his suspension of the writ of habeas corpus in the spring of 1861, authorizing army commanders to declare martial law while allowing civilians to be tried in military courts. In May 1863, the defiant former Ohio lawmaker denounced the "wicked and cruel" war started by "King Lincoln" and accused the nation's sixteenth president of "crushing out liberty and erecting a despotism"—a malicious statement that led to his arrest by General Ambrose E. Burnside, the recently deposed commander of the Army of the Potomac. Charging that Lincoln had launched "a terrible and bloody revolution," the maverick ex-legislator was subsequently jailed for the duration of the

6. Donald, *Lincoln*, p. 483.

7. Roseboom, *A History of Presidential Elections*, pp. 193-194

war, but Lincoln, who personally professed to have been pained by Valland-igham's arrest, later commuted his sentence, banishing his controversial antiwar critic to the Confederacy. Branded as a traitor in the North and received rather coldly in the South, "Valiant Val" later sought refuge in Canada where he ran, in absentia, for governor of Ohio in 1863, losing to the Union Party's John Brough by more than 100,000 votes.[8]

The odds-on favorite for the Democratic presidential nomination was George B. McClellan, the 37-year-old former general-in-chief of the Union army. McClellan had the powerful backing of financier August Belmont, railroad mag-nate Dean Richmond and industrialists William H. Aspinwall and Cyrus H. McCormick. Lincoln couldn't afford to take the Democrats lightly. Not only were they expected to be well-financed, they had also come very close to winning a majority in the 1862 mid-term congressional elections. Moreover, they also had a powerful set of issues—public weariness with the war and Lincoln's arbitrary use of executive authority.

John C. Fremont and the Radical Democrats

The beleaguered president also faced the likelihood of a serious third-party chal-lenge from John C. Fremont, the war hero and the first Republican presidential standard-bearer in history. Fremont, who had been removed from his command of the western military district by Lincoln in 1862, was still nursing a bitter grudge toward his commander-in-chief. A darling of the Radical Republicans, Fremont, who has more places in the American West named for him than anyone else in history, assembled a motley coalition of abolitionists and radical German-Americans into what initially appeared to be a formidable third party called the Radical Democratic Party (occasionally referred to as the Independent Republi-cans). About 400 Fremont supporters attended the party's national convention at Chapin Hall in Cleveland, Ohio, on May 31 and nominated the Pathfinder for the nation's highest office.

Wendell Phillips, the great social reformer and outspoken abolitionist, addressed the convention by letter, telling the delegates that Lincoln's reconstruc-tion policy "makes the freedom of the Negro a sham, and perpetuates slavery under a softer name."[9] In his ringing endorsement of Fremont, Phillips also

---

8.   Bill Kauffman, "Man Without a Country," *The American Enterprise* (March 2003), Volume 14, Issue 2, p. 43.

9.   McPherson, *Battle Cry of Freedom*, p. 716.

blasted the Lincoln administration as "a civil and military failure," arguing that the administration's avowed policy was ruinous to the North in virtually every respect.[10] Although a few lent behind-the-scenes support to the effort, hoping to dislodge Lincoln from the Union Party ticket, not a single prominent Republican took part in the Cleveland proceedings. A number of shrewd Democrats, on the other hand, managed to infiltrate the convention and were able to convince the politically naïve Fremont of the possibility of forging a coalition ticket with their party to defeat Lincoln.

Their handiwork was evidenced in the nomination of General John Cochrane of New York as Fremont's vice-presidential running mate. The 50-year-old Cochrane, who chaired the Cleveland convention, had been a states' rights Democratic congressman for two terms and was serving as attorney general of New York at the time of his nomination. Cochrane's nomination dismayed the White House. After all, he had only recently visited Lincoln and assured him that he would be attending the Cleveland convention for the sole purpose of trying "to forestall and break up" the bolting party.[11] No one, least of all Lincoln, expected him to be nominated.

Declaring that the southern "rebellion must be suppressed by force of arms, and without compromise," the Radical Democrats, in a particularly punitive mood, adopted a platform containing thirteen planks. Echoing Gerrit Smith's radical Liberty Party platforms of the 1840s and 1850s, the delegates called for a constitutional amendment to abolish slavery. They also asserted that Congress rather than the president must control reconstruction and urged, as "a measure of justice," the confiscation of Confederate lands for redistribution to soldiers and settlers. The party's platform also sharply denounced Lincoln's suspension of habeas corpus and suppression of free speech—the Democratic Party's main indictment of the administration. In addition, Fremont's followers advocated a single presidential term and the direct election of the president.[12]

Fremont accepted the new party's nomination, but rejected the party's proposal for the confiscation of rebel lands as too vengeful. In his letter of acceptance, the Pathfinder also indicated that he would be willing to withdraw from the race if the upcoming Union Party convention named a suitable candi-

---

10. Waugh, *Reelecting Lincoln*, p. 179
11. Ibid., p. 180.
12. Harold M. Dudley, "The Election of 1864," *Mississippi Valley Historical Review*. Vol. XVIII (March 1932); *New York Tribune*, June 1, 1864; Roseboom, *A History of Presidential Elections*, p. 196; McPherson, *Battle Cry of Freedom*, p. 716.

date—presumably, someone other than Lincoln—who would be willing to embrace the principles of the Cleveland convention.

Apparently struck by the number of people attending the Cleveland convention, Lincoln, who was clearly amused by the Radical Democratic proceedings, quickly dismissed Fremont's third-party candidacy with a passage from the Bible. "And everyone that was in distress and every one that was discontented gathered themselves unto him," Lincoln read aloud, "and he became a captain over them; and there were with him about four hundred men."[13] Others shared Lincoln's amusement. "What are they driving at?" wondered James Gordon Bennett of the *New York Herald*. Certainly not Fremont's election, he reasoned, especially with a platform as radical as the one they adopted. "What a precious piece of foolery it all is," concurred Henry Raymond of the *New York Times*, adding that the whole Cleveland affair bordered on "mental hallucination."[14]

Although many like Bennett and Raymond viewed the Radical Democrats as a bunch of political misfits and soreheads, it would have been a mistake to take Fremont's candidacy too lightly. Though something of a failure as a soldier, the former explorer was nonetheless an American legend known by everyone in the country. He was a household name long before anyone had heard of Abraham Lincoln. A larger than life personality, Fremont, at age fifty-one, was still a relatively young man in 1864, his chiseled features and dark blue eyes still resonating an air of youth that the country had fallen in love with more than a decade earlier. His appeal was widespread, ranging from such diverse personalities as Elizabeth Cady Stanton and former Pennsylvania governor William F. Johnston to William Cullen Bryant of the *New York Evening Post* and Manton Marble of the *New York World*. Everyone, of course, had his or her own agenda, including Marble, a dyed-in-the-wool Democrat who was using the movement as a means of splitting the Republican Party and defeating the despised Lincoln.[15]

Meanwhile, Lincoln's re-nomination seemed assured. Despite attempts by Bryant and a few of Lincoln's other adversaries to postpone the National Union Party's convention, the administration's forces convened in Baltimore only seven days after Fremont had been nominated in Cleveland. As it turned out, there wasn't much in the way of suspense at the Union convention. Salmon Chase, Lincoln's chief rival, had withdrawn from the race more than three months earlier, shortly after the Ohio legislature endorsed the president's re-election. A few

---

13. Donald, *Lincoln*, p. 503.
14. *New York Herald*, June 2, 1864, and the *New York Times*, June 2, 3, July 2, 1864, quoted in Waugh, *Reelecting Lincoln*, p. 181.
15. Waugh, *Reelecting Lincoln*, p. 176.

days earlier, Lincoln's managers had outmaneuvered Chase's supporters to secure an endorsement by the Indiana state convention. Embracing a platform calling for the complete suppression of the Confederate rebellion and for a constitutional amendment to end slavery, the Unionists unanimously nominated Lincoln for a second term.

In a stroke of genius, Lincoln skillfully arranged for the nomination of Andrew Johnson, a Tennessee Democrat, as his vice-presidential running mate. Johnson was nominated before the second ballot after garnering 200 votes on the first ballot to 150 for Hannibal Hamlin, Lincoln's colorless vice president, and 108 for New York's Daniel S. Dickinson, a pro-war former Democratic senator who enjoyed the support of Charles Sumner of Massachusetts. Shortly after Lincoln's election in 1860, Johnson sharply denounced the secessionists. "I would have them arrested and tried for treason," he declared, "and, if convicted, by the external God, they should suffer the penalty of the law at the hands of the executioner."[16]

Not everyone agreed with Lincoln's choice. "Can't you get a candidate for vice president without going down into a damned rebel province for one?" thundered Pennsylvania's Thad Stevens while Democratic newspapers denounced the National Union candidates as "a rail-splitting buffoon and a boorish tailor, both from the backwoods, both growing up in uncouth ignorance."[17] Though vilified as a traitor in the South, Johnson, who retained his seat in the U.S. Senate after his own state seceded from the Union, was named military governor of the state in 1862—a post in which he proved to be a fair-minded and able administrator. As military governor, Johnson granted amnesty to numerous Confederate sympathizers and pushed for an amendment to the state constitution outlawing slavery. Tennessee, it should be noted, was the only seceding state that ended slavery by its own action.

Although Lincoln was renominated without opposition, his re-election was still far from certain. The war wasn't going particularly well, to put it mildly, and the Union treasury was nearly depleted. The hard-drinking Grant took heavy casualties when he hurled his troops against Robert E. Lee's forces and General Sherman was making little if any headway in his struggle to capture Atlanta. Losses at Cold Harbor and the Wilderness, coupled with General Jubal Early's spectacular raid in early July, crossing the Potomac and nearly capturing Wash-

16. Whitney, *The American Presidents*, p. 152.
17. Roseboom, *A History of Presidential Elections*, p. 197.

ington—coming so close, in fact, that the Navy prepared a vessel to carry Lincoln to safety—didn't bode well for the beleaguered president.[18]

Confidence in the Union had fallen to an all-time low. There were many Republicans who continued to hold out some hope that a new convention could be held in the fall at which time the Union Party might dump Lincoln and name a new ticket. In fact, as late as September 1864—less than two months before the election—a questionnaire sent to Republican governors, leading editors and members of Congress found that a vast majority of the respondents agreed that Lincoln should be asked to step aside in favor of a new standard-bearer.

A behind-the-scenes effort to persuade both Lincoln and his Radical Democratic opponent John C. Fremont to withdraw from the race had taken shape during the hot summer months. Among others, the dump-Lincoln movement had the support of Ohio Senator Benjamin F. Wade and Rep. Henry Winter Davis of Maryland, both of whom had collaborated in the Wade-Davis bill, controversial legislation that would have required that more than half of those in the South who had voted in the 1860 elections to swear their allegiance and participate in drafting a new constitution before that state could be readmitted to the Union. Lincoln strongly disapproved of their bill and effectively killed it by a pocket veto.

The anybody-but-Lincoln drive also had the support of ex-Free Soiler Charles Sumner, influential *New York Tribune* editor Horace Greeley, Massachusetts Governor John A. Andrew, Sen. John Sherman of Ohio, as well as several other prominent political figures, not the least of whom included many of Salmon P. Chase's closest friends and supporters. Chase himself let it be known that he was available if a second Union Party convention needed a candidate.

Smelling blood, the Democrats confidently convened in Chicago on August 29 to nominate a presidential ticket. Union General George B. McClellan, who compiled a rather mediocre record on the battlefield, was heavily favored to win the party's nomination. McClellan, who had been fooled by Confederate "Quaker Guns"—logs painted to look like cannons—at both Manassas and Centerville, faced only token opposition from a small contingent of Peace Democrats backing 56-year-old Thomas H. Seymour, a former governor of Connecticut.

A somewhat controversial figure, Seymour's official portrait had been removed by the Connecticut state Senate in 1862 because of his strong opposition to the war. A former minister to Russia, Seymour fought for reconciliation with the South throughout the Civil War. As a member of the Connecticut assembly, Sey-

---

18. Nevins, *Fremont: Pathmaker of the West*, p. 576.

mour offered numerous peace resolutions in 1861 that were widely praised in the South, yet were overwhelmingly rejected by his state's legislature.

A handful of other delegates lined up behind reluctant New York Gov. Horatio Seymour, who had sharply criticized Lincoln's Emancipation Proclamation as a "bloody" and "barbarous" revolutionary act. The intrepid 54-year-old governor was also strongly opposed to conscription and at one point accused the Lincoln administration of padding draft quotas in predominantly Democratic districts. A polished conservative with thirty years of solid political experience under his belt, Seymour had rallied to the defense of Clement Vallandigham, the martyred Copperhead leader who was placed under arrest by a military tribunal in 1863.

As expected, McClellan, who had become the nation's second ranking general at age thirty-four, was easily nominated on the first ballot, garnering 264 votes to 38 for former Connecticut Gov. Thomas Seymour and a dozen for New York's Horatio Seymour. (Horatio Seymour, it should be noted, emerged as the party's presidential nominee four years later with the unenviable task of running against Civil War hero Ulysses S. Grant.) "Gentleman George" H. Pendleton, a 39-year-old Ohio congressman and a leader of the party's pre-Civil War peace wing, was chosen as McClellan's vice-presidential running mate. With McClellan not yet 38 years old, it was the youngest ticket ever nominated by a major political party.

The Democrats adopted a platform that included a peace plank heavily influenced by the indomitable Vallandigham of Ohio. Traveling incognito, the former congressman had recently returned from exile in Canada and became a delegate to the Democratic national convention from his home district in southwestern Ohio. Vallandigham's peace initiative called for an immediate "cessation of hostilities" and sharply condemned "four years of failure to restore the Union by the experiment of war."

As was the case with Fremont, Lincoln had removed McClellan from his post as commander of the Union forces in early November 1862. McClellan's hesitancy had irked Lincoln to no end. McClellan had been severely scolded by the president in April of that year. Lincoln's depiction of McClellan as having a bad case of the "slows" seems to have been right on target, as evidenced by the general's timid behavior at Antietam on September 17, the bloodiest day of the war. Numbed by the enormous casualties inflicted on his Union army, McClellan was reluctant to send in fresh troops commanded by William B. Franklin, thereby passing up a rare opportunity to cut Lee's demoralized army in half. McClellan's hesitation enabled the southern general's ragged and war-torn troops to retreat up the Shenandoah where they slowly began to regroup. Due to his extreme cautiousness, the irresolute McClellan unwittingly gave the Confederacy a new lease on life and, as a result, the bloody war dragged on for three additional years. Needless to say, Lincoln was furious.[19]

Lincoln had long believed that McClellan had his eyes on the presidency. In Lincoln's view, McClellan was the first military leader in history who was trying to rise to power by losing a war. Yet McClellan seemed every bit as reluctant a politician as he was a military leader. At first, the young West Point graduate was cool to the idea of challenging his former commander-in-chief, but after a great deal of soul-searching finally caved in to the pleadings of Democratic leaders. Deep down, McClellan believed that Lincoln was a tool of the vindictive Radical Republicans and that his re-election would usher in a period of even harsher treatment of the South—not only of the Confederate army but also of the region's civilian population.

While still in command of the Union army, McClellan had been highly critical of Lincoln's plans to issue an Emancipation Proclamation, believing that such a radical policy would quickly demoralize the ranks of the Union forces. The Union general was also sharply opposed to Lincoln's plans to confiscate the property of Confederate sympathizers. Moreover, McClellan was adamant in his belief that the war should be limited to military targets and should not be waged against civilian populations. Lincoln, of course, wanted the Army of the Potomac to strike more vigorous blows. McClellan refused. In a letter to Secretary of War Edwin M. Stanton, McClellan made it clear that he had no intention of supporting such a policy. He was relieved of duty four months later and was sent to Trenton, New Jersey, to await further orders. They never came.

During the autumn campaign, the former Union officer's military record was held up to ridicule and he was utterly unable to dissociate himself from the "follies of Chicago." On the one hand, he was under tremendous pressure from New York financier August Belmont, chairman of the Democratic National Committee, and other influential pro-war Democrats to take a decidedly hawkish stance, to emphasize that the restoration of the Union must be a condition of peace. On the other hand, dissident Democrat Clement Vallandigham and the Copperheads pressured him to take a more dovish position. To do otherwise, warned Vallandigham, would cost the Democratic ticket as many as two hundred thousand votes in the West—a figure that probably wasn't entirely off the mark. In the end, McClellan capitulated to Belmont and the War Democrats, stating in his September 8 letter of acceptance that he couldn't possibly look into the faces of his "gallant comrades of the army and navy who have survived so many bloody

---

19.   McPherson, *Battle Cry of Freedom*, pp. 536-545.

battles and tell them that their labors and the sacrifices of so many of our slain and wounded brethren had been in vain—that we have abandoned the Union for which we have so often periled our lives."

In repudiating the party's anti-war plank, McClellan alienated a portion of the party's peace element. However, many of the Peace Democrats remained loyal to the ticket, if for no other reason than to defeat Lincoln. Though clearly disappointed by McClellan's apparent about-face on the peace issue, Vallandigham and other Copperheads stumped, albeit half-heartedly, for the Democratic ticket in the fall. While some antiwar Democrats sat out the election altogether, another group of Peace Democrats, meeting in Columbus, Ohio, tried in vain to field a fourth-party ticket headed by Alexander Long, a one-term congressman from Cincinnati.

Though almost forgotten in history, Long was one of the most prominent antiwar Democrats in Congress, sharing that mantle with George H. Pendleton, also of Ohio, Maryland's Benjamin Harris, a two-term lawmaker who was later sentenced by a military court to three years at hard labor for providing shelter to two Confederate soldiers, Daniel W. Voorhees of Indiana, and former New York City Mayor Fernando Wood, a man who not only countenanced secession but suggested at the beginning of the war that New York City should also secede and become a free city—a proposal that simultaneously astonished and amused Lincoln.

Having been censured by the House of Representatives earlier that spring for uttering bitter peace-at-any-price sentiments, Long was initially opposed to McClellan's nomination, believing that the former Union general was the worst possible man to lead the Democrats against Lincoln. Such as they were, the obscure Ohio congressman had led the small but determined anti-McClellan forces at the Democratic convention in Chicago. "What has been the burden of our complaint against Mr. Lincoln and his administration?" he asked the delegates. "He has abridged the freedom of speech, he has arbitrarily arrested citizens and confined them in bastilles, and he has interfered with the freedom of elections." Yet in McClellan, he argued, the Democrats had chosen someone "who has gone farther in all three of these measures than Abraham Lincoln himself." Like other Copperheads, the 47-year-old Long, recognizing the futility of such an effort, decided not to mount an antiwar candidacy on a fourth-party ticket and, like fellow Ohioan Vallandigham, reluctantly threw his support to the Democratic nominee.[20]

20.   Waugh, *Reelecting Lincoln*, pp. 90, 289-290.

In the meantime, John Fremont's third-party candidacy took on even greater importance in August. It was widely believed that the Radical Democratic candidate would siphon enough votes from Lincoln to assure the president's defeat. Meeting at the home of David Dudley Field on August 14, Horace Greeley, Parke Godwin, Henry Winter Davis and twenty other prominent Republicans formed a committee to ask the president to withdraw from the race. Greeley believed that Lincoln was already beaten and should be replaced by Ulysses S. Grant, William Sherman or Benjamin F. Butler, the former military governor of New Orleans. Charles Sumner concurred, but cautioned the group that Lincoln's withdrawal must be "free and voluntary."

Lincoln, of course, had no intention of stepping aside and plans for a second Union Party convention vanished a few weeks later when Sherman's forces captured Atlanta on September 1, effectively crippling the Confederacy's ability to resist the Union army in the lower South. Robert E. Lee's fate had been sealed and Lincoln's popularity skyrocketed overnight. The Union cause had changed dramatically. Following the fall of Atlanta, Admiral David G. Farragut captured Mobile Bay, the hard-drinking Ulysses S. Grant was making considerable progress in Petersburg and General Philip Sheridan demolished Jubal Early's troops in the Shenandoah Valley. Many of Lincoln's radical detractors, including Horace Greeley, suddenly jumped on the president's bandwagon, swelling his campaign coffers and virtually assuring his re-election. Even Chase took to the stump on Lincoln's behalf in mid-September. The only question remaining was the size of his victory.

Fremont, whose candidacy failed to catch fire, officially pulled out of the race on September 22. In truth, the former general had been looking for a way out of the campaign for some time. Earlier attempts to negotiate a deal with McClellan and the Democrats had fallen on deaf ears. In exchange for the resignation of Postmaster General Montgomery Blair, an anathema to Fremont personally and to most Radical Republicans in general, the former explorer—a man who had crossed the continent on five occasions, including three times as an army officer—was able to save face while agreeing to withdraw from the contest. The popular Pathfinder, however, couldn't resist taking a parting shot at Lincoln in the process. Describing his administration as "politically, militarily, and financially a failure," Fremont faded, once and for all, from the public eye.[21]

John Cochrane, Fremont's vice-presidential co-star during their short-lived third-party campaign, also withdrew from the race and unenthusiastically

---

21.   Roseboom, *A History of Presidential Elections*, p. 200.

endorsed the sitting president. With the exception of abolitionist and labor reformer Wendell Phillips and a handful of others, most of Fremont's third-party adventurers followed their leaders back into the Republican fold and reluctantly supported Lincoln's re-election.

Reminding the voters of Lincoln's firmness in the face of secession, the Republicans portrayed the wartime Democrats as a treasonous lot, a misguided party that had been hijacked by fire-eating southerners during the secession crisis and a party that openly cooperated with Copperheads—a term applied indiscriminately to almost any northern Democrat who opposed Lincoln's policies—once the fighting started. They also dramatically reminded voters of the untold suffering of Union soldiers held in captivity in the South. McClellan and the Democrats were doomed.

Carrying twenty-two of the twenty-five states that remained in the Union, Lincoln swamped his Democratic rival by more than 400,000 votes, garnering 2,218,388 popular votes to the Democrat's 1,812,807. Lincoln amassed 212 electoral votes to McClellan's 21. McClellan carried only three states—Delaware, New Jersey and Kentucky. The National Union Party also gave Lincoln a huge majority in the 1864 congressional races, winning 145 seats in the House to the Democrats' 46. The Unionists also held a commanding majority in the U.S. Senate, holding 42 seats to only ten for the vastly outnumbered Democrats.

These were particularly lean years for Americans looking for alternatives to the Democrats and Republicans. In fact, the only person elected to Congress outside the traditional two-party system in 1864 was John R. Kelso, an Independent Radical Republican who defeated his two major party rivals in a hotly-contested House race in Missouri. The 33-year-old Kelso won his seat by narrowly edging out colorful Republican lawmaker Sempronius H. Boyd, a lawyer and former Springfield mayor, in a three-cornered race, garnering 3,841 votes to Boyd's 3,548. Kelso's hapless Democratic opponent was left in the dust, mustering only 400 votes in the three-way race. A graduate of Pleasant Ridge College, Kelso, who had served in the Union army earlier in the war, took his seat with the Union Party when the new Congress organized in March 1865.

The 1864 campaign essentially marked the end of John C. Fremont's public career. Though he lived for more than a quarter of a century following that campaign, the remainder of his life was sadly anticlimactic as he encountered one disappointing setback after another. Though he served briefly as territorial governor of Arizona in the late 1870s and had been mentioned as a possible presidential candidate on the National Union Greenback-Labor ticket as late as 1880, his political and personal fortunes had taken a nosedive. Gold found on his huge

Mariposa estate somehow slipped through his fingers and were it not for his wife's income as an author, he probably would have lived out the remainder of his life in abject poverty.[22]

As in 1864, minor party and independent activity was almost non-existent during the 1866 and 1867 mid-term congressional elections. Samuel F. Cary of Ohio was one of the few exceptions when he was elected to Congress as an independent in a special election in 1867 to fill a vacancy in the state's second congressional district caused by the resignation of Republican Rutherford B. Hayes, who stepped down to run for governor. Another exception was that of Lewis Selye of Rochester, New York. Running as an "Independent Republican," Selye, a 63-year-old newspaper publisher and former county treasurer, upset freshman GOP lawmaker Roswell Hart in the state's twenty-eighth congressional district, defeating the incumbent by more than 2,000 votes. Most independent and minor party hopefuls during this period fared rather poorly at the ballot box, as illustrated by Boston's Patrick R. Guiney, who ran unsuccessfully for Congress on the Workingmen's ticket that same year. Unable to overcome widespread anti-Irish prejudice in that city, the 31-year-old Guiney, an assistant district attorney and celebrated hero of Boston's Irish-Catholic "Fighting Ninth" regiment during the Civil War, barely garnered five percent of the vote against his major-party opponents in a race easily won by wealthy Republican Ginery Twichell, president of the Boston & Worcester Railway. Interestingly, Elizabeth Cady Stanton, the feminist and longtime woman's suffrage advocate, officially polled 24 votes in a bid for a seat in the U.S. House from New York's eighth congressional district. Stanton's 1866 candidacy occurred more than a half century before women were granted the right to vote.

During this period, a number of labor leaders seriously considered the idea of creating a national labor party. In August 1866, the National Labor Union, convening at its first congress in Baltimore, debated the issue of creating a new party independent of the Democrats and Republicans. It was a lively debate. "A new party of the people," declared delegate Edward Schlegel of the German Workingmen's Association of Chicago, "must be in the minority when it first comes into action." That's the way it has to be, he said. "Time and perseverance will give us victory; and if we are not willing to sacrifice time and employ perseverance, we are not deserving of victory." He then reminded the seventy-seven delegates in attendance that if it were not for the Free Soil Party's willingness to tough it out

---

22. Miller, *'If Elected…' Unsuccessful Candidates for the Presidency 1796-1968*, pp. 163-165.

in its early days, the Republican Party never would have become a reality and "Lincoln would never have been elected President of the United States."[23] Despite considerable opposition to the idea of forming a national labor party, the delegates voted to take steps to form such a party but failed to outline the specific steps necessary to bring such a party into existence, focusing, instead, on pushing for the adoption of an eight-hour workday.

'With Malice Toward None'

Coming shortly after the capture of Richmond, news of Robert E. Lee's surrender to General Ulysses S. Grant at the Appomattox Courthouse reached the nation's capital on the evening of April 9. The city—indeed, the entire North—was in a state of bedlam as jubilant citizens rejoiced in the Union victory. "The nation seems delirious with joy," wrote Gideon Welles in his diary. "Guns are firing, bells are ringing, flags flying, men laughing, children cheering, all, all are jubilant."[24]

President Lincoln, however, had little time to celebrate the conclusion of the nation's long national nightmare or to contemplate precisely how his administration would go about restoring the Union. An assassin's bullet made sure of that. Lincoln realized that postwar Reconstruction would be as difficult as anything he had encountered during the seemingly never-ending war. When an overflow crowd gathered outside the White House on the evening of April 10, filling the north portico, the carriageways, and the sidewalks, a dignified Lincoln, who was never particularly fond of giving extemporaneous speeches, refused to exult in victory and offered only a few low-keyed remarks before symbolically turning to a nearby band and asking them to play "Dixie"—one of his favorite tunes.

While no one knows with any certainty precisely how Lincoln would have brought about the reunification of the South, clues as to how the slain president might have handled the difficult issue of Reconstruction in the immediate aftermath of the war can be found in his December 1863 Proclamation of Amnesty and Reconstruction, the guiding principles of which were to accomplish reunion with the South as quickly as possible while ignoring calls for harsh treatment of that region. In his proclamation, Lincoln, while temporarily excluding high-ranking Confederate civil and military authorities from his edict, urged a general

23. Charlotte Todes, *William H. Sylvis and the National Labor Union*, (New York, 1942), pp. 60-61.
24. Oates, *With Malice Toward None*, p. 459.

amnesty for all those who voluntarily agreed to take an oath of loyalty to the United States while pledging to obey all federal laws pertaining to slavery. The sinewy president also laid out a detailed plan to allow the former states of the Confederacy to establish new governments and elect representatives to Congress when one-tenth of the electorate in those states that had participated in the 1860 presidential election had signed such an oath. Though Arkansas, Louisiana and Tennessee quickly complied with the terms, Congress, dominated by vindictive Radical Republicans such as Ohio's Benjamin F. Wade, strenuously objected to Lincoln's extraordinarily lenient proclamation.

Reading by candlelight from a second-story window on the evening of April 11—only seventy-two hours before brooding southern sympathizer John Wilkes Booth fatally wounded him at Ford's Theatre—Lincoln told a crowd of hundreds gathered on the lawn outside the White House that the nation faced a difficult road ahead, one "fraught with great difficulty." Recognizing that there were great differences "as to the mode, manner, and means of reconstruction," it was clear that the president, though perceptibly short on specifics that evening, yearned for a "righteous and speedy peace." Certainly, as biographer David Herbert Donald astutely noted, "Lincoln was not in favor of punishing the Confederates."[25]

Lincoln's death on the morning of April 15 stunned the nation. Although an attempt had been made on Andrew Jackson's life in the U.S. Capitol in 1835—the assailant's gun misfired twice—the notion that a president could be murdered in cold blood was simply unfathomable to nineteenth century Americans. A grieving and deeply shocked nation couldn't believe the news from Washington. The man whose heart had been broken by the most devastating and bloody war in American history had become, tragically, one of its final casualties. "Now," said a teary-eyed Edwin M. Stanton, "he belongs to the ages."[26]

After a heart-wrenching, nightlong vigil at Lincoln's bedside, Vice President Andrew Johnson was sworn in as the nation's seventeenth president on the morning of April 15, 1865. Like some of their beleaguered and bitter archenemies in the old Confederacy, the Radical Republicans spent little time mourning Lincoln's passing. Believing that "there will be no trouble now in running the government," as Ohio Sen. Benjamin F. Wade so tactlessly put it, the Radicals were pleased with the prospect of a Johnson presidency. After all, Johnson, unlike his predecessor, had used strong language in talking of punishing the southern aristocracy for their treasonous acts during the war. His rhetoric, moreover, led them

---

25. Donald, *Lincoln*, p. 582.
26. Ibid., p. 599.

to believe that the new president would be sympathetic to their plans for the harsh treatment of the defeated South. But they were badly mistaken.

As chief executive, Johnson was a fearless yet often reckless combatant for his beliefs and quickly became embroiled in one of the nastiest intra-governmental conflicts in the nation's history. Believing that the South should be treated as a wayward friend rather than a conquered enemy, Lincoln's 55-year-old successor couldn't quite swallow Thaddeus Stevens' belief that the South was some sort of foreign conquest, nor could he agree with Charles Sumner's assertion that the former slave states had committed suicide and deserved whatever fate Congress was willing to impose on them. Like Lincoln, Johnson advocated a "mild" reconstruction program for the South—in effect, turning the southern state governments over to their inhabitants while disenfranchising only the top leaders of the Confederacy. This policy, of course, angered the Radical Republicans in Congress. Led by Ohio's Benjamin Wade, the Radical Republicans, a growing bloc within the National Union Party's fragile coalition in Congress, favored a severe reconstruction policy that included empowering former black slaves and barring most former Confederates and their sympathizers from participating in government and politics.

Determined to carry out Lincoln's moderate plans for Reconstruction, Johnson further angered the Radicals by ending the Union's blockade of southern ports and announcing a general amnesty for Confederate soldiers, excluding high-ranking officers, elected officials and some wealthy southern aristocrats. He also established provisional governments in the former slave-holding states. Less than two months into his presidency, Johnson issued a series of proclamations enabling the former slave states to establish their own civil governments—measures that outraged Ohio's mean-spirited Wade and other leading Radical Republicans. The South, as one might expect, was generally pleased with Johnson's broadminded, non-vengeful policy of Reconstruction and quickly held state elections establishing new state governments. Within five months of Johnson's proclamation, the southern states elected their own governors, legislatures and members of Congress, including the U.S. Senate.

While none of this sat particularly well with the revenge-seeking Radicals, even the National Union Party's moderates were furious when Mississippi voters elected Democrat Benjamin G. Humphreys as governor in 1865. Humphreys, who had been expelled from West Point as a young cadet for participating in a Christmas Eve student riot in 1826, served in the Mississippi legislature in the late 1830s and early 1840s. A one-time anti-secessionist Whig, he served as a brigadier-general in the Confederate army and was later pardoned by President

Johnson. Re-elected in 1868, Mississippi's first post-war governor was forcibly removed from office later that year by the U.S. military.

But the Radical Republicans were most outraged when the Georgia legislature, in a proud yet defiant act, sent Alexander H. Stephens, the brilliant former vice-president of the Confederacy, to the U.S. Senate in 1865. Like Jefferson Davis, the 53-year-old Stephens had been captured by Union forces after the war, spending five months in a Boston prison. As vice president of the Confederacy, Stephens frequently disagreed with Jefferson Davis and led the opposition forces within the southern Republic. One of the South's greatest statesmen, in the early 1850s he thwarted rising secessionist sentiment and convinced southern lawmakers to accept Henry Clay's "Great Compromise." He later threw his support to the fledgling Constitutional Union Party in 1860 in a last-ditch effort to preserve the Union. Though vilified by the Radical Republicans, Stephens urged restraint and self-discipline upon the South during the period of Reconstruction. The Florida legislature followed suit, electing 31-year-old Wilkinson Call, a lawyer and ardent ex-Confederate, to the U.S. Senate. Congress, of course, refused to seat Stephens and Call and others elected from the former rebel states. It wasn't until 1868—and, in some cases, later than that—that the states in the Deep South were again represented in both houses of Congress.

The Radicals shouldn't have been surprised by the results of the post-war elections in the South. For that generation and for generations to come, most southerners refused to allow the memory of its heroic struggle fade away. Despite losing the war, its soldiers had fought valiantly and the South wasn't about to turn its back on those who had been in the frontlines—soldiers and politicians alike.

Perhaps even more unsettling to the Radicals than the election of so many ex-Confederates to Congress in 1865 was the fact that almost all of them had aligned themselves with the Democrats—including many former Whigs—thereby jeopardizing Republican control of the national legislature. Even more threatening to them was the fact that, with ratification of the Thirteenth Amendment, all of the former slaves in the South would now be counted in apportioning representation in the House of Representatives. Prior to its ratification, only three-fifths of the slave population had been counted for the purposes of congressional apportionment. In all likelihood, one could argue, Republican opposition to Johnson's Reconstruction program were as much the result of partisan political considerations as they were of any genuine fears that freed blacks would be mistreated under the rule of ex-Confederate officials.

But the Radicals had some legitimate reasons to be concerned with the return to power of so many former Confederates. Although they had grudgingly enforced the Thirteenth Amendment banning slavery, the newly elected southern legislatures wasted little time in approving the infamous "Black Codes," tough measures designed to keep African-Americans in their place. The toughest measures were originally enacted in Mississippi and South Carolina, stipulating that freed people could only rent in rural areas, thereby keeping former slaves on the plantations. In varying degree, the codes were later passed in other southern states. Among other things, these laws required blacks to sign annual employment contracts each January. Anyone who quit before their contract had expired forfeited any wages earned up to that point and were subject to arrest on vagrancy charges, punishable by fines, forced labor and whippings. The Black Codes also prohibited former slaves from making "insulting" comments to whites, forced young black mothers to return to the cotton fields, and, as preposterous as it sounds, even tried to regulate the sexual behavior of the new freedmen.

Enacted under Johnson's Reconstruction policy of administering a soft peace in the South, the Black Codes inflamed northern Radical Republicans who responded by passing the Civil Rights Act of 1866 to protect blacks in that region, incorporating this much-needed protection in the Constitution with the adoption of the Fourteenth Amendment. In an attempt to thwart the mean-spirited Radical Republicans from imposing even harsher treatment on the South, President Johnson vetoed 29 of their measures, 15 of which were overridden. Among those laws passed over his veto were the Freedmen's Bureau Act, which extended the life of the bureau providing education, medical care, land and jobs to thousands of former slaves; voting rights for African-Americans in the District of Columbia; and a series of Reconstruction measures that divided the South into five military districts, under the control of federal troops, and extended voting rights to African-Americans while disenfranchising countless white voters. Under these Radical Republican-sponsored measures, elected officials in the South were required to take an "ironclad oath" swearing that they had never knowingly collaborated with the Confederacy—thereby effectively eliminating the majority of the region's pre-war politicians from holding public office. As a precondition for reentering the Union, the southern states were also required to ratify the Fourteenth Amendment and adopt new state constitutions granting blacks the right to vote—an idea adamantly opposed by most southern whites.

As military governments replaced the civil governments set up by southern Democrats and as "Carpetbaggers," freed slaves and "scalawags"—those white southerners who joined forces with them—seized control of southern state legislatures, most whites in the South bitterly denounced Radical Reconstruction, resulting in the founding of the Ku Klux Klan in Pulaski, Tennessee, in 1866, a white supremacy organization ostensibly dedicated to resisting Reconstruction through random acts of terrorism.

Meanwhile, Johnson, a fearless and sometimes reckless fighter for what he believed in and whose mild Reconstruction policies had been sharply rebuked in the 1866 mid-term congressional elections, continued to spar with the Radical Republicans. The Radicals, as historian Eugene H. Roseboom noted, had established a virtual congressional oligarchy, "obsessed with a spirit of vengeance and a lust for power," seizing control of the federal government and establishing what amounted to "a party dictatorship."[27]

The Radicals detested Johnson and a House committee searched eagerly for grounds for impeachment, but moderate Republicans refused to go along when Radical Republican James M. Ashley, a one-time Free Soiler from Ohio, moved to impeach the president on a number of trumped up charges, including Johnson's alleged involvement in Lincoln's assassination and his purported sale of pardons.[28] Despite this setback, the Radicals persisted and finally got their chance when Johnson vetoed the Tenure of Office Act, a measure prohibiting the president from removing certain public officials from office without the advice and consent of the Senate. His veto was overridden. In February 1868, Johnson further infuriated the Radicals by firing Secretary of War Edwin M. Stanton, a Radical Republican who had been deliberately undermining his Reconstruction policies, and seeking to replace him with Ulysses S. Grant. While Stanton remained barricaded in his office surrounded by guards, the House responded quickly, voting 126-47 on February 24 to impeach Johnson for "high crimes and misdemeanors."

In all, the House approved eleven articles of impeachment, most of them dealing with Johnson's alleged violation of the Tenure of Office Act. With Chief Justice Salmon P. Chase presiding over his Senate trial, Johnson survived impeachment by a single vote on two occasions, largely the result of seven courageous Republicans, including Maine's William Pitt Fessenden, who risked their political careers by joining the Democrats in voting to exonerate the embattled chief executive. In doing so, they kept the vindictive Benjamin F. Wade of Ohio, the Radical Republican president pro tempore of the Senate—and thus next in line for the presidency—out of the White House. Many of those who voted to

---

27.   Roseboom, *A History of Presidential Elections*, pp. 209-210.
28.   Bailyn, *et al.*, *The Great Republic*, p. 542.

exonerate Johnson believed he was guilty of the charges, but couldn't stomach the idea of the 67-year-old Wade succeeding Johnson as president. A staunch supporter of women's suffrage and trade unionism, the rough and tumble Wade was so sure that Johnson would be convicted that he had already begun making his cabinet selections.

Seeking the Democratic presidential nomination in 1868, Johnson was deeply disappointed when the Democrats turned to Horatio Seymour on the twenty-second ballot at their national convention in New York's sparkling new Tammany Hall. Though overlooking the man in the White House, the Democrats adopted a platform that would have been ideally suited for the beleaguered president, including a call for amnesty for all former Confederates and a pledge to leave it up to the individual southern states to decide whether or not to grant suffrage to their black citizens. The Democrats, in sharp contrast to the party of Lincoln, also favored dismantling the controversial Freedmen's Bureau and other unpopular vestiges of Radical Reconstruction.

Although there had been some talk earlier that year of a possible independent labor party headed by Ohio congressman Samuel F. Cary, a 54-year-old former Union army general from Cincinnati, and the National Labor Union's William H. Sylvis as his vice-presidential running mate, a third-party ticket never materialized.[29] As such, the 1868 presidential election boiled down to a two-way race between Republican Ulysses S. Grant and Democrat Horatio Seymour, with the former prevailing by a margin of more than 309,000 popular votes.

The Republicans, meanwhile, continued to maintain their large majorities in Congress, holding 173 seats in the House of Representatives to 70 for the Democrats while claiming 61 seats in the U.S. Senate to only eleven for the hapless Democrats. Despite spirited independent campaigns conducted by Richard H. Dana, Jr., in Massachusetts, Minnesota's Ignatius Donnelly, New York's inimitable George F. Train and a handful of others, there were no independents elected to the 41st Congress.[30]

A distinguished Cambridge lawyer and best-selling author of *Two Years Before the Mast*, Dana had challenged Republican Benjamin F. Butler, a favorite of the

---

29. Todes, *William H. Sylvis and the National Labor Union*, p. 66. Sylvis had also been mentioned as a possible vice-presidential candidate on a Democratic ticket headed by reformer George H. Pendleton of Ohio, a leader of the party's pre-Civil War peace wing, and on a Republican ticket led by Salmon P. Chase, Secretary of the Treasury in the Lincoln administration. The longtime labor leader, however, disavowed any interest in seeking elective office, preferring to focus his time and energy on obtaining a shorter workday for American workers.

Radicals, in his bid for a second term from the fifth congressional district in Massachusetts. Dana, whose campaign was amply financed by banking and business interests, including the state's affluent cotton mill owners, ran as an "Independent Republican" in his bid to unseat the stormy and controversial Civil War general. A fascinating figure, the 53-year-old Harvard-educated lawyer, world traveler, and state legislator was less known for his role in founding the Free Soil Party in 1848 than for his later role as one of the government lawyers in the widely-watched treason trial of Confederate President Jefferson Davis twenty years later. An unabashed opponent of slavery, Dana was once severely assaulted on a Boston street while representing several fugitive slaves against federal authorities who sought to have them returned to their owners in the South. During the Civil War, he served as a U.S. attorney in Massachusetts and helped persuade the Supreme Court that the United States government had a right to establish a blockade of Confederate ports and to seize foreign vessels attempting to thwart the blockade. In 1876, President Grant nominated Dana as ambassador to Great Britain, but the U.S. Senate refused to confirm him, partly because Grant had failed to consult with the Republican leadership beforehand and partly due to the fact that the former Harvard instructor had been sued for plagiarism in connection with editing a legal textbook—a charge initially brought by Butler.[31]

A conservative aristocrat of Federalist heredity who harbored a visceral hatred for Butler, the 51-year-old Dana, a leading authority on maritime law, claimed during the 1868 congressional campaign that he was entitled to the support of the district's Republican voters because he had been a member of that party longer than his opponent, prompting a witty response from the general. "Judas was an older disciple than Paul, and for a time, while Paul persecuted the Christians, might have thought himself a better" disciple, Butler retorted, "but Dana should remember what happened to Judas." Secretly supported by Republican presidential standard-bearer Ulysses S. Grant and by the Republican National Committee, which paid General Judson Kilpatrick $200 a day to attack Butler's military record, Dana stumped vigorously in the district's working-class neigh-

---

30. Rebuffed by his own party, Donnelly was forced to seek re-election as an Independent Republican, garnering 33% of the vote while losing a three-cornered race to Democrat Eugene M. Wilson. See Martin Ridge, *Ignatius Donnelly: Portrait of a Politician* (St. Paul, 1962), pp. 115-122. The colorful George F. Train, running as an Independent Democrat, polled eleven percent of the vote in New York's fifth congressional district.

31. Howard P. Nash, Jr., *Stormy Petrel: The Life and Times of General Benjamin F. Butler 1818-1893* (Cranbury, N.J., 1969), p. 257.

borhoods, but committed a major *faux pas* when he told a predominately blue-collar audience that, as a former sailor, he, too, had once been "as dirty as any of you." Proving to be an inept campaigner, Dana garnered less than ten percent of the vote while the colorful Butler—more than doubling the vote of his Democratic challenger Judge Otis P. Lord, who waged an equally unimaginative and clumsy campaign—easily won a second term with nearly 66% of the vote.[32]

---

32. Ibid., pp. 247-249; Dick Nolan, *Benjamin Franklin Butler: The Damnedest Yankee* (Novato, CA, 1991), p. 332; Robert S. Holzman, *Stormy Ben Butler* (New York, 1954), p. 174, 207; William B. Hesseltine, *Ulysses S. Grant* (New York, 1935), p. 135.

11

The Liberal Republican Movement

❖

Reformers Versus Politicians

The 1872 presidential election marked the first of only two occasions in American history when a third party offered the most serious challenge to one of the country's two major parties. The other occasion, of course, was in 1912 when the Bull Moose Party's Teddy Roosevelt snorted and thundered against his Republican successor William H. Taft. In both instances, dissident members of the party in power—the Republicans—were responsible for creating the third-party movement that threatened the country's two major parties. The most significant difference between the Liberal Republicans of 1872 and Roosevelt's Progressive Party four decades later was that the Democrats, sensing the futility of trying to unseat the popular Ulysses S. Grant in a three-cornered race, took the unprecedented step of endorsing the Liberal Republican nominees rather than field a ticket of their own.

In May of 1872, a group of Republicans fed up with the widespread corruption in Ulysses S. Grant's administration and at odds with the president's harsh reconstruction policies in the South, met in Cincinnati to form a third party and nominate a rival ticket. To these insurgent Republicans, the Hero of Appomattox was now "Useless Grant."

Though personally incorruptible, Grant proved beyond any doubt that there was absolutely no correlation between one's competency on the battlefield and one's ability to govern a nation. In short, the former Union army general presided over one of the most corrupt and inept administrations in the country's history.

Upon taking office, Grant, who had failed in farming, real estate and as a U.S. Customs clerk before going to work in his father's leather goods store, assembled one of the least impressive and undistinguished administrations in U.S. history. His never-ending cabinet appointments even drew criticism from fellow Republicans. Grant's first Secretary of State, Elihu B. Washburne, though eminently qualified, resigned after only eleven days in office to become minister to France. His first choice for Secretary of the Treasury, wealthy campaign contributor Alexander T. Stewart, was disqualified due to an obscure conflict-of-interest law and was quickly replaced by the reticent George S. Boutwell of Massachusetts, a man of considerable experience and ability, who served for four years. But William A. Richardson, Boutwell's inept successor, was responsible for the misdeeds of one of the Treasury's special agents who inappropriately retained a staggering 50%—or $213,500—in delinquent taxes that he collected.

Things only got worse as the president, in a version of musical chairs, replaced one cabinet member after another. He named General John Schofield as Secretary of War, but changed his mind a week later and appointed General John A. Rawlins, an old war buddy, to fill the post. Rawlins died of tuberculosis six months later. William T. Sherman, Rawlins' replacement, lasted only a month and was replaced by William W. Belknap who resigned in 1876 rather than face impeachment for accepting bribes from traders at Indian posts. While awaiting Senate confirmation for chief justice of the Supreme Court, it was revealed that former Sen. George H. Williams of Oregon had suppressed an investigation of election fraud in his home state. An embarrassed Grant immediately withdrew his nomination. Adolph Borie, a wealthy Philadelphia businessman with no previous military experience, was named Secretary of the Navy, but resigned after only three months in office, complaining that he was only a "figurehead." The Navy Department, of course, was rampant with corruption. Political favoritism ruled everything from the hiring of workers in the nation's shipyards to awarding building contracts for new ships. Borie's successor was George M. Robeson of New Jersey, a man whose tenure was punctuated by a congressional investigation into charges of waste and extravagance. Grant's abysmal lack of judgment spilled over into other non-cabinet appointments, as illustrated by his nomination of a completely unqualified livery stable supervisor as minister to Belgium.

Scandal after scandal rocked Grant's years in the White House. The era of infamy began on Black Friday, the day marking the beginning of the notorious Gold Panic of 1869, when speculators Jay Gould and James Fisk tried to corner the gold market with the help of Grant's unscrupulous brother-in-law, 67-year-old Abel R. Corbin, who served as "jackal for this pair of lions." The two speculators paid the president's sleazy brother-in-law a tidy sum to use his influence in the White House to drive the price of gold up from $140 to $163.50 in a matter of only four days. Grant himself became an unwitting accomplice in their scheme when he attended a yachting party aboard one of Fisk's steamers, thus fueling speculation that the president was in their corner. During their short cruise on Fisk's Fall River line, Gould and the wily Fisk subtly pried information from Grant, who had consumed copious amounts of champagne and brandy, and were able to convince him not to sell off any more government-held gold. Grant later realized that he had been duped and ordered Secretary Boutwell to sell off $4 million in federal gold reserves on September 24—Black Friday. This ignited panic selling and the price of gold plummeted. Countless investors lost everything, several businesses were ruined and more the a few men took their own lives in its aftermath.

A congressional investigation into the Gold Panic exonerated Grant, but raised serious questions about his wife's involvement. During the investigation, Fisk contended that $500,000, or a third of the $1.5 million account set up for Corbin, was actually earmarked for First Lady Julie Grant. The investigation into charges of possible impropriety on the part of First Lady was later dropped by chivalrous congressmen at Grant's insistence, but charges against others in his administration, most notably that of the assistant Treasurer General, were pursued with vigor. Ironically, Rep. James A. Garfield of Ohio, who was later implicated in the Credit Mobilier affair, led the congressional investigation into the gold plundering scandal.

Corruption abounded. The Treasury Department, for instance, was simply infested with unscrupulous employees, especially among customhouse officers who routinely preyed on importers. The worst case was in New York where merchants who failed to make payoffs to customs officers had their shipments impeded. Those who refused to give in to the plunderers often had their shipments delayed and were subjected to tedious and time-consuming inspections. Crates and boxes that were not immediately removed from the docks were stored at exorbitant rates.

Other scandals followed, including the infamous "Whiskey Ring," in which hundreds of distillers and federal officials were accused of conspiring to pocket millions of dollars in liquor taxes. This scandal, which was uncovered by Treasury Secretary Benjamin H. Bristow in 1875, was probably the most embarrassing of the many that plagued the Grant administration, implicating the president's old friend John McDonald, head of the Internal Revenue Bureau in St. Louis. McDonald had once given Grant an expensive team of horses. Moreover, Grant's personal secretary was charged with taking a bribe from McDonald to put a halt to the investigation. As revelation after revelation of wrongdoing unfolded, Grant, who had dragged his feet at first, called for swift retribution, opposing all grants of immunity in exchange for testimony. "Let no guilty man escape," he insisted. McDonald was eventually found guilty and was sent to jail but Grant's personal secretary, Orville E. Babcock, was spared when the president intervened on his behalf. Reports also surfaced that Grant's oldest son, Frederick, a graduate of West Point, and the president's brother, Orvil Grant, were also somehow involved in the scandal, but nothing ever came of those stories.

Next came the notorious Credit Mobilier scandal, a story that was initially broke by the *New York Sun* in the heat of the 1872 presidential campaign. Executives of the Credit Mobilier holding company, it seems, had been skimming huge profits in the federally subsidized construction of the Union Pacific Railroad. In an effort to stave off a major congressional investigation into their corrupt practices, major stockholders in the Credit Mobilier of America had either given or sold shares at a deep discount to selected members of Congress. The scandal tarred several prominent Gilded Age politicians, not the least of whom included James G. Blaine of Maine, outgoing Vice President Schuyler Colfax and his successor, longtime Sen. Henry Wilson of Massachusetts. Rep. James A. Garfield, who was subsequently elected president in 1880, was also implicated in the scandal. Two members of the House were ultimately censured, including Republican Oakes Ames, a wealthy Massachusetts manufacturer who served as a kind of front man for Credit Mobilier during the scandal.

Later, of course, came the juicy Belknap Scandal, perhaps the most intriguing of all, involving high society, graft, rumors of suicide and impeachment proceedings. In that scandal, Secretary of War William W. Belknap was unanimously impeached by the House for allegedly accepting a $24,450 bribe in exchange for a lucrative trading post franchise at Fort Sill. The Indian traders involved in the bribe were given exclusive franchise to sell goods to Indians and soldiers at frontier posts. Belknap resigned rather than face trial. Later, his friends insisted that Belknap's wife had taken the bribe without his knowledge.

The scandals aside, Grant had deeply disappointed the nation's reformers when he failed to mention civil service reform in his first message to Congress in 1869, prompting the always quotable Henry Adams, the son of Lincoln's minister to Great Britain and the grandson and great-grandson of Presidents John Adams and John Quincy Adams who watched presidents come and go beneath the perch of his Lafayette Square window behind the White House, to remark that Grant was ushering in "a reign of western mediocrity."[1]

"Like all parties that have an undisturbed power for a long time," declared Sen. James Grimes of Iowa, a lifelong Republican and one of those who helped to found the Liberal Republican movement, the party had lost its way. It was "going to the dogs," he claimed. It was now the most "corrupt and debauched political party that has ever existed."[2] Scores of Republicans across the country agreed. There was little question that the Republican insurgents had a real issue in 1872, but given the vast patronage at his disposal, Grant controlled the Republican machinery and his nomination to a second term was all but certain. What the reformers needed was a party of their own.

Founded in 1870, the Liberal Republican Party was the brainchild of German-born Missouri Senator Carl Schurz. Schurz, who migrated to the United States after taking part as a student in the German revolution of 1848, was one of the most intriguing political figures in American history. Regarded as a "red Republican" because of his role in the revolution, Schurz was an ardent foe of slavery and had campaigned vigorously for Fremont and Lincoln in 1856 and 1860, respectively. The victorious Lincoln rewarded him with an appointment as minister to Spain in 1861. In 1865, after conducting an inspection of the South at President Andrew Johnson's request, Schurz recommended that voting rights be extended to blacks—a suggestion that wasn't exactly well received, especially in the former slaveholding states. The Missourian was later elected to the U.S. Senate, but soon split with Grant over the issue of corruption.

Under Schurz's leadership, a Liberal Republican-Democratic fusion ticket threw out the ruling Republican establishment in Missouri with the election of former Democratic Senator Benjamin Gratz Brown as governor in 1870. Brown, a lawyer and former newspaper editor who once fought a duel in defense of one of his editorials, was a veteran of the Free Soil movement and had advocated voting rights for women in the District of Columbia as early as 1866. In the 1870 gubernatorial campaign, Brown faced incumbent Gov. Joseph W. McClurg, a Radical Republican who had served three terms in the U.S. House, winning his first election on an Emancipationist ticket. McClurg was a vocal defender of the carpetbaggers—northerners who moved to the South after the Civil War to invest in abandoned or repossessed Confederate lands and who eventually won the lion's share of the political offices in that region. The former Union army officer, wrote the *St. Louis Dispatch*, embodied "all that is narrow, bigoted,

---

1.   Bailyn, *et al.*, *The Great Republic*, p. 573.
2.   Samuel Eliot Morison and Henry Steele Commager, *The Growth of the American Republic*, 2 vols. (New York, 1962), Vol. II, p. 69.

revengeful, and ignorant in the Radical [Republican] Party." Despite all the resources the Grant administration could muster on his behalf, McClurg went down to defeat, losing to Brown by more than 40,000 votes. Liberal Republican appeals to German-American voters in St. Louis and promises to enfranchise ex-Confederate Democrats proved too much for the Republicans. Moreover, McClurg's hateful views toward the South drove thousands of Missouri voters into the Democratic column for the next three decades and, in no small measure, helped to give birth to the Liberal Republican Party.

Following on Brown's electoral success, the Missouri reformers prepared to take their party national. Fed up with the corruption in the Grant administration, the state's Liberal Republicans met in Jefferson City on January 24, 1872, and formed a new party dedicated to reconciliation with the South, tariff reduction and civil service reform. The Missourians concluded with a call for a national convention to be held in Cincinnati, the "Queen City of the Ohio," on May 1, 1872. It was, as Schurz later recalled, "moving day." The call for a new party was met with sporadic enthusiasm in parts of the West and South and with guarded curiosity, if not suspicion, in the East.

Nationally, the seeds were being sewn for a Liberal Republican Party under the auspices of the Taxpayer's Union, a low-tariff lobby founded in 1871. It was through this organization that talk of a national third party began to percolate. When Grant stumbled over Santo Domingo, an open rebellion within the Republican ranks ensued, led by men like Schurz and Charles Sumner, the deposed chairman of the Senate Foreign Relations Committee. Third party sentiment boiled over when these men realized that Grant's re-nomination was inevitable.

It was no secret that Schurz himself was interested in the new party's presidential nomination, but his foreign birth prevented such a candidacy. As a consolation prize of sorts, the reformers named the Missouri lawmaker as the convention's chairman. There were plenty of other presidential hopefuls, however, not the least of whom was 64-year-old Charles Francis Adams, the "Great Iceberg," whose integrity and extraordinary talent was offset by his aloof, if not cold, demeanor. Adams, who had been the Free Soil Party's vice-presidential nominee almost a quarter of a century earlier, had retired from public life in 1868. His long record of public service included a stint as Lincoln's ambassador to England, arriving in that country just as it was announcing its support of the Confederacy in the Civil War.

Supreme Court Justice David Davis, who had been nominated by the tiny Labor Reform Party several months earlier, also threw his hat into the ring and was widely regarded as an almost prohibitive favorite. Unlike some of his potential rivals, the heavy-set jurist had plenty of money to spend on the race. Three-term Senator Lyman Trumbull of Illinois also entered the race. The 58-year-old Trumbull had served as chairman of the Judiciary Committee for ten years and was responsible for framing the historic thirteenth amendment, as well as the landmark Civil Rights Act of 1866. He earned the wrath of the Radical Republicans by casting one of the seven Republican votes that spared Andrew Johnson from conviction during the president's impeachment trial in 1868. Neither a radical nor a reformer, Trumbull was nevertheless acceptable to a large number of Liberal Republicans. His candidacy, however, was severely hampered by the fact that he had to compete with Davis for support from the large Illinois delegation. His less than magnetic personality and his disdain for pressing the flesh also hindered his prospects for the nomination.

Salmon P. Chase, the nineteenth century version of Minnesota's Harold E. Stassen forever chasing the elusive brass ring, also caught the presidential bug but was essentially eliminated from serious contention due to declining health. Aside from Adams, the Supreme Court chief justice was probably the ablest candidate in the field. Chase, whose presidential ambitions had been shattered forever during his ill-fated bid to unseat Lincoln in 1864, had suffered a serious stroke in 1870, leaving his speech a bit slurred and unable to write as effectively as he had in the past. Yet refusing to give up the ghost, the former Ohio governor more or less acquiesced to his supporters—a group that included such luminaries as New York's John Van Buren, longtime editor Murat Halstead, and former Cincinnati congressman Alexander Long—telling them that if they believed his "nomination will promote the interests of the country, I shall not refuse the use of my name." Chase's daughter Kate, still longing to play hostess in the White House, dutifully arranged an elaborate party in her father's honor in Washington on the eve of the Liberal Republican convention, ostensibly to show how much her father's health had improved since his devastating stroke a few years earlier. The *New York World* noted that Chase looked "so much his old self" and the *New York Herald*, a paper that supported him during his failed bid for the Democratic presidential nomination in 1868, reported that Chase seemed "to have discovered the fountain of youth," appearing as robust and lucid as he was ten years earlier.[3]

Yet not everyone was sold on the hardy perennial. Party founder Carl Schurz, who had always been suspicious of Chase's motives, cruelly commented that his "futile efforts to appear youthfully vigorous and agile were pathetically evident."[4]

---

3.   Frederick J. Blue, *Salmon P. Chase: A Life in Politics* (Kent, OH, 1987), pp. 316-319.

Most Liberal Republican delegates apparently agreed as Chase's candidacy stalled at the starting gate. Tragically, the 65-year-old ex-Liberty and Free Soil Party leader died less than a year after the 1872 presidential election.

Massachusetts Sen. Charles Sumner, a founder of the Free Soil Party, was also in the hunt. Sumner, who represented two different third parties in the U.S. Senate over a period of more than two decades—serving as a Free Soiler from 1851-55 and later as a Liberal Republican in 1873-74—was considered Grant's greatest nemesis. As chairman of the Senate Foreign Relations Committee, the 61-year-old Harvard-educated lawyer tried to control U.S. foreign policy, blaming Great Britain for prolonging the Civil War by giving aid and comfort to the Confederacy. Having made a complete break with Grant over the administration's treaty to annex the Dominican Republic, the fiery Sumner was removed from his powerful chairmanship in 1871. Sumner, whose loyalty to the Liberal Republican movement was tenuous at best, was once regarded as the most prominent figure in the Republican Party, if not in all of American politics. However, he was considered too self-righteous and abrasive and was not seriously considered by the delegates in Cincinnati. Despite his declining health, however, the former Harvard Law School lecturer was nominated for governor of Massachusetts on the Liberal Republican ticket later that year, but declined, opting instead to remain in the U.S. Senate where he continued to serve until his death in March 1874.

A number of other candidates were also interested in the party's presidential nomination, including Missouri Gov. Ben Gratz Brown, New Jersey Gov. Joel Parker, the reluctant vice-presidential nominee of the upstart Labor Reform Party, Gov. John MacAuley Palmer of Illinois and Andrew G. Curtin, a former governor of Pennsylvania. The 55-year-old Curtin nearly became Grant's vice-presidential running mate four years earlier. Former Ohio Gov. Jacob D. Cox, who once tried to segregate his state's African-American population, was also in the race. Cox had served as Grant's first Secretary of the Interior, a post in which he successfully resisted patronage and rewarded merit. He resigned from the cabinet over a policy dispute with Grant in 1870. The 43-year-old Cox had warned the Liberal Republicans that ambiguities on the issues "are the life of decaying parties, but the death of new ones."

Also seeking the nomination was dark-horse candidate Horace Greeley, the colorful yet highly controversial editor of the *New York Tribune*. Greeley was initially flattered when well-known journalist Alexander K. McClure, who had been Lincoln's most trusted advisor in Pennsylvania, suggested his name as a possible

---

4. Ibid., p. 317.

vice-presidential candidate on a ticket headed by Justice David Davis. Incidentally, McClure, who was elected to the Pennsylvania State Senate as a "Citizens Party" candidate later that same year—the only independent in the Pennsylvania Senate—supported Davis on all six ballots at the Liberal Republican convention. For his part, Greeley was slow in coming around to the third-party movement. It wasn't until March 20, 1872, that he finally issued a statement fully endorsing the Liberal Republican Party.

From this crowded field only Adams and Chase were given a realistic chance of defeating Grant. Nobody really took Greeley seriously. William Larimer, a one-time abolitionist and former state senator from Kansas, was the first to suggest the journalist's name as a presidential possibility. Among those who were soon echoing Larimer's suggestion was the fiery and highly erratic Cassius M. Clay of Kentucky, an antislavery crusader and distant relative of the late Henry Clay. Clay, who once ran for governor of Kentucky on an "Anti-Slavery" third-party ticket, was angry with the president for removing him from his diplomatic post in Russia. Theodore Tilton, the well-known editor of the *Independent*, also championed Greeley's long-shot candidacy.

Born in Amherst, New Hampshire, of English and Scotch-Irish parents, Greeley, who was something of a child prodigy, learned to read at the age of three and was apprenticed as a printer while in his early teens. Moving to New York City, he later became the founding editor and publisher of the *New Yorker* and the prestigious and influential *New York Tribune*, from whose pages he championed women's rights, favored land reform and labor, opposed slavery, criticized the war with Mexico and denounced big business. He was also a sharp critic of the death penalty and dabbled in the causes of utopian Fourierism—socialist settlements established by followers of French social philosopher Charles Fourier—and vegetarianism. He was also an unabashed protectionist. "If I were king of this country," he declared in 1870, "I would put a duty of $100 a ton on pig-iron and a proportionate duty on everything else that can be produced in America."[5] An enthusiastic American expansionist, Greeley is perhaps best remembered for his advice—"Go West, young man, and grow up with the country."

Evincing a crusading journalist's interest in politics, Greeley had served one term in Congress as a Whig in the late 1840s, briefly filling a vacancy.[6] In Congress, Greeley wasted little time scouring House members for alleged abuses,

---

5. Miller, *'If Elected…' Unsuccessful Candidates for the Presidency 1796-1968*, p. 204.
6. The vacancy occurred when the Whig Party's James Monroe successfully challenged the election of Democrat David S. Jackson in the 1846 congressional election.

including the prevalent practice of padding one's travel expenses. Even Honest Abe, a fellow Whig, found himself a target of one of Greeley's assaults. Lincoln, it seems, had charged the government for more than 1,600 miles in travel costs whereas the distance between Washington and Lincoln's home in Springfield, Illinois, was less than half that distance. The journalist-turned-politician said that Lincoln collected $676.80 in excess mileage. "The usually traveled route for a great many members of the last Congress was an exceedingly crooked one," Greeley quipped, "even for politicians." Greeley's criticism of his House colleagues won him few friends. "I have divided the House into two parties," he said, "one that would like to see me extinguished, and the other is one that wouldn't be satisfied without a hand in doing it."[7]

As publisher of the enormously influential *New York Tribune*, the 61-year-old Greeley employed a wide range of writers, including none other than Karl Marx, the father of socialism, who served as the *Tribune's* chief European correspondent during the 1850s. Greeley, too, had been one of the founders of the Republican Party in the 1850s and from the pages of his *New York Tribune* had popularized the Republican slogan, "Vote yourself a farm." He also played a critical role in the election of House Speaker Nathaniel P. Banks of Massachusetts in 1856. Banks, of course, was the only third-party Speaker of the House or Representatives in American history. During that marathon process, Greeley personally worked the cloakroom in search of votes for his compromise candidate and was twice physically assaulted by Rep. Albert Rust, a burly Arkansas Democrat, and was threatened with bodily harm by several other congressmen from slaveholding states. The intrepid journalist refused to back down and his persistence eventually enabled the Know-Nothing and Republican antislavery forces to gain control of the House under Speaker Banks.

Greeley's influence as a writer and lecturer waned somewhat after the war, but he was still capable, on occasion, of writing with his old fire, in what the erudite Edwin L. Godkin described as "an English style, which, for vigor, terseness, clearness, and simplicity, has never been surpassed."

A radical abolitionist leader of New York's Republican Party, Greeley was cool to Lincoln's re-election bid in 1864 and vigorously promoted John C. Fremont's short-lived third party candidacy. Fearing a Copperhead victory and a premature end to the war, the New York journalist later regretted his actions and eventually endorsed Lincoln, saying that he saw "no difference between their triumph [the

---

7.   Glyndon G. Van Deusen, *Horace Greeley: Nineteenth Century Crusader* (New York, 1964), p. 127.

Copperheads] and that of the outright rebels." At the close of the war, Greeley called for magnanimity on the part of the North, urging amnesty for the ex-Confederates and suffrage for the former slaves. It was a genuine appeal to both sections of the country, an effort to "clasp hands across the bloody chasm," as he later described it. He infuriated many northerners a few years later when he posted bail for the imprisoned Jefferson Davis. Greeley was also one of the few who came to the aid of destitute First Lady Mary Todd Lincoln following the president's assassination, imploring his readers to donate to "the late President's grieving widow and fatherless sons." Greeley enthusiastically supported Grant against Democrat Horatio Seymour in 1868, but soured on the incompetent former Union army general shortly after he took office.

There is little question that Greeley's awkward appearance militated against him. His metal-rimmed spectacles perched on the small nose of his round, whiskered face and the long silver locks flowing from the back of his balding head, made him an easy target of cartoonists. The most vicious of these was penned by the talented Thomas Nast, a Grant partisan, who savagely portrayed the eccentric journalist in a cartoon shaking hands with John Wilkes Booth while standing over Lincoln's grave.[8]

After leaving his full-time duties at the *Tribune* in December 1868, Greeley embarked on an extensive lecture tour. One of his stops was in Montreal, Canada, where he spoke on the subject of "presidentitis"—a condition that he apparently failed to recognize in his own hero, Henry Clay, who reached for the glittering prize no fewer than five times between 1824 and 1848. Daniel Webster, he told a Quebec audience, was a great moral leader but he failed in one important respect—"he wanted to be President and I don't." Chief Justice Salmon P. Chase, he said, made the same mistake. "General Lewis Cass died at about 82 and up to the day of his death he wanted to be President," Greeley continued. Without mentioning Clay, Greeley said that once one catches the disease, "he lives and dies in the delusion." Grant, he concluded, had been elected precisely because he did not long for the office of the presidency.

Greeley, of course, was an ambitious man himself and possessed a never-ending lust for public office. He would have welcomed re-election to Congress in 1850 and was willing to stoop for his party's nomination for lieutenant governor of New York four years later. He ran unsuccessfully for William Seward's seat in the U.S. Senate in 1861 and lost a second bid for the state's other Senate seat two years later. A perennial candidate of sorts, Greeley also waged unsuccessful cam-

---

8.   Ibid., p. 414.

paigns for Congress in 1868 and 1870, interspersed by a doomed bid for the state comptrollership in 1869. Needless to say, Greeley's numerous campaigns for public office by no means enhanced his prestige.

As such, nobody really gave Greeley much of a chance at the Liberal Republican convention, including the journalist himself. For all his intelligence, idealism and journalistic wit, he was regarded as too erratic, ill tempered and thoroughly lacking in political savvy to be taken seriously. His fortunes improved dramatically, however, when his entire New York delegation, overcoming a spirited challenge from ardent free traders, was seated despite the fact that the convention had rejected to so-called unit rule.

The Liberal Republican convention opened at Cincinnati's great Music Hall on May 1. Stanley Matthews, a former judge and one-time editor of the antislavery *Cincinnati Herald*, served as temporary chairman and Missouri's Carl Schurz was named permanent chairman. The convention hall was packed with anti-Grant politicians and other reform-minded Republicans. There were some Democrats, too, including 59-year-old John Cochrane, the former New York attorney general who had served briefly as John C. Fremont's vice-presidential running mate on the aborted Independent Republican ticket in 1864. Cochrane had turned down President Grant's offer of an ambassadorship to Uruguay and Paraguay three years earlier.

"Parties cannot live on their reputations," said Matthews on accepting the party's mantle as temporary chairman. "It was remarked, I believe, by Sir Walter Raleigh, in reference to the strife of ancestry, that those who boasted most of their progenitors were like the plant he had discovered in America, the best part was underground." The time had come, Matthews declared, that the American people "will no longer be dogs to wear the collar of a party." Yet, curiously, as George Washington Julian later pointed out, Matthews, like so many of those who had traveled to Cincinnati, scurried back to his master, collar and all.[9]

After disposing of routine business, the convention turned to the question of a presidential nominee. Without a doubt, the man to beat in Cincinnati was Justice Davis, a man who already one nomination under his belt and stood a fighting chance of also winning the Democratic nomination. There were, to be sure, some sporadic anti-Davis rumblings among the delegates, but there was no organized opposition to be found. A few delegates felt that Davis was really a Democrat in sheep's clothing. Moreover, Lincoln's one-time campaign manager had alienated

---

9.   Julian, *Political Recollections*, pp. 338, 340. Matthews supported the Republican ticket in the general election.

some hard-money liberals by supporting greenbacks and had angered some Liberal Republicans by favoring amnesty for southerners by upholding Missouri's test oath. There were also a few delegates who were deeply bothered by the flabby jurist's apparent willingness to use his seat on the bench as a steppingstone to the White House.

Despite these misgivings, it pretty much looked like clear sailing for Davis. Charles Francis Adams, who was on his way to London at the time of the Liberal Republican convention, didn't even have a coterie working on his behalf in Cincinnati and Trumbull, of course, couldn't be bothered with the mundane work involved in winning a presidential nomination. Suddenly, as if out of the blue, the opposition appeared, effectively derailing the highly paid, liquor-induced Davis bandwagon just before the convention opened.

In a conspiracy that ultimately backfired, four powerful liberal editors agreed to publish unflattering articles about Davis, each attacking the ambitious Supreme Court Justice from a different angle. All four articles, according to their plan, were reprinted in the host city's widely read *Commercial* on the eve of the convention. Dubbed "the Great Quadrilateral," the four editors were Murat Halstead of the Cincinnati *Commercial*, Horace White of the *Chicago Tribune*, Samuel Bowles of the *Springfield Republican*, and Henry Watterson, an ex-Confederate soldier and editorial light of the Louisville *Courier-Journal*.[10] With Schurz acting as their mentor, the four men agreed that the nominee should be either Lyman Trumbull, White's candidate, or Charles Francis Adams, who was favored by Bowles and Schurz. Adams was unquestionably the ablest of those suggested. He would, as Schurz argued, appeal to the country's "loftiest instincts." Referring to the Labor Reform convention that nominated Davis as a "gang of execrable dead beats," Watterson agreed that either Adams or Trumbull should be the candidate. The four conspirators were joined in their effort to "kill off" Davis by Whitelaw Reid of Greeley's *New York Tribune*.

The cabal succeeded in paralyzing Davis, but little did they realize at the time that their scheme would boomerang, resulting in the nomination of Horace Greeley, a staunch protectionist and one of the most unlikely and eccentric presidential candidates in history.[11]

---

10. Donald E. Greco, "Liberal Republican Party 1872," *The Encyclopedia of Third Parties in America*, Vol. II, pp. 334-338. Edwin L. Godkin of *The Nation*, who deplored the split in the Republican Party that year as the greatest disaster since Bull Run, adamantly refused to join his colleagues in the press in supporting the Liberal Republican movement.

11. Roseboom, *A History of Presidential Elections*, p. 228.

To almost everyone's surprise—including his own—the cantankerous newspaperman finished a strong second in the presidential balloting, tallying 147 votes on the first ballot to 203 for Charles Francis Adams. Trumbull garnered 110 votes; Brown, 95; Davis, the one-time presumptive nominee, 92 ½; Curtin, 62; and 2 ½ delegates supported the ailing Salmon P. Chase of Ohio. Possibly as part of a deal with Greeley's managers, Brown, a seasoned politician, dramatically withdrew from the contest and threw his support to the unsuspecting Greeley (a blow to Chase's strategists) and the New York journalist, who later claimed to be personally unaware of any "bargain," forged into the lead on the second ballot. But the aloof Adams went ahead again on the third ballot and stayed there until the sixth ballot. This was all the more remarkable considering that Adams had made no attempt whatsoever to win the party's nomination. Unlike the other contenders, he had neither an organization nor a spokesman in Cincinnati's Music Hall.

Trumbull's vote rose to 156 on the third ballot but dropped to 81 by the fifth ballot. On the next ballot, only a handful of diehard delegates stuck with the Illinois lawmaker. Davis' support began to erode on the fifth ballot when his vote was nearly sliced in half. With the Trumbull and Davis candidacies quickly dissipating, Greeley, picking up considerable new support in the South and West, took a ten-vote lead—334 to 324 for Adams. Incredibly, the crotchety New York journalist was within twenty-six votes of winning the party's nomination. Minnesota, which had supported Trumbull up to that point, then switched nine votes to him and Pennsylvania switched 32, putting Greeley over the top. A frenzied stampede followed and Greeley finished with 482 votes to 187 for Adams. Curiously, prior to the rush to Greeley, perennial hopeful Salmon P. Chase, in a last-ditch effort to slow the Greeley juggernaut, had quietly picked up support, reaching thirty-two votes on the final ballot. The aging Trumbull, a man who disdained the give-and-take of politics, garnered nineteen votes on the final ballot and Davis, done in by the "Great Quadilateral," received a paltry six votes.

To Greeley's diehard supporters—and there were many—it was as though the celestial skies had opened. The Quadrilateral, on the other hand, was stunned into disbelief. Bowles, Halsted and Shurz couldn't believe that there plan had backfired. Horace White looked like an "iceberg," as Watterson later described it. The mortified Watterson, who once wrote that Greeley had enough infectious influence to make "two pestilent men," was as pale as a ghost. Here they were, the great reformers, Watterson later recalled, "hoist by their own petard." Not a single one of them, even in his worst nightmare, imagined that a convention of free traders would possibly nominate an ardent protectionist like Greeley.

A free-for-all developed in the race for the party's vice-presidential nomination. No fewer than nine candidates were in the hunt, including Benjamin Gratz Brown of Missouri, Lyman Trumbull of Illinois and George Washington Julian of Indiana, who had been the Free Soil Party's vice-presidential nominee twenty years earlier. Cassius M. Clay of Kentucky, a former Whig who served as minister to Russia during the Lincoln and Johnson administrations, was also in the race, as were Nebraska Sen. Thomas W. Tipton, Illinois Gov. John M. Palmer and Gilbert C. Walker, the Democratic governor of Virginia. James M. Scovel, a 39-year-old former schoolteacher and chairman of the Liberal Republican Party in New Jersey, also received votes on the first ballot. Missouri's Gratz Brown, a one-time Free Soiler, who led Trumbull by 79 votes on the first ballot, captured the nomination on the second ballot, receiving 435 votes to Trumbull's 175 and 75 for Walker.

The highlight of the convention had been the fiery keynote address by Carl Schurz, one of the country's most gifted speakers. Calling for an "infusion of a loftier moral spirit" in the nation's political life, Schurz urged his fellow Liberal Republicans to rise above petty considerations and bickering. Defeating Grant was not the most important thing, he said. America didn't just need another president—it needed a better president. It was not enough, he intoned, to merely nominate an "honest and popular man." The country needed a statesman.

Ironically, Schurz was among the most disappointed of those who departed from Cincinnati at the convention's close. While professing confidence in Greeley's personal integrity, he was so infuriated by the convention's outcome that he unleashed an eleven-page letter threatening to bolt from the new party that he had done so much to create on the grounds that the reform movement had fallen victim to "political huckstering" and had been captured by "politicians of the old stamp."[12]

As expected, the Liberal Republicans, comprised largely of reformers, newspaper editors and an assortment of anti-Grant politicians including New York Sen. Reuben E. Fenton, Gov. John M. Palmer of Illinois and George Washington Julian of Indiana, focused most of their attention on political corruption, and the need for civil service reform. The new party took direct aim at Grant in the platform, accusing his administration of using the federal government "as a machinery of corruption" and charging that the Republican President had "interfered with tyrannical arrogance" in the political affairs of states and local municipali-

---

12. Earle Dudley Ross, *The Liberal Republican Movement* (Seattle, 1970) reprint, pp. 107-108.

ties. The party's platform, shaped in large part by Schurz, sharply denounced the "notoriously corrupt and unworthy men in places of power" and called for a single presidential term. It also demanded amnesty for former Confederate soldiers and an immediate end to the administration's vindictive Reconstruction policy in the South, including the withdrawal of all federal troops from that region. The Liberals also endorsed "equal and exact justice for all, of whatever nativity, race, color, or persuasion, religious or political." Other than a somewhat ambiguous plank of the important tariff issue, the Liberal Republican platform essentially steered clear of most economic issues.

Reaction to Greeley's unexpected nomination ranged from the incredulous to the starry-eyed. The *New York World*, which favored Charles Francis Adams, was dumbfounded, expressing its disappointment that a party founded by revenue reformers had nominated a zealous protectionist like Greeley. The *World* held out some hope that Greeley would siphon Republican votes in a three-way race for the presidency and urged the Democrats to nominate their own ticket, contending that Greeley was the country's "most conspicuous and heated opponent of the Democratic Party"—a not altogether inaccurate portrayal. "No two men could look each other in the face and say 'Greeley' without laughing," wrote one newspaper, while another suggested that there had been too much thinking and not enough drinking at the Cincinnati convention. Connecticut's Gideon Welles, resembling a Hebrew prophet, summed up the feeling of many Liberals when he said that it would have been difficult to find anyone more unsuitable and objectionable than Greeley, quickly adding that anyone was preferable to Grant. "A crooked stick may be made available to beat a mad dog," he quipped.[13]

The *Nation*, claiming that some of Greeley's New York supporters at the convention were "the worst political trash to be found anywhere," was also astonished and appalled by the news of Greeley's nomination and quickly deserted the Liberal Republican movement. Edwin L. Godkin, the sagacious editor of that publication, wrote that, "a greater degree of incredulity and disappointment…has not been felt…since the news of the first battle of Bull Run." *Harper's Weekly*, which was solidly in Grant's corner, was even more harsh, stating that Greeley was "totally destitute" of sound judgment and unfit for the presidency. It was inconceivable to its editors that Greeley could possibly replace Grant in the White House.

On the opposite end of the spectrum, Greeley's nomination was greeted with unrestrained euphoria. Greeley's own New York *Tribune* was ecstatic. Frank

---

13.   Van Deusen, *Horace Greeley: Nineteenth-Century Crusader*, p. 406.

Leslie's *Illustrated Newspaper*, a Democratic journal, bubbled with enthusiasm, claiming that Greeley was the real founder of the Republican Party and, more than anyone else, represented reform, purification and peace." And Samuel Bowles' *Springfield Republican*, while urging the regular Republicans to dump Grant, argued that Greeley's popularity was no myth, even his detractors had "a warm spot for him in their hearts."

In the meantime, President Grant was re-nominated by acclamation at the Republican national convention at Philadelphia's Academy of Music in early June. To no one's surprise, it was a pre-arranged love-in for the Hero of Appomattox. Massachusetts Senator Henry Wilson defeated scandal-tarred Vice President Schuyler Colfax by a margin of 364 ½ to 321 ½ to become Grant's new running mate. Paying lip service to the reformers, the Republicans endorsed a civil service plank and strongly supported civil rights for everyone. The 60-year-old Wilson, a one-time abolitionist editor of the *Boston Republican*, had served as chairman of the 1852 Free Soil convention that nominated John P. Hale for the presidency and was later elected to the U.S. Senate by a coalition of Free Soilers, Know-Nothings and Democrats before embracing the Republican banner during Lincoln's campaign in 1860. As an old antislavery veteran and former shoemaker, Wilson was expected to strengthen the ticket by drawing labor and African-American votes. The Republicans also endorsed a revenue tariff and applauded Grant's handling of Reconstruction.

Grant and Wilson were also nominated by a National Working Men's convention, which met in New York City two weeks earlier. The so-called "Working Men's" assemblage was a Republican machination designed, in part, to offset Justice David Davis' nomination at the Labor Reform Party's national convention in February and present Grant and Wilson as the true candidates of America's working class. The president, after all, had surrounded himself with wealthy men such as retailer Alexander T. Steward and railroad financier Jay Gould during his first term and badly needed a way to remind Midwestern farmers, former slaves and Union soldiers of his own working-class roots. Delegates from thirty-one states participated in the Working Men's national convention, giving the president 204 votes on the first ballot to five for Horace Greeley. Sen. Wilson was also an easy first ballot winner, receiving 160 votes to twenty-five for Edwin D. Morgan of New York in the vice-presidential balloting. Morgan, 61, was a former senator and governor and at the time was serving as chairman of the Republican National Committee. Vice President Schuyler Colfax, badly damaged by his role in the Credit Mobilier scandal, received a pathetic twenty-four votes. Wilson's nomination, like Grant's, was then made unanimous, enabling the "Galena Tan-ner" and the "Natick Shoemaker" to run under a labor-oriented banner in the general election. The Working Men's convention also adopted a platform calling for, among other things, a reduction in the national debt, enforcement of an eight-hour day and other laws benefiting the working class, including low interest rates.

In the meantime, several leading Liberal Republicans, including Schurz, were decidedly unhappy with the Cincinnati convention, especially those who didn't trust an ardent protectionist like Greeley. In New England, free traders Edward Atkinson and David A. Wells, who were working diligently to put another candidate in the field, issued a call for a meeting at Steinway Hall in New York City on May 30th to protest the "betrayal" of the Cincinnati convention. An all-out effort was made to recruit Schurz to their cause, but the Missouri lawmaker, while keenly interested in their maneuvers, remained publicly aloof.

At the May 30th meeting of the Free Trade League, chaired by William Cullen Bryant, the poet and longtime editor of the *New York Evening Post*, the tariff reformers urged the nomination of an independent reform ticket. The meeting exceeded all expectations. During the meeting, there was sustained applause when Charles Francis Adams was mentioned as a possible candidate. The demonstration in his behalf convinced Schurz and others in attendance that the Massachusetts diplomat might soon enter the race as an independent.[14]

Curiously, the tiny Anti-Secret Society Party, an offspring of the old Anti-Masonic Party, had already nominated the aging writer and historian for the nation's highest office. Meeting in Oberlin, Ohio, on May 21, this little-remembered group nominated the unsuspecting former diplomat for the presidency and tapped General Charles H. Howard as his vice-presidential running mate. Howard, 34, declined the nomination and was replaced on the ticket by publisher Joseph Lorenzo Barlow of Illinois, an ordained Baptist minister. Adams, however, was unceremoniously dumped from the ticket shortly after the party learned that he was a Royal Arch Mason. Embarrassed, the third party then quickly withdrew from the 1872 canvass.[15]

Meanwhile, a panic-stricken Greeley feared that his candidacy was about to unravel. "I'll do anything, go anywhere," he pleaded to Watterson. "It shan't be said that I have thrown any stumbling blocks in the way." Watterson assured Greeley that he had nothing to fear. He was right. Mass defection was avoided

---

14. Ross, *The Liberal Republican Movement*, pp. 110-112.
15. James T. Havel, *U.S. Presidential Candidates and the Elections: A Biographical and Historical Guide* (New York, 1996), Vol. I, p. 41.

when Schurz, hardly a Greeley enthusiast, quickly arranged a conference of various reforms groups, including dozens of Greeley men and Democrats, at the Fifth Avenue Hotel in New York on June 20. Described as a "solemnly farcical" affair, the two-day conference accomplished little, other than to stifle an all-out anti-Greeley revolt.

In any case, approximately sixty participants listened as speaker after speaker, each anxious—or desperate, for that matter—to rally behind anyone who could "beat Grant," spoke in favor of Greeley's fledgling candidacy. Trumbull of Illinois, conceding that many in attendance might have preferred someone other than Greeley, cautioned that it was too late to consider other possibilities and that for the good of the country they should all unite behind the Cincinnati nominee. John Forsyth of the *Mobile Register* followed with a half-hearted endorsement of Greeley. Former Connecticut Gov. James English, a wealthy manufacturer, also spoke for Greeley, as did aging former Sen. Lafayette Foster of the same state. Horace White of the *Chicago Tribune*, biting his tongue and demanding that Greeley keep his mouth shut during the autumn campaign, and Henry Watterson, who rarely passed up an opportunity to fire his harpoon in Grant's blubber, were among many others who spoke on the New York journalist's behalf. Even Josiah B. Grinnell, the young Vermont clergyman who had been advised by Greeley years earlier to "Go West, young man, go West," was their to defend his mentor. Grinnell had traveled from Iowa to speak for Greeley.

Schurz also addressed the gathering, giving a somewhat pathetic speech on Greeley's behalf. As late as that morning, the Missouri lawmaker was still contemplating a move to dump the New York journalist and replace him with a new Liberal Republican standard-bearer. In a low, conversational tone, Schurz admitted that Greeley was not his first choice, nor was he the right man for the country, but there was no other way to defeat Grant. Sprinkling the field with independent candidates, he argued, would only help to insure Grant's re-election. Greeley, he said, was a bitter pill, but one that must be swallowed if the nation's reform forces were to have any chance at all of unseating Grant.

Despite the parade of pro-Greeley speakers, few minds had been changed. The *New York Evening Post*, the *Nation*, the *New York World* and a number of German-language newspapers remained strongly opposed to Greeley. In fact, there were several in attendance who wanted to stop the Democratic stampede to Greeley by urging the Democrats to nominate the aging and aloof Charles Francis Adams, or possibly former congressman William S. Groesbeck of Ohio, at their national convention in Baltimore.

Despite Schurz's quick action, a small group of free traders, including Ohio's Jacob D. Cox and Parke Godwin of the *New York Evening Post*, nevertheless attempted to launch an Independent Liberal Republican ticket. Some of these bolters wanted to nominate editor William Cullen Bryant for the presidency, but the longtime journalist wasn't interested in mounting what would have almost certainly been a forlorn campaign for the nation's highest office. Meeting in secret, twenty-three delegates to the Fifth Avenue conference reassembled on June 22 and, claiming that "undue devotion to party" had "greatly damaged the Republic," proceeded to nominate former Ohio lawmaker William S. Groesbeck, a champion of civil service reform, for president. Frederick Law Olmsted, a brilliant and extraordinarily prolific landscape architect and visionary city planner whose magnificent works extended from Canada to Texas and from Sandy Hook to the Golden Gate, was named for the vice presidency. The Independent Liberal Republicans called for equal civil and political rights for all and an end to political patronage. The renegade Liberals also called for civil service reform, free trade and affirmed their belief that the people are best governed when governed least.[16]

The Independent Liberal Republicans, or "Opposition Party," as they were briefly described, included the likes of wealthy industrialist Edward Atkinson of Massachusetts and Judge George Hoadley of Cincinnati, a close personal friend and law partner of Salmon P. Chase. Oswald Ottendorfer, an anti-Tammany alderman and publisher of the German-language *New Yorker Staat-Zeitung*, and Simon Sterne, a New York lawyer and civic reformer, were also active Liberal Republican defectors. Like Schurz, Ottendorfer participated as a student in the liberal uprisings in the German-speaking countries of Europe in 1848, playing an active role in the revolt against the Metternich government in Vienna, the war against Denmark and in the rebellions in Saxony and Baden. Under threat of arrest, he fled to Switzerland before migrating to the United States, arriving on America's shores in 1850. A philanthropist, there is little question that the social-minded Ottendorfer would have put his money and considerable influence in the nation's German-American community behind an independent challenge to Grant and Greeley in 1872.

The short-lived Groesbeck-Olmsted pairing was arguably the most impressive ticket nominated that year. Of all the presidential candidates who have skipped lightly over the American political landscape, the former Cincinnati congressman is perhaps one of the least remembered. The 56-year-old Groesbeck, a distinguished-looking dark-haired man with a long, narrow face and ruggedly protrud-

---

16. Ross, *The Liberal Republican Movement*, pp. 124-125.

ing nose, was an attorney who had graduated first in his class at Miami University in Oxford, Ohio, in 1834. Having built a lucrative law practice, he ran unsuccessfully for Congress as a Democrat in 1854, but was elected two years later, winning with 43% of the vote against stiff Republican and Know-Nothing opposition. He was narrowly defeated for re-election in 1858, largely because he wavered on the all-important Kansas-Nebraska Act, apparently costing him countless votes among anti-Nebraska Democrats in his district.

Groesbeck was a delegate to the failed Peace Convention of 1861 before winning a seat in the Ohio Senate three years later. In 1866, he was a delegate to the National Union midterm convention and later served on Andrew Johnson's legal defense team during his widely publicized impeachment trial in 1868. It was his brilliant and eloquent speech, arguing that the president had the legal authority to remove Secretary of War Edwin Stanton, a favorite of the Radical Republicans, which probably saved Johnson's presidency. In defending the beleaguered president, the former Ohio lawmaker won the admiration of the Senate and the country. His speech was widely praised by *The Nation* and other leading publications of the time.

Frederick Law Olmsted, Groesbeck's vice-presidential co-star, was arguably the most impressive candidate nominated for the presidency or the vice presidency by any party that year. Born in Hartford, Connecticut, in 1822, Olmsted was the son of a prosperous merchant. He attended the prestigious Phillips Academy before going to work for a French dry-goods importer in New York, but quickly grew tired of that mundane work. A restless young man, he attended engineering lectures at Yale during the following year, but quickly grew bored with that too. In pursuit of adventure, Olmsted, like so many youth of that era, sailed before the mast en-route to China and the West Indies, a yearlong voyage that awakened him to different cultures and scenery.

Upon his return to the United States, Olmsted took up farming, working as an apprentice on a farm near Oswego, New York, before deciding to branch out on his own. He first operated a small farm in Guilford, Connecticut, and later managed the larger Ackerly farm on Staten Island, which his father purchased for him. He enthusiastically pursued his agricultural activities for several years before his literary interests turned his attention to new endeavors.

Following a second trip overseas—this time to Europe—Henry J. Raymond of the *New York Times* hired the young Olmsted to conduct an extensive tour of the South to write about the economic and social conditions of that region. Olmsted's curiosity on the subject of slavery had been piqued following a lengthy discussion with abolitionist William Lloyd Garrison when he visited Olmsted on his farm a few years earlier. Olmsted's letters to Raymond were printed in the *Times* and were later published as *A Journey in the Seaboard Slave States*, a book first published in 1856. Two subsequent journeys through the South on horseback followed—one to Texas with his brother, John, and a solitary trip from New Orleans to Richmond. Olmsted's observations on these journeys were later published as books. His writings portrayed the South—black and white alike—as a poor, indolent and backward society. Such were the fruits of bondage, he wrote, noting that the subsistence level of slaves and poor whites in that region discouraged the development of a large manufacturing base in the South. Certainly no raving abolitionist, Olmsted's writings were credited to some degree with preventing the pot from boiling over during this increasingly divisive period. A more objective writer on the subject probably couldn't have been found. "If any adventurer upon the South possessed open-mindedness," wrote one of his biographers, it was certainly Olmsted. Unlike some of his antislavery contemporaries, he wrote in a dispassionate, reasoned style—something that was terribly lacking during that period—preferring a calm examination of the facts to the kind of hyperbole offered by abolitionists and proslavery advocates alike. Though personally opposed to slavery, he had no political agenda. While viewing slavery as an unfortunate yet ingrained social institution, the young New York writer in no way blamed the ordinary people of the South for its existence. If anyone was to blame for the increased antislavery agitation of the 1850s, it was the "conceit, avarice, and folly" of wealthy slave owners.[17] Acclaimed at the time as the most accurate depiction of conditions in that region during the antebellum period, an abridged version of Olmsted's works later appeared as *The Cotton King*, a two-volume edition published in 1861, shortly after the outbreak of hostilities between the North and the South.

During the war, the noted landscape architect served as secretary of the U.S. Sanitary Commission, a quasi-public investigative and advisory organization responsible for the hygienic conditions of Union army camps. The commission—an early version of the Red Cross—relied heavily on volunteers, mostly women, to provide bandages, clothing, food and medicine to Union troops, including lodging for furloughed soldiers returning from the battlefield. Sanitary inspectors routinely instructed soldiers on such things as camp drainage, water supplies, cooking, and the proper placement of latrines. The Army Medical Bureau, however, steadfastly resisted the commission's leaders and volunteers. By

---

17.   Broadus W. Mitchell, *Frederick Law Olmsted: A Critic of the Old South* (Baltimore, 1924), pp. 69-71.

early 1862, the Sanitary Commission had become a national power of sorts and used its newly found influence to challenge the Medical Bureau's antiquated seniority system, which constantly held back promising young and highly-skilled surgeons. Olmsted personally attacked Army Surgeon-General Clement A. Finley as "a self-satisfied, supercilious, bigoted blockhead" who clung to his position of authority only because he was "the oldest of the old mess-room doctors." Olmsted's constant gnawing and persistent criticism led indirectly to Lincoln's appointment of new Surgeon-General William Hammond, a dynamic and energetic 33-year-old neurologist, in the spring of 1862.

Olmsted resigned from the commission the following year, the result of an injury sustained before the war. A benevolent and compassionate man with a penchant for public service, he helped organize the Southern Famine Relief Commission at the close of the war and later founded the New York State Charities Aid Association. Largely as a result of his extensive pre-war travels, Olmsted unexpectedly found himself a famous man and was soon named editor of the prestigious *Putnam's Magazine*. He later worked briefly as an associate editor of Edwin L. Godkin's *The Nation*, one of the country's most influential political periodicals. One of the most prominent champions of the nineteenth-century city beautification movement, Olmsted was appointed superintendent of Central Park in New York City in 1857 and, in partnership with noted London-born landscape architect Calvert Vaux, designed the 800-acre park in Manhattan, which was then considered the most beautiful public park in the United States. A man of considerable charm who was perfectly capable of bridging the usually wide gap between politics and the arts, Olmsted was soon besieged with other commissions and designed public parks in Buffalo, Chicago, Detroit, Milwaukee, Montreal, St. Louis and elsewhere. Among many other notable works, he also designed the landscaping on the Capitol grounds in Washington, D.C., as well as the Niagara Reservation at Niagara Falls. His planning and design of the 1893 World's Fair in Chicago was considered by many to be his most spectacular achievement. In addition, the country's leading post-Civil War landscape architect designed many university campuses across the country, including that of Stanford University in Palo Alta, California. In 1865, he was named as the first commissioner of Yosemite National Park. A most remarkable man, Olmsted earned post-graduate degrees from Yale, Harvard and Amherst universities and held law degrees from both Harvard and Yale. He was also a founder of the Metropolitan Museum of Art and the American Museum of Natural History in Central Park.

While much of Republican-controlled press spoke admirably about Groes-beck's short-lived candidacy, welcoming any development that would further divide the opposition, the *Chicago Times* strongly urged the Democrats to endorse the former Ohio lawmaker's candidacy at their Baltimore convention.[18] However, Groesbeck, who later endorsed Greeley, eventually declined the Inde-pendent Liberal Republican nomination, leaving most of the free traders associ-ated with the independent movement looking in vain to the Democrats for salvation, only to be disappointed. Olmsted, of course, also graciously refused the honor.

Eager to nominate anyone with even the slightest chance of defeating Grant, the Democrats convened at Ford's Opera House in Baltimore on July 9 and somewhat unenthusiastically endorsed the Greeley-Brown ticket. Greeley's nom-ination marked the first and only time in American history that a major party fas-tened its wagon to a third-party horse. Outnumbered in the House and holding only 17 of 74 seats in the U.S. Senate, the Democrats, anxious to shed their "trai-tor" image, desperately wanted to return to the White House after a twelve-year absence, even if it meant supporting a man like Greeley who never seemed to tire of pummeling their proud party.

Francis P. Blair, Jr., of Missouri laid most of the groundwork for Greeley's nomination in Baltimore. A former slave owner who had organized the Free Soil Party in Missouri, Blair had been the Democratic candidate for vice president in 1868. There was, to be sure, at least some opposition to Greeley at the Baltimore convention. A number of newspapers tried desperately to stop the shotgun wed-ding at the altar. Inarguably, the strongest opposition came from Manton Mar-ble's *New York World*, which enthusiastically supported Adams and made no pretense about its objection to Greeley, a man who in the past had denounced the Democrats as "traitors, slave-whippers, drunkards and lecherous beasts." A longtime rival of Greeley's *Tribune*, the *World* wanted a Democrat of good stand-ing, prompting the *New York Times*, a paper solidly in Grant's corner, to sarcasti-cally suggest that nothing short of Jefferson Davis would be acceptable to its rival newspaper. (Out of the public eye, the ex-president of the Confederacy had been released from prison in 1867 and was working for a Memphis insurance company that eventually went bankrupt.)

Despite the opposition of Marble's powerful newspaper, a handful of southern Bourbons and such party stalwarts as Delaware's Thomas Bayard and Charles O'Conor of New York, the controversial editor faced only token opposition in

18. *Chicago Times*, June 24, 1872.

Baltimore. Although considerable pro-Adams sentiment among the Democrats had been echoed in the weeks leading up the party's national convention, the aging diplomat did not want the nomination, preferring the quiet dignity of retirement to the awesome burdens and responsibilities of the presidency. In fact, the distant Adams was deeply relieved, though somewhat surprised, when he learned of Greeley's nomination by the Liberal Republicans a few months earlier.

Meanwhile, some of Justice David Davis' Democratic friends had urged him to seek their party's nomination, assuring him that the nomination was his for the asking. But Davis, depressed by the treatment he received in Cincinnati, refused to consider such an undertaking. "There was never a grand opportunity so recklessly thrown away, as at [Cincinnati]," he lamented. Unable to persuade any prominent Democrat to challenge the New York journalist for the party's nomination, Greeley's detractors marshaled their small forces behind the last-minute candidacies of Jeremiah S. Black, an eccentric, emotionally-charged and absent-minded former attorney general and secretary of state in the Buchanan administration, and the somewhat feeble 72-year-old former Sen. James A. Bayard, Jr., of Delaware, an ex-Whig who had briefly donned a Republican hat.

It was a sight to behold as August Belmont, the conservative financier who had long despised Greeley as a wild-eyed socialist, gave a welcoming speech to the Democrats arriving in Baltimore. Like other conservative Democrats, Belmont, who initially favored Charles Francis Adams, said that he would vote for his "deadliest enemy" to rid the country of Grant—and so he did.

The presidential balloting was a mere formality. Greeley's name was placed in nomination by ex-Barnburner and one-time Republican Sen. James R. Doolittle of Wisconsin. A close personal friend and staunch supporter of the late Abraham Lincoln, the 57-year-old Doolittle joined the Democratic Party when the Radical Republicans turned their guns on him for supporting Andrew Johnson's relatively mild reconstruction policies and for voting against the president's impeachment. Greeley, as expected, was easily nominated on the first and only ballot, garnering 686 votes to 21 for Black and 16 for the aging Bayard. Two other anti-Greeley votes were cast for former Ohio congressman William S. Groesbeck, the nominee of the Independent Liberal Republicans, and seven delegates abstained.

It was one of the most puzzling presidential nominations of all time. After all, Greeley was an anathema to most Democrats. Only a year earlier, for instance, the New York journalist said that he would vote for Grant before he would support *any* Democrat. Moreover, it was Greeley who once said that all Democrats might not be rascals, but that all rascals were Democrats, and it was the same Greeley, forever waving the "bloody shirt," who had time and again viciously assailed the Democrats as a treacherous and traitorous party. Yet, incredibly, the Democrats not only enthusiastically endorsed Ben Gratz-Brown, Greeley's vice-presidential running mate on the Liberal Republican ticket, but also accepted verbatim the party's vaguely worded platform, prompting Delaware's James Bayard to complain that it had been "forced down our throats without mastication or digestion." In perhaps the shortest nominating convention in American history, the entire Democratic proceedings lasted only six hours.

Once the aging journalist secured the nominations of the Liberal Republican and Democratic parties, a deeply disappointed David Davis, sensing the futility of a third-party candidacy, formally declined the Labor Reform Party's presidential nomination, which had been offered to him in February. In doing so, the obese judge and close friend of Lincoln left the fledgling labor party in a lurch.

Although the hour was late, the Labor Reformers, still determined to field their own ticket in the presidential sweepstakes, quickly scurried about for a suitable replacement. Almost immediately, the headless third party found itself being wooed by Colonel Blanton Duncan, a wealthy Kentuckian and self-proclaimed leader of the so-called "Straight-Out" Democrats.[19] In a letter sent to party leader Horace H. Day on July 10, Duncan asked if there couldn't be some sort of merger between the two organizations to fight "the monopolists and spoils-men in the two Radical parties." Upset that the Labor Reformers had nominated Davis in the first place, Day was more than receptive to Duncan's overture. Perhaps excited by rumors that the Straight-Out Democrats might offer their party's nomination to a "well-known Pennsylvanian"—possibly popular Gov. John Geary, a one-time frontrunner for the Labor Reform nomination—the Brooklyn philanthropist responded quickly to Duncan's overture, assuring him that the nation's working people had been entirely ignored by the Grant and Greeley-led parties. Hoping to create a lasting People's Party, Day said that a union with the Straight-Out Democrats would be "hailed by the Labor Reform Party with hope and joy." Geary's candidacy, of course, never materialized, yet the desperate Labor Reformers joined the Straight-Out coalition with almost reckless abandon—anything, after all, was preferable to Grant or Greeley.

In the meantime, speculation that the Straight-Out Democrats intended to nominate New York lawyer Charles O'Conor for the presidency began to surface. The son of impoverished Irish immigrants, O'Conor, a prominent attorney with deep loyalties to the South, was strongly opposed to Greeley's coalition candidacy. O'Conor, a lifelong Democrat, may have unintentionally fueled the rumor by granting an interview prior to the scheduled Straight-Out Democratic convention in Louisville. In his amiable yet enigmatic manner, O'Conor, who met privately with Tammany sachem Samuel J. Tilden the previous evening, refused to directly answer any political questions during the interview, telling the disappointed *New York Times* reporter that he "must keep out of the papers, if possible." The only thing he knew about his pending nomination by the Straight-Out Democrats, he said with a mischievous grin, was what he had read in the newspapers.

At a hastily called second convention in Philadelphia attended by 158 delegates from twenty-seven states in late August, the Labor Reformers gave their official blessing to the Straight-Out Democratic movement by endorsing O'Conor's rumored candidacy. Though billed as a secret meeting, the Labor Reform proceedings and O'Conor's tentative candidacy were widely reported in the press. The *New York Times*, for instance, ran several stories on the party's lively convention. Chairman William H. Irving of Ohio gave a lengthy address, which was frequently interrupted by cheers, denouncing those in the movement who were attempting to sell-out the Labor Reformers to either Grant or Greeley and urging the delegates to nominate their own ticket. The Labor Reformers then named a

---

19. A fascinating character, the ubiquitous Duncan lived in Louisville, Kentucky, until sometime in the early 1890's when he relocated with his wife to Los Angeles, settling in what is now Manhattan Beach. A little-known political adventurer of sorts, his footprints can be found not only in the "Straight-Out" Democratic and Labor Reform parties of 1872, but also later in the Greenback and Populist parties. He even ran for Congress on the Greenback ticket from Louisville in 1878. During the Civil War, Duncan, then living in Columbia, South Carolina, owned a large engraving and printing company where he printed money for the Confederacy until the end of the war. He had been a delegate to the Kentucky Secession Convention in 1861 and later organized and commanded a battalion that eventually became part of the 1st Kentucky Infantry Regiment. At the beginning of the war, his regiment served under Stonewall Jackson and saw action in Northern Virginia. Duncan mustered out of the army as a colonel in 1862 and immediately starting printing money for the Confederacy. A wealthy lawyer, Duncan also owned land in Mississippi, which he leased out to tenant farmers. All kinds of legends and folklore surround Duncan, who died in 1902. Some stories allege that just before the end of the Civil War, Jefferson Davis sent him to England to obtain funds for the Confederacy and while there exchanged cotton for gold, but by the time he returned the war was already over and he quietly moved to California with—of course—all of the gold as well as a few slaves. By then, Confederate money was worthless. Other stories suggest that when he arrived in California he built a large oceanfront plantation house high on a hill, complete with an oil-fueled lighthouse or beacon from which he could signal incoming ships. This fable contends that he also built an underground secret tunnel from the house to the sea and went into the smuggling business.

thirty-man delegation to attend the Straight-Out Democratic convention in Louisville with specific instructions to urge the nomination of Charles O'Conor for president and Eli Saulsbury of Delaware, for vice president. The 54-year-old Saulsbury, who had occasionally engaged in political rivalry with two of his brothers, had served as a state senator for four terms and as governor of Delaware from 1866-71.

Meanwhile, a separate Labor Reform group, led by Andrew C. Cameron, editor of the *Workingman's Advocate*, the official organ of the National Labor Union, held a conference in Columbus, Ohio, and decided that it was "inexpedient at this late day" to nominate another ticket. In retrospect, Cameron's group was right. Numbering only a dozen, this faction of the Labor Reform Party recognized that by this time the party's nomination was virtually worthless. Not only had the party wasted too much time on Davis, it was also badly divided. In its stronghold of Massachusetts, for example, the party had already split into two hostile groups—one faction led by Wendell Phillips and a second faction headed by machinist Ira Steward, the indefatigable president of Boston's Eight-Hour League, and George E. McNeill, chief deputy of the Massachusetts Bureau of Labor Statistics, a department he had labored long and hard to create. McNeill, who was later active in the Knights of Labor and the American Federation of Labor, published a history of the American labor movement in 1887. Similar splits in other states had also seriously weakened the party, possibly beyond repair.

The Straight-Out Democrats

The Greeley-Grant race provided the nation's Simon-pure Democrats and conservatives without a real choice in the 1872 presidential election. A number of "Straight-Out" Democrats—those who were adamantly opposed to their party's coalition with the Liberal Republicans—intended to rectify the situation by fielding a ticket of their own. The Straight-Out or "Bourbon" Democrats, as they were called, were not without prominent backing. The movement enjoyed the support not only of men of the caliber of Alexander H. Stephens of Georgia, but also of able men such as Senator Graham N. Fitch of Indiana, a former professor of medicine. This wasn't the first time that Stephens, no insignificant figure in national politics, dabbled on the periphery of the entrenched two-party system. Twenty years earlier he supported a fragile independent Whig-Nativist American ticket that desperately tried to run an ailing Daniel Webster for president. The reluctant Webster, of course, died less than a month before the election. Alfred P. Edgerton, a former Ohio congressman, and William Ferry, owner of the Ottawa Iron Works, a large Michigan machine shop and foundry, also joined the Straight-Out movement. Interestingly enough, so, too, did three former mayors of Grand Rapids, Michigan. Others attracted to the Straight-Out movement included ex-General Samuel Bell Maxey of Texas, a former Confederate commander of the Indian Territory military district and superintendent of Indian affairs, who ran for Congress that year on the Straight-Out Democratic ticket.

The movement also attracted the support of young journalist Mark M. "Brick" Pomeroy, the colorful ex-Copperhead who later emerged as one of the most influential leaders in the Greenback Party. In addition to Pomeroy's New York City-based *Democrat* and a few other Copperhead organs in and around New York City, the Straight-Out Democrats also received the support of at least seventeen other newspapers, including Wilbur Storey's *Chicago Times* and Alexander Stephens' Atlanta *Sun*, the Savannah *News* and the Quitman *Banner*—three of at least six Georgia newspapers that vigorously supported the O'Conor movement that year. The Long Island *Independent and Press* and Carl Daenzer's German-language *Anzeiger* in St. Louis also championed the Straight-Out cause. Interestingly, Daenzer's publication was one of at least three newspapers in Missouri—birthplace of the Liberal Republican Party—that longed for a purified Democratic ticket in 1872. Philanthropist Oswald Ottendorfer's widely-read German newspaper, the *New Yorker Staats-Zeitung*, also wholeheartedly supported the unadulterated Democratic movement.[20]

The Straight-Out Democrats believed that they could provide a stronger challenge to the scandal-ridden Grant than the Greeley-Brown ticket and were convinced that they would outpoll the Liberal Republicans in a three-cornered race for the White House. The potential was certainly there. Hundreds of thousands of Democrats across the country had serious reservations about Greeley and spirited Straight-Out Democratic state conventions were held in Georgia, Illinois, Indiana, Maryland, Missouri, New Jersey and elsewhere. Holding aloft the time-honored Democratic banner of Jefferson, Madison and Jackson, the New Jersey convention, attended by 75 delegates, sharply denounced the party's national convention in Baltimore. Having nominated "an uncompromising and unrepentant radical" like Greeley, the New Jersey Democrats insisted that the Baltimore proceedings were "invalid and void" and didn't truly represent the party's rank-and-file voters. Lambasting "overshadowing corporations," corruption in Con-

---

20.   For a partial list of these newspapers, see the *New York Times*, August 2, 1872.

gress and "imbecility in the Executive" branch, the New Jersey Straight-Out Democrats urged the party faithful to rally behind a separate ticket boldly committed to "the preservation of the Constitution, and the unity, and prosperity and peace of the country."

Anti-fusion Democrats in Georgia met in Atlanta on August 21 and ratified a platform, written by Alexander H. Stephens, containing a strong states' rights plank. A particularly enthusiastic Straight-Out convention also took place in Springfield, Illinois, where about one hundred delegates criticized the Baltimore "sell out" and decided to nominate a separate statewide ticket, sending chills down the spines of state and national party leaders who had already publicly committed themselves to the Democratic-Liberal Republican union.

The Straight-Out Democrats of Missouri, where the Liberal Republican movement first leaped onto the pages of American history, met in Jefferson City in late August and named a delegation to the Louisville convention. There was considerable discontent with Greeley in that state. Greeley's campaign, opined the *St. Louis Democrat*, was "like the boy who took a run of a half mile to jump a creek, and then let down before he got to it." The newspaper predicted that if Greeley's fortunes didn't improve soon, the Democratic standard-bearer would be forced to drop out of the race and the national party would have no choice but to rally behind the Louisville nominees.

Led nationally by the affable and articulate Blanton Duncan, the dissident Straight-Outs were determined to preserve the integrity of the Democratic Party's long history. The defeated South was again part of the country and it wasn't, in their view, a region that deserved the kind of harsh punishment being meted out by the president and vindictive men in Congress like Pennsylvania's Thaddeus Stevens and Ohio's Benjamin Wade. "The Straight-Out movement," Duncan insisted, was a "protest against radicalism." Horace Greeley, he said, supported "every obnoxious law" passed by Congress regarding control of the South and Ulysses S. Grant, as the nation's chief executive, had enforced them.

In the meantime, Greeley's supporters insisted that the Straight-Out Democrats were "Grant's sideshow," a Republican-financed ploy to split the Democratic vote—a charge that wasn't completely unfounded. The Liberals alleged that a claim against the government was hurried through the Interior Department after Duncan boasted that he could get 800,000 Democrats to vote against Greeley. Henry Watterson's *Louisville Courier-Journal* alleged that the Republicans had financed the party's Louisville convention. Duncan denied that he had received any funds whatsoever from the GOP and explained that he had personally paid for most of the convention's expenses as "a donation to the cause." The genial Duncan, a heavy-set man, had also been viciously attacked in the pages of Watterson's newspaper and by some of Greeley's supporters as an organizer of the Know-Nothing Party in the 1850s—a charge that he adamantly denied. In a well-publicized letter-to-the-editor, Duncan stated that he had voted against the Know-Nothing Party in 1854 when most of those who were now leading Greeley's campaign in Kentucky had supported the dark-lantern conspiracy.

There is some evidence, however, that President Grant may have smiled favorably on Duncan's undertaking in 1872. William E. Chandler, chairman of the Republican National Committee, apparently authorized money and manpower to assist the Straight-Out Democrats, using what he called "blowers and adventurers" to whip up support for the Louisville convention and to create Democratic divisions in the South, especially in Georgia, Kentucky and Texas, where Grant's prospects were marginal at best. In Pennsylvania, moreover, Chandler's national committee donated $1,000, the Republican state committee reportedly gave $1,800 and party leader J. Donald Cameron chipped in another $1,000 to send a delegation to Louisville. Another $500 was coughed up to send a band from Philadelphia to entertain the Straight-Out delegates.

Not all reaction to the Straight-Out Democratic movement was negative, however. The *Pittsburgh Dispatch*, a Democratic-leaning newspaper, reported that many Democrats felt that O'Conor was a better choice for president than the "vacillating political trickster put up at Baltimore." In late August there were similar press reports from western Ohio. In that area, a growing number of rural Democrats were leaning toward the Louisville nominees, causing a great deal of anxiety in the Greeley camp. A few local observers were convinced that the Liberal Republican campaign would collapse altogether in that region. Similarly, a number of Irish-owned newspapers in New York City and Boston hauled down the tattered Greeley banner and hoisted O'Conor's flag.

Of course, there weren't any scientific polls in those days. Newspaper editors and pundits frequently relied on the observations of reporters to gauge public opinion. One such "poll," taken by a *New York Times* correspondent who had traveled by rail from New York to Cheyenne, Wyoming, shortly before the Straight-Out Democratic convention in Louisville, reported that, while Grant was favored by more than 68% of the 473 people surveyed on his trip, Greeley, with sixteen percent, was in a virtual dead-heat with O'Conor for second place. Seventy-three of those interviewed, or more than fifteen percent, indicated a preference for the Louisville nominee.

More than 600 Democrats traveled to Louisville in early September to take part in the Straight-Out Democratic convention. There wasn't a Grant operative in sight, quickly disproving Greeley's contention that the whole thing had been part of a scheme by the Republicans to split the Democratic vote. The Republicans played only a small role, if any. Most of those in attendance were dyed-in-the-wool Democrats, unflinching in their devotion to their party.

The convention got off to a good start. Blanton Duncan's opening address brought forth the kind of spontaneous enthusiasm that had been sorely lacking in Baltimore, the kind that hadn't been heard since 1868 when the Democrats enthusiastically nominated New York's Horatio Seymour on the twenty-second ballot. The rousing cheers continued as temporary chairman Levi Chatfield, a former New York state attorney general, denounced the sell-out in Baltimore. Silence filled the hall as Michigan's William Ferry approached the rostrum to read a much-anticipated sealed letter from Charles O'Conor, the party's nominee-in-waiting.

O'Conor's lengthy letter, in which he sharply repudiated Greeley's nomination in Baltimore, was frequently interrupted by thunderous applause. His letter was a ready-made platform for the Straight-Out Democrats and was essentially adopted as such. In it, O'Conor criticized protectionists and free traders alike, and said the size of government bureaucracies could be reduced by four-fifths. Sounding more and more like a candidate, the conservative New York attorney advocated a pay-as-you-go policy and denounced the practice of government borrowing, saying that it is "the very life-blood of aristocratic rule, for it fetters labor as the bond-slave of capital." By eliminating the government's ability to borrow, he said, society could virtually abolish "that most shocking of all national crimes and calamities"—namely, war.

Needless to say, O'Conor's letter was enthusiastically received, especially his sharp denunciation of the Baltimore convention. Delegates cheered wildly and waved their hats in the air as O'Conor cast Greeley to the gods. Caught up in the ecstasy of the moment, most delegates ignored O'Conor's concluding remarks. And even those who heard him say that he wished to remain in private life, dismissed such talk as the words of a modest man who didn't want to appear to be too ambitious or anxious.

The jubilant delegates returned to their hotel rooms in the nearby Galt House, giving little thought to what O'Conor had actually said in his closing remarks and giving even less consideration to whom his prospective vice-presidential running mate might be.

The Straight-Out Democrats reconvened the following morning and, as if to show that they weren't engaged in mere "child's play" agreed to appoint a national committee consisting of two members from every state. The convention then proceeded with its presidential nomination. O'Conor's name was offered for nomination by acclamation, but there were a few shouts of "nay," at which point convention leaders, hoping to "smoke out the traitors," ordered a roll call of the states.

O'Conor, as expected, received 600 votes on the first ballot to four for Ohio's "Gentleman George" Pendleton, the Democratic vice-presidential nominee four years earlier. Apparently, a handful of mischievous Greeleyites had smuggled their way into the Louisville hall. Pendleton, of course, was supporting Greeley and had no interest in the Straight-Out proceedings. The only other disruption occurred when the irrepressible George Francis Train, who was still searching for a presidential nomination of his own, tried to protest the vote of the Nebraska delegation. The flamboyant, self-styled adventurer was shouted down and, amid physical threats, picked up his hat and scurried out of the hall, leaving his dignity behind.[21]

Prior to the convention, there had been some speculation that the Straight-Out Democrats would offer their vice-presidential nomination to former congressman James Knott of Kentucky, a 42-year-old lawyer and educator who possessed a great gift for satire. As Missouri's attorney general, he was imprisoned in 1862 for refusing to take the oath of allegiance to the federal government. There was also some talk of possibly nominating Alexander H. Stephens of Georgia, the ex-vice president of the Confederacy. Lingering antebellum emotions still ran high.

To the surprise of many, relative Democratic newcomer John Quincy Adams II of Massachusetts, the eldest son of Charles Francis Adams, was then nominated for the vice presidency. A favorite of the southern Bourbons in attendance, the 38-year-old Adams was nominated on the third ballot, narrowly defeating

---

21. Thornton, *The Nine Lives of Citizen Train*, pp. 221-227. Desperate for a presidential nomination—*any* nomination—Train, who hopped from one convention to another that year, immediately rushed out and rented the Louisville Opera House, where he promptly had himself nominated as the Citizens Party candidate. Exuding confidence, he actually expected to win presidency that year, believing that three years of active campaigning would result in a landslide victory against Grant. After refusing to join forces with Equal Rights Party candidate Victoria Woodhull earlier that summer, the flamboyant promoter and erratic adventurer proceeded to wage a full-scale campaign, describing himself as "The Man of Destiny" who would, among other things, speed up settlement of the West, ease the country's immigration laws—enabling twenty million immigrants to enter the country—and trounce Great Britain in the battle for trade with the Orient, thereby making the United States the world's premier economic power.

Ohio Democrat Alfred P. Edgerton and Virginia's James Lyons. A former prosecuting attorney from Richmond, Lyons had served in the Virginia legislature as a Whig in the 1850s. In addition to serving as defense counsel for Jefferson Davis during his trial following the Civil War, the 70-year-old lawyer also represented former First Lady Julia Gardiner Tyler in her highly publicized divorce suit in 1868.

In an extremely close contest, Adams' supporters had to overcome charges that their candidate had led a silver-spoon life and—equally damning—had descended from a family of haughty Federalists. His critics charged that Adams was just an ordinary young man with no special talent for public life. His only asset was his name. These charges, of course, were painfully true, and for a while it appeared as though the party might turn to the 59-year-old Edgerton, who most recently had been the Democratic candidate for lieutenant governor of Indiana in 1868

A strong opponent of slavery, Edgerton had vigorously opposed rescinding the Missouri Compromise and the Kansas-Nebraska Act during his two terms in Congress from his Toledo district in the early 1850s. His political career spanned more than four decades, ending with his unceremonious removal from the U.S. Civil Service Commission by President Cleveland in 1889—the very man who had appointed him to that post three years earlier. A seasoned politician, the former antislavery lawmaker came within six votes of capturing the Straight-Out vice presidential nomination.

In winning the party's nomination, Adams, a former trial judge, became the fourth member of the Adams dynasty to have been nominated for national office. While he eventually declined the party's nomination, Adams was nevertheless an ideal candidate for the lily-white Democrats in Louisville. After all, he bolted from the Democratic national convention earlier that year over the currency question and his illustrious name was sure to draw national attention to the Straight-Out ticket.

Advised by telegraph of his nomination, Charles O'Conor refused to accept the honor. The delegates were stunned. There was some talk of possibly naming an Adams-Edgerton or Adams-Lyons ticket, but party leaders decided to offer the party's top spot to Judge Lyons of Virginia, the convention's presiding officer. He, too, declined, but not before charging O'Conor with "moral cowardice." It was then decided to let the ticket stand.

Despite the reluctance of its candidates, the Straight-Out, or "Taproot" Democratic ticket, as it was sometimes called, was a pairing that just might turn some heads. For a short period, it appeared as though Democrats throughout the land might give them a second look. After all, both of its candidates were held in high esteem. O'Conor, of course, had a long and distinguished legal career. He never sought public office, but it often sought him. His piercing gray eyes and neatly groomed white beard that fringed the chin of his finely sculpted Irish face was a familiar sight in the upper-echelon of Tammany circles. He was, more than anything else, a Democrats' Democrat. Against his own wishes, he had been the party's nominee for lieutenant governor of New York in 1848. He was teamed up that year with tart-tongued gubernatorial candidate Reuben Walworth, the aging ex-chancellor of New York. Walworth and O'Conor fared rather poorly in that race, finishing nearly 104,000 votes behind the Whig Party's Hamilton Fish and almost 9,000 votes behind the Free Soil ticket headed by lawyer and railroad executive John A. Dix.

Yet as a lifelong admirer of the South, O'Conor had always been somewhat open to the idea of third party or splinter politics and had been an enthusiastic supporter of John C. Breckinridge's candidacy on the Southern Democratic ticket in 1860. Arguing that slavery was the "main pillar of our strength and an indispensable element of our growth and prosperity," O'Conor sympathized with the South throughout the Civil War by defending, in vain, the legality of secession. After the war, he served without compensation as senior counsel for Confederate President Jefferson Davis when he was charged with treason. Like Gerrit Smith and Horace Greeley, he even helped to post bail for the imprisoned Davis.

A conservative and stern man with an "inflexible temper," O'Conor was widely respected as a man of unwavering principles. He was an exceptional lawyer, possessing the kind of lucidity, conciseness and logic that established him as one of the ablest members of the New York bar. His arguments, according to one contemporary, "were beautiful examples of art." O'Conor first gained notoriety while representing actor Edwin Forrest's wife in a widely-publicized divorce trial in which the philandering actor tried to avoid what appeared to be a reasonable financial settlement. The New York lawyer also gained considerable attention in several fugitive slave cases in which he argued skillfully on behalf of the property owners, winning him, if not the admiration, at least the begrudging respect of abolitionist lawyers who conceded the brilliance of his legal arguments.

Shortly after the 1872 campaign, O'Conor, serving as counsel to the reform-minded Committee of Seventy, also achieved a great deal of fame as one of the prosecutors of William Marcy Tweed, the corrupt Tammany Hall boss who was convicted of swindling New York state out of $6 million. Later, O'Conor served as Samuel Tilden's counsel in the disputed presidential election of 1876.[22]

It was precisely O'Conor's sympathy for the South that landed him the Straight-out Democratic nomination in 1872, for this movement was largely comprised of southern Democrats like Blanton Duncan, who simply couldn't stomach Liberal Republican Horace Greeley. Greeley, after all, had been one of the country's most outspoken abolitionists prior to and during the Civil War and had favored equality and civil rights for African-Americans.

John Quincy Adams II, O'Conor's running mate, was a former state legislator who had served on Massachusetts Gov. John Andrew's staff during the war-between-the-states. A Harvard-educated lawyer, Adams was the first member of his family to cast his lot with the Democrats, joining the party in 1867 when he ran unsuccessfully for governor of Massachusetts. In that contest, the young Adams polled nearly 42% of the vote—the party's best showing in a gubernatorial contest in nearly a quarter of a century. It was the first of six unsuccessful gubernatorial campaigns, one of which was mounted on a similar "Straight-Out" Democratic ticket in 1879.

Though his change of party was characteristic of his independent nature—Adams reveled in lost causes—it was not made lightly. He did it solely for moral reasons. A staunch Lincoln supporter, Adams was angered by the Republican Party's harsh treatment of the South during the period of Reconstruction. He watched helplessly as the horror of Reconstruction spread throughout the South. By 1867, military tribunals, northern carpetbaggers, scalawags and former slaves replaced most of the local governments and state legislatures in much of the Old Confederacy. Thousands of ex-Confederates had been disenfranchised. The Radical Republicans, he believed, sought to punish the South even more. Indeed, from 1867 to 1877 they more or less controlled every state in the region with an iron fist. The vindictive and rapacious Radicals attempted to fasten black supremacy upon the defeated Confederacy, seeing to it that black lieutenant governors were installed in Louisiana, Mississippi and South Carolina. African-Americans, moreover, dominated the South Carolina legislature for a short while and Mississippi actually had two black U.S. Senators during this period—Hiram R. Revels, a Quaker-educated clergyman, and Blanche Bruce, an ex-slave who had been tortured by his master's son. Moreover, fifteen African-Americans were elected to the U.S. House of Representatives, including South Carolina's Robert DeLarge who was elected amid charges of voting irregularities on the part of Radical Republicans. The mean-spiritedness of the Radical agenda

---

22.   Miller, *'If Elected…' Unsuccessful Candidates for the Presidency 1796-1968*, pp. 213-214.

was vividly reflected by the fact that not a single African-American held an office of similar consequence in the North.

Moreover, extravagant spending and rampant corruption during this period marred virtually every state administration in the South, precisely because the old planter class and ex-Confederate military leaders—those who had been in positions of responsibility prior to the Civil War—were barred from holding office. Under the tutelage of the vengeful and largely inept Radicals, state coffers were frequently looted and taxes skyrocketed. The public debt of most southern states doubled and, in some cases, quadrupled during this period.

Adams was fond of reminding his audiences that his grandfather had predicted that when the great slavery struggle came to an end, "there must come a great constitutional party or anarchy." The younger Adams, who received a single vote for president from a South Carolina delegate at the 1868 Democratic convention, felt that the Democratic Party would be that "great constitutional party" that his grandfather had spoken of. His father, Charles Francis Adams, apparently shared the same view. Repulsed by the actions of the Radical Republicans, the longtime diplomat said while traveling abroad that the majority party—the Republicans—left little alternative "to anyone who will interest himself in the country's fate."

The O'Conor-Adams ticket was certainly an impressive one. In a lament of sorts, Edwin L. Godkin's *Nation* magazine, hardly enthusiastic about Grant and unwilling to reconcile itself to Greeley, described the Straight-Out Democratic ticket as one of "the highest character, and of great ability, whom we might all be proud to see in the highest places of government." But like most other liberal periodicals of the day, the *Nation* told its readers that the Straight-Out duo was the work of a "handful of wretched hacks" and was not a practical alternative in the election.

As it turned out, it was a moot point. O'Conor and Adams declined the Straight-Out Democratic nominations. Despite rejecting their respective nominations, both men were quickly punished for having been named at the Louisville convention. Though James O'Brien's Apollo Hall faction remained loyal to O'Conor, the Tammany Society in New York reportedly wanted his resignation, while Democrats in Massachusetts threatened to expel Adams.

For the next several weeks, the headless Straight-Out Democrats tried in vain to coax the New York lawyer into the race, but he refused to budge. On September 10, Major William Moreau of Indiana and seven others visited O'Conor for three hours at his office on Wall Street. At one point during their meeting, it appeared that O'Conor might be inching toward an acceptance, expressing sympathy for the Louisville convention while sharply lambasting Greeley as a "candidate of the corruptionists." He also criticized those Democrats who argued that the party must support Greeley as the lesser of two evils. If this was the case, he said, then the Democrats were doomed. He also dismissed those who claimed it was too late to launch a new ticket. Fifty days, he said, was plenty of time for an "awakening."[23] In the end, however, the New York lawyer refused to run. Still undeterred, the Bourbon Democrats entered electoral slates pledged to O'Conor and Adams in twenty-three states with 244 electoral votes—enough, theoretically at least, to put the reluctant O'Conor in the White House.

---

23. *New York Times*, September 11, 1872.

12

The Prohibition and Labor Reform Parties

✦

New Political Movements Begin to Take Shape

The nation's oldest third party and America's third oldest political party, the Prohibition Party was founded in early September 1869 at a convention attended by 500 delegates from nineteen states and the District of Columbia. Held at Farwell Hall in Chicago, the three-day meeting was the result of more than two years of tireless organizing on the part of John Russell, a Methodist minister and editor of Detroit's *Peninsular Herald*. For years, Russell was one of the lone voices advocating the formation of a national Prohibition Party. Described as the party's apostle St. Paul, Russell clearly played the largest role in shaping the party's early philosophy.[1] "We will be as harsh as truth, and as uncompromising as justice," he told the enthusiastic gathering in Chicago. "Urge us not to use moderation in a cause like the present. We are in earnest—we will not equivocate—we will not excuse—we will not retract a single inch, and we will be heard."[2]

But Russell wasn't alone in advocating a new party dedicated to the cause of temperance. Frustrated by the failure of the country's two major party's to embrace the temperance cause, the half-hearted enforcement of existing local prohibition laws and the founding of the United States Brewers' Association in 1864, a number of others were also clamoring for a new political party during this period, including antislavery activist and political gadfly Gerrit Smith, James

---

1. Roger Storms, *Partisan Prophets: A History of the Prohibition Party* (Denver, 1972), pp. 4-5.
2. John Kobler, *Ardent Spirits: The Rise and Fall of Prohibition* (New York, 1973), p. 83.

Black of Pennsylvania, Dr. William Ross of Illinois and Jonathan H. Orne, the tireless leader of the Good Templars and a former local elected official from Marblehead, Massachusetts. Ross, who helped to found the Illinois Prohibition Party several months earlier, was regarded as one of the greatest temperance speakers in the country and had led the floor fight for those advocating the formation of a new party at the Chicago convention.

Prior to its founding there were, to be sure, several local temperance parties already in existence, most notably Gerrit Smith's single-issue Anti-Dramshop Party in New York, which had been founded in 1842 and revived nearly three decades later, and Neal Dow's Temperance and Maine Law parties. Other temperance parties, such as James Black's Prohibition Party in Lancaster County, Pennsylvania, had also been active in the 1850s. Local temperance parties also existed in Connecticut, Georgia, Indiana and Ohio. Some of these parties even competed in statewide elections. As early as 1855, for example, temperance parties in Connecticut and Georgia fielded gubernatorial candidates.

Unlike some of the other local prohibition parties sprinkled across the American landscape during this period, Neal Dow's Temperance and Maine Law parties had been particularly successful in outlawing the manufacture and sale of alcoholic beverages in Maine. The son of Quaker parents, Dow was a wealthy businessman with a social conscience. He had inherited his family's tannery business at a young age and also dabbled in real estate, banking and railroads. A one-time Federalist and Whig, he was strongly influenced by jeweler James Appleton, one of the country's earliest prohibition advocates. A resident of distillery-ridden Salem, Massachusetts, Appleton, a descendant of the Massachusetts colony's first brewer, was the first to advance the idea of statutory prohibition of the manufacture and sale of liquor, petitioning the Massachusetts legislature in 1831.[3] Appleton moved to Portland, Maine, in 1833 and was elected to the state legislature three years later. No stranger to third party politics, Appleton, a staunch foe of slavery, was a frequent candidate for governor of Maine on the old Liberty Party ticket.

Convinced that the state's large woodlands and lucrative lumber trade with the West Indies gave Portland and Bangor stills a relatively inexpensive supply of

---

3.   Ibid., p. 47. Believing that 75% of the nation's crime and poverty was directly linked to liquor consumption, Appleton proposed a law fixing the minimum amount of liquor that could be purchased at any one time at thirty gallons—the intent being that to have to carry home such a large quantity every time someone wanted a drink or two would prove too burdensome. To no one's surprise, the Massachusetts Senate tabled Appleton's petition.

rum and molasses, Dow headed a successful drive among Portland employers to eliminate the traditional morning and afternoon liquor breaks for employees. As Overseer of the Poor, he came to believe that liquor was a leading cause of poverty. He organized the Maine Temperance Union in the hope of re-instilling old-fashioned Yankee moral values and succeeded in putting the issue of prohibition on the state's front burner. A somewhat pious man, Dow hoped to raise the productivity of Portland's large Irish labor supply.

Running on an anti-liquor platform, Dow was elected mayor of Portland in 1851 and was re-elected four years later. As mayor, he persuaded the Maine legislature to enact the "Maine Law," outlawing the manufacture and sale of alcoholic beverages in the Pine Tree State. Prohibition succeeded in that state largely because of the formation of the Dow's Maine Law Party in 1853. Quickly eclipsing the dying Whig Party as the major opposition to the Democrats, the new party primarily stressed two issues—defense of the Maine Law and opposition to the Kansas-Nebraska Act. Curiously, Dow, described as a "hellishly energetic" man, did little to help the Prohibition Party when he stood as its presidential standard-bearer in 1880. Like many other dry advocates of that era, it seems he never completely severed his ties with the Republican Party.

Another precursor to the national Prohibition Party was James Black's Prohibition Party of Lancaster, Pennsylvania. A descendant of Scottish immigrants who settled in America in 1790, Black was born in Lewisburg, Pennsylvania, on September 23, 1823. He had his first and last encounter with "demon rum" at the age of sixteen when, as a mule driver on the Pennsylvania and Union canal, he became violently ill when he tried to match drink for drink with some of the older men on the job. He immediately became an enemy of the liquor trade. Admitted to the Lancaster County bar in 1846, Black often rubbed shoulders with some of the area's leading attorneys, including men like Thaddeus Stevens and James Buchanan, the future president. Black was an early organizer of the Washingtonian Society, a temperance group founded in Baltimore in 1840, and of the National Temperance Society in 1865.[4] Originally a Democrat, Black switched parties in 1854, briefly becoming a Republican and served as a delegate at the party's first national convention in 1856 that nominated John C. Fremont for president. He also founded his own temperance party during this period. His Lancaster County Prohibition Party, founded in 1855, actually elected two state legislators on its ticket. Black was also instrumental in the founding of Ocean City, New Jersey, as a seaside paradise for Methodists.

Russell, Dow and Black were three of the more prominent individuals in the temperance movement who looked to the newly founded Republican Party in the

1850s as a beacon of humanitarian, Christian reform. Reconciled to the fact that slavery was the paramount issue of the day, they fervently believed that the Republicans would champion their cause as soon as the slavery issue was settled. It was ultimately a vain hope; immediately following the Civil War, the GOP increasingly became the instrument of corporate interests—a trend that continues to this day—as well as the tool of the vengeful Radicals seeking harsh Reconstruction in the South. Republicans like Dow and Black had nowhere to turn. With its large ethnic "wet" base, most early temperance advocates viewed the Democratic Party with disdain.

Antislavery activist Gerrit Smith of New York also played a role in the party's founding. Smith, of course, wasn't the only old Liberty Party veteran to join forces with the Prohibitionists. In fact, Smith advocated that the new party should be called the Anti-Dramshop Party, after his own temperance party in New York. That way, he reasoned, their opponents would be called the "Dramshop Party," thus stigmatizing them with a "suitable and infamous name." Among the other well-known abolitionists who eventually embraced temperance as the great reform issue once slavery had been abolished was William Goodell, the 77-year-old newspaper editor and founder of both the Liberty Party and the Liberty League, the latter of which opposed not only slavery, but tariffs, land monopolies, secret societies and the liquor trade.

According to party historian D. Leigh Colvin, Abraham Lincoln also agreed that temperance was the next major issue to be dealt with, reportedly making a comment to that effect on the very day of his assassination. "After reconstruction," the president purportedly told a friend, "the next great question will be the overthrow and suppression of the legalized liquor trade."[5] Indeed, Lincoln had

---

4.   It was somewhat curious that the Washingtonian Society named itself after George Washington, especially given the late president's fondness for alcohol. The nation's first president even had a distillery installed at Mount Vernon. Unlike the Bible-beating evangelist Lyman Beecher—the country's most powerful temperance orator—and the Reverend Justin Edwards of Andover's Congregational Church, the Washingtonians didn't view temperance as a religious issue, nor did they seek to outlaw drinking. Employing a psychological device not unlike that employed by Alcoholics Anonymous a century later, the Washingtonians insisted on a public confession and a voluntary pledge to refrain from consuming intoxicating liquors. Within two years of its founding, the Washingtonian Society garnered 23,000 pledges in New York, New Jersey and Pennsylvania, 30,000 in Kentucky and an estimated 60,000 in Ohio.

5.   D. Leigh Colvin, *Prohibition in the United States: A History of the Prohibition Party and of the Prohibition Movement* (New York, 1926), p. 60.

been impressed with the soundness of the Maine Law and wrote the first draft of a bill that was eventually passed by the Illinois legislature and submitted to a referendum of the people in 1855. Although the liquor industry long disputed these facts, there is plenty of evidence that Lincoln, who was running for the U.S. Senate that year, gave a number of speeches favoring the prohibitory law during the ensuing referendum. Consistent with this view, Lincoln's Whig supporters that year had adopted a dry plank and scornfully blasted the Democrats as "the Whiskey Party."[6]

In the two years following its founding, the Prohibition Party entered a number of candidates in local races in Maine, Massachusetts, New Hampshire, Illinois, Ohio, Michigan and Minnesota. Illinois was the first state to organize.[7] At a meeting of roughly two hundred delegates to the state's Temperance Convention in Bloomington in early December 1868, the third-party forces, led by Dr. William Ross, rejected the idea that the GOP would eventually adopt prohibition as a major issue. Overcoming a spirited challenge from the vocal Republicans in attendance, the Illinois temperance leaders formed a "Prohibition Party" and adopted a platform declaring war on the liquor trade.

The leaders of the Illinois convention proved prophetic in ignoring the pleas of those who insisted that the Republican Party would eventually embrace the temperance cause. The Republicans had no such plans. Following the new party's strong showing in the 1870 Illinois congressional races—in which one Prohibitionist came within 1,880 votes of unseating a six-term Republican incumbent in a three-way race—the panic-stricken GOP-dominated legislature, in attempt to appease the state's growing dry constituency, passed an anti-liquor civil damage law in early 1872. Brewers were so incensed by this severely punitive law that they threatened political retaliation. Afraid of alienating their large German and

---

6.   Kobler, *Ardent Spirits*, pp. 52-53. On the other hand, Lincoln never endorsed compulsory prohibition. "Prohibition will work great injury to the cause of temperance," he remarked in 1840. "It is a species of intemperance within itself, for it goes beyond the bounds of reason in that it attempts to control a man's appetite by legislation and makes a crime out of things that are not crimes," adding that compulsory legislation "strikes at the very principle upon which our Government was founded." When asked several years later where he stood on the issue, the former Whig congressman said: "I am not a temperance man, but I am temperate to this extent—I don't drink."

7.   Prohibitionists in Ohio were the first to run a candidate for governor, polling 696 votes in that state's 1869 gubernatorial contest won narrowly by Republican Rutherford B. Hayes, the future president. Several months earlier, a Prohibition ticket had been entered in Cleveland's municipal election.

Irish "wet" constituents, Illinois Republicans allowed Herman Raster, editor of the *Illinois Staats-Zeitung* and a longtime spokesman for brewery interests in the state's northwest region, to add a personal liberty plank to the party's state platform. Raster and others had threatened to bolt to Carl Schurz's Liberal Republican Party if their demands weren't met. Later that year, the Republican national convention adopted a resolution drafted by Raster designed to pacify the powerful liquor industry. It was no coincidence that Raster had been strategically placed on the party's platform committee.

In Maine, the short-lived Temperance and Maine Law Party nominated Nathan G. Hitchborn, a federal marshal, as its candidate for governor. Hitchborn polled 4,735 votes, or roughly five percent of the vote in his uphill campaign—a total never again equaled by the Prohibition Party in that state. Wendell Phillips, president of the American Anti-Slavery Society—an organization he felt shouldn't be disbanded until blacks had been granted the right to vote—polled an astonishing 21,946 votes for governor of Massachusetts on a Prohibition-Labor Reform ticket in 1870. Approximately 8,000 of his votes were cast on the Prohibition ticket. The following year, the Prohibitionists in that state nominated Judge Robert C. Pitman for governor. A former state senator, Pitman had sponsored several prohibition measures during his two terms in the legislature and was largely responsible for the reenactment of the state's prohibitory law in 1869. During Pitman's 1871 campaign, the Prohibitionists elected Reverend George H. Vibbert to the Massachusetts legislature—the first partisan Prohibitionist ever elected to a state legislative office.[8]

As previously mentioned, the fledgling party also had an impact in Illinois as early as 1870. In the state's second congressional district, Prohibitionist Jonathan C. Stoughton, polling nearly 38% of the vote, came within 1,880 votes of unseating six-term Republican John F. Farnsworth, a man with radical leanings during Reconstruction, in a three-cornered race. And Prohibitionist George W. Minier's vigorous campaign in the state's heavily Republican eighth district, encompassing the city of Bloomington and Lincoln's hometown of Springfield, enabled a Democrat to sneak into office for the first time in eight years. Minier garnered 1,175 votes in that race, or slightly more than four percent of the vote.

The Prohibition Party held its first presidential nominating convention in Columbus, Ohio, on February 22, 1872. Several prominent figures were mentioned as possible candidates, including U.S. Supreme Court Justice David Davis, Massachusetts Congressman Benjamin F. Butler, the ostentatious and

---

8.   Colvin, *Prohibition in the United States*, pp. 87-88.

controversial Union army general, and ailing U.S. Chief Justice Salmon P. Chase. Pennsylvania's Simeon B. Chase and hardly perennial Gerrit Smith were also considered possibilities. These were all giants. Salmon P. Chase and Justice Davis were actively seeking the Liberal Republican Party's presidential nomination that year. President Grant's name, of course, was never considered—most temperance voters were appalled by the president's reputed drinking habits. To almost everyone's surprise, the delegates turned to two of the party's founding members and nominated the relatively obscure 48-year-old James Black for president and John Russell for vice president. Russell's name was one of a half-dozen proposed for the vice presidency.[9]

Born in Geneseo, New York, in 1822, Russell moved to Michigan with his family when he was sixteen. He later entered the Methodist Episcopal ministry. Long active in the Order of Good Templars, Russell headed that temperance organization in Michigan for a dozen years and served as head of the worldwide Order in 1871 and 1872. Known as the "Father of the Prohibition Party," Russell had advocated a separate temperance party in his newspaper as early as 1867 and served as chairman of the party's national committee during its infancy from 1869-72. A prolific writer, he contributed numerous articles to temperance newspapers throughout the country. Russell, who lived to the ripe old age of ninety, remained active in party affairs until his death in November 1912, frequently seeking public office on the party's ticket in Michigan.

Before adjourning, the inexperienced Prohibitionists passed a platform so verbose that most newspapers ignored it altogether. In addition to a call for national prohibition through a constitutional amendment, the party's platform advocated an end to the "spoils" system through civil service reform, regulation of public utilities, fair treatment for labor and women's suffrage. The right of all citizens to vote, regardless of race, was also endorsed, as was a liberal immigration policy.

During the Columbus convention, the delegates named Simeon B. Chase of Pennsylvania to replace Russell as the party's new national chairman. Prior to switching parties, Chase, who had been an organizer of the Republican Party in Pennsylvania in the 1850s, was regarded as a likely future governor of Pennsylvania. Widely respected, Chase had served several terms in the state legislature from his rural Wyoming County district, including a brief stint as Speaker of the Pennsylvania House. Chase proved to be an exceptionally able presiding officer for the new party.

---

9.   Storms, *Partisan Prophets*, p. 7.

In addition to the Black-Russell ticket, the Prohibitionists slated several other noteworthy candidates in the 1872 elections, including former U.S. Senator Francis Gillette, the party's gubernatorial candidate in Connecticut. A dignified man, Gillette was valedictorian of his Yale class of 1829. He abandoned his study of law as a young man and pursued the life of a farmer. He was twice elected to the Connecticut House of Representatives, quickly identifying with the legislature's antislavery bloc. In 1838, he supported a voting rights amendment to remove the word "white" from the state constitution. The antithesis of a professional politician, the 65-year-old Gillette was certainly no stranger to third-party politics. Like slavery foe Samuel E. Sewall in neighboring Massachusetts, Gillette had been the Liberty Party's candidate for governor in 1841 and ran repeatedly for that office on the Liberty and Free Soil tickets over the next twelve years.

Gillette's persistence finally paid off in 1854 when he was elected to the U.S. Senate by a coalition of Whigs and Free Soilers in the Connecticut legislature. He reached Washington just in time to vote against the Kansas-Nebraska Act. Later, he was active in the formation of the Republican Party in Connecticut and lent his considerable energy to the antislavery and temperance movements. In fact, the basement of his home in Hartford was used as a way station in the Underground Railroad. Among other things, he was a founder of the American Temperance Life Insurance Company, later known as Phoenix Mutual. He was also active in educational reform and served as chairman of the Board of Trustees of the State Normal School upon its founding in 1849. Gillette's son, William—who later stumped for Teddy Roosevelt's Bull Moose Party—was a well-known actor, impresario and playwright who appeared on stage as Sherlock Holmes on no fewer than 1,300 occasions.

Party chairman Simeon B. Chase of Pennsylvania was another notable Prohibition gubernatorial candidate that year. He had forfeited a promising future in Pennsylvania politics when, as a matter of principle, he joined the fledgling anti-liquor party. Although the former Republican Speaker of the Pennsylvania House polled only 1,250 votes in 1872, his candidacy paved the way for future generations of Pennsylvania Prohibitionists. Beginning with Chase, the Prohibitionists competed in twenty-one consecutive gubernatorial campaigns in the Keystone State through 1950, playing a pivotal role in the election of progressive Republican Gifford Pinchot in 1930.

The Labor Reformers

The Prohibitionists weren't the only ones to challenge the two major parties in the 1872 presidential election. The largely forgotten Labor Reform Party also entered the fray. The Labor Reform Party was an offshoot of William H. Sylvis' National Labor Union, an organization founded six years earlier to unify and coordinate the efforts of various workers' groups across the country. A skilled propagandist and superb speaker who was more interested in cooperatives and currency reform than in the traditional labor issues such as hours and wages, Sylvis had recruited an estimated 640,000 members by 1868—a figure that has been highly disputed by some labor historians. The National Labor Union, remarked one scornful observer, was made up of "labor leaders without organizations, politicians without parties, women without husbands, and cranks, visionaries, and agitators without jobs."[10] The National Labor Union, which declined sharply following Sylvis'death in 1869, was the first national federation of trade unions in the United States.

The Labor Reform Party's roots dated back to Andrew Cameron's *Workingmen's Advocate*, which was published in Chicago and Cincinnati from 1863-77. A printer who was active in the Typographical Union, Cameron, who was widely regarded as the greatest labor editor of his time, had advocated the creation of an independent labor party as early as April 1866. The party grew out of the National Labor Union's 1867 convention when it passed a resolution stating that the time had come for the nation's industrious classes to "cut themselves aloof from party ties and predilections" and organize a National Labor Party. The party opted out of the 1868 presidential campaign but passed a Declaration of Principles, closely modeled after the Declaration of Independence. The Declaration, which dealt extensively with currency reform, called for the abolition of the national banking system, calling upon the federal government to set interest rates. The party also advocated the creation of a Department of Labor; an eight-hour workday; and government control of the railroads, water transportation and telegraph communications. The new party also urged the cooperation of everyone—blacks and whites, male and female alike—to unite and assist in making its principles a reality.

Campaigning with little money and virtually no editorial support, the fledgling party made a significant showing shortly after its founding when Edwin M. Chamberlin, a Harvard-educated attorney, polled 13,567 votes—or nearly ten

---

10.   Bailyn, *et al.*, *The Great Republic*, pp. 579-580.

percent of the total—against Republican William Claflin and Democrat John Quincy Adams II in the 1869 Massachusetts gubernatorial contest. It was an auspicious start for the fledgling Labor Reform Party. Campaigning on a platform calling for the incorporation of trade unions, the establishment of a bureau of labor statistics, an eight-hour workday and the abolition of convict labor, the Labor Reformers, comprised largely of members of the Knights of St. Crispin, the shoemakers' union, elected twenty-seven members of the lower house, as well as four state senators. The brief three-week campaign was nothing short of extraordinary and immediately put the new party on the political map.

Buoyed by its strong showing in the campaign and hoping to gain the support of the intellectual community, the Labor Reformers nominated the great orator and abolitionist Wendell Phillips for governor the following year. Phillips was initially reluctant to actively run for public office. "I have no wish to be governor of Massachusetts," he said, "and flattering as is this confidence, I thoroughly dislike to have my name drawn into party politics, for I belong to no political party."[11] Nevertheless, Phillips eventually acquiesced and waged a vigorous campaign against long odds, frequently speaking in the first person singular and almost always sounding pontifical. This alarmed many of his longtime friends and supporters, including a few who accused him of being overly ambitious. "His egotism increases every day," observed Fanny Garrison Villard, daughter of William Lloyd Garrison, "and now he talks as if he alone abolished slavery."[12] Phillips assured his friends that he wasn't interested in public office, that his campaign was merely an educational effort. "Born of six generations of Yankees," he replied, "I knew the way to office and turned my back on it thirty years ago."[13]

At his wife's urging, Phillips, a Harvard-educated lawyer, abandoned his legal career years earlier and had devoted all of his time and energy to the antislavery cause. Deeply moved by a proslavery mob that had viciously attacked abolitionist William Lloyd Garrison in Boston in 1835 and by the 1837 murder of antislavery editor Elijah Lovejoy in Alton, Illinois, Phillips quickly emerged as one of the most sought after abolitionist speakers in the country.[14] His informal, collo-

---

11. Bartlett, Irving H., *Wendell Phillips: Brahmin Radical* (Boston, 1961), p. 351.
12. Ibid., p. 355.
13. Sherwin, Oscar, *Prophet of Liberty: The Life and Times of Wendell Phillips* (New York, 1958), p. 585.
14. In a widely criticized speech, Massachusetts Attorney General James T. Austin said that Lovejoy had died a fool's death and compared his murderers to the men who threw tea into Boston harbor shortly before the War of Independence. See Lorenzo Sears, *Wendell Phillips, Orator and Agitator* (New York, 1909).

quial delivery was heard time and again on the Lyceum circuit and his speeches were frequently reprinted in northern periodicals.

Like his close friend Garrison, Phillips initially eschewed the idea of participating in electoral politics. His influence was felt far and wide. Among other things, he sharply opposed the Mexican War and, later, the Compromise of 1850, publicly urging defiance of the Fugitive Slave Law. He once referred to Lincoln as "that slave hound from Illinois" and "a first-rate second-rate man." Phillips also criticized Lincoln's emancipation policies during the Civil War and opposed the president's re-election in 1864, arguing that the federal government owed the former slaves more than simply their freedom. Long suspicious of Lincoln, Phillips believed that the ex-slaves were also entitled to public education, land, and full civil rights. The latter demand caused a falling out with Garrison in 1864, shortly after the aging abolitionist proposed dissolving the American Anti-Slavery Society. Undeterred, Phillips fought to keep the organization in existence until voting rights had been extended to black males. As such, the lawyer-turned-activist kept the abolitionist society alive, serving as its president until the passage of the Fifteenth Amendment in 1870, giving African-American males the right to vote.

During this period, Phillips turned much of his considerable energy and talent to other issues, including temperance, women's suffrage and the abolition of the death penalty. He was also active in the eight-hour movement and became a strong proponent of monetary reform, making him an ideal candidate for the Labor Reformers.

Phillips crafted the party's platform that year, declaring war on a system which "enslaves the workingman" and "robs labor and gorges capital." Among other things, his platform demanded an eight-hour day and an end to the forced importation of cheap Chinese labor. His forward-looking platform also urged equal pay for women—a radical notion in those days.

Running as a fusion candidate, Phillips campaigned arduously in his one and only bid for public office, delighting audiences throughout the commonwealth with his stirring eloquence and high-browed principles. He took to the campaign trail with zeal, attacking Democrats and Republicans alike for their failure to address the pressing issues of the day—labor reform and temperance. "The Democratic Party proposes nothing," he said, while the Republicans offered even less. "The Republican Party is an honorable party," he quipped, "but as the old critic said of the man who was praising his ancestors, 'If you judge it by the present canvass, its great merit rests, like the potato, underground.'" Resting on its laurels, the party "puts forth no effort for the future," he said.[15] Running on the

Labor Reform and Prohibition tickets, Phillips received 21,946 votes, or 14.5%, against Republican William Claflin and Democrat John Quincy Adams II (who was making the second of six unsuccessful bids for the governor's office). Despite his setback, there were several pockets of support for Phillips throughout Massachusetts, including the city of Lynn where he captured nearly 45% of the vote. While the party lost most of its seats in the state legislature that year, it nevertheless succeeded in persuading lawmakers in the Bay State to create the nation's first Bureau of Labor Statistics.

When Phillips refused to run for office again the following year, the Labor Reformers again turned to Edwin Chamberlin. The party also nominated an African-American for state attorney general. Phillips presided over the party's state convention and actively stumped for its ticket in the autumn campaign. In the 1871 gubernatorial contest, the 36-year-old Chamberlin received a disappointing 6,848 votes—a sharp decline from his previous showing in 1869 and that of Wendell Phillips in 1870. Phillips attributed the party's decline to employer intimidation—a charge that was undoubtedly true. But the size of the party's defeat that year can also be attributed to the sharp decline in union membership in New England during that period, especially among the once powerful Knights of St. Crispin.

Despite the short-lived success of the Labor Reform Party in Massachusetts, labor-oriented minor parties enjoyed a modicum of success in other parts of the country during this period, most notably in the election of James Blackmore as mayor of Pittsburgh on a Workingmen's ticket in 1868.

Meanwhile, the National Labor Reform Party went ahead with plans for the 1872 presidential campaign. Meeting in Washington in early 1871, a committee headed by Samuel P. Cummings, leader of the Knights of St. Crispin, recommended a national convention to be held in October of that year. It was later decided to postpone the convention until February 1872. A second group called for a national convention to be held on July 4, 1872, but National Labor Union president Richard F. Trevellick, a currency reformer who later served as national chairman of the Greenback Party, said the group had no authority to act separately.

Possibly by design, the party's national convention was held in Columbus, Ohio, at the same time that the Prohibitionists were holding their national convention in the same city. Convening on February 21, the Labor Reform convention was attended by delegates from 17 of the nation's 38 states. Curiously, only

15. Sherwin, *Prophet of Liberty*, pp. 579-580.

about twenty-five of the delegates in attendance were affiliated with organized labor. One of them was John Siney, a leading figure in the early history of the coal miners' union. By 1872, most trade unions had severed ties with the party's chief sponsor, the National Labor Union. Only the Crispins, weakened by strike losses, had bothered to send delegates to the National Labor Union's sixth conference in 1871. The Labor Reform Party's convention was comprised mainly of the politically naïve, the vast majority of whom had never attended a national convention before.

Despite the fact that labor was noticeably underrepresented at the party's national convention, the names of no fewer than nine presidential candidates, including the National Labor Union's Horace H. Day, a wealthy Brooklyn philanthropist, were considered at the Columbus gathering. Two of the biggest names considered were Pennsylvania Governor John W. Geary and Supreme Court Justice David Davis, whose name was simultaneously being bandied about by the infant Prohibition Party.

On the surface, Geary appeared to be the prohibitive favorite. An independent-minded politician who had ties to both major parties, the 52-year-old Geary had pursued successful careers in law and civil engineering and had served as a Mexican War officer, leading an assault at Chapultepec, before entering politics. As San Francisco's first mayor back in 1850, Geary had subdued countless outlaws in that wide-open city. He also served as governor of the Kansas Territory (1856-57) when that region was on the verge of civil war over the slavery issue. As territorial governor, Geary, an imposing man who stood almost six-foot-six, calmly ended the Kansas uprising in only three weeks time, largely by dismissing the proslavery militia and replacing it with federal troops. A former teacher and farmer, he had also served as chairman of the Democratic National Committee during the Polk administration and fought in the Union army at Chancellorsville, Gettysburg and other battles during the Civil War. Wounded at Cedar Mountain, he received a hero's welcome when he returned home to his western Pennsylvania farm. Resuming his political career, he was elected governor of Pennsylvania as a Republican in 1866, defeating his Democratic opponent by 17,000 votes. He was re-elected, albeit by a smaller margin, in 1869. As governor of the Keystone State, Geary exerted his independence by vetoing no fewer than 390 bills.

Although considered the frontrunner, Geary faced serious opposition from Horace H. Day of New York. A leading currency reformer, the 58-year-old Day was a strong advocate of producers' cooperatives and was one of the real movers and shakers in the National Labor Union, the first nationally-organized federation of unions. Day, who served as vice president of the organization, had been pushing for an eight-hour day for working people since the close of the Civil War. Earlier in his life, Day had been a successful businessman, owning, among other things, the Niagara Water Power Company. A leading industrialist of his era, he also built the Power Canal at Niagara Falls. For more than twenty years, the Brooklyn philanthropist owned a company that manufactured rubber products, but his New Jersey-based rubber business collapsed in 1852 following a protracted legal battle with Charles Goodyear over production rights. A devoted currency reformer, he was also the author of *The Financial System Unmasked and Dissected*, which was published in 1872.

There was also a strong movement to draft Supreme Court Justice David Davis, a ten-year veteran of the nation's highest court, as the party's presidential standard-bearer. A man seemingly with little in common with the Labor Reformers, Davis had been working quietly for the presidential nominations of the Liberal Republican and Democratic parties, which were scheduled to hold their national conventions in May and July, respectively.

Ohio's Thomas Ewing, Jr., an ex-Union army officer and former chief justice of the Kansas Supreme Court, was also regarded as a serious contender. On the eve of the convention, his name was one of the four or five names leaked to the press by party leaders as a possible nominee. Ewing's father had been a U.S. Senator on two occasions and served as Secretary of the Treasury in the Harrison and Tyler administrations and as Secretary of the Interior during Zachary Taylor's short-lived presidency. The younger Ewing started his public career at a very early age, serving as private secretary to President Taylor when he was barely nineteen years of age.

Ewing, 42, was an easy-going man with a gracious style, whose lofty ideals usually left a strong impression. An eloquent opponent of slavery, Ewing, a graduate of Brown University, is credited with exposing the fraudulent voting that took place in Kansas under the Lecompton constitution in January 1858. The public outcry that ensued prevented Kansas from being admitted to the Union as a slave state. In 1861, Ewing was named the first chief justice of the Kansas Supreme Court and represented his adopted state at the failed Peace Convention that year. He resigned from the court to recruit the 11th Kansas Volunteers during the Civil War and took part in several serious engagements, resulting in a promotion to the rank of brigadier-general. He was later brevetted major general for his stubborn resistance at Pilot Knob, in which a thousand men under his command courageously held a fort against 7,000 rebel soldiers.

Ewing is perhaps best remembered for his infamous Order No. 11, resulting in the savage depopulation of communities bordering Kansas. In an attempt to quell the ruthless pro-slavery guerillas led by William Clarke Quantrill and others, an enraged Ewing ordered the forcible removal of civilians in four Missouri counties bordering Kansas, leaving those communities a virtual wasteland for years to come.

After the war, Ewing practiced law in Washington, D.C., and turned down offers to serve as President Johnson's Secretary of War and Attorney General. Like his father, Ewing was a lifelong Whig who later switched parties in protest of the nation's harsh Reconstruction policies. He returned to Lancaster, Ohio, in 1870 and quickly emerged as a leader of the greenback wing of the Democratic Party. Ewing, who later served two terms in Congress, ran unsuccessfully for governor of Ohio in 1879, narrowly losing to wealthy Republican banker Charles Foster in a race that drew considerable national attention.

Geary outpolled his rivals on the convention's first ballot, receiving 69 votes to 59 for Brooklyn's Horace H. Day and 47 for the dark-horse Davis. Social agitator Wendell Phillips, the Boston aristocrat, received a disappointing thirteen votes; Gov. John McAuley Palmer of Illinois (who later emerged as the Gold Democratic nominee for president in 1896), garnered eight votes; seven were cast for New Jersey Gov. Joel Parker; and six delegates voted for former Indiana congressman George Washington Julian. The 55-year-old Julian, who presided over part of the convention for two days, was a seasoned minor party veteran. He had been the Free Soil Party's vice-presidential candidate twenty years earlier. Two other potential candidates whose names had been frequently mentioned—Liberal Republican Missouri Gov. Ben Gratz-Brown and Ohio's Thomas Ewing, Jr.—weren't placed in nomination.

After considerable jockeying, Justice Davis was nominated on the third ballot, garnering 201 of the 211 votes cast. Governor Joel Parker of New Jersey, who was widely regarded as an incorruptible politician, was then nominated for the vice presidency on the second ballot, receiving 112 votes to 57 for Edwin Chamberlin of Massachusetts and 22 for Ohio's Thomas Ewing. Chamberlin, who chaired the convention, led on the first ballot, garnering 72 votes to Parker's 70 and 31 for Ewing. Civil War General Absolom M. West of Mississippi received eighteen votes and ten delegates voted for 41-year-old William G. Brien, a physician and lawyer from Nashville, Tennessee. Like Davis, Parker's nomination was later made unanimous.

The 57-year-old Davis, a graduate of Yale Law School, was one of Lincoln's closest friends. He had served in the Illinois legislature as a Whig and presided over the pioneer eighth judicial circuit for fourteen years. The acknowledged leader of the Lincoln forces at the 1860 Republican convention, Davis labored tirelessly for Lincoln's nomination and election that year. Eager for an appointment to the Supreme Court, the ambitious lawyer watched patiently as Lincoln appointed two others—Noah H. Swayne and Samuel Miller—to the nation's highest court before finally choosing his old friend to fill a vacancy in 1862.

Davis, who remained on the bench until 1877, generally supported the court's nationalistic bent in judicial interpretation. Occasionally, however, he displayed a great deal of independence and courage as evidenced in 1866 when he delivered the highly unpopular opinion in the *Milligan* case, holding that the military trial of Lambdin Milligan, an Indiana Copperhead who had been sentenced to death for conspiring to aid and comfort the rebels and for inciting insurrection, was unconstitutional. In his ruling, Davis argued that military courts couldn't try civilians in non-combat areas where civil courts were functioning. As a result, Milligan and other conspirators were later set free. The Republican press widely criticized Davis' opinion, but Democratic newspapers generally commended him for his courageous ruling.

Davis was a most unlikely champion of the working class. After all, he accumulated a great deal of wealth by profiting from the misfortune of others—namely, by purchasing farms at tax sales and mortgage foreclosures. Moreover, as executor of Lincoln's estate, the 325-pound Supreme Court Justice tied up the late president's estate for more than two-and-a-half years in an attempt to deny Mary Todd Lincoln of her timely inheritance following her husband's assassination in 1865. In the meantime, the debt-ridden former First Lady, who was then living on a $130 monthly stipend, was forced to return jewelry that she acquired while in the White House and was forced to sell an elegant lace dress valued at $3,500 just to make ends meet.

It was generally believed that the wealthy Davis only aligned himself with the fledgling labor party as a springboard to the upcoming Liberal Republican and Democratic conventions. Nevertheless, the selection of the rotund Supreme Court justice was a shrewd maneuver by the new party, demonstrating that it had a keen understanding of the game of politics. In nominating the seemingly incongruous Davis, who in February appeared likely to capture either the Liberal Republican or Democratic nomination—and possibly both—certainly gave the little Labor Reform Party a great deal of instant credibility.

Joel Parker, Davis' vice-presidential running mate, was a man of unquestionable integrity. Given the scandal-a-day environment in Washington, he was an ideal choice. A former assemblyman and county prosecutor, Parker, a Princeton graduate, was elected governor of New Jersey as a Democrat in 1862, defeating the Union Party's Marcus L. Ward by nearly 15,000 votes. A tall and dignified man, Parker was an outspoken critic of federal encroachment, believing that the seceding states during the Civil War had been unnecessarily driven to secession by uncompromising and misguided northern abolitionists. He was also a harsh critic of Lincoln's Emancipation Proclamation and believed that it would make peace impossible. Nevertheless, he wholeheartedly supported the war effort and provided troops for the Union cause. Unable to succeed himself, Parker returned to his private law practice in 1866.

In 1868, Parker received thirteen votes for president on the first ballot at the Democratic national convention in New York and was again elected governor of the Garden State in 1871, narrowly defeating his Republican opponent. Hardly an intellectual giant and not a particularly imaginative politician, Parker, whose name was bandied about a few months later as a possible Liberal Republican and Democratic coalition candidate for the presidency, was nevertheless an honest man without so much as even a hint of scandal in his record. As such, he was a solid choice for the fledgling Labor Reform Party—especially given the rampant corruption in the Grant administration.

Denouncing monopolies and unwholesome greed, the Labor Reformers adopted a somewhat visionary platform calling for paper money to be issued directly by the government rather than private banks. This currency was to be legal tender for all debts, public and private. They also contended that the national debt should be honored without mortgaging the future earnings of workers and the issuance of tax-exempt bonds at exorbitant rates was roundly condemned. The party's platform, written without Davis' consent, also called for prohibiting cheap Chinese immigrant labor, the establishment of an eight-hour workday and the abolition of contract labor in the nation's prisons. One plank called for a general amnesty for former Confederate leaders. Perhaps the most interesting position of all was the party's call for a capital levy on wealth instead of a tax on general prosperity to finance future wars.

Davis, whose friends had tried desperately to have the convention postpone its decision until May, was somewhat taken aback by the radical Labor Reform nomination. Most of his friends and close advisors argued that no one could possibly run on the kind of left-wing platform adopted by the Labor Reformers. In a carefully worded missive that subtly avoided an outright acceptance of the party's nomination, the Supreme Court justice thanked the third party for bestowing such an honor on him and, borrowing a line from South Carolina's William

Lowndes a half-century earlier, told them "the Presidency is not an office to be either solicited or declined."

A number of leading Labor Reformers, including Horace H. Day and Ezra Wood, remained opposed to Davis' nomination. Day announced his intention of supporting the upcoming Women's Rights convention and its nominees. Moreover, several local labor committees called for a new convention.

Nevertheless, the little-remembered Labor Reformers nominated a presidential ticket to be reckoned with—at least momentarily. When Davis formally declined the party's nomination some four and a half months later, the short-lived Labor Reform Party died in the ambers of a smoldering coalition with the so-called "Straight Out" or Bourbon Democrats.

13

Victoria Woodhull and the Emergence of Feminist Politics

❖

Free Love, Spiritualism and Equal Rights in the 1872 Presidential Campaign

In addition to the reluctant Davis, Groesbeck and O'Conor candidacies and the little-noticed debut of the Prohibition Party—a third party that would outlive every minor party in American history—the 1872 presidential campaign also featured the first female candidate for the nation's highest office. She was Victoria Claflin Woodhull, one of the most controversial and legendary women of her time. Nominated by her own Equal Rights Party, which consisted mainly of spiritualists and various offbeat personalities who flocked to her cause, the 32-year-old Woodhull was not only the first woman to seek the presidency, but up to that point in history she was also the youngest person ever nominated for the presidency.[1]

Though written out of history for more than a century, Woodhull's bold bid for the presidency in 1872 was far from "the most uproarious farce that the lunatic fringe has yet produced," as described by a freelance journalist in the 1950s.[2] Claiming that women, as citizens of the United States, were enfranchised by the fourteenth and fifteenth amendments to the Constitution, Woodhull declared

---

1. In 1972, the Socialist Workers Party nominated 31-year-old Linda Jenness, a secretary from Atlanta, Georgia, for the nation's highest office. The little-known Trotskyite candidate appeared on the ballot in eighteen states that year, garnering roughly 65,000 votes.

2. Gerald W. Johnson, "Dynamic Victoria Woodhull," *American Heritage* (June 1956), Vol. VII, Number 4, p. 91.

her candidacy in the pages of the *New York Herald* on April 2, 1870—more than two full years before the election. "While others argued the equality of woman with man, I proved it by successfully engaging in business; while others sought to show that there was no valid reason why women should be treated, socially and politically, as being inferior to man, I boldly entered the arena of politics and business and exercised the rights I already possessed," she asserted. Arguing that neither the Democrats nor the Republicans had a major issue to put before the electorate in 1872, Woodhull said that she had the one issue that would capture the imagination of the nation's voters—women's suffrage. "The blacks were cattle in 1860," she argued. "A Negro now sits in Jeff Davis's seat in the United States Senate." Women, she eloquently insisted, should be afforded the same right.[3]

Because her announcement received so little attention, Woodhull was forced to declare her candidacy again in the pages of her own journal, *Woodhull and Claflin's Weekly*, on November 19, 1870. Woodhull was three years shy of constitutional eligibility when she initially declared her candidacy and still wasn't old enough to assume the presidency when she was formally nominated at the raucous Equal Rights Party convention at Apollo Hall near New York City's Madison Square on May 10, 1872.

Reaching out to the suffragists, labor organizers, temperance advocates, financial reformers and fellow spiritualists, the feminist pioneer issued a call for a national convention to be held in New York City in the spring of 1872. Coming at a time when the women's suffrage movement had grown lethargic, badly divided over strategy and tactics, Woodhull's candidacy, while generally ignored or viewed with skepticism, nevertheless managed to receive at least a scintilla of positive coverage in the mainstream press. In a highly favorable editorial, the *New York Herald*—the paper in which she made her original announcement—glowingly approved of her short platform and predicted that "the lady broker of Broad Street," possessing "novelty, enterprise, courage and determination" would roll up "the heaviest majority ever polled in this or any other nation" if women were granted the right to vote.[4]

Not everyone, however, was so easily impressed. "You will see by her hodgepodge weekly that Mrs. Woodhull and her followers are preparing for a great

---

3.　Lois Beachy Underhill, *The Woman Who Ran for President: The Many Lives of Victoria Woodhull* (New York, 1995), pp. 77-79.

4.　Ibid., p. 80.

political splurge," groaned aging abolitionist William Lloyd Garrison, a man who deplored electoral politics.[5]

In the weeks and days leading up to the Equal Rights convention, Woodhull kept a frantic schedule, addressing the American Labor Reform League on May 5 and speaking to the American Anti-Usury Society at the Cooper Institute the following day. Ferrying across the Hudson River, she also spoke to the esoteric Spiritualist Society of New Jersey two days later.

The spiritualists were an integral part of Woodhull's overall campaign strategy. She believed that if politicized the spiritualists, acting in unison, could defeat both major parties. Spiritualism, after all, was a mid-nineteenth century phenomenon and had tens of thousands of practitioners in the United States. The spiritualist movement had quickly swept through England and most of Europe in the 1850s, but was slow to take hold in the United States. But that changed in the late 1860s and early 1870s. As incredible at it sounds, spiritualist congregations in this country eventually numbered almost as many as any respectable Protestant denomination. Its devotees included not only people like Woodhull and aging financier Cornelius Vanderbilt, but also Mary Todd Lincoln, the grieving former First Lady who frequently indulged in séances. Moreover, a number of prominent intellectuals, including an occasional congressman, novelist or celebrity, also declared their adherence to spiritualism. It was, Woodhull believed, a constituency that could only be ignored at one's peril.

At one time in the late 1860s and early 1870s, there were more than a hundred spiritualist publications in the United States. Many of these periodicals had a decisive political slant, advocating such issues as peace, prohibition, women's equality and better treatment of the nation's black and Native American populations. Some of these publications also advocated socialism. On a deeper level, these early spiritualists believed in a kind of psychic oneness—a grand scheme involving all matter, both living and dead.

As the titular head of the American Association of Spiritualists—she was no longer an active practitioner—the Equal Rights standard-bearer tried her best to synthesize spiritualism with her own brand of socialism. Though her influence alone probably had little to do with it, spiritualism retained an unmistakable influence within the native-born American Left, especially in the Socialist Party, well into the 1900s.

Despite her hectic schedule in the weeks leading up to the Equal Rights convention, Woodhull had to take time out to make funeral arrangements for her

---

5.   Ibid., p. 204.

first husband, Canning Woodhull, whom she had supported—emotionally and financially—in the years following their divorce. Hopelessly addicted to morphine and alcohol, her ex-husband died on April 7 at the age of forty-eight.

On the eve of her own national convention, Woodhull addressed the National Woman Suffrage Association gathering at Steinway Hall in New York City on May 9, addressing that organization over Susan B. Anthony's vigorous objections. "The eyes of the world are upon this convention," Woodhull said. "Its enemies have sneered and laughed at the idea of combining reformers for any organized action. They say that women don't know enough to organize, and therefore are not to be feared as political opponents." Denouncing suffrage leaders opposed to her candidacy as elitists, Woodhull exhorted the delegates to adjourn to nearby Apollo Hall to help inaugurate a new party and nominate a presidential ticket.[6]

Much to her surprise, Woodhull's suggestion was greeted with unexpected enthusiasm, catching Anthony, the Suffrage convention's presiding officer, and several other suffragist leaders completely off guard. Anthony desperately banged her gavel on the podium repeatedly, ruling her feminist rival out of order. When that didn't work, Anthony resorted to an old political trick—ordering the lights in the hall turned off, forcing the delegates to leave the building.

Despite the fact that the Equal Rights Party had been conceived, organized and personally financed by Woodhull, her nomination was by no means a foregone conclusion. Aligning itself with Woodhull's third-party movement, the Radical Club of San Francisco had recommended the nomination of former Indiana congressman George W. Julian, the outstanding abolitionist and one-time Free Soil Party candidate for vice president. The 55-year-old former lawmaker had introduced legislation for a Sixteenth Amendment granting suffrage to women in 1869, but his bill eventually died in the House Judiciary Committee. A number of other candidates were also seeking the party's nomination. Even the spiritualists, providing the largest bloc of delegates to the convention, were seemingly split on the question of a nominee. While most of them supported Woodhull, who had been elected president of the American Association of Spiritualists in September 1871, a number of spiritualists leaned toward one of two other possible candidates—Andrew Jackson Davis, "the Poughkeepsie Seer" who supposedly delivered 157 lectures over a fourteen-month period while in a trance, and Robert Dale Owen, a prominent social reformer. An American devotee of

---

6.   Ibid., p. 205.

Swedish mystic and philosopher Immanuel Swedenborg, Davis advocated drastic reforms to curb financial manipulation and return democracy to the people.

Born in Glasgow, Scotland, in 1801, Owen had published New York's *Free Enquirer* for several years, a paper that advocated a more equitable distribution of wealth, emancipation and other social issues, before returning to his native Indiana. A former teacher, he had served two terms in Congress as a Democrat in the 1840s, representing a congressional district that included New Harmony, Indiana, a communal-type town founded by he and his father in 1825. In Congress, Owen introduced legislation to resolve the Oregon boundary dispute and authored legislation creating the Smithsonian Institution in Washington, D.C. Defeated for re-election in 1846, he later successfully advocated liberal divorce laws and property rights for married women in the Indiana constitutional convention of 1850. He also served as ambassador to Italy under President Franklin Pierce. While there, the former congressman embraced spiritualism. Hoping to find a scientific basis for spiritualism, he worked tirelessly, but largely unsuccessfully, to elevate it above cult status. A prolific writer, two of his books—*Footfalls on the Boundary of Another World*, published in 1860, and *The Debatable Land Between This World and the Next*, published twelve years later—raised a number of eyebrows, but convinced few readers that there was any real connection between the living and the dead.

Despite the credulousness of his spiritual writings, Owen still exerted some political influence. Salmon P. Chase credited Owen's 1862 letter on emancipation as having had more influence on Lincoln than anything else he had read on the subject. A free-thinking septuagenarian, Owen was revered by almost everyone assembled in Apollo Hall, especially the spiritualists, but his Scottish birth all but eliminated him from serious consideration. Then again, Woodhull was ineligible on two counts herself—her gender, as well as her age.

A number of suffragists believed that 57-year-old Elizabeth Cady Stanton, a relative moderate, was a more dignified choice and would therefore have a much wider appeal than the controversial Woodhull. Nobody objected more strenuously to Woodhull's nomination at the time than Susan B. Anthony. Often portrayed as "a vinegary old maid," Anthony was precisely that when it came to Victoria Woodhull. She was enormously jealous of Woodhull—and with good reason. The 51-year-old former schoolteacher deeply envied her rival's youth, beauty, intellect and money. She also had nothing but contempt for the spiritualist movement. Lacking the charisma of a Stanton or Woodhull, Anthony was often left to do the movement's unrewarding labor—raising money, stuffing envelopes, circulating petitions and organizing a never-ending series of afternoon teas and suffrage meetings. Having given up a teaching career—one of the few professions open to middle-class women in those days—Anthony believed that several others, including Stanton and recent convert Isabella Hooker, sister of the better known Harriet Beecher Stowe and minister Henry Ward Beecher, were far more deserving of the Equal Rights Party's presidential nomination than the younger and more attractive Woodhull.[7]

In a not so thinly-veiled attack on Woodhull at the Women's Suffrage convention, the aging spinster, green with envy, said that Woodhull "came to Washington with a powerful argument and with lots of cash behind her, and I bet you cash is a big thing with Congress." The delegates laughed and cheered. Hoping to tear apart Woodhull's carefully stitched quilt of socialists, spiritualists, labor reformers and temperance advocates—a combination that could potentially play havoc in the 1872 presidential campaign—Anthony went on to say that she had been asked by several New York newspapers if she was aware of Woodhull's family background. This, of course, was a subtle reminder that Woodhull's parents had worked in a traveling medicine show, that Victoria was somehow unworthy of the honor suffragists had just bestowed upon her. "Long live Miss Anthony," shouted one delegate, but Woodhull's endorsement stood.

Anthony's intense dislike, if not hatred, of Woodhull manifested itself many years later when she virtually wrote Woodhull out of the history of the women's suffrage movement in a three-volume collaboration with Stanton and Matilda Joslyn Gage. For all intents and purposes, those books became the historical record of the early women's rights movement.

Woodhull also faced other opposition at the Equal Rights convention. Socialists affiliated with Karl Marx's International Workingmen's Association, for instance, were promoting Wendell Phillips while the dry forces were pushing the candidacy of George Francis Train, a wealthy yet eccentric merchant and self-styled political reformer. A few leaders from the Labor Reform Party were also there to press for the nomination of David Davis, who had been nominated by their party in Columbus, Ohio, a few months earlier. Earlier, there was even a suggestion that the new party should nominate the Reverend Henry Ward Beecher, Woodhull's one-time lover. Beecher, a respected editor and writer, received a great deal of national fame in the abolition movement. Regarded as one of the most popular preachers of his day, overflow crowds routinely flocked to Beecher's Plymouth Church in Brooklyn Heights every Sunday to hear his sermons.

---

7.   Ibid., pp. 190-191.

Of all her potential challengers, Susan B. Anthony's suffragists were not Woodhull's greatest concern. More than anyone else, George Train, a brilliant and flamboyant businessman, was probably Woodhull's greatest threat. Not only did he have some name recognition, his campaign was also amply funded. While spiritualists and suffragists alike undoubtedly preferred him to either Grant or Greeley, the mercurial New Yorker wasn't the first choice of either faction at the Apollo Hall convention.

An outspoken champion of women's rights, the 43-year-old businessman and self-styled promoter announced his candidacy for the presidency in 1869—long before Woodhull joined the race. Except for two brief interludes—joining the French Communists in 1870 and beating the record of Jules Verne's famous fictional hero by two years by making a trip around the word in eighty days—Train had been campaigning for the presidency almost non-stop for three years. Without question, he was the most fascinating of all the colorful characters, including Greeley and Woodhull, who sought the presidency in 1872.

George Francis Train was an extraordinary human being, a man whose life, according to one biographer, would have provided full and adventurous lives for nine ordinary men.[8] Born in Boston in 1829, Train was raised by his maternal grandmother in Waltham, Massachusetts, after his siblings and parents succumbed to yellow fever while living in New Orleans in the early 1830s. He ran away from home when he was fourteen and took a job in a Cambridge grocery store before landing a job as a shipping clerk in a mercantile firm owned by a relative, Enoch Train. As an apprentice to his uncle, one of Boston's leading ship owners, Train was instrumental in building the last of the nation's glorious clipper ships, including the immortal *Flying Cloud*, while still a teenager. An enterprising young man, he moved to Australia in 1853 and started his own shipping firm, purportedly earning commissions amounting to $95,000 in his first year—a staggering sum in those days. Incredibly, while in scarcely populated Melbourne he nearly became president of the so-called Five-Star Republic during its fanciful but short-lived independence movement from Great Britain. He left Australia in 1855 and traveled extensively throughout Europe and the Orient. While in Paris, Train made contacts with Queen Maria Cristina's Spanish entourage. The Queen's banker later provided him with the funds to build the Atlantic and Great Western Railroad in Ohio, a four hundred-mile railway connecting the ports of Erie with the Ohio and Mississippi rivers.

---

8.   Willis Thornton, *The Nine Lives of Citizen Train* (New York, 1948), p. 313.

Dubbed "Express" Train and "Spread-Eagle" Train by his contemporaries, the flamboyant showman moved to London in 1858 and pursued a new venture, introducing British investors to the idea of building street railways in London, Australia, and the United States. His investors, however, were turned off by his fiery pro-Union speeches at the outset of the Civil War and his funding eventually dried up. Subsequently, almost every door was slammed in his face. But Train characteristically remained confident, telling British Prime Minister Benjamin D'Israeli, "You go to India by your Suez Canal; I'll go home, build a railway across the continent, and beat you to the goal."

True to his word, Train, a tall, handsome man with dark curly hair and a quicksilver temper, immersed himself in the building of the great Union Pacific Railroad, breaking ground in Omaha, Nebraska, on December 2, 1863. He invested heavily in land on which Nebraska now stands and at one point his title was estimated to be worth $30 million. The far-sighted entrepreneur even played a role in the infamous Credit Mobilier scheme that eventually damaged the careers of several Gilded Age politicians, including Vice President Schuyler Colfax.

During this period, Train lectured frequently and authored numerous books, including *Young America in Wall Street* (1858); *Spread-Eagleism* (1859); and a four-volume edition titled *Train's Union Speeches* (1862). An entertainer through and through, Train delighted his audiences with his off the cuff remarks and stories of his various exploits. He also spoke frequently about what he would do as president—an office he first sought in 1864. A self-made man, Train was by this time relatively wealthy and had built an extravagant villa in Newport, Rhode Island, where he lived lavishly on more than one hundred thousand dollars a year.

A "stormy petrel" of sorts, Train was arrested in Boston in 1862 for disturbing a public gathering and, to almost everyone's astonishment, later emerged as a leader of the French Commune in 1870 where he barely escaped assassination. A man of numerous causes, he championed, among other things, the Irish independence movement, prohibition and women's rights. Not quite in the pantheon of spellbinding orators—he was certainly no Wendell Phillips—Train could be a pretty good speaker when he wanted to be. His pro-Union speeches during the Civil War almost always attracted larger audiences than those of other propagandists, such as well-known abolitionist Frederick Douglass.

Train was also no stranger to politics. He ran unsuccessfully for governor of Kansas on a women's suffrage platform in the mid-1860s and had polled more than eleven percent of the vote as an independent candidate for Congress from

New York in 1868. In the latter campaign, Train, who was certainly no intellectual slouch, garnered 2,583 votes in a three-cornered race won by Democrat John Morrissey, an inarticulate racist and stereotypical Tammany thug who had been educated in the city's barrooms and brothels. Train also made abortive attempts for the Democratic presidential nomination in 1864 and 1868.

During this period, the notorious political and economic adventurer also became something of a greenback enthusiast to help speed along the post-Civil War boom. "Give us greenbacks we say," he demanded in 1867, "and build cities, plant corn, open coal mines, control railways, launch ships, grow cotton, establish factories, open gold and silver mines, erect rolling mills...Carry my resolution and there is sunshine in the sky."[9]

Though later regarded as something of an eccentric—not to mention a source of continual amusement—Train was a non-conformist in almost every sense of the word. More than a few considered him a "semi-lunatic," yet he preferred to think of himself as an "aristocratic loafer."[10] He loved nothing more than to shock the country's conservative prejudices—among other things, he once strolled down the street naked just to see what kind of sensation it would stir. He also gave Sunday evening lectures, ridiculing the Bible in an Ingersollian style long before the country ever heard of "the great agnostic" Robert G. Ingersoll.

A relentless publicity seeker, Train had an uncanny knack for getting his name in the newspapers. When he was 61 years old, he traveled around the world in sixty-seven days, breaking the previous record set by Nellie Bly. Two years later, he broke his own record, making the trip in just sixty days. His record-breaking around-the-world trips reportedly became the inspiration for Jules Verne's classic, *Around the World in Eighty Days.*

Proudly styling himself as "Champion Crank," Train was declared insane by no fewer than six courts of law during his lifetime. Toward the end of his life, the elderly Train lived simply, residing in a modest three-dollar-a-week boarding house and supposedly surviving on a daily diet consisting of a handful of peanuts and a glass of water. He rarely spoke with other adults, but was frequently seen on one of the worn-out benches in Madison Square Park, a benign, kindly old man who enjoyed reading stories to groups of curious children. When he died in 1904, more than 2,000 children trudged through the snow on a bitter January night to drop flowers on his coffin.

---

9.   Irwin Unger, *The Greenback Era: A Social and Political History of American Finance, 1865-1879* (Princeton, New Jersey, 1964), pp. 45-46.
10.   Mary Gabriel, *Notorious Victoria: The Life of Victoria Woodhull, Uncensored* (Chapel Hill, 1998), p. 189.

Largely forgotten today, Train was still a man of some consequence in 1872. His name could be found in the histories of finance, railroads, politics and women's rights. He had circled the globe on no fewer than five occasions and had lectured in virtually every major city in the world.

Advocating a mild form of reconstruction, Train was the first person to announce his candidacy for president in 1872. His declaration came shortly after President Grant allowed a Cuban arms vessel to sail out of New York harbor in May 1869. An enthusiastic backer of the Irish independence movement, Train, a simmering teakettle of emotion, was angry that the United States somehow managed earlier to stop a similar Fenian arms vessel shortly after it departed from the outskirts of Canada yet couldn't stop the gun-running Cuban ship. Convinced that this latest steamer was carrying arms and men to Cuba as part of an "English intrigue" and was in violation of international law, Train, who made his protest known on the front page of the *New York Times*, demanded that President Grant "seize" the Cuba-bound ship. The president, of course, ignored Train's admonition and the eccentric merchant was soon in the race for Grant's job.

During his three-year campaign, the erratic self-promoter traveled extensively throughout the country, lecturing to groups both large and small. He also published his own newspaper, *The Train Ligne*. Charging admission to his lectures, Train raised an impressive $90,000 during his campaign—far more than any other independent or third party presidential aspirant that year. Though he was eventually nominated for president by his own self-styled Citizens Party convention, Train unsuccessfully sought the Democratic, Labor Reform, Liberal Republican and Straight-Out Democratic nominations that year. His luck, as it turned out, wasn't any better at Woodhull's Equal Rights convention.

At least 668 delegates and alternates from twenty-six states and four territories convened in Apollo Hall on Friday morning, May 10. The convention hall was draped with huge and colorful banners reading GOVERNMENT PROTECTION AND PROVISION FROM THE CRADLE TO THE GRAVE and THE UNEMPLOYED DEMAND WORK. James D. Reymart, a well-known New York lawyer, civic reformer and close personal friend of Woodhull's, presided over the convention. While the convention attracted a wide assortment of offbeat personalities—representing "nearly every 'ism' known to the world," as one New York newspaper described it—it also drew a large number of respected and noted public figures, including Judge Alfred G. W. Carter of Cincinnati, a short, heavyset man who had labored tirelessly for women's suffrage.[11]

---

11.   Ibid., pp. 170-171.

Among the delegates in attendance were such unorthodox individuals as Ada Ballou, a little-known suffragist and eloquent spiritualist lecturer, and Moses Hull of Vineland, New Jersey, a one-time abolitionist and free-thinker who wrote extensively on the subject of free love. Spiritualist Caroline Hinckley Spear, a graduate and former faculty member of Penn Medical University in Philadelphia, a non-traditional medical school founded by Quakers, was also in attendance. So, too, was spiritualist leader and poet Horace Dresser. Belva Lockwood, who had just been accepted to law school, was also a delegate. Lockwood, of course, wasn't a spiritualist, but a dedicated teacher and staunch women's rights activist. She later ran for president on the Equal Rights Party ticket in 1884 and 1888.

The list of delegates, as Woodhull biographer Lois Beachy Underhill wrote, was a "collection of American originals." There were internationalists such as Theodore Banks, who served on the party's executive committee, as well as agrarian reformers and a handful of eclectic capitalists and communists. Included in this assembly of unique Americans were men like Presbyterian minister Ezra H. Heywood, a self-styled financial reformer from Massachusetts. A one-time Garrisonian abolitionist, the 43-year-old Heywood broke with the antislavery movement over its support for the Civil War. A prolific writer, Heywood published the *Word*, a libertarian monthly from which he actively promoted labor reform, temperance and free speech. Like Woodhull, Heywood considered marriage a form of slavery and wrote extensively about the free-love movement, resulting in his arrest on various obscenity charges by Anthony Comstock, the Victorian enforcer of decency, on no fewer than five occasions.[12]

Another delegate, Dr. E. B. Foote of New York City, author of the best-selling *Medical Common Sense*, which sold a quarter of a million copies during a ten-year period, had also been arrested on obscenity charges for selling birth control devices through the mail. Foote's son later coined the word "contraception."

The festive convention opened with a choir singing "Hail, Columbia," followed by welcoming remarks by the convention's temporary chairman. The jubilant delegates, hardly stifled by the sweltering ninety-one degree heat hanging over the city, quickly got down to business. The first order of business was that of naming their new party. Woodhull originally favored "Cosmo-Political Party," a name suggested by Stephen Pearl Andrews, but later seized upon the title "Equal Rights Party" as a more appropriate name. Rejecting the suggestion of an Oregon delegate who wanted the new party to be called the "Human Rights Party," the delegates adopted the Equal Rights Party as its official name. The party, however,

---

12. Underhill, *The Woman Who Ran for President*, pp. 206-207.

has occasionally been referred to as the People's Party or, less frequently, as the National Radical Reformers.

New York's James D. Reymart was then named permanent chairman of the convention and, following a vigorous discussion, the party's platform committee adopted a document presented by Colonel James Harvey Blood, Woodhull's second husband and alter ego, as the party's official platform. Blood, who married Woodhull in July 1866, was a former Union army officer and accountant who had worked briefly as a city auditor in St. Louis. A dark-haired man with neatly clipped sideburns, Blood, who usually looked after Woodhull's financial affairs, had a new role on this day—serving as his wife's convention manager.

The platform he presented, though most likely written by Woodhull's intellectual guru and ghostwriter Stephen Pearl Andrews, was a sophisticated document containing twenty-three planks, including women's suffrage, a graduated income tax, full employment, regulation of the nation's monopolies and the nationalization of railroads and other major industries. The Equal Rights Party also called for public ownership of the nation's land, water and mineral resources. The platform—which clearly wasn't stitched together by rank amateurs—also included a forward-looking proposal for the establishment of a universal government with international arbitration powers to prevent future wars. A demand from temperance forces inside Apollo Hall for a strong prohibition plank calling for total abstinence was rejected in favor of a watered-down resolution discouraging the consumption of intoxicating liquors.

When the convention reconvened at eight o'clock that evening, Woodhull, a petite, attractive woman with piercing blue eyes and fine features, wearing an expensive black dress with a fresh rose pinned to her collar, slowly walked to the podium. The hall grew quiet. "Go where we may in the land," the 34-year-old candidate began, "we see despotism, inequality, and injustice." Delivering one of the most eloquent and moving convention speeches of all time—second only, perhaps, to Eugene McCarthy's magnificent nominating speech for Adlai Stevenson at the Democratic national convention in 1960—Woodhull for the next hour exhorted the delegates in Apollo Hall to join the second American Revolution, a political, social, industrial, economic and sexual revolution. "Let us have justice though the heavens fall!," she concluded. The delegates then erupted with such spontaneous and boisterous cheers, chanting her name over and over again, that it nearly deafened unsuspecting passersby outside the hall. Within moments, Woodhull was unanimously nominated for the presidency. In the pandemonium that ensued, no other names were placed in nomination. Everyone in the hall, it seems, was caught up in the excitement of the moment. "Victoria! Victoria! Victoria!"[13]

After discussing several possibilities, the delegates, at the urging of New Jersey's Moses Hull, then selected well-known slavery foe Frederick Douglass as Woodhull's vice-presidential running mate. "We have had the oppressed sex represented by Woodhull," shouted Hull from the convention's floor, "we must have the oppressed race represented by Douglas."[14] The delegates then adopted the slogan, "Women's, Negroes' and Workingman's Ticket" in his honor. The colorful Benjamin F. Butler of Massachusetts, Elizabeth Cady Stanton, Radical Republican Benjamin F. Wade of Ohio, Chief Spotted Tail of Wyoming—a man of remarkable intelligence and extraordinary foresight who had once nearly been buried alive—and Laura De Force Gordon, a 33-year-old spiritualist lecturer, attorney and newspaper publisher from California, were also among the dozen or so names mentioned as possible vice-presidential candidates. Woodhull concurred with the convention's choice. She had been an admirer of the former slave-turned-emancipator dating back to the national suffrage convention of 1869.

It was widely speculated that the 54-year-old Douglass, who had escaped from slavery when he was twenty, was the son of a slave woman and her white master. He was inarguably the most influential African-American leader of the nineteenth century, a compelling if unique voice for social justice. Considered brilliant but complex, Douglass had served as an advisor to President Lincoln on two occasions. During the Civil War, he labored long and hard as a propagandist for the Union cause. After the war, he traveled widely as a lecturer on racial issues, national politics and women's rights.

His nomination, however, later proved somewhat embarrassing to Woodhull and the Equal Rights Party. An exuberant Woodhull made the mistake of telling the press that Douglass' letter of acceptance would be read at the party's ratification meeting at the Grand Opera House, but the black abolitionist, who was preoccupied in New Orleans, never acknowledged his nomination. As Woodhull soon found out, Douglass had no intention of abandoning the party of Lincoln and actively campaigned for Grant's re-election that year.

Meanwhile, the press virtually ignored Woodhull's nomination. The stingy pro-Grant *New York Times*, for example—a paper that devoted countless column

---

13. Ibid., pp. 3-4.
14. Johanna Johnston, *Mrs. Satan: The Incredible Saga of Victoria Woodhull* (London, 1967), pp. 146-147.

inches and tens of thousands of words that year to the aborted Straight-Out Democratic movement that ended up without a candidate—devoted only six short paragraphs to the Apollo Hall convention, a meager 407 words. Most newspapers ignored it altogether.

Wasting little time, Woodhull's Equal Rights Party got down to serious business following the convention. The party's executive committee, headed by Colonel Blood, came up with a unique idea—one that was probably dreamed up by Woodhull herself. The committee suggested issuing interest-free bonds redeemable only if and when the party came to power. It was a shrewd idea—the funds would not have to be repaid if Woodhull lost. The bonds were to be printed on the highest quality bank paper and would bear the name of the candidate, as well as the party's banner, featuring "the Goddess of Liberty on a field of white, with the words 'Equal Rights' underneath." This novel approach seemed to work at first as Woodhull's supporters immediately purchased some $1,600 in bonds and pledged another $4,700 to the cause. Woodhull confidently told the press that she expected the party to raise $100,000 within a few days.[15]

Curiously, Woodhull immediately began transferring all of her personal and business affairs under the auspices of the Equal Rights Party. It was agreed that the party would pay for her private residence, which wasn't to exceed $1,000 per month and would also double as the party's national headquarters. Her newspaper and brokerage firm were also placed under the umbrella of the Equal Rights Party. Her actions, of course, would be blatantly illegal under today's restrictive federal election laws, but in those days things were quite different and such commingling of funds wasn't all that unusual. After all, Grant's re-election campaign was being financed, in part, by funds received from the scandalous Whiskey Ring. No questions of impropriety were ever raised. If the Equal Rights Party provides "that excellent woman with a comfortable house, at a rent not less than twelve thousand dollars [per year]," contemptuously observed the *New York Times*, "we have no personal reason to complain."[16]

Despite such sarcasm, the one-time Queen of Wall Street was off and running. Woodhull's blatant disregard for the social mores considered appropriate for women in nineteenth century America was largely the product of her unusual childhood. Raised in a family of mesmerists and spiritualists, she often accompanied her parents in a traveling medicine show. With such an unorthodox

---

15. Underhill, *The Woman Who Ran for President*, pp. 209-211.
16. Ibid., p. 210; *New York Times* reprinted in *Woodhull & Claflin's Weekly*, June 1, 1872.

upbringing, it is hard to imagine the feminist pioneer eagerly adapting to the social niceties of that era. The victim of the irresponsible and profligate whims of her alcoholic father and, later, of the myriad shortcomings of her first husband, Woodhull's fiercely independent spirit was earned the hard way.

Born poor but beautiful, Victoria and her sister, Tennessee Claflin, were able to charm Commodore Cornelius Vanderbilt, the great railroad magnate and philanthropist, with their supposed spiritual powers. One of the richest men in the world, Vanderbilt even asked Tennie to marry him, but she refused. Nevertheless, the aging Vanderbilt proved to be a valuable investment counselor to the two ambitious young women. With Vanderbilt's help and guidance, Victoria and Tennessee proceeded to amaze Wall Street's male-dominated world with incredibly profitable investments in stocks and bonds. Before long, the two young women opened their own brokerage firm, earning them the well-deserved title of "Queens of Wall Street."

Woodhull was soon an immensely wealthy woman. She claimed to have come out a "winner" during the Gold Panic of 1869 when more than a dozen Wall Street firms and hundreds of other companies faced financial ruin. Though slightly prone to exaggeration, Woodhull estimated her net worth at $700,000—or more than $6 million by today's standards—by the end of 1869. Approximately, one-seventh of that, she said, had been earned as a clairvoyant, most of which she speculated on the gold market.

The two sisters eventually soured on Wall Street and started a muckraking campaign through the pages of their own newspaper, denouncing speculators for cheating and swindling the nation's rich, middle and laboring classes. Along with anarchist philosopher Stephen Pearl Andrews, Victoria and Tennessee launched *Woodhull and Claflin's Weekly*, a publication inspired by socialist, libertarian and utopian ideas, in May of 1870. From its pages, the controversial Woodhull voiced her opinions on a wide range of topics, the first of which was her sharp denunciation of Wall Street speculators.

The 61-year-old Andrews, a frequent guest at Woodhull's many soirees, served as her political mentor, metaphysical theorist, ghostwriter and sounding board—in short, a kind of one-man brain trust. A radical reformer and pioneer sociologist, Andrews, known as "the Pantarch"—a nickname he gave his idealized semi-anarchist society—held degrees in law and medicine and was perhaps best known for his anarchist work, *The Science of Society*. Most New Yorkers, however, probably remembered him from a lively three-way debate he had with essayist and critic Henry James, Sr., and Horace Greeley in the *New York Tribune* on the subject of free love. As an abolitionist living in the slaveholding state of Texas in the early 1840s, Andrews and his wife and infant child barely escaped with their lives in the middle of the night when an unruly mob attacked their home.

An eccentric philosopher, Andrews was easily recognizable in intellectual circles, his flowing white beard, stern eyes and hawk-like nose resembled that of "an Old Testament prophet." He was familiar with thirty-two languages and spoke several of them fluently. As a noted linguist, he also developed Alwato, which was intended to be a universal language not unlike Esperanto, an artificial language developed by Russian scholar Ludwig Zamenhof in the late 1880's. Andrews also developed a phonetic technique for teaching illiterate people to read and was the first to introduce English inventor Isaac Pitman's shorthand system in the United States. Andrews also founded a utopian community on Long Island years earlier, but it eventually failed, as did a second communal living experiment a few years later.

In Woodhull, Andrews saw an opportunity to advance his own ideas and immediately set out to radicalize the nation's first woman stockbroker. Woodhull, to be sure, was dazzled by Andrews and viewed him as an invaluable intellectual resource. It was an unlikely, but harmonious alliance. The Pantarch, indeed, proved invaluable and before long Woodhull found herself heading New York's Section 12 of Karl Marx's First International—a most incongruous role for a former denizen of Wall Street. Her section was largely a collage of self-styled reformers and women's rights advocates. In this role, the Claflin sisters published the first English translation of Marx's famous *Communist Manifesto* in December 1871. Yet Marx and his dogmatic and narrow-minded U.S. supporters scoffed at Woodhull's "free love" and spiritualist beliefs and her group, along with several French sections, was later expelled from the International.

In May of that year, Woodhull, introducing a broader, humanitarian reform agenda to the American electorate, delivered her celebrated "Great Secession Speech," in which the stockbroker-turned-radical reformer urged women to avoid affiliating with either major party. If Congress fails to give women the right to vote, she asserted, "we shall proceed to call another convention...and erect a new government..." Those were fighting words.[17]

Overcoming the strenuous opposition of Susan B. Anthony, Woodhull was endorsed for the presidency by the National Woman's Suffrage convention in Washington, D.C., in January 1872. As the featured speaker at that gathering, the one-time Wall Street broker urged her fellow feminists to cast off their Democratic and Republican shackles, "which have become a stench in the nostrils of

17.   Ibid., pp. 125-126.

all thoughtful people."[18] Elizabeth Cady Stanton, agreeing that it was time to make the two major parties "tremble," was among those who lent their support to Woodhull's uphill candidacy that year. Stanton, who tried unsuccessfully to run for Congress as an independent in 1866, understood all too well the difficulties Woodhull would encounter.

On the eve of the Labor Reform Party's national convention in Columbus, Woodhull gave her famous "Impending Revolution" speech to an overflow crowd at New York City's Academy of Music. Determined to win over the city's labor element to her new party, Woodhull, beaming with confidence, lashed out at the inequitable distribution of wealth and attacked the country's most affluent citizens, including her old friend Vanderbilt.

"A Vanderbilt may sit in his office and manipulate stocks, or make dividends, by which, in a few years, he amasses $50 million from the industries of the county, and he is one of the remarkable men of the age," she said indignantly. "But if a poor, half-starved child were to take a loaf of bread from his cupboard, to prevent starvation, she would be sent first to the Tombs and thence to Black-well's Island." "Is it right," she asked, "that the millions should toil all their lives long, scarcely having comfortable food and clothes, while the few manage to control all the benefits?" A society that permits such arbitrary distributions of wealthy, she concluded, "is a disgrace to Christian civilization."[19]

It was a momentous speech. The feisty feminist had come full circle, from successful venture capitalist to undaunted Christian socialist, yet most New York newspapers ignored her brilliant speech to the Academy's standing-room only audience. Among the leading dailies, only the Democratic *World* covered it, sparsely devoting a dozen lines to her compelling and profound remarks on the emancipation of the working classes, the evils of monopolies and the relationship of Christianity to politics. The powerful New York press, which spared no ink in its coverage of her arrest later that year for allegedly sending obscene material through the mails, could apparently find no space for Woodhull's sharp condemnation of the Vanderbilts, the Astors, and capitalism in general.

Not to be denied, the self-styled socialist forged ahead. By this time, Woodhull was something of a celebrity in American socialist circles. She was the head of New York's Section 12 of Karl Marx First International, which was represented in the United States by the International Workingmen's Association. It had several sections in New York, including Section 9, comprised primarily of

---

18. Ibid., p. 189.
19. Ibid., pp. 194-195.

German, émigré socialists and Section 12, dominated by the Claflin sisters. Section 12 had grown out of Stephen Pearl Andrews' New Democracy, an organization that sought to unify various reform elements. With the help of novelist Marie Stevens Howland, a veteran of the textile mills in Lowell, Massachusetts, Andrews built Section 12 into an influential section promoting economic and political rights for women within the International Workingmen's Association.

Not surprisingly, other Marxists, with some justification, denounced Woodhull and her sister as "bourgeois intellectuals" and "parlor radicals" whose flamboyant and divisive personalities were damaging to the country's fledgling socialist movement.[20] Section 9, whose predominately foreign-born members were generally more conservative in matters of morality than their counterparts in Section 12, was eventually able to persuade the General Council of the First International in London to expel Woodhull's group from its membership. Woodhull's group, along with several French sections that were expelled at the same time, later sought re-entry into the International but their requests were denied. Ever loyal to the controversial and lively Woodhull, the socialists in Section 12 refused to go quietly into the night and, causing a breakup of the First International in the United States, declared its independence from the First International at a meeting in Philadelphia on July 9, 1872, at which time they called for the establishment of a democratic, pluralistic American section independent of the European Marxists and direct political action through Woodhull's newly-formed Equal Rights Party.

Through the pages of her provocative journal, published under the masthead, "Progress! Free Thought! Untrammeled Lives!" Victoria stunned the nation in 1871 by combining her strong belief in women's rights with an outspoken advocacy of "free love," a widely misunderstood concept. "Free love" did not promote promiscuity, as many of her critics charged, but rather the absence of any legal ties between consenting adults. Woodhull believed that marriage enslaved women and constrained individual freedom. Not surprisingly, her writings during this period were peppered with frontal assaults on the sanctity of the family. Not surprisingly, the feminist gadfly was roundly criticized for having the audacity to express such views. Cartoonist Thomas Nast depicted her as "Mrs. Satan" in *Harper's* magazine and she was soon viewed by a large segment of the American population as a mirror of socialism's infidel status.

Despite growing public indignation and outrage, Victoria courageously plowed ahead, cleverly preempting Susan B. Anthony and the leaders of the

---

20. Ibid., p. 197.

National Women's Suffrage Association, who had long sought an opportunity to present their case to Congress. With the aid of congressmen William Loughridge of Iowa, Indiana's George W. Julian, and the unflappable Benjamin F. Butler of Massachusetts—the latter of whom probably drafted her "Memorial" presented to the House Judiciary Committee and no doubt delighted in helping Victoria upstage the entire women's rights movement—Woodhull beat them to it, becoming the first woman to ever testify before a congressional committee and the first person to testify on behalf of female suffrage. Incredibly, she also managed to arrange a private meeting with President Grant in his White House office, further infuriating Susan B. Anthony and other suffrage leaders.

Using the pages of her weekly, Woodhull boldly told her readers that her name alone destined her for the nation's highest office. "Was there not another Victoria already reigning in Britain?" she asked. "Is it true that a Victoria rules the great rival nation," she asked rhetorically in her acceptance speech, "and it might grace the amity just sealed between the two nations [the treaty settling the *Alabama* claims] and be a new security of peace, if a twin sisterhood of Victoria were to preside over the two nations."[21]

Pubic reaction to the feminist pioneer's candidacy was anything but supportive. The chauvinistic Horace Greeley—a presidential rival—quipped: "Gibbery, gibbery, gab, the women had a confab, and demanded the rights to wear the tights. Gibbery, gibbery, gab." Reaction from others, though less colorful than Greeley, was even more indignant.[22] "The career of Victoria Woodhull cannot but be entertaining as she gains public attention by hook or by crook," sneered the *New York Times*. "Mrs. Woodhull, with an ambition worthy of a female Napoleon, goes for the presidency and strikes immediately at the White House."[23]

'A Monstrous Conspiracy'

Tragically, Woodhull's short-lived candidacy was marred by one setback after another. First, her running mate, Frederick Douglass, refused to accept the party's nomination. Then came a public humiliation when the Grand Opera House, objecting to "the class of people" expected to attend, cancelled a scheduled campaign kick-off rally. (Woodhull rescheduled the meeting at the Cooper

---

21.   Miller, *'If Elected...' Unsuccessful Candidates for the Presidency 1796-1968*, p. 211.
22.   Ibid., p. 211.
23.   Underhill, *The Woman Who Ran for President*, pp. 7-8.

Institute, where she made a short but impassioned plea for support from the city's working-class voters.) A third setback occurred when Gov. William B. Washburn of Massachusetts refused to allow Woodhull to campaign in Boston, saying that one "might as well have the undressed women of North Street on stage there."[24] Making matters worse, her campaign funds quickly dried up and her weekly publication was running in the red to the tune of three hundred dollars a week. "Newsmen were being bribed to exclude it from their stands," she asserted, and postal workers refused to deliver it. She and Tennie were forced to suspend publication on June 22.[25]

A concerted effort, it seems, was also made to drive the controversial third-party aspirant and her family from New York City. Shortly after accepting her party's nomination, Woodhull's family was evicted from their home and the candidate's attention was diverted to the more immediate task of finding a landlord who was willing to risk his reputation by renting to the controversial gadfly.

When well-known Brooklyn minister Henry Ward Beecher, an adulterously adventurous preacher and one of Woodhull's former lovers, refused to come to their aid, Victoria and Tennessee decided to publish a wickedly sensational story alleging that the minister had been involved in a torrid affair with the wife of Theodore Tilton, the highly-esteemed editor of the *Independent*, one of the country's leading periodicals. Over the years, Beecher, son of the fire-breathing Lyman Beecher and brother of best-selling author Harriet Beecher Stowe, had been romantically involved with several women in his congregation. Woodhull also published a second article describing the sexual depravity of Luther C. Challis, a prominent Wall Street broker. Her explosives article resulted in a protracted legal battle during which Victoria and her sister were arrested under the country's prudish Comstock laws prohibiting the sending of so-called obscenity through the mails.

In the meantime, Woodhull's presidential candidacy came to a screeching halt. She had been distracted for nearly six weeks, spending most of that time trying to find housing for her family. No longer viewed as a front for Vanderbilt's market intentions, her brokerage firm, Woodhull, Claflin & Company, went belly up. In August, Woodhull was publicly humiliated yet again when she was sued by creditors and had to testify that she didn't even own the clothes she was wearing. She was virtually penniless. Exactly what happened to the small fortune she had amassed a few years earlier remains a mystery.

---

24. Miller, *'If Elected…' Unsuccessful Candidates for the Presidency 1796-1968*, p. 211.
25. Underhill, *The Woman Who Ran for President*, p. 218.

In any case, Woodhull eventually found lodging at the Gilsey, a moderately priced hotel. However, when the proprietor learned of her identity, he asked her to leave. She refused. Then one evening, following a long day at the office, Woodhull returned to the hotel to find all of her possessions piled outside the hotel's door. A security guard had been hired to keep her out. She spent hours walking the city's streets with her two frightened children in tow, trying desperately to find a place to stay. Finally, at one o'clock in the morning, she took her tired children to her office where they all slept on the floor. She and her children eventually moved in with another of Woodhull's sisters.

Throughout this ordeal, Woodhull watched helplessly as her former supporters abandoned the Equal Rights Party in droves. "The inauguration of the new party, and my nomination, seemed to fall dead upon the country," she later lamented.[26] Theodore Tilton, a one-time admirer, understandably wanted nothing to do with Woodhull and actively supported Horace Greeley's candidacy. Tilton's motives, of course, weren't entirely unselfish. He hoped to succeed Greeley as the editor the *New York Tribune* if the longtime editor was able to defeat Ulysses S. Grant.[27] Educator Belva Lockwood, another early supporter who later ran for president herself on an Equal Rights ticket in 1884 and 1888, also stumped for Greeley. Frederick Douglass, as mentioned previously, campaigned vigorously for Grant. So did—of all people—Wendell Phillips, who apparently reasoned that at least Grant hadn't mistreated the Indians. Most women's rights activists, including Elizabeth Cady Stanton, also refused to support Woodhull. The envious Susan B. Anthony, who was still angry that an interloper—especially a controversial outsider like Woodhull—had been endorsed at the women's suffrage convention in January, was fined $100 for attempting to cast a straight Republican vote in 1872. It served her right.

Woodhull and her sister, Tennie, spent Election Day in cell number eleven of the Ludlow Street jail, awaiting a preliminary hearing on federal obscenity charges. Five members of the paper's staff were also jailed, including Colonel Blood and Stephen Pearl Andrews. They were already behind bars in the notorious Jefferson Market Prison, one of the worst prisons in the country. All of the newspaper's staff members, except Blood, were released for lack of evidence. Like his wife and her sister, Blood faced months of legal harassment.

Meanwhile, bail for Victoria and Tennessee had been set at a rather exorbitant $8,000 each. George F. Train, the rich eccentric and Woodhull's one-time rival

26. Ibid., p. 218.
27. Gabriel, *Notorious Victoria*, p. 174.

for the Equal Rights Party nomination, generously offered to put up their bail, but the two women proudly declined. Woodhull's attorney had already advised the women that if they were released they would almost certainly be arrested again on other charges. Nevertheless, Victoria and Tennessee appreciated his willingness to help. As Woodhull herself later explained, Train, "like a true knight errant flew to our side as a champion."[28]

Aside from James D. Reymart, Woodhull's attorney, the inimitable Train was one of the few people who tried to assist the outcast feminist during the many trials and tribulations she faced that year. In an effort to prove their innocence, Train published numerous passages from the Bible in an attempt to show that Victoria's language in the Beecher case was well within acceptable standards. His writings, however, were deemed defamatory and he, too, was arrested on obscenity charges and spent the next six months in jail. He was eventually released after being declared harmlessly insane and spent the remainder of his life as a "professional crank."

No longer a candidate, Woodhull never expressed a personal preference for either Grant or Greeley. She knew both men personally but suggested in her revived *Weekly* of November 2 that the winning candidate should be brought to trial for illegally serving as president by refusing to allow women—a majority of the American people—the right to vote. Election officials failed to tally even a single vote for the "free love" champion, thereby ending the brief but colorful political career of the celebrated spiritualist. Woodhull divorced Blood in 1876 on the grounds of adultery, the only valid reason for divorce in New York in those days. It was most likely a mutual decision, but it's clear that James Blood was deeply wounded by their permanent separation. Unlike his ex-wife, he remained committed to the idea of third-party politics and languished as a radical writer for the *Greenback Labor Chronicle* in Auburn, Maine, for several years before that newspaper eventually collapsed. He was something of a minor celebrity in Maine because of his previous marriage to Woodhull. However, he rarely spoke of her other than to say that the "grandest woman in the world went back on me."[29] Though still deeply in love with Woodhull, Blood eventually remarried and set off for the Gold Coast of Africa where he died in 1885, while still a relatively young man.

Long out of the public eye, Woodhull and her sister moved to Britain in 1877. The twice-divorced, one-time presidential candidate eventually married John

---

28. Thornton, *The Nine Lives of Citizen Train*, p. 227.
29. Johnston, *Mrs. Satan*, p. 251.

Biddulph Martin, a prosperous English banker, and settled into a more "respectable" existence. Martin, an honors graduate at Oxford, had everything going for him—affluence, power and social standing. He provided Woodhull with the kind of comfortable life that had escaped her in the United States. Tennessee Claflin, Victoria's equally flamboyant sister, also settled into a new life of nobility as Lady Cook, the wife of a wealthy and elderly widower who had a deep interest in spiritualism. During a séance, it seems, Tennie claimed to have received a message from Cook's late wife advising him that he should marry her. Lonely and eager for companionship, the retired importer and art collector asked for Tennie's hand in marriage. As buoyant and insouciant as ever, Tennie thoroughly enjoyed her new life, dividing her time between the couple's magnificent home on the Thames and their palatial estate in Portugal, not far from Lisbon.

Despite her new life of respectability and wealth, Victoria still longed for the public spotlight. With the assistance of her husband and daughter, she launched *The Humanitarian*, a somewhat conservative periodical loosely modeled after her *Woodhull & Claflin's Weekly* that mixed sociology, politics, women's rights, economics, and fiction. She evidently also missed the rough and tumble of American politics. Though now living in Great Britain, it came as something of a surprise when she again sought the U.S. presidency on two occasions, running briefly in 1880 and waging a concerted and dignified campaign against Grover Cleveland and Benjamin Harrison in 1892. While her 1880 campaign appeared to consist of little more than publishing a supplement to the September issue of *The American Traveler* in London, her bid for the presidency in 1892 appears to have been a more spirited effort.[30] Promising to inaugurate "a system of education which will waken people to the responsibility of creating a race of gods instead of inferior human beings," Woodhull was nominated at a small convention of former supporters held at the Willard Hotel in Washington, D.C. Spending several months in the United States that year, the Humanitarian Party standard-bearer gave numerous interviews and issued press releases on an almost daily basis. She described her campaign as an "educational" effort and predicted that there would be a woman president before too long. As in 1872, however, Woodhull was painfully aware that she couldn't possibly be elected. "The truth is that I am too many years ahead of this age and the exalted views and objects of humanitarianism can scarcely be grasped as yet by the unenlightened mind of the average man," she sighed.[31]

---

30. Barbara Goldsmith, *Other Powers: The Age of Suffrage, Spiritualism, and the Scandalous Victoria Woodhull* (New York, 1998), pp. 440-441.

Outliving her husband by thirty years, Woodhull died an extremely wealthy woman in 1927, only a few months shy of her eighty-ninth birthday. As she requested, her ashes were scattered over the Atlantic Ocean, providing a link between her two countries. At the time of her death, Woodhull's estate was valued at approximately $14 million in current dollars.

For all intents and purposes, the American electorate didn't really have an alternative to the two major parties in 1872. The Prohibition Party, experiencing the birth pangs common in a new party, was only able to offer a ticket in six states—Connecticut, Michigan, New Hampshire, New York, Ohio and Pennsylvania. The headless Straight-Out Democrats and the Labor Reformers were saddled with a candidate who refused to run and the Independent Liberal Republicans never mounted a campaign. Moreover, Victoria Woodhull, languishing in a jail cell with her sister Tennie, was legally barred from the contest.

The erratic yet colorful George F. Train also dropped out of the race in the closing days of the campaign. After returning from a month-long trip to Europe in September—hardly a practical way to wage a presidential campaign—he enthusiastically returned to the campaign trail and, in fact, was in the middle of a harangue on the steps of a Wall Street banking firm when someone handed him a newspaper containing the news of Woodhull's plight. Stopping in the middle of a sentence, he rushed down the steps and out of the presidential picture.[32]

So, for better or worse, it was Greeley or Grant—arguably, two of the most unfit men to ever seek the nation's highest office. It was also one of the nastiest campaigns in American history. "We have watched eight successive campaigns," wrote the *New York Observer*, "and we are quite sure for total depravity, this beats them all."[33]

Relying heavily on his reputation as a war hero, Grant remained aloof during the campaign, spending most of the summer at his vacation home in Long Branch, New Jersey. It was left to his subordinates to explain away the myriad scandals that plagued his first four years in office. Although an economic depression was just around the corner, the Republican incumbent benefited tremendously from a relatively vibrant economy. Grant also enjoyed the support of big business, Union army veterans and former slaves who were unwilling to abandon the party of the Great Emancipator, Abraham Lincoln.

---

31. Johnston, *Mrs. Satan*, pp. 286-288; Underhill, *The Woman Who Ran for President*, p. 293.
32. Thornton, *The Nine Lives of Citizen Train*, p. 227.
33. *New York Observer*, September 26, 1872.

Though it was somewhat unseemly for a presidential candidate to take to the campaign trail in those days, Greeley abandoned his role of "Sage of Chappaqua" and took his campaign for honesty and reform across the country, denouncing the Republicans for "waving the bloody shirt"—something he had done repeatedly in the past. Supported by most of the nation's large non-partisan newspapers, "Uncle Horace," as he was affectionately dubbed, donning his familiar white hat and wrinkled suit, jumped into the campaign with both feet, delivering a major speech in Portland, Maine, in August. Between September 19 and 29, the New York journalist delivered almost two hundred speeches in the crucial swing states of New Jersey, Pennsylvania, Ohio, Indiana and Kentucky.

Despite a concerted effort on his part, Greeley's campaign, which looked so promising in the spring, never really caught fire in the fall. Historians and pundits have generally praised his stump speeches for their magnanimity. "Greeley's speeches were marvels of impromptu oratory," wrote Henry Watterson, "mostly homely appeals to the better sense of the people, convincing in their simplicity if the North were in any mood to listen and to reason."[34]

Yet it is equally true that some of his speeches simply served to confound and, in some cases, anger the electorate. "If anyone could send a great nation to the dogs," opined the New York Times, "the man is Greeley."[35] Speaking in Pittsburgh on September 19, the aging Liberal Republican candidate alienated Union veterans by accusing them of "rekindling the bitterness and hatred" of the Civil War. In Louisville, he characterized African-Americans as "ignorant, deceived and misguided" and, while speaking in Jefferson, Indiana, he foolishly suggested that his opposition to slavery might have been a "mistake." Greeley, of course, was deeply disappointed, if not bitter, about the lack of support he was receiving from the black community, especially given his long track record in the abolitionist movement. Frederick Douglass, inarguably the best-known African-American leader in the country, enthusiastically endorsed Grant and was given the honor of heading the Republican electoral ticket in New York.[36] The only real token of support Greeley received from African-Americans came from a convention of Liberal Republican Colored Men at Weissiger Hall in Louisville on September 25. In endorsing Greeley's candidacy, that convention sharply denounced "the villainy" of Reconstruction and urged African-American voters to rid themselves of their "vampires," not the least of whom was Ulysses S. Grant.

---

34.   Henry Luther Stoddard, *Horace Greeley: Printer, Editor, Crusader* (New York, 1946), p. 312.
35.   Boller, *Presidential Campaigns*, p. 128.
36.   Ross, *The Liberal Republican Movement*, p. 165.

The performance of Ben Gratz-Brown, Greeley's vice-presidential running mate, was equally disastrous. While attending commencement exercises at Yale, his alma mater, an obviously drunk Brown said that universities in the dynamic, exciting West were better institutions of higher learning than schools in the backward East. Apparently intoxicated, Brown made a similarly embarrassing appearance in New York City when he fainted in public, prompting the irreverent *Nation* to sardonically observe that Brown could as easily represent the nation's temperance voters as Greeley represented the country's reformers.

Lured to public office like a moth to a flame, Greeley was time and again singed by the experience. His presidential campaign proved to be no different, but this time he was not merely seared but burnt to a crisp. The campaign was an altogether exasperating experience for the aging journalist, both politically as well as personally. Saddened by the death of his ailing wife shortly before the election and worried sick about his diminishing control of his beloved *Tribune*, Greeley watched almost helplessly as the Republicans, hoping to destroy his fragile coalition candidacy, dredged up many of his earlier diatribes against the Democrats, particularly his 1866 description of that party as "the traitorous section of northern politics." His numerous eccentricities, most notably his vegetarianism, his flirtation with Fourierism and his tenuous connection with feminist gadfly Victoria Woodhull were all used against him. Moreover, his association with Tammany Hall and its nefariously corrupt former "Boss" William Marcy Tweed also undermined his candidacy.

Despite the uphill battle facing him, Greeley canvassed the country with enthusiasm from the rear of his campaign train, calling again and again for reform and change. In mid-July, shortly after receiving the Democratic nomination, it appeared as though Greeley might actually win. Greeley-for-President clubs mushroomed across the country. From the moment of his nomination, recalled Alexander K. McClure of the *Philadelphia Times*, "everything pointed to Greeley's election and a tidal wave that would sweep Greeley seemed certain, but in August the great business interests of the country became alarmed and Greeley's popularity ebbed to a humiliating defeat."[37]

Greeley's fortunes had turned quickly. State elections in North Carolina in August and the September elections in Vermont and Maine spelled trouble for the Democrats. In the two New England states, the Republicans piled up larger than usual majorities. Rumors abounded. The Philadelphia *Sunday Republic* reported in early September that a move was afoot in Democratic circles to dump

---

37. Stoddard, *Horace Greeley: Printer, Editor, Crusader*, p. 311.

Greeley and replace him with Straight-Out nominee Charles O'Conor, or possibly somebody else. Things were also not going particularly well on the campaign trail as union veterans jeered and hissed the New York journalist at virtually every stop and a rock was thrown through the window of his train while campaigning in Ohio, nearly hitting him.

Vastly outspent by the Republicans, Greeley found it increasingly difficult to keep up with the never-ending charges and innuendos hurled in his direction. He was damned as a traitor and belittled as a fool. Things were so bad, he quipped at the end of the campaign, "that I hardly knew whether I was running for the presidency or the penitentiary."[38] No major candidate for the presidency had ever been as vilified as was Horace Greeley during the 1872 campaign. Yet the Liberal Republican standard-bearer persevered. Out on the edge of darkness, with his whole life collapsing before him, a deeply grieving Greeley tried in vain to point the country in a new direction. But few listened.

The country opted instead for four more years of incompetence, corruption and scandal. Capturing 286 of 349 electoral votes, President Grant carried every state in the North and most of the South, easily trouncing his Liberal Republican rival while garnering 3,597,132 votes to Greeley's 2,834,125.[39] He even carried Greeley's home state of New York by more than 53,000 votes. Despite his anti-slavery reputation, Greeley nevertheless managed to carry the border states of Kentucky, Maryland and Missouri and won convincingly in Georgia, Tennessee and Texas. A switch of only 908 votes in Virginia would have also put that state in his column.

Hundreds of thousands of ex-Copperheads in the North and Bourbon Democrats in the South refused to go to the polls, thereby contributing to Greeley's overwhelming defeat. In addition to blaming the Bourbon Democrats, George Washington Julian attributed Greeley's defeat to the "unscrupulous and desperate hostility" of the Republicans, a party for which Greeley "had done more than any other man, living, or dead."[40]

The result proved fatal for Greeley, both figuratively and literally. Blaming himself for the overwhelming Liberal Republican-Democratic debacle, the deeply dejected journalist said that his "horrible record" had "paralyzed" the fragile coalition. He suffered a mental breakdown shortly after the election and died on

38. Boller, *Presidential Campaigns*, p. 129.
39. The electoral votes of Arkansas were not counted due to a technicality and Congress rejected Louisiana's eight electoral votes because of disputed results—a prelude of things to come.
40. Julian, *Political Recollections*, p. 348.

November 29, only twenty-four days after the election. His death touched the nation, provoking an outpouring of affection from Democrats and Republicans alike. Even his harshest critics paid tribute to the fallen journalist. Greeley had been "hunted to his grave by political assassins whose calumnies broke his heart," said Indiana's Julian. "He was scarcely less a martyr than Lincoln, or less honored after his death, and his graceless defamers now seemed to think they could atone for their crime by singing his praises."[41] Incredibly, several newspapers suggested that Greeley's electors should cast their votes for Grant in the Electoral College to "lift the Administration out of partisanship." Greeley's electors, however, were too bitter for that sort of magnanimous gesture and divided their electoral votes between four candidates, with Indiana's Thomas A. Hendrick's receiving the majority. Ben Gratz-Brown of Missouri, Charles J. Jenkins of Georgia and Supreme Court Justice David Davis also received votes. Apparently believing that a dead Greeley would be more useful to the country than "Useless" Grant, three Georgia electors dutifully cast their ballots for the late *Tribune* editor, but Congress refused to count their votes.

Prohibitionist James Black, a small-time railroad lawyer and ardent foe of hard cider, did not actively campaign in the 1872 presidential contest, relying instead on John Russell's *Peninsular Herald* for publicity. One hundred thousand copies of Russell's pamphlet, "An Adequate Remedy for a National Evil," were distributed throughout the country. Despite endorsements from seven college presidents and numerous clergymen, the vast majority of dry voters ignored the Prohibition Party during its maiden campaign and cast their ballots for Greeley, an outspoken champion of temperance dating back to the 1850s. Black was never a factor in the contest, polling only 5,608 votes nationally. The party's best showing was in Michigan, where Black and Russell polled six-tenths of one percent of the vote.

Like Russell, James Black remained active in the Prohibition Party for the rest of his life and served as chairman of the party's national committee from 1876 to 1880. At the time of his death in 1893, he had the largest collection of prohibition materials in the country, which he bequeathed to the National Temperance Society, an organization that he had helped to create.

The Straight-Out Democrats, who had named electoral slates pledged to Charles O'Conor and John Quincy Adams II in twenty-three states, polled a pitiful 29,489 votes nationally. In some jurisdictions, the Straight-Out Democrats were aided by local Republicans anxious to distribute ballots for the Bourbon

---

41. Ibid., p. 351.

ticket, hoping that O'Conor would siphon votes from traditionally Democratic voters.[42] Despite his poor showing nationally, there were a few pockets of support for the Straight-Out Democratic ticket sprinkled across the country, especially in towns and cities with sizable Irish-American populations. O'Conor ran strongest in Georgia where at least six newspapers endorsed the Straight-Out movement. The most influential of these was the Atlanta *Sun*, owned by Alexander Stephens, who earlier had commented that the choice between Grant and Greeley was like choosing between "hemlock and strychnine."[43] The *Sun* had carried on a lively debate with the Atlanta *Constitution* throughout the autumn campaign. O'Conor garnered 3,999 votes in Georgia, or slightly less than three percent of the total. He also made a similar showing in Oregon, polling just below three percent, and polled over two percent of the vote in Delaware and Texas.

In Missouri, birthplace of the Liberal Republican-Democratic fusion experiment, there were still a few Democrats who opposed coalition at any cost and nearly one out of every hundred voters took a Straight-Out ballot on November 5, giving O'Conor 2,439 votes in that state. One of his strongest showings in the nation, in fact, occurred in Osage County, Missouri, just east of Jefferson City, where Straight-Out Democratic electors garnered a whopping 31% of the vote.

The Straight-Out Democrats of Pennsylvania, meeting in Harrisburg on October 16, opted against naming electors for O'Conor and urged all honest Democrats to stay home on Election Day. This was a blow to the state's tiny Labor Reform Party, which expected to support O'Conor and had already nominated a full slate of statewide candidates, including labor leader William P. Schell for governor. When the Straight-Out Democrats dropped out of the picture, the dispirited Labor Reformers failed to follow through with a campaign.

The reluctant O'Conor was nevertheless a factor of sorts in several small towns and cities across the country, occasionally polling the difference between his major party rivals. In Crawford County, Illinois, for example, the New York lawyer received 184 votes—or eight percent of the county's total—while Greeley lost in Crawford by only 74 votes. One of O'Conor's strongest showings in the country occurred in rural Union County in northeast Oregon, where he garnered a respectable 16.5% of the popular vote. Moreover, in heavily Republican Tillamook County, Oregon, the Straight-Out standard-bearer actually ran even with Greeley.

---

42. Ross, *The Liberal Republican Movement*, pp. 148-149.
43. William Gillette, "Election of 1872," Arthur M. Schlesinger, Jr., ed., *A History of American Presidential Elections*, 4 vols. (New York, 1971), Vol. II, p. 1318.

Despite Grant's overwhelming victory, the Liberal Republican-Democratic fusion campaign was not a complete washout as fusion candidates won gubernatorial races in Georgia, Missouri and Florida. In Missouri, Silas Woodson, a former Kentucky legislator and circuit court judge, became the state's eighteenth governor. Educated in a typical one-room schoolhouse, the 54-year-old Woodson defeated Republican John B. Henderson, a one-time states' rights Democrat who later introduced the emancipation amendment to the Constitution. Henderson had been one of the "honorable seven" who courageously went against his own party and spared President Andrew Johnson during his impeachment trial.

In most states, however, Liberal Republican gubernatorial candidates went down in flames, including those in Kansas, Mississippi and Vermont. In Illinois, Gustavus Koerner, the state's most prominent German-American politician and the Liberal Republican candidate for governor, lost to Republican Richard J. Oglesby by more than 40,000 votes and in New York, ex-Free Soiler Francis Kernan, a Catholic, lost to Republican John A. Dix, another former member of the Free Soil Party, by a margin of 445,801 to 392,350. In Massachusetts, antislavery advocate Francis W. Bird, the "Sage of Walpole," lost to Republican William Washburn, a wealthy banker, by an overwhelming margin of 133,900 to 59,626. Bird, who was nominated after Charles Sumner refused to run, was regarded as a leading Republican before switching to the Liberal Republican Party. He had served as an advisor to several leading Republican statesmen, including Sumner, after whom he named one of his sons.

For a brief period prior to the party's disintegration, the Liberal Republicans also claimed seven seats in the U.S. Senate, including that of Massachusetts Sen. Charles Sumner. The Liberal Republicans also took some solace in the fact that their coalition with the Democrats on the congressional level helped to elect no fewer than fifty-one members of the House, including fourteen of their own—up from two in the previous Congress. Liberal Republican coalition tickets ran strongest in Georgia, Maryland and Missouri, winning nine of thirteen House seats in the latter state.

The Prohibitionists, Straight-Out Democrats and Labor Reformers, as well as a handful of independents also competed in gubernatorial campaigns that year. By far, the most impressive independent candidacy occurred in West Virginia where incumbent Gov. John J. Jacob, a Democrat, was forced to run for re-election as an independent after his own party refused to re-nominate him. The 41-year-old Dickinson-educated lawyer, who was endorsed by the state's Republican Party, prevailed in the campaign, defeating Democrat Johnson M. Camden by more than 2,500 votes.

In Indiana, the Straight-Out Democrats met in the state Senate chamber in Indianapolis on September 19 and, hoping to "reorganize and re-baptize" the state Democratic Party, nominated a full slate of candidates, including former congressman Alfred P. Edgerton for governor. William C. Moreau was named for one of the state's two at-large seats in Congress. This Straight-Out ticket, perhaps more than any other, was of particular concern to Horace Greeley and the regular Democrats. Indiana, after all, was a crucial swing state, without which Greeley could not possibly hope to win the presidency. Tremendous pressure was put on Edgerton to withdraw from the race. He eventually did, but it was more out of disappointment in his failure to capture the Straight-Out Democratic nomination for vice president in Louisville earlier in the month, than out of any profound concern for Greeley's candidacy.

In Illinois, the Straight-Out Democrats tapped former Senator Sidney Breese for governor. Breese, who for years made his livelihood as a muckraking newspaper editor, was a longtime adversary of the late Stephen A. Douglas and had served in the U.S. Senate from 1843-49 where he chaired the Public Lands Committee. The 72-year-old Breese, who was a state Supreme Court justice at the time of his nomination, wasn't really a factor in the race as former Republican Gov. Richard J. Ogelsby trounced his Liberal Republican-Democratic rival by more than 40,000 votes. In Connecticut, former Sen. Francis Gillette, the Prohibition Party's candidate for governor, ran well ahead of his party's national ticket and easily polled the difference between his major party rivals.

Though the Liberal Republican movement outlived Greeley and tenuously clung to life in parts of the South for a few years following the 1872 presidential election, the Labor Reform and Equal Rights parties died quiet deaths on or before Election Day. The Prohibition Party was the only minor party to survive the Grant landslide and, remarkably, has competed with pluck and a prayer in every presidential election through the year 2000.

While the Republicans won an overwhelming majority in the 1872 congressional elections—increasing their majority in the Senate and increasing their huge majority over the out-of-power Democrats in the House—there were at least ninety independent and third party candidates for Congress that year, excluding at least sixteen Liberal Republicans.[44]

---

44.   Dubin, *United States Congressional Elections, 1788-1997*, p. 228. The Republicans claimed 200 seats at the opening of the 43rd Congress to 83 Democrats, five Conservatives, three Liberal Republicans and one Independent Democrat.

The most prominent among them was Andrew Johnson, the 63-year-old ex-president who waged a spirited but forlorn independent campaign for Tennessee's newly created at-large seat in the U.S. House of Representatives. Seeking vindication, the tailor-turned-politician had tired of his passive life in Greenville, saying that the town was "as lifeless as a graveyard." Having narrowly failed in a bid for the U.S. Senate in 1869, Lincoln's successor was more anxious than ever to return to Washington.

Facing formidable opposition from Republican Horace Maynard, a one-time member of the Know-Nothing Party, and Democrat Benjamin F. Cheatham, a popular Confederate general, Johnson, who had endorsed Liberal Republican Horace Greeley for president earlier in the year, lashed out at the corrupt Grant administration, military rings and the two old parties, asserting that he was ready once again to fight for the people and the Constitution.

In one of the most forensic campaigns in Tennessee history, the former president delivered some of the finest stump speeches ever heard in the Volunteer State. However, his late start, coupled with the abusive and negative attacks heaped on him by his opponents, worked against his independent candidacy. Maynard, who had seconded Johnson's name for the vice presidency at the 1864 Union Party convention in Baltimore, charged that the former president was responsible for the wrongful execution of Mary Surratt in the assassination of Abraham Lincoln. Surratt, to be sure, had some knowledge of the conspiracy, but her direct involvement in Lincoln's murder was never proven. In fact, it is still debated by historians to this day. Cheatham's diehard Confederate supporters, who heckled Johnson at every opportunity, also raised the same issue. Hampered by an unusually late state and damaged by the criticism surrounding Surrat's execution, the former president finished a distant third in the race, garnering 37,903 votes, or roughly twenty percent of the vote, to Maynard's 80,250 and 66,106 for Cheatham.

In addition to Johnson's candidacy, several other independent and minor party candidates also waged noteworthy congressional campaigns that fall. Among them was William J. Hynes, an Irish-born lawyer form Little Rock. Running on the satellite Black and Tan Republican ticket, the 29-year-old Hynes was narrowly elected to Congress in a hard-fought race for the at-large seat in Arkansas, defeating his regular Republican opponent by 437 votes. Hynes, who was defeated in a bid for re-election two years later, took his seat in the House as a Liberal Republican.

One of the most interesting races involving a third-party candidate that year occurred in New York City's ninth congressional district in Manhattan where

John Hardy, a Scottish-born former alderman and one-time Copperhead, was nearly elected to Congress on an anti-Tammany "Apollo Hall" ticket against strong Democratic and Republican opposition. Prior to joining the reform movement, the 37-year-old Hardy, a graduate of the City College of New York, had moved freely in Tammany circles, serving in the state assembly and winning a seat on the Board of Alderman on five occasions. A lawyer, he also served briefly as clerk of the Common Council while much of the plundering was taking place under Tammany Hall's notoriously corrupt "Boss" William Marcy Tweed.

In his congressional race, Hardy was pitted against Democrat "Big Judge" Michael B. Connolly, Tammany's handpicked candidate, and Republican David Mellish, a former schoolteacher and reporter for the *New York Tribune*. With his patriotism called into serious question, it proved to be a difficult campaign for the Apollo Hall candidate. Time and again, Hardy was raked over the coals for having delivered a "virulent Copperhead speech" opposing Lincoln's call for troops in April 1861. Shortly after the outbreak of the war, Hardy joined with five other lawmakers in boldly voting against Lincoln's request for Union troops from New York—a rare act of defiance in the North at the time.

The former assemblyman faced a few more blind swipes of the pruner's knife when the *New York Times*, which was supporting Hardy's Republican opponent, claimed that the former alderman had not only been a sympathizer in the anti-draft riots in New York City in the summer of 1863, but had been the mob's chief "emissary" and spokesman. That charge, of course, was utter nonsense and Hardy vigorously denied the accusation. Antiwar sentiment had been festering in America's largest city for years—with or without Hardy's involvement. Moreover, Tammany Hall had done virtually everything in its power, including registering fictitious voters—a common machine practice in those days—to defeat Lincoln in 1860, enabling Democrat Stephen A. Douglas to carry the city by a comfortable 29,300 votes. Shortly after Lincoln's election, Mayor Fernando Wood—one of the most erratic political figures in the city's history—seriously flirted with secession, proposing in a speech to council members that New York City should secede from the Union and establish a free and independent city modeled after the ancient city-states. That way, the Tammany leader fumed, the city could preserve its uninterrupted trade with its "aggrieved brethren" in the South.

Moreover, a significant Copperhead presence had operated within the city throughout the Civil War and Democratic newspapers had been hammering away against proscription, suggesting that white working men would be forced to risk their lives to free southern slaves who would then migrate North to take their jobs. Even Horatio Seymour, the state's popular Democratic governor, warned the Lincoln administration in a Fourth of July speech that "the bloody and treasonable doctrine of public necessity can be proclaimed by a mob as well as by a government." By the summer of 1863, New York City, with its crowded Irish tenements, rampant crime, high unemployment and declining wages, was a tinderbox.

A longshoremen's strike in June, in which African-American stevedores under police escort replaced striking Irish workers, inflamed tensions even further. Four days of intense rioting ensued, leaving at least 105 people dead, including the lynching of six blacks. Countless others were severely beaten. The vast majority of those killed, however, were antiwar protesters slain by Lincoln's Union soldiers. Property damaged exceeded two million dollars. In the mayhem, the first floor of Horace Greeley's *Tribune* was gutted, the city's Colored Orphan Asylum was burned to the ground, and more than 100 other properties were set ablaze, while another 250 buildings were ransacked and damaged. The riots were finally quelled after several Union regiments from Pennsylvania fired at the rioters with the same deadly force they had used in Gettysburg against the Confederate army only two weeks earlier.

All of this, incredibly, was laid at Hardy's feet during his third-party bid for Congress in 1872. Despite the negative publicity directed at him by the *New York Times* and other leading daily newspapers, the Apollo Hall candidate put up a valiant fight. Though falsely portrayed as a "ringer" for the discredited Tammany machine, Hardy came within 773 votes of winning a seat in Congress, polling 7,068 votes to 7,841 for Republican David Mellish. Tammany Democrat Michael Connolly, a corrupt former magistrate, was left in the dust, garnering 5,847 votes.

Hardy became something of a perennial candidate for Congress thereafter, occasionally running as an independent and at other times as a Democrat. In 1874, he polled an astonishing 37% of the vote in a heated three-cornered race as an independent against popular Democrat Fernando Wood, the enigmatic Tammany politician and former three-term mayor. Hardy waged another strong campaign on an "Anti-Tammany" ticket in 1878, again losing to the erratic and unpredictable former mayor by a mere 797 votes. Hardy's persistence finally paid off in 1881 when he won a special election to fill a vacancy following Fernando Wood's unexpected death in February of that year. He served in Congress as a Democrat for three years before losing his seat in 1884.

The 1874 Mid-Term Elections

With the country in the midst of a serious economic downturn, the Republicans took it on the chin during the 1874-75 mid-term elections as the Democrats, a party that had been previously outnumbered in the U.S. House by a margin of 200 to 83, captured a 70-seat majority. It was the first Democratic majority in the House of Representatives since before the Civil War. In addition to three Independent-Republicans, William H. Felton, an independent Democrat from Georgia, Anti-Monopolist Lucien L. Ainsworth of Iowa, Independent Reformer William B. Anderson of Illinois, and the Independent Reform Party's George W. Cate, William P. Lynde and Samuel Burchard of Wisconsin, also held seats in the 44th Congress. A former state legislator and longtime circuit court judge from rural Portage County in upper Wisconsin, Cate was elected on a Reform-Democratic fusion ticket, defeating incumbent Republican Alexander S. McDill by two votes out of a total of 19,090 votes cast.

The three Independent-Republicans elected in 1874 included Dudley C. Denison, a cousin of the late Salmon P. Chase of Ohio. Denison, a former state legislator and U.S. district attorney for Vermont, defeated four-term Republican incumbent Luke P. Poland in a four-way race to capture the seat in the state's second congressional district. Poland, who had served briefly in the U.S. Senate, chaired the House committees that investigated the Ku Klux Klan, the Credit Mobilier scandal and the corrupt Carpetbag administration in Arkansas. Former sheriff and Charleston alderman Edmund W. Mackey of South Carolina and Guilford Wiley Wells, a transplanted New Yorker and George Washington University-educated lawyer from Mississippi, were also elected to Congress as independent or breakaway Republicans.

Three independents were also elected to the U.S. House of Representatives that year, including former Speaker of the House Nathaniel P. Banks of Massachusetts who had lost his seat to Republican Daniel W. Gooch two years earlier. Running without a party label, the 58-year-old Banks garnered nearly 65% of the vote to regain his seat. The newly elected independents also included John R. Goodin of Kansas, a former state legislator and district court judge from Humboldt, and Julius H. Seelye of Massachusetts, a former minister and professor of moral philosophy at Amherst College. The 50-year-old Seelye, a graduate of the Auburn Theological Seminary, had served as pastor of the First Reformed Church in Schenectady, New York, before accepting a teaching position at Amherst. Running as an independent, Seelye polled nearly 42% of the vote in defeating Republican Charles A. Stevens and Democrat Henry C. Hill. Seelye didn't seek a second term in 1876 and, instead, was named president of Amherst College—a position he held until 1890. As president of the college, the longtime educator inaugurated what is believed to have been the first instance of student self-government at an American institution of higher learning. In 1884, he was considered for the American Prohibition Party's presidential nomination.

Candidates running outside the traditional two-party system also waged viable campaigns in several other House districts, including in Pennsylvania's twenty-third congressional district where Pittsburgh lawyer Samuel A. Purviance, an aging Whig ex-congressman and former Pennsylvania attorney general, mounted a political comeback. Running as an independent, the 65-year-old Purviance, a former prosecuting attorney and longtime Republican National Committee member, garnered over 21% of the vote against his major-party opponents in a race won by Democrat Alexander G. Cochran, a 28-year-old Columbia Law School graduate. In Illinois, the Independent Reform Party's Rolla B. Henry received over nineteen percent of the vote in a three-way race won by Democrat William A. Sparks, a former state senator who later battled land speculators, cattlemen, land-grant railroads and their lackeys in Washington as President Cleveland's commissioner of the U.S. General Land Office from 1885-88. In his losing effort, the little-remembered Independent Reform aspirant garnered an eye-opening 4,023 votes to 8,723 for Sparks and 7,932 for incumbent Republican James S. Martin.

Independent and third-party candidates also waged competitive races in several gubernatorial campaigns during this period, not the least of which was Thomas F. Campbell's strong showing in Oregon's 1874 governor's race. Running as an independent, Campbell garnered more than a quarter of the vote against popular Democratic incumbent La Fayette Grover and his Republican opponent. In California, former congressman and agricultural innovator John Bidwell, nearly outpolling his Republican rival, made a similarly strong showing the following year in a three-way race won by Democrat William Irwin. In Massachusetts, the Temperance Party's John I. Baker received 9,124 votes—more than five percent of the total—in a race decided by 5,300 votes and in Rhode Island, industrialist Rowland Hazard, running as an independent, outpolled his major party rivals but was denied the governorship when the election was eventually decided by the state legislature.

14

The Birth of the Greenback Party

✦

Agrarian and Currency Reformers Enter the Fray

Continued rampant corruption in the Grant administration cost the Republicans dearly in the 1874 mid-term congressional elections. While losing control of the House that year, the party's majority in the U.S. Senate was trimmed by eighteen seats. Continued wrongdoing in the Grant administration loomed as the major barrier to continued GOP control of the White House as the 1876 presidential contest got underway. Other factors, including continued carpetbag misrule in the South and an economic downturn, were also working against the majority party.

The greatest threat to continued Republican rule came once again from the Liberal Republicans, a group that one might have thought would have faded away with the disastrous Greeley candidacy of 1872. A conference of some 200 leading Liberal Republicans at the Fifth Avenue Hotel in New York City on May 8, 1876, made it clear that they had every intention of fielding their own ticket again if the two major parties waffled on the critical issue of governmental reform. Led by Missouri's Carl Schurz, the aging Charles Francis Adams of Massachusetts and William Cullen Bryant of the *New York Evening Post*, the reformers warned both major parties against nominating anyone who was not a tried and true reformer.

Most reformers favored Benjamin H. Bristow of Kentucky for president. Prior to being forced out of the Grant administration, the 44-year-old Bristow was widely credited with breaking up the infamous tax-dodging "Whiskey Ring." Years earlier, Bristow had been a strong proponent of the Thirteenth Amendment, outlawing slavery, and actively supported Lincoln's re-election in 1864. As

U.S. Attorney for Kentucky in the late 1860s, he fought the state's powerful Ku Klux Klan to a standstill, obtaining twenty-nine convictions—including a murder conviction—against its members. The Liberal Republicans also looked favorably on several other potential candidates, including Charles Francis Adams and Ohio Gov. Rutherford B. Hayes. In no uncertain terms, the Liberal Republicans made it clear they wouldn't support a third term for Grant, nor were they likely to support New York's Roscoe Conkling or Indiana Sen. Oliver Morton—two other leading contenders for the Republican presidential nomination.

The regular Republicans seemed to get the message, even if the impervious Grant didn't. Virtually blind to criticism, the 54-year-old president, who thoroughly enjoyed life in the White House and his summer vacations in Long Branch, was seriously entertaining the idea of running for a third consecutive term until House Republicans, by an overwhelming 233 to 18 vote, nixed the idea.

When the GOP convened in Cincinnati's Exposition Hall on June 14, Bristow was one of ten or so candidates seeking the party's presidential nomination. The Kentucky lawmaker, however, received only 113 votes on the first ballot and the race eventually developed into a two-man battle to the death between James G. Blaine, the "Plumed Knight" of Maine, and Ohio Gov. Rutherford B. Hayes, a civil service reformer. A dark-horse candidate, Hayes was nominated on the convention's seventh ballot, narrowly defeating his rival. William Wheeler, a scrupulously honest New York lawmaker who refused to accept a salary increase in 1873 when Congress approved an eleventh-hour "pay grab," was nominated for the vice presidency. While remaining discreetly silent on Grant's mishandling of Reconstruction in the South, the Republicans, throwing a bone to the Liberals, adopted a platform condemning the spoils system.

The Democrats, meeting in St. Louis two weeks later, nominated Gov. Samuel J. Tilden of New York for the presidency and named Gov. Thomas A. Hendricks of Indiana as his vice-presidential co-star. A confirmed bachelor, the wealthy and cultured 62-year-old Tilden had a sterling reputation, the result of successfully taking on the larcenous Tweed Ring in New York City and for later smashing the state's notoriously corrupt Canal Ring. Longing for a return to the White House for the first time in sixteen years, the Democrats called for civil service reform, the repeal of the Resumption Act of 1875 and an end to wasteful government spending.

Plans for a Liberal Republican nominating convention to be held in Philadelphia in late July were called off when party chairman Ethan Allen, shortly after consulting with party leaders, strongly urged the Liberals to support Hayes.

Hayes, he said, favored the Liberal Republican agenda—namely, civil service reform, a single presidential term and a return to specie payment (i.e., hard currency, such as gold and silver). With the notable exceptions of Charles Francis Adams and Henry Watterson of the *Louisville Courier-Journal* who broke ranks and supported Democrat Samuel J. Tilden, most Liberal Republicans enthusiastically embraced Hayes' candidacy and so ended the short-lived Liberal Republican saga. While the short-lived Liberal Republican Party exited the stage, a new and unrelated political movement made its national debut.

The Greenback Party

To help finance the Civil War, the Union treasury issued $450 million in paper money, or greenbacks. Greenbacks did not include gold and silver certificates, but were merely promises by the federal government to honor payment of wartime debts. Unfortunately, the massive issuance of greenbacks caused farm prices to skyrocket and triggered runaway inflation.

Following the war there was a prolonged and sometimes acrimonious debate in both major parties between those who hoped to continue printing paper money and those who wanted to limit the amount of greenbacks in circulation. Debtors, most notably farmers, wanted to continue the inflationary policy of issuing "cheap money" backed by neither gold or silver because it enabled them to pay their debts in money worth less than when they initially borrowed it. Some of the greenback advocates even went so far as to suggest that it would be downright "un-American" to abandon paper money and return to the antiquated gold standard. One of those who made this argument was the ambitious financier Jay Cooke. "Why," he asked, should this great country "be stunted and dwarfed—its activities chilled and its very life blood curdled—by these miserable 'hard coin' theories, the musty theories of a bygone age?"[1]

As early as 1841, antebellum economist Edward Kellogg had advanced the idea that a flexible supply of paper money served the interests of workers and farmers while hard currency only benefited the wealthy. Kellogg intensified his crusade for paper currency in 1849 with the publication of his treatise, *Labor and Other Capital*, a book described by labor leader Robert Schilling as "the Bible of the early currency reformers." Kellogg, a successful dry goods merchant in New York City who was forced to suspend his business during the Panic of 1837, was convinced that a flexible money supply—known as "inter-convertibil-

---

1.   Bailyn, *et al., The Great Republic*, p. 575.

ity"—would destroy the money monopoly, enabling debtors to free themselves while eliminating speculation in land and poverty.[2] Some twenty years later, Alexander Campbell, the father of the Greenback Party, popularized Kellogg's theory. In 1864, Campbell published *The True American System of Finance*, a primer on Kellogg's theory. During the Panic of 1873, Campbell's writings found a large and attentive audience among the nation's hard-pressed farmers who were confronted with ever-declining agricultural prices and tight credit. Some American manufacturers, especially iron makers who profited handsomely from an inflated currency—helping them to broaden their markets—were also opposed to the idea of resuming the gold standard.

Many others, however, believed just the opposite. Wall Street strenuously demanded an end to the issuance of greenbacks and Secretary of the Treasury Hugh McCulloch, who wasted little time asking Congress for authority to retire them as a first step toward resumption, believed that gold and silver were the only true measure of value.[3] "My chief aim," he told his subordinates in March 1865, shortly after taking office, is to "institute measures to bring the business of the country gradually back to the specie basis, a departure from which...is no less damaging and demoralizing to the people than expensive to the government." McCulloch, a banker and something of a racist who once suggested that gold and silver were the only true regulators of trade and were "prepared by the Almighty for this very purpose," then proceeded to quietly fund a large block of interest bearing legal tenders, including an assortment of other quasi-monetary notes. Congress quickly responded to McCulloch's annual report in December, pledging cooperation with the Secretary's efforts to bring about a contraction of the country's paper currency. [4] Other leading "hard money" advocates during this period included Edward A. Atkinson, a public-spirited cotton manufacturer from Massachusetts and David A. Wells, the influential former chairman of the Special Revenue Committee.[5] But there were many others also clamoring for a return to specie payments, including conservative *laissez-faire* economist William Graham Sumner of Yale, who portrayed the issuance of greenbacks during the Civil War as a great wartime mistake. "Whatever strength a nation has is weakened by issuing legal tender notes," he wrote in *A History of American Currency*. "All history

2.   Ralph R. Ricker, *The Greenback-Labor Movement in Pennsylvania* (Bellefonte, Pennsylvania, 1966), pp. 24-25.

3.   U.S. Treasury, *Annual Report of the Secretary of the Treasury on the State of the Finances for the Year 1865*, pp. 9-14.

4.   Unger, *The Greenback Era*, p. 41; Hugh McCulloch, *Men and Measures of Half a Century* (New York, 1900), p. 201.

shows that paper money with a forced circulation is not a temporary resource," but rather "a mischief easily done but most difficult to cure."[6] Similarly, banks and other creditors stood to lose from inflation and were almost universally opposed to paper money.

For all practical purposes, Greenbackism, as a political movement, actually began as early as 1866 when western farmers demanded that retired greenbacks should be put back into circulation, thereby creating an inflationary currency. Several Democratic politicians, most notably Henry Clay Dean of Iowa and Allen G. Thurman, George Pendleton, Samuel F. Cary and Clement L. Vallandigham of Ohio, picked up the cause and began demanding an increased paper currency as a way of retiring the nation's huge Civil War debt while aiding debt-ridden farmers in the west. It wasn't long before the *Cincinnati Enquirer* took up the issue as a way of wresting control of the Democratic Party from the eastern establishment under the control of Wall Street financier August Belmont and New York City's powerful Tammany Hall organization.

The original Greenback movement was first put to the test in Ohio's hotly-contested 1867 gubernatorial campaign when "sound money" Republican Rutherford B. Hayes narrowly defeated Democrat Allen G. Thurman. Following his razor-thin defeat, Thurman and other Ohio Democrats decided that the issue was too radical and modified it as a plan to specifically pay down the nation's war debts. Known as the "Ohio Idea," it was then adopted as a major plank in the Democratic national platform of 1868. Though initially denounced by the Republicans, the issue picked up steam and Congress eventually passed legislation suspending the authority of the Secretary of Treasury to remove greenbacks from circulation.[7]

The Panic of 1873 brought the currency issue to the forefront when the Republicans decided to resume gold payments with the passage of the Resumption Act. This legislation, which was to take effect in 1879, brought howls of pro-

---

5.   Ibid., pp. 127-131. In 1875, Wells published *The Cremation Theory of Specie Resumption*, advocating a drastic program of burning half a million greenback dollars every week—an idea first proposed by Harvard professor Francis Bowen. Bowen, a professor of Natural Religion, Moral Philosophy and Civil Polity, believed that the use of paper money had "done even more harm to the morals of the country than to its commerce, its reputation, and its financial well being."

6.   William Graham Sumner, *A History of American Currency* (New York, 1874), p. 202.

7.   Reginald C. McGrane, *William Allen: A Study in Western Democracy* (Columbus, Ohio, 1925), pp. 179-182; Davis R. Dewey, *Financial History of the United States* (New York, 1934), p. 348.

test from the debt-ridden Midwest, providing the spark for a series of reform-minded third parties in various states and leading to the founding of the nationally organized Greenback and Anti-Monopoly parties. Though never important factors in presidential elections, these parties attracted able men like James B. Weaver of Iowa, Edward Allis of Wisconsin, the colorful Ignatius Donnelly of Minnesota and William "Roaring Bill" Allen of Ohio and served as a springboard for the politically potent Populist Party of the 1890s.

The depression following the Panic of 1873 witnessed a large number of mortgage foreclosures, falling prices, a sharp rise in unemployment (during the winter of 1873-74, nearly one-fourth of all laborers in New York City were out of work) and a significantly reduced money supply. During this period, most greenback advocates worked within the two major parties to promote the issuance of cheap paper money, but made little headway.

Frustrated by the inability of the two major parties to end the depression, agrarian leaders in the Midwest launched a number of statewide third parties and, with a modicum of success, challenged the Democrats and Republicans for control of state, county and local offices in more than a dozen states in 1873 and 1874. These parties adopted various names in different states. In Illinois, Kansas and Wisconsin, they were known as the Independent Reform Party; in Indiana, the party was simply called the Independent Party; in Michigan, the National Reform Party; in Missouri, the People's Party; in Iowa and Minnesota they were called the Anti-Monopolist parties; and in California the movement was known alternately as the People's Independent or Anti-Monopoly Party. In Oregon, Nebraska and Georgia, the insurgents were simply known as "Independents."

The agrarian third-party movement, which had been embraced by California's Newton Booth, the U.S. Senate's leading insurgent, was not to be taken lightly. "It is idle to talk of the failure of a movement which has gained the political control of the states of Wisconsin and California; which is dictating terms to the old parties in Iowa and Kansas; which has carried a majority of the counties of Illinois" and was threatening to do the same in Michigan, Minnesota and elsewhere, cautioned Horace White's *Chicago Weekly Tribune* in January 1874. The significance of the farmer's movement, the paper continued, was that it offered to those "who have sought and failed to secure it in the old dividend-paying parties, an opportunity to accomplish something for the benefit of the country at large—not for the farmers merely, but for all who live by their industry, as distinguished from those who live by politics, speculations and class-legislation."[8]

---

8.   *Chicago Weekly Tribune*, January 28, 1874.

In Illinois, where railroad regulation was the dominant issue, the Independent Reform Party, under the leadership of Willard C. Flagg, president of the State Farmers' Association, took part in fusion campaigns with Democrats or Republicans and captured local offices in fifty-three of the state's sixty-six counties in the 1873 elections. In neighboring Wisconsin, the highly successful Independent Reform Party played a pivotal role in the election of Democrat William R. Taylor, a pro-Grange governor and the first Democrat elected to that post in eighteen years. In 1874, the Independent Reformers in that state also captured three congressional seats and held thirty-five seats in the state House and fifteen seats in the state Senate.[9]

The Grange, also known as the "Patrons of Husbandry," was not overtly political—and only marginally partisan. Founded in 1867 by Minnesotan Oliver H. Kelley, an Elk River homesteader and Mason claiming to be "as full of public spirit as a dog is full of fleas," the Grange quickly swept across rural America, in many ways laying the groundwork for the Greenback-Labor and Populist parties of the 1870s and 1890s. The order included women as equal members but was initially racially exclusive to placate its southern membership. Among other things, the order sought legislation to loosen credit for small farmers and legislation regulating railroad and warehouse rates. A colorful figure, Taylor vigorously tried to push through Granger-supported railroad legislation and stunned the citizens of his state when he celebrated a court decision favorable to the Grangers by blasting a salvo of artillery from the state capitol.[10]

In Iowa, the Anti-Monopoly Party supplanted the Democrats as the only opposition to the entrenched Republicans—a party that dominated politics in that state since before the Civil War. Uniting with the down-and-out Democrats in Des Moines in August 1873, the Anti-Monopolist Party was made up primarily of Grange farmers, including many who had previously considered themselves loyal Republicans. Virtually mirroring their counterparts in Illinois, the Iowans demanded the regulation of railroad rates and when the Republican-controlled legislature refused to enact such legislation, the Anti-Monopoly Party was born. That autumn, the Iowa Anti-Monopolists nominated Jacob G. Vale for governor, pitting the former independent against Republican incumbent Cyrus C. Carpenter, who himself was a prominent Granger. During the campaign, the

9.   Fred E. Haynes, *Third Party Movements Since the Civil War* (New York, 1916, reprint, 1966), p. 60. The three Reform Party congressmen were William P. Lynde, Samuel D. Burchard and George W. Cate.

10.   Solon J. Buck, *The Agrarian Crusade: A Chronicle of the Farmer in Politics* (New Haven, 1920), p. 38.

Anti-Monopoly Party appeared disorganized, financially strapped and lacking effective leadership, except perhaps in a few instances at the local level. Despite these drawbacks, the new party surprised virtually everyone when Vale garnered 44% of the vote—a significantly larger share of the vote than the Democratic candidate had managed two years earlier and a larger percentage of the vote than any Democratic gubernatorial candidate dating back to 1859.

Even more impressive, the Iowa Anti-Monopolists elected eight state senators and forty-nine representatives to the Republicans' fourteen and forty-eight, respectively. The almost even split in the lower house of the legislature resulted in a deadlock in the battle for Speaker of the House, with the Republicans finally winning control on the 142nd ballot under a compromise whereby the Anti-Monopolists were guaranteed a number of committee chairmanships and other legislative offices. The following year, the party claimed a seat in Congress when Lucien L. Ainsworth, a nominal Democrat, was elected on the Anti-Monopoly ticket, narrowly defeating his Republican opponent.

Agrarian third parties also had a modicum of success in other states. In Kansas, which was later a stronghold for the Union Labor and Populist parties, the Independent Reform Party captured nine state Senate seats and twelve House seats in 1874. In addition to the party's impressive showing in Wisconsin where the party won fifty seats in the state legislature, the Independents in Oregon also won numerous legislative and local elections while its gubernatorial candidate, Thomas F. Campbell, received more than a quarter of the vote against his Democratic and Republican opponents.

In California, Republican Gov. Newton Booth, looming as a hero to the state's hard-pressed farmers and others disenchanted with the two-party system, formed his own People's Independent Party, an anti-monopoly party that attracted broad support from Democrats and Republicans alike. Hoping to use his creation as a springboard to the U.S. Senate, Booth's third-party made impressive gains in 1873, winning hundreds of local and state legislative races, often at the expense of the Republicans. Pioneer John Bidwell, who traveled to California in the first wagon train from Missouri in 1841 and later served in Congress as a Unionist, garnered more than twenty-four percent of the vote against his major party rivals as the gubernatorial candidate of Booth's fledgling Independent Party in 1875, enabling Democrat William Irwin to waltz into office with barely half the vote. California Republicans were furious, bitterly denouncing Booth, who resigned as governor earlier that year to take his seat in the U.S. Senate as an Anti-Monopolist, as a treacherous man who had sabotaged his former party. The *California Alta* was equally angry, calling Booth's Independent Party "a mushroom which grew in a night on a dunghill of aspersion, slander, and prejudice."

William H. Felton, a physician-turned-farmer who later entered the Methodist ministry, spearheaded a similar movement in Georgia. A longtime advocate of public education and penal reform, Felton, a "picturesque figure of fiery eloquence" who had served as a surgeon in the Civil War, emerged as the leading independent Democrat in the state, denouncing the state's reactionary and corrupt Bourbon machine with his typical fiery eloquence. Influenced to a certain extent by the budding Granger movement, which first appeared in Georgia in 1872, Felton ran for Congress as an independent Democrat in 1874 from the "bloody seventh" congressional district, an isolated area of small farmers and few blacks in the state's rural mountainous western region. While Granger influence was far weaker in the south than in the Midwest, it found a willing adherent in Felton. "Men talk of the improvement of business, the revival of business, and all that," he declared, yet "the rich are growing richer and the poor are growing poorer from day to day."[11]

Taking on former governor and multimillionaire railroad executive Joseph E. Brown's powerful Democratic organization was a daunting task, one that lesser men certainly would have shied away from. With the help of his wife, Rebecca, the 51-year-old Methodist minister and farmer, denouncing his opponent as a tool of the "Atlanta ring" and blasting the entrenched Bourbon machine at every opportunity, exposed his Democratic opponent's role in a fraudulent bond scheme, forcing Brown's machine to replace its original candidate with a less seedy character. But neither the replacement nor Brown's considerable influence and money were able to prevent Felton from squeaking out a narrow 82-vote victory. He was re-elected as an independent Democrat in 1876 and 1878, defeating Brown's handpicked candidate in both contests. Emory Speer, another Independent Democrat, joined Felton in Congress after defeating the machine's candidate to win one-time Know-Nothing and Constitutional Unionist Benjamin H. Hill's seat in Georgia's ninth congressional district encompassing the mountains in the state's northeastern region. Felton was defeated in his bid for a third term in 1880.

Though he later served in the state legislature where he worked tirelessly to reform the state's brutal convict labor system while continuing to wage his one-man war against the conservative Bourbon machine, Felton tried unsuccessfully to regain his seat in Congress on four occasions, the last time as a Populist in

---

11.   C. Vann Woodward, *Tom Watson: Agrarian Rebel* (London, 1938), pp. 68-69.

1894. (In 1922, Rebecca Latimer Felton, Felton's 87-year-old widow, who had worked closely by her husband's side during his stormy public career, became the first woman ever to serve in the U.S. Senate, if only for two days, when she was appointed to the late Thomas E. Watson's seat until a successor could be elected and sworn in. A longtime writer for the *Atlanta Journal*, she was a longtime champion of good government, penal reform, temperance and woman's suffrage.) Nevertheless, as one writer pointed out, the issues brought to the forefront by the Feltons were essentially the same as those championed by the Greenbackers and by the Populist Party a few years later. The eleven planks on which they campaigned in 1882—a year when Felton lost narrowly in a bid to regain his old House seat—included a strong anti-monopolist stance; opposition to the state's antiquated convict lease system; and an end to sectional prejudices. The Georgia Independents also supported universal public education, bimetallism, and full payment of the public debt—both state and national—as rapidly as possible.[12]

Georgia's Independent Democratic movement continued to flourish until the early 1880s. In the state's 1880 gubernatorial campaign, the Independents put up novelist and former U.S. Sen. Thomas M. Norwood against incumbent Democrat Alfred H. Colquitt, whose administration was so rife with corruption that it had set off a wave of insurgency unequalled in the state's history. A young Thomas E. Watson, the great Populist leader who was not yet twenty-four years of age, was among those who stumped for the former senator, likening Norwood and the Independent Democratic cause to a "gathering cloud that would rain happiness in the presence of the sun of principle and the bow of heaven as a promise of good government."[13] Watson's two lifelong idols—the legendary Alexander H. Stephens, who was then confined to a wheelchair, and former Sen. Robert Toombs, who had been instrumental in overthrowing Carpetbag rule a few years earlier—also supported the Independent movement that year.[14] Despite waging a vigorous campaign, Norwood, who was something of an ineffectual public speaker, was nevertheless defeated by more than 54,000 votes, losing to Colquitt by a margin of 117,803 to 63,631.

Two years later, the Independent Democrats nearly succeeded in convincing the aging Alexander H. Stephens, the state's most revered politician, to be their candidate in the governor's race. The Georgia governorship, they believed, would certainly be a fitting tribute to his long and distinguished career. With a political

12. Anna Rochester, *The Populist Movement in the United States* (New York, 1943), pp. 36-37.
13. William W. Brewton, *The Life of Thomas E. Watson* (Atlanta, 1926), pp. 148-149.
14. Woodward, *Tom Watson: Agrarian Rebel*, p. 78.

career that spanned nearly five decades, Stephens served in the Georgia legislature for six years and in Congress for eight terms. He also served as vice president of the Confederacy from 1861-65, a position in which he often found himself at odds with President Jefferson Davis. As early as 1850, he warned Congress that "whenever this government is brought in hostile array against me and mine, I am for disunion openly, boldly, and fearless. I am for revolution." Having spent five months in a Boston prison after the Civil War, Stephens nevertheless urged restraint and discipline upon the South during the difficult days of Reconstruction. In 1866, the venerable Georgia lawmaker was elected to the U.S. Senate, but wasn't allowed to take his seat because he represented a "rebel" state. He later returned to the U.S. House of Representatives, serving from 1873 until his retirement in 1882.

The 70-year-old Stephens, a frail, gnarled figure then confined to a wheelchair, was committed to neither party but had been quietly encouraging the Independent Democrats. He still commanded a significant following and easily could have tipped the balance to the Independents, enabling the insurgents, once and for all, to oust the entrenched Bourbons. When word got out that Stephens might accept their nomination, the regular Democrats, hoping to avoid a calamity, asked the aging statesman to head their ticket in the gubernatorial race, begging him to accept for the sake of party unity. In a fatal blow to the Independents, Stephens, who had been privately communicating with Brown and Colquitt, accepted the nomination, thereby effectively killing the insurgent movement. Denouncing Stephens as a tool of the Bourbon machine, the deeply disappointed Independent Democrats rallied behind Lucius J. Gartrell, a 61-year-old former congressman and brigadier-general in the Confederate army. Gartrell, whose candidacy had also been endorsed by the state's "Lilly White" and "Black and Tan" Republican factions, was simply no match for the popular Stephens, losing by the overwhelming margin of 107,649 to 44,893.

In Minnesota, the ubiquitous Ignatius Donnelly launched the short-lived Anti-Monopoly Party and, reluctantly endorsed by the Democrats, won a seat in the state Senate. A number of other Anti-Monopolists also won seats in the legislature that year. Denounced by Republican newspapers as the "Potato Bug Party"—consisting, they said, of agricultural parasites—the Anti-Monopolists, under Donnelly's fiery leadership, immediately launched an assault on the state's corporate interests, beginning with a call for a major investigation of Minnesota's lumber industry and introducing legislation requiring insurance companies doing business in the state to invest locally. The Anti-Monopolists also tried unsuccessfully to break-up a high-interest loan monopoly operating in the state by increasing the amount of funds available to rural farmers, thereby preventing a drain of rural funds to financial centers in the East. Like most of the other measures sponsored by the Anti-Monopolists, this measure was ultimately blocked by the Republican-controlled legislature.

Frustrated by the apparent unwillingness of the Democrats and Republicans to adopt an inflationary monetary policy, dozens of farmers from the West and the South joined a few labor leaders and a handful of political reformers at a meeting in Indianapolis in November 1874 and proposed the creation of a new political organization committed to clean government and currency reform. The Indianapolis group also called a second meeting in Cleveland four months later. Representatives from sixteen states attended the Cleveland convention. It was here that the National Independent—or Greenback Party, as it was more commonly known—was formally launched. Before adjourning, party leaders called for a national convention to be held in Indianapolis the following spring.

The party's leadership at this time included Alexander Campbell, an Illinois congressman, and the highly literate Ignatius Donnelly, a former lieutenant governor of Minnesota. A transplanted Philadelphian, Donnelly was also a former three-term Republican member of the U.S. House and had been deeply involved in the Granger movement. Donnelly, who waged the first of several third-party campaigns a few years earlier, could be found in the forefront of most agrarian and third-party movements over the next quarter of a century. Other notable Greenback leaders included James Buchanan, a 300-pound Indianapolis attorney who was described by the *Chicago Tribune* as the new party's "political Moses," editor Marcus "Brick" Pomeroy of Chicago and ex-congressman Moses W. Field of Michigan, the man who issued the call to the party's historic 1876 national convention. Buchanan, the author of the so-called "Indiana Financial Plan," made a comfortable living as a lawyer before turning his attention to financial matters following the Panic of 1873. The 29-year-old Buchanan was also publisher and editor of *The Sun*, an Indianapolis weekly primarily devoted to agrarian interests. A shrewd and ambitious man, Buchanan purchased the newspaper, in part, to promote his U.S. Senate ambitions.

There were also a number of other men—now long forgotten—who were instrumental in launching the Greenback Party, including Ezra A. Olleman, a prosperous merchant who, as an associate editor of the *Indiana Farmer*, played a major role in founding the party in Indiana. While he eventually had a falling out with other Greenback leaders in the state, Olleman, a one-time cabinetmaker and former Republican state legislator, had a lasting influence on the Greenback movement as a result of his conspicuous editorial work for the *Indianapolis Sun*, which he co-owned with James Buchanan. German-born Robert Schilling of the Coopers' International Union was also among those who helped to launch the Greenback Party.

Mark Pomeroy was perhaps the most interesting of the many colorful characters that flocked to the Greenback banner. A newspaper publisher, propagandist, former Copperhead, ex-Democrat and sometime humorist, "Brick" Pomeroy was a moderately successful journalist from LaCrosse, Wisconsin, who later moved to New York City where he founded *Brick Pomeroy's Democrat*, a sensationalist newspaper with a relatively large circulation. After his New York paper failed, Pomeroy relocated to Chicago in 1875 and, shortly after breaking with the Democratic Party, began editing a Greenback journal the following year. Over the course of the next few years, he personally organized some 8,000 Greenback Clubs throughout the country.

On May 17, 1876, 239 delegates, representing nearly half the states in the Union, convened at the Academy of Music in Indianapolis. The convention, which was chaired by Thomas J. Durant, a veteran Fourierist and former wartime attorney general of Louisiana, heard opening remarks by temporary chairman Ignatius Donnelly who exhorted the delegates to oppose the "disastrous" policies of both major parties which had done little to pull the country out of its three-year depression. Emphasizing a centennial theme—1776 to 1876—Donnelly argued that the founding fathers had established a nation in which individuals should "outweigh the dollar." It was preposterous, he claimed, for Congress to haggle over Jefferson Davis's future and other colossal diversions while the real issues—namely, the economy and economic opportunity for all—were being obfuscated by the major parties.

No fewer than eight candidates were considered for the party's presidential nomination, including Justice David Davis of Illinois. Remembering all too well how the Supreme Court justice had left the Labor Reform Party in a lurch four years earlier, delegates from the East quickly dismissed Davis's name from consideration. Other names considered by the delegates included California's Newton Booth, James W. Singleton, a 64-year-old former state legislator from Quincy, Illinois, and "General" Robert F. Wingate, a little-known monetary reformer from Missouri.

William Allen of Ohio, a 73-year-old Democrat whose political career spanned the antebellum and post-Civil War periods, was also seriously considered to head the Greenback ticket in 1876. As a sixteen-year-old boy, Allen, who was raised a poor orphan, made a perilous journey on foot across the Alleghenies in the dead of winter to find his half-sister's home in Ohio. Elected governor of

Ohio in 1874 after spending a quarter century on the political sidelines, "Rise Up" Allen—a nickname given to him by the *Cincinnati Commercial's* Murat Halstead—initially served in Congress for one term back in the early 1830s when he defeated his Whig opponent, Gen. Duncan McArthur, by a single vote, becoming, at age twenty-nine, the youngest member of the House. Interestingly, he later married McArthur's daughter. Allen also served two terms in the U.S. Senate where, as a staunch expansionist, he chaired the Foreign Relations Committee and served as President Polk's leading spokesman during the war with Mexico. A vociferous advocate of "Fifty-four Forty or Fight" in the Oregon controversy with Great Britain, he resigned his chairmanship after the Senate ratified the Oregon treaty, dividing the region at the forty-ninth parallel. Allen was also considered a possible compromise candidate for president at the 1848 Democratic national convention and, as an unabashed Peace Democrat, was a bitter critic of the Lincoln administration during the Civil War.

Prior to making his spectacular reappearance in politics in 1874, the aging Ohioan had devoted the previous twenty-five years of his life to farming. During his remarkable political comeback that year, the septuagenarian astonished nearly everyone by waging a highly energetic campaign, vigorously denouncing the widespread corruption in the Grant administration. A fiscal conservative of sorts, Allen also blasted the national administration for raising taxes and for pushing legislation "for the benefit of corporations, cliques, and rings." One of the country's foremost advocates of an irredeemable paper currency, Allen, whose name was closely identified with the so-called "Ohio idea," was nearly everyone's second choice for president at the Greenback Party's national convention and, according to historian Fred E. Haynes in *Third Party Movements Since the Civil War*, was apparently waiting in the wings in the event that Peter Cooper declined the party's nomination. Allen's name, interestingly enough, was later placed in nomination at the Democratic national convention in St. Louis.[15]

Despite a relatively crowded field, the convention ultimately turned to wealthy New York industrialist Peter Cooper, the brilliant 85-year-old inventor and founder of the Cooper Union, as its presidential standard-bearer. An old Jacksonian in the Loco-Foco tradition, Cooper received 352 votes on the first ballot to 60 for congressman Alexander Campbell of Illinois, 58 for former Pennsylvania Gov. Andrew G. Curtin and 31 for Ohio's William Allen. Cooper's nomination was then made unanimous. Interestingly, Cooper's son-in-law was

---

15.   Haynes, *Third Party Movements Since the Civil War*, p. 113; *The Weekly Iowa State Register* (Des Moines), May 26, 1876.

Abram Hewitt of New York, the highly capable chairman of the Democratic National Committee. Hewitt was also Cooper's business partner. Even more intriguing was the fact that Edward Cooper, the industrialist's reform-minded son who later became mayor of New York City, served as Democrat Samuel J. Tilden's campaign treasurer during the 1876 presidential campaign. The younger Cooper, then a member of New York City's Irving Hall reform faction, had worked closely with Tilden and Hewitt in cleansing Tammany Hall of the notorious Tweed Ring. Despite his son and son-in-law's close ties to the Democratic standard-bearer, Cooper enthusiastically embraced the fledgling Greenback Party and promised to contribute generously to the party's autumn campaign.

His age notwithstanding, the tall, lantern-jawed, white-bearded philanthropist was a most unusual candidate. A man far ahead of his time, Cooper was an exceedingly rich Republican, but spoke like a tried and true radical financial reformer. Lending an air of dignity and respectability to the radical party, he was an ideal standard-bearer for the fledgling Greenback movement. "The dealers in money," he said, sounding nothing like a Republican, had always, "since the days of Moses, been the dangerous class." The country, he observed on another occasion, was quickly developing "an aristocracy of wealth, the worst form of aristocracy that can curse the prosperity of any country" and predicted that there would be "a whirlwind precipitated upon the moneyed men of this country."[16] Like other financial reformers of his time, Cooper also argued that the par value of greenbacks and gold could be achieved through the extension of full legal tender status for greenbacks. "This return to specie payments may be made without such injury, by honoring the currency in every way," he said, "by making it exclusively the money as well as the legal tender of the country; by receiving it for all forms of taxes, duties and debts to the government, as well as payment of all private debts..."[17] Though lacking a formal education himself, the generous entrepreneur established the Cooper Institute (later renamed Cooper Union) in New York City in 1859 to provide education for the city's growing working-class population. Thousands of laborers enjoyed the privileges of its free library and reading room. Having struggled as an apprentice to a coach builder, earning between twenty-five to seventy-five dollars per year, Cooper eventually saved enough

---

16.   Peter Lyon, "The Honest Man," *American Heritage*, Vol. X, Number 2 (February 1959), p. 5.

17.   *The Great Campaign*, Aug, 1, 1876, as quoted in Gretchen Ritter, *Goldbugs and Greenbacks: The Antimonopoly Tradition and the Politics of Finance in America, 1865-1896* (Cambridge, 1997), pp. 100-101.

money to strike out on his own and purchased a shearing cloth machine, making a small fortune in the process.

One of the most interesting and decent men to ever seek the presidency, Cooper, who was raised in the wilderness of the Hudson River Valley near Peekskill, was apprenticed to a carriage maker when he was seventeen, earning about twenty-five dollars a year. Though ashamed of his own lack of education, polish and urbanity, Cooper nevertheless strived to improve the quality of life for others. "I was always fussing and contriving," he said later, "and was never satisfied unless I was doing something difficult—something that had never been done before, if possible." Among other things, he tried to convert the power from the tides of the East River in New York into compressed air as a means of powering the city's ferries from New York to Brooklyn. He also invented the first lawn mower, a rotary steam engine, as well as an endless chain mechanism for hauling boats along the new Erie Canal. Yet none of these early inventions brought him any fame or fortune.[18]

But that all changed in 1821, just before the country's initial manufacturing boom, when Cooper purchased a glue factory and in virtually no time at all dominated the nation's glue industry. He was quickly dubbed the "Glue King" and before long the self-made industrialist was earning close to $100,000 a year. Cannily investing his new fortune in real estate, especially in Manhattan, Cooper's net worth exceeded $123,000 by 1833 and more than $1.1 million by 1856. During this period, the wily New York inventor built *Tom Thumb*, the famous single-cylinder, one-horsepower steam locomotive capable of pulling a train around short curves. Not long after that, he constructed an iron factory in New York City and later converted it into a highly profitable rolling mill. In 1854, he built the largest rolling mill in the United States, from which the first structural iron for fireproof building was produced, earning him the coveted Bessemer gold medal in 1870 for his role in developing the American iron trade. Ever a visionary, Cooper also contributed large sums of money to important public projects, such as the laying of the Atlantic cable in 1866.

More than anything else, wrote Peter Lyon, Cooper was "the conscience of his times," a troubled social thinker and beloved philanthropist, firmly believing that wealth brought with it a grave social responsibility. "The production of wealth," he insisted, "is not the work of any one man, and the acquisition of great fortunes is not possible without the cooperation of multitudes of men; and...therefore the individuals to whose lot these fortunes fall...should never lose sight of the fact

---

18.   Lyon, "The Honest Man," p. 7.

that as they hold them by the will of society expressed in statute law, so they should administer them as trustees for the benefit of society as inculcated by moral law."[19] The altruistic businessman firmly believed that no one had a right to accumulate or horde large personal fortunes—a seemingly perverse outlook in the Gilded Age, a period rife with greedy and arrogant robber barons such as Cornelius Vanderbilt, Jay Gould, Jim Fisk, and Daniel Drew, the unscrupulous Vanderbilt rival who bilked the Erie Railroad out of an estimated nine million dollars and then used that money to manipulate bank credit, stock prices, and the foreign exchange before being irrevocably ruined in the Panic of 1873.

In addition to his numerous inventions and commercial enterprises, Cooper was also a dedicated reformer, finding time to push for compulsory education as a leading member of the Public School Society and working to solve the problem of juvenile delinquency as a member of the New York Juvenile Asylum. He was also responsible for a free milk dispensary for the underprivileged and labored tirelessly to free New York voters from the grip of Tammany Hall, frequently serving as chairman of various civic-minded good government groups. But his most significant contribution was undoubtedly the establishment of the Cooper Union for the Advancement of Science and Art, an institution he founded at the age of sixty-eight. Though initially disparaged by George Templeton Strong and other prominent New Yorkers as a half-million dollar "folly" cynically established to avoid taxes, Cooper's institute of higher learning was an overnight success. With a night school offering a curriculum that included instruction in chemistry, mathematics, physics, music, and mechanical and architectural drawing, the Cooper Institute, as it was called in those days, enjoyed an enrollment exceeding three thousand people a week. But it was as a center of contemporary thought, a forum for new and exciting ideas, that the Cooper Union was best known. It was there, in the winter of 1860, that Abraham Lincoln delivered a speech that he himself later acknowledged had catapulted him to the presidency. The Union's great hall was filled to capacity time and again over the years to hear such luminaries as Susan B. Anthony, Mark Twain, Horace Greeley, Robert Ingersoll, Victoria Woodhull, Henry Ward Beecher, Thomas Huxley and others.

The Greenback Party's vice-presidential nomination was initially offered to Sen. Newton Booth of California, a soft-money advocate who trounced Missouri's Robert F. Wingate on the first ballot, garnering 412 votes to the Missourian's 45. But Booth, a popular figure who made a personal fortune selling provisions to miners during the California gold rush, declined the offer. The

19.   Ibid., pp. 5-6.

party then turned to the somewhat nationally obscure former Ohio congressman and Union army general Samuel F. Cary. The 62-year-old Cary, a popular Cincinnati reformer, graciously accepted the new party's vice-presidential nomination and promised to campaign vigorously for the Greenback ticket. Privately, several party leaders were hoping that the aging Cooper would step aside and allow Cary to serve as president in the unlikely event that the Greenback candidates finished ahead of Tilden and Hayes in the general election.

Cary, a graduate of Miami University in Oxford, Ohio, had given up a comfortable law practice in 1845 to devote all of his time and energy to philanthropic pursuits and the prohibition cause, serving for a period as head of the Sons of Temperance in North America. He also edited several prohibition newspapers during this period, including the *Ohio Temperance Organ*, and was a much sought after temperance speaker, addressing groups in towns and cities in twenty-six states, as well as large audiences in England, Ireland, Scotland and Wales. His speeches were often enlivened with healthy doses of sarcasm—which quickly became his trademark.

Turning to politics, Cary, who had earlier turned down a seat on the Ohio Supreme Court, actively campaigned for Whig William H. Harrison in 1840 and took part in subsequent Whig and Republican campaigns. He served as a recruiting officer in the Union army during the Civil War and was later commissioned as a general. With solid labor support, he was narrowly elected to Congress in a special election as an independent in his heavily Republican district in 1867, defeating his Republican opponent by 959 votes in a three-way race. In Congress, Cary served on the education and labor committees and delivered a particularly powerful speech on labor, winning him accolades from various labor leaders across the country. He also won the respect of many of his Democratic colleagues by opposing President Johnson's impeachment in 1868. Refusing to cling to any party label for very long, Cary eventually became a Democrat and was that party's candidate for lieutenant governor of Ohio in 1875. Like his presidential running mate, the former Ohio lawmaker was deeply committed to the greenback cause, believing that wartime inflation had only benefited the rich. "For every disaster of the war, every time our boys were driven back from the field, it only added to the gains of the Moneyed Power," he said.[20]

In addition to encouraging woman's suffrage, federal regulation of interstate commerce and a graduated income tax, the Greenback platform, viewing the

---

20. *The Great Campaign*, September 5, 1876, as quoted in Gretchen, *Goldbugs and Greenbacks*, p. 102.

Resumption Act of 1875 as a plot to further enrich eastern bankers, demanded the immediate repeal of that law and called for the issuance of greater amounts of paper money to provide relief to America's beleaguered farmers and struggling industries. The party's platform also opposed the sale of government bonds to purchase gold and silver as a substitute for issuing legal tender notes.

Given his advanced years, Cooper was unable to actively campaign, but a concerted effort was made on his behalf by hundreds of enthusiastic supporters. His campaign posters, bearing an impressive portrait of the bespectacled and bearded candidate, asserted: "National prosperity cannot be restored by enforcing idleness on a large portion of the people." Except for a large contribution from Cooper, the fledgling party was woefully short on funds throughout the campaign. It was also so poorly organized that it failed to name presidential electors in twenty of the nation's thirty-seven states. Moreover, the new party was given only scant attention in the mainstream media, which focused most of its attention on the razor-thin contest between Democrat Samuel J. Tilden of New York and Republican Rutherford B. Hayes of Ohio. So it wasn't surprising, therefore, that Cooper's candidacy was "greeted with a chorus of catcalls and horselaughs from every influential newspaper editor in the country, and the jeers persisted throughout the campaign."[21]

Despite its shoestring budget, the Greenback Party put up a brave fight during its maiden campaign—churning out countless pieces of literature from the party's headquarters in Union Square and distributing thousands of pamphlets through the numerous Greenback Clubs sprinkled across the country. Somewhat secretive in nature, the clubs had been organized in the summer of 1875 by Mark Pomeroy, a former Copperhead and radical editor of *Pomeroy's Democrat* and *The Great Campaign*, whose writings were often peppered with anti-Semitic slurs, slander, and threats of violence.[22] In addition to Pomeroy's publications, the Greenback ticket also received enthusiastic backing from J. A. Noonan's Chicago-based *Industrial Age*, Donnelly's *Anti-Monopolist* of St. Paul and James Buchanan and Ezra A. Olleman's *Indianapolis Sun*, the country's first full-fledged Greenback newspaper.[23]

21. Lyon., "The Honest Man," p. 106.
22. Gretchen, *Goldbugs and Greenbacks*, p. 134.
23. The *Industrial Age*, which folded shortly after the 1876 election, was founded in 1873 by S. M. Smith, secretary of the Illinois Farmers' Association, and J. A. Noonan, a Wisconsin anti-monopolist who had long been active in the fight for railroad regulation.

In addition to Cooper's candidacy, about a dozen or so Greenback candidates sought seats in Congress that year. Among them was Maine's irrepressible Solon Chase who campaigned on an "Inflationist" ticket, Minnesota's Ignatius Donnelly and independent Representative William B. Anderson of Illinois, the latter of whom garnered an impressive 26% of the vote on the Greenback ticket against two major party opponents in an unsuccessful bid for a second term. A lawyer and former state senator, Anderson had narrowly defeated a Democratic incumbent and a Republican rival in 1874 to narrowly win a U.S. House seat from the state's nineteenth congressional district. Congressman John R. Goodin of Kansas, a former judge and newspaper editor who sought re-election on an Independent Greenback ticket, also waged a spirited campaign that year, losing to his Republican challenger by roughly 4,500 votes. Like Chase, many of the Greenback candidates ran under various banners, including a few who filed as independents.

Hardly discouraged by its initial foray into national politics, the Prohibition Party also competed in the 1876 presidential campaign. Coming off a relatively strong showing in Connecticut where it polled five percent of the vote in that state's 1874 elections, the Prohibitionists had plenty of reason to be optimistic. In addition to its impressive showing in the Constitution State, the party nearly captured the Rhode Island governorship in 1875 when Rowland Hazard, the party's gubernatorial candidate, amassed an impressive 8,724 votes—a plurality—against stiff Democratic and Republican opposition. A mill owner, Hazard was deeply concerned with his employees' welfare and had introduced one of the first profit-sharing plans in the nation's history. Unfortunately, Hazard, who also ran as an independent, was denied the governorship when the Democrats and Republicans in the state legislature passed him over for one of their own, naming Republican Henry Lippitt as the state's twenty-ninth governor. Lippitt had finished 356 votes behind Hazard in the popular vote. Moreover, in 1874 the Temperance Reform Party was founded in California, a state that later proved to be fertile ground for the dry advocates.

The Prohibition Party's national convention met on May 17, 1876, in Cleveland and nominated 43-year-old Green Clay Smith, a former Union army officer, for president. During the Civil War, Smith defeated troops commanded by the legendary Confederate General Nathan Bedford Forrest at Rutherford Creek. Smith's father was a noted Indian fighter who served under Gen. William Henry Harrison in the battle of Tippecanoe and later served as Harrison's aide-de-camp during the battle of the Thames in 1813. The younger Smith served as a volunteer during the Mexican War and graduated from Transylvania University in

Lexington, Kentucky, in 1849, before earning his law degree from the same school in 1852. During the Civil War, Smith, who was wounded in Lebanon, Tennessee, in 1862, was promoted to the rank of brigadier-general. Smith served two terms in Congress and nearly became Abraham Lincoln's vice-presidential running mate on the Union Party ticket in 1864, losing to Tennessee's Andrew Johnson by a single vote in preliminary caucusing. In 1866, President Johnson appointed him as the second territorial governor of Montana and he served in that capacity until 1868, a period that saw the Indians under the great Sioux chief Sitting Bull and the legendary Lakota warrior Crazy Horse scattered and subdued under the terms of the treaty of Ft. Laramie. The following year, Smith entered the Baptist ministry in the nation's capital, where he remained until his death in 1895.

The Prohibitionists named Gideon T. Stewart, a longtime local officeholder in Huron, Ohio, and a man who devoted nearly sixty years of his life to the temperance cause, as the party vice-presidential candidate. At different times, Stewart, who was responsible for inserting a women's suffrage plank in the party's platform in 1872, served as editor of the *Toledo Blade* and the *Toledo Commercial* and, during the Civil War, owned the *Dubuque Times* in Iowa—the only Union daily newspaper in the northern half of the state. A prolific writer, Stewart, who later chaired the party's national committee, also served three terms as county auditor and was twice the Prohibition Party's candidate for governor of Ohio.

Changing its name to the Prohibition Reform Party, the teetotalers adopted a platform calling for the immediate enactment of prohibition. They also called for the abolition of polygamy and denounced lotteries and gambling. The far-seeing Prohibitionists also decried the inhumane treatment of the nation's prisoners and urged the direct election of the U.S. Senate.

Two other minor parties also competed in the 1876 presidential election. The more significant of the two was the American National Party, a distant offspring of the original Anti-Masonic Party.

American National Party

Founded in Syracuse, New York, earlier in the year by the National Christian Association, the American National Party also entered the 1876 presidential campaign. Meeting in Pittsburgh's Liberty Hall on June 8, 1875, this little-remembered party nominated Reverend James B. Walker of Illinois for president. Walker was chosen after such notables as Charles Francis Adams and abolitionist

Jonathan Blanchard, the president and founder of Wheaton College who had given the party's keynote address, declined to run. The relatively obscure Donald Kirkpatrick of Syracuse, New York, was chosen as Walker's vice-presidential co-star. Kirkpatrick, 46, was a past president of the National Christian Association and longtime member of the Anti-Secret Society Association.

Proclaiming that the United States was a "Christian nation and not a heathen nation, and that the God of the Christian Scriptures is the author of civil government," the American National Party adopted a platform containing eleven principles, including support for liquor prohibition, legislation to curb monopolies, the direct election of the president and vice president, the elimination of secret societies and monopolies, and the fair and just treatment of American Indians. It also favored a return to specie payment, the elimination of the Electoral College, and urged a greater emphasis on arbitration in settling international disputes. The predominately Protestant party also called for Bible study in the nation's public schools.[24]

The American National Party was clearly Blanchard's brainchild. A graduate of Middlebury College, the 65-year-old Blanchard, who had once debated Stephen A. Douglas on the question of slavery, was the longtime publisher of *The Christian Cynosure*, a publication devoted to the denunciation of secret societies. A combative personality with strong convictions, Blanchard's opposition to slavery was so strong that as a young man he quit Andover Academy because he felt the school's administration was too tolerant in its views toward slavery. As a young man, he also dabbled a bit in the anti-Masonic movement. In February 1837, he met Thaddeus Stevens, the famous fugitive slave defender and antislavery lawmaker from Pennsylvania, who was then a member of the Anti-Masonic Party. "Mr. Stevens," he said, "if you can turn your Anti-Masons into abolitionists, you will have a party whose politics will not bleach out. The slaveholders will not 'possum' like Freemasons, but will die game."[25] On several occasions, the Presbyterian minister was roughed up by irate mobs angered by his violent denunciations of slavery. Moreover, his lectures in support of temperance and opposition to secret societies often drew considerable antagonism. In the autumn of 1867, Blanchard and a group of others met in the town hall in Aurora, Illinois, to discuss the evils of secret societies. It was from that meeting that the National Christian Association was born.

---

24. Casson, Doug, "American National Party, 1874-1880," *The Encyclopedia of Third Parties in America*, Vol. I, pp. 145-147.
25. Griffin, *Their Brothers' Keepers*, p. 162.

From the outset, it was clear that Blanchard's long-forgotten post-bellum party was hoping to revive the issue of anti-Masonry. "Freemasonry must be destroyed if the country is to be saved," declared Blanchard in his keynote address at the 1875 Pittsburgh convention. "That fellowshipping Freemasonry is disintegrating the church," he said, adding that voting for Masons was equivalent to "voting for men who in practice deny the first principles of Republican government." The *Christian Cynosure*, the organization's monthly magazine—which, incidentally, was continually published from 1868 to 1983—dredged up countless old charges against the Masons, including the timeworn fable of the Illuminati conspiracy.[26]

The author of numerous theological works, James B. Walker was pastor of the local Congregational Church and a professor of moral philosophy at Wheaton College. Raised on a frontier farm near Pittsburgh, the 71-year-old Walker once walked nearly 300 miles from Pittsburgh to Philadelphia where he landed a job in a print shop. As a young man, he practiced law and later published the *Western Courier* in Ravenna, Ohio.

Inspired by Ohio clergyman and abolitionist Theodore D. Weld, Walker threw himself wholeheartedly into the antislavery cause and gained some notoriety in 1839 with the publication of his book, *The Philosophy of the Plan of Salvation*, which was used extensively as a textbook in the United States and was later translated into several languages. In 1840, Walker established *The Watchman of the Valley*, a religious newspaper in Cincinnati. Though his ardent antislavery views aroused considerable hostility, he struggled, often at great personal risk, to keep his publication alive for a few years before being named pastor of the Congregational Church in Mansfield, Ohio. His Mansfield congregation, comprised largely of abolitionists and temperance reformers, prospered under his leadership. In 1865, Walker was elected to the Michigan state Senate and later taught intellectual and moral philosophy at Wheaton College in Illinois. He also served as pastor of the town's Congregational Church. A widower, Walker and his first wife had adopted and raised thirteen orphans.

The second of these minor parties, if it can be described as such, was something called the Imperialist Party, which purportedly nominated little-known William Washington of Nashville, Tennessee, for the nation's highest office. Apparently envisioning himself as "Emperor of the World," it came as no surprise

---

26. Seymour Martin Lipset and Earl Raab, *The Politics of Unreason: Right-Wing Extremism in America, 1790-1970* (New York, 1970), p. 77.

when this fringe candidate failed to receive any officially recorded votes in the election.

Although both major parties agreed on most issues that year—hard money, an end to Reconstruction, civil service reform and honest government—the campaign was nevertheless a down and dirty affair. During the fall campaign, the Democrats blasted the Republicans for the lingering corruption of the Grant administration, while the Republicans waved the "bloody shirt," labeling the Democrats as the party of treason and rebellion. The aging Charles Francis Adams endorsed Tilden while Missouri's Carl Schurz actively campaigned for Hayes. As Election Day approached, Tilden was regarded as a slight favorite.

While the Prohibition Reform and American National parties were hardly factors in the disputed 1876 presidential contest, the same thing cannot be said of the fledgling Greenback Party. In a little-known yet odd twist of fate, the Greenback Party played a decisive role in the outcome as Republican Rutherford B. Hayes narrowly defeated Democrat Samuel Tilden, despite the fact that Tilden had garnered 254,235 more popular votes than his Republican rival. Official returns gave Tilden 4,288,546 popular votes to 4,034,311 for Hayes. Greenback Party candidate Peter Cooper, running strongest in the Midwest, polled 75,973 votes, or slightly below one percent of the national total. The aging iron manufacturer ran strongest in Kansas where he polled over six percent of the vote. He also received over three percent of the vote in Illinois and Iowa and nearly the same amount in Michigan.

Exactly how many votes were cast for the Greenback standard-bearer but were never counted, as labor leader Terence V. Powderly charged, remains a mystery. According to Powderly, hundreds and possibly thousands of Cooper's votes were never counted—a familiar occurrence in those days. In his autobiography, Powderly maintained that while the local Greenback Club in his district boasted more than three hundred members, only three votes were counted for Cooper on Election Day. As a member of the local election board explained to him, it made "no sense in throwing good votes away on weak, foolish, unknown, and unnecessary third parties" and, given the fact that it was a Democratic district, it was customary for local election officials to credit those "foolish" votes to the Democratic ticket. Powderly later discovered that the same practice occurred in other districts and wasn't necessarily confined to the same party. In other words, in predominately Republican districts, many of Cooper's votes were credited to Hayes.[27]

---

27.   Ricker, *The Greenback-Labor Movement in Pennsylvania*, pp. 31-32.

Despite editorial endorsements from more than forty newspapers, Prohibitionist Green Clay Smith—who, for lack of a single vote, nearly became Lincoln's successor on April 15, 1865—garnered a dismal 9,737 votes. The campaign of 1876 provided the first real evidence of massive vote fraud against the Prohibition Party in New York. Incredibly, in New York City, as in Buffalo and Albany, not a single vote was recorded for the party's presidential ticket, despite the fact that several party leaders lived in those cities and rallies had been held in each of them. Corrupt or incompetent state election officials credited Smith with only 2,369 votes in the Empire State—probably only a fraction of the actual number of votes cast for him. Running strongest in New York, the American National Party's James B. Walker, whose candidacy was virtually ignored by the mainstream press, polled 2,508 votes nationally.

In one of the most controversial presidential elections in American history—perhaps second only to the 2000 presidential election in which the U.S. Supreme Court essentially handpicked the country's 43d president—Hayes was later awarded 185 electoral votes to Tilden's 184. The people had elected Democrat Samuel J. Tilden on November 7, 1876, but it was Rutherford Hayes who took the oath of office four months later.

Although overlooked by most historians, the fledgling Greenback Party played a crucial, if not decisive, role in that stolen election, unwittingly helping to put Rutherford B. Hayes in the White House. On election night, Democrat Tilden, a boyhood friend of the late Martin Van Buren, went to bed thinking he had won the election, while Hayes retired for the night almost certain of his defeat. The following morning most newspapers reported that Tilden had won the election. But Republican national chairman Zachariah Chandler and a few of his friends at the *New York Times* weren't about to give up control of the White House without a fight. Determined to swing the electoral votes of Florida, Louisiana and South Carolina—three states still under carpetbag rule—into the Hayes column, thereby tipping the scales in the Republican's favor, John C. Reid of the *Times* and an exhausted Chandler sent telegrams to Republican leaders in those states asking them to hold their states for Hayes. If they could hang on, Hayes would be the next president. Confident that the carpetbaggers could hold the three states in question—especially since the Republicans controlled the election boards tasked with certifying the returns in those states—Chandler then announced publicly that Hayes had received 185 electoral votes to Tilden's 184.

Both parties immediately dispatched party leaders with mouths full of promises and pockets full of money into the three disputed states to get a closer look at the situation. On November 10, Ulysses S. Grant, the lame-duck incumbent, sent additional troops into the contested states "to preserve peace and good order" and to guarantee that the local election boards remained "unmolested" while tallying the official results. "Should there be any grounds of suspicion of fraudulent counting on either side," he ordered, "it should be reported and denounced at once. No man worthy of the office of President would be willing to hold the office if counted in, placed there by fraud; either party can afford to be disappointed in the result, but the country cannot afford to have the result tainted by the suspicion of illegal or false returns."[28]

As in the disputed and highly controversial presidential election of 2000 where hanging chads, butterfly ballots, inept voters, farcically incompetent election supervisors and the U.S. Supreme Court turned America's democracy on its face, the situation in Florida was considered the most contentious of the four disputed states in 1876. On November 27, the state's canvassing board, deliberately excluding the returns of two Democratic precincts in Baker County, gave Hayes a 43-vote statewide plurality. Within nine days, that margin mysteriously swelled to 924 votes. The Democrats argued that the canvassing board should simply have counted votes, instead of deciding which ballots to count, arguing that a full counting of all the ballots cast would have given Tilden a 1,700-vote majority. The Florida Supreme Court ordered the canvassing board to meet on December 27, but it refused to do so. The Florida attorney general, a Democrat, appeared by himself and certified Tilden's electors. The board then convened shortly thereafter and certified the Republican electors. On January 1, 1877, the Florida Supreme Court then rejected the canvassing board's certification and the Democratic governor and the Democratic-controlled legislature then certified Tilden's victory. When the state Supreme Court decided to delay ruling on a challenge to the Republican certification, two sets of election returns were sent to the Democratic-controlled U.S. House of Representatives, which refused to participate in a joint session with the Republican Senate. It was then that Congress decided to appoint a bipartisan Electoral Commission to resolve the disputed electoral votes.

Another disputed state was Oregon in the Far West. On election night, Hayes had clearly carried the state's popular vote—garnering 1,050 more popular votes than Tilden—but one of his three electors had been declared ineligible because he was a U.S. postmaster. (The constitution prohibits federal officeholders from serving as electors.) Hoping to offset some of the "palpable frauds" that had taken place in Florida, Louisiana and South Carolina, Democratic national chairman

---

28. Roy Morris, Jr., *Fraud of the Century: Rutherford B. Hayes, Samuel Tilden, and the Stolen Election of 1876* (New York, 2003), p. 174.

Abram Hewitt, Peter Cooper's son-in-law, convinced Oregon's Democratic governor to replace the disqualified Republican elector with a Democrat. The governor then certified the highest Tilden elector as the Republican's replacement.

Meanwhile, in the three southern states, it soon became apparent that bribery, forgery, intimidation and good old-fashioned ballot box stuffing had occurred on a massive scale—and neither party was without blame. Democrats had intimidated African-American voters to keep them away from the polls while Republicans, backed by federal troops, encouraged blacks to vote—early and often. In a free and fair election, Tilden probably would have carried Florida and Louisiana and Hayes probably won a majority in South Carolina. After a recount, Louisiana's vote was still very much in question and South Carolina sent two sets of returns to Washington, one for Hayes and one for Tilden. From Florida came three tallies, two favoring Tilden and one favoring Hayes.

Consequently, when Congress met in December 1876 it had a bona-fide constitutional crisis on its hands. With the Senate controlled by the Republican and the Democrats enjoying a majority in the House—and neither body willing to allow the other to decide the outcome—Congress resolved the impasse by agreeing, after weeks of rancorous debate, to establish an Electoral Commission to determine which candidate had actually won the disputed votes in Florida, Louisiana, South Carolina and Oregon. The Democrats agreed to this "deal," but only after being assured that Hayes, if elected, would withdraw federal troops from the South, thereby leaving the state governments in the hands of southern whites. The Senate approved the bill establishing the Electoral Commission by a vote of 47-17 and the House gave its consent by a margin of 191-86.

The bipartisan commission was comprised of five senators, five House members and five Supreme Court justices. Seven of its members were Republicans and seven were Democrats. Justice David Davis, the corpulent Illinoisan who was highly regarded by both parties and considered the most politically independent of all of the judges on the nation's highest court, was expected to be the fifteenth member. At the last minute, however, Davis was elected to the U.S. Senate by a coalition of Greenback and Democratic lawmakers in the Illinois legislature—a move that probably cost Tilden and the Democrats the presidency. Although the Greenback Party's presidential ticket garnered only 17,207 votes in Illinois—or roughly a quarter of the votes cast for the state's Independent Reform Party two years earlier—the party held eight seats in the state legislature. Holding the balance of power in that body, the Greenback lawmakers were instrumental in electing Davis to the U.S. Senate, unwittingly removing him from the electoral commission that ultimately decided the 1876 presidential election.

Many Greenbackers, of course, had long admired Davis and several of them, including Minnesota's Ignatius Donnelly, actually hoped that he would be the one to carry the party's banner in the presidential campaign that year. Coincidentally, Davis was elected to the U.S. Senate, narrowly defeating longtime Republican Sen. John A. Logan, on the very afternoon that Congress approved the Electoral Commission. Most historians agree that as a member of the commission, Davis almost certainly would have supported Samuel Tilden in that hotly disputed and controversial election. Ironically, Tilden's own nephew, Colonel William T. Pelton, was one of those who convinced Democrats in the Illinois legislature to join with the Greenbackers in supporting Davis's candidacy, believing that in doing so it would embolden the Supreme Court justice to support Tilden in the disputed presidential contest. In charge of printing and distributing millions of pieces of campaign literature from the party's Literary Bureau in New York City during the campaign, Pelton, of course, had no way of knowing that Davis, who had every intention of remaining on the Court until March 5—the day of the president's inauguration—would refuse his place on the commission as a result of winning the Senate seat.

Meanwhile, Justice Joseph P. Bradley, a six-year veteran of the Supreme Court, replaced Davis on the commission. Bradley, who had been appointed by Ulysses S. Grant in 1870, was considered the most independent of the remaining justices, all of whom were Republicans. As such, the Rutgers-educated jurist had the support of the Democratic congressional leadership and, for the most part, was expected to rule in an impartial and nonpartisan manner. However, he hardly lived up to Democratic expectations, siding with the Republicans on each and every crucial issue that came before the commission. By a vote of eight to seven, the highly partisan Electoral Commission awarded the twenty disputed electoral votes from Florida, Louisiana and South Carolina to Hayes. By the same margin, they also gave him Oregon's hotly contested third elector, giving the Republican presidential standard-bearer a total of 185 electoral votes to Tilden's 184. The House formally approved Hayes as the nation's nineteenth president just fifty-six hours before his inauguration was scheduled to take place. As was the case 124 years later when Democrat Al Gore clearly defeated George W. Bush, there's little doubt that the presidency had been stolen. A majority of the American people had clearly voted for Democrat Tilden, but it was Hayes who took the oath of office on March 5, 1877.

Unlike Bush's controversial election, ushering in one of the most nefarious and deceitful administrations in U.S. history, Rutherford B. Hayes, one of the most high-minded and principled men to ever occupy the White House, proved to be a rather innocuous president. He kept his word to the Liberal Republicans and the American people and didn't seek a second term in 1880. While he wasn't particularly daring or dynamic, Hayes was a competent chief executive and clearly had the country's best interests at heart. During his term in office, the result of what one historian described as "the most flagrant misuse of power in the nation's history," Hayes nevertheless tried his level best and, unlike his predecessor Ulysses S. Grant, his administration was free of even the remotest hint of scandal.

Like Republican George W. Bush a century and a quarter later, Hayes, who was dubbed "His Fraudulency," was never entirely able to overcome the stigma surrounding the controversial election that landed him in the White House. In much the same way that John Quincy Adams had been saddled by charges of a "corrupt bargain" with Henry Clay in 1824, Hayes found it difficult, if not impossible, to set the nation's agenda during his four years in office. The Democrats, enjoying a thirteen-seat majority in the House of Representatives during his first two years in office and a somewhat slighter majority during the final two years of his administration, effectively blocked most of the legislation proposed by the well-meaning Harvard-educated president.

Yet, as historian Roy Morris, Jr., keenly observed, leaders in both major parties were responsible for the election's outcome. "By formally acquiescing to what modern historian Paul Johnson has aptly termed 'a legalized fraud,'" wrote Morris, "leaders of both parties in Congress heedlessly fostered an atmosphere of mutual suspicion, antagonism, and hatred that lingered over the political landscape for the better part of a century."[29]

Within two months of his inauguration, Hayes made good on the apparent "bargain" or compromise that landed him in the Executive Mansion by withdrawing all but a handful of federal troops from Louisiana and South Carolina, effectively ending Reconstruction and consequently disenfranchising African-American voters in the South for years to come. In addition to restoring white supremacy in that region, the two-party compromise, as historian Howard Zinn recently pointed out, essentially "doomed blacks in the South to semi-slavery," redeployed federal troops from the former Confederacy to drive Indians from their ancestral lands in the West, while subjugating millions of working-class people all over the country to "ruthless corporate power." Behind the Hayes-Tilden debacle was a hard, cold fact. "The Republican Party and the Northern industrial-financial interests that dominated it," wrote Zinn, "were no longer inter-

---

29. Morris, *Fraud of the Century*, p. 3.

ested in the fate of the former slaves."[30] The beleaguered president was also rocked by the railroad workers' strike of 1877 when he was forced to send in federal troops to quell the strike efforts in West Virginia, Maryland, Pennsylvania, Illinois, Missouri and California, where he authorized three naval warships to stand by just off the coast of San Francisco.

On the positive side, the Ohio born and bred president tried to instill integrity and honor in government, but was thwarted time and again by Congress. His attempts to initiate civil service reform failed miserably as congressional Democrats and Republicans alike repeatedly turned a deaf ear to his pleas. His widely publicized firing of Chester Arthur, the powerful Collector of the Port of New York, drew a firestorm of protest from Republican bosses, especially among the Stalwarts. Yet, Hayes tried to surround himself with the best and the brightest of his generation and it is interesting to note that four of the most prominent men in his cabinet—Secretary of State William M. Evarts, Secretary of Interior Carl Schurz, Attorney General Charles Devens and Postmaster General David M. Key—were ex-Liberal Republican reformers who had supported Horace Greeley against Grant in 1872.

Haunted throughout his four-year tenure by the questionable and controversial circumstances that put him in the White House, Hayes was never given the traditional "honeymoon" grace period usually afforded American presidents. From the outset, his critics—Democrats and Republicans alike—displayed an almost crushing invective against him. Despite his sterling reputation, innuendos and investigations dominated his four years in office. The Democrats, of course, believed that Tilden was the rightful heir to the Executive Mansion and the mean-spirited Republican Stalwarts, dubbing Hayes a "Half-Breed," had serious misgivings about the titular head of their party, particularly on patronage matters.

Likewise, pundits and observers never tired of pummeling the Republican president, the worst example of which was Ohio journalist and scholar Donn Piatt's inflammatory editorial published shortly before Hayes was sworn in as the nation's nineteenth president. As the election slowly escaped Tilden's grasp, Piatt, who was then editor of the weekly *Washington Capitol*, completely lost his temper, thrusting his pen at the thieves who stole the election, excoriating the "bayonet-backed" carpetbaggers and the "coarse, brutal and ignorant" president surrounded by his "sycophantic pimps." Once again, he believed, the American

---

30.   Howard Zinn, "Disputed Elections, Concealed Facts," *The Progressive*, Vol. 65, Issue 2 (February 2001).

people had taken back their government only to be swindled by the corrupt and unsavory powers-that-be. Incredibly, Piatt, a staunch Democrat and Tilden supporter, wrote that if the president-elect "can ride in safety from the executive mansion to the Capitol to be inaugurated, we are fitted for the slavery that will follow [his] inauguration." Those were dangerous words in a jittery nation already filled with cries of "Tilden or Blood!" While protesting that he never advocated killing anyone, Piatt's explanation was hardly reassuring, insisting a short while later that the people must "take up arms...and use them in the open field." A former Hamilton County common pleas court judge who once tried to enlist slaves into the Maryland militia during the Civil War, Piatt was subsequently indicted on charges of "inciting insurrection" but the charges were later dropped. (Curiously, the longtime journalist later grew to admire Hayes and approved of most of his policies.)[31]

As late as 1879—three years into his term—a Democratic House investigating committee headed by congressman Clarkson Potter, a New York lawyer who later served as president of the American Bar Association, issued a report stating that Tilden had been unfairly cheated out of the presidency.

Ironically, in his last State of the Union address, the 58-year-old lame duck president called attention to the plight of the former slaves in the South—the very people who had been disfranchised by the alleged "bargain" that landed him in the White House—and urged that their voting rights be restored. Hayes lived in quiet retirement after leaving the White House, spending most of his time on charitable activities

Meanwhile, leaders of the Greenback Party were hardly discouraged by Peter Cooper's relatively poor showing in the campaign of 1876. Even if they were, their spirits almost certainly soared when the party, under the leadership of D. B. Sturgeon, a Toledo physician, captured traditionally Republican Lucas County, Ohio, in the 1877 off-year elections. Sturgeon was one of two Greenback candidates elected to the lower house of the Ohio legislature. The results had stunned nearly everyone—including the party's national leaders.[32] In all, Greenback candidates garnered more than 187,000 votes in 1877, including several who did much better than expected, especially in Wisconsin where industrialist Edward P. Allis garnered 26,116 votes out of approximately 175,000 votes cast in that state's gubernatorial race. The same was true in Pennsylvania, where the United Green-

---

31. Mark Wahlgren Summers, *The Press Gang: Newspapers and Politics, 1865-1878* (Chapel Hill, 1994), pp. 298-299, 306.
32. Unger, *The Greenback Era*, p. 376.

back-Labor Party, under the leadership of party chairman Franklin Dewees, a Pottsville lawyer and former Democrat, and vigorously supported by John M. Davis' *National Labor Tribune*, received considerable attention when James L. Wright, the party's candidate for state treasurer, polled a whopping 52,854 votes—or almost ten percent of the statewide total. Supported by Terence V. Powderly's increasingly potent Knights of Labor, the little-known Wright garnered 20,000 of his votes in three of Pennsylvania's sixty-seven counties—Lycoming, Luzerne and Schuylkill. Climaxing the party's remarkable showing in the Keystone State that year, the United Greenback-Labor ticket swept blue-collar Luzerne County, winning virtually all of the contested local races in that county with a larger vote than the combined totals of the Democratic and Republican parties.[33]

Buoyed by their success, Toledo's Sturgeon and other Ohio Greenbackers immediately planned for a national convention to discuss the country's dismal state of affairs. Among those signing the call for a national convention to be held in Toledo in February 1878 were such leading insurgents as Alexander Campbell, Peter Cooper, Thomas J. Durant, Moses Field, Wendell Phillips, Ignatius Donnelly, Solon Chase and James B. Weaver. Western Pennsylvania's Thomas Armstrong, editor of the *National Labor Tribune*—the voice of the Amalgamated Iron and Steel workers—and a prominent member of the Knights of Labor, was also among those who sponsored the meeting.

Assembling at Toledo's Wheeler Opera House on a cold and blustery day in late February, the conference, which was chaired by Pennsylvania's Dewees, closely resembled the party's 1876 national convention in Indianapolis, leaving one with a strong sense of *déjà vu*. Some 1,100 delegates from twenty-eight states attended the Toledo convention. Most of the old Greenbackers were there, including Richard Trevellick of Michigan, Robert Schilling, Marcus "Brick" Pomeroy, Samuel F. Cary, Cooper's vice-presidential running mate in 1876, and the mysterious Blanton Duncan, the Kentucky businessman who had tried to forge an alliance between the Labor Reformers and the "Straight-Out" Democratic movement in the waning days of the Grant-Greeley race in 1872. Knights of Labor founder Uriah S. Stephens, the 56-year-old tailor and former abolitionist who had actively campaigned for Fremont in 1856 and Lincoln in 1860, was also in attendance and, perhaps more than anyone else, was responsible for the inclusion of the word "labor" in the party's name. For the most part, the only

---

33. Ricker, *The Greenback-Labor Movement in Pennsylvania*, p. 39. Interestingly, more than a quarter of the party's 187,095 votes in 1877 were cast in Pennsylvania.

new faces in Toledo were those from organized labor who had only recently been politicized in the wake of the labor upheaval of the previous summer. Like Stephens, trade unionists Trevellick, Schilling and John Siney, the dynamic leader of the Pennsylvania anthracite miners, played an important role in the Toledo convention, critically bridging the gap between the newer labor delegates and the older monetary reformers.[34]

While organized labor played a significant role in the convention, it was clear that the original Greenback element still had the upper hand in determining the party's platform. As the prolific historian Philip S. Foner pointed out, it was Edward P. Allis of Wisconsin and Eben Moody Boynton of Massachusetts, both wealthy manufacturers, who, along with Walter P. Groom of the New York Board of Trade, really controlled the proceedings.[35] Differing little from the party's platform of 1876, the Toledo convention, among other things, called on Congress to supply enough money for the full employment of labor, the taxation of federal bonds, government-issued paper money without bank intermediaries, the adoption of a graduated federal income tax, homestead legislation, government subsidies for agriculture, and the exclusion of Chinese labor. The party's main focus remained on what the delegates perceived as a financial system that took from the many to enrich the few. Overcoming the vigorous objection of Thomas Buchanan, editor of the *Indianapolis Sun* and brother of Indiana Greenback leader James Buchanan, the party also jettisoned Alexander Campbell's proposal for an "inter-convertible bond." Once the centerpiece of the greenback philosophy, the Kellogg-Campbell bond formula had long since given way to more urgent demands for the "immediate and absolute" repeal of the Resumption Act. The delegates also formally changed the party's name to the "National Party," but it was more commonly known from then on as the Greenback-Labor Party.[36]

That spring, the party scored stunning victories in Maine, New York, and Michigan, winning some 200 of 700 races for town assessor in the latter state alone.[37] Before the year was out, the Greenback-Labor Party polled a staggering 1,060,000 votes nationally, winning hundreds of state legislative seats across the country and capturing thirteen seats in Congress, a majority of them on fusion tickets.[38] Though falling short of its goal of holding the balance of power in Con-

---

34. Unger, *The Greenback Era*, pp. 376-377.
35. Foner, *History of the Labor Movement in the United States*, Vol. I, p. 483.
36. Unger, *The Greenback Era*, p. 376-377; Peter H. Argersinger, "The Greenback Party, 1873-1886," *The Encyclopedia of Third Parties in America*, Vol. II, p. 273.
37. Ibid., p. 379.

gress, its members quickly formed a "Greenback bloc" in the House that included future Vice President Adlai E. Stevenson, a "soft money" leader from Illinois and the grandfather of the erudite and witty Democratic presidential standard-bearer in 1952 and 1956. "Uncle Adlai," as he was affectionately known, had served a previous term in the House in the mid-seventies as a Democrat. The party also made serious inroads in New England, where labor leader Thompson H. Murch of Maine, secretary of the granite cutters' union, was sent to Congress by defeating Republican incumbent Eugene Hale and Democrat Joseph H. Martin. George W. Ladd, another Greenbacker, was also elected to Congress from that state, upsetting Republican House member Llewellyn Powers, a former county prosecutor, by a margin of 12,921 to 10,095.

Other Greenback members of Congress included Alabama's William M. Lowe, a former lieutenant-colonel in the Confederate army; Gilbert De La Matyr, a Methodist Episcopal minister from Indiana whose candidacy on the Greenback ticket led to his forced retirement from the pulpit; Iowa's James B. Weaver and Edward H. Gillette, editor of the *Iowa Tribune*; Nicholas Ford, a state legislator from Missouri; Albert P. Forsythe, leader of the Illinois Grange; Daniel L. Russell, a political maverick who later served as governor of North Carolina; lawyer and pro-labor writer Hendrick B. Wright and Dickinson-educated lawyer Seth H. Yocum of Pennsylvania; George Washington Jones, a former lieutenant-governor of Texas; and Bradley Barlow, a banker and railroad executive from Vermont. A few of these candidates, including Murch and Ladd of Maine, Vermont's Barlow and Forsythe of Illinois, were elected without the aid of a fusion campaign with one of the major parties.

The Greenback-Labor Party also nearly captured two other U.S. House seats that year when inventor Eben Moody Boynton came within 113 votes of unseating Republican George B. Loring, a surgeon-turned-politician, in a tight three-way race in Massachusetts, and lawyer Charles N. Brumm fell 192 votes short of defeating his Democratic rival in a three-cornered contest in eastern Pennsylva-

---

38.   Despite its tremendous showing that year, the party also suffered a number of disappointments, not the least of which was Joseph A. Labadie's relatively poor showing in Detroit's mayoralty race. Known as the "Gentle Anarchist," Labadie, a poet and labor agitator who spent a lifetime involved in an array of labor and social reform movements—the Knights of Labor, the Socialist Labor Party, the Greenback-Labor Party, the eight-hour and single-tax movements, as well as playing an active role in the defense of the Haymarket martyrs, to name but a few—polled only several hundred votes in his mayoralty campaign. See Carlotta R. Anderson, *All-American Anarchist: Joseph A. Labadie and the Labor Movement* (Detroit, 1998).

nia's thirteenth congressional district, encompassing the state's anthracite region.[39] The party also threw a scare into Republican lawmaker Russell Errett in western Pennsylvania when Pittsburgh's David Kirk, a Scottish-born oilman waging the first of two unsuccessful bids for Congress, finished a strong second in a hotly-contested four-way race. Kirk, who served as temporary chairman of the party's state convention in Philadelphia earlier that year, had lost his personal fortune in the early 1870's when discriminatory freight rates virtually wiped out his refinery and oil yard in Franklin, Pennsylvania. He became an avid Greenbacker shortly thereafter. In a second bid for a seat in the U.S. House in 1880, the hard-luck Kirk again came up short, losing to a Republican in a different district by 546 votes out of more than 35,000 votes cast.[40]

In all, Greenback-Labor congressional candidates finished ahead of one of their major party rivals in more than three-dozen House races around the country in 1878, including spirited but unsuccessful campaigns by party founder Alexander Campbell in Illinois and by the venerable Solon Chase in Maine. An avowed inflationist and chairman of the state party, Chase had campaigned vigorously that year for one of Maine's five House seats, polling a remarkable 8,472 votes while losing to an entrenched four-term Republican. Chase's Democratic opponent was left in the dust. In Michigan, Charles C. Comstock, a sixty-year-old furniture manufacturer and former mayor of Flint, waged a surprisingly strong race in that state's fifth congressional district, losing to a two-term Republican lawmaker by a margin of 15,893 to 15,273. The Democratic candidate polled a paltry 3,468 votes. Comstock was finally elected to Congress on a Democratic-Greenback Labor fusion ticket in 1884.

Solomon G. Kitchen, an influential and wealthy former state senator and ex-Confederate soldier, also waged a hard-fought campaign for the U.S. House on the Greenback ticket in Missouri's third congressional district, garnering nearly 35% of the vote in a three-way race won by Democrat Lowndes H. Davis. A Confederate hero of sorts, Kitchen had amassed more than $100,000 in real estate—a considerable fortune in those days. Wounded at Byram's Ford, his Missouri regiment provided the largest number of soldiers in Gen. John S. Mar-

---

39.   Brumm was eventually elected to Congress on the Greenback-Labor ticket in 1880 and was re-elected in 1882. He served five more terms as a Republican over a period of a quarter of a century, before resigning in 1909 to take a seat on the Common Pleas Court in Schuylkill County—a judgeship he held until his death in 1917. Interestingly, the former Greenback lawmaker emerged as the Bull Moose Party's candidate for governor of Pennsylvania in 1914 when he was in his late seventies.

40.   Ricker, *The Greenback-Labor Movement in Pennsylvania*, p. 44.

maduke's Brigade during Sterling Price's bloody efforts to redeem Missouri from Union forces in 1864.

Remarkably, Greenback candidates drew approximately twelve percent of the vote in statewide elections that year. In Pennsylvania, which provided the largest "straight" Greenback vote in the country that year, gubernatorial candidate Samuel R. Mason, a lawyer and outspoken currency reformer, polled an impressive 81,758 votes, or nearly 12%, in a race decided by fewer than 23,000 votes and longtime Judge Daniel Agnew of Beaver County garnered 99,316 votes in a three-cornered race for his seat on the Pennsylvania Supreme Court. A member of the state's highest court since 1863, Agnew, who failed to win re-nomination by the Republicans earlier that spring, issued a sharply-worded attack on the powerful Quay-Cameron Republican machine late in the campaign.

However, the Greenback-Labor campaign in Pennsylvania wasn't without its difficulties. The marriage of convenience between the currency reformers who originally made up the old Greenback Party and the labor advocates who had recently joined the party in Toledo wasn't quite as idyllic as national party leaders had hoped. Beginning with the rejection of Scranton's Terence V. Powderly as permanent chairman, the party's state convention in Philadelphia's Concert Hall earlier that spring was a contentious and raucous affair that nearly split the party asunder. Believing that the election of a Greenback-Labor governor was within the realm of possibility, a heated four-way battle for the party's gubernatorial nomination ensued, with Mason, lumberman William H. Armstrong, Victor E. Piollet, leader of the Pennsylvania Grange, and Hendrick B. Wright, a longtime spokesman for labor in Congress, each throwing his hat in the ring. Armstrong and Mason were former Republicans while Piollet and Wright were ex-Democrats.

After considerable bloodletting in which the labor group, headed by Uriah S. Stephens, Powderly and *National Labor Tribune* editor Thomas Armstrong of Pittsburgh, was pitted against the currency reformers led by William Armstrong and others, Mason—an attorney for the Pennsylvania Railroad, as it later turned out—was nominated on the second ballot, garnering 115 votes to Wright's 57 and 24 for Thomas Armstrong. Two diehard delegates stuck with the relatively obscure Piollet, who was hoping to emerge as a compromise candidate. Christopher Shearer, a former building contractor, was nominated for lieutenant governor, but later declined. The party also nominated James L. Wright, a Philadelphia tailor and longtime activist in the anti-monopoly movement, for Secretary of Internal Affairs. Much to the chagrin of Stephens, Armstrong and other labor leaders, the party's platform included few labor demands, save for a plank calling for a shorter workday and higher wages.[41]

Were it not for the heroic intervention of John Siney of the Miners' union, the Greenback-Labor convention would have split in two. "There are but two parties in the field," he reminded the delegates, "the party of the skinners and the skinned, the party of the robbers and the robbed. Come then," he pleaded, "let us work together as laborers, as greenbackers, as all opposed to the rule of politicians of either the Republican or the Democratic Party."[42]

Though falling short of his goal of obtaining at least 150,000 votes, Mason, who said the party's objective was to carry the state's legislative ticket and "put an anti-Cameron man in the U.S. Senate," carried Lawrence County in western Pennsylvania and ran a close second to his Democratic rival in the party's stronghold in the anthracite region of Schuylkill County. Moreover, Greenback-Labor candidates in the Keystone State won dozens of county races that year and eighteen Greenback or Greenback fusion candidates were elected to the state legislature, including one state senator—John Parker of Schuylkill County, a former blacksmith and editor of the *Mahoney Record*.[43] In municipal elections held earlier that year, Greenback or Greenback-Labor candidates won mayoralty races in no fewer than three Pennsylvania cities—Meadville, Titusville and Scranton. One of those elected was Terence V. Powderly, the neurasthenic leader of the Knights of Labor who defeated a joint Democratic and Republican citizens' ticket to become mayor of Scranton.[44] His election stunned the *Scranton Republican*, a paper that had strongly urged voters to defeat Powderly's "Molly Maguire ticket" and dreaded the city's future "with a succession of Powderlys" in the mayor's office and "a non-taxpaying irresponsible rabble in power."[45] Ironically, Powderly—who later served as an honorary vice president of the American Bimetallic League—eventually drifted toward conservatism, switching his political affiliation to Republican and stumping vigorously for his longtime friend William McKinley in his heated 1896 presidential campaign against Democratic-

41. Ricker, *The Greenback Labor Movement in the United States*, pp. 43-48.
42. Foner, *History of the Labor Movement in the United States*, Vol. I, pp. 484-485.
43. Schuylkill County was long a Greenback-Labor stronghold. It gave 1,426 votes, or nearly six percent, to Ben Butler during the 1884 presidential campaign and as late as 1886, when the national party was on its deathbed—and long after county Republicans stopped fusing with Greenbackers in state and local races—Schuylkill voters sent John Tahaney to the state legislature on the Greenback-Labor ticket.
44. Ricker, *The Greenback Labor Movement in Pennsylvania*, pp. 43, 51-69.
45. Foner, *History of the Labor Movement in the United States*, Vol. I, p. 484.

Populist William Jennings Bryan. Conducting a speaking tour of the nation's industrial centers during that tumultuous campaign, the one-time radical labor leader vigorously defended the GOP's protective tariffs and "sound money" policy—resulting in an appointment as McKinley's immigration commissioner the following year.

The results in New York, where the party was called the United Workingmen and Greenback Party, were even more spectacular. That spring, the new party outpolled the Democrats in Rochester and Syracuse and elected mayors in Auburn, Elmira, Oswego and Utica. It also elected supervisors in no fewer than seventeen counties, mostly in rural upstate New York. But as in Pennsylvania, the Greenback and labor elements also experienced turmoil at their state convention in Syracuse that spring, essentially dividing the party between urban workers and the old Greenback faction centered in the state's rural areas. As in neighboring Pennsylvania, the party adopted few labor demands in its platform.

In heavily Republican Massachusetts, Benjamin F. Butler, the controversial former Union army general, running on the Greenback and Democratic tickets, came within 25,000 votes of defeating Republican Thomas Talbot in that state's gubernatorial campaign. Butler, who didn't declare his candidacy until August, had threatened to cut deeply into the Republican Party's large working-class constituency, especially among Irish voters in Boston, as well as in some of the state's larger towns. The deeply worried Republicans brought in some of their big guns to lure back the labor vote, including Missouri's Carl Schurz and conservative Democratic Sen. Francis Kernan of New York, a Catholic and one-time Free Soiler who crossed party lines in an effort to defeat Butler.

Spirited gubernatorial campaigns were also waged in Kansas, Maine, Michigan, Nebraska and Texas. In Maine and Texas, Greenback-Labor candidates actually finished ahead of one of their major party rivals and the party nearly accomplished the same feat in Michigan when its gubernatorial candidate, Henry S. Smith, the Greenback mayor of Grand Rapids, garnered 73,313 votes while running a close third in that staunchly Republican state, roughly 5,000 votes behind the Democratic nominee. In Maine, Greenback candidate Joseph L. Smith, a businessman and ex-Republican, garnered nearly a third of the vote while finishing second in that state's gubernatorial race, some 26,000 votes ahead of Democrat Alonzo Garcelon, a former mayor of Lewiston. Official results gave popular three-term Republican Governor Selden Connor 56,559 votes to Smith's 41,371 and 28,218 for Garcelon, a Union army physician who served in the first battle of Bull Run and later witnessed the horrible carnage at Antietam—a bloody confrontation that took the lives of more Americans in a single day than the War of 1812, the Mexican War, and the Spanish-American war combined.

Incredibly, the Greenbackers captured sixty-four seats in the state House to sixty-five for the Republicans and only twenty-two for the Democrats. Since no candidate received a majority, the election was decided by the fusion-dominated state legislature, which eventually settled on Democrat Garcelon who had finished third in the popular balloting. There was even more confusion in the 1879 gubernatorial campaign when the Greenback Party's Smith garnered nearly 35% of the popular vote to 49.5% for Republican Daniel F. Davis. Garcelon again finished a distant third, receiving less than sixteen percent of the popular vote. As in 1878, the gubernatorial election was again decided by the legislature.

During the chaotic days and weeks that followed, Garcelon, charging that the GOP had engaged in fraud and bribery during the election, illegally maneuvered to unseat a number of Republican legislators and install Democratic-Greenback fusionists in their place, but was eventually overruled by the State Supreme Court. After weeks of political wrangling and infighting—a period in which, according to some sources, as many as seven different men claimed the title of governor or acting governor—the Republicans were able to seat a majority in the legislature and elected Davis governor. Emotions, fueled by sensational newspaper coverage, were super-charged during the twelve-day standoff and was it not for the level-headedness, courage and calm demeanor of former governor Joshua L. Chamberlain, an ardent Lincoln Republican who was in charge of the state militia during the crisis, civil war probably would have ensued. It seems that Republican Senator James G. Blaine, determined to "rescue" his party, set up an armed camp of Republicans at his home next to the state Capitol building. Garcelon responded in kind, assembling nearly one hundred men armed to the teeth around the state capitol. Meanwhile, the Democratic and Greenback-Labor parties, joining forces, quickly raised their own army, which was headquartered in a downtown Augusta hotel.

Armed confrontation seemed almost inevitable. Realizing that he had bit off more than he could chew, a panicked Garcelon then called in the state militia, headed by the former governor. Chamberlain, a former four-term governor who was then president of Bowdoin College, managed to keep the peace by persuading the lame-duck Democratic governor to replace his hired army with members of the city's police department. A target of assassination himself, Chamberlain, who kept the militia outside the city limits for the duration of the showdown, later uncovered a plot to kill Blaine and promptly warned the senator. Blaine, realizing the seriousness of the situation, had a sudden change of heart and immediately called on his own people to disarm, urging his fellow Republicans to wait for the Supreme Court to decide the matter—a position advocated by Chamberlain throughout the crisis. In the meantime, Joseph L. Smith, the Greenback candidate for governor, declared himself the winner and tried to strip Chamberlain of his duties and have him arrested, but the former governor—who remained unarmed throughout the ordeal—refused to back down. The harrowing twelve-day crisis came to an end when the Maine Supreme Court seated a Republican majority in both the House and Senate, which in turn installed Davis as governor.

To avoid the possibility of a gubernatorial election again being decided by the legislature, the Greenback-Labor and Democratic parties united behind the candidacy of former state attorney general Harris M. Plaisted, a Republican-turned-Greenbacker, in the following year's gubernatorial election. A former Union army officer who had served briefly in the Maine legislature, Plaisted—who was one of only three Greenback governors in American history—later edited and published Augusta's *New Age*, from which he championed William Jennings Bryan and the cause of bimetallism. The only fusionist governor in Maine's history, Plaisted narrowly defeated Davis in the 1880 gubernatorial election. The unexpected Greenback victory in ordinarily Republican Maine sent shock waves through Wall Street, resulting first in a sharp decline in the market followed by feverish buying and selling.[46] By this time, the Democrats had been relegated to third-party status in Maine and James Weaver, in a congratulatory telegram to Plaisted, blasted the Democrats for attempting to claim his victory as their own. "It is most amusing to see the Democratic leaders masquerading behind the Greenback Party and calling our victory a Democratic boom—a Democrat couldn't come within 40,000 votes of victory," he said. "The Democrats in Maine showed their good sense by voting the Greenback ticket."[47]

Similarly, things weren't entirely bleak for the Prohibitionists during this period. The party won several local offices in the 1877 off-year elections and, fusing with the Republicans, helped elect General Charles C. Van Zandt, a former Speaker of the Rhode Island House of Representatives, to the first of three terms as governor of that state. In Massachusetts, Judge Robert C. Pitman again ran for governor on the Prohibition ticket that year, garnering an impressive 16,354

46. James Ford Rhodes, *History of the United States from the Compromise of 1850 to the McKinley-Bryan Campaign of 1896* (New York, 1920), Volume 8, p. 132.

47. Mark A. Lause, *The Civil War's Last Campaign: James B. Weaver, the Greenback-Labor Party & the Politics of Race & Section*, p 153; Chicago *Weekly Express*, Sept. 28, 1880; Winamac *Greenback Journal*, Sept. 25, 1880.

votes—or nearly nine percent of the total—against incumbent Republican Alexander H. Rice and Democratic challenger William Gaston. Pitman, a former state senator, was the author of *Alcohol and the State*, a book described by Prohibition historian D. Leigh Colvin as one of the finest books ever written on that topic.[48]

---

48.   Colvin, *Prohibition in the United States*, p. 87.

15

The Workingmen's Party of the United States

❖

The Nation's Original Marxist Party

On the early morning of September 18, 1873, as President Grant dozed in a guest room at financier Jay Cooke's palatial estate in Philadelphia, his host quietly left his mansion and traveled to Center City to padlock the doors of his bank. It seems that Jay Cooke and Company, with a branch in New York City, the nation's financial hub, had overextended its investment in Northern Pacific Railroad stock. The collapse of Cooke's bank was the latest in a series of lesser bank failures earlier in the month. By closing the doors to his bank, Cooke, who earned an estimated ten to twelve million dollars selling Treasury bonds during the Civil War, set off the Panic of 1873—the third of seven major depressions in American history.

The latest depression wiped out hundreds of small businesses and brought hunger and death to countless working people while, curiously, the fortunes of the Astors, Vanderbilts, Rockefellers and Morgans kept growing. Throughout the decade-long economic crisis of the 1870s, Andrew Carnegie was building up his steel empire and John D. Rockefeller's Standard Oil Company was virtually wiping out all of its competitors in the oil industry.

Unemployment and homelessness were prevalent throughout the land. In Chicago some 20,000 unemployed workers marched on City Hall, demanding food, clothing and housing before being beaten back by police officers. In early 1874, things were so bleak in New York that an estimated 90,000 homeless workers, seeking food and shelter, regularly spent one or two nights a month in any one police station before moving on to another one. In January of that year, New York City police officers used clubs to stave off a huge crowd of unemployed and hungry workers marching on City Hall. All hell broke loose. Many of the marchers, including women and small children, were trampled underfoot in the ensuing stampede while many others were mercilessly clubbed by mounted police officers.

The hopelessness of the situation—the anxiety and utter despair experienced by millions of jobless men and women—was tragically illustrated five years later, in 1878, when the SS *Metropolis*, carrying scores of job-seeking Americans to South America where they hoped to find work, sank with all aboard. An hour after news of the steamship tragedy reached Philadelphia, hundreds of hunger-bitten workers besieged the local office of the steamship agent, clamoring to replace the drowned workers.[1]

This was also a period of tremendous labor upheaval. Throughout this period, employers frequently hired "scabs"—usually immigrants desperate for work and willing to drudge for relatively low wages—to replace striking workers. In 1874, for example, mine owners in Pittsburgh's bituminous coal region hired hundreds of Italian immigrants, most of whom spoke little if any English, to replace striking miners—leading to the murder of three of the scabs. Jurors, however, exonerated the accused miners, creating friction and lingering bitterness between the Italian immigrants and the coal miners. Nowhere, however, was the situation as tense and violent as it was in the anthracite coal region of Pennsylvania, where Irish coal miners, belonging to a secret society called the Ancient Order of the Hibernians, were accused of committing random acts of intimidation and violence—including murder—against several mine owners and their superintendents. Dubbed the "Molly Maguires," two-dozen of them were convicted and sentenced to death on the testimony of a paid informer, James McParlan, a detective for the Pinkerton Agency, which had been hired by the Philadelphia and Reading Coal and Iron Company. Despite a few poorly organized protests and demonstrations on their behalf, nineteen "Mollies" were eventually executed.

Against this backdrop, the country's first nationally organized socialist party was founded through a merger of four groups. These included Karl Marx's recently disbanded First International in Chicago and three Lasallean organizations—the Workingmen's Party of Illinois, the Social Political Society of Cincinnati and the Social Democratic Workingmen's Party of North America. Of these four groups, the Social Democratic Workingmen's Party, with 1,500 members, was by far the largest. Founded in 1874, this party, which was headed by Adolph Strasser—president of the Cigar Makers' International Union who later played

---

1.   Zinn, *A People's History of the United States*, p. 238.

an active role in the formation the American Federation of Labor. The Democratic Workingmen's Party regularly ran candidates for local office during its brief
history, but with generally disappointing results. The party moved gradually
toward acceptance of the principles of Marx's First International and by early
1876 began discussing a possible merger with nineteen American sections of the
International.

Numerous socialist groups from around the country, including the Social
Democratic Workingmen's Party, sent delegations to the party's founding convention in Philadelphia in July 1876, hoping to reconcile the differences between
the Lassalleans, who favored direct political action, and Marxists, who felt that
the party's first aim should be to organize the nation's working class into trade
unions. The Lassalleans, as they were dubbed, were followers of playwright Ferdinand Lassalle, a veteran of the 1848 French Revolution and founder of Germany's Democratic Socialist Party. Calling itself the Workingmen's Party of the
United States (WPUS), the left-wing party adopted a Declaration of Principles
calling for "the emancipation of the working classes," trade union organization
and "the abolition of class rule." Heavily influenced by the Marxists, the party's
platform also advocated a system of cooperative production in which all labor
would become the common property of society. The Lassalleans, however, won a
majority of seats on the party's national executive committee and their leader,
Philip Van Patten, was elected national secretary. Although the new party generally frowned on electoral activity, the Lasalleans were eventually successful in
pushing through a provision allowing sections to participate in local elections if
conditions warranted.

"Success and long life to the Workingmen's Party of the United States," trumpeted *The Socialist*, a New York-based newspaper, when the short-lived party was
founded in the summer of 1876.[2] Almost immediately, the Workingmen's Party
of the United States attracted a number of well-known labor leaders to its banner,
including Albert Parsons, a former confederate soldier and self-taught intellectual
who was sentenced to death and hung on a scaffold in November 1887 for allegedly conspiring in the Haymarket Square tragedy. Parson's wife, Lucy, a Texas-
born woman of Spanish and Indian ancestry, was also active in the party. The
couple's mixed marriage forced them to flee from Texas and they eventually settled in Chicago in 1873. A frequent contributor to the International Working
People's Association (IWPA) weekly publication *Alarm*, Lucy Parsons, a tireless

---

2.   Philip S. Foner, *The Workingmen's Party of the United States: A History of the First
     Marxist Party in the Americas* (Minneapolis, 1984), p. 7.

working-class revolutionary, spent a lifetime struggling for the rights of the poor, unemployed, homeless, women, children, and minorities. In one of her best-known and most significant writings, she encouraged workers and the unemployed to resort to acts of violence against the rich. An undaunted anarchist for most of her life, she later published *Freedom*, a short-lived newspaper that condemned the racist lynching of blacks in the South, briefly joined Eugene V. Debs' Social Democracy, and was a founding member of the Industrial Workers of the World, also known as the Wobblies. Despairing of the rising tides of capitalism and fascism in the late 1930s, Parsons formally joined the Communist Party in 1939—three years before her death in a house fire at the age of eighty-nine. The Marxist party also attracted the support of socialist *wunderkind* Peter J. McGuire, a social and labor activist who led his predominantly Irish slum-tenant following in New York in dramatic public demonstrations demanding relief in the early 1870s. McGuire, who later advocated pure and simple trade unionism, organized the first English-speaking branch of the Socialist Labor Party.

Other notable figures drawn to the new party included Samuel Gompers, who later founded the American Federation of Labor, leftist J. P. McDonnell, secretary to Karl Marx in the International Workingmen's Association, as well as Peter H. Clark, the country's first known African-American socialist. The principal of an African-American high school in Cincinnati, Clark, a gifted speaker and brilliant organizer, was a former Republican who once dabbled in the Liberal Republican movement before joining the Workingmen's Party in late March 1877. The following year, the 48-year-old educator was the party's nominee for state superintendent of schools, running ahead of the entire Workingmen's ticket.[3]

Among those influential in the party's early development were Philip Van Patten, who served as the party's first national secretary until 1883, and Friedrich Sorge, head of the International Workingmen's Association and a frequent correspondent of Marx and Engels. Adolph Douai, Laurence Gronlund, British-born Thomas J. Morgan, George A. Schilling, Otto Weydemeyer and Adolph Strasser, head of the Cigar Maker's Union and later a founding member of the American Federation of Labor, were also among the cavalcade of the American Left's leading lights who were influential in the country's first labor-oriented political party. Interestingly, many of those who flocked to the Workingmen's Party were exiles of the German revolution of 1848. Of those, Adolph Douai, a free-thinker and ardent supporter of women's suffrage who once edited the *San Antonio Zeitung*, an abolitionist newspaper in Texas, was perhaps the best known of the "Forty-

---

3.   Ibid., p. 101.

Eighters" who found refuge in the fledgling WPUS. Born in Germany in 1819, Douai, who once established a kindergarten in Boston—the first kindergarten in America—later served as co-editor of the socialist *New Yorker Volkszeitung*, a position he held from 1878 until 1888.

Due to its large German composition, the Workingmen's Party published two German-language weekly newspapers, the *Arbeiterstimme* in New York and the *Vorbote* in Chicago. In addition, J.P. McDonnell edited the party's English-speaking newspaper, *The Socialist* (later renamed the *Labor Standard*), which was inherited from the short-lived Social Democratic Workingmen's Party of North America.

Within a year of its founding, the Workingmen's Party of the United States found itself playing a prominent role in the great railroad strike of 1877—particularly in St. Louis and Chicago, but also in several other cities. Although its national leadership refused to actively participate in the series of strikes that were sweeping the nation, advising workers against the "futility" of unplanned revolts, hundreds of party activists took part in the wave of labor unrest that rocked the country that year. During the long, hot summer of that year, railroad workers, protesting a ten percent cut in their already meager wages, uncoupled several locomotives at the Baltimore and Ohio railway yard in Martinsburg, West Virginia, idling six hundred freight trains. Within days, the strike spread to Pittsburgh and then to ten other states. New Jersey's railroad traffic came to a virtual standstill. In New York, a militia was quickly organized and in Ohio, the strike spread from Lake Erie to the Ohio River. Moreover, Indiana was in a state of suspended animation and dozens of other communities were poised for similar labor demonstrations.

In Chicago and St. Louis, members of the Workingmen's Party of the United States did the bulk of the work, distributing thousands of leaflets and organizing dozens of demonstrations and rallies. The fiery Albert Parsons demanded the nationalization of the railroads in a dramatic speech at a Chicago rally attended by some 6,000 people. Things quickly turned violent and twenty-one people were killed in confrontations when strikers from the city's freight yards, factories, stockyards and crewmen from ships docked in Lake Michigan clashed with police during the course of the next two days.

In the most violent incident of the strike, Pennsylvania Governor John Hartranft sent state militia units from Philadelphia to clear railway tracks of a large group of strikers in Pittsburgh, a city without any discernible Workingmen's Party presence. Twenty-six people were killed in the ensuing melee. The state's brutal action naturally infuriated the strikers and their sympathizers. Under assault, the militia took refuge in the city's roundhouse, which was set on fire shortly thereafter by the enraged strikers. The soldiers, fearing for their lives, fled the city at dawn, leaving the strikers in control. After the militiamen retreated, the strikers destroyed an estimated $5 million of railroad property.

Having succeeded in calling a general strike that virtually cut off all city services while stopping the shipment of goods to the city, the Workingmen's Party in St. Louis actually replaced City Hall as the center of government for five days. Mayor Henry C. Overstolz, a wealthy German-born businessman who frequently feuded with the local party bosses, was initially sympathetic to the strikers and had refused to put down the strike. For a brief moment, St. Louis was governed by the party's "Executive Committee," which issued permits to move and distribute food and other basic commodities.

However, the party's success in St. Louis was short-lived as police, militia and heavily armed federal troops eventually quelled the strike. Police raided the party's headquarters and arrested seventy people, including most of the party's executive committee. The Burlington Railroad fired more than 130 strike leaders and party leader Laurence Gronlund, a Danish-born Fabian socialist whose 1884 book *Cooperative Commonwealth* assailed capitalism's competitive, cruel and wasteful nature, later influencing a precocious generation of American-born socialists, was charged with treason but never tried.

Following the bitter and violent railroad strike, the party experienced a rapid increase in membership. By 1878, it claimed 7,000 members throughout the country, mostly skilled craft workers. The lingering depression coupled with the party's growing membership and publicity from its role in the railroad strike caused the Workingmen's Party to reconsider the question of electoral activity. With the Lasalleans solidly in control at the party's first national convention in Newark, New Jersey, in December 1877, the WPUS reversed its original position and encouraged electoral participation. Adopting the slogan, "Science the Arsenal, Reason the Weapon, the Ballot the Missile," the party's constitution and platform were radically altered with an emphasis placed on mobilizing workers at the ballot box. The party also changed its name to the Socialistic Labor Party (later shortened to Socialist Labor Party). The party's organizational structure remained virtually intact with Philip Van Patten continuing to serve as national secretary.

Shortly thereafter, however, the party lost a number of its most prominent members, including Marxists J. P. McDonnell and Friedrich Sorge, both of whom were adamantly opposed to the party's participation in electoral politics. McDonnell and Sorge led most of the party's militant trade unionists into the

International Labor Union (ILA) where they worked closely with eight-hour advocates such as Ira Steward and George O'Neill. Samuel Gompers, a young cigar maker who later founded the American Federation of Labor, also left the organization to concentrate on building the labor movement.

Meanwhile, the WPUS enjoyed a modicum of success at the ballot box in 1878-79, most notably in Cincinnati, Chicago and St. Louis. Campaigning under the banner of the Socialist Labor Party, the left-wing party elected three state representatives and succeeded in sending party member Sylvester Artley to the Illinois Senate. Moreover, Socialists John McAsliff and party founder George A. Schilling—one of the party's most gifted speakers and a man of considerable influence in Chicago labor circles—garnered nearly ten and twelve percent of the vote, respectively, in bids for U.S. House seats from Illinois in the 1878 mid-term congressional elections. In addition, four aldermanic candidates, running on a "municipal socialism" platform strikingly similar to that later advocated by the Socialist Party of Eugene Debs and Norman Thomas, were elected in Chicago earlier that year. Moreover, Ernst Schmidt, a popular physician and noted Marxian scholar, garnered more than 12,000 votes in a bid for mayor on the party's ticket the following spring. The party also polled 9,000 votes in Cincinnati's 1878 municipal election and polled 7,000 votes in St. Louis, electing five school board members and two aldermen in the latter city.

In addition to fielding a gubernatorial ticket in New York in 1879, the Socialist Labor Party also put up local tickets in Boston, Cleveland, Denver, Detroit and New Orleans during this period. Earlier, a "Workingmen's" ticket, heavily influenced by the SLP and comprised largely of trade unionists, garnered more than sixty percent of the vote in an 1877 municipal campaign in Louisville, Kentucky. The party's early success in Chicago, St. Louis and elsewhere convinced party leaders that they were about to duplicate the phenomenal success of the Social Democratic Party in Germany—a party that captured a dozen seats in that country's 1877 elections. (Founded in 1875 by socialists Ferdinand Bebel and Wilhelm Liebknecht, the German Social Democratic Party was so successful from the outset that Chancellor Otto von Bismark, fearing a socialist insurrection, introduced draconian anti-socialist laws banning party meetings and publications—legislation that remained on the books in Germany until 1890.)

Nobody was more impressed by the Workingmen's Party's early electoral success than the leaders of the Greenback Party, who began to view the fledgling party as a potential ally. By 1880, the Socialist Labor Party boasted as many as 12,000 members in almost one hundred and forty branches throughout the country. Moreover, it had already won local elections in Chicago, St. Louis, Milwaukee, and New Haven, as well as posting victories in a host of smaller towns and cities across the nation, including Jeffersonville, Indiana, where the SLP elected two councilmen and came close to winning that town's mayoralty race.[4]

As the country prepared for the 1880 presidential election, the Socialist Labor Party, convening in Allegheny City, Pennsylvania, in late December 1879, nominated 57-year-old Caleb Pink of New York for the presidency over two other candidates. A prominent Brooklyn land reformer and self-styled spiritualist, Pink had been the Socialist Labor Party's candidate for governor of New York earlier that year and, along with national secretary Philip Van Patten and the party's national executive committee, later played an instrumental role in bringing about the party's union with the Greenback-Labor Party during the 1880 presidential campaign.[5]

By 1881, membership in the Socialist Labor Party dwindled to approximately 2,600—and even that might have been a somewhat inflated figure. By then, the country's meager socialist forces were sharply divided between three competing elements—the Socialist Labor Party, with its emphasis on the ballot box; the emerging craft unions with their emphasis on hours and wages; and the assorted radical social revolutionary and anarchist organizations sprinkled across the country.[6] Meanwhile, hundreds of German revolutionaries, hoping to escape Bismark's anti-socialist crackdown in that country, immigrated to the United States in the early 1880s, eventually leading to the creation of the militant International Working People's Association (IWPA) in 1883. Section after section of the Socialist Labor Party defected and joined the IWPA, leaving the SLP a virtual shell of its former self. Both organizations had a large following among German immigrants and when one failed the other prospered. By the end of 1883, the

---

4.   Lause, *The Civil War's Last Campaign*, p. 40. "By 1880," wrote Lause in his brilliant study of the Weaver campaign of that year, "the party claimed 100,000 votes—an exaggeration close enough to the truth to go unchallenged."

5.   Morris Hillquit, *History of Socialism in the United States*, (New York, 1971), pp. 241-242; Frank Girard and Ben Perry, *The Socialist Labor Party 1876-1991: A Short History*, (Philadelphia, 1991), pp. 6-7. A referendum, which included Caleb Pink's name along with two lesser-known candidates, was later rejected by the party's rank-and-file membership, which was overwhelmingly opposed to running a separate SLP ticket in 1880.

6.   Ira Kipnis, *The American Socialist Movement 1897-1912* (New York, 1952), p. 10. This scholarly book contains an excellent history of the socialist movement in the United States from its inception through its decline following the presidential election of 1912. According to Dr. Kipnis, at one time there were more than 150,000 dues-paying socialists in the country, as well as hundreds of socialist publications.

IWPA boasted a membership of 7,000 while the Socialist Labor Party could claim only 1,500—a far cry from the estimated 7,000 members enjoyed by the Workingmen's Party of the United States, its precursor, only a few years earlier.

Though the Workingmen's Party of the United States formally survived only a little more than a year—from July 1876 to December 1877—in reality, as the late Philip S. Foner keenly observed, "it has had the longest life of any radical party in the United States"—and is second only to the Prohibitionists in minor-party longevity. Beginning with the Socialistic Labor Party (now the Socialist Labor Party, a party that is still in existence today) and through the organizational splits, which initially gave birth to the Social Democratic Party of Eugene V. Debs and Victor Berger before evolving into the Socialist Party USA in 1901. It was from that party that subsequent splits eventually led to the founding of the present-day Communist Party in 1919.[7]

"Sand-Lot Mobocracy"—California's Workingmen's Party

The "terrible" seventies also saw the rise of the Workingmen's Party of California, a third-party that wrought considerable havoc in that state during the tumultuous period of the late 1870s. Although the Panic of 1873 helped worsen conditions, Californians had been feeling a severe economic pinch dating back to the 1860s when the state's once-abundant gold mines began drying up. As the gold mining industry collapsed, production of mining equipment in San Francisco's once-bustling foundries and machine shops grinded to a halt and the city began to resemble a ghost town. Wages and prices fell dramatically and real estate values plummeted. Conditions deteriorated even further in 1869 with the completion of the transcontinental railroad, a period when thousands of worker were let go by the Central Pacific Railroad. No longer needed, these workers swelled the ranks of San Francisco's unemployed, estimated to be more than seven thousand of the city's 149,000 citizens.

San Francisco, of course, wasn't the only area hurting in the Golden State. In the rural Sacramento Valley, a future Workingmen's Party stronghold, wheat prices dropped sharply and sheep sold for the remarkably low price of a dollar apiece. Elsewhere in the state, the economy was only slightly better. By 1877, poverty was clearly on the rise as California experienced a whopping 451 business failures.

---

7.   Foner, *The Workingmen's Party of the United States*, p. 7.

Unfortunately, laborers, farmers and businessmen alike began blaming the recent influx of Chinese immigrants for their economic woes. The first Chinese arrivals had settled in San Francisco in the late 1840s. By 1870, California's Chinese population numbered more than 49,000 and by 1880 that figure swelled to a staggering 75,132. Most of these immigrants were from the port city of Canton, China, and more than half of them made San Francisco their home.

During this period of rampant immigration, a number of so-called "anti-coolie" associations, such as the Workingmen's Protective Association and the Industrial Reformers, a group founded in February 1870, began sprouting up in the Bay Area and in other parts of California, presumably to make life a living hell for the unwanted Chinese immigrants.

Reacting to the growing anti-Chinese sentiment, politicians in both major parties were only too willing to pass local ordinances and legislation designed to thwart the state's burgeoning Chinese population. Legislation denying the unwanted arrivals the right of citizenship and suffrage sailed through the state legislature, as did laws restricting their access to the courts and the right to send their children to public schools. As mean-spirited as these statutes were, most of the anti-Chinese legislation approved during this period had little affect. Efforts to curb Chinese immigration, which was legally protected by the Burlingame Treaty of 1868, failed miserably.

Unable to stem the flow of legal Chinese migration to the city, San Franciscans watched helplessly as its Chinese population continued to mushroom. By 1876, manufacturers in the city, eager to hire employees who were willing to work for extraordinarily low wages, employed approximately 14,000 Chinese workers. Thousands of other Chinese immigrants toiled in agriculture and on irrigation and reclamation projects.

With little or no economic improvement in sight, anti-Chinese tensions often grew ugly, occasionally resulting in outbreaks of violence. One incident that shocked the nation occurred in Los Angeles in 1871 when a frantic mob brutally lynched nineteen Chinese residents in the city's Calle de Los Negros section. More than 150 men were subsequently indicted. In a travesty of justice, only six of the men served any jail time and none of them served more than six months. In March 1877, the country was again stunned when five men, claiming to be acting under orders from the Workingmen's Protective Association, attacked a group of Chinese workers on a ranch, shooting them and leaving them to burn to death in their cabin.

Founded by the bold, enriched by gold, by the 1870s California had turned cold and San Francisco, its world-class city, had become a center of discontent and rebellion. During the great railroad strike of that year, the nation's first major—and bloodiest—labor uprising, riots broke out in Maryland, Pennsylvania, Virginia and West Virginia and eventually spread to ten other states. Learning of the spontaneous labor uprising, leaders of the San Francisco branch of the WPUS called for a mass meeting to express solidarity with their striking brethren back East. Ten days after it started, when railway workers in Martinsburg, West Virginia, resisted wage cuts by refusing to go to work, the "reign of rabble" had finally reached the West Coast.

In San Francisco, however, the strike took on an unexpected twist when rioters, not content to merely lash out at railroad magnates such as Jay Gould, vented their anger and frustration by turning on another longtime nemesis—the Chinese. This unruly mob smashed storefront windows in Chinatown, burned a Chinese laundry to the ground and destroyed fifteen washhouses. Ironically, the riots of July 1877 erupted during a peaceful demonstration of the Workingmen's Party of the United States (WPUS). Much to its credit, the WPUS, a socialist organization with roots in the Marxian International Workingmen's Association that eventually led to the founding of the Socialist Labor Party, never embraced an anti-Chinese policy. In fact, the party strongly contended that Chinese workers were essentially slaves, not unlike the average American worker. In its official newspaper, the *Labor Standard*, the WPUS urged laborers to fight for "the abolition of the coolie system" and, after that, the abolition of capitalism itself. "Organize, organize, organize," the party urged, "but *don't kill the coolie!*"

Alarmed by the unprovoked violence, concerned property owners and merchants quickly organized a "Committee of Safety" and formed a vigilante "Pick Handle Brigade" to keep the peace. Mayor Andrew Jackson Bryant, a businessman, fully supported their action. The committee also had the support of Gov. William Irwin who immediately requested military assistance from President Hayes. After conferring with the White House, the Secretary of the Navy dispatched the *Lackawanna, Monterey* and *Pensacola* from the Mare Island naval yard. For a week, the three warships were anchored off the San Francisco coast, prepared, if necessary, to assist the vigilantes. During the weeklong standoff, the protestors threatened to destroy the wharves of the Pacific Mail Steamship Company where Chinese immigrants first stepped onto American soil. On the afternoon of July 27, Chinese immigrants under heavy vigilante and police protection, landed in San Francisco. That evening, lawless protestors torched the steamship company's lumberyards, setting off a showdown between the unruly rioters and the Pick Handle Brigade at a nearby bluff. The demoralized demonstrators were dispersed after a two-hour battle and calm was restored to the city the following day.

The July riots caused a great stir among workers in San Francisco and Oakland. Shortly thereafter, labor organizer John G. Day and businessman Denis Kearney founded the Workingmen's Party of California. A Canadian-born carpenter of Irish descent, Day presided over a meeting of the Workingmen's Trade and Labor Union of San Francisco—an organization founded shortly after the July riots—from which the party was launched. Ironically, Kearney had earlier served as a vigilante in the Pick Handle Brigade. Envisioning themselves as the leaders of a powerful new political party comprised of the state's growing ranks of unemployed and discontented laborers, the radical Kearney—who urged workers to buy muskets in the aftermath of the July riots—served as the party's president and Day served as vice president. Kearney's bold and controversial rhetoric drew the wrath of several San Francisco newspapers, drawing attention to the party that it probably wouldn't have otherwise received. A few nights later, Kearney delivered an even more inflammatory speech. Urging workers to join his party, the sandlot orator promised to rid the country of "cheap Chinese labor." Even death, Kearney said, was "preferable to life on a par with the Chinaman." The slogan, "The Chinese Must Go!" became the party's clarion call.

Proposing "to wrest the government from the hands of the rich and place it in the hands of the people, where it properly belongs," the California Workingmen's Party also warned workers against the dangerous encroachments of capital and promised to break-up land monopolies.[8] According to Kearney, a "golden lobby" consisting of "land grabbers, bloated bondholders, railroad magnates, and shoddy aristocrats," controlled Congress. He urged California workers to join his party and "meet fraud with force."

Kearney, who was born in Ireland in 1847 and orphaned at the age of eleven, went to work as a cabin boy when he was quite young, earning his keep on American vessels sailing the trans-Atlantic. He first set foot in San Francisco when his ship docked there in 1868. He continued to sail on coastal steamers for the next four years before purchasing a small freight business in San Francisco. He became a naturalized citizen in 1876.

A short, stocky man with a slight mustache, Kearney had turned a tremendous profit as a drayman, enabling him to acquire some relatively expensive property. Politically, Kearney was unmistakably a conservative during this period of his life and in 1876 he even marched in a torchlight procession for Republican presiden-

---

8.   Foner, *History of the Labor Movement in the United States,* Vol. I, p. 490.

tial candidate Rutherford Hayes. A social conservative, the hard-working and thrifty businessman was strongly opposed to the use of tobacco and vigorously supported the temperance movement.

Though lacking a formal education, Kearney assiduously read the works of Darwin and Spencer and regularly attended the Sunday meetings of the city's Lyceum of Self-Culture debating club. Speaking in a thick Irish brogue, Kearney used the Lyceum forum not only to hone his own speaking skills but also to defend capitalism. As a debater, he initially defended the Chinese and occasionally lashed out against the working classes—the very people he sought to represent in his new political party. His audiences, however, generally regarded him as an arrogant bore whose emotional speeches lacked logic and substance.

Kearney's sudden transformation—adopting a vehemently anti-Chinese and pro-labor stance—undoubtedly confused many of those who had heard his Sunday afternoon speeches. In fact, earlier he tried to join the Workingmen's Party of the United States, but was rejected as an enemy of the working class.[9] Precisely what triggered his sudden change of heart is subject to debate. Some believed that he had grown bitter because he suffered substantial losses in the stock market while others were convinced that he was merely a demagogue waiting to happen and the widespread anti-Chinese sentiment sweeping the city gave him an opportunity to fulfill that role. There was nothing subtle about Kearney. On one occasion, he declared that "when the Chinese question is settled, we can discuss whether it would be better to hang, shoot, or cut the capitalists to pieces." Kearney viciously attacked the enemies of his fledgling party, particularly the millionaires who lived on San Francisco's famous Nob Hill. "The dignity of labor," he said, "must be sustained, even if we have to kill every wretch that opposes it." Predicting that "a social revolution" would soon "convulse the country," party co-founder John G. Day, echoed similar remarks, stating that desperate times call for desperate measures and that every citizen had a right to a musket. Despite his inflammatory language, Kearney, whose harangues, parades and public demonstrations kept the city in a constant state of turmoil, quickly became the idol of thousands of working-class San Franciscans.

While denounced by most of his contemporaries and historians as a classic demagogue, single-tax economist Henry George provided perhaps the most compelling explanation of Kearney's powerful emotional appeal. Comparing him to Cincinnatus—the ancient Roman dictator who gave up his position and power sixteen days after it was granted to return to a life of farming—George believed

---

9.   Ibid., p. 490.

that Kearney's appeal derived from his ability to lead people while not appearing to be driven by personal ambition. Like Cincinnatus, Kearney intended to return to his dray after leading the people to victory, observed the insightful journalist, who was then dabbling in California's Land Reform League while putting the finishing touches on *Progress and Poverty*—the *Uncle Tom's Cabin* of the 1880's. "These things," wrote George, "the style of his oratory, the prominence he had attained, his energy, tact, and temperance, gave him command." While denouncing politicians and attacking his rivals, Kearney, who was usually dressed in rough work clothes, appealed not only to prejudice and petty jealousies, but also to the personal ambitions of his working-class followers. The blue-collar laborers who followed him into the Workingmen's Party, George noted, "flattered themselves with the idea that *they* were the men of whom sheriffs, and supervisors, and school-directors, and senators, and assemblymen were to be made, and they brought to the new party and to the support of Kearney all the enthusiasm which such a hope called forth."[10]

Shortly after launching the Workingmen's Party of California, Kearney, Day and H. L. Knight, the party's secretary, were indicted on conspiracy charges for trying to incite a riot. They were eventually acquitted, but not before the city's Board of Supervisors enacted an infamous gag law, effectively curtailing the party's freedom of speech. The Supervisors' attack on basic liberties helped to swell the party's ranks as countless San Franciscans, viewing the Workingmen's Party as a movement to protect the civil rights of all Americans, flocked to the xenophobic party in record numbers.

In the meantime, Kearney's third party movement rapidly expanded beyond San Francisco's borders. Chapters were established in Los Angeles, Sacramento, Santa Barbara, San Luis Obispo and elsewhere. The party held its first statewide convention—a highly secretive affair—in San Francisco in mid-January 1878, and ratified a platform opposing Chinese labor and monopolies, while favoring an eight-hour workday. While calling for a restriction of 640 acres on the amount of land any individual could own, the Workingmen also demanded the abolition of the Electoral College, as well as the direct election of U.S. Senators. The platform's most curious plank, however, was the one dealing with malfeasance in office, which was punishable by life imprisonment without the possibility of pardon.[11]

---

10. Neil Larry Shumsky, *The Evolution of Political Protest and the Workingmen's Party of California* (Columbus, Ohio, 1991), p. 173.

11. Fine, *Labor and Farmer Parties in the United States, 1828-1928*, p. 66.

The Workingmen's Party experienced its first taste of victory immediately after the convention when John W. "Barebones" Bones defeated his Democratic and Republican opponents in a special election for the state Senate in Alameda County. A month later, in another special election, the fledgling party elected a candidate to the Santa Clara County assembly. In March, the party scored several spectacular victories in municipal elections in Oakland and Sacramento. In Oakland, the party joined a fusion campaign with the Democrats to elect Washburne R. Andrus, a carpenter, as mayor of that city. Workingmen's candidates were also elected to the posts of city attorney and police judge, while two others won seats on the city council. During the next two weeks, the party won municipal races in Berkeley, Haywood, Nevada City, Redwood City and Santa Cruz. In December, the Workingmen's Party, continuing to makes its presence felt, captured twelve of fifteen city council seats in Los Angeles, as well as a handful of other city offices.

Shortly thereafter, Kearney's third-party movement found itself smack-dab in the middle of a heated campaign to frame a new state constitution. Electing fifty-one delegates to the constitutional convention in the June 19 primary, the Workingmen's Party, though vastly outnumbered, was able to sway considerable influence over the proceedings. Among other things, the party was responsible for the inclusion of a measure calling for an eight-hour day on all public works programs. The Workingmen were also responsible for measures barring Chinese immigrants from seeking employment on government projects and prohibiting corporations from hiring Chinese laborers.

Kearney and other party leaders stumped vigorously throughout the state for passage of the proposed constitution. Despite concerted opposition from most of the state's leading newspapers, banks, railroads, utilities, manufacturing and mining companies, California voters ratified the new constitution by a vote of 77,959 to 67,134.

Promising to enforce the new constitution, the Workingmen's Party slated William F. White of Santa Cruz, one of the state's most distinguished pioneers, for governor and nominated Oakland Mayor Washburne Andrus for lieutenant governor in the heated California gubernatorial contest in 1879. A native of Limerick, Ireland, White, who was a brother-in-law of New York Democrat William Bourke Cockran and the father of Stephen Mallory White (who later represented California in the U.S. Senate as a Democrat in the 1890's), had been a delegate to the state constitutional convention of 1849. In a spirited three-way race, the Workingmen's candidate polled over 27% of the vote while losing to Republican George C. Perkins. Perkins garnered 67,965 votes to Democrat Hugh J. Glenn's

47,667 and 44,482 for White.[12] Despite losing the gubernatorial race, Kearney's party managed to elect Robert F. Morrison as Chief Justice of the California Supreme Court, as well as five of the six associate justices. Incredibly, the Workingmen's Party also elected a state railroad commissioner, ten state senators—compared to only seven for the Democrats—and sixteen assemblymen, thirteen of whom represented assembly districts in and around the party's stronghold of San Francisco. The radical labor party also registered a stunning victory in that city's mayoral contest when it elected Baptist minister Isaac S. Kalloch to the city's top elective post. Although it failed to win any seats on the board of supervisors, the party was also successful in the city attorney, treasurer, auditor, tax collector and sheriff's races, while winning several judgeships and school board seats, as well as three minor elective posts.

In addition, the Workingmen's Party nearly elected a congressman in the state's first congressional district that year, when San Francisco attorney Clitus Barbour, finishing a strong second in a bitterly contested three-way race, came within 1,625 votes of unseating two-term Republican lawmaker Horace Davis. The Workingmen's James J. Ayres, moreover, garnered 10,527 votes, or nearly 28% of the vote, while finishing a close third in the neighboring fourth congressional district.

As remarkable as it was, the success of Kearney's third-party movement was incredibly and inexplicably very short-lived. Regarded by many as ruffians, the party's popularity declined sharply over the next two years. By 1881 only four Workingmen were re-elected to the state assembly—and all four of them were elected with Democratic support. While the party's rapid decline in San Francisco was partly the result of Mayor Kalloch's turbulent administration, other factors had also contributed to its sudden demise.

Believing that there were "more wicked people" in San Francisco than anywhere else, Kalloch, a 47-year-old native of Maine left his pulpit in Leavenworth, Kansas, in 1875 and headed West, hoping to convert San Francisco's immoral population. Shortly after arriving in the city, he built the city's Metropolitan Temple—the largest Baptist church in America—and began converting the city's sinners. Kalloch's state-of-the-art church, which included libraries, reading rooms, gymnasiums and nurseries, was different than most other houses of worship and liberal-minded Kalloch was unlike most other Baptist ministers. He was

12.   Royce D. Delmatier, Clarence F. McIntosh, and Earl G. Waters, eds., *The Rumble of California Politics 1848-1970* (New York, 1970), pp. 88-89. A Colusa wheat rancher, Hugh J. Glenn had also been nominated by the short-lived New Constitution Party, a new party sponsored by the *San Francisco Chronicle*.

rather open-minded, accepted Darwinian theories and questioned the infallibility of Scripture. He routinely criticized what he described as "fashionable churches" that catered to the wealthy, calling them "toys for grown-up people as much as a carriage or a box at the opera." While denouncing those churches that catered to the rich and powerful while excluding indigent and working-class parishioners, Kalloch firmly believed that houses of worship should be open to everyone—rich and poor alike.

The golden-voiced Kalloch, who initially opposed Kearney's Workingmen's Party, soon aligned himself with Kearney's nascent party, unexpectedly announcing his support for the fledgling party on July 4, 1878. It was a sudden conversion, "like Saul of Tarsus," as one contemporary writer described it. After all, Kalloch had frequently criticized Kearney from his pulpit and had even talked about suppressing the anti-Chinese movement with "bayonets and Gatling guns." In making his dramatic announcement, the flamboyant Baptist minister, who already had his eye on the mayor's office, prayed that the rights of labor should be respected and that the Chinese must go. In his fiery sermon, he also said that "the grasping spirit of remorseless monopoly" must be controlled. From that moment on, Kalloch, who had earned an honorary master's degree from Colby and Colgate universities, frequently denounced San Francisco's Chinese population as a nuisance from his pulpit at the corner of Fifth and Jessie streets.

Before long, the Metropolitan Temple was the church of choice for thousands of workingmen as they began packing its hall every Sunday. In the meantime, Kalloch quickly became one of the party's most popular leaders and in 1879 he was nominated for mayor on the party's ticket. Having survived two gunshot wounds at the hands of the *San Francisco Chronicle's* Charles De Young, the Baptist minister-turned-politician swept past his Republican rival in the general election, garnering 20,069 votes to his opponent's 19,550. A large sympathy vote clearly made the difference in the race. During the campaign, Kalloch, who had been viciously attacked as a womanizer and worse in De Young's newspaper, sharply denounced the editor and his family from the pulpit. Seething with anger, De Young fired two shots from a derringer outside of Kalloch's Temple on August 23, seriously wounding the mayoral candidate. The minister-turned-politician eventually recovered, but was bedridden for the remainder of the campaign.

Promising that he would never steal, get drunk "or do any other dishonorable act," the newly elected mayor fully recovered from the August shooting, but that hardly signaled the end of the bitter Kalloch-deYoung feud, a rivalry that intensified significantly once Kalloch took office. Charges and countercharges were traded like backhand shots at a world tennis championship. The whole affair ended tragically on April 23, 1880, when Milton Kalloch, the mayor's son, in an apparent fit of rage, fatally gunned down De Young at the *Chronicle's* business office. The younger Kalloch, who worked as a clerk in his father's office, believed that the editor had libeled his father by calling him a corrupt politician and an adulterer. Although there were several witnesses to the murder, the mayor's son was later acquitted by a sympathetic jury.

During his two-year term, Kalloch, who was charged with malfeasance in office, constantly sparred with the Board of Supervisors and had to fend off several impeachments attempts. Although the Workingmen had elected the mayor, not one of their candidates was elected to the Board of Supervisors, resulting in a badly divided administration. As a consequence, San Francisco's government was virtually paralyzed during Kalloch's term in office. When President Rutherford B. Hayes visited the city in 1880—the first president to ever visit California while in office—the city's supervisors refused to include the mayor on the official welcoming committee.

While the embattled Baptist minister fought off efforts to oust him from office, party leader Denis Kearney tried unsuccessfully to influence the Workingmen's bloc in the state legislature. His fiery style and abusive behavior didn't go over very well with most legislators and he was eventually barred from the assembly chambers. Republican Maurice C. Blake, a former state legislator and judge of the municipal criminal court, replaced Kalloch as mayor in 1881. Out-of-town newspapers rejoiced when Mayor Kalloch and his "Hoodlum" party went down to defeat in San Francisco.

There were, to be sure, other factors that contributed to the party's untimely demise. One of those was Charles J. Beerstecher's role as the party's sole member of the state's powerful railroad commission. In 1877, Beerstecher, whose father had participated in the German revolution of 1848, headed the German-speaking section of the Workingmen's Party of the United States in San Francisco. Like many WPUS members in California, Beerstecher allied himself with the Workingmen's Party of California shortly after it was founded and in the spring of 1878 introduced a resolution at the party's state convention recognizing the Workingmen's Party of the United States as "a kindred organization," committed to the emancipation of the working-class.[13] A delegate to the state constitutional convention in 1878, Beerstecher was elected to the state Railroad Commission on

---

13.   Shumsky, *The Evolution of Political Protest and the Workingmen's Party of California*, p. 207.

the Workingmen's ticket the following year. Despite his longtime advocacy of socialism, once in office he was universally viewed as a pawn of the powerful railroad interests.

A more significant contributing factor in the party's collapse, however, was Kearney's apparent willingness to strike a deal with "Blind Boss" Chris Buckley, a saloon owner and shrewd Democratic leader who rebuilt his demoralized party on the ruins of the Workingmen's Party. In late 1879, Kearney agreed that the Workingmen's Party would support Democratic candidates for national office in exchange for Democratic support in state and municipal elections. Kearney, who was hardly an astute politician, was apparently unaware that there wouldn't be any municipal elections held in 1880 due to provisions in the new state constitution—a fact that hadn't escaped the perspicacious Buckley. As a result, most of the party's membership enthusiastically supported the Democratic ticket in 1880—helping Democrat Winfield S. Hancock narrowly carry the state against Republican James A. Garfield—and, consequently, never returned to the Workingmen's fold. Fusing with the Democrats, Kearney's party also apparently made the difference in at least two U.S. House races that year, providing the margin of victory for Democrat Campbell P. Berry in the state's third congressional district in 1879 and enabling Civil War General William S. Rosecrans—a man Lincoln once described as "confused and stunned like a duck hit on the head" following the disaster at Chickamauga in the autumn of 1863—to narrowly defeat Republican Horace Davis in California's first congressional district the following year.[14] Of course, not all of the Workingmen were pleased with Kearney's decision to enter into a fusion campaign with the Democrats and quickly threw their support to the fledgling Greenback-Labor Party. One of those was Stephen Maybell of San Francisco. Maybell, who was one of the sixteen Workingmen elected to the California assembly in 1879, decided to run against Davis and Rosecrans on the Greenback ticket, but wasn't a factor in the outcome.[15]

As his San Francisco-based party slowly began to disintegrate, Kearney also flirted with the Greenback-Labor Party, vigorously pushing for Benjamin Butler's presidential nomination in 1880 and serving as sergeant-at-arms at the party's national convention in Chicago that year. He was hissed and booed at that convention when he protested that he had not traveled 2,600 miles to Chicago to listen to women talk about suffrage, facetiously referring the matter to "a

---

14. For Lincoln quote, see McPherson, *Battle Cry of Freedom*, p. 675.

15. Rosecrans narrowly defeated Davis, garnering 21,005 votes to the Republican lawmaker's 19,496. The Greenback-Labor Party's Stephen Maybell received 683 votes, or less than two percent of the total.

convention of the daughters of Eve, to meet in Chicago in fifty years."[16] A few years later, he also stumped for Butler and the short-lived Anti-Monopoly Party. The notorious sandlot agitator, who tried unsuccessfully to revive the Working-men's Party in 1883, retired from politics shortly thereafter. His rabid opposition to Chinese immigration, however, continued unabated. He spent the winter of 1887-88 in New York and Washington, D.C., campaigning against what he described as the "mongolization" of America, urging Congress to adopt legisla-tion totally excluding Chinese immigration. Both major parties, of course, had adopted strong anti-Chinese immigration planks in their respective 1880 plat-forms, but shied away from the issue by the mid-1880s. Moreover, anti-Chinese sentiment had virtually evaporated by then, even in California. The sandlot ora-tor was simply out of touch. Kearney, who had inherited a fortune from his uncle in the early 1890s, joined an exodus to the East Bay shortly after his San Fran-cisco residence was destroyed in the earthquake and fire of 1906, settling in Alameda where he died the following year. When asked shortly before his death how he reconciled his wealth with his previous radical politics, Kearney responded rather nonchalantly. "Oh, you know, somebody has to do the work."[17]

The Workingmen's Party of the United States and Kearney's Workingmen's Party of California were not the only new parties to take shape during this period. A number of other third-party movements, including the Farmers' Alliance in upstate New York, also sprang into existence in the late 1870s. One of the more intriguing of these short-lived parties was the National Liberal Party, founded by the National Liberal League, a forerunner of the modern San Diego-based National League for the Separation of Church and State. Led by such notable freethinkers as Francis E. Abbott, longtime land reformer and abolitionist Elizur Wright and Robert G. Ingersoll, the great agnostic, and later by Milwaukee women's rights activist Juliet H. Severence, most of the League's membership,

16.   Lause, *The Civil War's Last Campaign*, p. 65.
17.   Delmatier, McIntosh, and Waters, *The Rumble of California Politics 1848-1970*, p. 93.

having shifted dramatically to the Left, was eventually absorbed into the larger Greenback-Labor movement.[18]

18. Lause, *The Civil War's Last Campaign*, pp. 36, 44, 168-169. The National Liberal League was founded at the Centennial Exposition in Philadelphia on July 4, 1876, to promote an anticlerical and freethinking agenda. In 1878, the league, then led by Ingersoll, launched the National Defense Association against the Comstock prosecutions, especially that of Presbyterian minister Ezra H. Heywood, an anarchist and one-time Victoria Woodhull supporter who was sentenced to two years of hard labor for advocating free love and sexual emancipation for women.

16

The Iowa Insurgent

✦

The Greenback-Labor Party at High Tide

The Greenbackers were generally sympathetic to the Workingmen's Party of the United States, as well as to Denis Kearney's fledgling third-party movement in California. It was only natural, therefore, that a kind of fusion should take place on a national scale. Along with hundreds of labor organizers and currency reformers, more than a thousand members of the Greenback Party, representing twenty-eight states, gathered in Toledo, Ohio, in the winter of 1878 and adopted a platform denouncing the tax-exempt status of government bonds, the Resumption Act and wasteful government spending. Other planks adopted at the Toledo conference called for the elimination of bank notes and the issuance of all money by the federal government. The group also supported the coinage of silver on the same basis as gold, a shorter workday, the creation of a federal bureau of labor, the abolition of prison labor for private profit, and the enforcement of stricter immigration laws, including closing the nation's borders to Chinese immigrants.

At its 1880 national convention held in Chicago, the Greenback-Labor Party expanded its platform to include the adoption of an income tax, unlimited coinage of silver and gold, women's suffrage and several other progressive measures, including an eight-hour workday, curtailment of child labor and a sanitary code for industry. The delegates also endorsed planks opposing monopolies, especially of railroads, land and banking.

The national Greenback convention that year—a cacophony of discordant voices representing almost every reform movement in the country—was held in historic Exposition Hall, the site of the Republican national convention, which had just concluded the previous day. When delegates began filing into the hall around noon on June 9, some of them were surprised to see portraits of Republican Party founders still adorning the walls. Large portraits of Benjamin F. Wade,

Charles Sumner, Joshua R. Giddings and other prominent Republican figures hung on adjoining sides of the hall and a huge visage of Abraham Lincoln was draped over the north end of the hall. Following a protracted floor fight, a 187-man delegation representing the radical Union Greenback Party was seated, as was a 44-person delegation from the Socialist Labor Party. The National Woman Suffrage Association, led by Matilda Jocelyn Gage, was also represented with at least a half-dozen delegates. Several smaller yet vocal delegations, including one representing the Eight-Hour League, were also seated at the Greenback convention.

The delegates laughed and cheered when the minister giving the invocation thanked God that Jesus was a carpenter. The minister reminded the delegates that many prayers had been said for the Democrats and the Republicans over the years, but none had ever been answered. "We come to Thee, O, Lord," he said, "on our own hook."[1] Another minister, Gilbert De La Matyr, a 55-year-old Greenback congressman from Indianapolis, was named temporary chairman, presumably because he had the loudest voice in the hall. De La Matyr, who was once denounced as a "communist of the most dangerous type" by some of his critics, presided ably over the proceedings, but was later replaced by permanent chairman Richard F. Trevellick of Michigan, a leader in the Knights of Labor, the country's largest labor organization.[2] Trevellick, who organized no fewer than fifty unions during his long career in the labor movement, had served alternately as president of the International Union of Ship Carpenters and Caulkers and as president of the Detroit Trades' Assembly. Long regarded as an "old warhorse" of the labor movement, the 51-year-old British-born Trevellick, a ship carpenter from Detroit and veteran of William H. Sylvis' National Labor Union, was elected permanent chairman on the convention's second day.

The delegates listened intently to addresses by a member of the Canadian parliament and a leader of that country's Currency Reform League. While extending sympathy and encouragement to the Greenback-Labor Party, both speakers urged the fledgling party to fight for the adoption of a legal circulating currency.[3] The convention also heard a rousing speech from Denis Kearney, the flamboyant leader of the California Workingmen's Party. In his speech, Kearney thanked God that even the Republicans had the wisdom to finally reject Ulysses S. Grant. (The former president, in a bid for an unprecedented third term, had unsuccess-

---

1. *New York Times*, June 10, 1880.
2. Lause, *The Civil War's Last Campaign*, pp. 64-65.
3. *New York Times*, June 10, 1880.

fully sought the Republican presidential nomination earlier that year.) Amid cheers, Kearney also predicted that Republican presidential candidate James Garfield would poll less than one-third of the vote in California, Nevada and Oregon. Kearney, however, was booed when he complained that "he had not traveled 2,600 miles to waste time in Chicago hearing the women talk"—a reference to a woman's suffrage plank that had been offered by Susan B. Anthony.[4]

The convention's greatest suspense, as expected, occurred in the battle for the party's presidential nomination. In all, the names of no fewer than nine candidates were placed in nomination. Among them was Thompson H. Murch of Maine who was nominated by a delegate from Tennessee wistfully claiming to be the nation's only surviving Confederate private. An ex-sailor and stonecutter, the 50-year-old Murch, a Greenback congressman, withdrew his name form consideration before the balloting began. Other candidates considered by the Greenback delegates were the stormy Ben Butler of Massachusetts, publisher Solon Chase, a former state legislator and chairman of the Greenback Party in Maine, Alexander Campbell, the aging former congressman from Illinois, and 56-year-old Edward Allis of Wisconsin. Known as "Uncle Solon," the 58-year-old Chase, who briefly attended the U.S. Military Academy before being rejected for physical reasons, served in the Maine legislature as a Republican in the early 1860s and later published the *Greenback Labor Chronicle*. He single-handedly organized the Greenback Party in Maine—creating one of the party's most effective statewide organizations in the country. "Inflate the currency," he once said, "and you raise the price of my steers and at the same time pay the public debt. Resumption means falling prices and shrinkage of wages."[5] A wealthy manufacturer and patron of the arts, the cultured Allis had been the Greenback Party's candidate for governor of Wisconsin in 1877, garnering nearly fifteen percent of the vote. A native of upstate New York, the wealthy industrialist had started with a tannery and eventually built it into the Reliance Iron Works—the largest industrial plant in the country.

Amid rousing cheers, Chicago's Seymour F. Norton placed the name of Alexander Campbell, a former mine operator who had come "from the ranks of the people," in nomination. A sentimental favorite, the 65-year-old Campbell was described as having been "summoned by the immortal Lincoln to Washington to consult on the finances of the country" during the Civil War. Little-known Benjamin E. Woolf of New York, a 44-year-old London-born musician and drama

---

4.   Haynes, *Third Party Movements Since the Civil War*, p. 136.
5.   Ibid., p. 128.

critic, also briefly sought the nomination and there was talk of a possible "favorite-son" candidacy by Henly James, the longtime leader of the Indiana Grange. Placed in nomination by a delegate from Indiana, Woolf, speaking from the convention floor, withdrew from the contest shortly before the balloting began and heartily endorsed James B. Weaver of Iowa.

In the days leading up to the party's national convention, there was plenty of speculation that Ben Butler of Massachusetts might emerge as the party's presidential standard-bearer. Hoping for lightning to strike, Horace Binney Sargent, an honors graduate from Harvard and longtime leader of the Massachusetts Grand Army of the Republic, brought the Massachusetts delegation to Chicago firmly committed to the controversial Butler. More than a few other delegates, including California's Denis Kearney, the blustery leader of that state's Workingmen's Party, believed that with the former Union army general at the head of the ticket, the GLP could deny the Democrats and Republicans a majority in the Electoral College and throw the election into the House of Representatives, thereby forcing the two old parties, at a minimum, to make concessions to the insurgents. In a best-case scenario, they reasoned, Democratic lawmakers would overwhelmingly prefer their man to Republican James A. Garfield and—theoretically, at least—Butler could wind up as the nation's twentieth president. Though he was keenly aware of such speculation, the ex-general, who spent an estimated $275,000 of his own money in losing bids for governor of Massachusetts during the previous two years, apparently wasn't ready for another campaign—at least not in 1880. Butler, who was still licking his wounds from his back-to-back gubernatorial losses in 1878 and 1879, spent the better part of the year mending political fences back home and, much to the chagrin of the Greenback leadership, later endorsed Democrat Winfield Scott Hancock in the general election.

Despite a laundry list of candidates, the race eventually boiled down to a three-way contest between James B. Weaver of Iowa, Pennsylvania's Hendrick B. Wright and popular *Irish World* columnist Stephen D. Dillaye of New York, the presidential standard-bearer of the party's radical Union Greenback faction. The 47-year-old Weaver, an Iowa lawyer and Greenback congressman who had served in the Union army during the Civil War, rising spectacularly from private to lieutenant and finally to brigadier general before the end of the war, was generally regarded as the party's frontrunner.

With Butler remaining characteristically aloof, the 72-year-old Wright, publisher of the pro-labor *Anthracite Monitor*, emerged as Weaver's most serious challenger. A self-seeking philanthropist, Wright, then serving in his last term in Congress, annually distributed thousands of loaves of bread to his working-class constituency in northeast Pennsylvania. Considered a demagogue by his detractors, Wright had chaired the 1844 Democratic national convention in Baltimore and was a serious candidate for the party's vice-presidential nomination that year. Before joining the Greenback movement, the longtime Pennsylvania lawmaker had been a delegate at six of the seven succeeding Democratic national conventions. Originally elected to Congress in 1852, Wright had served in the U.S. House on four separate occasions, his last two terms (1877-81) as a member of the Greenback-Labor Party.

A frail, sixty-year-old Harvard-educated attorney and author, Dillaye had been nominated for president by a small majority at the National Union Greenback-Labor convention at the Masonic Hall in St. Louis in early March. Nearly 250 delegates from twenty states attended that convention, including such noteworthy figures as Patrick Ford of the *Irish World*, temporary chairman Lafayette Chesley of New Hampshire, former National Greenback gubernatorial candidate Hugo Preyer of Ohio, and Missouri's Ira S. Hazeltine. A former state representative, the 59-year-old Hazeltine was elected to Congress on a Greenback-Labor/Republican fusion ticket later that year. The St. Louis gathering also attracted Iowa's Horace A. Spencer, an old friend of James B. Weaver, and atheist writer and lecturer Kersey Graves, a prominent leader of the National Liberal Party in Indiana. Led by Marcus "Brick" Pomeroy and Ralph E. Hoyt of Indianapolis, the Union Greenback-Labor Party boasted more than 8,000 organized Greenback clubs across the country. They also claimed two million members—a figure apparently even more inflationary than their economic philosophy.[6]

James B. Weaver, whose name was placed in nomination by Iowa Congressman Edward H. Gillette, chairman of the committee on resolutions, was nominated on the first ballot, receiving 224 ½ votes to Wright's 126 ½ and 119 for the little-remembered Stephen D. Dillaye. Ninety-five delegates voted for Benjamin Butler, the former Union army officer from Massachusetts who enjoyed the enthusiastic support of California's Denis Kearney and Missouri's Joshua A. Bodenhamer, editor of the Carthage *People's Press*. Maine's Solon Chase—who was placed in nomination as "God's pillar of the soil, the farmer's friend"—was the choice of 89 delegates; Wisconsin's Allis received 41 votes; and twenty-one delegates voted for the beloved Alexander Campbell. Weaver's nomination was then made unanimous by acclamation.

---

6.   *New York Times*, March 5, 6, 1880; Lause, *The Civil War's Last Campaign*, pp. 49-50.

In a battle of ex-Confederates, 62-year-old Barzillai J. Chambers of Texas—often mistakenly referred to as "Benjamin" Chambers—defeated Mississippi's Absolom M. West by a margin of 403 to 311 on the first ballot to win the party's vice-presidential nomination. Like Weaver, Chambers' nomination was then made unanimous. Placed in nomination by Butler enthusiast Horace Binney Sargent of Massachusetts, the 62-year-old West had been elected to the U.S. House of Representatives as an anti-secessionist in 1865, but Congress refused to seat any of the elected members from the South that year, except in the case of those from Andrew Johnson's home state of Tennessee. As a member of the Greenback Party's platform committee, the chauvinistic West had irritated a number of radicals earlier in the convention's proceedings by his steadfast opposition to woman's suffrage, as well as his unsuccessful attempt to block a plank calling for an eight-hour workday. A former Union Whig member of the Mississippi legislature, West, a wealthy planter and former president of the Mississippi Central Railroad, reappeared on the national scene four years later as Ben Butler's vice-presidential running mate on the ill-fated Anti-Monopoly ticket.

The Chicago delegates approved a forward-looking platform calling for the issuance of greenbacks as full payment for the public debt and the abolition of the privately-owned national banking system. While opposing the Burlingame Treaty, which allowed for the importation of cheap Chinese labor, the party supported the enforcement of an eight-hour workday; the abolition of convict and child labor; the establishment of Bureau of Labor Statistics; a graduated income tax; and, at the insistence of socialist Peter J. McGuire, the convention adopted an SLP-inspired "land plank" and approved, by a vote of 528-125, a resolution declaring "that every citizen of due age, sound mind, and not a felon, be fully enfranchised"—referring the resolution to the respective states with a favorable recommendation. The party also placed a de-emphasis on the military and sharply criticized the "action of the old parties in fostering and sustaining gigantic land, railroad, and money corporations and monopolies" and in granting them powers that should rightfully belong to the government.[7]

Having secured the endorsement of the Socialistic Labor Party while absorbing the remnants of the National Liberal League and the short-lived Workingmen's Party of the United States, the Greenback-Labor ticket, representing a diverse agrarian and working-class constituency, was ideally positioned to mount a serious challenge to the country's two old and corrupt parties. Given the party's vast left-wing composition, it was of little surprise that Weaver's nomination was

---

7.   Haynes, *Third Party Movements Since the Civil War*, p. 137.

widely denounced in the mainstream press, the most vicious criticism of which emanated from the *New York Times*, a newspaper then solidly in the Republican camp. It was only fitting that this "assemblage of lunatics" should nominate an indefatigable "agitator and inflationist" like Weaver, intoned the *Times* shortly after Weaver received the Greenback-Labor nomination. "He is in favor of unlimited currency, a free division of all property, and a return to the primitive system of money under which anything is money which men agree to call by that name." Similar criticism was offered by most of the mainstream press. "A more biased evaluation of Weaver's political philosophy could scarcely have been offered to the American public," wrote historian Herbert Clancy. "Faced with a barrage of such propaganda, Weaver had about as much chance of winning the presidency in 1880 as a Chinaman had of receiving a royal welcome in California" that year.[8]

Born in Dayton, Ohio, in June 1833, Weaver was raised on farms in Ohio and Iowa. His family settled in rural Iowa when he was ten years old. Given his rural upbringing, he was understandably sympathetic to the plight of farmers during the post-Civil War period. An idealist with a quick mind, a persuasive speaking style and a love for public debate, the Iowa insurgent was tailor-made for a leadership role in the nation's budding agrarian movement that flourished between 1870 and the turn-of-the-century.

After establishing himself as a moderately successful attorney in Bloomfield, Iowa, Weaver entered politics when he was barely twenty-three years old. Having been drawn to the abolitionist movement after reading Harriet Beecher Stowe's classic, *Uncle Tom's Cabin*, as well as Horace Greeley's biting antislavery editorials in the *New York Tribune*, Weaver cut his political teeth in the newly-founded Republican Party by actively supporting John C. Fremont's candidacy in 1856.

Receiving a lieutenant's commission in the Union army shortly after enlisting, Weaver personally took part in the bloody battles of Fort Donelson and Shiloh. He also helped to quell sporadic pro-Confederate violence in his home state. After the war, he returned to his private law practice and soon discovered that his military record was a valuable political asset. He was elected district attorney of Iowa's second judicial district in 1866 and was appointed federal assessor of internal revenue by President Andrew Johnson the following year.

Despite his meteoric rise in state Republican politics—he was still in his early thirties—Weaver slowly grew disillusioned with the party of his youth. By temperament an activist, Weaver believed that the GOP was no longer the party of

---

8.   Herbert J. S. J. Clancy, *The Presidential Election of 1880* (Chicago, 1958), p. 164.

great men like Fremont and Lincoln. Like many other western agrarians, he felt that the Republican Party had abandoned farmers in favor of big business. Declining farm prices, high railroad rates and the federal government's deflationary currency policies were harming the nation's farmers. Land grants to railroads, he believed, were robbing farmers of their rightful share of the most productive public lands in the West.

Though unhappy with the general direction of the Republican Party, Weaver remained loyal to the GOP during his unsuccessful bid for his Congress in 1873. After losing the Republican nomination for governor two years later, the bearded ex-Civil War general grew increasingly disenchanted with his party, but nonetheless remained steadfastly loyal to the party of the Union and supported Republican Rutherford B. Hayes rather than Peter Cooper, the aging Greenback candidate, in the disputed 1876 presidential election. By the summer of 1877, however, Weaver concluded that it was "impossible" to remain within his party. Distressed by the federal troops sent to squash the striking railroad workers earlier that summer, the Bloomfield lawyer finally acknowledged, in an August letter, that he could no longer "remain silent and withhold my protest against what I consider to be a gigantic wrong. I shall act with the Independents."[9] As such, he campaigned successfully for Congress on the Greenback ticket in 1878, defeating incumbent Republican Ezekiel S. Sampson by more than 2,000 votes. During that campaign, Weaver called for an expanded and flexible national currency to inflate the declining incomes of his rural constituents. Some of his former allies, growing increasingly uncomfortable with his outspoken criticism of GOP policies, were probably relieved by Weaver's departure. One of the original thirteen Greenbackers elected to Congress in 1878, Weaver, who had an impeccable reputation and was considered one of the most honest politicians of that era, quickly distinguished himself in the U.S. House by working tirelessly to promote the Greenback Party's economic program.

In his July 3 letter of acceptance, Weaver said that the Greenback-Labor Party was poised "to strike a decisive blow for industrial emancipation." Describing the party's platform as "comprehensive, reasonable, and progressive," the former Republican lawmaker criticized the system of funding the public debt through the nation's banks as an idea "borrowed from the English monarchy" and said there was no excuse for funding those bonds, "except to perpetuate the debt as the basis of an iniquitous banking monopoly." It must be apparent to all, he continued, that "the great moneyed interests" were in complete control of the gov-

---

9.   Lause, *The Civil War's Last Campaign*, p. 36.

ernment and were "fast swallowing up the profits of labor and reducing the people to a condition of vassalage and dependence." He also denounced the donation of public lands to large corporations and urged the prohibition of "Chinese servile laborers." One of the party's grand missions was "to banish forever from American politics that deplorable spirit of sectional hatred," which, he added, was being fostered by the two old parties.[10] Grounding his campaign in the Democratic principles "of Jefferson and Jackson, and the pure Republicanism of Abraham Lincoln and Thaddeus Stevens," Weaver also urged a free ballot, "a fair count, and equal rights for all classes, for the laboring man in the Northern factories, mines, and workshops, and for the struggling poor, both black and white, in the cotton fields in the South."[11]

Barzillai Chambers, Weaver's vice-presidential running mate, was born in rural Kentucky and had enlisted in the Mexican War when he was twenty years old, serving as an aide-de-camp to his uncle. In 1839 he became a surveyor on the Texas frontier and worked in that capacity for eight years. As the elected district surveyor of the "Old Robertson Land District" in 1847, Chambers lived totally surrounded by Indians "with no actual white settlers" in the area, serving the new settlers as a surveyor, merchant, farmer, and private banker.[12] During this period, he also served on the board of alderman in Cleburne, Texas.

Perhaps influenced by Texas Sen. Louis Wigfall, one of Jefferson Davis' staunchest critics who argued incessantly for conscription, Chambers, who was hardly an ardent secessionist, made enemies in Richmond as an outspoken foe of the Confederate Exemption laws during the Civil War, which allowed wealthy southerners to buy their way out of the army by buying substitutes, thereby giving rise to the old adage: "A rich man's war but a poor man's fight." Among those exempted under Confederate law were state officials, railroad and river workers, some industrial laborers, telegraph operators, miners, hospital personnel, clergymen, teachers and apothecaries. The exemption laws also allowed the sons of those with more twenty slaves to avoid conscription. The South, as Pulitzer prize-winning author James M. McPherson noted, soon had more ministers than there were parishes and an abundance of apothecary shops with "a few empty jars, a cheap assortment of combs and brushes, a few bottles of 'hair-dye' and 'wizard oil' and other Yankee nostrums" popped up everywhere.[13]

---

10.   Haynes, *Third-Party Movements Since the Civil War*, pp. 138-140.
11.   Hesseltine, *Third-Party Movements in the United States*, pp. 142-145.
12.   Lause, *The Civil War's Last Campaign*, p. 50.
13.   Ibid., p. 50; McPherson, *Battle Cry of Freedom*, pp. 430-431.

During this period, Chambers became an admirer of Patrick Cleburne, an Irish-born Confederate general from Arkansas who, in 1864, took the unusual step of advocating emancipation of southern slaves who agreed to fight for the Confederacy. Following the war, Chambers, who was twice widowed, returned to farming and, enthusiastically embracing the Greenback cause, became a respected authority on economic matters. The former Confederate colonel first came to public attention in 1868 with a newspaper article critical of the country's interest-bearing national debt. Turning to politics, he ran unsuccessfully for the Texas legislature as a Democrat in 1876 and again as a Greenback candidate two years later. He also served on the executive committee of the Greenback Party's national committee and briefly published *The Chronicle*, a Cleburne-based Greenback newspaper. (The town of Cleburne, Texas, incidentally, was founded by Chambers and named for Patrick Cleburne.)

Chambers delivered only a few speeches during the 1880 campaign and those were under the auspices of the Socialistic Labor Party. One of those was in St. Louis a few weeks after the Chicago convention. Speaking at Tivoli Hall in that city, the former Confederate soldier described himself as "a farmer...in full sympathy with all the laboring element of the country." "We are a band of brothers," he told the wildly cheering radicals, "knowing no South, no North, no East and no West." Looking over the largely socialist crowd, he said that he was "satisfied that the Communists and Socialists were a body of men battling for human rights." Badly injured in a fall from a train platform in Texas the following Thursday, his active participation in the campaign was thereafter limited to writing letters to newspapers, including what one supporter described as exchanging "sledge-hammer blows" with the editor of the *Dallas Herald*. Though he seriously considered dropping out of the race since to do otherwise "would add no strength to the party," his friends urged him to stick it out. At least one opposition paper found humor in the vice-presidential candidate's misfortune. "We are sorry for the General," quipped the Mobile *Daily Register*, "but must remind him that his platform is a very rickety one to stand on."[14]

As the 1880 presidential election approached, a number of Stalwarts—those true-blue Republicans who were angered by President Hayes' decision to withdraw federal troops from the southern states, thereby enabling the Democrats to again take control of the South—scouted about for a candidate who could restore the party to its post-war glory days under Ulysses S. Grant. They didn't have to look too far. They soon found their man—ex-President Grant himself.

---

14.   Ibid., pp. 90-91, 193; *Mobile Daily Register*, July 17, 1880.

Returning from a leisurely three-year tour of Europe and Asia, the former President was greeted with honor and respect as huge crowds gathered to see the Hero of Appomattox. Newspaper accounts of his trip helped restore much of his popularity and the Stalwarts, led by the powerful Roscoe Conkling, New York's imperious political boss, were busy glossing over the ex-president's past blunders and lining up support for his unprecedented comeback.

Still a relatively young man at fifty-seven, Grant at first seemed reluctant to run but eventually yielded to pressure from family, friends and supporters. In New York, the Republican state convention pledged its support to the former two-term president and in Pennsylvania, J. Donald Cameron, son the aging Simon Cameron, put the entire delegation of the Keystone State in the Grant column. Likewise, Illinois Sen. John A. Logan was lining up his state's large GOP delegation for the former president.

Remembering that Grant had presided over a rogue's gallery of corruption during his two terms in office, not everyone—including the Hayes administration—was excited by the prospect of the ex-president's return to power and opposition leaders, clinging to the "No third term" argument, quickly rallied behind the candidacy of Ohio's John Sherman, brother of the famous General William Tecumseh Sherman and author of the Resumption Act. Others disenchanted with the idea of a Grant comeback threw their support to former Illinois Representative Elihu Washburne, who had served briefly as Grant's Secretary of State in 1869, and Sen. George F. Edmunds of Vermont. Minnesota's William Windom, who later resigned from the U.S. Senate to briefly serve as Garfield's Secretary of the Treasury before returning to that body, was also in the hunt, but was given almost no chance of success. The names of a number of favorite-son candidates were also floated about, including that of longtime congressman George F. Hoar of Massachusetts, who ended up chairing the party's national convention. But the only one with a realistic possibility of stopping Grant was James G. Blaine of Maine, but the former Speaker of the House remained aloof—a fact that hardly discouraged his loyal lieutenants from rounding up delegates on his behalf.

Despite a spirited effort to gloss over Grant's past mistakes, there were many in the GOP who were not reassured and continued to view the former president with scorn and often with downright contempt. They didn't buy the argument that the ex-president was now wiser and more experienced, or that he alone could atone for Hayes' obvious shortcomings by protecting African-Americans in the South and reviving Republicanism in that region. As such, his opponents organized "No third term" clubs throughout the country and, under the leadership of former Sen. John B. Henderson of Missouri, held a convention in St. Louis in May—less than a month before the Republican national convention in Chicago—to devise a strategy for stopping the Grant juggernaut.[15]

The Republican convention, which was held at Exposition Hall in Chicago a week before the Greenback-Labor Party assembled there, turned out to be a real free-for-all. Grant led in the early balloting, garnering 304 votes on the first ballot to 284 for the reluctant Blaine, 93 for Sherman, 34 for Edmunds, 30 for Washburne and ten for Minnesota's Windom. Actually, Grant, whose foreign travels had been chronicled in John Russell Young's best-selling book *Around the World with General Grant,* led on the first thirty-five ballots and came within 66 votes of becoming the only president in American history up 'til then to be nominated for an unprecedented third term. Grant's political comeback, however, was derailed when the Sherman and Blaine forces combined to settle the stalemate, rallying behind the dark-horse candidacy of James A. Garfield, a nine-term congressman from Ohio who served as the official spokesman for the convention's anti-Grant forces and who, in that role, used his considerable parliamentary skills to outmaneuver the Conkling forces in the selection of the convention's temporary and permanent chairmen. As chairman of the rules committee, the Ohio lawmaker had also introduced a rule allowing delegates to vote individually rather than as a unit—thereby dooming Grant's chances. Garfield was nominated on the thirty-sixth ballot. The Conkling forces stuck with Grant throughout the convention, giving the ex-President 306 votes on the final ballot to Garfield's 399 and 42 for Blaine. In a show of unity, the Garfield forces allowed Grant's New York backers to name the vice-presidential candidate. They suggested Chester A. Arthur, the deposed collector of the Port of New York. Dubbed the "Gentleman Boss" of that city's Republican Party, Arthur, who had never been elected to public office, easily defeated Elihu B. Washburne of Illinois on the convention's only ballot, garnering 463 votes to Washburne's 193 and a scattering of ninety for several favorite-son candidates.

The Republican platform that year was pretty much a repeat of the one approved in 1876. Undoubtedly influenced by growing anti-Chinese sentiment, the Republicans added a plank condemning the influx of Chinese immigration, but the issue of civil service reform, which had caused so much contention between the Hayes administration and the party's Stalwarts, wasn't even mentioned.

---

15. Roseboom, *A History of Presidential Elections,* pp. 253-254.

The Democrats, who hadn't won the White House since 1856, met in Cincinnati three weeks later and plucked General Winfield Scott Hancock of Pennsylvania from a crowded field of eighteen or nineteen candidates that included Delaware's Thomas F. Bayard, Allen G. Thurman of Ohio, Supreme Court Justice Stephen J. Field, former congressman Henry Payne of Ohio and Illinois Representative William R. Morrison. Hancock received 171 votes on the first ballot—less than one-quarter of the total. Bayard finished second with 153 votes with Payne, Thurman, Field, and Morrison, an ex-California gold miner who had been seriously wounded in the siege of Fort Donelson during the Civil War, running far behind. Hancock's vote increased to 320 on the second ballot before obliging delegates began switching their votes to him, giving him 705 votes—and the nomination.

Hancock knew little about public policy but had been regarded as a fair-minded military governor of Texas and Louisiana in 1868. A 56-year-old graduate of West Point, the Pennsylvania native saw action in the Mexican War and in the Kansas border skirmishes of the mid-1850s before entering the Civil War as a brigadier-general in the Union army. He had been widely praised for his role at Antietam and Gettysburg, where on the battle's second day he turned the fighting in the Union's favor. As early as 1868, the Democrats had considered Hancock as a serious presidential possibility. In fact, he had briefly taken the lead on the eighteenth ballot at the party's national convention that year before the delegates turned to veteran politician Horatio Seymour of New York. Hancock had also been a serious contender for the Democratic nomination in 1876, before ultimately losing to New York's Samuel J. Tilden. Unlike many ex-Union officers, Hancock was highly regarded in the South, largely as a result of his roles as military governor of Louisiana and Texas where, much to his credit, his relatively moderate policies contrasted sharply with the rather vindictive congressional mandates for that region.

The Democrats named William H. English, a wealthy banker and former congressman from Indiana, for the nation's second spot and adopted a platform condemning Chinese immigration and advocating civil service reform. The Democrats also sharply denounced the Republicans for their role in the "great fraud" of 1876—a reference to Hayes' disputed victory over Democrat Samuel Tilden, a man many people expected to be nominated again in 1880.

The Prohibitionists, meanwhile, met in Cleveland, Ohio, on June 17 and nominated Neal Dow of Maine for the presidency. One hundred and forty-two delegates from a dozen states took part in the proceedings. At the time of his nomination, Dow was vacillating on whether or not to make a complete break with the Republican Party. Like Garfield, Hancock and Weaver, Dow, too, had served as a general in the Union army during the Civil War. His vice-presidential running mate was Henry A. Thompson, president of Otterbein University in Ohio. The delegates restored the party's former name and adopted a platform consisting of thirteen planks, focusing almost exclusively on the liquor question.[16]

A little-known American Party also competed in the 1880 presidential campaign. This party nominated John Wolcott Phelps, a lanky and somewhat cranky former Union army general, for president and named former Senator Samuel C. Pomeroy of Kansas as his vice-presidential running mate. Pomeroy, who lost his seat in the U.S. Senate amid a scandal in 1872, did not actively campaign for the ticket. The party's platform included a plank that specifically called for the elimination of the Masonic Order. "Expose, withstand, and remove secret societies, Freemasonry in particular," it asserted, "and other anti-Christian movements, in order to save the churches of Christ from being depraved." This late nineteenth century anti-Masonic party also called for justice for American Indians and a tariff that would provide "equal protection to all classes of industry." Moreover, the tiny American Party agreed with the Prohibitionists on the liquor question and was in general agreement with the Greenback-Labor Party on the issues of currency reform and land monopolies.[17]

A one-time abolitionist, the bearded, 67-year-old Phelps was the author of several books. According to his biographer, he was also convinced "that the Masonic Lodge was the cause of many of the country's evils."[18] A graduate of the U.S. Military Academy, Phelps saw action against the Creeks and Seminoles and fought bravely in the Mexican War. At the outbreak of the Civil War, he served as commander of Vermont's first regiment and was later promoted to the rank of brigadier-general, gallantly leading the force that captured Newport News and commanding the expedition that seized Ship Island, Mississippi, proving vital to the Union army's capture of New Orleans.

Phelps abhorred slavery and had a fierce dislike for the wealthy southerners who owned them. With the same sort of zeal that motivated John Brown at

---

16. *Cleveland Leader*, June 18, 1880; *New York Times*, June 18, 1880.
17. Clancy, *The Presidential Election of 1880*, pp. 165-166; *Appleton's Annual Cyclopaedia and Register of Important Events of the Year 1880* (New York 1881), Vol. V, p. 697; Robert Morris, *William Morgan; or, Political Anti-Masonry: Its Rise, Growth and Decadence* (New York, 1883), pp. 373-374.
18. Cecil H. C. Howard, *Life and Public Services of Gen. John Wolcott Phelps* (Brattleboro, 1887), p. 36.

Harper's Ferry, Phelps actively sought to liberate slaves during the war, ordering his men to undertake numerous raids on southern plantations and carry any slaves found back to the safety of their federal camps. Inaugurating his own emancipation proclamation of sorts, he also took it upon himself to raise and train several companies of fugitive slaves and envisioned dispatching them into active combat duty. Phelps was an excellent, if not somewhat fanatical, commander and was widely liked by his troops—black as well as white—and had few equals as a drillmaster, competently barking out orders in his high-pitched, shrill voice to as many as five regiments at once. Unlike other Union generals in the South who preferred to live in abandoned mansions, the austere Phelps considered his tent quite sufficient and if former slaveholders seeking the return of their slaves found his closed quarters unbearably hot or too crowded, the better. A man of unwavering principle and conviction, he never once returned a slave who had come to him seeking refuge, despite countless pleas from their former owners.[19]

Under the command of the ubiquitous Benjamin F. Butler, Phelps was with Captain David Farragut's fleet when it broke through the Lower Mississippi and captured New Orleans in the spring of 1862. While performing garrison duty at Camp Parapet in Carrolton, about seven miles northeast of New Orleans, Phelps, having successfully recruited five regiments of about three hundred African-American "contrabands"—fugitives who had escaped slavery and sought refuge in Union camps—asked Butler, his commanding officer, for arms, saying that it was his hope to raise three black regiments for defense of his position, which was then viewed as vulnerable. It wasn't necessarily an outlandish request, especially considering the fact that his men were dying at the rate of two to three a day. When Butler, refusing to provide arms, directed the grizzled army officer to employ the ex-slaves in clearing trees and brush away from the area in front of his line of defense, Phelps was livid, telling Butler that he wasn't "willing to become a slave driver" and threatened to tender his resignation. "Phelps has gone crazy," Butler told his superiors. "He is as mad as a March Hare on the 'nigger question.'" Butler tried to calm the agitated general, but to no avail. In the end, Phelps resigned his commission and returned to his farm in Brattleboro, Vermont, not long before he was branded an outlaw by the Confederacy.[20]

Back in Vermont, Phelps resumed his one-man crusade against the Masons with the same ferocity that he displayed toward the slaveholders. He enthusiasti-

---

19.   Richard S. West, Jr., *Lincoln's Scapegoat General: A Life of Benjamin F. Butler 1818-1893* (Boston, 1965), p. 176.

20.   Nolan, *Benjamin Franklin Butler: The Damnedest Yankee*, pp. 194-198; West, *Lincoln's Scapegoat General*, p. 180.

cally accepted the American Party's presidential nomination in 1880, saying that he was proud to carry the party's banner "whether accompanied by a few or many." He urged the North and South to unite in opposition to the Masons, an organization he denounced as "an English device of a barbarous age." The American Party standard-bearer, who had been an ardent anti-slavery advocate, also claimed that the Masons were a more insidious danger to the Republic than the so-called "slave power" had ever been—and that was a mouthful for someone who despised slavery as much as he did.

Phelps and Pomeroy received votes under four separate party designations that year—"Anti-Masonic" in California, Illinois and Pennsylvania; "Anti-Secret" in Kansas; "National American" in Michigan; and "American" in Rhode Island and Wisconsin.

As promised in his letter of acceptance in July, James B. Weaver, the Greenback-Labor Party's standard-bearer, waged a vigorous campaign, traveling some 20,000 miles from Arkansas to the northeastern corner of Maine and from Lake Michigan to Mobile, Alabama. One of the hardest working candidates in American history and the first to take his campaign directly to the people, the former Iowa congressman gave more than 100 speeches, shook hands with an estimated 30,000 people and routinely drew crowds ranging from 3,000 to as many as 30,000, including large rallies at Boston's famous Faneuil Hall in early September and at Cooper Union in New York City later in the month. Despite a heroic effort, his candidacy was virtually blacked-out by the mainstream press. As Haynes pointed out, it was as though there was "a conspiracy of silence on the part of the newspapers of the old parties." The GLP standard-bearer was also the target of dirty tricks, including a forged letter that appeared in the *New York Star* claiming that he was in the pay of the national Republican Party—a charge that was sharply refuted by *The Weekly Iowa State Register*, a Republican newspaper.[21]

While acknowledging that his candidacy would hurt the Democrats in some regions of the country, Weaver denied that his effort was aimed at punishing one party more than the other. "My candidacy is the severest stab the Republican Party ever received," he said in September while campaigning in upstate New York, "and it also damages the Democrats. I do not care a fig which suffers the most from it."[22]

For Weaver and the Greenback-Labor Party the road to the White House seemed to wind through Alabama, Maine, Arkansas, Indiana, Colorado, West

---

21. Haynes, *Third-Party Movements Since the Civil War*, pp. 140-141.
22. Lause, *The Civil War's Last Campaign*, p. 147.

Virginia and Ohio. The tiny Greenback-Labor Party in Alabama—never a strong Greenback state—took part state elections in August, while Maine and Arkansas voters would go to the polls in September and those in Indiana, Colorado, West Virginia and Ohio would cast ballots in October. The best chance—perhaps the *only* chance—for a strong Greenback-Labor turnout in November was to build momentum in some of the earlier contests. As such, Weaver barnstormed through Alabama, the first state to vote, stumping in Scottsboro, Huntsville, Courtland and Birmingham during the second week of July before sneaking back to Iowa for a brief weekend of rest and relaxation. Returning to Alabama a few days later, Weaver was attacked by the Democratic newspapers in the state as a Republican "in disguise"—and worse.

Angered by reports that local Democratic election officials in the South had uniformly "counted out" votes for Greenback candidates in the past, Weaver adopted a new stump speech, one that overshadowed the issue of currency reform. This was a national issue, he warned, for "if you strike down a free ballot in Alabama, you strike it down in Iowa and New York, and in every other state in the Union as well," adding that he would rather be shot right then and there than "fail to warn my countrymen of the danger that threatens our free institutions in Alabama or elsewhere."[23] Despite Weaver's concerted efforts in the heart of Dixie, the Democrats piled up a record vote—and a questionable one, at that—as Democratic Gov. Rufus W. Cobb slaughtered the Reverend James M. Pickens, the Greenback Party's gubernatorial hopeful, by a margin of 134,905 to 42,363. Weaver and other Greenback leaders were convinced that there had been massive vote fraud in Alabama. Pointing out that Pickens had the Greenback-Labor nomination, the Republican endorsement and the support of many disaffected Democrats, Weaver lamented that no one's vote in Alabama was worth anything unless he is a Democrat. "The thing is absurd," he fumed, and "a terrible outrage on the civilization of the age."[24]

Discouraged by the events in Alabama but not willing to give up entirely on the South, Weaver headed to Arkansas next where at a rally in southwestern Nevada County he was introduced by GLP gubernatorial candidate W. P. Parks, an ex-Confederate soldier who had lost a leg in the battle of Shiloh—the same

23. Ibid., pp. 94-97.
24. Ibid., pp. 105-107. The margin of victory for Cobbs was greater than the total turn-out in the previous year's hotly contested election and even some Democratic newspapers winced when they reported the obviously padded returns. Disgusted by the alleged Democratic vote tampering, one Alabamian complained that southerners now lived "under a despotism more dreadful than the Russian autocracy."

battle Weaver had fought in. "The boys in gray are with you in Arkansas, and we are fighting for freedom and the flag in Arkansas," said the one-legged veteran. "We know now that the war was the rich man's war and the poor man's fight." Deeply moved, Weaver gave one of his best speeches of the campaign, telling the audience of nearly 10,000 that the Greenback-Labor Party's convention in Chicago had dug "a grave across the Mason and Dixon's line. In that grave we put a coffin," he said. "In that coffin we put the bloody shirt and the war issues, and covered it over gently…We buried it there forever." As proof that it meant business, Weaver reminded the audience that the Greenback-Labor Party was the first party since the war to nominate a former Yankee solider and a former Confederate solider on the same ticket.[25]

Despite spending two weeks in the state, the Arkansas Greenback-Labor Party remained moribund—indeed, it was trounced in the September election and delivered a negligible 4,079 votes for Weaver in November. Things looked even worse in other parts of the South, especially in Mississippi where threats of violence against the insurgents were occasionally carried out, as was the case of a Greenback candidate for sheriff of Yalobusha County, who was gunned down in the streets of Coffeeville in broad daylight. Things got even uglier later in the campaign when the nephew of former Confederate Brigadier-General Absolom M. West, the Greenback Party's candidate for the U.S. Senate, was murdered by Bourbon assailants who also shot the editor of the *Holmes County Times*, a local newspaper sympathetic to the insurgent movement.[26] Violence aside, one-party Mississippi had always been a difficult place for the Greenbackers. In an earlier campaign, authorities there had arbitrarily invalidated Greenback ballots because the Goddess of Liberty had been printed on the reverse side of the party's official ballot. Originally planning to campaign in Mississippi, Georgia, Missouri and Texas, Weaver abandoned his southern strategy altogether and focused his attention in the following weeks in the northeast, particularly in the widely-watched governor's race in Maine, where voters were scheduled to go to the polls on September 13.

Maine got its first taste of Greenback-style politics shortly after news of the Resumption Act reached the state in 1875, when old Solon Chase—one of the most colorful characters in the movement—dressed in coarse clothing and his customary white hat, crisscrossed the state telling voters how the redemption of the nation's paper money at face value in gold would adversely affect the value of

25.   Ibid., pp. 113-114.
26.   Ibid., pp. 205-206.

their steers, colts, hogs and other livestock. Not many paid attention to Chase at first as the Greenback Party garnered fewer than 600 votes in the September 1876 election, but within two years the Greenback Party, garnering about one-third of the votes cast, sent two members to Congress—Thompson Murch and George W. Ladd—and attained a balance of power in the state legislature, while nearly capturing the governor's office. A grassroots organization virtually unparalleled anywhere else in the country, the Greenback-Labor movement in Maine struck fear in the dominant Republicans and inspired the long-dormant Democrats, who had been out of power for more than a quarter century, to seek fusion with the insurgents.

In 1879, the Greenback gubernatorial candidate polled nearly 35% of the vote—about 21,000 votes behind the successful Republican candidate and more than 26,000 votes ahead of incumbent Democrat Alonzo Garcelon—in a race that remained in dispute for several weeks before the state Supreme Court ultimately decided in favor of the Republicans in mid-January 1880. After that bitter experience, the Democrats—whose candidate had briefly seized the statehouse with about a hundred armed men in the aftermath of the bitter 1879 election—were anxious to take part in a fusion effort with the insurgents. But not all of the Greenbackers favored such a marriage. "For twenty years," complained one Greenbacker, "a set of silk stocking lawyers have led the Democratic Party of this state to the slaughter" and now they were attempting to carry their craft into the Greenback-Labor Party by promising to bankroll the joint "Union" ticket and saturating the state with Democratic speakers in an effort "to steal the Greenback-Labor Party, bag and baggage."

Despite spirited efforts by the fiery Solon Chase, who didn't want to see "five years of hard work being wiped out as with a sponge," and other party members who were adamantly opposed to fusion, the Greenback-Labor Party's state committee, meeting in Bangor in June, endorsed cooperation with the Democrats on a "Union" fusion ticket headed by gubernatorial candidate Harris M. Plaisted, a former state legislator and one-time Union army officer.[27] The Democrats also tried to extend the fusion arrangement to the presidential campaign in November, but most of the state's Greenbackers balked, keenly aware that Weaver had no interest in sharing electors with Hancock in Maine or anywhere else.

As it was, fusion with the Democrats in the September state elections came with a heavy price as several leading insurgents—mostly ex-Republicans—returned to their former party. Among those disgusted by the Democratic-

---

27.   Ibid., pp. 137-138.

Greenback Labor alliance was the party's state chairman, E. H. Gove, who almost immediately announced his support for Garfield in the presidential election.

With far more cash than the financially-strapped Greenbackers, the Democrats, who had promised to raise a $50,000 war chest for the fusion ticket, were the dominant partner in the so-called "Union" campaign, financing tours of the state by such leading insurgents as Ben Butler of Massachusetts, Samuel F. Cary of Ohio, and New Haven *Union* editor Alexander Troup of Connecticut, all of whom had close ties with the Greenback-Labor Party—and each of whom, to Weaver's bewilderment, endorsed Democrat Winfield Scott Hancock in that year's presidential contest.[28]

Though staunchly opposed to fusion, Weaver, like Chase, personally thought highly of Plaisted—he actually considered him "a straight out Green-backer"—and threw his support to the Union ticket. Plaisted's success, he declared, "will be a solid Greenback victory, wholly without Democratic significance."[29] As in Alabama and Arkansas, Weaver, beginning his tour of the state at a grand torchlight procession in Lewistown on August 30, again conducted a whirlwind campaign, stumping for Plaisted and other Greenback-Labor (Union) candidates throughout the Pine State. Although campaigning for the fusion ticket, Weaver, who was usually hissed and booed by Democrats in the audience, pulled no punches when it came to criticizing the Democrats, denouncing the party's apparent electoral fraud in Alabama and southern "bulldozing" in general. Scoffing at any fusion "half horse and half alligator," Weaver insisted that there shouldn't be any "fusion between two parties diametrically opposed to each just for the purpose of electing somebody."[30] As such, he refused to share the platform with Hancock's supporters and even boycotted a much-publicized "Union" campaign rally at Bangor on September 4 that featured Benjamin Butler and other prominent Democratic speakers. Pursuing his own agenda, Weaver campaigned vigorously in Augusta, Ellsworth and Belfast, where in the latter town he encountered one of the most enthusiastic receptions of the entire campaign, including an overflow crowd of at least 1,500 who turned out to hear him speak

---

28. Under Troup's leadership, the Greenback-Labor Party of Connecticut had forced the state's generally conservative Democratic Party to seek fusion with the insurgents in 1878, prompting a group of disgusted Democrats associated with Yale University to consider running a rival ticket that year. See *New York Times*, October 14, 1878; Unger, *The Greenback Era*, p. 379.

29. Lause, *The Civil War's Last Campaign*, p. 138.

30. Ibid., p. 146.

at Hayford Hall—a speech that, according to Plaisted, ultimately determined the outcome of the gubernatorial race.[31]

While in New England, Weaver also stumped in Vermont, Massachusetts and Connecticut, where the relatively conservative Alexander Troup and his influential New Haven *Union* had turned its back on the Greenback cause shortly after party leaders in that state adopted several radical measures that had been rejected at the party's national convention in Chicago, including a Socialist Labor Party-inspired "land plank," sanctions against usury, a graduated income tax and other left-wing measures. Following a rally in New Haven, Weaver hurried back to Maine to assist Plaisted in his stretch run before heading to New York.

Weaver learned of Plaisted's victory while campaigning in Albany, New York, where a local Workingmen's Party formed the nucleus of the local Greenback-Labor Party.[32] Speaking to reporters the following day, Weaver, while conceding that the Democrats contributed to the victory, insisted that the results in Maine were "a genuine, straight out Greenback victory"—and nothing less. He also categorically denied an Associated Press story that the newly elected governor planned to stump for Hancock.[33]

Plaisted's razor-thin victory in Maine was the high point of the Weaver campaign. Thereafter, the former Iowa congressman was forced to circle the wagons, hoping for a strong GLP showing in Illinois, Kansas, Michigan, Missouri, Wisconsin, and, of course, his native Iowa. He spent the final weeks of the campaign stumping in Indiana, Illinois, and Iowa. Accompanied by his fourteen-year-old son, Weaver barnstormed through Indiana, drawing crowds ranging from 1,800 to an estimated 30,000 in Terre Haute.[34]

---

31. Ibid., pp. 145-146.
32. Plaisted defeated incumbent Gov. Daniel F. Davis by the slimmest of margins, garnering 73,713 votes to the Republican's 73,544. In addition, the Greenback-Labor Party's Thompson H. Murch and George W. Ladd, running on fusion tickets, were re-elected to Congress, but the party was disappointed when Frank M. Fogg of Auburn, the radical editor of the *Greenback Labor Chronicle* and the man who had hired Victoria Woodhull's ex-husband to write for that paper, was narrowly defeated in his bid for a seat in the U.S. House from the state's second congressional district. The party also suffered a heartbreaking loss in the neighboring third congressional district when party member William Philbrick, waging his second campaign for Congress, fell 467 votes short of unseating Republican lawmaker Stephen D. Lindsey.
33. Lause, *The Civil War's Last Campaign*, pp. 151-152; *Elmira Sunday Morning Telegram*, Sept. 19, 1880.

Remaining adamantly opposed to fusion, the Greenback-Labor standard-bearer told voters in Aurora, Illinois, that he would "suffer my right arm to wither before I will help to take the Greenbackers into the camps of either of these old parties." Denouncing Democrats and Republicans alike, the Iowa congressman said that if he could destroy the Democratic Party he would do so "in an instant." He felt no less strongly about the GOP. "God knows if I could blow the Republican Party and its leadership to perdition I would put a ton of dynamite under them and touch it off." The two major parties, he said, were so similar on the great economic issues facing the country that a "Lowell shoemaker can't make a bristle stiff enough to run between them." He also accused the two major parties of disenfranchising hundreds of thousands of voters through "bulldozing" and restoration of the poll tax, charging that the latter measure had disenfranchised 70,000 voters in Virginia and as many as 120,000 in Massachusetts. When a war breaks out, he observed, these same citizens are the first ones expected to serve in the army. "Wars are always the poor man's fight, you know, and the rich man profits by their blood every time—every time, but when it comes to saying there shall be justice between capital and labor in this country they strike down a poor man and call him an infamous tramp. I say that is subversive of the principles of American liberty, and the country cannot stand long that will endure it." He also spoke out in favor of woman's suffrage, saying that it was wrong for a nation to disenfranchise at least fifty percent of its population, "and that confessedly the better half, our wives and our daughters."[35]

In early October, Weaver also had to fend off charges that he and his fellow Greenback-Laborites had been conspiring with the Republicans for months. It was, as historian Mark Lause pointed out, "a well-engineered, last minute scandal"—and one that undoubtedly proved costly for the Greenback Labor standard-bearer. The charges, which were made by Dyer D. Lum, assistant secretary of the Greenback National Committee and a recent convert to the Socialist Labor Party, were splashed on the front pages of Democratic newspapers throughout the country. In a letter to Greenback-Labor congressman Thompson Murch of Maine on October 1, Dyer announced his resignation from the campaign, contending that the Greenback-Labor Party's campaign had been "manipulated in the interest of the Republican Party" and that Weaver's campaign expenses were being borne in large measure by the Republican National Committee.[36]

34. Frederick Emory Haynes, *James Baird Weaver* (Iowa City, 1919, reprint 1975), p. 167.

35. Lause, *The Civil War's Last Campaign*, pp. 193-198.

A former congressional clerk for Pennsylvania House member Henrick Wright's Select Committee on the Depression of Labor, the 40-year-old Lum, a Union army combat veteran and political columnist for the *Irish World*, was a former member of the Massachusetts Labor Reform Party and had been the Greenback-Labor Party's candidate for lieutenant governor of Massachusetts on a ticket headed by Wendell Phillips in 1877. Among other things, Lum charged that George O. Jones, chief fundraiser for the Greenback-Labor campaign, had been delivering Greenback members of Congress to the Republicans on a per capita basis and had allegedly accepted $5,000 from the Garfield campaign. He also accused Weaver of taking $900 to $1,000 from Jones while campaigning in Alabama and several hundred dollars while stumping in Arkansas and that the Greenback-Labor standard-bearer was specifically paid by the Republicans to "denounce fusion in Maine." Though Lum's allegations "reeked of 90-proof Alabama Bourbon," as Lause so delightfully put it, a number of insurgents who had already split from the Greenback-Labor Party seized upon Lum's allegations as justification for their defections. Among them was Alexander Troup of the *New Haven Union* who declared that he now had "the clearest evidence that could be desired" of Weaver's true intent. Stephen D. Dillaye of New York, who had been defeated at the Greenback-Labor convention in Chicago, joined the chorus, calling Weaver "a traitor" and complaining to Lum that almost every Greenback newspaper in the country edited by a former Republican was "full of abuse of Hancock," while steadfastly opposing almost every attempt at fusion between the Democrats and the Greenbackers.[37]

The Republicans, of course, had little to say about these charges other than to denounce them as "absurd and ridiculous." They realized that the growing rift between the Democrats and the Greenback-Labor Party could only help to benefit their candidate, likely winning few converts to Hancock and driving at least as many insurgents into the Garfield campaign. The insurgents, on the other hand, had plenty to say. Seymour F. Norton's *Chicago Express*, which referred to Lum as "a characterless adventurer," sharply denounced the allegations and George O. Jones, the party's chief fundraiser, described Lum as "a drunken little loafer" and called his charges "a blackmailing job," adding that Lum had intimated that the whole story might be stopped for a certain price. While admitting that Jones had given him several hundred dollars to help defray his campaign expenses, Weaver

---

36.   Ibid., p. 185; Haynes, *James Baird Weaver*, pp. 167-168; *New York Herald*, Oct. 2, 1880; *New York Tribune*, Oct. 2, 1880.

37.   Ibid., pp. 185-188.

called the charges "base, treacherous, and false in all of its essential features" and to prove his point released a detail accounting of his campaign's expenses, proving beyond a doubt that the large sums of money Lum had spoken about clearly never passed through the coffers of the Greenback-Labor Party's presidential campaign. The third-party candidate also asserted that he had "never requested, either directly or indirectly, personally or through another, contributions from the Republican committee, its agents or friends; nor have I the promise or hope of receiving any money from such source." He also reminded voters that he had been equally critical of both major parties throughout the campaign. "I am making an open fight for the integrity of my party and the welfare of the people against both the old rotten organizations," he declared."[38]

Lum's real motives in 1880 have never been clearly delineated. A fascinating yet somewhat erratic figure on the fringe of American politics, Lum had once written extensively for the *Banner of Light*, a spiritualist newspaper, and was among those who endorsed Victoria Woodhull's call for an Equal Rights Party in 1872 before dabbling in Buddhism and plunging more deeply into the eight-hour and labor reform movements, culminating, subsequently, in the ranks of the Greenback-Labor Party. Like most others attracted to the Greenback-Labor movement, Lum, who had twice been captured by the Confederates during the Civil War, was highly critical of both major parties, believing the Republicans to be "the party of nascent imperialism" and denouncing the Democrats as a party wholly "without principle, without leadership, without aim, save in the all-absorbing one of the spoils." In 1879, Lum, writing under the pseudonym of "Gurth," accepted an assignment as the Washington correspondent of the *Irish World*. He also churned out articles for *Evolution*, a liberal monthly, as well as individualist anarchist Benjamin R. Tucker's *Radical Review*, frequently writing about labor, financial, and land reform issues, as well as third-party politics.[39]

A descendant of abolitionists Lewis and Arthur Tappan, Lum was not completely satisfied with the reformist aims of the Greenback movement and joined the more revolutionary-minded Socialist Labor Party during the summer of 1880. (Ironically, he joined the Socialist Labor Party out of disgust with Weaver's

---

38. Ibid., pp. 187-191; Haynes, *James Baird Weaver*, pp. 169-170. Weaver reported that he had received a total of $1,695 for the campaign, $800 of which had been provided by Jones. Of that total, Weaver contributed $570 to help pay expenses incurred by Greenback-Labor organizations in various states. The remaining $1,125, he said, went toward paying his own expenses—and even that amount fell short of his actual expenditures.

39. Ibid., pp. 191-193; *Irish World*, May 8, 25, 1878; Jan. 10, April 3, June 19, 1880.

candidacy at precisely the same moment that a number of SLPers were leaving that Marxist party due to their dissatisfaction with the party's support of the Greenback-Labor presidential standard-bearer.) Prior to joining the SLP, Lum, as secretary of the Greenback-Labor Party's credentials committee, fought hard to have members of the Socialist Labor Party accepted as delegates to the party's national convention in Chicago. Despite the SLP's endorsement of Weaver's candidacy, there's little question that Lum was personally disappointed in the Iowa lawmaker's nomination that year, believing that the party was more interested in immediate electoral success than in promoting its radical economic principles.[40]

Curiously, Lum spent part of the ensuing autumn researching Democratic presidential candidate Winfield Scott Hancock's role in the investigation of Lincoln's assassination and, in the course of his research, apparently visited and interviewed the family of Mary Surratt, one of the conspirators sentenced to death for her alleged role in Lincoln's murder. Many people in the South felt that Surratt, who was hanged on July 7, 1865, had been unfairly tried and convicted—and certainly didn't deserve to be put to death. According to Washington lawyer Warwick Martin, a member of the Greenback-Labor Party's national committee, Lum hoped to publish an article in the *Irish World* detailing Hancock's presumably sinister involvement in Surratt's death—the first woman in American history to be executed—in an attempt to embarrass the Democratic standard-bearer in the South, the Democratic Party's strongest region. When the *Irish World* refused to run the story, Martin further speculated that Lum might have tried to peddle his potentially damaging article to Republican newspapers, but they, too, apparently had little interest in publishing it.[41]

Frustrated with spiritualism and the labor reform movement, the one-time bookbinder later became ensconced in the anarchist movement, joining the International Working People's Association and working closely with Albert Parsons and other leading radicals. He later played an important role in defending the Haymarket Square martyrs. As editor of *The Alarm*, a Chicago-based anarchist publication with a large following among German anarchists sympathetic to notorious revolutionary Johann Most—the brilliant editor and speaker and unquestionably the leading anarchist in the United States—Lum also worked feverishly to unite the individualistic and native-born "Boston anarchists" with the more radical and predominately immigrant and collectivist "Chicago anar-

---

40.   *Irish World*, June 26, July 3, 1880; Lum letter to Terence V. Powderly, Sept. 15, 1880, Powderly Papers, Catholic University, Washington, D.C.
41.   Lause, *The Civil War's Last Campaign*, p. 189.

chists" during the heady days of labor unrest in the mid-1880s through the disintegration of the anarchist movement in the early 1890s, but with little success. During this period, he also fell in love with libertarian writer Voltairine de Cleyre, one of the most neglected figures in American radicalism and with whom he carried on a long-distance relationship until his death in 1893. Lum later worked as a writer for the American Federation of Labor (AFL) where he occasionally attacked the same radicals he had once tried to mobilize. From time to time, he also tried to revive anarchism by stirring things up, including getting involved in several bomb plots and applauding young anarchist Alexander Berkman's attempt to assassinate Henry Clay Frick, the hard-driving manager of Andrew Carnegie's Homestead steel plant and an implacable enemy of labor unions. Speaking at a rally in New York City in defense of Berkman, the longtime anarchist and agitator said that "the lesson for capitalists to learn is that workingmen are now so desperate that they not only make up their minds to die, but decide to take such men as Frick to St. Peter's gate with them."[42] Frustrated and increasingly despondent by his unsuccessful attempts to revive anarchism in the aftermath of a massive government crackdown on radicals, the lonely and financially destitute anarchist and one-time Greenbacker, having grown steadily dependent on alcohol and opium, died of a drug overdose in New York's Bowery the following spring.

Widely publicized by Democratic newspapers, Lum's charges, whether true or not, had a devastating effect on Weaver's candidacy as contributions to the Greenback-Labor campaign virtually dried up following the allegations. Seymour F. Norton's *Chicago Express*, for instance, reported contributions of only $105.05 following the false disclosures, compared to some $1,700 raised for the campaign prior to Lum's damaging charges.[43]

While barely having time to refute Lum's charges, Weaver was again put on the defensive with the publication of a forged letter, purportedly to have been written by him to Greenback Congressman Edward H. Gillette in early September. In the bogus letter, which was published by the *New York Star* in late October, Weaver supposedly indicated that since most Greenbackers would probably return to the Republican Party, the GLP's only chance for success in the election would be to siphon votes from the Democratic ticket in the remote hope of throwing the presidential contest into the House of Representatives "where our chances would all be equal." The handwriting on the letter didn't even remotely

---

42. *New York Times*, Aug. 2, 1892.
43. Lause, *The Civil War's Last Campaign*, p. 193.

match that of Weaver's, but that didn't prevent mischievous Democratic newspapers from giving the story wide circulation. Apparently concocted by Democrats who were embittered by Weaver's refusal to take part in fusion campaigns with their party in Maine and elsewhere, the letter was immediately denounced by the candidate as an obvious forgery—an assertion corroborated by Gillette, who emphatically denied that he had ever received such a letter.[44]

The election returns from Ohio, West Virginia, and Indiana in October further dampened Weaver's prospects of making a strong showing against the entrenched establishment parties. In West Virginia, where the party picked up several seats in the state legislature, GLP gubernatorial candidate Napoleon B. French finished a distant third, polling roughly eleven percent of the vote, and in Indiana, the party's birthplace and a state where Weaver expended a great deal of time and energy, all eleven Greenback-Labor candidates for the U.S. House of Representatives went down to humiliating defeat, including incumbent GLP lawmaker Gilbert De La Matyr. One of the party's most powerful speakers, the longtime Methodist minister, who had been sharply denounced as a dangerous radical, polled less than six percent of the vote in Indiana's seventh congressional district. Moreover, Richard Gregg, the party's gubernatorial candidate, garnered a disappointing 14,881 votes, or barely three percent of the total, against Republican Albert Gallatin Porter and Democrat Franklin Landers in a race decided by fewer than 7,000 votes.[45]

If things weren't already bad enough, Weaver's candidacy was also hampered by a number of major defections from the Greenback-Labor Party. Among those who abandoned the party and supported the Democrats that year were such leading insurgents as Samuel F. Cary, the party's vice-presidential candidate in 1876, Benjamin F. Butler of Massachusetts, Alexander Troup, publisher of the *New Haven Union*, and the sagacious and splendidly colorful Ignatius Donnelly of Minnesota. Blanton Duncan, the brilliant, eccentric and somewhat mysterious Kentuckian, also supported the Democratic ticket, as did Pennsylvania congressman Hendrick B. Wright and Marcus M. "Brick" Pomeroy, the controversial publisher and mover and shaker in the Union Greenback clubs. New York Union Greenback club chairman Uri Mulford, a Methodist Episcopal minister, also endorsed Hancock late in the campaign, asserting that Garfield and the other Republican "authors of the prevailing debt nursing and labor-crushing financial

---

44. Haynes, *James Baird Weaver*, pp. 170-171.
45. De La Matyr, who stumped vigorously for Weaver during the autumn campaign, garnered only 2,135 votes, or less than six percent of the total, to Republican Stanton J. Peelle's 17,610 and Democrat Casabianca Byfield's 16,806.

system will feel our blows."[46] Moreover, rumors that Peter Cooper, the Greenback Party's aging and beloved presidential standard-bearer four years earlier, had also defected were strongly denied by the GLP's leadership.

Despite these defections, a number of leading insurgents rallied to Weaver's side, campaigning arduously for the Greenback-Labor ticket. Among those who stood by their party's standard-bearer in the waning weeks of the campaign were such outstanding Greenback leaders as Col. Seymour F. Norton, Rep. Gilbert De La Matyr of Indiana, Absolom M. West of Mississippi and Ralph E. Hoyt, the tireless leader of the Union Greenback Clubs who refused to follow Brick Pomeroy in supporting the Democratic nominee.[47] Even Stephen D. Dillaye, Weaver's leading opponent in Chicago, experienced a change of heart and retracted his earlier support of the charges made by Lum.[48]

During the autumn campaign, Garfield and the Republicans benefited enormously from Hancock's glaring lack of political experience. The Democratic standard-bearer was roundly criticized for suggesting that the tariff question was a local matter—although in the context in which he made it he wasn't entirely incorrect. *Harper's Weekly*, among others, belittled his statement as aimless, unintelligent and absurd. The Republicans then leveled a charge that bordered on the edge of the ridiculous, if not over the edge, when they asserted that Hancock's son had married a rebel sympathizer. It was a ludicrous campaign smear—Hancock's loyalty to the Union was never in question. On a lighter note, the Republicans also issued an outrageously humorous pamphlet on Hancock's record of "Statesmanship and Political Achievements" that contained seven blank pages. It wasn't entirely off the mark. On national issues, Hancock appeared to be woefully ill prepared to assume the nation's highest office.

Trying to salvage the election, the red-faced Democrats desperately fought back on the issue of corruption, reminding voters that Garfield had once received $329 from Credit Mobilier, the Union Pacific Railroad's corrupt holding company, insisting that it was a bribe and not a loan, as the Ohio congressman had adamantly maintained. The Democrats also tried to get some additional mileage out of the fact that President Hayes had removed Chester Arthur as head of the New York Customs House on the grounds that the New York City "boss," who was responsible for doling out more than one thousand federal jobs, embodied everything that was wrong with the age-old practice of patronage. Abuses

46. *Chicago Weekly Express*, November 9, 1880, as quoted in Lause, *The Civil War's Last Campaign*, p. 204.
47. Lause, *The Civil War's Last Campaign*, p. 196.
48. Ibid., pp. 203-204; *Chicago Weekly Express*, Nov. 2, 1880.

abounded and Arthur's presence on the Republican ticket in 1880 was proof, they claimed, that the GOP wasn't really serious about ending the corrupt spoils system.

In the closing days of the campaign, General Weaver, who had predicted earlier that the Greenback-Labor Party would elect anywhere from twenty-five to fifty congressmen, concentrated his energies in his home base of northeastern Iowa in what historian Mark A. Lause described as the campaign's "final line of defense."[49] In an election eve address, Weaver reminded his audience that he had given more than a hundred speeches "from Arkansas clear up to the northeast corner of Maine, and midway from the east side of Lake Michigan to the bay of Mobile" over the course the campaign. He also predicted that he would receive somewhere between 600,000 and 1,500,000 votes—an astounding showing for a relatively new party. "We are coming Father Abraham, more than 600,000 strong," he declared, paraphrasing the wartime song. "Vote your conscience instead of your party," he urged his followers, "for I say to you, as my last words, that if we cannot tone up the American people to that point where they will vote their conscience, as their conscience dictates, instead of their party, the nation is a failure." The former Union army general then issued his final command. "Now for a general assault along the whole length of the enemy's lines."[50]

A record 78.4% of the American electorate turned out in the 1880 presidential election. In the razor-thin contest that year, Republican James A. Garfield narrowly defeated Democrat Winfield Scott, garnering 4,446,158 popular votes to Hancock's 4,444,260—a difference of only 1,898 votes. The Greenback-Labor Party's James Weaver polled a respectable 305,997 votes. Like most other minor party presidential candidates in American history, Prohibitionist Neal Dow and the American Party's John Phelps weren't really factors in the election. In fact, the vast majority of voters weren't even aware that they were running. Dow, the reluctant Prohibition Party candidate, received 9,674 votes in sixteen states and the little-known Phelps brought up the rear with a scant 707 votes. The Republicans won a 22-seat majority in the congressional elections that year, while the Greenback-Labor Party claimed ten seats. Virginia's Readjuster Party also held two House seats in the 47th Congress.

With fewer than 2,000 popular votes separating the two major party candidates, the campaign of 1880 was, until then, the closest presidential election in American history. In the end, Garfield received 214 electoral votes to 155 for

---

49. Ibid., p. 200.
50. Ibid., p. 206.

Hancock. As expected, New York's thirty-five electoral votes determined the outcome with the Empire State giving Garfield a 21,033-vote majority over his Democratic rival. If the state had voted for Hancock, as it did for Tilden four years earlier, Hancock would have enjoyed an Electoral College majority of 190 to 179. Hancock, who received all 138 electoral votes of the Solid South, carried twenty of the thirty-eight states that took part in the election. On election night, an exhausted Hancock went to bed around 7 p.m., but was awakened by his wife around five in the morning with news of his defeat. "That is all right," he told her, "I can stand it," and turned over and fell back to sleep. Nevertheless, like Tilden in 1876, the former Union army general went to his grave in 1886 believing that he had been cheated out of the presidency.[51]

Were it not for a return to relative prosperity and the success of the Resumption Act, the Greenback-Labor Party's Weaver probably would have made a much stronger showing in the 1880 presidential campaign. Though he ran a relatively strong race in Texas, where he garnered nearly twelve percent of the vote, and in his native Iowa, where he received one of every ten votes cast, Weaver polled only 3.3 percent of the vote nationally. Despite polling the difference between Garfield and Hancock in three states—California, Indiana and New Jersey—Weaver was disappointed that his candidacy didn't have a greater impact, but nevertheless put on a brave face, telling his supporters that Greenback-Laborites had "reason to feel proud of the result" and promising to continue the fight "until we are victorious." "We did not expect to elect our presidential candidate," he told a *Chicago Tribune* reporter shortly after the election, "but we expected to establish ourselves as a party to be respected"—and in that, the former Union army officer felt that his insurgent candidacy had been successful.[52]

Moreover, Weaver's total would have exceeded 375,000 votes nationally if the 68,696 to 69,453 votes cast for Greenback electors on the "Union" fusion ticket in Maine—a state that had just elected a Greenback-Laborite as governor—had been proportionally allocated to both parties instead of being dishonestly credited entirely to Hancock, whose Democratic electors received anywhere from 3,700 to 4,300 fewer votes than the Greenback-Labor electors on that ticket.[53] As it turned out, Weaver was credited with only the 4,409 votes received by the highest elector on Solon Chase's militantly straight-out Greenback-Labor electoral

---

51. Clancy, *The Presidential Election of 1880*, pp. 242-243.
52. *The Weekly Iowa State Register*, November 19, 26, 1880, as quoted in Haynes, *James Baird Weaver*, pp. 175-178.
53. Lause, *The Civil War's Last Campaign*, p. 210.

ticket in that state. A number of Greenback publications believed the Weaver's national showing had been vastly underreported. After listing the totals for Garfield and Hancock, one obviously incredulous GLP newspaper wrote, "Weaver—well, let's see, did the Greenbackers vote? Guess not," and while both major parties were guilty of massive vote fraud that year, Patrick Ford's *Irish World* said that Greenback-Labor voters "may rest assured that no opportunity was lost or no compunction felt in slaughtering us."[54]

Far from being laid to rest, General Weaver, who survived the bloody battles of Fort Donelson and Shiloh during the Civil War, would be back to fight another day. So, too, would the Greenbackers or, more precisely, their descendants—the Anti-Monopolist, Union Labor and Populist parties. And though it must have seemed remote to them at the time, their influence would one day be felt in numerous programs eventually adopted by the country's two major parties.

The Republicans regained control of the House of Representatives for the first time in eight years, winning 152 seats to 130 for the Democrats. The Greenback-Labor Party claimed ten seats and the Readjusters were successful in two of Virginia's nine House races. The U.S. Senate, meanwhile, was evenly divided between the two major parties in the 47th Congress, with Virginia Readjuster William C. Mahone and Anti-Monopolist Newton Booth of California holding the balance of power.

Four incumbent Greenback lawmakers lost their seats in Congress that year, including Adlai Stevenson in Illinois, Edward H. Gillette in Iowa, Hendrick B. Wright in Pennsylvania and Indiana's Gilbert De La Matyr. Four other Greenback congressmen, including James B. Weaver and Pennsylvania's relatively youthful Seth H. Yocum, who moved to Johnson City, Tennessee, where he opened a tannery and later served as mayor, didn't seek re-election that year. Moreover, in Iowa—where Greenback strength fell by approximately 15,000 votes from two years earlier—Weaver was unable to keep his own congressional seat in the party's column as fusionist John C. Cook, his successor on the Greenback-Labor ticket, was narrowly defeated by Republican Marsena E. Cutts, losing to the longtime state legislator in a hotly-disputed race by a mere 106 votes out of nearly 36,000 votes cast. Judge Cook, a Democrat, was later awarded the seat in the closing days of the 47th Congress.

Running as a Democrat, Adlai Stevenson of Illinois was narrowly defeated in his bid for another term, while Iowa's Gillette, a close ally of Weaver running on a Democratic-Greenback fusion ticket, lost by more than 3,000 votes to Republi-

---

54. Ibid., p. 208.

can John A. Kasson, a highly-regarded diplomat and one-time Free Soiler who played a key role in drafting the 1860 Republican platform on which Lincoln sought the presidency. In Pennsylvania's twelfth congressional district, Republican Joseph A. Scranton, a wealthy newspaper publisher, trounced the Greenback-Labor Party's Hendrick B. Wright in a three-way race, thereby closing out the aging congressman's long political career—a vocation, incidentally, that spanned nearly fifty years. The 73-year-old Wright, a longtime publisher of the pro-labor *Anthracite Monitor*, died the following September. In Indiana's seventh district, Gilbert De La Matyr, the erstwhile and colorful Methodist Episcopal minister who served as the party's temporary chairman at its national convention earlier that year, garnered less than six percent of the vote against his major party opponents. Returning to the ministry, De La Matyr moved to Denver, Colorado, shortly after losing his seat. He later settled in Akron, Ohio, where he served as pastor of that city's First Methodist Episcopal Church until his death in 1892.

Joining the party's five incumbents who were re-elected that year—Lowe of Alabama, Murch and Ladd of Maine, Ford of Missouri and Jones of Texas—were five new Greenback-Labor congressmen, including three from Missouri. These included Charles N. Brumm and James Mosgrove of Pennsylvania and Ira S. Hazeltine, Theron M. Rice and Joseph H. Burrows of the Show Me State. Except for Pennsylvania's Mosgrove, who ran as a Democratic and Greenback candidate, the others were all elected on Greenback-Republican fusion tickets. In addition, the Greenback-Labor Party played a decisive role in the election of Brooklyn minister John Hyatt Smith in New York's third congressional district. Smith, a political independent who was supported by the Democratic and Greenback parties, upset an incumbent Republican to win his House seat. Similarly, in California, the Workingmen's Party's endorsement of retired Union army general William S. Rosecrans enabled the Civil War hero to narrowly defeat incumbent Republican Horace Davis in that state's first congressional district. Rosecrans, to almost no one's surprise, took his seat in Congress as a Democrat.

The newly elected Greenback congressmen were a diverse group. Pennsylvania's Mosgrove, a 58-year-old iron manufacturer and banker from Kittanning, ran unsuccessfully for Congress on the Greenback-Labor ticket in 1878, garnering over 31% of the vote against stiff Democratic and Republican opposition. A lifelong Democrat, Mosgrove accepted the Greenback Party's nomination that year largely because he sympathized with the party's financial doctrines. Running with Democratic and Greenback support, he narrowly captured the seat two years later, defeating the Republican incumbent by 757 votes. A lawyer and farmer, Missouri's Ira S. Hazeltine was a former Republican state legislator and delegate to the 1860 Republican national convention that nominated Lincoln for president. Hazeltine also owned the largest apple orchard in Greene County, Missouri. Theron M. Rice, a Union army veteran, was a teacher-turned-lawyer and circuit court judge from Tipton, Missouri, and Joseph H. Burrows, who was born in Manchester, England, was a forty-year-old ordained minister who had served briefly in the Missouri legislature. In addition to these, Virginia's robust and progressive Readjuster Party won two of that state's nine congressional seats, sending ex-Confederate officers John Paul and Abram Fulkerson to Congress. Both men had previously served in the Virginia Senate.

James A. Garfield, the nation's twentieth president, served as the country's chief executive for only two hundred days before dying from gunshot wounds suffered at the hands of Charles J. Guiteau, an unbalanced religious fanatic. From the beginning, Garfield's tragic and short-lived presidency was hampered by a drag down, knockout struggle with New York Republican boss Roscoe Conkling, the head of that state's powerful Stalwart faction, over the issue of patronage. Garfield prevailed in that bout while the New Yorker sulked. The New York lawmaker was so angered by Garfield's refusal to acquiesce to him on patronage matters in the Empire State and by the president's apparent concessions to James G. Blaine and his "Half-Breeds," that he willingly gave up his seat in the U.S. Senate. Other leading Stalwarts were equally angered by Garfield's snub. His willingness to play hardball with Conkling and the Stalwarts earned the young president accolades from pundits across the country while significantly enhancing the respect and prestige of the office of the presidency. No longer would the country's chief executive have to take orders from unscrupulous, power-hungry machine bosses.

Tragically, an assassin's bullets ended Garfield's life before he could capitalize on his surging popularity. On the morning of July 2, 1881, while entering the Baltimore and Potomac railroad station in Washington, D.C., where he was to board a train bound for Massachusetts to attend the twenty-fifth reunion of his alma mater at Williams College, Garfield was shot once in the back and once in the arm by crazed gunman Charles Guiteau, who shouted, "I am a Stalwart and Arthur is President now!"[55]

Garfield was rushed back to the White House where physicians worked feverishly to save his life, but weren't able to locate and remove the bullet lodged in his back. (X-rays were still fourteen years in the offing.) Still a relatively young man at forty-nine, Garfield clung to life for more than two and a half months. After

---

55. Whitney, *The American Presidents*, p. 178.

lingering near death for more than eight weeks, the nation's twentieth president, seeking relief from the oppressive humidity blanketing the nation's capital that summer, asked to be moved to a seaside cottage in Elberon, New Jersey, a resort community, where he died on September 19, 1881.

Vice President Chester A. Arthur succeeded Garfield as the nation's twenty-first chief executive. Though a few detractors later claimed that Arthur was ineligible for the presidency because he had actually been born in Canada and that his Irish-immigrant father had switched his birthplace and birth date with that of a younger son who had died as an infant, Arthur was nevertheless sworn into office at his home in New York City the following day.

The Democrats regained control of the House in the 1882 mid-term elections, holding a sizeable majority over the Republicans. The GOP, however, clung to a four-seat majority in the U.S. Senate. No fewer than forty-five House members went down to defeat that year—the second largest number of incumbents to lose their seats in nearly a quarter of a century. Virginia's Readjuster Party held four seats in the U.S. House of Representatives and Minnesota's venerable Knute Nelson initially took his seat in the 48th Congress as an Independent Republican. Two independents—newspaper editor and former state legislator Thomas P. Ochiltree of Texas and Mississippi's James R. Chalmers, a former Confederate brigadier-general who played a conspicuous role in Nathan Bedford Forrest's brilliant military campaigns in Mississippi, Tennessee and Kentucky during the Civil War—also served in the forty-eighth Congress, along with Iowa Greenbacker Luman H. "Calamity" Weller and Pennsylvania's Charles Napoleon Brumm, who was narrowly re-elected that year on a Greenback-Republican fusion ticket. Brumm's victory, as it turned out, was of little consolation to Greenback-Labor leaders as the 44-year-old Luzerne County lawmaker took his seat with the Republicans when the 48th Congress organized in early 1883. In addition, two Independent Democrats—John F. Finerty of Illinois and Oscar Turner of Kentucky—and Theodore Lyman of Massachusetts, an independent Republican running on a fusion ticket, defeated major-party opponents to win seats in the House that year, while former congressman William H. Felton, running as an Independent Democrat, came close to regaining his old seat in Georgia's seventh congressional district. Moreover, Tyre York, a 46-year-old surgeon and former state legislator, was elected to Congress from North Carolina on the Liberal Party ticket, narrowly defeating his Democratic rival in a three-cornered race that included an Independent Republican aspirant.

The election of seven third-party congressmen and two independents that year was indicative of the growing discontent with the entrenched two-party system.

In at least eight House races that year, unsuccessful independent or third party candidates finished ahead of one of their major-party rivals. Excluding major party candidates who were cross-endorsed by one or more of the minor parties, independent and third-party candidates for Congress garnered a whopping 1,084,074 votes in the 1882 mid-term congressional elections. Nearly a third of those votes were cast for the 164 candidates representing the Greenback-Labor Party while nearly 100,000 voters cast ballots for the Prohibition Party, which fielded candidates in approximately ninety House districts that year.[56]

Despite the relatively large vote cast for congressional candidates running outside the traditional two-party system, 1882 turned out to be a particularly tough year for the Greenback-Labor Party. Not only had James B. Weaver failed to regain his old seat in the U.S. House from Iowa, but five of the party's ten incumbent congressmen, including Thompson H. Murch of Maine and Missouri's Nicholas Ford, also went down to defeat while two other Greenback lawmakers decided not to seek another term. Making matters worse, William M. Lowe, a 40-year-old Greenback congressman from Alabama, died in Huntsville three weeks before the election.

The Greenback-Labor Party didn't fare much better in other contests around the country. Labor leader Thomas Armstrong, the party's candidate for governor in Pennsylvania, didn't come even remotely close to matching the party's vote total in the preceding gubernatorial election and the party's overall vote in the Keystone State dropped dramatically, including in its former strongholds among farmers in western Pennsylvania and in the state's bituminous coalfield regions. During the campaign, Armstrong, the longtime editor of the Knights of Labor's *National Labor Tribune,* the voice of the Amalgamated Association of Iron and Steel Workers in western Pennsylvania, was forced to deny charges that his campaign was being financed by the Republicans, who were then facing unexpected opposition from an Independent Republican ticket headed by maverick Republican John Stewart, a state senator from Chambersburg. Put on the defensive for much of the campaign, Armstrong and Terence V. Powderly, the party's candidate for lieutenant governor, finished some 20,000 votes behind the Independent Republican ticket, polling a dismal 23,996 votes, or slightly more than three percent of the total. In the end, the Greenback-Labor candidate garnered less than a third of the votes cast for Samuel R. Mason, the party's gubernatorial candidate in 1878. In addition, the eight state Senate and forty-nine House candidates fielded by the party that year went down to defeat, leaving the disheartened

---

56. Dubin, *United States Congressional Elections,* pp. 257-263.

Greenback-Laborites without any representation in the Pennsylvania legislature.[57]

One of the Greenback congressmen opting against another term in Congress in 1882 was the colorful George Washington Jones of Texas, a two-term incumbent who gave up his relatively safe seat in the House to run unsuccessfully for governor of Texas on a Republican-Greenback fusion ticket. It was the first of two unsuccessful campaigns waged by the rural lawyer against Democrat John Ireland, a popular former Confederate army officer. Jones was born in Alabama and raised in Tennessee before settling with his parents on the Colorado River, not far from Bastrop, Texas. Admitted to the Texas bar in 1851, he was elected to the Texas legislature two years later. In 1856, he was district attorney of Bastrop County, an office he held until the beginning of the Civil War. Not without controversy, Jones, who was considered a heavy drinker—a binge drinker, to be more accurate—reputedly shot and killed a fellow attorney during this period, but was apparently never charged in the incident.

A Unionist and strong supporter of Stephen A. Douglas, Jones nevertheless enlisted as a private in the Confederate army shortly after the outbreak of the war—"a foolish undertaking," he said at the time, "but I will fight it out with my people." During the war, he was promoted to the rank of colonel. After the war, Jones, who had resumed his law practice in Bastrop, was elected lieutenant governor of Texas, garnering nearly 85% of the vote against Republican Livingston Lindsay, a radical unionist who later served on the Texas Supreme Court. Following the passage of the Military Reconstruction Act of 1867, Texas was placed under military command, creating an almost impossible situation for Gov. James W. Throckmorton who frequently clashed with Gen. Charles Griffin, the military commander of the Texas district. Among other things, Throckmorton, citing his state's opposition to the Fourteenth Amendment, refused to provide additional protection for the state's African-American citizens when ordered to do so by Griffin. He and his lieutenant governor also adamantly refused to publicly support the policies of Radical Reconstruction that had been so harshly imposed on the South. Regarded as impediments to Reconstruction, Major Gen. Philip H. Sheridan, commander of the Fifth Military District, forcibly removed Throckmorton and Jones from office in July 1867.

After a failed attempt in 1876, Jones was elected as a Greenback member of Congress from the state's fifth congressional district two years later. He was reelected in 1880, narrowly defeating his Democratic rival by 233 votes. Despite

---

57. Ricker, *The Greenback-Labor Movement in Pennsylvania*, pp. 102-104.

waging a vigorous campaign, the Greenback congressman came up short in his 1882 bid for the Texas governorship, losing to Democrat John Ireland by a margin of 150,811 to 108,988. In a rematch against Ireland two years later, Jones, then running as a Republican, garnered less than thirty percent of the vote in a three-way race in which the Greenback Party's nominee siphoned off more than 23,000 votes. The former lawmaker mounted one last political comeback at the age of seventy when he unsuccessfully ran for Congress as a Populist.

Although the Greenback-Labor Party captured only two seats in the U.S. House in 1882—and both of those were the result of fusion efforts—the party waged competitive races in several districts across the country and took part in at least a dozen other successful fusion campaigns. In Iowa, former Greenback congressman Edward H. Gillette garnered nearly 23% of the vote in an unsuccessful bid to win back his old House seat in the state's seventh congressional district and Charles H. Moody of Kansas received almost thirty percent of the vote in a bid to unseat Republican John A. Anderson. In Nebraska, Anti-Monopoly Party candidates waged strong campaigns in the state's three congressional districts, with one of the candidates polling over 38% of the vote while finishing a close second in a three-cornered race. In all, the Greenback-Labor Party fielded candidates in more than half of the nation's congressional districts in the 1882 mid-term elections. That figure includes seven "Anti-Monopoly" candidates—three from Illinois, three from Nebraska and one Anti-Monopoly Democrat in New York—one Working Men's Party candidate in Pennsylvania and a fusion campaign between the Greenback-Labor Party and the Readjusters in Virginia, as well as a similar fusion ticket with the Democrats in Michigan, a Greenback stronghold. Moreover, Greenback congressional candidates provided the most significant opposition to a major party candidate in at least ten House races across the country.

In Texas, Eben L. Dohoney, a well-known former state senator and father of that state's landmark Homestead legislation in 1871, polled almost 37% of the vote on the Greenback ticket in an unsuccessful attempt to unseat longtime Democratic congressman Charles A. Culberson—one of the state's most powerful political figures. One of the most intriguing and influential characters in Texas history, Dohoney, a staunch temperance activist, switched parties with unusual frequency, jumping from the Democrats to the Greenback Party and then to the Prohibition Party and finally to the Populists in the early 1890s. A popular vote getter on whatever ticket his name happened to appear, Dohoney once garnered more than 200,000 votes in an unsuccessful bid for chief justice of the Texas Court of Criminal Appeals.

George Washington Jones and Eben L. Dohoney notwithstanding, the Greenback Party in Texas, consisting largely of dissenting Democrats, Republican businessmen interested in specie speculation, heavily indebted farmers, and African-American voters who no longer felt welcome in the party of Lincoln, had a rich and colorful history. By 1878, there were some 482 Greenback Clubs organized around the state, including seventy predominately black clubs.

The Greenback Party of Texas held its first statewide convention in Austin in March of that year and convened again on August 7 in Waco, where it approved a platform and nominated a full slate of candidates. The party's platform, closely mirroring that of the national party, urged the federal government to issue greenbacks as full legal tender and to redeem treasury notes and bonds with such paper currency. Among other things, the party also called for government regulation of the railroads, pay cuts for public officials, an end to the state's convict labor laws and the establishment of a tax-supported public school system. The Greenback ticket that year was headed by William H. Hamman, a lawyer, oil prospector and former brigadier-general in the Confederate army, as its nominee for governor. The 48-year-old entrepreneur ran a respectable second in the gubernatorial race, garnering more than 55,000 votes against Democrat Oran M. Roberts, while finishing far ahead of the nominal Republican candidate.

That same year, the Greenback Party of Texas nominated John C. Mitchell for the U.S. Senate—a politically provocative move in post-Reconstruction Texas. Mitchell, a 41-year-old African-American farmer, had previously served in the state legislature. The Texas Greenbackers easily replaced the Republicans as the state's second party when it won a dozen seats in the state legislature and elected George W. Jones to Congress that year.

During this period, the party attracted some of the state's most picturesque political figures, not the least of whom was Sam Evans of Fort Worth, "The Great Aginner"—a nickname given to him because he had opposed so many legislative issues. Agreeing with the Greenback Party's call for an increase in paper currency, Evans, a veteran state lawmaker who served in the Texas House and Senate, abruptly quit the Democratic Party and joined the Greenback movement while he was in the legislature. In the legislature, Evans, who was convinced that huge corporations in the East were trying to squeeze out the country's small farmers, consistently opposed almost every bill that favored big business. Evans also believed that the railroads should be publicly owned and consistently fought the private development of railroad lines across Texas during a period when most of the state's leaders were actively encouraging the railroads to lay tracks through the rapidly-developing regions of Dallas and Fort Worth. In one of his many unsuccessful proposals, Evans, who later flirted with the Union Labor and Populist parties, introduced legislation opposing the gold standard. "Eastern bankers control gold, and this impoverishes the small people and farmers," he maintained. "Texas should be in the forefront of sponsoring free coinage of silver and unlimited issuance of paper money backed initially only by the integrity of our federal government."

Another of those attracted to the new party was James S. Rains, a former Missouri state senator and one-time Democrat, Know-Nothing and Constitutional Unionist who relocated to Texas during the Civil War. Relieved of his command in the Confederate army in the fall of 1862, Rains later recruited a unit of men in Missouri when General Sterling Price made his infamous raid there in 1864, guiding them back to Arkansas where they joined the Confederate army. In the mid-1870s, Rains became an organizer for the Grange and eventually joined the fledgling Greenback Party, serving as its candidate for lieutenant governor in his adopted state in 1878. The 63-year-old Rains was just beginning a speaking tour on behalf of James B. Weaver and the Greenback ticket in 1880 when he suddenly died of a stroke.

Twenty of the 140 delegates to the party's 1880 convention in Austin were African-Americans—a testimony to the party's diversity in that state. General Hamman ran for governor again, but placed a distant third in the race with only 33,699 votes, finishing some 30,000 votes behind the Republican candidate and more than 132,000 votes behind the incumbent Democrat. The party also lost eight seats in the state legislature. Although Jones was re-elected to Congress that year, the party was clearly on the decline. By 1882, the party was only a shell of its former self and made no nominations, but encouraged its members to support Jones' fusion candidacy in the governor's race. Shortly thereafter, most of its members returned to their former parties. Sadly, only twenty delegates showed up at the party's 1884 state convention in Waco.

The Greenback-Labor Party ran candidates in fifteen of the seventeen states holding gubernatorial elections in 1882 and, with the exceptions of Minnesota and North Carolina, the party also fielded candidates for the highest statewide office up for election in every state that wasn't holding a gubernatorial contest that year. In one of the most closely-watched races in the country, 64-year-old Charles Robinson, the physician-turned-politician who had served as the first governor of Kansas two decades earlier, mounted a comeback on the Greenback-Labor ticket, garnering 20,933 votes in a three-cornered race narrowly won by Democrat George W. Glick. By all accounts, Robinson's twelve percent share of the vote cost Republican John P. St. John—who later emerged as the Prohibition Party's presidential standard-bearer—an unprecedented third term as governor.

Despite its rather abysmal showing in the 1882 mid-term elections, Greenback-Labor members had plenty to cheer about when the voters of Michigan put one of their own in the governor's office. Along with Harris M. Plaisted of Maine and the stormy Benjamin Butler of Massachusetts, 67-year-old Josiah W. Begole, an amiable and highly principled businessman and banker, was one of only three Greenback governors in American history. Like his counterparts in Maine and Massachusetts, Begole was swept into office on a Democratic-Greenback fusion ticket. Remarkably, he was also the only man outside the Republican Party to win the Michigan governorship in nearly thirty years.

The Greenback-Labor Party, which was strongest in the western and northern counties of the Lower Peninsula, had been making headway in the state for several years. Led by labor leader Richard Trevellick of Detroit, the party first flexed its considerable political muscle in the 1878 gubernatorial contest when Grand Rapids Mayor Henry S. Smith garnered nearly 75,000 votes in a three-way contest, running only slightly behind his Democratic rival. This was a far cry from the 8,207 votes cast for William Sparks, the party's gubernatorial candidate in 1876. Continuing to gain momentum, the Michigan Greenbackers elected eighteen members to the state legislature in 1880—a year when the party's overall vote nearly equaled that of the Democrats. Begole's victory that year was all the more astounding given the fact that there was also an anti-fusion Greenback candidate in the race—Waldo May, a little-known currency reformer who ran as a "Straight Greenback" candidate. Despite May's presence in the race, Begole defeated the sitting Republican governor by a margin of 154,269 to 149,697. Prohibitionist Daniel P. Sagendorph polled 5,854 votes and 2,006 votes, or less than one percent of the total, were cast for dissident Greenback aspirant Waldo May.

Of French descent, Begole was the oldest of ten children and had been educated in an old log schoolhouse in rural Mount Morris, New York. Seeking his fortune, the 21-year-old adventurer traveled west and settled in the wilderness of the Michigan Territory in the summer of 1836. He eventually established a five hundred-acre farm in what is now the outskirts of Flint, Michigan, which was then a small trading post and where he established one of the region's largest sawmills. A staunch antislavery advocate, Begole joined the Republican Party as a young man and served in various local offices, including that of county treasurer. During the Civil War, he took an active part in recruiting soldiers and supplies for the Union army, but was deeply affected when his oldest son was killed by a Confederate bullet near Atlanta toward the end of the war.

Having being elected to the state Senate in 1870, Begole won a seat in Congress as a Republican two years later, defeating his Democratic opponent by a comfortable margin. As one of seventeen farmers in the U.S. House, he served on the agriculture committee where he worked diligently to improve conditions for the nation's farmers. A staunch advocate of paper money, he also supported the re-monetizaton of silver and other currency reform measures, all of which went down to defeat during the 43rd Congress. His work in these areas, however, earned him the respect and admiration of Greenback leaders in Michigan and throughout the country. Unfortunately, he was defeated in a bid for re-election two years later, losing narrowly to George H. Durand, a former congressman and founder of the Genesee County Bar Association.[58]

The largely forgotten Michigander was a decent and compassionate man and, as one newspaper reported, was utterly "incapable of bearing malice, even against his bitterest enemies." He was also a man of considerable wit and wisdom. His true character was revealed in 1881, shortly after a devastating fire raged through several counties in northeast Michigan, destroying virtually everything in its wake. When local authorities in Port Huron and Detroit haggled over the distribution of disaster relief funds, delaying much-needed aid to the ravaged communities, Begole stepped in and personally offered financial assistance. "Let no man suffer while I have money," he said.

Though given little chance in the 1882 gubernatorial campaign—one newspaper said that the Michigan Republicans were "too strong to be beaten by a combination of Democrats and Greenbackers"—Begole surprised everyone, including himself, when he upset David H. Jerome, the heavily favored Republican incumbent, by more than 4,500 votes. True to his Greenback principles, the new governor wasted little time establishing a Bureau of Labor Statistics and during his tenure Michigan enacted child labor legislation prohibiting the employment of children under the age of fourteen—one of the first laws of its kind in the country. Under Begole's watch, the state legislature also passed a law requiring compulsory education for all children under that age. In addition, the Greenback governor pushed for a stringent law preventing large insurance companies from engaging in price-fixing practices, then a relatively common occurrence. One of his biggest accomplishments was the construction of an insane asylum in

---

58.   Durand, a former mayor of Flint, received 17,758 votes to Begole's 16,122. The Prohibition Party's Erastus C. Harrington garnered 1,023 votes.

Traverse City. Unfortunately, his efforts to bring about much-needed changes in the state's convict labor system and his attempt to place a prohibition amendment to the state constitution on the statewide ballot were blocked by the Republican-controlled legislature.

Long interested in prison reform, Begole appointed newspaperman and prison-reform advocate Elihu H. Pond as warden of the Jackson Prison in 1883. Pond, a former state senator, had been fighting to stop the practice of selling admission tickets to morbid curiosity seekers who apparently had nothing better to do than gape at convicts as though they were animals. Unable to overcome the many obstacles placed in his path by the Republican-controlled legislature, the amiable and aging Greenbacker was narrowly defeated in his bid for re-election in 1884, losing by fewer than 6,000 votes to Republican Russell A. Alger, a wealthy lumberman who later served as McKinley's Secretary of War, in a three-cornered race in which the Prohibition Party's David Preston polled an astonishing 22,207 votes, or nearly six percent of the total.

The Independent Republican Movement

A largely forgotten political development during this period was the short-lived Independent Republican movement, a precursor of sorts to the "Mugwumps" who provided critical support to Democrat Grover Cleveland in the 1884 presidential campaign against James G. Blaine, the GOP's badly tarnished nominee. More precisely, the Independent Republican movement was a spirited but largely unsuccessful protest against the bossism and arrogance of Stalwart leaders such as New York's Roscoe Conkling and Pennsylvania's J. Donald Cameron, son and protégé of Republican leader Simon Cameron. The elder Cameron, of course, was less than a sterling example of integrity. "An honest politician is one who, when he is bought, will stay bought," he once said. The younger Cameron was the first in the Cameron-Quay-Penrose Dynasty that dominated politics in the Keystone State for more than fifty years.

Nationally, more than a dozen reform-minded Republicans ran for Congress on the "Independent Republican" label in the 1882 mid-term elections. Included among the Republican reformers were men like Theodore Lyman of Massachusetts, a zoologist and founder of the Reform Club of Boston and Wisconsin's Elisha Keyes, the "Bismark of Western politics." The son of a wealthy former mayor of Boston, Lyman was a cultured, witty man of considerable charm. Having graduated near the top of his class at Harvard in 1855, Lyman spent the early part of the Civil War years abroad, collecting artifacts for the Museum of Comparative Zoology. Science, it seems, was of much greater interest to him than the hostilities between the North and the South. In fact, Lyman was so appalled by the abolitionists in the years leading up to the war that he hadn't even bothered to vote for Lincoln in 1860. Moreover, he didn't enlist in the Union cause until sometime in 1863 when, following a short stint as a volunteer on Massachusetts Gov. John Andrew's staff, he served as a lieutenant colonel in General Meade's headquarters. Politicized by the war, Lyman turned to politics shorter after the war-between-the-states. Having defeated the Republican incumbent in his 1882 House race, Lyman, who had campaigned on a "Civil Service Reform-Democratic" fusion ticket, retired from Congress after only one term due to declining health.[59]

Keyes was quite a different story—President Fillmore had named him as a solicitor in the Post Office when he was in his early twenties. Unlike Lyman, Keyes was hardly a reformer. A former mayor of Madison, Wisconsin, he was very much a political insider, serving as chairman of Wisconsin's delegation to the Republican National Convention in 1872 and 1876 and ruling the state party with an iron rod from 1867-1877 before attempting a comeback as a so-called "reform" candidate.

The list of Independent Republican House candidates also included the venerable Knute Nelson of Minnesota, a conservative former state senator who had been wounded and captured at Port Huron during the Civil War, and Maine's Nelson Dingley, Jr., publisher of the *Lewiston Journal*. A regular Republican, Dingley was endorsed by the state's independents during the 1882 mid-term election. (In Maine, the Independent Republicans fielded a nearly complete slate of candidates, but fared poorly in the September election.) In Missouri, self-styled reformer Gustavus Sessinghaus waged a spirited campaign for the state's eighth congressional district seat, polling nearly 36% of the vote in a four-way race. A German-born member of the St. Louis school board, Sessinghaus had successfully contested Democrat Richard G. Frost's disputed election in 1880, but served only two days in the 47th Congress before the House adjourned.

Nowhere, however, was the Independent Republican movement more profoundly felt than in Pennsylvania. In that Republican stronghold, the Independent Republicans fielded no fewer than six candidates for Congress, as well as a plethora of state legislative candidates. They also nominated a separate gubernatorial ticket headed by state Sen. John Stewart of Chambersburg. Widely

---

59. *Boston Transcript*, September 10, 1897.

regarded as an independent-minded and incorruptible lawmaker, Stewart siphoned enough votes from the regular Republican ticket in the 1882 campaign to enable young Democrat Robert E. Pattison to squeeze into office. A reform-minded city controller of Philadelphia, the 32-year-old Pattison, who had been reelected to a second term as controller as a result of hard-hitting exposés on corruption in Philadelphia newspapers in 1880, was the first Democrat elected governor of the Keystone State in a quarter century.[60]

The Independent Republican movement in Pennsylvania essentially grew out of Republican legislator Charles S. Wolfe's independent "anti-machine" campaign for state treasurer in 1881, eventually mushrooming to the point that it genuinely threatened the GOP's longstanding domination of Pennsylvania politics. Of Pennsylvania Dutch ancestry, the 36-year-old Wolfe, a graduate of Harvard Law School, was regarded as one of the most astute men in the state legislature. Among other things, he was an early temperance advocate, proposing a resolution to prohibit the sale or use of liquor in the House cloakroom—then a common practice. He also established a reputation as something of a political reformer and led the investigation in a celebrated corruption case in 1876 that resulted in the expulsion of two members of the state legislature. An archenemy of Cameron and later of Matthew Quay, the much-despised and much-feared powerful Pennsylvania Republican boss, Wolfe worked diligently to defeat Cameron during his bid for re-election to the U.S. Senate in 1878. In fact, he was one of five Republicans who voted with the Democrats against Cameron, but it wasn't enough to prevent the aging lawmaker's return to office that year. Two years later, Wolfe was one of fifty-six Republican lawmakers who refused to take part in the Republican caucus for the U.S. Senate and played an important role in the election of John I. Mitchell, an independent-minded Republican, against Cameron's handpicked candidate.

During his campaign for state treasurer, Wolfe denied charges that he was out to wreck the Republican Party. He was running, he insisted, to end bossism and to restore the cause of true Republicanism. "A little strong medicine now is better, in my judgment," he said, "than either boss success or Republican disaster" in the future. Waging a vigorous campaign, Wolfe scared the daylights out of the Republican machine that year, polling a respectable 49,984 votes to Republican Silas Bailey's 265,295 and the Democratic candidate's 258,431.

---

60. Nathaniel Burt and Wallace E. Davies, "The Iron Age 1876-1905," *Philadelphia: A 300-Year History*, p. 497.

In the aftermath of Wolfe's unsuccessful candidacy, the state's Independent Republicans established their own state committee, an organization wholly separate from Cameron's corrupt machine. Spearheaded by William W. Alcorn of Philadelphia's Citizens' Committee of One Hundred, the independent movement quickly attracted a large number of prominent Republicans, including John Welsh, president of the National Board of Trade and a former ambassador to Great Britain. A highly influential Philadelphia businessman, Welsh proved to be a phenomenal fundraiser. One of the earliest and most persistent Independent Republican organizers was Wharton Barker, an iron manufacturer and chairman of the Industrial League who had openly supported Wolfe in 1881. Barker, who later ran for president as a Populist during that party's waning years, was an emphatic protectionist. U.S. Senator John Mitchell stumped for the ticket in the state's northern counties. Former congressman William H. Koontz and William M. Dorr, a prominent lawyer and newspaper editor, also lent their support to the fledgling Independent Republican movement, as did Mayor Charles W. Miller of Meadville and former Erie County Judge Henry Souther. Judge J. W. Cochran of Cameron County, a wealthy lumber dealer, also threw his support to the independent movement.[61]

Like Wolfe, Stewart's independent candidacy in 1882 caused Cameron and the Republican leadership many sleepless nights. Several newspapers predicted that Stewart's candidacy would siphon enough votes to throw the election to Democrat Pattison—a prediction that was right on the mark. One nervous Stalwart newspaper predicted that Stewart would poll 75,000 votes, thereby virtually assuring a Democratic victory. In the early summer, Maine's James G. Blaine, one of the party's most popular figures, intimated that he was sympathetic to the Independent Republican movement and that he would actively campaign on their behalf.[62] Stewart, after all, had campaigned arduously for Blaine in 1876 and 1880. Poor health—at least that was the excuse given—apparently prevented the "Plumed Knight" from taking an active part in the campaign.

Blasting the "personal despotism" and corruption of the Cameron-led machine, Stewart ran a vigorous campaign, defending a great political party that had been, in his words, "prostituted" for "base and ignoble purposes." After failing to convince GOP leaders to hold a new state convention for the purpose of nominating a new gubernatorial ticket, the Chambersburg lawmaker barnstormed the state, drawing large and enthusiastic crowds, particularly in Harris-

---

61. *New York Times*, July 28, 1882.
62. Ibid., October 19, 1882.

burg and Wilkes-Barre, and recruiting local Republican officials at virtually every stop. Meanwhile, the regulars grew increasingly desperate. Leading out-of-state Republicans, including Senators Benjamin Harrison of Indiana, Ohio's John Sherman and George F. Edmunds of Vermont—the latter two who were actively seeking the party's presidential nomination in 1884—refused to travel to Pennsylvania to stump for the regular organization.[63] Playing up the "tariff scare" among manufacturers, the unsavory Simon Cameron suggested that Stewart's candidacy was being financed by free traders—a dubious charge, especially considering that the movement's key figures, such as Wharton Barker, Joseph Wharton and John Welsh, had close ties to the state's manufacturing interests and were generally regarded as staunch protectionists.[64] Regular Republican nominee James A. Beaver, a staunch Stalwart who hobbled around the state with a cane and had actively supported Grant's bid for an unprecedented third term in 1880, made the ludicrous charge that wealthy New Yorkers were buying up the state's coal lands and that only his election could prevent it from continuing, while the chairman of the Republican state committee, in a particularly loathsome ploy reminiscent of the Know-Nothings of three decades earlier, appealed to voters' prejudices by claiming that a number of Catholics were employed as clerks in Pattison's Philadelphia office.

Coming within 59 votes of carrying tiny Tioga County, Stewart's whirlwind campaign netted a respectable 43,743 votes to Democrat Robert Pattison's 355,791 and Republican James Beaver's 315,589.[65] Though they had no intention of "slaughtering" the state's Republican congressional delegation—as some of the state's partisan Republican newspapers charged—the Independent Republicans were also a factor in several U.S. House races in the state.[66] William McMichael, a popular Union army officer during the Civil War, garnered 40,995 votes while waging an energetic and spirited campaign, polling the difference between his major party rivals in a heated battle for the state's at-large congressional seat. Moreover, incumbent GOP lawmaker Cornelius C. Jadwin received a third of the vote in the state's 15th congressional district, finishing a close second in a race won by Democrat George Post. Running as an Independent Republican, Jadwin, a 47-year-old pharmacist from Honesdale, garnered 9,101 votes to Post's 11,555 and regular Republican Edward Overton's 5,675. Moreover, John

---

63. Ibid., September 27, 1882.
64. Ibid., August 24, 1882.
65. Greenback-Labor candidate Thomas Armstrong garnered 23,996 votes and the Temperance Party's Alfred C. Petit received 5,196.
66. *New York Times*, August 12, 1882.

McCleery, the Independent Republican nominee in the state's 14th congressional district, polled the difference between Republican Samuel F. Barr and his Democratic rival in a race decided by only 145 votes. Though the Independent Republicans failed to win many seats in their own right, their presence in the general election, splitting the vote in traditionally Republican districts throughout the state, enabled the Democrats to take control of the Pennsylvania House for the first time since 1876. Their presence also helped the Democrats win twelve of the state's twenty-seven congressional seats—compared to only eight seats won during the 1880 congressional elections.

Nationally, the Independent Republicans claimed three seats in the 48th Congress—Nelson Dingley in Maine, Theodore Lyman in Massachusetts and the highly popular Knute Nelson in Minnesota. The party had also endorsed Wisconsin's John Winans, a Janesville lawyer and independent-minded member of the state legislature. A Democrat, Winans eked out a narrow victory over his Republican opponent in a tight four-way race where the Prohibition and Greenback candidates combined for nearly 8.5% of the vote. The Independent Republicans had clearly provided Winans' margin of victory in that razor-thin contest.

In all, roughly 125,000 votes were cast for Independent Republican congressional candidates in the 1882 mid-term elections. Despite the party's relative success in a handful of races, most Independent Republican candidates fared poorly, the most disastrous results occurring in Maine where the party's gubernatorial candidate, Warren N. Vinton, polled less than two-tenths of one percent of the vote, finishing dead last behind the Greenback Party's Solon Chase and Prohibitionist William T. Eustis.

The Independent Republican movement fizzled out shortly after the 1882 campaign. There was, to be sure, some occasional sniping by insurgent Republicans in the years that followed. In 1885, for example, the Independent Republicans in Pennsylvania threatened to run a candidate against the much-despised and much-feared Republican boss Matthew S. Quay in the state treasurer's race, but their threat proved to be empty. Most of the Republican insurgents, such as Minnesota's Knute Nelson, returned to the regular Republican fold. Nelson, of course, retained a fiercely independent streak, occasionally going against his party as evidenced by his support of a federal income tax and low tariffs and his sponsorship of legislation creating the Commerce and Labor Department in 1902. Pennsylvania's Charles Wolfe and others, however, found new political homes. Wolfe later cast his lot with the fledgling Prohibition Party and waged a spirited campaign for governor on its ticket in 1886, polling a respectable 32,458 votes in that contest.

The Readjuster Movement in Virginia

Launched by former Confederate hero William C. Mahone in Richmond in late February 1879, the Readjuster Party of Virginia was one of the most successful statewide third parties in American history, eclipsed perhaps only by Minnesota's left-wing Farmer-Labor Party of the 1920s and 1930s. Founded as a result of a longstanding dispute over the state's mounting public debt following the Civil War, the Readjusters, a proto-Populist movement, played a major role in Virginia politics for nearly a decade. Third parties, of course, were nothing new in Virginia. Two separate and distinct Conservative parties flourished in the Old Dominion prior to the emergence of the Readjuster movement. In addition, Virginians elected three Know-Nothing congressmen, including ardent states' righter Alexander R. Boteler, in the 1850s.

The first of the two Conservative parties, adhering to a strict states' rights philosophy, was largely comprised of anti-Van Buren Democrats. This party, operating independently of the national Democrats, elected two congressmen in 1838. The second and far more successful Conservative Party, created in opposition to radical Republican Reconstruction in the late 1860s, was a vital force in Virginia politics for more than a decade and a half before finally aligning itself with the national Democratic Party in 1883. The latter-day Conservatives, who took their name in deference to the large number of former Whigs who joined their party in droves in the aftermath of the Civil War, sent no fewer than five congressmen to Washington in 1869 and elected Gilbert C. Walker, a 36-year-old transplanted New Yorker, governor that same year. An attorney and wealthy industrialist, Walker defeated Virginia's incumbent Republican Henry Horatio Wells by more than 18,000 votes to effectively end provisional Republican rule in that state. The second Conservative Party also elected John W. Johnston and Robert E. Withers to the U.S. Senate in 1870 and 1875, respectively. A physician and former Confederate army officer, Withers was the founder of the *Lynchburg News*, while the white-bearded Johnston, a former circuit court judge, had served in the Virginia legislature prior to the war. At least ten Conservatives also held seats in Congress between 1870 and 1877.

Demanding that Virginia's huge debt incurred during the Civil War and the period of Reconstruction should be significantly scaled back, William Mahone, aided by a serious economic depression, bolted from the Funder-dominated Conservative Party and led the Readjusters to a sweeping victory in the 1879 statewide elections, capturing 56 of the 100 seats in the state House of Delegates and 24 of the 40 seats in the state Senate. Described by one historian as the "most successful interracial democratic political movement in the postwar South," most of the Readjuster support came from African-American voters, as well as from poor whites living in the western part of the state.[67] Interestingly, Mahone himself once estimated that the party's membership included about 110,000 blacks and roughly 65,000 whites.

The son of a saloonkeeper, Mahone's rise to political power was nothing short of spectacular. A graduate of the Virginia Military Institute, his ability to lead and command didn't go unnoticed by Robert E. Lee and, as a result, he quickly rose to the rank of major-general during the Civil War. Wounded during the second battle of Manassas, Mahone founded the Norfolk & Western Railroad shortly after the war. Though he eventually lost most of his personal fortune during the depression of 1873, he also purchased the *Richmond Whig*, a daily newspaper, during this period. The "Railroad Ishmael," as he was dubbed, won a seat in the U.S. Senate as a Readjuster in 1880 and briefly held the balance of power between the evenly divided Democrats and Republicans in that body.[68] He was later branded a "traitor" when he formally joined the Republican Party a few years later, eventually becoming that party's undisputed boss in Virginia.

Other prominent Readjusters included Harrison H. Riddleberger, a former Democrat who, like Mahone, also served in the U.S. Senate as a Readjuster, and William E. Cameron who was elected governor on the Readjuster ticket in 1881—a year when the party again won majorities in both chambers of the legislature. A 38-year-old newspaper editor and lawyer, Riddleberger was the sponsor of legislation that finally settled Virginia's longstanding and divisive debt issue. An influential ally of William Mahone, the Shenandoah Valley lawmaker was also largely responsible for directing patronage to build up the fledgling party organization. Cameron, an editorial writer of immense influence, was a popular three-term mayor of Petersburg, a city with a majority African-American population. Another prominent Readjuster was John E. Massey, a fiery Baptist preacher and farmer who served as lieutenant governor, state auditor, and state superintendent of public instruction. Largely because of Mahone's hostility toward him, "Parson Massey," a former Conservative and self-described "father of the Read-

---

67. Jane Dailey, *Before Jim Crow: the Politics of Race in Postemancipation Virginia* (Chapel Hill, 2000), p. 5.

68. The Democrats and Republicans each held thirty-seven seats in the U.S. Senate. Former Supreme Court Justice David Davis of Illinois held the other seat. The rotund Illinoisan had been elected to the U.S. Senate as an independent in 1877, but was expected to align himself with the Democrats.

juster movement," never fulfilled his dream of serving as governor or possibly in the U.S. Senate.

Following its initial showing the previous year, the Readjusters had high hopes as the 1880 presidential election approached. Rejecting overtures from the Democrats, Republicans and the Greenback-Labor Party, the Readjusters, under Mahone's leadership, ran their own slate of presidential electors committed to Democrat Winfield Scott Hancock during the 1880 presidential election, but finished a distant third in the statewide balloting. Despite their relatively poor showing, the Readjusters managed to elect two congressmen that year—John Paul and Abram Fulkerson, both of whom were regarded as moderates.[69]

The party, however, quickly rebounded from the experience of 1880. In addition to sending Mahone to the U.S. Senate and putting Cameron in the governor's chair in 1881, Readjuster candidates captured five of the state's nine U.S. House seats in the 1882 congressional elections. The party's success, of course, was no accident. Given choice committee assignments in the U.S. Senate and ample patronage powers from President Chester Arthur—who, unlike his predecessors Hayes and Garfield, welcomed Readjuster support—Mahone was a ruthless political boss, demanding complete loyalty and generosity. Among other things, state employees living in Richmond were expected to contribute five percent of their salaries to the party's coffers and federal employees were required to donate no less than two percent of their annual salaries to the party. Businesses receiving state contracts were also expected to give generously to the Readjuster war chest. Mahone, who was never particularly popular among the party's rank-and-file, also cleverly gerrymandered the state's congressional districts to assure the election of candidates sympathetic to the Republican administration—in one instance going so far as to squeeze 187,000 whites into one district and suggesting that it was equivalent to 132,000 people living in a predominately black district. In a few short years, Mahone, though lacking much in the way of personal

---

69. The pro-Hancock Readjuster ticket garnered only 31,507 votes to the national Democrats' 96,449 and the GOP's 84,020. (See Renan Levine, "Readjuster Party of Virginia, 1877-1883," *The Encyclopedia of Third Parties in America*, Vol. II, p. 483.) Earlier that year, Mahone had toyed with the idea of fielding an independent slate of presidential electors and later, when it appeared likely that former President Ulysses S. Grant would capture the Republican nomination for a third term, proposed a Readjuster-Republican fusion ticket consisting of six Readjusters and five Republicans, but that idea was later rejected by the Republican state convention. Mahone's electoral ticket was ultimately ignored by the Democratic National Committee, which threw its support to the Funders' Democratic electors.

magnetism, had built a political machine that was the envy of his rival Conservatives.[70]

During Cameron's administration, the Readjusters successfully repudiated a
third of the state's prewar debt and floated low-interest bonds to pay the remaining debt. Though it wasn't finally settled until 1918, the debt issue was virtually
removed from the state's front burner—at least as a contentious political matter—when the U.S. Supreme Court validated the Riddleberger Act in 1883. In
its ruling, the nation's highest court ordered the state to pay a total debt of about
$21 million through the issuance of new interest-bearing bonds known as "Rid-
dlebergers." The remaining one-third of the state's pre-Civil War debt was to be
assumed by West Virginia, which at the beginning of the war had been part of
Virginia.

But that year also marked the beginning of the end for the progressive, multi-
racial party. Having completely fused with the Republicans, the Readjuster campaign of 1883 was an unmitigated disaster, beginning with a bloody race riot a
few days before the election outside the Danville Opera House, which left several
people dead.[71] Successfully portraying the riot as a "race war" instigated by blacks
while falsely suggesting that this was the sort of thing that voters could expect to
happen as a result of race-mixing or when African-Americans were given positions of authority, the race-baiting Democrats easily swept the 1883 elections,
thereby ending the party's brief and eventful control of Virginia politics.

When the party mysteriously petered out in 1887—not long before implementation of the notorious Jim Crow laws officially sanctioning the social and
political disenfranchisement of millions of blacks in the South—it left a progressive legacy. Among other things, the forward-looking Readjusters increased corporate taxes, abolished the whipping post, eliminated the one-dollar poll tax and
reduced real estate taxes across-the-board by approximately twenty percent, or
nearly $13,000,000. The party also increased appropriations for public education
by more than $200,000 a year over the amounts spent during the period of Con-
servative Party domination from 1870-77 and provided funding for the construction of an African-American college at Petersburg. Many Readjusters, including

---

70. Charles Chilton Pearson, *The Readjuster Movement in Virginia* (New Haven, 1917),
     p. 156.
71. The riot was believed to have been triggered by state Senate candidate William E.
     Sims, a Yale-educated Scalawag-turned-Readjuster, who delivered a passionate
     speech to a large following of African-American supporters in racially-tense Danville
     the week before the election. Sims, a former Confederate soldier, had lost narrowly
     in a bid for Congress on the Readjuster ticket the previous year.

Mahone, remained politically active as Republicans following the party's baffling disappearance while others returned to the Democratic fold. Mahone ran unsuccessfully for governor on the Republican ticket in 1889, losing to Democrat Philip W. McKinney by 42,000 votes.

17

John P. St. John & "Beast" Butler

◆

The Prohibition and Anti-Monopoly Parties in 1884

The topsy-turvy and razor-thin presidential contest of 1884 between Democrat Grover Cleveland and Republican James G. Blaine marked the first of two campaigns in the party's history that the Prohibitionists played a major, if not decisive, role in determining the outcome of a presidential election. Invigorated by a relatively strong showing in the 1882 mid-term elections, the Prohibitionists, hoping, in the words of their national party chairman to "strike a crushing blow at one wing of the liquor army," nominated former two-term Kansas governor John P. St. John for president. The party's vice-presidential candidate was William Daniel, a former state senator from Maryland and founding president of that state's Temperance Alliance.

Born in Brookville, Indiana, St. John, the son of an alcoholic father, had to fend for himself at an early age—joining the California gold rush, voyaging as a sailor to Hawaii, Central and South America and later enlisting as an Indian fighter, an occupation in which he was twice wounded. Possessing an innate thirst for knowledge, he read as much history and biography as he could lay his hands on. He also began studying law while living in a miner's cabin. St. John later moved to Charleston, Illinois, and began practicing law. Serving as a lieutenant colonel of one of that state's regiments during the Civil War, he settled in Kansas after the war and launched his political career shortly thereafter, eventually winning a seat in the state Senate as a Republican. While in the legislature, he earned a reputation as a strong proponent of prohibition. For years, the state's Prohibition Party asked him to be its candidate for governor, but St. John repeatedly turned them down, believing that the Republican Party would ultimately take up the "dry" cause.

St. John finally agreed to run on the Prohibition ticket, but only on the condition that his own party refused to add a prohibition amendment to the state constitution. Much to his delight, the Republican Party not only embraced prohibition but also nominated him for governor in 1878. He was easily elected that year, garnering nearly 54% of the vote and was re-elected by an even wider margin two years later. As governor, St. John pushed through the prohibition amendment, making Kansas the first state in the nation to adopt such a measure (shortly thereafter, Maine followed suit by passing its own prohibition amendment).

In 1882, St. John fell victim to the "wets" within his own party and narrowly lost his bid for a third term, losing to Democrat George W. Glick by 8,000 votes in a three-cornered race with the Greenback Party's Charles Robinson. Nevertheless, the former Kansas governor continued to cling to the notion that the national Republican Party would eventually embrace the issue of prohibition. However, a number of incidents leading up to the 1884 presidential election made it clear that the GOP had no intention of championing the prohibition cause.

The first of these incidents occurred during the party's platform committee hearings when Frances Willard, the dynamic young president of the Woman's Christian Temperance Union and activist extraordinaire who much preferred hunting and horseback riding to housework, pleaded with the Republican hierarchy to present a forthright position on prohibition. Willard was given a rather cold reception and a copy of the WCTU memorandum that she had presented to the platform committee was later found on the floor stained with tobacco juice. The tobacco-stained memo was photographed and subsequently appeared in a number of temperance periodicals across the nation, enraging a significant portion of the GOP's prohibitionist base.

The nation's temperance forces were further alienated from the Republican Party when that party's nominees, James G. Blaine and John A. Logan, suggested that tax revenues for liquor sales might be used to help fund public education—a policy, according to D. Leigh Colvin, that was "exceedingly distasteful to persons of moral discernment." But the incident that really galvanized the Prohibitionists in 1884 took place in the Maine state elections in September of that year. Maine was the scene of a spirited, hard-fought campaign to add a prohibition amendment to the state's constitution. When Blaine, a native of the state, arrived at his polling place he refused to take the ballot containing the question on the constitutional amendment. News of his indifference spread through the temperance ranks like wildfire.

Dismayed by Blaine's actions and upset that Willard had been given such short shrift at the Republican convention, St. John decided to seek the Prohibition Party's presidential nomination. "I will condemn such cowardice, such disregard of the best interest of the people with my voice and vote," he said in aligning himself with the nation's largest minor party.

But the former Kansas governor wasn't alone. At least four others were also considered for the party's presidential nomination that year, including General Clinton B. Fisk of New Jersey and party chairman Gideon T. Stewart, a former newspaper editor, lawyer, and perennial Prohibition candidate for public office in Ohio. A former Whig, the sixty-year-old Stewart ran for the Ohio State Supreme Court on no fewer than ten occasions between 1869 and 1899. There was also a flurry of activity on behalf of James Black of Pennsylvania, the party's aging presidential standard-bearer in the 1872 campaign. However, no one ran harder for the nomination than Richard H. McDonald, a 64-year-old physician from San Francisco. McDonald had been the party's candidate for governor of California in 1882. McDonald's campaign for the party's presidential nomination, however, encountered rough sailing when it was learned that he had once worked in a whiskey distillery in Kentucky and by more recent charges that he had manufactured and sold a medication containing alcohol—a charge that his supporters tried to refuted by pointing out that every bottle sold included a temperance tract attacking the liquor industry.

Having rescheduled their national convention until after the Democratic and Republican conventions had adjourned, the Prohibitionists—then calling themselves, courtesy of Frances Willard, the Prohibition Home Protection Party—convened in Pittsburgh on July 23-24 and, following a motion by new national committee chairman John B. Finch, unanimously nominated John P. St. John for the nation's highest office. More than seven hundred delegates and alternates from thirty-one states and territories attended the gathering at Pittsburgh's Lafayette Hall.

Frances E. Willard, the public-spirited leader of the Woman's Christian Temperance Union who later worked closely with Terence V. Powderly and the Knights of Labor while slowly embracing Populism and eventually drifting toward socialism—a path also taken by the Populist Party's Mary E. Lease—was among those who gave seconding speeches for St. John. A devoted Prohibitionist at the time, Willard had urged the party to change its name to the Prohibition Home Protection Party a few years earlier and was believed to have been the one responsible for the adoption of the white rose as the party's emblem.[1] Willard's speech was followed by such a loud and prolonged applause, observed one reporter, that it seemed like it would never stop. Clara A. Hoffman of Missouri gave one of the seconding speeches. Hoffman's speech, though somewhat over-blown, may have been the most eloquent, describing the former Kansas governor as "the Lion-hearted, leading the crusade of the nineteenth century, not to the rescue of the empty sepulcher of our risen and ascended Lord from Moslem hands, but to rescue and reclaim the temple of the soul where should ever dwell the spirit of the Crucified."[2]

Fifty-eight-year-old William Daniel, who served as temporary chairman of the convention, was named as St. John's vice-presidential running mate after Clinton Fisk and George P. Rogers, a former local public officeholder from New London, Connecticut, withdrew from the race. Born on remote Deal's Island in Somerset County, Maryland, Daniel was a graduate of Dickinson College where he had studied law. He was first elected to the Maryland House of Delegates in 1853 before winning a seat in the state Senate on the Know-Nothing ticket in 1857. He resigned the following year, moved to Baltimore, and became an ardent anti-slavery Republican. Known as the "Little Giant," he was also a member of the Maryland State Constitutional Convention in 1864 that grappled with the ques-tion of emancipation of the state's slave population and eight years later became the first president of the Maryland State Temperance Alliance, serving in that capacity until 1884. Under his leadership, thirteen of Maryland's twenty-three counties outlawed the sale and consumption of liquor under the state's local option laws. An able attorney—he maintained a law practice in Baltimore from 1858 to 1897—Daniel personally drafted many of those laws, defended them in court and frequently prosecuted violators.[3]

In addition to the many comprehensive reforms advocated in previous years, such as women's suffrage, the party's platform included several new planks sup-porting, among other things, veterans' pensions and a protective tariff. As usual, the Prohibitionists also took a swipe at the two major parties, condemning the Republicans for doing nothing in the twenty-four years that they had controlled the White House and Congress to curb the baneful liquor traffic and criticizing the Democrats for blocking the creation of a commission of inquiry to study the effects of such traffic. Claiming that the liquor industry was costing the nation

---

1.   J. C. Furnas, *The Life and Times of the Late Demon Rum* (London, 1965), p. 287. Willard also named her new collie puppy after the party, or "Hib" for short.
2.   Colvin, *Prohibition in the United States*, pp. 155-157.
3.   Ibid., p. 157.

eight hundred million dollars a year while dragging families into poverty, destroying lives and filling up the country's jail cells, penitentiaries, insane asylums and hospitals with its victims, the Prohibition platform, as in the three previous presidential campaigns, once again called for a constitutional amendment prohibiting the importation, exportation, manufacture and sale of alcoholic drinks.

The presidential election of 1884 was one of the most acrimonious and exciting campaigns in American history. Both major party candidates, to be sure, had somewhat tarnished records, although one was of a personal nature while the other involved a candidate's public conduct. Democrat Grover Cleveland's reputation, for example, had come under close scrutiny after the *Buffalo Evening Telegraph* reported the "sordid" story of Maria Halpin, who alleged that Cleveland had fathered a son to her ten years earlier. For his part, Cleveland accepted responsibility for the child and made some financial arrangements for his upbringing. He later had the boy placed in an orphanage due to the mother's alleged negligence. The young boy was eventually adopted. In any case, the story was carried in Republican-owned newspapers throughout the country. Republican James G. Blaine, a former Speaker of the House of Representatives, was no saint himself. His earlier shady transactions with railroad interests surfaced time and again during the campaign.

Given the negative publicity heaped on both major party candidates, the Prohibition Party was positioned to make significant gains in 1884. Seeking "to make the party a force that should be felt," St. John, sporting what one writer described as "the finest pair of handlebar mustaches west of St. Louis" concentrated the bulk of his effort in the larger states, especially New York.[4] The former Kansas governor realized that the Empire State's thirty-six electoral votes would be crucial in what was shaping up to be an extremely close contest between Cleveland and Blaine. As such, St. John made at least forty-one appearances in the state during the campaign. He also made seventeen campaign stops between Illinois and Massachusetts and was greeted by overflow audiences in at least six major cities. His vice-presidential running mate, William Daniel, stumped in eight southern states and conducted a swing through New England, Illinois and Wisconsin.

For the first time in its history, active party chapters were established in states throughout the country. Prominent statewide tickets bolstered the fledgling party's uphill campaign for the White House. In Massachusetts, Julius H. Seelye,

---

4.   Furnas, *The Life and Times of the Late Demon Rum*, p. 273.

a former congressman and president of Amherst College, was the party's gubernatorial candidate and James B. Hobbs, former president of the Chicago Board of
Trade, stood as the party's candidate for governor in Illinois. In Wisconsin, the
party slated Samuel D. Hastings for governor. A proven vote getter, Hastings was
a former four-term state treasurer.

Perhaps the most significant work done at the state level during this period
was in Indiana, where party member Eli Ritter, a Civil War hero and lawyer who
established the legal basis for prohibition in the courts, put together a first-rate
organization that would pay huge dividends for the party for years to come. The
father of Halsted Ritter—one of only a handful of federal judges ever convicted
and removed from office—and Mary Ritter Beard, the well-known suffragist and
women's rights activist, the elder Ritter was best known in Prohibition circles for
having won a reversal in federal court of a state Supreme Court ruling in *Haggart
v. Stehlin*, establishing a legal precedence that saloonkeepers didn't enjoy the
same rights as other business owners because of their potential harm to the moral
tone of a community. He also gained some fame a few years later by prosecuting
voting fraud cases against some of Indiana's major political bosses. Although Ritter's organizing efforts came too late to directly benefit St. John's candidacy that
year, his efforts nonetheless laid the groundwork for subsequent Prohibition campaigns, making Indiana, historically, one of the party's strongest and most
dependable states.[5]

There's little question that St. John's candidacy posed a genuine threat to the
GOP's prospects that year, especially since the Republicans were already badly
divided by the departure of the independent and reform-minded "Mugwumps."
Derived from an Algonquin Indian word meaning "big chief," the term was originally used derisively but was later worn as a badge of honor by the independent-
minded Republican reformers, whose ranks that year included Daniel DeLeon,
the Columbia University professor who later guided the Socialist Labor Party as
its longtime intellectual guru and autocratic leader.

The Prohibition strategy—a long shot, to be sure—was to try to throw the
presidential election into the House of Representatives by pulling off an upset
victory in heavily populated New York. The situation in that state was both complex and volatile, to say the least. Like Anti-Monopolist Benjamin Butler, St.
John made an all-out effort there and party leaders were convinced that a large
number of temperance supporters who usually voted Republican would support
the former Kansas governor as a way of scolding Blaine. The Republicans, of

---

5.   Storms, *Partisan Prophets*, p. 14.

course, were keenly aware of this possibility and, through the auspices of the Republican National Committee, secretly financed the campaign of the Anti-Monopoly Party's Butler in an attempt to siphon Democratic votes from Grover Cleveland.

The Republicans had repudiated President Chester Arthur on the fourth ballot at their national convention in Chicago in early June, opting instead for Blaine, considered by many to be the most popular Republican of his generation. In addition to unseating a sitting president of his own party, Blaine had also swept past several other notable candidates on his way to securing the GOP nomination. Among those pushed aside were Senators George F. Edmunds of Vermont, John A. Logan of Illinois, John Sherman of Ohio and Connecticut's Joseph R. Hawley, a former editor of the *Hartford Courant*. In addition, two other prominent Republicans, whose names had the potential of galvanizing a deadlocked Chicago convention, were never serious factors in the race—Robert Todd Lincoln, the forty-year-old son of the late president who was then serving as Secretary of War, and William T. Sherman, the venerated Civil War general. Lincoln and Sherman didn't actively seek the GOP's nomination, but both received a scattering of votes at the convention. Stalwart John A. Logan of Illinois, who had traveled the path of military glory to political prominence, was named as Blaine's vice-presidential running mate. A one-time leader of the Grand Army of the Republic, the nation's most powerful veterans' group, the 58-year-old Logan was one of the congressmen named to conduct impeachment proceedings against Andrew Johnson in 1868.

The GOP platform repeated many of the same vague pledges made in earlier platforms, but its tariff plank was decidedly more protectionist than in the past. The Republicans also called for an international agreement to fix the relative value of gold and silver; endorsed railroad regulation; the creation of a labor bureau; extension of civil service reform; and improvement of the Navy. The Republicans also eulogized Garfield who was assassinated in 1881 and, though casting him into political oblivion, heaped praise on Arthur's administration.

President Arthur, who had high hopes of winning the presidency in his own right, was deeply disappointed at being rejected by his own party. As the fourth vice president in American history to assume the office of chief magistrate following the death of a president, Arthur was anxious to put his own stamp on the White House by replacing almost all of Garfield's cabinet officers in the months following his swearing-in as the nation's twenty-first president in the early morning hours of September 20, 1881. Secretary of War Robert Todd Lincoln was the only Cabinet officer who was asked to stay on. Even James G. Blaine was eventually replaced as Secretary of State.

To the surprise and delight of the nation's leading political reformers, the new president confounded many in his own party by proposing a sweeping reform of the country's civil service system in his first annual address to Congress in December 1881. Despite his own mediocre record on patronage—a record marked by the old adage "to the victor go the spoils"—Arthur signed the Pendleton Civil Service Act into law thirteen months later. This was particularly galling to party bosses, such as New York's Roscoe Conkling, who believed they had found refuge in Arthur's bosom. Saddled with a Democratic majority in the House following the 1882 mid-term elections, Arthur was unable to get Congress to act on many of his proposals. His appeals for federal aid to education had fallen on deaf ears. So, too, did his suggestion that since the country was experiencing a wave of prosperity, marked by a $109 million federal surplus, Congress should abolish all internal revenue taxes except those on tobacco and alcoholic beverages. As the nation's chief executive, Arthur used his veto power sparingly, but flexing what little muscle he had, he vetoed legislation excluding Chinese immigration and a bill calling for $19 million in river and harbor improvements that he felt was riddled with pork for special interests. Congress, however, was able to override both vetoes.

During the course of his "accidental" presidency, the former "Gentleman Boss" of New York City alienated almost every element of New York's Republican establishment, especially the power-hungry Stalwarts who received little in the way of patronage and spoils from their old leader. Likewise, the powerful New York duo of Roscoe Conkling and Thomas C. Platt, a wealthy banker and Conkling protégé, were personally excluded from Arthur's administration. In the spring of 1881, both men resigned from the U.S. Senate in a huff after Garfield appointed James G. Blaine, their archenemy, to head the State Department and then refused to give them any control over patronage in New York, excluding them from sharing in the biggest prize of all—the New York Customhouse. By this time, Conkling had lost all respect for Garfield—and his disdain for the administration continued into Arthur's years as president. Compared to Arthur's presidency, he once sighed, "the administration of Hayes becomes respectable, if not heroic."[6] Shortly after resigning from the Senate, Conkling, whose abrasive nature offended many politicians and voters alike, looked to the New York legislature for vindication, but the state's lawmakers refused to return him to the U.S.

---

6.   Degregorio, *The Complete Book of U.S. Presidents*, p. 32.

Senate. The man who Blaine once described as possessing an "overpowering tur-key-gobbler strut," then walked off the political stage forever. He later turned down offers to serve on the U.S. Supreme Court.

Unwittingly or not, Arthur also offended a number of prominent Republicans outside of New York, including Ohio's John Sherman and James G. Blaine of Maine, the latter being somewhat put off by Secretary of State Frederick T. Frel-inghuysen's seeming disregard for many of the policies he established during his tenure in the State Department. The independents, or so-called "Mugwumps," were the only group that might have been predisposed to supporting the belea-guered president—but even they didn't trust him enough to lend their critical support in his uphill battle for the party's nomination.

The Anti-Monopolists

The late nineteenth century saw the rise of the "robber barons," men like J.P. Morgan, John D. Rockefeller, Andrew Carnegie and the circumspect Jacob Schiff. Their advent in the business world accompanied the emergence of the modern corporation. While no one could argue that the tremendous increase in productivity and the introduction of new forms of energy, new materials and new inventions fostered by the industrial revolution, were certainly beneficial to the nation, many worried about the growing concentration of wealth spawned by these emerging financial and industrial giants. Though many Americans contin-ued to revere men like Thomas Edison, George Westinghouse and other fathers of the Industrial Age, a number of others were becoming increasingly concerned with the social by-products of industrialism—namely, the presence of concen-trated wealth and economic power, with its ability to influence and corrupt not only politics, but society in general. The fear, suspicion and envy engendered by this massive concentration of wealth soon found its political expression in the growing anti-monopoly movement.

Prior to the mid-1880s, the anti-monopolists could always find some refuge in the Grangers or Greenbackers. By the early eighties, however, it was becoming increasingly clear that the growing economic power of monopolies and financial trusts had to be resisted in a more direct manner. Good old-fashioned, honest American competition was nearly dead, or so they believed, having been mortally wounded by greedy, power-hungry business tycoons like Rockefeller and Schiff who were gobbling up one enterprise after another.

This renewed wave of anti-monopoly agitation began in early 1881, shortly after Henry Demarest Lloyd published a story critical of the Standard Oil monopoly in the pages of the *Atlantic Monthly*. The magazine article formed the basis for his best-selling book *Wealth against Commonwealth*. Shortly thereafter, a number of other journalists took up the cause and before long the anti-monopoly movement was a force to be reckoned with.[7]

The leading anti-monopolist critics of the day included economist Henry George and Edward Bellamy, America's best known and most influential utopian socialist. George's *Progress and Poverty*, published in 1879, and Bellamy's *Looking Backward*, published nine years later, alerted a large segment of the American population to the dangers of business mergers and the problems associated with the nation's trusts.

In *Looking Backward*, Bellamy wrote about a lone survivor of capitalist Boston in the late 1880s who was suddenly awakened in the year 2000, after more than a century of sleep, to discover that American society had undergone a profound and peaceful revolution. Private ownership of the means of production had been abolished and a new society, free from exploitation, poverty, war, crime, corruption and pollution, had been created. While Bellamy's book was denounced as radical and dangerous, it nevertheless reached a large audience. Bellamy, a lifelong resident of Chicopee Falls, Massachusetts, had struck a chord.

Henry George made his celebrated case against economic concentration in the opening of his book *Progress and Poverty*, a financial opus that, according to biographer Edward J. Rose, was destined to be the *Uncle Tom's Cabin* of the 1880s. Like Harriet Beecher Stowe's book, the single-tax economist also addressed the issue of slavery—wage slavery—and it was the monopolist and landowner who was the Simon Legree of George's book.[8] "So long as all increased wealth which modern progress brings goes but [to] build up great fortunes, to increase luxury and make sharper the contrast between the House of Have and the House of Want, progress is not real and cannot be permanent," wrote George. "The reaction must come."[9]

One such reaction was the creation of the short-lived Anti-Monopoly Party in the summer of 1883. The culmination of nearly twenty years of progressive politics laid the foundation for this hardy and forward-looking party, the outgrowth of hundreds of local anti-monopolist reform efforts in the Midwest, Northeast, and the South, dating back to the establishment of the National Labor Union in 1865 and the fledgling Labor Reform Party of the early 1870s.[10] Holding its

---

7.   Haynes, *Third Party Movements Since the Civil War*, p. 147.
8.   Edward J. Rose, *Henry George*, (New York, 1968), pp. 60-61.
9.   Henry George, *Progress and Poverty*.
10.   Ritter, *Goldbugs and Greenbacks*, p. 53.

national convention in Chicago on May 14, 1884, the Anti-Monopolists endorsed the principles of the Declaration of Independence and sounded the alarm against the "giant monopolies," especially those in the banking and transportations industries, which had "inflicted countless wrongs upon the toiling millions of the United States." The party's platform also called on Congress to "protect the man who earns his bread by the sweat of his face" by establishing a bureau of labor statistics empowered to settle labor disputes by arbitration rather than brute force, enforcing an eight-hour day and prohibiting the importation of cheap foreign labor. The Anti-Monopolists also called for the timely payment of the nation's public debt, the direct election of U.S. senators, the enactment of a graduated income tax, and an end to the prevailing practice of providing large land grants to corporations. In a sweeping appeal to the nation's farmers to assist in the overthrow of monopolies, the party's platform sharply denounced widespread corporate and railroad discrimination against farmers and demanded "the fostering care of government" to protect them.[11]

Meeting at the Hershey Music Hall, the Anti-Monopoly Party, with delegates representing twenty-one states and territories, as well as the District of Columbia, chose the controversial Benjamin F. Butler of Massachusetts for president. Marked by equanimity, the Anti-Monopoly convention easily nominated Butler on the first ballot, giving him 124 of 132 votes to a scattering for Allen G. Thurman of Ohio and the inimitable Solon Chase of Maine. John F. Henry, who succeeded temporary chairman Alson J. Streeter of Illinois, chaired the one-day affair. The ambitious Butler, who did not immediately accept the nomination—delaying his formal acceptance for nearly two months—nevertheless hoped that the Anti-Monopoly and Greenback nominations would enhance his chances of winning the Democratic presidential nomination in July. The Anti-Monopolists left open the vice-presidential slot, but later accepted as Butler's running mate the choice of the dying Greenback Party. In many respects, Butler, who had once been described as the "Mephistophiles of American politics," was the ideal candidate for this new party.[12]

The former governor of Massachusetts, after all, had laid down the gauntlet against the Democrats and Republicans some six years earlier when he professed his independence from both major parties. "I have left the old parties," he asserted in a speech in Maine in August 1878. "I belonged to the Democratic

---

11. Myra Burt Adelman, "Anti-Monopoly Party 1884," *The Encyclopedia of Third Parties in America*, Vol. I, p. 179.
12. *Chicago Daily Tribune*, November 13, 1874, quoted in Haynes, *Third Party Movements Since the Civil War*, p. 151.

Party until it attempted to destroy the Union, and was with the Republican Party until it deserted its founders the laboring-men," he continued. "The capitalists now hold the Republican Party bound hand and foot." The former Union army general, who was then running for governor of Massachusetts on the Greenback-Labor ticket, was particularly critical of the GOP, a party he had been identified with for more than a decade following the Civil War. President Hayes, he charged, had violated virtually every pledge he made during his 1876 campaign and had betrayed African-Americans in the South, adding that President Grant's efforts to strengthen public credit a few years earlier was nothing short of "a swindle."[13] He had also endeared himself to party leaders with his testimony against the powerful Standard Oil Trust before a congressional committee in 1880 and by his consistent condemnation of the polarization of wealth—an issue he rarely veered from dating back to his days as military governor of New Orleans when he placed a punitive levy on the wealthy citizens of that city to help feed the poor.[14]

The Greenback-Labor Party, in a state of serious decline following its drubbing in the 1882 mid-term congressional elections, convened at English's Opera House in Indianapolis two weeks later and also named Butler as its presidential candidate. As expected, the former general wasn't exactly given a free ride at the Greenback gathering. A number of delegates wanted to nominate Jesse Harper for president while still others looked to Ohio's John Seitz, a former state legislator and former Greenback gubernatorial candidate, to lead the party's ticket against Cleveland and Blaine in the general election. A venerable leader of the Greenback Party in Illinois, Harper was the man who had placed Abraham Lincoln's name in nomination at the Republican national convention in 1860. The 55-year-old Seitz, who twice ran for Congress on the Greenback ticket, withdrew from the race shortly before the Indianapolis convention. Others were talking up the name of aging Supreme Court Justice David Davis—the man who left the Labor Reform Party high and dry in 1872—but his potential candidacy failed to excite the party's rank-and-file. Despite a spirited effort on the part of Harper's supporters, Butler easily defeated the crusty 61-year-old journalist by a vote of 323 to 98 on the first ballot, with two delegates opting for Maine's Solon Chase and one voting for Edward Allis of Wisconsin. The rapidly disintegrating party made only one significant contribution to the 1884 campaign, that of naming Absolom M. West, a former Confederate general from Mississippi, as Butler's

13.   Ritter, *Goldbugs and Greenbacks*, p. 143; Haynes, *Third Party Movements Since the Civil War*, p. 150.

14.   Hans L. Trefousse, *Ben Butler: The South Called Him Beast!* (New York, 1957), p. 250.

vice-presidential running mate. The 66-year-old West, who served in the Mississippi legislature as a Union Whig prior to the war-between-the-states, had been the Greenback-Labor candidate for the U.S. Senate in 1880. In deference to the older party, the Anti-Monopoly Party's executive committee added West's name to their national ticket. As in the Weaver-Chambers ticket of four years earlier, the Greenback-Labor Party again had a ticket comprised of ex-Union and Confederate officers.

Continuing to weigh his options, Butler did not immediately accept the two minor party nominations. "Is not my record as a Greenbacker for twenty years sufficient without a formal pledge to you which would cause me to pointed at as a man who bids for the nomination?" he asked when urged to accept the Greenback Party's nomination in Indianapolis.[15] To many party activists, his coy response must have seemed like a case of *déjà vu*, eerily reminiscent of the way Judge David Davis of Illinois treated the Labor Reformers following their convention in 1872.

On the other hand, the self-styled financial reformer never lost his enthusiasm for the greenback cause, as expressed in a letter written nearly two years earlier. "The greenback is money, and is within the control of the government as all money is within its control...There is a practical difficulty with making the greenback nominally receivable for duties at the Custom House, because customs duties have been pledged by law to be received in gold as security for the interest on the national debt. That pledge of course cannot be broken. But gold certificates are received instead of gold, because they are the same thing. And the greenback, as long as it is equal to gold, or as now at a premium above it, will be received in the same way...I believe all thoughtful men are Greenbackers, and that the people will rise up *en masse* at any attempt to destroy the greenback."[16] Those words were music to the ears of Greenback enthusiasts throughout the country.

Encouraged by Tammany boss John Kelly, the irrepressible former governor of Massachusetts, hoping that lightning would strike, decided to seek the Democratic presidential nomination, but was virtually chased out of Chicago by the party's southern delegates who bitterly recalled his corrupt military rule of New Orleans during the Civil War.[17] The South, of course, wanted nothing to do with its old enemy. "We may be willing to eat crow," said one Georgia delegate,

---

15.   Haynes, *Third Party Movements Since the Civil War*, p. 149.
16.   Butler letter to H. G. Hinckley, Oct. 19, 1882, quoted in Holzman, *Stormy Ben Butler*, p. 215.

"but we'll be damned if we'll eat turkey buzzard."[18] Butler, who attended the convention as an at-large delegate from Massachusetts, was one of several candidates who actively sought the Democratic nomination that year. In addition to the former Massachusetts governor, the field also included Delaware's Thomas F. Bayard, Allen G. Thurman of Ohio, and Rep. Samuel J. Randall of Pennsylvania. The leading candidate, of course, was New York Gov. Grover Cleveland, a 47-year-old reformer who had incurred the ever-lasting enmity of Tammany Hall by aligning himself with young Teddy Roosevelt in a drive for municipal reform in New York City. A former sheriff and mayor of Buffalo where he put an end to corrupt street-cleaning and sewer contracts, the short, jolly, heavyset and blue-eyed governor was backed by reformers of all shapes and colors, including the "Mugwumps"—a group of independent Republicans who were generally unhappy with their party's nomination of James G. Blaine—in his drive for the Democratic nomination. His candidacy, however, offended the party's protectionists, led by longtime Representative and former Speaker of the House Samuel J. Randall of Philadelphia, a potential Butler ally who had gained some fleeting fame several years earlier with his slogan, "Retrenchment and Reform."[19]

In the meantime, "Cockeyed" Ben Butler was named, almost unanimously, as an at-large delegate to the Democratic national convention and a majority, though not all, of the Massachusetts delegation was committed to him on the first ballot.[20] Arriving in Chicago a day late, Butler was greeted at the railway station by 3,000 union members who had organized a parade complete with brass bands, huge portraits bearing his likeness and countless transparencies emblazoned with the words, "THE WORKINGMAN WELCOMES BUTLER," "BUTLER WILL SWEEP THE COUNTRY" and "LABOR NEEDS A

---

17. Roseboom, *A History of Presidential Elections*, p. 266; Plympton letter to Butler, June 20, 1884, Butler Papers, quoted in West, *Lincoln's Scapegoat General*, p. 383. Realizing that the Democrats were in a good position to win for the first time in more than twenty years, Butler hoped to take advantage of the considerable factionalism and feuds within the party to capture the nomination. In vying for the party's nod, the aging general dispatched his trusted advisor and campaign manager Noah A. Plympton to round up delegates pledged to him in several western states. On June 20, Plympton advised him that the situation was fluid, but that his chances hinged primarily on his ability to make inroads against Cleveland in New York. "A great deal depends on smashing Cleveland and that done we have a chance," he told Butler.

18. Robert S. Holzman, *Stormy Ben Butler*, pp. 215-216.

19. Trefousse, *Ben Butler: The South Called Him Beast!* p. 251.

20. West, *Lincoln's Scapegoat General*, p. 383.

STATESMAN." Later, a spontaneous crowd estimated at 20,000 gathered outside his hotel room to hear him speak.[21]

Though he realized by then that his own chances of capturing the party's nomination were almost nonexistent, the retired general was determined to deny Cleveland that honor. Hoping for a deadlocked convention, Butler and Tammany Hall's John Kelly tried to create a stampede for dark horse candidate Thomas A. Hendricks of Indiana by bribing the ticket taker at the convention hall to honor only the counterfeit tickets that they had distributed, thereby packing the convention's gallery with men who were paid to cheer every time Hendricks's name was mentioned. Their scheme almost worked as the deafening cheers and roars at every mention of the former Indiana governor's name nearly shook the convention hall to its foundation.

During the proceedings, Butler, further damaging his already slim prospects, antagonized the Democrats by calling for a high, Republican-style tariff, arguing that such a tariff was the only way to protect the jobs of laborers in New York, New Jersey, Connecticut, Massachusetts and elsewhere. However, the party's platform committee, beholden to moneyed interests, struggled for thirty-six hours to phrase a plank that didn't completely alienate Butler and his motley crew of Greenback followers. Their effort at crafting such a plank reminded the former Union army general of a "western hunter who tried to shoot his rifle at something he saw dimly stirring in a bush, so as to hit it if it was a deer and miss it if it was a calf."[22]

In his minority report, Butler proposed that workers should be allowed to "organize for their own protection," not unlike the way capital was permitted to incorporate and combine for its own protection. He also criticized the nation's monopolies for dividing the country into two classes—"the very rich and the very poor"—and denounced the importation of cheap foreign labor. "America ought never to be a Lazar house for the reception of pauper labor of other countries," he declared. Despite cheers from the prim Frances Willard and colorful feminist and actress Anna Dickinson who made up a small but noisy contingent of Butler supporters in the convention's gallery, the general's speech, given late in the evening, swayed few delegates and his minority report was overwhelmingly rejected by a vote of 712 ½ to 97 ½. "If you refuse to stand by the workingmen," Butler defiantly shouted as his time expired, "God help you, I cannot."[23] Having difficulty

---

21.   *New York Herald*, July 6, 1884, quoted in West, *Lincoln's Scapegoat General*, p. 386; Nash, *Stormy Petrel*, p. 293.
22.   West, *Lincoln's Scapegoat General*, p. 387.
23.   Ibid., pp. 387-388.

finding anyone of any stature who was willing to place his name in nomination, Butler realized that his candidacy was doomed and quietly withdrew from the race. Fending off Hendricks and Delaware's Thomas F. Bayard, Cleveland was easily nominated on the second ballot. Hendricks was chosen as Cleveland's vice-presidential running mate. Hailing from a crucial swing state, the 64-year-old Hendricks had been Tilden's vice-presidential partner in the disputed election of 1876.

After nearly a quarter of a century of uninterrupted Republican control of the White House, the Democrats embraced a platform that was more "platitudinous" than substantive, calling for, among other things, civil service reform and fair elections. They also issued a lengthy yet ambiguous position on the critical tariff issue. Acknowledging that the current tariff system was riddled with abuses, the Democrats pledged not to harm domestic industries and recommended that luxury items should be taxed more heavily than basic necessities.

Butler's brief flirtation with the Democrats angered a number of Anti-Monopolist and Greenback-Labor activists, including a dispirited group of Greenbackers in Morgantown, Kentucky, who denounced his "betrayal" of their party as having "no parallel since the days of Judas Iscariot and Benedict Arnold."[24] It wasn't until long after the Democratic convention in Chicago in July—and fully three months after his nominations by the smaller Anti-Monopoly and Greenback-Labor parties—that Butler, always a lone wolf in American politics, finally indicated that he would actively campaign on the joint third-party tickets. Butler, who would have done nearly anything to derail Cleveland's nomination—possibly even supporting his old foe Bayard—viewed the New York governor's nomination as a victory for the country's free traders. "Looking at the men who gathered around Mr. Cleveland and at the doctrines they entertained," he recalled, "I thought I foresaw great danger to the country in his election."[25]

Considered abrasive, egotistical and driven by insatiable ambition, the 65-year-old Butler was one of the most controversial, yet colorful, third party personalities in American history. He was also one of the best-known public figures of his time and during the Civil War was in the news perhaps more than any other man except for Ulysses S. Grant and Abraham Lincoln. A judge who knew him well once told John Hay, Lincoln's private secretary, that Butler was the "smartest damned rascal that ever lived."[26] Butler always commanded atten-

24. Ibid., p. 391.
25. Benjamin F. Butler, *Butler's Book: Autobiography and Personal Reminiscences of Major-General Benjamin F. Butler* (Boston, 1892), pp. 982-983.
26. Holzman, *Stormy Ben Butler*, p. 141.

tion—and not just from the commentators, satirists, and cartoonists who loved nothing more than to sling arrows at him. He was "always a radical, who appealed to men's discontent," wrote the *Review of Reviews* shortly after his passing. A shrewd and sometimes unscrupulous criminal lawyer, he nevertheless possessed "brilliant and noble qualities, and he was a man of intense democratic instincts in an environment of intellectual, moral and social aristocracy."[27] Butler, observed the *Boston Globe* shortly after his death in 1893, "will assuredly rank among the famous and commanding figures of the nineteenth century," a man who was "not merely part of the career of the nation, but was in a peculiar sense a real maker of our history."[28]

Vilified by some for his radical political views, he was a hero to countless others. The editor of the *Albany Evening Post* described Butler as "the ablest man, lawyer and statesman" in all of New England and John W. McClure, the editor of the *Philadelphia Times*, hailed him as the only reform governor in the country who truly grasped the country's volatile political situation and the only one "who has advanced one step on the road to the White House," while the *Detroit Evening Press* observed that Butler's candidacy in 1884 would be "a formidable one," adding that thousands of voters in states across the country revered him as a "model leader and the bravest and boldest champion of popular rights," a man who would certainly "stir things up" in a way that hadn't been seen since the days of Andrew Jackson's presidency.[29]

Butler's peculiar appearance, radical politics, contentious style and frequent party switching, however, made him a favorite target of political pundits and cartoonists, especially Thomas Nast, the brilliant cartoonist for *Harper's Weekly*.[30] What stood out the most about his physical appearance were his eyes, which were blatantly crossed and embellished with a drooping left eyelid—a defect since birth. Standing only five foot four, Butler's huge head and otherwise unprepos-

---

27. John Hay, *Lincoln and the Civil War in the Diaries and Letters of John Hay* (New York, 1939), p. 115.

28. *Boston Globe*, January 12, 1893.

29. West, *Lincoln's Scapegoat General*, pp. 381-383.

30. Butler forcefully protested when Nast did an engraving for use as a frontispiece in James Parton's favorable biography, *General Butler in New Orleans*. When the talented cartoonist depicted the Union army general in full military regalia with a sword, seated and leaning awkwardly against a table on the veranda of the St. Charles Hotel in New Orleans while surrounded by a group of furtive-looking aides, Butler, who usually wasn't self-conscious about his appearance, complained that "such a cutthroat as that will keep people from buying the book."

sessing appearance belied the powerful role he played in American politics. "The truth," remarked one Washington observer during Butler's congressional career, is that his "big head contains a good share of the brains of the House, and he possess qualities that would make him a leader in any cause he might espouse."[31] "It is too bad that Butler has been biographically neglected," wrote historian George F. Milton in 1941, "for in war as in peace he was a P. T. Barnum character. Gross in body, he was unscrupulously clever in mind and incorrigibly political in purpose."[32] Popular writer and humorist Mark Twain was also among those who poked fun at Butler's appearance. "The forward part of his skull looks raised like a water-blister," Twain wrote irreverently. "He is short and pursy—fond of standing with his hands in pants pocket and looking around to each speaker with the air of a man who has half a mind to crush them and yet is rather too indifferent. Butler is dismally and drearily homely. When he smiles it is like the breaking up of a hard winter."[33] A Richmond newspaper was even harsher than the irreverent humorist, describing Butler as "the beastliest, bloodiest poltroon and pickpocket the world ever saw."[34] The controversial Union army general evoked strong emotions, even in death. When former Massachusetts Supreme Court Judge Ebenezer R. Hoar, a longtime foe, was asked if he planned to attend Butler's funeral in the winter of 1893, he replied, "No, but I am in favor of it."[35] But not everyone heaped abuse on the former Union general. "Butler is a man fashionable to abuse," observed President Ulysses S. Grant, "but he is a man who has done the country great service, and who is worthy of its gratitude."[36]

The great-grandson of Revolutionary War General Joseph Cilley, Butler was born on November 5, 1818, and was raised by his widowed mother in Nottingham, New Hampshire. His father had died of yellow fever in the West Indies when young Ben was only four months old. A sickly young man, Butler weighed only ninety-seven pounds when he graduated from Maine's Waterbury College (now Colby University) in 1838, at age twenty. The scrappy lawyer-turned soldier-turned politician was admitted to the Massachusetts bar two years later and began practicing law in the city of Lowell shortly thereafter, quickly establishing himself as one of the best—though perhaps not the most scrupulous—criminal

---

31. Underhill, *The Woman Who Ran for President*, p. 96.
32. George Fort Milton, *Conflict* (New York, 1941), p. 54.
33. Nash, *Third Parties in American Politics* (Washington, D.C., 1959), p. 169.
34. Butler, *Butler's Book*, p. 568.
35. Don C. Seitz, *The "Also Rans"* (New York, 1928), p. 319.
36. John Russell Young, *Around the World with General Grant* (New York, 1879), Vol. II, p. 304.

lawyers in the state and the nation. Adept at introducing favorable testimony and keeping damaging evidence out, he was a devastatingly effective lawyer and almost impossible to defeat in a courtroom. Butler was admitted to practice before the U.S. Supreme Court in 1845, becoming, at the age twenty-seven, one of the youngest lawyers ever to earn that distinction. Coincidentally, Abraham Lincoln, then thirty-six, was also admitted to practice before the high court during the same session.

An immensely gifted lawyer and politician, Butler had an even greater knack for making money and was worth more than seven million dollars at the time of his death in 1893—a tidy sum in those days. During the Civil War, it was often said that if Butler were president he would make millions for himself during the first three months of his presidency, but would probably win the war in the next three months.[37]

An unapologetic and consistent champion of the social underdog, Butler gave his first political speech on behalf of Martin Van Buren during the 1840 presidential campaign, but was so disgusted by the outcome of that election that he swore off politics—at least for the time being. Within a few years, however, he was back in the game and throughout the 1850s played an active role in reform politics and was instrumental in organizing a coalition of Democrats and Free Soilers that eventually toppled the entrenched Whig Party in Massachusetts. Running on a platform espousing a ten-hour workday, Butler was elected as a Democrat to the Massachusetts legislature in 1852, representing a predominately Catholic and Democratic constituency in the city of Lowell. He won in the face of corporations' warning employees that they would be fired if they voted for him.[38]

As a legislator, Butler worked arduously for a shorter workday and, though unsuccessful in having legislation mandating a shorter workday passed by the state legislature, there's little doubt that his immense personal pressure played a crucial role in the decision by the state's factory owners to voluntarily reduce the typical workday from fourteen to eleven hours. As a newly-elected state lawmaker, Butler, a man of tremendous patience and a wickedly long memory, enraged the state's nascent Know-Nothing movement by sponsoring a measure to provide compensation for the destruction of the Ursuline Convent in Charlestown, a Catholic teaching academy for young women that had been burned to the ground by an unruly Protestant mob some eighteen years earlier. The wanton

---

37.   Waugh, *Reelecting Lincoln*, pp. 106-107.
38.   Foner, *History of the Labor Movement in the United States*, Vol. I, p. 214.

destruction of property and assault on a group of defenseless women and small children appalled and horrified the nation, including a large segment of the usually diffident Boston Brahmins who, led by Harrison Gray Otis, sharply denounced the mob's action and recommended a reward for the capture of those responsible. Meeting at Boston's fabled Faneuil Hall, the Brahmins also urged the enforcement of stringent measures to prevent similar rioting in the future. Even Lyman Beecher, whose antipathy toward Roman Catholicism had done much to fan the flames of hatred, denounced the burning of the convent from his Boston pulpit the following Sunday. Although thirteen men were eventually arrested, including eight who were held on arson charges, only one person was convicted—a youth sentenced to life imprisonment—but he was promptly pardoned when Catholics in Boston petitioned for his release.[39] Butler's legislation, which was eventually approved by a legislative committee and passed by the Massachusetts House of Representatives, encountered serious opposition when militant Know-Nothing forces pressured the state Senate to defeat the measure. By then, the *Boston Pilot*, a Catholic newspaper, admitted that the convent issue was dead and the Ursulines, tragically, would never be compensated for their losses.[40]

Butler, who later became something of a perennial gubernatorial aspirant, was the Democratic nominee for governor of Massachusetts in 1859, finishing a distant second in a three-cornered race against Republican Nathaniel P. Banks and the Know-Nothing Party's George N. Briggs, a former Whig congressman and governor.

The following year Butler, who was then widely perceived as a conservative, was nominated for the same office by the state's Breckinridge Democrats, but ran poorly, garnering fewer than 6,000 votes and finishing far behind Republican John A. Andrew, Democrat Erasmus D. Beach and the Constitutional Union Party's Amos A. Lawrence. Butler, of course, supported John Breckinridge against Lincoln and Douglas in the presidential election that year. Butler, who attended every Democratic convention since 1848, was pledged to Stephen A. Douglas of Illinois at the party's national convention in Charleston, South Carolina, in the spring of 1860. Possessing little enthusiasm for Douglas whose policies he didn't entirely agree with, Butler nevertheless stuck with the Illinois lawmaker through seven ballots before switching to Jefferson Davis, whom he subsequently supported on fifty-seven ballots. His real preference was Horatio Seymour of New York or James Guthrie of Kentucky, a former Secretary of the

---

39. Billington, *The Protestant Crusade*, pp. 85-87.
40. *Boston Pilot*, April 23, 1853.

Treasury in the Pierce administration. When Seymour remained above the fray, it was Butler's hope that a deadlocked convention would eventually turn to the Kentuckian, but Guthrie's candidacy was lost in the shuffle when southern Democrats bolted the convention in protest over the party's moderate platform.

Butler then joined other northern conservative Democrats and the southern bolters in nominating Buchanan's vice president, John C. Breckinridge, at the breakaway convention of Southern Democrats at Baltimore's Maryland Institute while the regular Democratic convention was still in session. The Breckinridge-led party, among other things, demanded the strict enforcement of the Fugitive Slave Law. During the pre-war period, Butler's personal attitude toward slavery was ambiguous. He displayed no outward hostility toward slave owners and contended on several occasions that slavery was constitutional, no matter how violently the abolitionists preached against it. On the other hand, he was somewhat aloof regarding the enforcement of the controversial Fugitive Slave Law, telling more than one audience that it was highly unlikely they would ever find him racing around the countryside chasing runaway slaves.

As might have been expected, Butler was greeted with hostility and criticism when he returned to his home district in Massachusetts following the Democratic conventions of that year. After all, he had repeatedly voted for Jefferson Davis in a desperate attempt to stop Douglas, the man his district had specifically instructed him to support. When he prepared to issue a statement about his role at the convention, a crowd of more than six thousand angry Democrats showed up, jeering and booing him so loudly that he was unable to address the crowd. He was also hung in effigy and severely criticized in the ever-hostile press. Postponing his speech for two weeks, giving the mob-like atmosphere plenty of time to cool off, Butler defiantly embarked on his quixotic gubernatorial campaign on the doomed Breckinridge Southern Democratic ticket—one of at least seven unsuccessful tries for the Massachusetts governorship.

Commissioned as a general in the Union army during the Civil War, "Old Cockeye," as he was called, was widely credited with single-handedly preserving Maryland as a Union state (though much of the credit actually belongs to Thomas Hicks, the state's Know-Nothing governor at the time). During the Fort Sumter crisis, Butler, a brigadier general, rushed his Massachusetts militia unit to Washington to protect the nation's capital and shortly thereafter led his troops in the capture of Baltimore. Lincoln was impressed by Butler's loyalty and initiative and quickly promoted him to the rank of major general and put him in charge of Fort Monroe in Virginia. When runaway slaves began appearing at the fort seeking protection from their former slaveholders, Butler refused to return them to their owners, issuing a statement to the effect that slaves were to be treated as "contraband of war"—an idea that originated with Gen. John Wolcott Phelps of Vermont—and then setting them free. In this respect, Butler, as one of his biographers asserted, was probably more deserving than Lincoln of the title "Great Emancipator," for while Lincoln and Congress dithered, Butler set thousands of black slaves free.

In 1861, the irrepressible Union army officer was granted permission to organize six New England regiments—a role that put him sharply at odds with Republican Gov. John Andrew of Massachusetts. Andrew repeatedly expressed his concern that Butler was recruiting too many Democrats as officers, but Lincoln, who was anxious to unite pro-war Democrats with the Republicans in defense of the Union, supported Butler in his confrontations with Andrew. After leading an unauthorized yet highly successful march on Baltimore, securing that city for the safe passage of Union troops, Butler's army was later sent to the Mississippi coast before capturing New Orleans in May 1862.

As military governor of occupied New Orleans, the celebrated war hero received considerable notoriety for his confiscation of southern property and his rather harsh treatment of intractable southerners, earning him the sobriquet "Beast Butler." In one incident, he ordered the execution of a man who had torn down the American flag. In addition to seizing the posh St. Charles Hotel and using it as his headquarters, the controversial Union army officer also confiscated $800,000 from the Dutch consulate, insisting that the funds were intended for the purchase of Confederate war supplies. Pro-Confederate journalist Alexander Walker, who was one of those arrested and sent to Ship Island where he was confined to a small hut with seven other leading southern citizens, vividly described the squalid conditions of the Confederate prisoners under Butler's command. The prisoners, he said, were given wretched and unwholesome rations and many of the condemned soldiers were subjected to hard labor while compelled to wear ball and chains. Jefferson Davis accused Butler of "inciting African slaves to insurrection" by arming them for war and denounced the former Massachusetts lawmaker as "an outlaw and common enemy of mankind" who should be hanged immediately if captured. Butler, of course, was one of the few Union military commanders who favored the recruitment of black regiments and had established a unit of African-American soldiers called the First Regiment Louisiana Native Guards. Later, he united thirty-seven black regiments to form the Twenty-Fifth Corps and arranged for them to learn to read and write—actions that won the affection of Radical Republicans in Congress, while horrifying the Confederates.

Butler's infamous order to treat southern women who dared to insult his Union soldiers—who, incidentally, indulged in uncontrolled looting of the city—as "women of the town plying their trade," did not sit well in the South. In memory of his army's widespread looting of the city, Butler's enemies would forever refer to him as "Spoons Butler." (Rumor had it that Butler himself swiped silver from various dinner tables while serving as military governor.)

Despite the negative publicity surrounding him, Butler's tenure in New Orleans left a positive lasting impression on a large number of the city's inhabitants, mostly the poor. When he first arrived with federal troops in New Orleans, Butler found thousands of unemployed workers facing famine and starvation, unable to afford basic necessities such as bread and flour, the latter of which was selling for a staggering fourteen dollars a barrel. "It appears that the need of relief to the destitute poor of the city requires more extended measures and greater outlay than have yet been made," he said in issuing his general order. "It becomes a question in justice upon whom this burden should fall." Then, answering his own question, stated that it clearly should fall "upon those who have brought this great calamity upon their fellow citizens"—the New Orleans aristocracy.[41]

A man who learned everything while forgetting nothing, Butler knew exactly who they were. Shortly after Farragut's fleet entered the lower Mississippi, Butler's troops, searching for enemy assets, came across a list containing the names of wealthy New Orleans businessmen who had contributed a total of $1,250,000 to a Confederate defense fund. The list also revealed exactly how much each person had contributed. "The subscribers to this fund, by this very act, betray their treasonable designs and their ability to pay at least a much smaller tax for the relief of their destitute and starving neighbors," Butler bellowed. He then levied a tax on all of those who had contributed to the fund, assessing each of them a tax equal to twenty-five percent of their original contribution to the "treasonable" defense fund. Sparing no one loyal to the Confederacy, he also levied special assessments of $100 to $500 against cotton brokers who had publicly urged Louisiana farmers not to bring their cotton to the city, raising a considerable amount to help feed the city's hungry and homeless citizenry.[42]

In addition to levying a similar tax on Confederate bondholders, the Union army general also placed strict price controls on food. He was relentless. "The poor must be employed and fed, and you must disgorge," he bluntly told the city's affluent residents. "It will never do to have it said, that while you lie back

---

41.   Nolan, *Benjamin Franklin Butler: The Damnedest Yankee*, p. 175.
42.   Ibid., p. 175.

on cushioned divans, tasting turtle, and sipping the wine cup, dressed in fine linen, and rolling in lordly carriages, that gaunt hunger stalked in the once busy streets, and poverty flouted its rags for the want of the privilege to work." New Orleans' wealthiest citizens disgorged to the tune of $350,000—all of which was distributed to the city's poorest inhabitants, including more than 9,700 families that had gone hungry for months prior to Butler's arrival. In all, $70,000 worth of food was distributed monthly to feed the poor; $2,000 a month was spent to support five asylums for orphans and widows; and an additional $5,000 a month was given to the city's Charity Hospital. Butler, who always had a soft spot for blue-collar workers, also employed more than a thousand men to clean the city's streets and repair its badly dilapidated wharves.[43]

Butler's activities as a relief administrator won him the everlasting affection of many of the city's ordinary folks—a large number of whom eventually declared their allegiance to the Union. But his policy of getting tough with the rich earned him the everlasting condemnation of New Orleans' wealthier citizens. It was a little known fact, too, that Butler personally dug deep into his own pocket to help various Catholic charitable institutions in New Orleans.

Yet Butler, who had displayed a rare talent for antagonizing almost everyone, including the Lincoln administration, was stunned when he was removed from his command in New Orleans and replaced by Gen. Nathaniel P. Banks, the former Know-Nothing Speaker of the House. Though Secretary of War Edwin M. Stanton had signed the peremptory order relieving him of his command, the general realized that the unexpected directive had Secretary of State William H. Seward's fingerprints all over it.[44]

Putting his personal feelings aside, Butler graciously greeted his successor with the roar of a full artillery salute as the new commander of the occupying army passed the forts on the lower Mississippi on his way to New Orleans and then welcomed him with an honor guard at the city's wharf. After briefing Banks and turning over all of his records, the general decided to stay in the city a few days

---

43. Foner, *History of the Labor Movement in the United States*, Vol. I, pp. 328-329. (See also Howard P. Johnson, *New Orleans Under General Butler*, unpublished doctoral dissertation, Yale University, 1937.)

44. Nolan, *Benjamin Franklin Butler: The Damnedest Yankee*, p. 221; Holzman, *Stormy Ben Butler*, pp. 109-110. Though a definitive reason was never given for his removal, a Seward biographer wrote that the Secretary of State had grown tired of spending almost half his time dealing with complaints from foreign ministers regarding Butler's administration in New Orleans. See Thornton Kirkland Lothrop, *William Henry Seward* (Boston, 1898), p. 373.

before returning North. Responding to pleas from the family of Pierre Soulé, Butler asked Secretary Stanton to free the imprisoned 61-year-old rebel firebrand and allow him to live in Boston on parole for the remainder of the war. Shortly after arriving in the city, Butler had arrested Soulé, a former Democratic senator and sheriff of New Orleans, on charges of "flagrant treason" and then sent him North to be imprisoned in Boston's Fort Warren prison, where he had been languishing ever since. A short man about the size of Napoleon with jet-black hair, the French-born Soulé had made the mistake of defiantly obstructing Butler's orders by smuggling beef from the city's relief committee to feed Confederate troops at Camp Moore, leaving the poor inhabitants of New Orleans to go hungry. Informed that the wife of General Pierre Beauregard—the man who coined the lasting phrase "Butler the Beast"—was gravely ill in her New Orleans home, Butler, in another humanitarian gesture, sent a letter of sympathy to the Confederate general along with a pass guaranteeing him safe passage to the city and back.[45]

Despite these humanitarian gestures toward his southern antagonists, at least one notable Confederate leader expressed considerable ill will toward the departing military governor. In a proclamation marking the change of command in the city, President Jefferson Davis—a man Butler had voted for fifty-seven times at the Democratic national convention two years earlier—ordered that the Massachusetts general was to be summarily hanged if he fell into Confederate hands. In spelling out the list of "crimes" committed by Butler, Davis pointed out that he had recruited a number of black regiments for the Union war effort during his

---

45. Nolan, *Benjamin Franklin Butler: The Damnedest Yankee*, pp. 154, 223. Though a committed secessionist dating back to at least 1850, Soulé, curiously enough, was one of the few prominent politicians in the South to have supported Stephen A. Douglas during the 1860 presidential campaign, organizing anti-machine Democrats and Know-Nothings for the Illinois senator. One of the most intriguing figures in Louisiana politics, his support for the Northern Democrat in that race probably had more to do with his longstanding rivalry with Sen. John Slidell, a staunch Breckinridge supporter, for control of the state's Democratic Party than any deeply-held philosophical affinity for Douglas' policies. A reckless champion of slavery expansion, Soulé had served as Franklin Pierce's minister to Spain, but resigned after denouncing that country's monarchy and becoming the administration's scapegoat for their mishandling of the controversial Ostend Manifesto—which he had drafted—regarding the acquisition of Cuba. At the time of his arrest, Soulé, who had once wounded the French ambassador in a duel, was active in the Southern Independence Association, a highly secretive secessionist society sworn to resist the reestablishment of the Union, regardless of the outcome of the war.

tenure in the South. This was entirely unacceptable. The ex-slaves, Davis stormed, had "not only been incited to insurrection by every license and encouragement, but numbers of them have actually been armed for a servile war—a war in its nature far exceeding the horrors and most merciless atrocities of savages."[46]

But it was Butler, as usual, who had the last word. "I have not been too harsh," he told the citizens of New Orleans in his farewell address. "I might have smoked you to death in the caverns as were the Covenanters of Scotland by a royal British general, or roasted you like the people of Algiers were roasted by the French; your wives and daughters might have been given over to the ravisher as were the women of Spain in the Peninsular War, and your property turned over to indiscriminate plunder like that of the Chinese when the English captured their capital; you might have been blown from the mouths of cannons as were the sepoys of Delhi—and yet kept within the rules of civilized war as practiced by the most polished and hypocritical capitals of Europe. But I have not done so."[47]

A lesser man might have retired from the army following the kind of sharp rebuke Butler had received at the hands of the wily William H. Seward. Yet Butler decided to stick it out and eventually accepted an assignment to command Fort Monroe in Virginia—again. This was good news for President Lincoln, who feared what might have happened politically if a sulking Butler had returned to Lowell. Lincoln had a lot to be worried about. After all, Butler, who was one of the few Union commanders who hadn't been involved in a major bloodbath or who had recklessly engineered a calamity, was widely revered in the North. Only a fool would have ignored the large and growing sentiment favoring a Butler presidential candidacy. The fact that Jefferson Davis wanted to hang him only increased Butler's popularity, especially at a time when else little was going right for the North in the increasingly protracted, costly and bloody war. Butler had already proven himself to Lincoln by securing Baltimore in a quickly and brilliantly executed maneuver, as well as during his first tour of Fort Monroe when he refused to return escaped slaves on the grounds that they were "contraband" of war, thereby opening the way for the eventual emancipation of slavery. Not only had Butler implemented an efficient occupation of New Orleans, conducted several successful military operations, recruited a number of African-American regiments while freeing thousands of slaves and providing for them, but he did all of this with relatively meager forces—far less troop strength than that enjoyed by

---

46. Ibid., p. 223.
47. Holzman, *Stormy Ben Butler*, p. 110.

other Union generals. Remarkably, Butler accomplished all of this and still managed to return $500,000 to the federal coffers.[48]

Though this period marked the height of his wartime popularity, Butler's military career took a nosedive from this point on as he bungled one major operation after another. His first major setback occurred in the spring of 1864 when, after leading his troops from Fort Monroe up the St. James on an approach to Richmond from the rear, he apparently dallied, allowing the enemy to reinforce the city with troops from North and South Carolina. He also failed to move on Petersburg, apparently bluffed by Confederate George E. Pickett—who had lost two-thirds of his men at Gettysburg a year earlier—into thinking that the city was more heavily fortified than it actually was. A more daring general might have captured Richmond or Petersburg, but Butler accomplished neither. His troops were "completely shut off from further operations directly against Richmond as if it had been in a bottle, strongly corked," wrote a disappointed Ulysses Grant in his official report.[49] With his 12,000 troops bottled up on Bermuda Hundred about twelve miles from the city, effectively cut off from any action, Butler's dream of winning the war by capturing Richmond had come to an abrupt end. Adding insult to injury, he later failed miserably during a planned joint naval and land assault on Fort Fisher in Wilmington, North Carolina, in late December, prematurely abandoning the operation and leaving seven hundred of his men stranded on the beach to be rescued later by Admiral David D. Porter. Butler was sharply criticized for his hasty departure. "In doing this," said Grant, "Butler made a fearful mistake." A greater example of "timidity and inefficiency in American military history, not excepting Hull's surrender," couldn't be found anywhere, said a Massachusetts congressman.[50]

Expressing serious doubts about Butler's military abilities, especially after his unsuccessful campaigns in Richmond and Petersburg as well as his failure to capture Fort Fisher in December 1864, General Ulysses S. Grant relieved him of his command in early January 1865. Although a distraught Butler blamed his removal on Grant's West Point staff, saying they were doing everything in their power to vilify and abuse him, Butler's dismissal was widely hailed. The *New York World* said it was the "best emancipation proclamation Mr. Lincoln has yet made."[51]

---

48.   Nolan, *Benjamin Franklin Butler: The Damnedest Yankee*, pp. 226-227.
49.   Holzman, *Stormy Ben Butler*, p. 121.
50.   Ibid., pp. 149-152.
51.   Ibid., pp. 152-153.

Ironically, less than a year earlier the sky appeared to be the limit for the colorful union army general, both politically as well as militarily. Having clearly been radicalized by the war, the one-time Breckinridge Democrat had become the talk of the country. Moreover, a presidential boom had developed on his behalf as early as 1863, coinciding with the publication of James Parton's favorable biography detailing his administration in New Orleans—a book that became something of a bestseller in the North. His popularity seemed to skyrocket every time an opponent heaped abuse upon him, as was the case when Fernando Wood, a fiery Copperhead and former mayor of New York City, introduced a resolution in the U.S. House calling for an investigation into Butler's conduct in New Orleans, and again when Kentucky's aging and enfeebled Garrett Davis clumsily pressed for a similar investigation in the U.S. Senate.[52]

Recognizing that the war wasn't going particularly well and that Lincoln was hemorrhaging politically, Butler did little to discourage those who were urging him to seek the nation's highest office in 1864. Several newspapers, including Horace Greeley's *New York Tribune*, were promoting him as a possible alternative to Lincoln while supporters back home in Massachusetts were actively promoting his candidacy. Even more fortuitous was the growing list of prominent Republicans opposed to Lincoln's re-nomination. The list included such outstanding Republican leaders as Lyman Trumbull, Zachariah Chandler, Salmon P. Chase, Henry Winter Davis, Horace Greeley, Ebenezer R. Hoar, Parke Godwin, Wendell Phillips, Thaddeus Stevens, William Curtis Noyes, financier J. Murray Forbes, Massachusetts Governor John A. Andrew, and the radical Benjamin F. Wade of Ohio, all of whom, at one time or another, expressed their desire to see someone other than Lincoln occupy the White House. Chase, as usual, was already off chasing his elusive dream, which he would do again in 1868 and 1872. Except for Forbes, Andrew and the conservative Hoar of Massachusetts, all of whom undoubtedly preferred Lincoln to Butler, most of those mentioned probably would have been inclined to support Butler in a race against Lincoln for the Republican nomination.[53] No one realized more than Butler that Lincoln's re-election prospects were probably doomed. Expressing serious reservations about any Democrat who might replace Lincoln, the general began

---

52. Trefousse, *Ben Butler: The South Called Him Beast!* pp. 158-161. When Davis brought the issue up in the Senate, Butler pressed for an official investigation and issued a ringing challenge to have every act of the Kentucky lawmaker's political life scrutinized, at which point the Kentucky lawmaker dropped the matter.

53. Nash, *Stormy Petrel*, p. 203.

sounding more and more like a candidate. "I think Lincoln is beaten," he told his wife, "but who can be nominated at Chicago that will not lose the country?"[54]

"Lincoln drifts," said Wendell Phillips in a speech in Massachusetts, "Butler steers." Countless other radical Republicans concurred. Those looking for a more vigorous prosecution of the war had to look no further than Fort Monroe to find a man who wouldn't be afraid—as Lincoln was—to "hang traitors, confiscate their property, do justice to loyal men, and retaliate the wrongs even of Negroes."[55] Meanwhile, Butler, who was keeping a close eye on political developments, began wooing the press in earnest, inviting reporters aboard his steamer and lavishing them with their own accommodations. Yet, almost simultaneously, stories about his devastating military blunders of the previous month began hitting the newsstands, leading some to suspect that they were deliberated planted to derail a potential groundswell for the traitor-hanging general at the National Union Party convention in Baltimore.

In the meantime, Butler had been sounded out as a possible vice-presidential running mate on Lincoln's ticket—a ploy more than likely designed to neutralize the popular general. According to the story, which was later corroborated by Simon Cameron and respected journalist Alexander McClure, Butler wasn't very receptive to the idea, jokingly telling Cameron, Lincoln's emissary who had recently returned from Russia, that he would only accept the second spot on the ticket if the beleaguered president assured him that he would "die or resign within three months" of his inauguration. "Ask him what he thinks I have done to deserve to be punished at forty-six years of age by being made to sit as presiding officer of the Senate and listen for four years to debates more or less stupid in which I could take no part or say a word, or even be allowed to vote upon any subject which might concern the welfare of the country, except when my enemies might think my vote would injure me in the estimation of the people, and therefore by some parliamentary trick make a tie upon such questions so that I might be compelled to vote."[56]

Though intended as a lighthearted reply, Butler's reference to Lincoln dying within three months of his second inauguration turned out to be a prophetically grisly response considering that Lincoln was assassinated only forty-two days into his second term. Under the tragic circumstances, Butler—and not Andrew Johnson—would have become America's seventeenth President. Lincoln, who

---

54.   Waugh, *Reelecting Lincoln*, p. 272.
55.   Ibid., p. 162.
56.   Butler, *Butler's Book*, p. 634.

once described Butler as "full of poison gas as a dead dog," was reportedly amused by the general's comment. Nevertheless, Lincoln believed that Butler, as the first prominent Democrat to enthusiastically support the war effort, would add considerable strength to the National Union ticket, especially in New England.[57]

Coincidentally, backers of Treasury Secretary Salmon P. Chase, who was then campaigning hard to unseat Lincoln, had also approached Butler about the possibility of a vice-presidential candidacy that year, but the feisty general made it clear that he had no interest in serving as anyone's vice president. "I will not be a candidate for any elective office whatever until the war is over," he said, adding that it was nothing personal against the Ohioan. It turned out to be a moot point as Chase's candidacy fizzled out shortly thereafter.[58]

Along with those of other Radical Republicans, Butler's hopes were dashed in early June when Lincoln, benefiting from an overwhelming desire against swapping horses in midstream, was easily nominated at the Union Party convention at Baltimore's Front Street Theatre. The war coalition party adopted a platform calling for the "utter and complete extirpation of slavery" by constitutional amendment and named Andrew Johnson, a prominent War Democrat from Tennessee, as Lincoln's vice-presidential running mate.

But that wasn't the end of it. Butler's name surfaced again later in August—nearly two months after Lincoln had been nominated at the National Union convention in Baltimore—when several leading Republicans, including such luminaries as Ohio's Salmon P. Chase, Charles Sumner of Massachusetts and New York City Mayor George Opdyke, considered holding another convention to replace the increasing unpopular president who appeared, by almost all accounts, to be badly trailing Democrat George B. McClellan. Coming on the heels of the Wade-Davis manifesto, blasting Lincoln's timid reconstruction policy and his veto of a radical reconstruction bill authored by the fiery Benjamin Wade of Ohio and Maryland's Henry Winter Davis—radical malcontents of his own party—it was clear that insurrection was afoot. "Mr. Lincoln is already beaten. He cannot be elected. We must have another ticket to save us from utter overthrow," lamented the *New York Tribune's* Greeley. Butler, who was then being mentioned as a possible replacement for Secretary of War Edwin Stanton, was one of those Greeley proposed as a possible replacement for Lincoln. "In order to save the country you must make Old Ben Butler President," declared

---

57. Nolan, *Benjamin Franklin Butler: The Damnedest Yankee*, p. 263. When asked whom Lincoln should name as a vice-presidential running mate, Butler offhandedly suggested Andrew Johnson of Tennessee.

58. Ibid., p. 263.

one radical. Ben Wade and others echoed the same thing.[59] Butler, of course, monitored the developments with keen interest. His supporters canvassed the country and Sarah Butler, convinced that her husband was the only man who could save the country, urged him to come home and take charge of his campaign.[60] But it was all for naught. The last-minute movement to replace Lincoln fell apart shortly after the dissenters issued a call for a new national convention to be held in Cincinnati on September 28—less than six weeks before the election. By then, the war had turned considerably in Lincoln's favor.

Though he took no active part in the 1864 canvass except to obligingly endorse the Republican ticket in Massachusetts, Butler was summoned to Stanton's office in Washington in early November and was told that he was being sent to New York to quell expected interference in the election. According to reports, a well-organized seditious plot—far exceeding the draft riots of the prior year—was apparently afoot to undermine Lincoln's campaign in New York City. Masterminded by rebels and sympathetic Copperheads, the plan was to intimidate and drive as many Republican voters away from the polls as possible to ensure an overwhelming victory for McClellan in the nation's most populous city. Several thousand rebels were expected to lead the movement. If such a plan ever existed, it was foiled by Butler's presence. Though he personally thought the reports were vastly exaggerated, Butler—concerned that a large military presence would in itself be intimidating—unobtrusively placed soldiers dressed in plain clothes at every polling precinct in the city. He also set up a command center, complete with telegraph lines connecting directly into his headquarters at the Hoffman Hotel. With an estimated five thousand men under his command, he stationed gunboats discreetly around Wall Street and some of the worst parts of the city and had a brigade of infantrymen ready to land on the Battery if things got out of hand. Remarkably, there were almost no irregularities in the election, other than the fact that an embarrassed and angry August Belmont, the Democratic national chairman, was disenfranchised for having placed a bet on the election. The election went off without a hitch. Despite an unusually heavy turnout under rainy conditions, the city experienced one of its most tranquil elections in history.[61]

Butler's on-again, off-again candidacy in 1864 hardly damaged his relationship with Lincoln. The president had often sought his advice and Butler, ignor-

---

59. Waugh, *Reelecting Lincoln*, p. 270.
60. Trefousse, *Ben Butler: The South Called Him Beast!* p. 162.
61. Waugh, *Reelecting Lincoln*, pp. 348-350.

ing the traditional military chain of command, frequently visited Lincoln at the White House. In the spring of 1863, the two men had talked extensively about a wide range of issues, including the possibility of enlisting and organizing all of the Union's black troops under the umbrella of the Army of the Potomac. They also talked about the colonization of the country's African-American population, a favorite topic of Lincoln's. Butler told the president that it would never work, that the vast majority of blacks would resist such efforts. Thinking outside the box, Butler also encouraged the commander-in-chief to consider secretly landing an army of white soldiers somewhere in the South for the purpose of recruiting black slaves into a formidable army and equipping them with "spears and revolvers" that could then be used to terrorize the entire region. During their conversation, Butler also criticized Lincoln's policy of clemency for deserters. Butler, who believed that all Union army deserters should summarily be put to death, argued that the Union army's front lines were continually being depleted by soldiers who deserted in order to re-enlist in other corps merely to take advantage of bonuses being offered for such enlistments. Realizing that Lincoln personally didn't have the heart to condemn deserters to death, Butler advised the war weary president to relieve himself of the burden by delegating such responsibility to his top military leaders, but Lincoln wouldn't budge. "The responsibility would be mine, all the same," he said sorrowfully.[62]

While organizing a number of black regiments during the war, Butler also commissioned roughly seventy-five African-American soldiers as officers in Louisiana's Native Guard regiments—an astounding fact given that only thirty-two others blacks, mostly surgeons and chaplains, were commissioned in the 149 black regiments and artillery batteries raised by the entire Union army during the war. Unfortunately, nearly all of those commissioned by Butler who hadn't been killed or discharged due to war-related injuries were later forced out of the service by Butler's successor, Major-General Nathaniel P. Banks, the former Know-Nothing Speaker of the House who believed that only whites were qualified to serve as officers—even in black regiments.[63]

Butler's military record gained him considerable favor among Radical Republicans during the war and he was elected to Congress on the Republican ticket in 1866, polling in excess of 76% of the vote against his hapless Democratic rival. He was re-elected against somewhat stiffer opposition two years later, garnering

---

62. Butler, *Butler's Book*, pp. 577-580.
63. Edward A. Miller, Jr., "Garland H. White, black army chaplain," *Civil War History*, Vol. 43, Issue 3, 1997.

65% of the vote while defeating Democrat Otis P. Lord and Richard H. Dana, who was running as an independent. According to one reporter, Butler's behavior during Andrew Johnson's impeachment trial was the only thing that saved him in his bid for a second term that year. "The radicals owed it to themselves not to desert the man who had shown himself Mr. Johnson's bitterest enemy," wrote on of Butler's biographers.[64] Butler served four consecutive terms in the House and was instrumental in framing legislation that established military rule in the South. In Congress, he was a vociferous and unrelenting critic of Andrew Johnson, sharply denouncing the president's attempts to veto the extension of the Freeman's Bureau, the Civil Rights Act and the Reconstruction Acts. During a speech before a large audience in Brooklyn shortly after his election in 1866, the Massachusetts congressman referred to the president as "King Andrew the Indecent." His drunkenness, vicious harangues and usurpation of power, Butler told the crowd, were all high crimes and misdemeanors and warranted impeachment.[65]

In the House, Butler vehemently argued that southern plantations should be forcibly taken from their owners and divided among former slaves—a proposal that delighted some of his fellow Radical Republicans. Throwing all caution to the wind, he further explained that he had no qualms taking the wealth of those responsible for the war to feed the innocent poor, the people who had suffered most during the unnecessary war. He also maintained that the Civil War had been a war of the rich against the poor, a war of the landowner against the laborer and that it was really "a struggle for the retention of power in the hands of the few against the many."

In 1867, Butler joined with Benjamin F. Loan, a Radical Republican congressman from Missouri, and Ohio Representative James M. Ashley in recklessly claiming that Vice President Andrew Johnson had been somehow involved in the conspiracy to assassinate Abraham Lincoln and accused Johnson of tampering with John Wilkes Booth's diary. Eighteen pages of the diary had been cut out, Butler said, and it was Johnson who stood to profit most from Lincoln's assassination. Despite the ensuing publicity, Butler's special committee established to investigate the assassination wasn't able to come up with any hard evidence tying Johnson to the conspiracy. Butler's committee poured over hundreds of letters from individuals claiming to have important knowledge about the assassination, but found nothing. "We felt it a duty to the country that nothing should be said

---

64.   Holzman, *Stormy Ben Butler*, p. 174.
65.   *New York Herald*, Nov. 25, 1866.

or done to give a foundation for any such suspicion against its President"—certainly not without overwhelming proof. Though committee members were never able to ascertain exactly where the vice president was when John Wilkes Booth dropped a card off at his Kirkwood House residence a few blocks from Ford's Theatre about an hour before Lincoln was shot, Butler later said that he was thoroughly convinced that Johnson had no role in the assassination. "Speaking for myself," he wrote in his lengthy memoirs nearly a quarter of a century later, "I think I ought to say that there was no reliable evidence at all to convince a prudent and responsible man that there was any ground for the suspicions entertained against Johnson."[66]

Unlike Edwin M. Stanton and many others at the time, Butler also never believed that Jefferson Davis, who spent the better part of two years shackled in chains at Fort Monroe, had incited Lincoln's murder. Butler long regretted the fact that Davis had been placed in chains. "I do not know how far I should have been stirred in the direction of putting Davis in chains had I stood beside the deathbed of Mr. Lincoln as did Stanton," he recalled, but there was never any proof that the former leader of the Confederacy had somehow incited the conspirators to assassinate the president.[67]

During Johnson's impeachment trial later that year, the ever controversial Butler accused the beleaguered president of bribing two Republican senators to switch their votes at the last minute—a charge that was never proven. At the suggestion of the ailing Thaddeus Stevens, Butler, who had personally authored the tenth article of impeachment, served as the lead House prosecutor during Johnson's removal trial. His poor performance in the role, however, has often been cited as one of the key factors in Johnson's ultimate acquittal. During the trial, the Secretary of the Navy accused Butler and other members of the prosecutorial team of playing "the part of buffoons," displaying "levity in a matter of the gravest importance to the nation." Butler, however, took his role seriously, questioning virtually every statement entered into the record by the President's counsel. Leaving nothing to chance, it was even alleged that he had spies rifle through the wastebaskets of the opposing counsel. He was also confident—perhaps overconfident—of the trial's outcome. "The removal of the great obstruction is certain," he declared shortly before the verdict was announced. "Wade and prosperity are sure to come with the apple-blossoms"—a reference that Ohio's Benjamin Wade—the Senate president pro tem and the next in line for the presi-

---

66. Butler, *Butler's Book*, pp. 930-931.
67. Ibid., p. 915.

dency—would soon be the next president of the United States. Wade, of course, shared Butler's view and was so confident of Johnson's conviction that he had already begun to select his cabinet.

Yet when Johnson was acquitted by a single vote on May 26, Butler, refusing to acknowledge defeat, immediately formed a congressional committee to investigate the possibility that several senators had accepted bribes in exchange for their vote of "not guilty." Convinced that Johnson's men had tampered with the jury—in this case, the U.S. Senate—Butler had messages impounded at every telegraph office in Washington and ordered financial institutions to provide detailed analyses of member's bank accounts. In July, Butler's committee indirectly charged four senators with corruption and three others were tainted with suspicion. Butler's co-managers refused to sign their names to the report.

The Massachusetts congressman later focused his attention on the Ku Klux Klan, leading to the passage of the Ku Klux Act of 1871, which gave the president the power to suspend the writ of habeas corpus in states where Klan activities had caused disturbances. It was Butler, after all, who had taken the House floor in 1868, dramatically waving the torn and blood-stained shirt of a federal tax collector who had been whipped by the Ku Klux Klan in Mississippi, thereby giving the Republican Party one of its most powerful propaganda weapons of all time. The symbolic "bloody shirt" was used effectively in Republican presidential campaigns for the next two decades. Riding through the night, the white-robed Klan had terrorized thousands of black citizens during this period, inflicting countless acts of violence against them in an effort to intimidate and keep them from the polls. Southern whites, Butler said at the time, believed that they were justified in these outrages because they wanted to insure white governments in their respective states. President Grant used the legislation, which included punishment by fine and imprisonment, several times in an attempt to curtail and control Klan activities in the South.

The controversial former Union army general was an unsuccessful candidate for the Republican gubernatorial nomination in 1871 and again in 1872, losing to William B. Washburn, a wealthy banker, both times. During this period, a number of Massachusetts Republicans were growing leery of Butler's increasingly radical stands. Likewise, Butler himself was growing disillusioned with the Republican Party, a party drifting toward conservatism that failed to keep pace with his increasingly turgid progressive beliefs. By the early 1870s Butler was advocating, among other things, cheap money, women's suffrage, labor reform and the adoption of an income tax—ideas well outside the mainstream of Republican thought. The last straw came when he publicly opposed the efforts of Boston's Brahmins to expand the civil service system in order to eliminate corruption. A concerted effort to remove him from office succeeded when he was defeated in a bid for a fifth House term in 1874, losing to Democrat and Liberal candidate Charles P. Thompson by nearly a thousand votes.

Returned to Congress as a Republican in 1876 when he defeated Democratic incumbent John K. Tarbox in a contentious three-way race, Butler briefly flirted with the young Greenback Party but soon returned—uninvited, of course—to the Democratic fold and waged unsuccessful campaigns for governor of Massachusetts in 1878 and 1879 on Greenback-Democratic fusion tickets.[68] Viewed as one of the country's leading spokesmen for currency reform and labor, Butler received some unexpected help during his 1878 campaign from San Francisco's radical labor leader Denis Kearney, head of that state's fledgling Workingmen's Party and a man whose street corner appeal to laborers paid innumerable political dividends. Kearney, of course, was scouting about for someone to lead the Workingmen and Greenback parties in the 1880 presidential campaign—and Butler was the first name on his short list of possibilities. Campaigning in Boston, the California demagogue hailed the former Civil War general as a "liberator of the people" and denounced the regular Democrats, who were then backing one of their own against Butler on a so-called "Straight-Out" Democratic ticket, as "lop-eared mackerel." He also implied that if Butler were not elected, Beacon Street and Back Bay would run with blood, forcing the Greenback-Labor candidate to disclaim him. While Kearney was stumping for Butler, the *New York Graphic* proposed a Butler-Kearney ticket in 1880.[69] Despite Kearney's spirited efforts, Butler lost that race by more than 25,000 votes.

In 1878, the Massachusetts congressman, always a step ahead of his colleagues, introduced a bill that would have provided up to $1,250 plus the cost of transportation to families that had expressed an interest in taking up farming on public lands in the West. Designed to ease the country's growing unemployment problem, Butler's legislation garnered strong support from labor, but was promptly denounced as a radical and "communistic" proposal and eventually died in committee.[70]

---

68. Hoping to derail Butler's political comeback, Ebenezer F. Hoar, one of his staunchest enemies, ran as an Independent Republican, siphoning more than eight percent of the vote in the three-cornered race. It wasn't enough, however, to prevent Butler's victory. Butler garnered 12,100 votes in the seventh district race to the incumbent Democrat's 9,379 and 1,955 for Judge Hoar, the failed spoiler.

69. Delmatier, McIntosh and Waters, eds., *The Rumble of California Politics 1848-1870*, pp. 84-85.

Butler was finally elected governor of Massachusetts on his *seventh* try in 1882. Talk about persistence. Campaigning on a Democratic-Greenback fusion ticket that year, he defeated his Republican opponent by nearly 14,000 votes. Butler's administration, while controversial, probably drew more criticism than it actually deserved. Many residents of the Bay State, particularly Boston's upper-crust Brahmins, were embarrassed by the "spoon-stealing" general's election and Harvard University, breaking its time-honored tradition, refused to grant Butler an honorary doctorate degree that had been bestowed on virtually every previous governor of the state. Despite his utter disdain for the Ivy League school, Butler, ironically, had enrolled his son Paul at Harvard, not because he "deemed it the best school in the country," but rather because he didn't want his son's career "hindered, as his father had been, by the fact that he was not a graduate of Harvard."[71]

As governor, the dynamic and controversial Civil War general actually compiled a half decent record, cracking down on graft and corruption, modernizing the state administration and reorganizing its budgeting and purchasing procedures. He also crusaded for woman's suffrage and mandatory shorter working hours—issues that he had championed for nearly two decades. He also conducted an investigation into the state's Tewksbury Almshouse, an institution for paupers, where investigators found that depraved officials were selling the bodies of its indigent residents to medical schools. To the consternation of many, Butler also named George L. Ruffin, a highly qualified African-American lawyer, to the bench—the first black judge in the history of Massachusetts. It wasn't until seventy-six years later, in 1958, that another black in that state was finally appointed as a full-time member of the bench. Butler also appointed Michael J. McCafferty, the state's first Irish-Catholic judge. McCafferty had a long career on the bench, serving with distinction until his retirement.[72]

Largely because of his unabashedly progressive record, most "respectable" citizens in Massachusetts, viewing their governor as an unpredictable radical who was hopelessly disgracing the state's good name, agreed that something had to be done to prevent Butler's re-election. Moreover, they feared that if Butler were re-

---

70. Foner, *History of the Labor Movement in the United States,* Vol. I, pp. 444-445.

71. Holzman, *Stormy Ben Butler,* p. 212. Butler contemptuously held Harvard second only to West Point as the worst institutions of higher education in the country. "The less of West Point a man has the more successful he will be," he once said. Curiously, as Holzman pointed out, Butler nevertheless "sent one of his sons to each of the despised institutions."

72. Ibid., p. 212; Butler, *Butler's Book,* pp. 974-975.

elected he would almost certainly emerge as a leading contender for the Democratic presidential nomination in 1884 and were determined to prevent that from happening. While most anti-Butler Democrats sat out the 1883 campaign, the Republicans, smelling blood, pulled out all the stops in an effort to defeat the unconventional and quarrelsome governor.

With most of the state's bankers and leading businessmen arrayed against him, the campaign for re-election was a particularly difficult one for the seasoned campaigner—a race Butler later described as "a very bitter and fatiguing" experience. In addition to pouring tons of money into the campaign to unseat Butler, political reformer Moorfield Story, a leading figure in the Mugwump movement, authored a particularly negative campaign pamphlet filled with inaccurate newspaper quotations and misquotations attributed to the governor over a period of years, and Charles Francis Adams, speaking for an aroused citizenry of Beacon Hill, railed against the ex-Union army general to an overflow crowd in Boston's Faneuil Hall. Henry Adams, the erudite son of Lincoln's minister to Great Britain, offered to campaign against Butler and even the young Henry Cabot Lodge, then establishing himself as a writer of some promise, enthusiastically threw himself into the battle. Butler's mortal enemies George F. Hoar, a longtime Republican member of the U.S. Senate, and his older brother Ebenezer, a former congressman who had served briefly as attorney general in the Grant administration, also did everything in their power to end Butler's political career.

Growing increasingly desperate, Butler and the Democrats trotted out the issue of the Tewksbury Almshouse—an institution long mismanaged under a succession of Republican governors—publishing a grotesquely graphic campaign pamphlet filled with disturbing illustrations of inmates being eaten by rats, babies being sold to medical schools, and sandals supposedly made out of tanned human skin. But such sensationalism had little impact on the voters of Massachusetts that year. When all the votes were counted, Butler was narrowly defeated in his bid for a second term, losing to popular Republican congressman George D. Robinson by a margin of 160,092 to 150,228. Not taking his rejection by the voters of Massachusetts particularly well, Butler blamed his narrow defeat on the Democratic Party's "rum element" in Boston, alleging that the Republicans had bribed traditionally Democratic Irish voters to vote against him—a charge not entirely without merit. He also attributed his setback to a scarcity of ballots for him at polling places caused by a mechanical breakdown of the printing press used to print his ballots the night before the election. Following his defeat, most observers believed that "Brave Old Ben's" political career was over. But Butler had other ideas. Though outwardly coy about his ambitions, he still longed for one more public office—the presidency.[73]

For nearly two decades, Butler enthusiasts had been urging the former Massachusetts governor to run for president and when the opportunity presented itself at an informal conference of anti-monopoly and labor organizations in Chicago on March 4, 1884, the former Union army general finally agreed to take the plunge. Declining farm prices coupled with a string of bank failures, presaging a possible economic panic earlier that year, convinced the former governor that his candidacy was not necessarily a hopeless undertaking. In fact, he believed that the 150,000 votes cast for him in the 1883 gubernatorial campaign—an increase of almost 40,000 votes over his 1878 and 1879 showings and 17,000 more than he had received in his successful campaign a year earlier—was something of a mandate, even in defeat. It certainly wasn't his Waterloo, as many observers suggested. There was a certain "tidal wave" quality to his showing that give him hope that not only would Massachusetts go Democratic in 1884, but that his own political future still held some promise—a belief that was echoed by the *Boston Globe*.[74] Shortly before formally entering the race as a third-party candidate, Butler explained his political philosophy to a throng of some 3,000 laborers in Providence. "Politics," he said, "should be the highest exhibition of the human intellect in favor of the greatest number of men and for the greatest good of the greatest number."[75]

---

73. West, *Lincoln's Scapegoat General*, pp. 381-382; Butler, *Butler's Book*, p. 981; Trefousse, *Ben Butler: The South Called Him Beast!*, pp. 249-250.

74. Butler letter to Charles A. Dana, December 3, 1883, Butler Papers, (Library of Congress); Trefousse, *Ben Butler*, p. 250; *Boston Globe*, July 6, 1884. The *Globe's* editors described the former governor as "the first choice of the 150,000 Democrats" in Massachusetts and, arguably, "of the working people everywhere," adding that African-Americans in the South had "not forgotten" his friendship, especially "at a time when they sorely needed friends."

75. *New York Sun*, August 30, 1884, quoted in West, *Lincoln's Scapegoat General*, p. 396.

18

Spoilers

❖

Third-Party Candidates Wreck Havoc on the Two-Party System

After failing to parlay the Anti-Monopoly and Greenback-Labor nominations into an even more magnificent prize at the Democratic national convention in Chicago later that summer, Butler eventually took to the stump as the candidate of the "People's Party," the moniker he gave to the consolidated minor parties supporting his candidacy. In a lengthy address, published on August 12, Butler denounced the two old parties and said that he would actively undertake a short, hard-hitting, and decisive campaign beginning in mid-September.[1]

Believing that he might throw the election into the House of Representatives, the turbulent former Union army general cunningly devised a scheme for altering the outcome in the Electoral College by advancing the idea of "fusion" tickets—then a common practice in American politics—consisting of the Anti-Monopoly and Greenback-Labor parties and whichever major party was considered weaker in a given state. The minor and major party coalitions in those states would then name a common list of electors on a fusion ticket with the understanding that, in the event that the fusion ticket carried the state, the electoral votes from that state would be cast in proportion to the number of votes actually received by each of the presidential candidates. In predominately Democratic West Virginia, for example, voters supporting the fusion ticket would have the choice of two ballots, one supporting Butler and his electors and one for Republican James G. Blaine with the same set of electors. If the fusion ticket carried the state, West Virginia's six electoral votes would then be proportionately divided between Blaine and Butler. In traditionally Republican states, Butler hoped to

---

1.   Howard P. Nash, Jr., *Stormy Petrel*, p. 295.

fuse with the Democrats, with the electoral votes in those states proportionately divided between himself and Democrat Grover Cleveland.[2]

Butler's scheme wasn't nearly as preposterous as it might have appeared at first blush. The idealistic Charles A. Dana of the *New York Sun*, long a Butler admirer and a man who was hoping to "shake things up in Washington," believed that the plan might be "entirely feasible" and went so far as to optimistically predict that Butler-Cleveland fusion tickets would carry such traditionally Republican strongholds as Connecticut, Indiana, and New Jersey, and would have a fighting chance in critically important states such as Illinois, Massachusetts, Michigan, New Hampshire, Ohio, and Wisconsin. Moreover, Dana, whose newspaper lost nearly half of its circulation as a result of its unwavering support of Butler during the 1884 campaign, believed that a Greenback-Republican fusion ticket, relying heavily on Butler's widespread appeal to African-American voters, would make serious inroads in the solidly Democratic South and had a reasonable chance of carrying Florida, Louisiana, Mississippi, North Carolina, South Carolina, Virginia and West Virginia.[3]

Although ex-Confederate Col. William H. Parsons of Mississippi had unofficially launched Butler's third-party bid for the White House in a "rabble-rousing" speech in Washington, D.C., a few months earlier, Butler formally kicked-off his campaign on August 29 with a trip to Harrisburg, Pennsylvania, where he received an endorsement of sorts from the aging Simon Cameron—the man who twenty years earlier had traveled to Fort Monroe to offer Butler the vice-presidency on Lincoln's ticket and a man Butler had once represented in a highly-publicized extortion case. The Anti-Monopoly candidate then attended a Grangers' picnic at nearby Williams Grove where, donning a straw hat, he exhorted the farmers in attendance to support his new People's Party and replace the old parties. Appearing at the Masonic Temple in New York the following evening, Butler was greeted with a band playing "Hail to the Chief" while the audience of several hundred spontaneously cheered his arrival, waving hats, canes, umbrellas and handkerchiefs and applauded enthusiastically as the Greenback-Labor candidate launched into a hard-hitting anti-monopoly speech.[4]

---

2.   West, *Lincoln's Scapegoat General*, pp. 392-393.
3.   Ibid., p. 393; Holzman, p. 219; Butler, *Butler's Book*, p. 983. Except in Michigan, where Butler polled more than 42,000 votes and where the Cleveland-Butler fusion ticket nearly toppled Blaine, the fusion effort failed miserably as Greenback-Laborites were unable to convince their major-party counterparts in Indiana, New Jersey and West Virginia to join in fusion campaigns.
4.   Ibid., pp. 395-397.

Butler embarked on a two-week swing through the Midwest in early September, campaigning in the old Greenback strongholds of Michigan, Illinois, Minnesota, Iowa, Nebraska and Kansas. Large and enthusiastic crowds greeted him everywhere he appeared. He drew 10,000 in Grand Rapids, Michigan, and another 10,000 turned out to hear him excoriate the Democrats and Republicans in Des Moines a few days later. He also defended his fusion strategy in Des Moines, telling his large audience that if the People's Party failed to break up the "useless and offensive" major parties, the country would be saddled with mediocre politics for years to come. "I have them in my power," he said, referring to his fusion strategy, "and I am using them for their own destruction. In their place the people will build up a new party. Don't ask me for an apology for being a humble instrument in accomplishing that."[5] Speaking at the fairgrounds in Omaha a few days later, Butler said that a man could "steal $3,000,000 of pork in Chicago and go unpunished," while someone who steals enough to support his family is sent to jail. He also said that the cry of overproduction should be changed to a cry of under-consumption. "People are starving while Nebraska granaries are overflowing with grain. The railroads will not allow grain and consumers to be brought together" to end hunger in the country, he said, urging Midwestern farmers to "liberate themselves as the abolitionists liberated the slaves."[6]

Returning to New York City on September 15, the mercurial candidate held a gargantuan rally in Union Square before heading to Lowville, New York, where an estimated five hundred wagons were packed around the speaker's stand. "The *New York World* accuses me of making a canvass in favor of Blaine," he told his large audience, "and when I went out in Michigan and fused with Cleveland's people to give him some electoral votes in a Republican state, they began abusing me because I was trying to help Cleveland." Such criticism, he said, strengthened his resolve. "They both abuse me so that I know I am pretty nearly right," he said confidently, adding that he was in the process of founding a party that would survive long after he was gone.[7]

A formal "notification" ceremony attended by a capacity crowd of 7,000 supporters and onlookers—and an estimated four times that many lining the flare-lit streets outside—was held at a skating rink in Lowell, Massachusetts, on the evening of September 21. The ceremony included a spectacular parade of laborers and Civil War veterans and was followed a few days later by the official found-

---

5. *Chicago Tribune*, September 4, 9, 1884.
6. *New York Herald*, September 10, 1884.
7. West, *Lincoln's Scapegoat General*, pp. 398-399; *New York Herald*, September 18, 1884.

ing of Butler's so-called People's Party in Worcester. Attorney Noah A. Plympton, Butler's long-suffering campaign manager, was named as the party's national president and, as might have been expected, Butler's own progressive agenda was adopted as the party's official platform.

Following a short excursion into New Hampshire, Butler held rallies at Faneuil Hall and the Tremont House in Boston and another one in Springfield before returning to New York for a series of major speeches in Brooklyn, Albany, Troy, Rochester, and Buffalo. Former state Senator Thomas F. Grady, a Tammany Democrat and close ally of John Kelly, accompanied Butler in his travels throughout the state. The former Massachusetts governor spoke to an enthusiastic crowd of 10,000 in a circus tent in Albany before rushing to address another large and boisterous crowd on the steps of the city hall building in nearby Troy. As he was leaving, dozens of supporters flocked around his carriage and a saloonkeeper handed him a glass of lager, which the third-party candidate gulped down with great gusto.[8]

It was during this campaign swing that Butler's campaign apparently developed a major financial crisis, one that nearly brought the campaign to a grinding halt. From the outset, Greenback-Labor and Anti-Monopoly leaders provided little in the way of financial support to Butler's fledgling candidacy, believing that the "millionaire lawyer" was quite capable of personally financing his campaign.[9] Indeed, his own campaign manager estimated that Butler generously spent $200,000 of his own fortune during the 1884 campaign.[10] Moreover, treasurer William A. Fowler, working out of the party's poorly staffed national headquarters at the Fifth Avenue Hotel in New York City, repeatedly had to borrow money from friends when emergencies arose and Francis D. Moulton, who Butler had skillfully defended in the famous Beecher trial several years earlier, borrowed heavily from his own company's credit line in order to lend the campaign $8,500 in much needed cash. In addition, several Greenback and Anti-Monopoly editors and party organizers were frequently forced to spend their personal funds during the campaign, often nearly spending themselves into bankruptcy.

Meanwhile, nervous Democrats had tried earlier to coax the third-party candidate out of the contest with promises of a position in a Cleveland administration. In fact, former Speaker of the House Samuel J. Randall of Pennsylvania, an old acquaintance, was sent to negotiate with Butler.[11] The Republicans, on the other

8.   Ibid., p. 401.
9.   At the time of his death in 1893, Butler's net worth was estimated at $7,000,000. See *New York Tribune*, January 12, 1893.
10.   *Buffalo Times*, August 23, 1890; West, *Lincoln's Scapegoat General*, pp. 393-394.

hand, did everything within their power to keep him in the race—including secretly financing his campaign. Tammany Hall's John Kelly, who personally couldn't stomach Grover Cleveland, was also suspected of surreptitiously aiding the former general's third-party candidacy. Though it is nearly impossible to discern exactly how much the Tammany chieftain had pledged to Butler's candidacy, it is known that when he switched to Cleveland late in the campaign, he reneged on the remaining $838 of Tammany's pledge to Butler's war chest.[12] Inarguably the most powerful Democrat in New York City, "Honest John" Kelly was certainly no stranger to third-party intrigue. In an attempt to punish the state's anti-Tammany Democratic governor, Kelly had personally challenged Lucius Robinson on a third-party ticket in 1879—a rather unusual move for a Tammany politician. Angered by Robinson's decision to remove a Tammany loyalist from the office of county clerk, the Tammany chieftain, displaying his legendary vindictive streak, waged a well-organized statewide campaign and polled 77,566 votes in that race, sending the reform-minded Democratic governor to an early retirement.[13]

Kelly again displayed a bull-sized taste for revenge in 1884, shortly after Gov. Grover Cleveland, who had already made it clear that he had no intention of steering patronage to Tammany Hall, suggested that Thomas F. Grady, leader of Tammany's legislative bloc in Albany, shouldn't be returned to the legislature on the grounds that he was obstructing his legislative program. Kelly was incensed, believing that the reform governor was determined to weaken his authority and essentially render Tammany Hall ineffective as a political force. As such, it came as no surprise when Kelly, who had coaxed Butler into the race for the Democratic nomination a few months earlier, arrived at the party's national convention

---

11. West, *Lincoln's Scapegoat General*, p. 389; Nash, *Stormy Petrel*, p. 295; M. P. Curran, *Life of Patrick A. Collins* (Norwood, MA, 1906), pp. 92-93. In an interview with the *Buffalo Times* in the summer of 1890, Plympton said that Butler had been offered the position of Attorney General, a foreign mission, or control of all of the political patronage in New England, but Butler refused to seriously consider any of them. The only one of the three positions that even remotely interested him was the post of ambassador to St. James, but the Anti-Monopoly standard-bearer, after discussing his options with his campaign manager, insisted that such an appointment would be "impractical" since the U.S. Senate would never confirm him and the British would never tolerate such an appointment.

12. Ibid., p. 394.

13. Robinson was defeated by Republican Alonzo B. Cornell, losing to the former Western Union telegraph executive by a margin of 418,567 to 375,790. Kelly's 77,000 votes had clearly made the difference.

in Chicago later that summer adamantly opposed to Cleveland's nomination. "I will not lift a hand for him," he crowed. "If he thinks he can be elected without me let him go ahead, but I will never help him." In a desperate attempt to derail Cleveland's candidacy, Kelly and his organization spread rumors that the New York governor harbored deep-seated anti-Catholic sentiments and was a confirmed drunkard—neither of which were true. Kelly also charged that the mayor of Chicago, a prominent Cleveland supporter, had packed the convention's galleries with Cleveland supporters. Speaking for Tammany Hall, Thomas F. Grady, who had been marked for defeat by Cleveland, and William Bourke Cockran, one of Tammany Hall's most gifted speakers, delivered long and ill-timed speeches viciously attacking the eventual nominee, prompting Wisconsin's gray-haired Edward S. Bragg to declare that the young men in his delegation loved Cleveland most "for the enemies he has made." All eyes then suddenly turned on Kelly and his Tammany delegation—a sizable bloc that had been rendered impotent by the convention's failure to dispose of the unit rule, thereby permitting individual voting by delegates. Despite the spirited opposition of Tammany delegates, the large New York delegation, voting under the party's unit rule, went solidly for Cleveland on the first ballot. When a last-ditch effort to stampede the convention for Indiana's Thomas A. Hendricks—a man viewed by reformers as something of a machine politician—met with devastating defeat on the second ballot, a reporter asked Kelly if he intended to support the Democratic nominee. "Get out of here," he growled. "I don't wish to talk to anybody."[14]

True to his word, Kelly initially refused to help the Democratic presidential ticket following the Chicago convention, focusing most of Tammany's efforts and resources on behalf of the organization's candidate for mayor while simultaneously secretly assisting Butler's looming third-party candidacy. After meeting privately with Cleveland on October 15, Kelly—much to Butler's chagrin—publicly threw the weight of his powerful Tammany organization behind the Democratic candidate. Yet, privately he still longed for Cleveland's defeat. As the returns trickled in on election night, a dejected Kelly was in a particularly gloomy mood, lamenting that he was finished as a political force in New York politics. "We are gone," he said, putting his hand to his head.[15]

While it is impossible to determine the precise amount of financial assistance Kelly and his Tammany organization actually provided to the Greenback-Labor

---

14. Oliver E. Allen, *The Tiger: The Rise and Fall of Tammany Hall* (New York, 1993), pp. 167-168; *The Nation*, July 17, 1884; Roseboom, *A History of Presidential Elections*, pp. 266-267.

15. Ibid., pp. 168-169.

candidate during the 1884 presidential campaign, there is little question that the Republican National Committee, hoping that Butler would siphon enough Democratic votes from Cleveland to throw the election to Blaine, provided ample support to the third-party ticket. These allegations, which were first brought to light by Patrick A. Collins, an Irish-born congressman and chairman of the Massachusetts Democratic Committee who later served as mayor of Boston, undoubtedly cost Butler countless votes among laborers who believed that he had struck a deal with the unsavory and corrupt Blaine in an effort to defeat the Democratic candidate.[16]

Moreover, there is plenty of evidence to suggest that Butler had personally lobbied the GOP for such assistance during a series of meetings with Secretary of the Navy William E. Chandler over the course of that summer, including once in late July when he accompanied Chandler, a longtime Blaine confidant, on the deck of the steamer U.S.S. *Tallapoosa* at the Portsmouth Navy Yard. It was there that Chandler and Edward H. Rollins, a former GOP senator from New Hampshire, urged Butler to accept the third-party nominations and to run hard against Cleveland as a quasi-Democrat. Butler later invited the Navy Secretary and his entourage to his cottage in Cape Ann where he was hosting a reunion of soldiers from the Thirty-first Massachusetts regiment that served with him during the Civil War. In exchange for actively stumping against Cleveland in New York, New Jersey and Connecticut, Butler was purportedly guaranteed control of federal patronage in New England if Blaine won the election—an extremely attractive offer that Butler would have found difficult to ignore.[17]

16. Holzman, *Stormy Ben Butler*, p. 217; Nash, *Stormy Petrel*, p. 296; Curran, *The Life of Patrick A. Collins*, pp. 92-93. Growing up as a young immigrant boy during the Know-Nothing period that swept New England in the 1850s, Collins, a victim of the Irish potato famine, had learned to combat intolerance at an early age and continued to fight prejudice and argue for assimilation of the Irish-American population throughout his long political career. One of the more colorful politicians of that era, Collins, a one-time American president of Charles Stewart Parnell's tenant farmer-based National Land League, served in Congress from 1883-1889 before, as he put it, making good on his escape from Washington. He later served as a fiscally conservative mayor of Boston from 1902-1905. Despite his staunch support of Cleveland during the 1884 campaign, the 40-year-old Collins was given little consideration for a federal appointment from the Democratic president, although he later served as U.S. consul-general in London during Cleveland's second term from 1893-1897.

17. West, *Lincoln's Scapegoat General*, pp. 394-395; Nash, *Stormy Petrel*, p. 295; Holzman, *Stormy Ben Butler*, p. 217; David Saville Muzzey, *James G. Blaine* (New York, 1934), p. 304; Curran, *Life of Patrick A. Collins*, p. 92.

Exactly what sort of financial assistance that Chandler, acting as a go-between with the Republican National Committee and Blaine's campaign, promised is uncertain, but in a September 24 letter to Chandler, the former Massachusetts governor reminded the Navy Secretary that his friends had "not even come up to the pittance which they promised in aid" and informed Chandler that he needed "at least $35,000 beyond what was understood, i.e., $5,000 a week." That some sort of bargain had been struck earlier between Chandler and Butler is entirely without question, but the exact details of that sordid arrangement still remain clouded in mystery, some 120 years after that extraordinary and turbulent campaign. In any event, a number of newspapers quickly picked up on the rumors and the Greenback-Labor candidate was mercilessly pilloried in the mainstream press. The *New York Times*, for instance, sharply denounced Butler's apparent "treachery," suggesting that every laborer who supported the Anti-Monopoly candidate would unwittingly become "the dupe of the basest conspiracy that has ever disgraced a presidential canvass in the United States." Pulling no punches, the traditionally Republican *Times*, which threw its support to Democrat Grover Cleveland that year, also referred to Butler as "the Benedict Arnold of American politics." Patrick J. Ford of the *Irish World*, who had already stumped for Butler in eight towns throughout New York, demanded to know if the charges were true and, if so, threatened to abandon the campaign.[18] *Harper's Weekly* later embellished the story a bit, telling its readers that Blaine had given Butler $25,000 down with a promise of an additional $25,000 to be paid in later installments—a charge that Butler furiously, but unconvincingly, denied.[19]

Despite Butler's strenuous refutations, the story was given a great deal of credence when William H. Parsons, a former newspaper editor and chairman of the Greenback-Labor Committee in Maryland, told reporters that when he approached Butler's campaign about the possibility of having the general make an appearance in Baltimore, he was referred by Butler's managers to the Republican National Committee, which, he was supposedly told, was directing the former governor's campaign. The Republicans, he said, informed him that they couldn't afford to send Butler to Maryland because it wasn't what they considered to be a "doubtful state."[20] A former confederate colonel who had toyed briefly with the idea of establishing a Confederate colony in British Honduras at

---

18. Ibid., pp. 399-401, 405-407; *New York Times*, October 19, 20, 1884. Buried under a stack of unread correspondence, Butler did not see Ford's letter until after the campaign was over.
19. *Harper's Weekly*, October 25, 1884.
20. West, *Lincoln's Scapegoat General*, pp. 404-405.

the close of the Civil War, Parsons, a former Mississippi legislator, was the older brother of Albert R. Parsons, who a few years later was one of those unjustly executed for his alleged role in the Haymarket Square bombing. Something of a health faddist, the 58-year-old Parsons, who offered to campaign for Butler in eight northern states, had also been one of the party's most enthusiastic supporters, establishing a freelance campaign of sorts on Butler's behalf in the nation's capital long before the former Union army general officially threw his hat in the ring.[21]

Butler had long considered Parsons something of an interloper and loose cannon and had advised his managers early on to have nothing to do with him. Yet the damaging statement made by Parsons, which received widespread coverage throughout the country, forced Butler to deny the former newspaper editor's allegations. "I have read Parson's statement," he said in prepared remarks in Syracuse on October 20. "There is not one word of truth in it." Nevertheless, the story continued to haunt Butler and the Anti-Monopoly Party during the final weeks of the campaign. A subsequent telegram from Parsons to Cleveland's national headquarters on November 1, in which the former Confederate officer challenged Blaine and Butler to open their books at the First National Bank of New York City, certainly didn't help matters.[22]

If that wasn't damaging enough, Butler was also severely criticized for renting a luxurious railroad car in an effort to canvass more of the nation's most populous state while saving time having to check in and out of hotel rooms. The ostentatious and gaily-painted boudoir car that he rented for $150 per day had comfortable dining and sleeping accommodations for a party of fifteen. The sleek sleeper-diner included what one reporter described as a "royal dining room" and "four magnificent sleeping rooms." According to newspaper reports, the luxury car was fit for a king with its majestic walls and ceilings covered with heavily embossed leather, a "lustrous nickel-plated" lavatory, and a writing desk made of carved Spanish mahogany. The car's costly tapestry provided the "people's candidate" with plenty of privacy and its bar was stocked with every kind of liquor imaginable, including a case and a half of expensive Medford rum—one of Butler's favorites. Butler eventually abandoned the railroad car in Elmira, not so much due to the ensuing criticism, but rather because time-consuming repairs had caused him to miss several important connections.[23]

---

21. Ibid., pp. 385, 404.
22. Ibid., pp. 405-406.

While these issues undoubtedly hurt Butler in the eyes of organized labor, at least one prominent labor leader stuck with him through thick and thin. "I am not a Butler man," said Samuel Gompers, the co-founder and first president of the American Federation of Labor. "I am no man's man. Butler is my man."[24] Despite the increasingly negative publicity swirling around his candidacy, the undaunted Union army general continued to wage a vigorous campaign against the two major parties, flaying at the Republicans as a party "kept alive by the cohesive power of public plunder" while maintaining that the desperately hungry Democrats—a party that hadn't occupied the White House in nearly a quarter of a century—had allowed monopolistic business interests, including the Erie Railroad and Rockefeller oil interests, to shape their platform.[25] He also told large groups of workingmen that if Cleveland were elected, they would starve.[26]

Following a second trip to the Midwest which included stops in Fort Wayne, Indianapolis, Cincinnati and Pittsburgh, Butler, who waged one of the most strenuous campaigns since the days of Stephen A. Douglas, returned to the crucial battleground state of New York where he spent the last two weeks of the campaign, delivering an average of two speeches a day. In those speeches, the Anti-Monopoly candidate appealed to New York's large Irish constituency by frequently "twisting the lion's tail" in colorful attacks aimed at the English monarchy, a tactic also used by Republican James G. Blaine. Relying heavily on a party-subsidized newspaper in New York City, Butler waged a vigorous campaign in the nation's most populous state and was expected to cut deeply into Cleveland's large Democratic base in New York City. He also continued to enjoy the support of Charles A. Dana of the *New York Sun*, one of the most principled editors in the country and a man who remained loyal to Butler until the bitter end. "Butler is a disturbing and health-giving force wherever he appears in politics," wrote Dana. "Many people do not agree with him and many heartily detest him; but the agitation which he brings is salubrious. He leaves the political atmosphere in a better state than when he finds it."[27]

---

23. Ibid., pp. 402-403; Holzman, *Stormy Ben Butler*, p. 218; Trefousse, *Ben Butler: The South Called Him Beast!* p. 253. "It did not seem to bother him that such ostentation was hardly fitting for a People's Party candidate," wrote Trefousse.

24. Samuel Gompers, *Seventy Years of Life and Labor* (New York, 1935), Vol. II, p. 78.

25. West, *Lincoln's Scapegoat General*, p. 403.

26. Holzman, *Stormy Ben Butler*, p. 218.

27. *New York Sun*, September 12, 1884, quoted in West, *Lincoln's Scapegoat General*, p. 407; Trefousse, *Ben Butler: The South Called Him Beast!* p. 253; Holzman, *Stormy Ben Butler*, p. 218; *Harper's Weekly*, Sept. 6, 1884.

In addition to the Butler and St. John candidacies, two other minor parties also fielded tickets in the 1884 presidential election. An American Prohibition Party briefly ran former U.S. Sen. Samuel Clarke Pomeroy of Kansas for president and the little-known Equal Rights Party nominated educator and women's rights activist Belva Lockwood for the nation's highest office.

The American Prohibition Party was a splinter group made up of disgruntled Prohibitionists. Declaring the United States a Christian nation, the party met in Chicago on June 19. Joseph L. Barlow, a Baptist minister from Connecticut, chaired the convention. Barlow, who had been captured by the Confederate Army at Harper's Ferry during the Civil War, had briefly served as Charles Francis Adams' vice-presidential running mate on the aborted Anti-Masonic Party ticket in 1872. Wasting little time, the American Prohibitionists easily nominated Pomeroy on the convention's first ballot, giving him 72 votes to a scattering of eleven votes for Jonathan Blanchard of Illinois, Prohibitionist John P. St. John and two others. John A. Conant, a little-known 55-year-old silk mill worker from Connecticut, was named as Pomeroy's vice-presidential running mate. In addition to calling for the total prohibition of intoxicating beverages, the American Prohibition Party adopted a surprisingly progressive platform calling for the abolition of the Electoral College and the direct election of the president; tariff reduction; women's suffrage; and the extension of civil rights to protect American Indians and Asians. The party also opposed the use of prison labor and sought to outlaw secret societies—a rather peculiar position considering that Pomeroy himself was a prominent member of a secret society.

It's hard to imagine a group of reformers nominating anyone more unsavory than Pomeroy. The former Kansas lawmaker, after all, had authored the infamous "Pomeroy Circular" in an attempt to embarrass President Lincoln during the 1864 campaign. Moreover, "Old Subsidy Pom," as he was derisively dubbed, was driven from public life in 1872 amid bribery and corruption charges. While seeking a third term in the U.S. Senate that year, it seems that Pomeroy had offered his opponent $7,000 to withdraw from the race. "The Pomeroy party," wrote the *New York Times*, "has actually eclipsed in absurdity the Blaine and Logan party." In its stinging editorial, the newspaper also reminded voters that the former Kansas lawmaker was a leading member of a secret society when he was driven out of public office, adding that it was the height of hypocrisy for Pomeroy to now emerge as a spokesman for a party espousing "morality, religion, and opposition to secret societies."[28] The paper's criticism turned out to be

---

28. *New York Times*, July 2, 1884.

unnecessary, as the aging former senator withdrew from the race shortly after receiving the party's nomination.

Belva Lockwood and the Equal Rights Party

A female-led Equal Rights Party also entered the race for the White House in 1884. The history of this relatively short-lived party is really the story of Belva Ann Lockwood, a brilliant teacher-turned-lawyer whose many crusades included the women's suffrage movement, temperance and world peace.

The party's founding, in fact, had been the result of a letter written by Lockwood to California suffragist and labor organizer, Marietta Stow, on August 10, 1884—less than three month's before the presidential election. Noting that the legal disenfranchisement of women didn't necessarily prevent them from seeking elective office, Lockwood asked rhetorically, "Why not nominate women for important places? Is not Victoria Empress of India? Have we not among our countrymen persons of as much talent and ability? Is not history full of precedents of women rulers?" She was clearly exasperated with the party of Lincoln and angered by Susan B. Anthony and Elizabeth Cady Stanton's continuing faith in the Republican Party. "It is quite time that we had our own party, our own platform, and our own nominees. We shall never have equal rights until we take them, nor respect until we command it."[29]

Inspired by Lockwood's letter, Stow set out with Clara Foltz, an obscure San Jose housewife and the first woman ever admitted to the California Bar, and other suffragists in that state to organize the National Equal Rights Party.[30] The party was organized quickly and, following an initial convention on August 23, met in San Francisco in late September 1884 and unanimously nominated Lockwood for the presidency. The delegates then chose Marietta Stow, who had chaired the gathering, as Lockwood's vice-presidential running mate, but only after longtime New York City woman's suffrage leader Clemence Sophia Lozier, a 71-year-old pioneer physician who had paved the way for the founding of the first women's medical college in New York, formally declined the honor. The 54-

---

29.   Jill Norgren, "Lockwood in '84," *The Wilson Quarterly*, Vol. 26, Issue 4 (Autumn, 2002).

30.   Foltz later insisted that Lockwood's nomination was a lighthearted joke on their part, but in *Equal to the Occasion: Women Editors of the Nineteenth Century West*, Stow's biographer, Sherilyn Cox Bennion, has made a pretty convincing case that the founding of the National Equal Rights Party—and Lockwood's candidacy—was indeed a serious effort.

year-old Stow, who served as editor of the *Woman's Herald of Industry and Social Science Cooperator*, had been an independent candidate for governor of California in 1882—more than three decades before women were finally granted the right to vote in state elections.

Reflecting Lockwood's progressive views, the Equal Rights Party adopted a platform calling for women's suffrage, prohibition, civil-service reform and the abolition of distinctions between men and women in property rights. The party also promised to enforce equal political rights for "every class of our citizens irrespective of sex, color or nationality" in order to make the United States "in truth what it has so long been in name, 'the land of the free and home of the brave.'" The party came out strongly in favor of citizenship for Native Americans and the allotment of tribal land. Staunchly opposed to the "wholesale monopoly of the judiciary" by men, Lockwood said that, if elected, she would appoint a reasonable number of women as U.S. attorneys, marshals and federal judges, including naming a competent woman to any vacancy that might occur on the United States Supreme Court. Among other things, the Equal Rights Party also denounced monopolies—promising that the nation's remaining public lands would go to the "honest yeomanry," and not the railroads—supported temperance, and called for the outlawing of war as an instrument of public policy. The party adopted a middle-of-the-road stance on the issue of tariffs, supporting neither high tariffs nor free trade. Recognizing the importance of sound bites—long before that term was coined—Lockwood argued that the party's platform should be brief enough that newspapers would be willing to publish it and that voters would take the time to read it.[31]

Lost in the shadow of such vaunted women's suffrage leaders as Elizabeth Cady Stanton and Susan B. Anthony, Lockwood is almost forgotten today and that's an injustice, for she was, as scholar Jill Norgren pointed out, "a model of courageous activism and an admirable symbol of a woman's movement that increasingly invested its energies in party politics."[32] A resident of Washington, D.C., Lockwood gained some notoriety in 1879 when she won the right for women to argue cases before the U.S. Supreme Court. An avid bicyclist—actually it was a tricycle, a mode of transportation then in vogue—Lockwood could frequently be seen pedaling down Pennsylvania Avenue in red stockings at speeds up to ten miles per hour. Her home on F Street, where she frequently played host

---

31. Norgren, "Lockwood in '84."
32. Ibid.

to the leading progressive women of that era, served as her national campaign headquarters.[33]

In many respects, the 53-year-old Lockwood, one of the few female trial lawyers in the country, was the ideal candidate for a party dedicated to the achievement of political and economic equality for women. The teacher-turned-lawyer, after all, had frequently been the victim of discrimination herself. As a young teacher, she discovered that her salary was less than half of what her male counterparts were receiving. Moreover, she had long been active in the feminist movement and, courageously, was one of the few members of the National Woman's Suffrage Association who had actively supported Victoria Woodhull's ill-fated third-party presidential bid in 1872. However, the Washington, D.C. firebrand wasn't the first woman approached by the fledgling third-party activists in 1884. Earlier, Stow had urged Abigail Scott Duniway, an Oregon newspaper editor, activist and founder of the Oregon State Women Suffrage Association, to accept the party's presidential nomination, but the fifty-year-old Duniway declined, believing that flaunting the names of women for high public office would undermine the woman's suffrage cause and would provide "unscrupulous opponents with new pretexts and excuses for lying about them."[34]

Undauntedly tossing her chapeau into the ring, the twice-widowed Lockwood proved to be an enthusiastic campaigner and was hardly discouraged that many prominent women's rights advocates, such as Anthony and Stanton—the first president of the National Woman's Suffrage Association—threw their support to Republican James G. Blaine because they mistakenly, if not foolishly, believed that women could achieve their goals within the two-party system. Moreover, a number of other women followed the lead of Frances Willard, the dynamic bellwether of the Women's Christian Temperance Union, in supporting the Prohibition Party's John P. St. John that year.

Much to her delight, the *Washington Evening Star* splashed the news of Lockwood's candidacy on the front page of its paper the day after she accepted the party's nomination, reprinting the entire text of her acceptance letter and platform. In an editorial the following day, the *Star* called the Equal Rights platform "the best of the lot" and editor Crosby Noyes lamented that it had not appeared earlier, saying that if it had "the other candidates might have had the benefit of perusing it and framing their epistles in accord with its pith and candor."[35]

---

33. *Washington Post*, July 6, 1952.
34. Norgren, "Lockwood in '84."
35. Ibid.

A ratification meeting was held at Wilson's Station in Maryland in mid-September at which time Lockwood, addressing a group of seventy-five supporters and journalists, gave her first speech of the 1884 campaign. In early October, the lady lawyer embarked on a campaign swing that included paid lectures in Baltimore, Philadelphia, New York, Cleveland, Louisville and Flint, Michigan, where she addressed an audience of 1,000—a crowd larger than the one that turned out the following night to hear Democratic congressman Frank H. Hurd of Ohio, who was then crisscrossing the state on behalf of Grover Cleveland. Addressing a crowd of five hundred at the Cleveland Opera House in mid-October, Lockwood assailed the Democrats on free trade, arguing that the nation's oldest party was "willing to risk our manufacturing interests in the face of the starving hordes of pauper labor in other countries" and ripped into the Republicans for supporting a high tariff that was equally injurious to American industry. Refusing to be portrayed as a single-issue candidate, the fashionably dressed and articulate third-party hopeful talked about a whole range of issues during the course of her spirited campaign, only occasionally talking about the role women had played in making the country "blossom as a rose."[36]

Impressed by the positive feeling created by a recent meeting of European leaders, Lockwood sent a letter to Democrat Grover Cleveland in late September, proposing a summit of all the presidential candidates in Wheeling, West Virginia. She later sent her proposal to her other rivals for the presidency. The idea, she said, was to bring all of the candidates for the presidency together for a serious discussion of the issues without the sort of rancor and negative attacks that had marked the campaign up to that point.[37] Unfortunately, her rivals didn't take her proposal very seriously.

Like her male rivals that year, Lockwood was subject to her fair share of ridicule, but it was really no worse than the abuse heaped on Cleveland ("Ma, Ma Where's My Pa"), and the treatment accorded Blaine and Butler, both of whom were severely savaged by cartoonist Thomas Nast, the brilliant German-born "Prince of Caricaturists." (Jeering at labor's support of Butler during the 1884 campaign, Nast sketched a cartoon of the former Massachusetts governor being carried into the White House by a procession of Irishmen and convicts.) Cartoonists for Frank Leslie's *Illustrated* and *Puck* mass-circulation newspapers, made fun of all the candidates, including the Equal Rights Party standard-bearer.[38]

---

36. Ibid.
37. *New York Times*, September 29, 1884.
38. Norgren, "Lockwood in '84"; *Harper's Weekly*, August 23, 1884.

The 1884 presidential campaign was a particularly nasty affair, turning less on the issues and more on the personality of the two major-party candidates. Scandals, moreover, were the order of the day. "The public is angry and abusive," wrote the usually contrary Henry Adams. "We are all swearing at each other like demons."[39] The liberal *Nation* magazine concurred, lamenting that partisan politics had "never before reached so low a depth of degradation" in this country.[40] The Republicans, refusing to give up the White House without a fight, took full advantage of a story that appeared in the *Buffalo Evening Telegraph* in July alleging that Cleveland had fathered an illegitimate child in 1874, casting aspersions on the Democratic nominee's morality. Cleveland didn't deny the allegations and admitted that he had made financial arrangements for the boy, eventually having him placed in an orphanage, from which he was later adopted by a good family. Nevertheless, the incident spawned the popular chant, "Ma, Ma, where's my Pa? Gone to the White House, Ha, Ha, Ha!" Cleveland, however, had his defenders, including Edwin L. Godkin of the *Nation*, who compared the New York governor to Benjamin Franklin and Alexander Hamilton—gifted, but certainly not perfect—and maintained that Cleveland would be a far more competent chief executive than a wheeler-dealer like Blaine.[41] The Democrats, meanwhile, assailed Blaine for his shady dealings with the railroad industry while in Congress, giving way to another popular campaign chant, "Blaine! Blaine! James G. Blaine! The Monumental Liar from the state of Maine!"[42]

Blaine's record, of course, left a lot to be desired. Regarded as one of the most corrupt politicians of his time, the former Speaker of the House was anything but a model of perfection. His earlier dealings with railroad interests had raised plenty of questions and provided ample material for the nation's political cartoonists, including the extraordinarily talented Bernhard Gillam of the satirical weekly *Puck*, who portrayed Blaine as the "tattooed man"—indelibly marked with the words "Bribery," "Little Rock" and "Mulligan Letters" on his body.[43] In 1869, it seems, Blaine had helped an Arkansas railroad secure renewal of a land grant. Working closely with Warren Fisher, a Boston broker, the Maine lawmaker arranged to sell the railroad's bonds but when the bond prices fell, Blaine refunded the investors' money by secretly selling the nearly worthless bonds to the unsuspecting Union Pacific Railroad at an exorbitant price. In 1876, Blaine,

39. Boller, *Presidential Campaigns*, p. 147.
40. *The Nation*, October 23, 1884.
41. Boller, *Presidential Campaigns*, p. 149.
42. Roseboom, *A History of Presidential Elections*, p. 272.
43. Boller, *Presidential Campaigns*, p. 153.

who was then being investigated for his role in the episode, intercepted letters furnished to a House investigating committee by James Mulligan, Fisher's bookkeeper. He then furnished the investigation committee excerpts from those letters that appeared to exonerate him. A second batch of letters—including one from Blaine to the bookkeeper asking him to burn the original—was uncovered during the 1884 campaign, causing a great deal of embarrassment and placing the Republican standard-bearer under a cloud of suspicion.[44]

For Prohibitionist John P. St. John—who many believed was a breath of fresh air compared to his Republican rival—the 1884 canvass was a difficult one. The Republicans were desperate and one of Blaine's managers offered the Prohibition standard-bearer a lucrative bribe to withdraw from the race—which St. John adamantly rejected.[45] In early September, the former steamboat worker-turned-lawyer and ex-Forty-niner was forced to deny that he was withdrawing from the race. "I saw the newspaper article charging me with the intention of selling out to the Republicans," he told reporters at the Sherman House in Chicago. Acknowledging that while he hadn't actively sought the Prohibition Party's nomination, he said he had no intention of dropping out. "I don't know that even this much of a denial is warranted by the nature of the statements set afloat," he said, "but I make it to put at rest all doubts." While St. John didn't harbor any illusions about actually being sworn in as America's twenty-second president in March of 1885, he nevertheless predicted that he would poll a million votes, auguring well for the party in future elections.[46]

Angered by bitter attacks from Republican editors, on October 20 St. John cancelled a speaking tour of New England, New Jersey, Pennsylvania and some of the western states and said that he was going to focus all of his energy in the state of New York—home of the largest block of electoral votes in the country—in an effort to render Blaine's defeat. Since most "dry" voters probably would have supported Blaine if St. John were not in the race, this last-minute change of strategy sent chills up the spines of the Republican managers. Stunned by this sudden turn of events, the Republicans could do little to stifle the former Indian fighter's all-out effort to play the role of spoiler in the nation's most populous state. "The Republican Party must now understand that they will have to come over to us, as the Whig Party had to come over to the Abolitionists," said

---

44. Roseboom, *A History of Presidential Elections*, pp. 269-270.
45. Storms, *Partisan Prophets*, p. 15.
46. *New York Times*, September 5, 1884.

party chairman John B. Finch. "If Blaine should be elected it means that the cause of prohibition would be pushed back twenty years."[47]

Enthusiastically endorsing Cleveland's candidacy, the so-called "Mugwumps" were another important factor in the razor-thin 1884 presidential contest. Headed by former Missouri senator and ex-Secretary of the Interior Carl Schurz and headquartered in a small, poorly manned office in New York City, the independents and a sprinkling of Republican bolters who joined the effort included such prominent intellectuals as Harvard President Charles W. Eliot and most of that school's faculty. An elite regiment of reformers opposed to the crass spoils of American politics in the Gilded Age, the Mugwumps called for fiscal responsibility in government, civil service reform, tariff reduction and maintenance of the country's gold standard. The Reverend Henry Ward Beecher, Charles Francis Adams, Jr., and longtime civil service reformers Edwin L. Godkin of the *Nation* and George W. Curtis, the longtime political editor of *Harper's Weekly*, were also among those who supported Cleveland against Blaine. Earlier that year, the 60-year-old Curtis, who had served as chairman of the National Civil Service Reform League in the aftermath of the Civil War, was a delegate to the Republican national convention that nominated Blaine. Their ranks also included young Columbia University instructor Daniel DeLeon, who later emerged as the indefatigable and autocratic leader of the Socialist Labor Party. During the campaign, DeLeon, a prize lecturer on constitutional law and Latin American diplomacy, wrote an eight-page pamphlet entitled, *A Specimen of Mr. Blaine's Diplomacy: Is He a Safe Man to Trust as President?* Although he drifted considerably leftward after the 1884 campaign—enthusiastically supporting the United Labor Party's Henry George in the 1886 New York City mayoralty race—DeLeon took a genuine liking to Cleveland and later named one of his sons after the Mugwump champion.[48]

As Election Day approached, it became increasingly obvious that the election would hinge on the outcome in heavily populated New York. All four candidates—St. John, Butler, Cleveland and Blaine—made an all-effort in the Empire State. Even Belva Lockwood waged a spirited campaign there. Prohibitionist John P. St. John actively campaigned in the state with the support of Frances E. Willard and the influential Women's Christian Temperance Union. John B. Gough, a majestically hirsute figure, reformed alcoholic, and perhaps the best

---

47. Ibid., October 21, 184.
48. Roseboom, *A History of Presidential Elections*, p. 269; Boller, *Presidential Campaigns*, p. 147; L. Glen Seretan, *Daniel DeLeon: The Odyssey of an American Marxist* (Cambridge, MA, 1979), pp. 23-24.

known temperance speaker in the world—delivering over 9,600 lectures in the United States, Canada, England, Ireland and Scotland—spoke at a rally for St. John sponsored by the Prohibition Club of Newburgh in New York City. John B. Finch, the party's young national chairman who doubled as the head of the Order of Good Templars, also spoke at the rally, telling the audience of more than five hundred that the liquor interests were firmly in control of both old parties. "The battle is simply a battle of self-defense for the upholding of the home and for the destruction of the vicious elements and vitiating tendencies of our civilization," he said. "The present attitude of firm temperance men has been precipitated by the fact that the liquor interest is absolutely in control of both the old parties, dictatorial, insolent, proud in its ascendancy. That gigantic interest," he concluded, "must be conquered or it will conquer the country."[49]

The Anti-Monopolist Party's Benjamin Butler, whose campaign was being surreptitiously financed by Tammany Hall's John B. Kelly, as well as by the Republican National Committee, also stumped aggressively in New York. Democrat Grover Cleveland, who made only two formal speeches during the campaign—one in Newark, New Jersey, and the other in Bridgeport, Connecticut—also made a concerted effort for the state's thirty-six electoral votes, campaigning vigorously in Buffalo and reviewing a parade of 40,000 in New York City during the campaign's closing days.[50] Likewise, the Republicans, hoping to tip the scales in Blaine's favor, pulled out all the stops. In addition to secretly financing Butler's third-party candidacy in an attempt to siphon Democratic votes from Cleveland, the GOP's propaganda machine spread rumors that Cleveland was a religious bigot—and worse.

The Republicans were cautiously optimistic about their chances in New York. After all, New York City's large Catholic population, estimated at close to half a million, seemed to favor Blaine, whose mother was Irish Catholic and whose cousin was the mother-superior of a local convent. Moreover, Blaine himself was known to occasionally "twist the British Lion's tail," much to the delight of all good Irishmen. Blaine, who was genuinely sympathetic to the Irish cause, had been endorsed by the *Irish Nation* and the widely-read *Irish World*.

Shadowed by the Prohibition Party's John P. St. John throughout the state, Blaine's managers were confident that his support among New York's large Irish-American population, many of whom were opposed to temperance, would easily offset any votes that were lost to the Prohibition ticket. Blaine's support among

---

49. Colvin, *Prohibition in the United States*, pp. 161-162.
50. Roseboom, *A History of Presidential Elections*, p. 272.

Irish-American voters, however, was severely eroded on October 29, otherwise known as "Black Wednesday." That morning at a meeting of several hundred Protestant ministers at the Fifth Avenue Hotel in New York City, Samuel D. Burchard, a Presbyterian clergyman, concluded his welcoming address by calling the Democrats the party of "Rum, Romanism, and Rebellion." Blaine, who attended the reception, apparently didn't hear Burchard's comments. Realizing the significance of Burchard's insensitive remarks, John B. Finch, the Prohibition Party's national chairman who happened to be present, quickly jotted them down. Standing behind him at the reception was Daniel Manning, leader of the Democratic Party in upstate New York who later served as Cleveland's Secretary of the Treasury. The unscrupulous Manning snatched the paper out of Finch's hand and hurried to the nearest telegraph office. The minister's tasteless remarks spread like wildfire as newspapers throughout the country carried Burchard's inflammatory comments and Blaine's apparent acquiescence. By the time Blaine tried to disavow the minister's incendiary remarks, the damage was already done. Thousands of Irish Catholic voters in New York City and elsewhere were too angry to listen to any explanation that the "Plumed Knight" had to offer.

"Black Wednesday" got even darker for the Republican standard-bearer that evening during a lavish fundraising dinner at New York's fashionable Delmonico's restaurant, attended by some of New York's wealthiest citizens, including John Jacob Astor, Jay Gould, Cyris W. Field, Russell Sage and several other millionaires. Though the country was in a depression at the time, Blaine, who ignored the advice of the GOP national chairman not to attend the fundraiser, extolled Republican prosperity in his post-dinner remarks. The following morning, Joseph Pulitzer's New York *World* featured a front-page headline and accompanying cartoon picturing "Belshazzar Blaine and the Money Kings" dining in opulent splendor while a hungry man and his ragged wife and child begged for scraps.

Col. Robert G. Ingersoll's refusal to speak on his behalf in New York also hurt Blaine considerably. The "great agnostic" had delivered one of the greatest nominating speeches in American history when he placed the "Plumed Knight" in nomination at the 1876 Republican national convention. Apparently snubbed by Blaine's managers, the eloquent 51-year-old former Union army officer, one of the most quotable men of his time, refused to stump for Blaine and was undoubtedly delighted by the fact that a man of the cloth helped Blaine go down to defeat when an agnostic like himself probably could have put him in the White House.[51]

If things weren't already bleak enough for the former lawmaker from Maine, Election Day rain clouds in upstate New York darkened his presidential prospects forever. A driving rain in that region made it extremely difficult, if not impossible, for many farmers to get to the polls. Unfortunately for Blaine, turnout in the cities—where most Democrats lived—was largely unaffected by the weather.

On Election Day, Democrat Grover Cleveland narrowly defeated the GOP standard-bearer by a margin of 4,874,621 to 4,848,936. The Prohibition Party's John P. St. John, who had waged one of the most vigorous campaigns in the party's history, garnered a somewhat respectable 153,128 votes nationally—nearly fifteen times greater than any previous Prohibition candidate for president. The former Kansas governor polled 26,016 votes in New York, or more than two percent of the total, clearly costing Blaine the state's thirty-six electoral votes and the presidency. (Blaine lost to Cleveland in the Empire State by a mere 1,047 votes out of more than 1,167,000 votes cast.) The Anti-Monopoly Party's Benjamin Butler, polling the difference between his two major-party rivals in Connecticut, Indiana, Massachusetts and New York, where he garnered 16,955 votes, received a relatively disappointing 175,300 votes nationally, or barely half the number of votes received by the Greenback-Labor Party's James B. Weaver in 1880. Butler garnered a respectable 42,252 votes, or 10.5% of the total, in Michigan, a former Greenback stronghold, and tallied 24,382 votes, or eight percent, in his home state of Massachusetts and more than six percent in the farm state of Kansas, where he received a somewhat impressive 16,341 votes. He also ran reasonably well in Maine and Colorado, receiving approximately three percent of the vote in both states. Although at least one source credits her with as many as 4,149 votes nationally, election officials apparently refused to officially count any votes for Belva Lockwood of the Equal Rights Party.[52]

---

51. Ibid., p. 273.
52. Miller, *'If Elected...' Unsuccessful Candidates for the Presidency 1796-1968*, p. 497; Jill Norgren, "Equal Rights Party, 1872-1880s," *The Encyclopedia of Third Parties*, Vol. I, p. 252; *New York Times*, Dec. 20, 1884. Although election officials refused to count votes cast for the Equal Rights Party electors, Lockwood appears to have received at least one quasi-official vote in the 1884 presidential election. According to the Illinois State Treasurer, a voter in Waukegan voted for the Equal Rights Party's electors, a slate that included several women. James H. Carr, a printer from Waukegan, Illinois, had prepared the ballot. Although his vote apparently wasn't included in the official canvass, Carr, who was one of Lockwood's electors in that state, told the State Treasurer that he had cast such a ballot for the feminist candidate on Election Day.

Though his biographer blamed his narrow defeat on the independent Republicans who supported Cleveland, James G. Blaine deeply regretted making the race. Both personally and politically, the whole campaign had been a disaster, he confided shortly after the election. "I ought to have obeyed what was really, my strong instinct against running," he told a close friend. "My regrets do not in the least take the form of mourning over defeat in the election, but over my blunder in ever consenting to run. It was the wrong year and gave to my enemies their coveted opportunities."[53]

Convinced that he would garner at least 1,500,000 votes, the Anti-Monopoly Party's Benjamin F. Butler was deeply disappointed by his meager showing.[54] He wasn't even able to play the role of spoiler; every vote that he siphoned from Cleveland was apparently offset by St. John's ability to slice into Blaine's total. Claiming that he had been cheated out of thousands of votes in New York—enough to have prevented Cleveland's election—when election officials fraudulently gave his votes to his Democratic rival in countless precincts in Brooklyn and New York City, Butler was initially inclined to launch a formal investigation into vote fraud in that state but dropped the idea when Tammany Hall's John Kelly, suffering from a severe bronchial condition and a myriad of other ailments, suddenly fell ill shortly after the election. Without Kelly's assistance, Butler maintained, it would have been next to impossible to bring in the necessary Democratic witnesses to prove his case. Nevertheless, Butler, who campaigned briefly for Republican Benjamin Harrison in the 1888 presidential campaign, was convinced that Cleveland—having carried the nation's most populous state by the slimmest of margins—had been elected by fraudulent means.[55] Given the immense amount of time and energy he expended in that crucial state, the nearly 17,000 votes officially recorded for Butler in New York was far below expectations, thereby lending some credibility to his allegation. Powerful Massachusetts Sen. George F. Hoar, Butler's longtime nemesis, and journalist Edward Stanwood, Blaine's brother-in-law, subsequently echoed these same charges. When Stanwood, a former editor of the *Boston Daily Advertiser*, again reiterated the charges a few years after Cleveland's death in 1908, William G. Rice and Francis L. Stetson, one of Cleveland's former law partners, examined the evidence and disproved the allegations—at least to the satisfaction of some.[56]

---

53. Rhodes, *History of the United States from the Compromise of 1850 to the McKinley-Bryan Campaign of 1896*, Vol. 8, p. 132.
54. West, *Lincoln's Scapegoat General*, p. 407.
55. Butler, *Butler's Book*, p. 984; Charles Edward Russell, *Blaine of Maine* (New York, 1931), p. 402; Holzman, *Stormy Ben Butler*, p. 219.

Ironically, Butler's total in New York might have been greater were it not for a bitter labor dispute between the *New York Tribune* and members of the International Typographical Union. The local union had declared an all-out war against Blaine because the *Tribune* had endorsed his candidacy and, as a result, most of the union's membership worked vigorously for Cleveland, instead of supporting Butler's pro-labor candidacy which they might have done under more favorable circumstances.[57]

On closer examination, the Anti-Monopoly ticket actually ran stronger in rural farming communities in the Midwest and in some parts of the South than among urban workers in the industrial northeast, especially in New York, where Butler had made such a concerted effort. In fact, more than 97,000 of his votes came from states in the Midwest and Far West. "General Butler and his platform appealed especially to wage-workers, but they received very little support from that quarter," observed longtime Knights of Labor leader Joseph R. Buchanan, adding that most of the former general's strength had come "from the farmers."[58] Buchanan's observation was correct; the traditional farming states of Arkansas, Colorado, Indiana, Kansas, Michigan, and Minnesota were among Butler's strongest states.

Despite the party's massive defeat in the presidential election, leaders of the Anti-Monopoly and Greenback parties nevertheless had something to smile about when the returns began trickling in—namely, the return of Iowa's James B. Weaver to Congress on the Greenback ticket after a four-year absence. The last Greenbacker to serve in Congress, Weaver narrowly defeated his Republican opponent by sixty-seven votes, garnering 16,684 votes to Republican Frank T. Campbell's 16,617. The party also provided the margin of victory for at least three Democratic House candidates running on fusion tickets in Michigan and made the difference in Democratic congressman William H. Neece's narrow victory in Illinois. Running on a joint Democratic and Anti-Monopoly ticket, the freshman lawmaker defeated his Republican challenger by a razor-thin 327 votes out of more than 36,500 votes cast. The Greenback Party also came within 153

56. Nash, *Stormy Petrel*, p. 297; George F. Hoar, *Autobiography of Seventy Years* (New York, 1903), Vol. I, p. 408; Edward Stanwood, *James Gillespie Blaine* (Boston, 1905); Edward Stanwood, "Election Superstitions and Fallacies," *Atlantic Monthly*, October, 1912, Vol. CX, p. 559; William Gorham Rice and Francis Lynde Stetson, "Was New York Vote's Stolen?" *North American Review*, January 1914, Vol. CXCIX, p. 79.

57. Ibid., p. 297.

58. Joseph R. Buchanan, *The Story of a Labor Agitator* (New York, 1903), p. 101.

votes of claiming one of West Virginia's four congressional seats when a Democratic incumbent narrowly defeated physician Andrew R. Barbee, a longtime party member and former colonel in the Confederate army. In mounting his second campaign for the seat, Barbee, a former state senator, ran on a Greenback-Republican fusion ticket.

Party leaders were also buoyed by the news of 27-year-old Benjamin Franklin Shively's election to Congress. Shively, a lawyer and journalist, was a former secretary of the National Anti-Monopoly Association. This joy, however, was somewhat offset by the news of Luman H. "Calamity" Weller's defeat in Iowa and by Charles N. Brumm's defection to the GOP in Pennsylvania. They were the only two Greenback candidates who had served in the previous Congress. Weller, who was once described by *The Iowa State Register* as "the greatest political crank that Iowa has yet produced, in any party or in any field outside of a lunatic asylum," was narrowly defeated in his bid for a second term, losing to his Republican rival by a slim 230 votes.[59] Despite his setback, the former Greenback congressman, a close friend of Minnesota's Ignatius Donnelly, remained active in the agrarian and third-party movements, serving as proprietor and editor of the *Farmers' Advocate*, a weekly newspaper based in Independence, Iowa, and as president of the nationally-organized Chosen Farmers of America. In 1901, he was the Populist candidate for governor of Iowa against popular progressive Republican Albert B. Cummins and his Democratic challenger, but ran rather poorly. Sometimes referred to as "Lemuel" Weller, he was also a member of the Populist Party's national committee from 1890 until his death on March 2, 1914—serving in that capacity longer than anyone else.

The Greenback Party also waged somewhat competitive gubernatorial races in Massachusetts, Missouri and Texas that year. In Massachusetts, the Greenback Party's Matthew McCafferty garnered 24,363 votes in a three-way won by Republican George D. Robinson—the man who unseated Butler a year earlier. In Missouri, former Greenback congressman Nicholas Ford, running on a Greenback-Republican fusion ticket, was narrowly defeated, losing to the illustriously-named Democrat John Sappington Marmaduke by a margin of 218,885 to 207,93, while in Texas the Greenback candidate garnered over seven percent of the vote in a three-cornered race easily won by incumbent Democrat John Ireland.

---

59. *The Iowa State Register* of November 17, 1882, as quoted in Haynes, *Third Party Movements Since the Civil War*, p. 187.

Though clearly on its last legs, the Greenback-Labor Party also continued to win occasional state legislative and local races, as was the case in Vermont's state elections in September when four Greenbackers were elected to the state House of Representatives—doubling its membership in that overwhelmingly Republican body.[60]

In addition to Weaver, at least one other candidate was elected to Congress on a third-party ticket in 1884. Running on an Independent Labor Party ticket, Michael Hahn, a former governor of Louisiana, was elected to the U.S. House of Representatives from the state's second congressional district in New Orleans, defeating his Democratic rival by a margin of 7,356 to 6,103.[61] Hahn, who served as governor of Louisiana during the federal occupation in 1864-65, had previously served one term in Congress as a "Unionist" in the early 1860s. He had also been elected to the U.S. Senate in 1865, but was refused his seat when Congress, in the aftermath of Lincoln's assassination, refused to seat any lawmakers from the South. As governor, Hahn's administration initiated Reconstruction in that state, laying the foundation for black enfranchisement and establishing an African-American public school system. A lawyer and former manager and editor of the *New Orleans Daily Republican*, the 54-year-old former governor took his seat with the Republicans when the 49th Congress convened. Unfortunately, he died midway through his term when he suffered a ruptured blood vessel near his heart.

For the first time in its fifteen-year history, the Prohibition Party had played a decisive role in determining the outcome of a presidential election. National chairman John B. Finch was ecstatic, stating that the Republican Party was destined for the political graveyard and predicting that the Prohibitionists would bury the whiskey Democrats in 1888. "Weakening Republican mass support gave some satisfaction to Prohibition Party leaders," wrote scholar Paul Kleppner. "They continually spoke of 'holding the balance-of-power,' and enumerated those states in which their total exceeded the margin of difference between the Democratic and Republican totals."[62]

The dry party, which fielded no fewer than 145 candidates for Congress in 1884, put up a strong fight in at least a half-dozen races across the country, including the battle for Rhode Island's second congressional district seat where Democrat Charles H. Page was eventually seated after winning a special election.

---

60. *New York Times*, September 6, 1884.
61. Ibid., November 6, 1884.
62. Paul Kleppner, "The Greenback and Prohibition Parties," in Schlesinger, et. al., *History of U.S. Political Parties* (New York, 1973), Vol. II, p. 1574.

In that race, Prohibitionist Alfred B. Chadsey had initially polled nearly ten percent of the vote against his major-party rivals. Prohibition candidates also waged spirited races for two of Michigan's eleven U.S. House seats, polling over six percent of the vote in the state's second and third congressional districts, respectively. In Wisconsin, John M. Olin, a brilliant Madison lawyer who did as much for the causes of temperance and women's suffrage as anyone in the state's history, polled a critically decisive 5.2% of the vote against "Fighting Bob" LaFollette and his Democratic rival in a race narrowly won by the legendary progressive lawmaker. In one of the closest House races in the country that year, the young Dane County district attorney defeated incumbent Democratic congressman Burr W. Jones, a plain-spoken and affable Madison attorney, garnering 17,433 votes to 16,942 for Jones and 1,885 for Olin. Moreover, James Black, the party's aging presidential standard-bearer in 1872, polled 10,471 votes, or slightly more than one percent of the total, in an unsuccessful bid for Pennsylvania's at-large seat in the U.S. House of Representatives.

For his part, St. John was hung in effigy and burned in more than one hundred communities across the country. Republican-inspired attacks on Prohibitionists intensified in the wake of the election and several ministers who were sympathetic to the fledgling third party were expelled from their pulpits. Incredibly, the name of St. John County in Kansas was changed to Logan County, in honor of Blaine's running mate, a fellow Kansan. During the debate over changing the county's name, one legislator reportedly prayed that St. John's name should be "obliterated from Kansas history." The hatred for St. John and the Prohibitionists, wrote party historian D. Leigh Colvin, was based on something deeper than Blaine's defeat. "The political regime feared that the Prohibition Party was about to start a landslide which would squarely divide the country on the prohibition question and destroy the old political organizations."[63]

Having played the role of spoiler, the Prohibitionists, easily eclipsing the Greenback-Labor Party as the country's leading third-party, were poised—or so it seemed—to play a larger role in American politics. In 1886, two Prohibitionists were elected to the state legislature in Vermont, as well as one in Illinois. One of the party's premier efforts that year occurred in tiny Delaware where James R. Hoffecker, running under the banner of the Temperance Reform Party, garnered nearly thirty-six percent of the vote against former Democratic congressman Benjamin T. Biggs in that state's gubernatorial contest. Twenty-seven newspapers in Ohio endorsed the party that year. The following year, two Prohibition Party

---

63.   Colvin, *Prohibition in the United States*, pp. 164-166.

candidates were also elected to the Massachusetts legislature, including one who was elected to the state senate.[64]

Like the Anti-Monopoly Party's Benjamin F. Butler, Belva A. Lockwood also claimed that 1,336 votes cast for her in New York were fraudulently tabulated for Democrat Grover Cleveland—providing him with the margin of victory in that crucial state. She also alleged that election officials in eight other states had failed to record votes that had been legally cast for her electors, including 379 in New Hampshire, 374 in Michigan, 1,008 in Illinois, 562 in Iowa, 318 in Maryland, and 734 in California. She also charged that "a large vote in Pennsylvania" was simply dumped into the waste basket as false votes" and that the entire electoral vote of Indiana—a state decided by 6,500 votes—had been "fraudulently and illegally counted" for Cleveland. In the years preceding the adoption of the Australian ballot in the early 1890's, it wasn't impossible for local election officials to stuff the ballot box or destroy ballots—and that was precisely what Lockwood claimed had happened.[65] Unlike Butler, however, Lockwood urged lawmakers to set aside the returns from New York and petitioned Congress for Indiana's fifteen electoral votes, arguing that the electors from that state had switched their votes from Cleveland to her at the last minute. That wasn't true, of course. It was all part of a prank engineered by the good old boys in the Hoosier State. It is uncertain whether Lockwood actually fell for it, or was merely going along in the spirit of political gamesmanship.[66]

---

64. Storms, *Partisan Prophets*, p. 17.
65. The United States was slow in adopting the secret ballot. South Australia adopted it in 1858 and the British Parliament, overcoming the waning influence of utilitarian philosopher John Stuart Mill—who believed that everyone's vote should be cast "under the eye and criticism of the public"—adopted the secret ballot in 1872. The first Australian-ballot law in the United States was enacted by the Kentucky legislature in 1880, but because the state's constitution still required viva voce voting in state elections, it only applied to municipal elections in Louisville. In 1888, Massachusetts became the first state to issue government-printed ballots in state and federal elections. By the early 1890s, thirty-three states had uniform ballots printed and distributed by the government and every state except Connecticut, Georgia, North Carolina, and South Carolina used such a ballot during the McKinley-Bryan presidential election of 1896. By 1942, forty-five of the nation's forty-eight states used the Australian ballot, while Georgia and Delaware used a modified version. South Carolina was the only state at the time that failed to provide government-printed ballots. See V. O. Key, Jr., *Politics, Parties, and Pressure Groups* (New York, 1952), pp. 649-651; Richard Winger, "History of U.S. Ballot Access Law for New and Minor Parties," *The Encyclopedia of Third Parties in America*, Vol. I, pp. 72-95.

Deeply disappointed that he hadn't made a stronger showing, Benjamin F. Butler returned to his law practice in Boston following the campaign. A new generation of voters unfamiliar with Big Bethel, New Orleans, and the "bloody shirt" made it clear to the general that his time had come and gone. The decisive setback essentially marked the end of his political career, although, in the 1888 presidential election he stumped briefly for Republican Benjamin Harrison in Michigan, a former Greenback stronghold—and a state where Butler nearly held the balance of power between Blaine and Cleveland four years earlier. During his brief appearance in that campaign it was clear that "Brave Old Ben" hadn't lost any of his old magic. When someone lowered a bunch of spoons on a rope while he was speaking under a tall tree, Butler, never missing a beat, quipped that they must have been some of the spoons that he neglected to get while he was in New Orleans. The crowd ate it up. Though hardly anyone noticed at the time, he also endorsed the Populist Party's James B. Weaver during the 1892 presidential campaign.

Although retired from the political arena, the ubiquitous Butler remained in the news and was frequently mentioned in coverage of the annual Butler Club dinners, held on the anniversary of his capture of New Orleans. He also occasionally sallied forth to agitate for the annexation of Canada or to speak out against free trade—two issues near and dear to his heart. In 1887, the former Massachusetts governor appeared before the U.S. Supreme Court on behalf of Haymarket Square defendants August Spies and Samuel Fielden, both of whom had been convicted of murder in the May 4, 1884, bombing that killed a police officer. One of the eight men condemned in the case was Albert Parsons, the younger brother of William H. Parsons who had caused Butler so much grief during the recent presidential campaign. Their case, which generated as much attention throughout the nation and the world as the infamous Sacco-Vanzetti case four decades later, had been appealed to the federal courts on the grounds that the Illinois courts had violated their constitutional rights of equal protection under the law. Lawyers for the defendants argued strenuously that a handpicked "hanging jury" had unjustly convicted the men, sentencing them to death. Their lawyers were absolutely right. The state's attorney later affirmed that "anarchy" was the real defendant in the case and Judge Joseph E. Gary, the presiding judge during the trial, "flaunted his bias against the defendants" at every opportunity.[67]

---

66.   Norgren, "Lockwood in '84."

67.   Nash, *Stormy Petrel*, pp. 298-299; Trefousse, *Ben Butler: The South Called Him Beast!* p. 254; West, *Lincoln's Scapegoat General*, p. 413; Dave Roediger, "Haymarket Incident," *Encyclopedia of the American Left* (Urbana, 1990), pp. 295-297.

During his court appearance, Butler argued that because his clients were foreigners (Spies, a German, had emigrated to the United States when he was seventeen, and Fielden, a textile worker, was an Englishman who arrived on America's shores in 1868), they were entitled to special privileges in addition to their constitutional rights, suggesting that both men should have been tried in accordance with laws pertaining to search and seizure and the right to a legal jury that were in force when applicable treaties between their respective countries and the United States had been ratified. The justices, believing that the men's fate had already been sealed, paid little attention to Butler while he vigorously pleaded their case and several of them read briefs or other documents while he spoke, barely acknowledging his presence. In the end, Butler's petition was denied on the grounds that he was trying to make a legal point that had not been made previously in any of the lower courts and, therefore, couldn't be raised for the first time in the Supreme Court. Along with three other Haymarket martyrs, the 32-year-old Spies, a newspaper editor and frequent candidate for office on the Socialist Labor Party ticket, was executed by hanging in November 1887, while the 37-year-old Fielden, an organizer for the International Working People's Association (IWPA) who had been injured in the Haymarket bombing, was later released from prison by Illinois Governor John Peter Altgeld, whose courageous and stinging pardon message acknowledged the gross injustice of the trial.[68]

The retired general, of course, was widely criticized in the press for defending the anarchists. "Don't misunderstand me, madam," he explained to a female critic. "I will defend upon proper occasion if his life is in question, even the editor of a newspaper who has abused me for twenty years if I think that there is a chance of saving his life."[69]

In 1889, Butler, who possessed a prodigious memory, became involved in a widely publicized feud with his old nemesis Admiral David D. Porter, an egotistical man given to considerable self-glorifying hyperbole. The son of the famous commander of the *Essex* during the War of 1812, Porter, though considered somewhat unscrupulous, was generally regarded as a competent, aggressive and resourceful career naval officer. He served as superintendent of the U.S. Naval Academy in Annapolis following the war and became Admiral of the Navy following Farragut's death in 1870. Butler could hardly stomach Porter and had even gone so far as to propose abolishing the grade of admiral during Grant's

---

68. Ibid., pp. 298–299; West, *Lincoln's Scapegoat General*, p. 413; Roediger, "Haymarket Incident," pp. 295–297; *Chicago Tribune*, November 11, 1887.
69. West, *Lincoln's Scapegoat General*, p. 413.

presidency, shortly after some unflattering letters Porter wrote about the Hero of Appomattox first surfaced.[70]

The revived feud, which had been smoldering for more than a quarter of a century, centered on the war records of the two men. Butler and Porter, of course, had been bitter enemies since they took part in a joint assault on heavily constructed Fort Jackson and Fort Saint Phillip on opposite sides of the Mississippi in the spring of 1862. Porter argued that his mortar shells, which lit up the Louisiana skyline like a massive Fourth of July fireworks display, was responsible for the fall of the two heavily fortified structures, but Butler claimed his infantry deserved credit for taking the forts. In retrospect, Admiral David G. Farragut, a sixty-year-old Tennessee native who went to sea at the remarkably young age of nine and saw action in the War of 1812, was the true hero in the capture of New Orleans, but it was left to Butler and Porter to fight over the scraps, battling for what little glory might be theirs for toppling the Confederate forts, some seventy-five miles downstream from the city. Butler wondered how Porter, whose "superbly useless bombardment" at the outset of the attack, could claim that *he* had captured the forts when his ships failed to fire a single shot at the forts for three days prior to their surrender. In his official report to Secretary of War Edwin M. Stanton only days after the engagement, Butler paid homage to Farragut for courageously leading his fleet past the forts en route to New Orleans, but sharply criticized Porter's mortar flotilla for withdrawing some miles downriver so as to avoid the Confederate ironclad *Louisiana*, which was lying moored off Fort Jackson.[71]

In their revived quarrel more than two decades later, the retired general again claimed that Porter had fled during the heated battle for control of the forts and to prove his point had an agent for the Department of the Navy search its archives for the long lost log of the admiral's flagship, the *Harriet Lane*, but the researcher came up empty-handed. This was proof, asserted Butler, that the admiral had either destroyed the log or had it safely hidden away to avoid unwanted scrutiny. A clearly rattled Porter offered a somewhat dubious explanation, claiming that the log had disappeared when Confederates captured his ship in Galveston seven months after the fall of New Orleans. The invective between the two men was heated and contentious, but the controversy eventually ended

---

70. Nolan, *Benjamin Franklin Butler: The Damnedest Yankee*, p. 139; Trefousse, *Ben Butler: The South Called Him Beast!* p. 254.

71. Holzman, *Stormy Ben Butler*, pp. 76, 219-220; Nolan, *Benjamin Franklin Butler: The Damnedest Yankee*, pp. 146-149; Richard S. West, Jr., *The Second Admiral* (New York, 1937), p. 342; McPherson, *Battle Cry of Freedom*, pp. 419-420.

when Porter succumbed to a heart attack and died in early 1891. Throughout it all, Butler seemed to relish in this type of personal confrontation. "The general looked well and was apparently not worried by the fight," reported the *Boston Globe*. "He had a sprig of mignonette and a big rose in his buttonhole, and he chewed on his gum with great zest. Age had not blunted his combative qualities."[72]

During this period, Butler also began work on his long-awaited memoirs, an 1,154-page tome published by a Boston publishing house in early 1892. Though hardly a brilliant polemicist, Butler was nevertheless a pretty good writer. His prose, as the editor of the *North American Review* once commented, had "all the vivacity and sparkling qualities of the best French writers."[73] Lucid until the end of his life, the retired general didn't want or need the help of a ghostwriter and, relying almost entirely on his own memory and wartime documents and letters, completed his manuscript during the first week of January 1892—a year before his death. It was a good thing that his memory was so sharp, for he had many enemies to remember," quipped one his biographers.[74] Poignant and pungently written, *Butler's Book* was scathing in its treatment of many of the general's contemporaries. "Probably no serious book ever written by a person of equal prominence contains so much bitter abuse and unmeasured invective as his autobiography," declared one writer.[75] Many of his contemporaries, however, applauded his literary effort. General Oliver O. Howard, a West Point professional who lost an arm during the bloody Battle of Fair Oaks and later commanded the Army of the Tennessee, found Butler's memoir "more intriguing than any novel."[76]

The controversial military governor of the Crescent City spared few of his wartime contemporaries in his lengthy treatise. He had particularly sharp words for Henry W. Halleck, Lincoln's inept but grandly titled "general in chief" and one of those who was responsible for relieving him of his duties in New Orleans, accusing the balding and paunchy West Point graduate of inconsistency, vanity and cowardice and describing him as "a lying, treacherous, hypocritical scoundrel with no moral sense."[77] A military scholar and dedicated disciple of Antoine Henry Jomini, Napoleon's brilliant Swiss-born strategist and an expert on the

---

72. Ibid., pp. 219-220.
73. West, *Lincoln's Scapegoat General*, 416.
74. Holzman, *Stormy Ben Butler*, p. 230.
75. Clarence Edward Macartney, *Lincoln and His Generals* (Philadelphia, 1925), p. 66.
76. *New York World*, January 12, 1893, quoted in Holzman, *Stormy Ben Butler*, pp. 220-221.

great Corsican's military campaigns—and whose works Halleck had once translated—the new general in chief, like McClellan, was a slow and indecisive commander, breathtakingly spending two months to creep from Shiloh to Corinth
only to discover when he finally reached his destination that the southern army
had already moved South with all of its provisions.[78] While Porter was described
as "a reckless, conscienceless, and impudent liar," Butler scornfully blasted
Gideon Welles, the crusty Secretary of the Navy—and one of the few who questioned the wisdom of removing Butler from his command in New Orleans—for
reducing the sentence of an officer that he had personally punished for running
away from the enemy. In Butler's eyes, Welles apparently thought that cowardice
was excusable. Though he wrote fondly of Admiral Farregut, Ulysses S. Grant
was one of the few other soldiers whose reputation on the battlefield escaped Butler's poison pen, but even he, in his role as the nation's eighteenth president, was
criticized as "a moral coward."[79]

Butler also savaged John Hay, Lincoln's personal secretary and the author of a
ten-volume biography on the slain president. Apparently disturbed by Hay's contention that Butler may not have been the originator of the phrase "contraband"
as applied to slaves during the Civil War, the former Massachusetts governor,
calling Hay's assertion "an emanation of malice and ignorance," said that he
knew more about his subject than his biographer could ever hope to know and
said that Lincoln's memory deserved better. "You can't weigh a load of hay with
fish scales, you know."[80]

Succumbing to pneumonia, Butler died in Washington on January 11, 1893,
almost a year after his book was published. His death made the front pages of
papers all over the country and thousands paid their respects when his body lay in
state in Lowell's Huntington Hall, while hundreds more trudged through knee-
deep snow on a stormy and bitterly cold January day to watch their hero being
laid to rest. He was buried with full military honors. Cannons were fired, fol-

---

77. Butler, *Butler's Book*, pp. 463, 871. Lincoln later denied that Gen. Halleck had any
     hand in Butler's removal. (See Lincoln's letter to I. N. Arnold, May 26, 1863, quoted
     in Angle and Miers, *The Living Lincoln*, p. 542.)
78. McPherson, *Battle Cry of Freedom*, p. 331; Bailyn, *et al.*, *The Great Republic*, pp. 488-
     489, 494.
79. Ibid., pp. 752, 1010; Holzman, *Stormy Ben Butler*, pp. 220-222; Nolan, *Benjamin
     Franklin Butler: The Damnedest Yankee*, p. 227; Richard Nelson Current, *Old Thad
     Stevens* (Madison, 1942), p. 32.
80. Butler, *Butler's Book*, pp. 260-264.

lowed by three volleys of musketry and a roll of muffled drums, at which point a shivering bugler played taps for the fallen Union army general.

Butler's death evoked an outpouring of emotion from all quarters. "In this section of the country Butler was the most cordially despised and hated man that ever lived," opined the *New Orleans Times-Democrat*.[81] "Old Ben Butler is dead!" gleefully shouted the *Nashville American*. "Early yesterday morning the angel of death acting under the devil's orders, took him from earth and landed him in hell. In all this southern country there are no tears, no sighs and no regrets. He lived only too long. We are glad he has at last been removed from earth and even pity the devil the possession he has secured."[82] Others weren't quite so harsh. "While he was alive we could not all agree with him," wrote the *Iowa State Register*, "but now that he is dead, we can all agree in paying him the tribute which is due him as a great and original character in American political history."[83] President Harry P. Judson of the University of Chicago said that Butler shouldn't "be dismissed as a mere demagogue," as some were prone to do, adding that the "historian who looks back a hundred years hence may assign Butler a very different place as an actual force in politics from that we should now be inclined to give him."[84]

Perhaps the most fitting—and moving—tribute was the one offered by the *New York Sun's* Charles A. Dana, the former assistant Secretary of War and a longtime personal friend of Butler. "For the last quarter of a century at least Benjamin Franklin Butler has stood out as the most original, the most American and the most picturesque character in our public life. He had courage equal to every occasion; his given word needed no brackets; his friendships and his enmities knew no variableness or shadow of turning; his opinions were never disguised nor withheld; his devotion to his country was without qualifications; his faith in the future of liberty and democracy was neither intoxicated by their victories nor disheartened by their defeats; his intellectual resources were marvelous; his mind naturally adhered to the poor and the weak; and his delight was to stand by the underdog in the fight." He had lived a full life, Dana concluded, "a life of energy

---

81. *Lowell Evening Star*, January 26, 1893, quoted in West, *Lincoln's Scapegoat General*, p. 421.

82. *Nashville American*, January 12, 1893, quoted in *The Washington Times*, August 22, 1998.

83. *The Weekly Iowa State Register*, January 13, 1893, quoted in Haynes, *Third Party Movements Since the Civil War*, pp. 151-152.

84. Harry Pratt Judson, "American Politics—a Study of Four Careers," *The Review of Reviews*, New York (March, 1893), Vol. VII, pp. 169-173.

and effort, of success and of failure and he has passed to the allotted reward while we who remain may well be grateful to heaven such a man has lived."[85]

While the Anti-Monopoly Party disappeared almost immediately following the 1884 presidential campaign, the Greenback Party continued to limp along for a few more years, largely as a paper organization. Apparently, it even managed to elect a member of the Mississippi legislature as late as 1891. The party fielded a little more than a dozen candidates in the 1886 mid-term congressional elections, but really wasn't a factor except in the case of James B. Weaver's successful bid for re-election in Iowa's sixth congressional district.[86] The party fared no better at the statewide level, polling insignificantly in several gubernatorial contests that year. In Pennsylvania, for instance, where Greenback-Republican congressman Charles N. Brumm continued to assist the party, the Greenbackers met with disaster when ex-Republican Robert J. Houston, the party's Irish-born candidate for governor, garnered a disappointing 4,835 votes, finishing far behind the Prohibition Party's Charles S. Wolfe.[87] The Pennsylvania organization, then led by Theodore P. Rynder, an insurance agent from Erie, merged with the fledgling Union Labor Party the following year. In its final days, the fading Greenback-Labor Party again attempted to launch a national ticket in 1888, but with little success. A presidential election without the Greenback Party, lamented party chairman George O. Jones in August of that year, "would be like the play of 'Hamlet,' without Hamlet." The eight delegates, including Jones, who convened in Cincinnati a month later were so disappointed by the small turnout that they merely drafted a statement of principles and went home—never to be heard from again.[88]

---

85. West, *Lincoln's Scapegoat General*, pp. 421-422.

86. In addition to providing the margin of victory in Weaver's hotly-contested race in Iowa and aiding Charles N. Brumm's re-election efforts in Pennsylvania, the Greenback Party's strongest congressional showings that year occurred in Arkansas, where a little-remembered preacher garnered over fifteen percent of the vote in a three-way race, and in Massachusetts, where the Reverend Willard Spaulding, running on a Greenback-Prohibition fusion ticket, received 2,663 votes—easily polling the difference between his major party rivals.

87. Ricker, *The Greenback-Labor Movement in Pennsylvania*, pp. 117-118. The Pennsylvania Prohibition Party had placed a Greenback plank in its 1885 platform. Wolfe garnered 32,458 votes in the 1886 gubernatorial campaign.

88. *Appletons' Annual Cyclopaedia*, 1891, p. 533, cited in Haynes, *Third Party Movements Since the Civil War*, p. 507n.

Selected Bibliography

Allen, Oliver E., *The Tiger: The Rise and Fall of Tammany Hall.* New York: Perseus Books Group, 1993.

Anbinder, Tyler, *Nativism & Slavery: The Northern Know Nothings & the Politics of the 1850s.* New York: Oxford University Press, 1992.

Angle, Paul M. and Earl Schenck Miers, eds., *The Living Lincoln.* Reprinted. New York: Barnes & Noble Books, 1992.

Bailyn, Bernard, David Brion Davis, David Herbert Donald, John L. Thomas, Robert H. Wiebe, and Gordon S. Wood, *The Great Republic: A History of the American People.* Lexington, MA: D. C. Heath and Company, 1981.

Baker, Jean H., *Ambivalent Americans: The Know-Nothing Party in Maryland.* Baltimore: Johns Hopkins University Press, 1977.

Baringer, William, *Lincoln's Rise to Power.* Boston: Little, Brown and Company, 1937.

Barnes, Gilbert Hobbs, *The Anti-Slavery Impulse 1830-1844.* Reprinted. New York: Harcourt, Brace & World, Inc., 1964.

Beals, Carleton, *Brass-Knuckle Crusade, The Great Know-Nothing Conspiracy: 1820-1860.* New York: Hastings House Publishers, 1960.

Bennett, David H., *The Party of Fear: From Nativist Movements to the New Right in American History.* Chapel Hill: University of North Carolina Press, 1988.

Billington, Ray Allen, *The Protestant Crusade 1800-1860: A Study of the Origins of American Nativism.* Reprinted. Chicago: Quadrangle Books, 1964.

Binkley, Wilfred E., *American Political Parties: Their Natural History.* New York: Alfred A. Knopf, Inc., 1947.

Black, James, *Brief History of Prohibition and of the Prohibition Reform Party*. New York: National Committee of the Prohibition Reform Party, 1880.

Blue, Frederick J., *Salmon P. Chase: A Life in Politics*. Kent, OH: Kent State University Press, 1987.

_____, *The Free Soilers: Third Party Politics 1848-54*. Urbana: University of Illinois Press, 1973.

Boller, Paul F., Jr., *Presidential Campaigns*. New York: Oxford University Press, 1985.

Brewton, William W., *The Life of Thomas E. Watson*. Atlanta: Published by the author, 1926.

Buck, Solon J., *The Agrarian Crusade*. New Haven: Yale University Press, 1920.

Buhle, Mari Jo, Paul Buhle, and Dan Georgakas, eds., *Encyclopedia of the American Left*. Urbana: University of Illinois Press, 1992.

Clancy, Herbert John, *The Presidential Election of 1880*. Chicago: Loyola U. Press, 1958.

Colvin, D. Leigh, *Prohibition in the United States: A History of the Prohibition Party and of the Prohibition Movement*. New York: George H. Doran Company, 1926.

Coulter, E. Merton, *Georgia: A Short History*. Chapel Hill: University of North Carolina Press, 1973.

Crenshaw, Ollinger, *The Slave States in the Presidential Election of 1860*. Reprinted. Gloucester, MA: Peter Smith, 1969.

Degregorio, William A., *The Complete Book of U.S. Presidents*. Fort Lee, New Jersey: Barricade Books, Inc., 2001.

Delmatier, Royce D., Clarence F. McIntosh and Earl G. Waters, eds., *The Rumble of California Politics, 1848-1870*. New York: John Wiley & Sons, Inc., 1970.

Diamond, Robert A., ed., *Congressional Quarterly's Guide to U.S. Elections*. First edition. Washington, D.C.: Congressional Quarterly Inc., 1975.

Donald, David Herbert, *Lincoln*. New York: Simon & Schuster, 1995.

Donovan, Herbert D. A., *The Barnburners*. Reprinted. Philadelphia: Porcupine Press, 1974.

Dubin, Michael J., *United States Congressional Elections, 1788-1997*. Jefferson, North Carolina: McFarland & Company, Inc., Publishers, 1998.

Dumond, Dwight Lowell, *The Secession Movement 1860-1861*. Reprinted. New York: Octagon Books, 1973.

Ewing, Cortez A. M., *Presidential Elections: From Abraham Lincoln to Franklin D. Roosevelt*. Norman, OK: University of Oklahoma Press, 1940.

Fine, Nathan, *Labor and Farmer Parties in the United States 1828-1928*. Reprinted. New York: Russell & Russell, 1961.

Fite, Emerson David, *The Presidential Campaign of 1860*. Reprinted. Port Washington, New York: Kennikat Press, Inc., 1967.

Fladeland, Betty, *James Gillespie Birney: Slaveholder to Abolitionist*. Ithaca, N.Y.: Cornell University Press, 1955.

Foner, Eric and John A. Garraty, eds., *The Reader's Companion to American History*. Boston: Houghton Mifflin Company, 1991.

_____, *Free Soil, Free Labor, Free Men: The Ideology of the Republican Party before the Civil War*. London, England: Oxford University Press, 1970.

Foner, Philip S., *History of the Labor Movement in the United States*, Volume 1. New York: International Publishers, Co., Inc., 1947.

_____, *The Workingmen's Party of the United States: A History of the First Marxist Party in the Americas*. Minneapolis: MEP Publications, 1984.

Frothingham, Paul Revere, *Edward Everett, Orator and Statesman*. Boston: Houghton Co., 1925

Furnas, J. C., *The Late Demon Rum*. London, England: W. H. Allen, 1965.

Gabriel, Mary, *Notorious Victoria: The Life of Victoria Woodhull, Uncensored*. Chapel Hill: Algonquin Books of Chapel Hill, 1998.

Gatell, Frank Otto, *John Gorham Palfrey and the New England Conscience*. Cambridge, MA: Harvard University Press, 1963.

_____, "'Conscience and Judgment': The Bolt of the Massachusetts Conscience Whigs," *The Historian*, 20 (1959), pp. 18-49.

Gienapp, William E., *The Origins of the Republican Party 1852-1856*. New York: Oxford University Press, 1987.

Gillespie, J. David, *Politics at the Periphery: Third Parties in Two-Party America*. Columbia: University of South Carolina Press, 1993.

Girard, Frank and Ben Perry, *The Socialist Labor Party 1876-1991: A Short History*. Philadelphia: Livra Books, 1991.

Glassner, Gregory K., *Adopted Son: The Life, Wit & Wisdom of William Wirt, 1772-1834*. Madison County, VA: Kurt-Ketner Publishing, Inc., 1997.

Goldsmith, Barbara, *Other Powers: The Age of Suffrage, Spiritualism, and the Scandalous Victoria Woodhull*. New York: Alfred A. Knopf, Inc., 1998.

Griffin, Clifford S., *Their Brothers' Keepers: Moral Stewardship in the United States, 1800-1865*. New Brunswick, New Jersey: Rutgers University Press, 1960.

Gusfield, Joseph R., *Symbolic Crusade: Status Politics and the American Temperance Movement*. Urbana: University of Illinois Press, 1963.

Hamilton, Alexander, James Madison and John Jay, *The Federalist Papers*. Edited by Clinton Rossiter. New York: Penguin Group, 1961.

Havel, James T., *U.S. Presidential Candidates and the Elections: A Biographical and Historical Guide*. 2 vols. New York: Simon & Schuster Macmillan, 1996.

Hayes, Melvin L., *Mr. Lincoln Runs for President*. New York: The Citadel Press, 1960.

Haynes, Fred E, *James Baird Weaver*. Reprinted. New York: Arno Press, 1975.

_____, *Third Party Movements Since the Civil War*. Reprinted. New York: Russell & Russell, 1966.

Hesseltine, William B., *The Rise and Fall of Third Parties: From Anti-Masonry to Wallace*. Washington, D.C.: Public Affairs Press, 1948.

_____, *Third Party Movements in the United States*. Princeton, New Jersey: D. Van Nostrand Company, Inc., 1962.

Hillquit, Morris, *History of Socialism in the United States*. Fifth edition. New York: Dover Publications, Inc., 1971.

Holli, Melvin G. and Peter d' A. Jones, eds., *Biographical Dictionary of American Mayors, 1820-1980*. Westport, CT: Greenwood Press, 1981.

_____, *The American Mayor: The Best & The Worst Big-City Leaders*. University Park, PA: Pennsylvania State University Press, 1999.

Holt, Michael F., *The Political Crisis of the 1850s*. New York: John Wiley & Sons, Inc., 1978.

_____, *The Rise and Fall of the American Whig Party: Jacksonian Politics and the Onset of the Civil War*. New York: Oxford University Press, 1999.

Holzman, Robert S., *Stormy Ben Butler*. New York: Collier Books, 1961.

Johnson, Gerald W., "Dynamic Victoria Woodhull," *American Heritage*, Vol. VII, Number 4 (June 1956), pp. 44-47, 86-91.

Johnston, Johanna, *Mrs. Satan: The Incredible Saga of Victoria Woodhull*. London, England: Macmillan, 1967.

Julian, George W., *Political Recollections 1840-1872*. Reprinted. New York: Negro Universities Press, 1970.

Key, V. O., Jr., *Politics, Parties, and Pressure Groups*. New York: Thomas Y. Crowell Company, 1952.

King, Willard L., *Lincoln's Manager: David Davis*. Cambridge, MA: Harvard University Press, 1960.

Kipnis, Ira, *The American Socialist Movement 1897-1912*. New York: Columbia University Press, 1952.

Kobler, John, *Ardent Spirits: the Rise and Fall of Prohibition*. New York: G. P. Putnam's Sons, 1973.

Krout, John Allen, *The Origins of Prohibition*. New York: Alfred A. Knopf, Inc., 1925.

Krushke, Earl Roger, *Encyclopedia of Third Parties in the United States*. Santa Barbara: ABC-CLIO, 1991.

Lause, Mark A., *The Civil War's Last Campaign: James B. Weaver, the Greenback-Labor Party & the Politics of Race & Section*. Lanham, MD: University Press of America, Inc., 2001.

Lawson, Elizabeth, *Lincoln's Third Party*. New York: International Publishers Co., Inc., 1948.

Lipset, Seymour Martin and Earl Raab, *The Politics of Unreason: Right-Wing Extremism in America, 1790-1970*. New York: Harper & Row, Publishers, 1970.

Lorant, Stefan, *The Glorious Buren: The American Presidency*. New York: Harper & Row, 1968.

Lyon, Peter, "The Honest Man," *American Heritage*, Vo. X, Number 2 (February 1959), pp. 4-11, 104-107.

Macy, Jesse, *The Anti-Slavery Crusade*. New Haven: Yale University Press, 1919.

Mazmanian, Daniel A., *Third Parties in Presidential Elections*. Washington, D.C.: The Brookings Institution, 1974.

McCarthy, Charles, "Anti-Masonic Party," *American Historical Association Report*. Washington, D.C., 1902.

McPherson, James M., *Battle Cry of Freedom: The Civil War Era*. New York: Ballantine Books, 1988.

Miller, John C., *The Federalist Era, 1789-1801*. New York: Harper & Row, Publishers, Inc., 1960.

Miller, Lillian B. and the staff of the Historian's Office, National Portrait Gallery, *'If Elected...Unsuccessful Candidates for the Presidency 1796-1968*. Washington, D.C.: Smithsonian Institution Press, 1972.

Mitchell, Stewart, *Horatio Seymour of New York*. Reprinted. New York: De Capo Press, 1970.

Morris, Roy, Jr., *Fraud of the Century: Rutherford B. Hayes, Samuel Tilden, and the Stolen Election of 1876*. New York: Simon & Schuster, 2003.

Mulkern, John R., *The Know-Nothing Party in Massachusetts: The Rise and Fall of a People's Movement*. Boston: Northeastern University Press, 1990.

Nash, Howard P., Jr., *Stormy Petrel: The Life and Times of General Benjamin F. Butler 1818-1893*. Cranbury, New Jersey: Fairleigh Dickinson University Press, 1969.

_____, *Third Parties in American Politics*. Washington, D.C.: Public Affairs Press, 1959.

Ness, Immanuel and James Ciment, eds., *The Encyclopedia of Third Parties in America*. 3 vols. Armonk, New York: M. E. Sharpe Inc., 2000.

Nevins, Allan, *The Emergence of Lincoln*. 2 vols. New York: Charles Scribner's Sons, 1950.

Nolan, Dick, *Benjamin Franklin Butler: The Damnedest Yankee*. Novato, CA: Presidio Press, 1991.

Nye, Russell B., *Midwestern Progressive Politics: A Historical Study of Its Origins and Development, 1870-1958*. New York: Harper & Row, Publishers, 1959.

Oates, Stephen B., *With Malice Toward None: The Life of Abraham Lincoln*. New York: Harper & Row, Publishers, Inc., 1977.

Overdyke, W. Darrell, *The Know-Nothing Party in the South*. Gloucester, MA: Peter Smith, 1968.

Parks, Joseph Howard, *John Bell of Tennessee*. Baton Rouge: Louisiana State University Press, 1950.

Potter, David M., *The Impending Crisis 1848-1861*. Completed and edited by Don E. Fehrenbacher. New York: Harper & Row, Publishers, Inc., 1976.

Ratner, Lorman, *Antimasonry: The Crusade and the Party*. Englewood Cliffs, New Jersey: Prentice-Hall, Inc., 1969.

Rayback, Joseph G., *Free Soil: The Election of 1848*. Lexington, KY: The University of Kentucky Press, 1970.

_____, *Martin Van Buren*. New York: Eastern Acorn Press, 1982.

Rayback, Robert J., *Millard Fillmore: Biography of a President*. Buffalo: Buffalo Historical Society, 1959.

Ricker, Ralph R., *The Greenback-Labor Movement in Pennsylvania*. Bellefonte, PA: Pennsylvania Heritage, Inc., 1966.

Riddleberger, Patrick W., *George Washington Julian: Radical Republican*. Indianapolis: Indiana Historical Bureau, 1966.

Ridge, Martin, *Ignatius Donnelly: Portrait of a Politician*. Reprinted. St. Paul: Minnesota Historical Society Press, 1991.

Ritter, Gretchen, *Goldbugs and Greenbacks: The Antimonopoly Tradition and the Politics of Finance in America, 1865-1896*. Cambridge, England: Cambridge University Press, 1997.

Rochester, Anna, *The Populist Movement in the United States*. New York: International Publishers Co., Inc., 1943.

Rose, Edward J., *Henry George*. New York: Twayne Publishers, Inc., 1968.

Roseboom, Eugene H., *A History of Presidential Elections: From George Washington to Richard M. Nixon*. New York: Macmillan Publishing Co., Inc., 1970.

Rosenstone, Steven J., Roy L. Behr and Edward H. Lazarus, *Third Parties in America: Citizen Response to Major Party Failure*. Princeton, New Jersey: Princeton University Press, 1984.

Ross, Earle Dudley, *The Liberal Republican Movement*. Reprinted. Seattle: University of Washington Press, 1970.

Schlesinger, Arthur M., Jr., and Fred Isabel, eds., *History of American Presidential Elections*. 4 vols. New York: Chelsea House, 1971.

_____, *History of U.S. Political Parties*. 4 vols. New York: Chelsea House, 1973.

Scrugham, Mary, *The Peaceable Americans of 1860-1861*. Reprinted. New York: Octagon Books, 1976.

Seretan, L. Glen, *Daniel DeLeon: The Odyssey of an American Marxist*. Cambridge, MA: Harvard University Press, 1979.

Sewell, Richard H., *Ballots for Freedom: Antislavery Politics in the United States 1837-1860*. New York: Oxford University Press, Inc., 1976.

_____, *John P. Hale and the Politics of Abolition*. Cambridge, MA: Harvard University Press, 1965.

Shumsky, Neil Larry, *The Evolution of Political Protest and the Workingmen's Party of California*. Columbus: Ohio State University Press, 1991.

Smith, Richard Norton, *Patriarch: George Washington and the New American Nation*. Boston: Houghton Mifflin Company, 1993.

Smith, Theodore Clarke, *The Liberty and Free Soil Parties in the Northwest*. New York: Russell & Russell, 1897.

Soule, Leon Cyprian, *The Know Nothing Party in New Orleans*. Baton Rouge: The Louisiana Historical Association, 1961.

Stedman, Murray S., Jr., and Susan W. Stedman, *Discontent at the Polls: A Study of Farmer and Labor Parties 1827-1948*. New York: Columbia University Press, 1950.

Stewart, James Brewer, *Joshua R. Giddings and the Tactics of Radical Politics*. Cleveland: Press of Case Western Reserve University, 1970.

Stoddard, Henry Luther, *Horace Greeley: Printer, Editor, Crusader*. New York: G. P. Putnam's Sons, 1946.

Storms, Roger C., *Partisan Prophets: A History of the Prohibition Party*. Denver: National Prohibition Foundation, Inc., 1972.

Thornton, Willis, *The Nine Lives of Citizen Train*. New York: Greenberg, 1948.

Todes, Charlotte, *William H. Sylvis and the National Labor Union*. New York: International Publishers Co., Inc., 1942.

Underhill, Lois Beachy, *The Woman Who Ran for President: The Many Lives of Victoria Woodhull*. New York: Penguin Books, 1995.

Unger, Irwin, *The Greenback Era: A Social and Political History of American Finance 1865-1879*. Princeton, New Jersey: Princeton University Press, 1964.

Usher, Ellis Baker, *The Greenback Movement of 1876-1884 and Wisconsin's Part in It*. Milwaukee: E. B. Usher, 1911.

Van Deusen, Glyndon G., *Horace Greeley: Nineteenth Century Crusader*. New York: Philadelphia: University of Pennsylvania Press, 1953.

Vaughn, William Preston, *The Anti-Masonic Party in the United States, 1826-1843*. Lexington, KY: The University of Kentucky Press, 1983.

Volpe, Vernon L., *Forlorn Hope of Freedom: The Liberty Party in the Old Northwest, 1838-1848*. Kent, OH: Kent State University Press, 1990.

Waugh, John C., *Reelecting Lincoln: The Battle for the 1864 Presidency*. Cambridge, MA: De Capo Press, 1997.

Weigley, Russell F., ed., *Philadelphia: A 300-Year History*. New York: W. W. Norton & Company, 1982.

West, Richard S., Jr., *Lincoln's Scapegoat General: A Life of Benjamin F. Butler 1818-1893*. Boston: Houghton Mifflin Company, 1965.

Whitman, Alden, *Labor Parties 1827-1834*. New York: International Publishers Co., Inc., 1943.

Whitney, David C., *The American Presidents*. Garden City, New York: Doubleday & Company, Inc., 1978.

Williams, John Hoyt, *Sam Houston: A Biography of the Father of Texas*. New York: Simon & Schuster, 1993.

Woodward, C. Vann, *Tom Watson: Agrarian Rebel.* London, England: Oxford University Press, 1938.

Zinn, Howard, *A People's History of the United States.* New York: Harper Collins, 1980.

Index

N

0-595-31723-5